Multicultural Law Enforcement: Strategies for Peacekeeping in a Diverse Society

Third Edition

Robert M. Shusta
Deena R. Levine
Herbert Z. Wong
Philip R. Harris

PEARSON
Prentice Hall

Pearson Education
Upper Saddle River, New Jersey 07458

Library of Congress Cataloging-in-Publication Data

Multicultural law enforcement / [Robert M. Shusta ... et al.].-- 3rd ed.
   p. cm.
 Includes bibliographical references and index.
 ISBN 0-13-113307-1
 1. Police-community relations--United States. 2. Discrimination in law
enforcement--United States. 3. Multiculturalism--United States. 4. Intercultural communication--United States. I. Shusta, Robert M.

HV7936.P8M85 2005
363.2'3--dc22

              2004012616

Executive Editor: Frank Mortimer, Jr.
Associate Editor: Sarah Holle
Managing Editor: Mary Carnis
Production Management: Pine Tree Composition, Inc.
Production Editor: Linda Duarte
Production Liaison: Brian Hyland
Director of Manufacturing and Production: Bruce Johnson
Manufacturing Buyer: Cathleen Petersen
Design Director: Cheryl Asherman
Printer/Binder: Phoenix
Cover Design: Carey Davies
Cover Illustration: Larry Williams / CORBIS

Pearson Education LTD
Pearson Education Singapore, Pte. Ltd
Pearson Education, Canada, Ltd
Pearson Education–Japan

Pearson Education Australia PTY, Limited
Pearson Education North Asia Ltd
Pearson Educaçion de Mexico, S.A. de C.V.
Pearson Education Malaysia, Pte. Ltd

10 9 8 7 6 5 4 3 2

ISBN 0-13-113307-1

To all our family members

Midge
Michael, Ilana, Kara
Janet
Phyllis, Michele

For their support and understanding of the value of this work

CONTENTS

CHAPTER 8: Law Enforcement Contact with Arab Americans and Other Middle Eastern Groups   220

CHAPTER 9: Law Enforcement Contact With Native Americans   253

PART 3: Multicultural Law Enforcement Elements in Terrorism and Homeland Security   281

FOREWORD

We are involved in some of the most challenging times in the history of law enforcement. Peacekeeping in a multicultural society in the 21st century calls for new strategies, skills, tools, and cultural knowledge on the part of those engaged in all aspects of the criminal justice system and homeland security. For decades, American communities and their agencies of law enforcement have struggled with peacekeeping challenges related to race, class, ethnicity, religion, sexual orientation, gender, and other demographic differences among our citizens. Today, such matters are more complex because of the diversity of our communities and the vast increase in numbers of immigrants, legal and illegal, as well as new threats from both foreign and domestic terrorists. Furthermore, today's "local" peacekeeping challenges are, oftentimes, multijurisdictional, regional, national, and global in scope.

Compared to a decade ago, contemporary law enforcement has improved resources to meet these challenges resulting from the diversity within our communities and the multicultural law enforcement aspects of peacekeeping. First, we have better educated, more competent, and diverse personnel in our agencies, as is evident here in our own Detroit Police Department. They benefit from continuing professional development in the acquisition of bilingual skills and cross-cultural awareness, contributing to an ability to interact and to work with people from a multitude of backgrounds. Second, the law and judicial processes have changed with respect to equal opportunity, affirmative action, racial profiling, and homeland security. Third, we now have instant access to helpful research and informational technology tools enabling us to be more sophisticated in our peacekeeping process.

That is why the publication of this third edition of *Multicultural Law Enforcement* is so significant. Over 95 percent of published books never enter into their second edition. Clearly, the authors have filled a gap in the law enforcement literature, and we readers are fortunate to now have access to the third edition. Since the book was first printed in 1995, this volume has established itself as a classic in the criminal justice field. Its adoption by police academies, criminal justice courses, and universities and colleges, in general, is testimony to its acceptance. *Multicultural Law Enforcement's* major sections effectively address the key multicultural needs of law enforcement, as practitioners in increasing numbers have discovered for themselves. The practical contents of the book provide critical information and insight that will improve police performance and professionalism. The subject matter herein, especially on culture specifics, continues to be on the leading edge.

This third edition of *Multicultural Law Enforcement* will enable agencies to prepare officers to form partnerships for effective community-based policing and to develop resources within criminal justice services for multicultural communities. Many of us have learned from the lessons of the past in terms of racial profiling, urban demonstrations, equal employment opportunity, terrorism, and homeland security, and we have developed strategies and implemented procedures to address, correct, and prevent the issues that caused them.

Here in the City of Detroit, we not only have a very diverse police force, but also seek continuous innovative and proactive ways for multicultural law enforcement strategies and community policing. For example, in the Detroit Police Department we have added to our basic Citizens' Police Academies concept. We now offer specialized academies to citizens based on the diversity reflected in our communities.

Because the southwest area of Detroit is home to a large Hispanic American population, large parts of which do not speak English, we have created an academy dedicated to non-English speaking Hispanic Americans. Similarly, we have developed an academy for our senior citizens that respond to their unique needs and perspectives. We are also proud of our successful police–community relations with the large Arab American and Chaldean population in Detroit.

I am impressed by the diversity and competencies of the authors of *Multicultural Law Enforcement*. In addition to the vast and cumulative experience of the four authors, each has sought additional cultural information and input from contributors from various other diverse backgrounds. This is why I feel confident in recommending this text. I encourage all who use it to take what you learn from the authors and translate the strategies, information, and tools of this exceptional work for the betterment of your communities and the larger society.

Chief Ella M. Bully-Cummings
City of Detroit Police Department

PREFACE

This third edition of *Multicultural Law Enforcement: Strategies for Peacekeeping in a Diverse Society* is a tribute to all our readers who enthusiastically received the first two editions. It is a textbook for police departments and academies and colleges and universities. It is also designed to assist all levels of criminal justice representatives in understanding the pervasive influences of culture, race, and ethnicity in the workplace and in multicultural communities. The text continues to focus on the cross-cultural contact that police officers and civilian employees have with coworkers, victims, suspects, and citizens from diverse backgrounds. The third edition also includes material on homeland security and the war on terrorism, as well as on racial profiling and hate crimes related to events on and after September 11, 2001. In addition, we have expanded the sections on community-based policing, undocumented immigrants and immigrant women, urban dynamics, women, and gays and lesbians in law enforcement. We include updated demographic data using the most current population estimates and projections available to date.

Throughout these pages, we stress the need for awareness, understanding of cultural differences, and respect toward those of different backgrounds. We encourage all representatives of law enforcement to examine preconceived notions they might hold of particular groups. We outline for police executives why they should build awareness and promote cultural understanding and tolerance within their agencies.

An increasing number of leaders in law enforcement agencies and their employees have accepted the premise that greater cross-cultural competency must be a key objective of all management and professional development. Demographic changes have had a tremendous impact not only on the types of crimes committed but also on the composition of the law enforcement workforce and the people with whom officers make contact. To be effective, police executives must understand the diversity in their workforces and in their changing communities. Professionalism today includes the need for greater consideration across cultures and improved communication with members of diverse groups.

In an era when news is processed and accessed immediately, the public is exposed almost daily to instances of cross-cultural and interracial contact between law enforcement agents and citizens. So, too, have community members become increasingly sophisticated and critical with regard to how members of diverse cultural and racial groups are treated by public servants. Employees of police departments and other agencies entrusted with law enforcement find that they are now serving communities that carefully observe them and hold them accountable for their actions.

This new edition has been updated and expanded to provide practical information and guidelines for law enforcement managers, supervisors, officers, and instructors. With cross-cultural knowledge, sensitivity, and tolerance, those who are charged with the responsibility of peacekeeping will improve their image while demonstrating greater professionalism within the changing multicultural workforce and community.

Robert M. Shusta, MPA   **Herbert Z. Wong, PhD**
Deena R. Levine, MA   **Philip R. Harris, PhD**

ACKNOWLEDGMENTS

This third edition has benefited from content expert contributions by the following people and organizations:

David Barlow, PhD, Associate Professor, Fayetteville State University, North Carolina

Danilo Begonia, JD, Professor, Asian American Studies, San Francisco State University, San Francisco, California

Deputy Chief Ondra Berry, Reno Police Department, Reno, Nevada

Patricia DeRosa, President, ChangeWorks Consulting, Randolph, Massachusetts

Ronald Griffin, Pastor, Pastor and Community Leader, Detroit, Michigan

Mitchell Grobeson, retired Sergeant, Los Angeles Police Department, Los Angeles, California

Ronald Haddad, Senior Deputy Chief, Detroit Police Department, Detroit, Michigan

Lubna Ismail, President, Connecting Cultures, Washington, DC

Sari Karet, Executive Director, Cambodian American Foundation, San Francisco, California

Kao T. Li, MS, MBA, Executive Director, Quincy Asian Resources, Inc., Quincy, Massachusetts

Sergeant Aaron T. Olson, Oregon State Police, Portland, Oregon

Glen Perry, Police Outreach Volunteer and Youth Case Manager, Immigrant and Refugee Community Organization, Portland, Oregon

Oscar Ramirez, PhD, Police and Court Expert Consultant, San Antonio, Texas

Jose Rivera, retired Peace Officer, Education Director—Native American Museum, Sausalito, California

Lourdes Rodriguez-Nogues, EdD, President, Rasi Associates, Boston, Massachusetts

Helen Samhan, Executive Director, Arab American Institute Foundation, Washington, DC

Victoria Santos, President, Santos & Associates, Newark, California

Reverend Onasai Veevau, Pastor and Pacific Islander Community Leader, San Mateo, California

Norita Jones Vlach, PhD, Professor, School of Social Work, San Jose State University, San Jose, California

James Zogby, Ph D, Director, Arab American Institute Foundation, Washington, DC

John Zogby, PhD, President, Zogby International, New York, New York

We owe special thanks to the following individuals for their helpful insights:

Kim Ah-Low, Georgia

Corporal Mohamed Berro, Michigan

Joe Canton, PhD, California

Chung H. Chuong, California

Captain S. Rob Hardman, USCG (Ret.), Virginia

Wilbur Herrington, Massachusetts

Jim Kahue, Hawaii

Chief Susan Jones, California

Judith Kaye, JD, Connecticut

Charles Marquez, Colorado

Lieutenant Darryl McAllister, California

Sarah Miyahira, PhD, Hawaii

Margaret Moore, Washington, DC

Dinh Van Nguyen, California

JoAnne Pina, PhD, Washington, DC

Eduardo Rodela, PhD, Washington, DC

Chief Darrel Stephens, North Carolina

George Thompson, California

We also wish to acknowledge those who were helpful in the production (research, writing, graphics, and editing contributions) of this edition:

Eric Eldon, student researcher, Palo Alto, California

Judi Lipsett, editorial assistance, San Antonio, Texas

Ilana Lipsett, researcher and writer, San Diego, California

Nathan Young, graphics, Pleasant Hill, California

Prentice Hall and the authors would like to thank the following for reviewing this edition:

Steven M. Christianson, Green River Community College, Auburn, Washington

Terry Miller, Valencia Community College, Orlando, Florida

Erik Laurentz, Tacoma Community College, Tacoma, Washington

Aaron T. Olsen, Portland Community College, Portland, Oregon

ABOUT THE AUTHORS

Robert M. Shusta, Captain ret., MPA, served over 27 years in law enforcement, and retired as a Captain at the Concord, California, Police Department. He has been a part-time instructor at numerous colleges and universities in northern California and at police academies. He is a graduate of the 158th FBI National Academy and the 4th California Command College conducted by POST. He served on state commissions responsible for developing and recommending to POST guidelines, policy, and training on cultural awareness and crimes motivated by hate.

Deena R. Levine, MA, has been providing consulting and training to organizations in both the public and private sectors since 1983. She is the principal of Deena Levine & Associates, a firm specializing in cross-cultural and communication workplace training as well as consulting on issues related to global business. She and her associates, together with representatives from community organizations, have provided programs to police departments, focusing on cross-cultural and human relations. She worked at the Intercultural Relations Institute, formerly at Stanford University, developing multicultural workforce training for managers and supervisors. She wrote an additional widely used text on the cultural aspects of communication, titled *Beyond Language: Cross-Cultural Communication* (Regents/Prentice Hall).

Herbert Z. Wong, PhD, an organizational psychologist, provides cultural awareness and diversity training to law enforcement officers on local, state, and federal levels nationwide. He is President of Herbert Z. Wong & Associates, a management consulting firm to over 300 businesses, universities, government agencies, and corporations, specializing in multicultural management and workforce diversity. In 1990, Dr. Wong cofounded and was President of the National Diversity Conference, which became the Society for Human Resource Management's Workplace Diversity Conference. He developed and provided the national Training-of-Trainers programs for the seven-part Valuing Diversity videotape series used in over 4,000 organizations worldwide. In addition, Dr. Wong has written extensive papers and publications on workforce diversity and multicultural leadership issues.

Philip R. Harris, PhD, is a management psychologist with extensive experience in both the criminal justice system and cross-cultural studies. President of Harris International, Ltd., in La Jolla, California, he is author/editor of approximately 40 volumes, including *Managing Cultural Differences* (6th ed., Butterworth-Heinemann) and *The New Work Culture* (2nd ed., Human Resource Development Press). A global consultant to over 200 systems, he has had as law enforcement clients the California POST Command College, the Office of Naval Research/USMC Corrections Officers, the U.S. Customs Service, the District of Columbia Police Department, and the Philadelphia Police Department Dr. Harris is listed in *Who's Who in America.*

Part 1

IMPACT OF CULTURAL DIVERSITY ON LAW ENFORCEMENT

Part One of *Multicultural Law Enforcement* introduces readers to the implications of a multicultural society for law enforcement, both within and outside the police agency. Chapter 1 discusses aspects of the changing population, and presents views on diversity.

The inclusion of three case studies in Chapter 1 exemplifies how the presence of different cultures can affect the very nature and perception of crime itself. The authors present the subject of prejudice and its effect on police work, providing specific examples of its consequences in law enforcement. They also discuss community-based policing and provide examples of departments with and without community partnerships. The chapter ends with suggestions for improving law enforcement in multicultural communities.

Chapter 2 discusses demographic changes that are taking place within law enforcement agencies, as well as reactions to diversity in the law enforcement workplace and responses to it. In addition to data on ethnic and racial groups, this chapter provides information on women, and on gay men and lesbians in law enforcement institutions across the country. The authors illustrate the realities of the new workforce and the corresponding need for flexibility in leadership styles.

1

Chapter 3 discusses challenges in recruitment, retention, and promotion of police personnel from various racial, ethnic, and cultural backgrounds. The authors present strategies for recruitment, emphasizing the commitment required by law enforcement chief executives and the need to look inward—that is, to assess the level of comfort and inclusion that all employees experience in a given agency. If the levels are not high, hiring, retention, and promotion will be difficult. Chapter 3 describes the pressing need facing all agencies to build a workforce of highly qualified individuals of diverse backgrounds and in which all people have equal access to the hiring, retention, and promotion processes.

Chapter 4 provides practical information highlighting the dynamics of cross-cultural communication in law enforcement. The chapter includes a discussion of the special problems involved when officers must communicate with speakers of other languages. We present typical styles of communication that people may display when they are uncomfortable with cross-cultural contact. The chapter now includes a section on the need for communication sensitivity post-9/11. In addition, it covers nonverbal differences across cultures, and to some of the communication issues that arise between men and women in law enforcement agencies. Finally, the authors present skills and techniques for officers to apply in situations of cross-cultural contact.

Each chapter ends with discussion questions and a list of references, including websites. The following appendices correspond to the chapter content in Part One:

A. Multicultural Community and Workforce: Attitude Assessment

B. Cultural Diversity Survey: Needs Assessment

C. Listing of Consultants and Resources

D. Self-Assessment of Communication Skills in Law Enforcement: Communications Inventory

Chapter 1

Multicultural Communities: Challenges for Law Enforcement

OVERVIEW

In this chapter we discuss law enforcement challenges related to the growing multicultural population in the United States. Chapter 1 begins with the need for an increased understanding of the diverse populations with which law enforcement officials interact. The discussion of our mosaic society incorporates a brief historical perspective on immigration. Three mini case studies illustrate the points of contact between a person's culture and a particular crime or offense. We present practical reasons why officers should have an understanding of the cultural backgrounds of the groups they commonly encounter. Next, we discuss how prejudice interferes with, but can be overcome by, the professional behavior of law enforcement officers. The authors discuss community-based policing, along with its implications for positive relations and contact with diverse immigrant and ethnic communities. The chapter ends with tips for improving law enforcement in multicultural communities.

COMMENTARY

> The 21st century will be the century in which we redefine ourselves as the first country in world history that is literally made up of every part of the world.
>
> —*Mr. Kenneth Prewitt, Director of the U.S. Census Bureau, 1998–2001*

Multiculturalism and diversity are at the very heart of America, and describe accurately the demographics of our nation. The word *multiculturalism* does not refer to a movement or political force, nor is it an anti-American term. A multicultural community is simply one that is comprised of many different ethnic and racial groups. The United States, compared to virtually all other nations, has experienced unparalleled growth in its multicultural population. Reactions to these changes range from appreciation and even celebration of diversity to an absolute intolerance of differences. In its extreme form, intolerance resulting in crimes of hate is a major law enforcement and criminal justice concern.

Law enforcement officials—those whose professional ideal is to protect and serve people equally from all backgrounds—must face the challenges and complexities of a diverse society. Although our nation has been enriched by diversity, many police procedures and interactions with citizens can be complicated by diversity. A lack of knowledge of cultural differences can result in inadvertent violation of individuals' rights as well as officer safety and risk issues. Officers, even more than others, must ensure that their prejudices are in check and that they refrain from acting on any biased thought—after all, bias is common to all human beings. The following quotes provide a national perspective on the mandate of law enforcement:

Initial Report of the United States of America to the United Nations Committee on the Elimination of Racial Discrimination

As a functioning, multi-racial [and multicultural] democracy, the United States seeks to enforce the established rights of individuals to protection against discrimination based upon race, color, national origin, religion, gender, age, disability status, and citizenship status in virtually every aspect of social and economic life.. . . . The federal government has established a wide-ranging set of enforcement procedures to administer these laws, with the U.S. Department of Justice exercising a major coordination and leadership role on most critical enforcement issues. (September 2000)

Interview with Deputy Chief Ondra Berry, Reno, Nevada, Police Department

Law enforcement is under a powerful microscope in terms of how citizens are treated. Minority and ethnic communities have become increasingly competent in understanding the role of law enforcement, and expectations of law enforcement for professionalism have been elevated from previous years. In an age when information about what happens in a police department on the East Coast speeds across to the West Coast in seconds, law enforcement officials must be aware. They must be vigilant. They must do the right thing. (Berry, personal communication, 2003)

INTRODUCTION

The United States has always been a magnet for people from nearly every corner of the earth, and, consequently, U.S. demographics continue to undergo constant change. In efforts to be both proactive and responsive to diverse communities, police officers and groups from many backgrounds around the country are working to become more closely connected in direct relationships promoted in community-based policing models. Leaders, both from law enforcement agencies and the community, have realized that they both benefit when each group seeks mutual assistance and understanding. The job of law enforcement requires a certain level of comfort and professionalism in interacting with people from all backgrounds whether one is working with community members to build trust or dealing with suspects, victims, and coworkers.

Through increased awareness, knowledge, and skills, law enforcement as a profession can increase its "cultural competence." Developing cultural competence is a process that evolves over time, requiring that individuals and organizations place a high value on the following (adapted from Cross, Bazron, Dennis, & Isaacs, 1989):

- Developing a set of principles, attitudes, policies, and structures that will enable all individuals in the organization to work effectively and equitably across all cultures

- Developing the capacity to:

- acquire and apply cross-cultural knowledge
- respond to and communicate effectively within the cultural contexts that the organization serves

The strategies one uses to approach and build rapport with one's own cultural group may very well result in unsuspected difficulties with another group. The acts of approaching, communicating, questioning, assisting, and establishing trust with members of culturally diverse groups require special knowledge and skills that have nothing to do with the fact that "the law is the law" and must be enforced equally. Acquiring knowledge and skills that lead to sensitivity does not imply preferential treatment of any one group; rather, it contributes to improved communication with members of all groups.

Individuals must seek a balance between, on the one hand, downplaying and even denying the differences of others, and, on the other hand, distorting the role of culture, race, and ethnicity. In an effort to simply "respect all humans equally," we may inadvertently diminish the influence of culture or ethnicity, including the role it has played historically in our society.

The Melting Pot Myth and the Mosaic

Multiculturalism, also referred to as cultural pluralism, violates what some consider to be the "American way of life." However, from the time our country was founded, we were never a homogeneous society. The indigenous peoples of America (the ancestors of the American Indians) were here long before Christopher Columbus "discovered" them. There is even strong evidence that the first Africans who set foot in this country came as free people, 200 years before the slave trade from Africa began (Rawlins, 1992). Furthermore, the majority of people in America can claim to be the children, grandchildren, or great-grandchildren of people who have migrated here. Americans did not originate from a common stock. Until fairly recently, America has been referred to as a melting pot, a term depicting an image of people coming together and forming a unified culture. One of the earliest usages of the term was in the early 1900s, when a famous American playwright, Israel Zangwill, referring to the mass migration from Europe, said, "America is God's crucible, the great Melting-Pot where all the races of Europe are melting and re-forming. . . . Germans and Frenchmen, Irishmen and Englishmen, Jews and Russians—into the Crucible with you all! God is making the American!" (Zangwill, 1908).

This first use of the term melting pot was not designed to incorporate anyone except Europeans. Did the melting pot ever exist, then, in the United States? No, it never did. Yet people still refer to the belief, which is not much more than a romantic myth about the "good old days." African Americans, brought forcibly to this country between 1619 and 1850, were never part of the early descriptions of the melting pot. Likewise, Native American peoples were not considered for the melting pot. It is not coincidental that these groups were nonwhite and were therefore not "meltable." Furthermore, throughout our past, great efforts have been made to prevent any additional diversity. Most notable in this regard was the Chinese Exclusion Act in 1882, which denied Chinese laborers the right to enter America. Early in the 20th century organized labor formed the Japanese and Korean Exclusion League "to protest the influx of

'Coolie' labor and in fear of threat to the living standards of American workingmen"
(Kennedy, 1986, p. 72). Immigration was discouraged or prevented if it did not add
strength to what already existed as the European-descended majority of the population
(Handlin, 1975).

Even at the peak of immigration (late 1800s), New York City exemplified how different immigrant groups stayed separate from each other, with little of the "blending"
that people often imagine took place (Miller, 2003). Three-fourths of New York City's
population consisted of first- or second-generation immigrants (including Europeans
and Asians); 80 percent did not speak English, and there were 100 foreign-language
newspapers in circulation. The new arrivals were not accepted by those who had already settled, and newcomers found comfort in an alien society by choosing to remain
in ethnic enclaves with people who shared their culture and life experiences.

The first generation of every immigrant and refugee group seeing the United
States as the land of hope and opportunity has always experienced obstacles in acculturation (i.e., integration) into the new society. In many cases, people resisted Americanization and kept to themselves. Italians, the Irish, eastern European Jews, the
Portuguese, Germans, and virtually all other groups tended to remain apart when they
first came. Most previously settled immigrants were distrustful and disdainful of each
newcomer group. "Mainstreaming" began to occur only with children of immigrants
(although some people within certain immigrant groups tried to assimilate quickly).
For the most part, however, society did not permit a quick shedding of previous cultural identity. History has never supported the metaphor of the melting pot, especially
with regard to the first and second generations of most groups of newcomers. Despite
the reality of past multicultural disharmony and tension in the United States, however,
the notion of the melting pot prevailed.

The terms mosaic and tapestry more accurately and idealistically portray a view of
diversity in America. They describe a society in which all colors and backgrounds contribute their parts to form society as a whole, but one in which groups are not required
to lose their characteristics in order to "melt" together. The idea of a mosaic portrays a
society in which all races and ethnic groups are displayed in a form that is attractive
because of the very elements of which it is made. Each group is seen as separate and
distinct in contributing its own color, shape, and design to the whole, resulting in an
enriched society.

Reactions to Diversity: Past and Present

Accepting diversity has always been a difficult proposition for most Americans (Miller,
2003). Typical criticisms of immigrants, now and historically, include "They hold on to
their cultures," "They don't learn our language," "Their customs and behavior are
strange," and "They form cliques." Many newcomers, in fact, have historically resisted
Americanization, keeping to ethnic enclaves. They were not usually accepted by mainstream society.

Are the reactions to newcomers today so different from people's reactions to earlier waves of immigrants? Let's look at reactions to the Irish, who by the middle of the
19th century constituted the largest group of immigrants in the United States, making

up almost 45 percent of the foreign-born population. Approximately 4.25 million people left Ireland, mainly because of the potato famine. Many of these immigrants had come from rural areas but ended up in cities on the East Coast. Most were illiterate; some spoke only Gaelic (Kennedy, 1986). Their reception in America was anything but welcoming, exemplified by the plethora of signs saying, "Jobs available, no Irish need apply," which could be seen frequently.

> The Irish . . . endure[d] the scorn and discrimination later to be inflicted, to some degree at least, on each successive wave of immigrants by already settled "Americans." In speech and in dress, they seemed foreign; they were poor and unskilled and they were arriving in overwhelming numbers. . . . The Irish found many doors closed to them, both socially and economically. When their earnings were not enough . . . their wives and daughters obtained employment as servants. (Kennedy, 1986, p. 18)

If this account were rewritten without specific references to time and cultural group, it would be reasonable to assume it describes contemporary reactions to newcomers. One could take this quotation and substitute Jew, Italian, or Polish at various points in history. Today, it could be used in reference to Cubans, Somalis, Afghans, Mexicans, Haitians, Serbs, or Ethiopians. If we compare immigration today with that during earlier periods in U.S. history, we find similarities as well as significant differences. In the past few decades, we have received people from cultures more dramatically different than those from western Europe. For example, many of our "new Americans" from parts of Asia or Africa bring values and languages not commonly associated with or related to mainstream American values and language. Middle Easterners bring customs unknown to many U.S.-born Americans. (For cultural specifics, refer to Chapters 5 through 9.) Many refugees bring scars of political persecution or war trauma, the nature of which the majority of Americans cannot even fathom. The relatively mild experiences of those who came as voluntary migrants do not compare with the tragedies of many of the more recent refugees. True, desperate economic conditions compelled many early European immigrants to leave their countries (and thus their leaving was not entirely voluntary). However, their experiences do not parallel, for example, war-torn eastern European refugees who came to the United States in the 1990s.

Disparaging comments were once made toward the very people whose descendants would, in later years, constitute much of mainstream America. Many fourth- and fifth-generation immigrants have forgotten their history (Miller, 2003) and are intolerant of the "foreign ways" of emerging immigrant groups. Every new group seems to be met with some suspicion and, in many cases, hostility. Adjustment to a new society is and has always been a long and painful process, and the first-generation immigrant group suffers, whether Irish, Jewish, Polish, Afghani, Laotian, Filipino, or Russian. It must also be remembered that many groups did not come to the United States of their own free will but rather were victims of a political or economic system that forced them to abruptly cut their roots and escape their homelands. Although grateful for their welcome to this country, such newcomers did not want to be uprooted. Many new Americans did not have any part in the creation of events that led to the flight from their countries.

DIVERSE SOCIETY

In *One America in the 21st Century: Forging a New Future,* data showed that although racially and ethnically diverse groups have made progress with respect to the indicators used to measure the quality of life, they still face barriers to full inclusion in American life. In the area of civil rights enforcement, the Advisory Board to the President's Initiative on Race (1998) made the following recommendations:

- Strengthen civil rights enforcement
- Improve data collection on racial and ethnic discrimination
- Strengthen laws and enforcement against hate crimes

A diverse society obviously makes any law enforcement officer or manager's job more difficult. Racial tensions, cultural background, and ethnicity are bound to complicate many police procedures and encounters with citizens. It would be naive to "preach" to law enforcement officers, agents, and managers about the value of diversity when day-to-day activities are complicated by diversity. But the longer it takes to understand the influences of culture and ethnicity on behavior, the longer every police procedure and encounter between the police and the multicultural public will remain complicated. At a minimum, there must be a basic acceptance of diversity on the part of all criminal justice representatives as a precursor to improving interpersonal relations and contact across cultural, ethnic, and racial lines.

The Overlap of Race, Culture, and Ethnicity

Before entering into a discussion of demographics of various minority and immigrant groups, we must mention how, in this 21st century, demographic estimates and projections are likely to fall short of counting the true mix of people in the United States. In the culture-specific chapters (i.e., Chapters 5–9) of this book, we discuss characteristics and law enforcement–related issues of Asian and Pacific Americans, African Americans, Latino and Hispanic Americans, Arab Americans and other Middle Eastern groups, and Native Americans. This categorization is merely for the sake of convenience; an individual may belong to two or more groups. For example, a black Latino, such as a person from the Dominican Republic or Brazil, may identify him- or herself as both black and Latino. Race and ethnic background (e.g., in the case of a black Latino) are not necessarily mutually exclusive. Hispanic is considered an ethnicity, not a race. Therefore, people of Latino descent can count themselves as part of any race. An individual who in the 1990 census counted himself or herself as black and now chooses both black and white is considered one person with two races in the 2000 census ("Multiracial Data in Census," 2000).

Law enforcement officials need to be aware of the overlap between race and ethnicity and that many individuals consider themselves to be multiracial. "Everyday, in every corner of America, we are redrawing the color lines and are redefining what race really means. It's not just a matter of black and white anymore; the nuances of brown and yellow and red mean more—and less than ever" ("Redefining Race in America," 2000, p. 38).

The United States, a heterogeneous society, is an amalgam of races, cultures, and ethnic groups and is commonplace. The first photo in the *Newsweek* article, "Redefining Race in America," shows a child whose ethnicity is Nigerian, Irish, African American, Native American, Russian Jewish, and Polish Jewish (from parents and grandparents). Her U.S. census category may be simply "other." When we interpret population statistics, we have to understand that the face of America is changing. In 1860 there were only three census categories: black, white, and quadroon (a person who has one black grandparent, or the child of a mulatto and a white). In the 2000 census, there were 63 possible options for marking racial identity, or twice that if people responded to whether or not they were of Hispanic ethnicity. The 2000 Census Director, Kenneth Prewitt, wrote the concept of classification by race is human-made, and endlessly complex.

> What is extraordinary is that the nation moved suddenly, and with only minimal public understanding of the consequences, from a limited and relatively closed racial taxonomy to one that has no limits. In the future, racial categories will no doubt become more numerous. And why not? What grounds does the government have to declare "enough is enough?" When there were only three or even four or five categories, maybe "enough is enough" was plausible. But how can we decide, as a nation, that what we allow for on the census form of today—63 racial groups or 126 racial/ethnic ones—is the "right" number? It can't be, nor can any other number be 'right.' There is no political or scientifically defensible limit. (Prewitt, 2001)

Changing Population

Changes in population characteristics between 1990 and 2000 have been dramatic. Exhibits 1.1 and 1.2 graphically present the relative sizes of various ethnic populations. According to population projections, by 2050, the non-Hispanic white population will

	1990	*2000*	*DIFFERENCE*	*PERCENT DIFFERENCE*
Hispanic Origin	22.4	35.3	13	58%
White, non-Hispanic	188.1	194.6	6.4	3.40%
Black, non-Hispanic	29.2	34	4.7	16.20%
Asian	6.6	10.1	3.5	52.40%
American Indian and Alaska Native	1.8	2.1	0.3	15.30%
Native Hawaiian and Other Pacific Islander	0.3	0.3	0	8.50%
Other Race	0.3	0.5	0.2	87.80%
Total	248.7	281.4	32.7	13.20%

Exhibit 1.1   Difference in Population by Race and Hispanic Origin: 1990 to 2000 (rounded to the nearest hundred thousand).
Source: U.S. Census Bureau, 2001
Notes: The 2000 data does not include persons who described themselves as being of more than one of the above racial categories, as the 1990 data did not include this option.

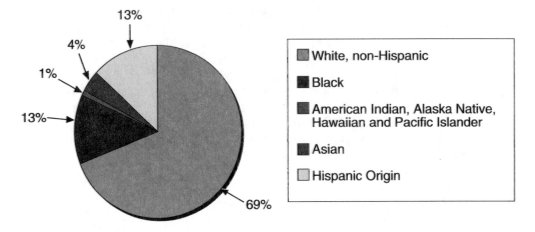

Exhibit 1.2   Resident Population by Race and Hispanic Origin: 2000.
Source: U.S. Census Bureau, Statistical Abstract of the United States: 2002.

decline to 53 percent from 70 percent in 2000. In 2050, 25 percent of the population will be of Hispanic origin, 15 percent will be black, 9 percent Asian and Pacific Islander, and 1 percent American Indian, Eskimo, and Aleut. The non-Hispanic white population will be the slowest-growing race group (see Exhibit 1.3). This demographic shift has already occurred in some large cities across the country and in a number of areas in California, where the minority has become the majority. This change has had a huge impact on many institutions in society, not the least of which is law enforcement.

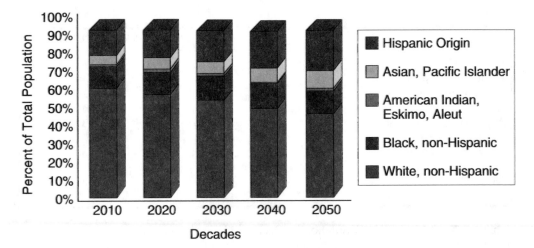

Exhibit 1.3   Resident Population by Race and Hispanic Origin Status—Projections: 2010 to 2050.
Source: U.S. Statistical Abstract of the United States: 2002.

Immigrants

Immigration is not a new phenomenon in the United States. Virtually every citizen, except for indigenous peoples of America, can claim to be a descendent of someone who migrated (whether voluntarily or not) from another country. Immigration levels per decade reached their highest absolute numbers ever at the end of the last century, when the number of immigrants surpassed 9 million from 1991–2000 (see Exhibit 1.4). In addition, immigrants from 1980 to the present have come from many more parts of the world than those who arrived at the turn of the 20th century (Exhibit 1.5). The U.S. Census Bureau reported in March 2002 that approximately 32.5 million U.S. residents (11.5 percent of the population) had been born in other countries.

Among the foreign born in 2002, 52.2 percent were from Latin America, 25.5 percent from Asia, 14.0 percent from Europe, and the remaining 8.3 percent from other regions of the world. The foreign-born population from Central America, including Mexico, made up more than two-thirds of the foreign born from Latin America and more than one-third of the total foreign born (see Exhibit 1.5). In terms of geographic distribution within the country, 11 percent of the foreign-born population lived in the

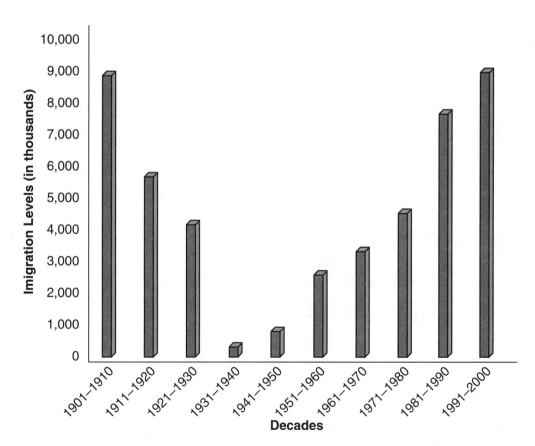

Exhibit 1.4 Immigration to America in the 20th Century.
Source: U.S. Census Bureau, Statistical Abstract of the United States: 2002.

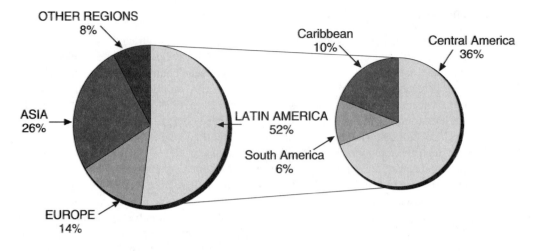

Exhibit 1.5   Emigration to America by World Region, 2002.
Source: U.S. Census Bureau, Current Population Reports, February 2003: "The Foreign Born Population in the United States: March 2002."

Midwest, 23 percent lived in the Northeast, 28 percent in the South, and 38 percent in the West (see Exhibit 1.6) (U.S. Census, 2002).

Even though most Americans, with the exception of the indigenous peoples, have been immigrants at some time in their lineage, anti-immigrant sentiment is common. Especially in a time of recession, many people perceive that immigrants are taking jobs away from "real Americans" (forgetting that legal immigrants are also "real" Americans). However, the issues surrounding immigration are not as clear-cut as they may at first appear. Despite the problems that are inevitably created when large groups of people have to be absorbed into a society, some immigrant groups stimulate the economy, revitalize neighborhoods, and eventually become fully participatory and loyal Ameri-

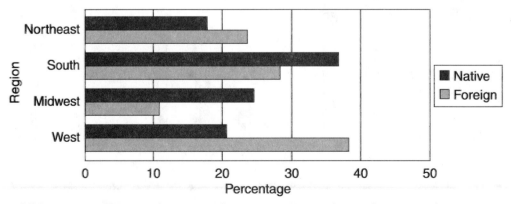

Exhibit 1.6   Distribution of Native and Foreign-Born Populations by Regional Percentages of Each Population.
Source: U.S. Census Bureau, Current Population Reports, February 2003: "The Foreign Born Population in the United States: March 2002."

can citizens. Nevertheless, if an officer has an anti-immigrant bias, negative attitudes may surface when that officer interacts with immigrants, especially under stressful circumstances. When officers are under pressure, negative attitudes become apparent and their communication may become unprofessional. Indeed, some citizens have claimed that officers with whom they have been in contact do not attempt to understand them or demonstrate little patience in communicating or finding a translator. (See Chapter 4 for a discussion of communication issues and law enforcement.)

In addition, officers must be aware of "racial flash points" that are created when immigrants move into economically depressed areas with large and diverse populations. Some people feel that immigrants' moving into certain urban areas displaces economically disadvantaged groups or deprives them of access to work. (It is beyond the scope of this chapter to discuss the validity, or lack thereof, of this sentiment.) Thus law enforcement representatives may see hostility between, for example, blacks and Korean or Arab immigrants in such cities as Los Angeles, New York, and Detroit. Although officers cannot be expected to solve these deep-seated problems, they may find themselves in situations in which they can serve as cultural mediators, helping each group to increase understanding and toleration of the other. For example, police can point out that the absence of a Korean grocer's smile or greeting of a customer is not necessarily a sign of hostility, but rather a cultural trait. (The behavior may also be an expression of distrust, but that is not always the case.) When a person complains that an Arab liquor store owner does not hire outside his or her community, officers can explain that it is usually because the business is a small, family-run operation in which employees are family members. Of course, not all problems are cultural, but with an understanding of immigrants' backgrounds, officers can help explain points of tension to members of other ethnic groups.

Furthermore, some behaviors may be common to more than one immigrant population, yet unfamiliar to officers working with these groups. As part of his community policing outreach, Sergeant Aaron T. Olson, a patrol supervisor with the Oregon State Police, established an ongoing police outreach to Portland area immigrants. The organization, called IRCO (Immigrant Refugee Community Organization), sponsors classes in which Sergeant Olson orients new immigrants and refugees on interaction with American police, and on how to use 911. What Sergeant Olson has learned directly from the immigrant community, he shares with the police officers he supervises and with other police departments. In addition, as a criminal justice instructor and multicultural trainer in a public safety academy, he has the opportunity to provide this invaluable information to college students and to new police and corrections officers. He teaches, for example, that:

> In the U.S., most police departments don't want the driver or passengers to exit their car and walk back to the police car. In other countries, like Cuba, Japan, Mexico, and Russia, it is expected that motorists exit their car and walk back to the police officer. I have learned this from translators and immigrants who have shared this from these outreach workshops. As a result of learning this information, I make it a practice to inform police officers of this specific behavior in the classes I teach at the public safety academy. (Olson, 2003)

The more direct contact officers have in ethnic and immigrant communities, the more knowledge they will gain about cultural differences that may have an impact on law enforcement.

Undocumented Immigrants

There are two major groups of undocumented immigrants: those who cross U.S. borders without having been "inspected" and those who enter the country with legal documents as temporary residents but have violated their legal admission status by extending their stay. Initially, Mexicans and other Latin Americans come to most people's minds when they hear the terms illegal alien and undocumented worker. Additionally, however, people from the Dominican Republic enter through Puerto Rico; since Puerto Ricans are U.S. citizens, they are considered legal. Therefore, officers may be in contact with "Puerto Ricans" who are actually from the Dominican Republic and have therefore come to the United States under an illegal pretext. (There is also the smuggling of Asians into the United States, and this includes women brought in for the sex trade.) People from other parts of the world may come to the United States on a tourist visa and then decide to remain permanently (e.g., Canadians).

Some undocumented "aliens" come to the United States hoping to remain legally by proving that they escaped their homeland because of political repression, claiming that if they were to return, they would face persecution or death (i.e., they are seeking asylum). People who are often deported as undocumented arrivals are those who come as "economic refugees" (i.e., their economic status in their home country may be desperate). Undocumented aliens generally have few occupational skills and are willing to take menial jobs that many American citizens will not accept. They fill economic gaps in various regions where low-wage labor is needed.

Outer appearances are not an accurate guide to who has legal status and who does not. Both illegal and legal immigrants may live in the same neighborhoods. In addition, the U.S. government has occasionally legalized significant numbers of some populations of formerly illegal immigrants, usually in recognition of special circumstances in those persons' home countries, such as large-scale natural disasters or serious political instability.

Illegal immigrants lack documents that would enable them to obtain legal residence in the United States. The societal consequences are far-reaching. Law enforcement officials, politicians, and social service providers, among others, have had to deal with many concerns related to housing, education, safety, employment, spousal violence, and health care. The illegal segment of the immigrant population poses some difficult challenges for law enforcement officials. Trojanowicz and Bucqueroux (1990) found that:

> [Illegal immigrants] pose a difficult challenge for police, because fear of deportation often makes them reluctant to report crimes committed against them—which also makes them easy prey. They can also fall victim to crimes related to their vulnerability—scams including extortion, fees for phony documentation. . . . Because so many arrive with little or no money and have difficulty making a living, undocumented aliens often cluster in low-income, high-crime areas. (p. 246)

The principal barrier to establishing trust with undocumented immigrants concerns their fears about being reported to the Immigration and Naturalization Service (INS). The argument supporting leaving illegal immigrants alone (unless they have committed a criminal act or are creating a disturbance) is based on the perspective that tracking down and deporting illegal workers is technically the job of the INS and not the police. Police department managements have to create policies related to turning in illegal immigrants to the INS. Sometimes the trust of the entire community (illegal and legal immigrants) is at stake. Donya Fernandez (2000), a language rights attorney in San Francisco, California, suggests that police departments make it known to immigrant communities when they have decided not to turn in illegal immigrants to the INS. When this is known, there may be less fear of the police when it comes to reporting crimes (Fernandez, 2000).

Undocumented Immigrants: Demographic Information

The Immigration and Naturalization Service (INS) estimated that by January 2000, there were over 7 million undocumented people living in the United States. In its 2003 report on the subject, the INS places the growth of this population at 350,000 annually. This figure is 75,000 per year higher than was estimated before the 2000 census, primarily because of improved means of counting this hard-to-track population.

In the above-noted report, California was estimated to have the highest number of unauthorized residents, with 2.2 million, 32 percent of the national total. After California, Texas, New York, Illinois, and Florida were the next four states with the largest numbers of unauthorized immigrants (see Exhibit 1.7). Mexico accounted for the

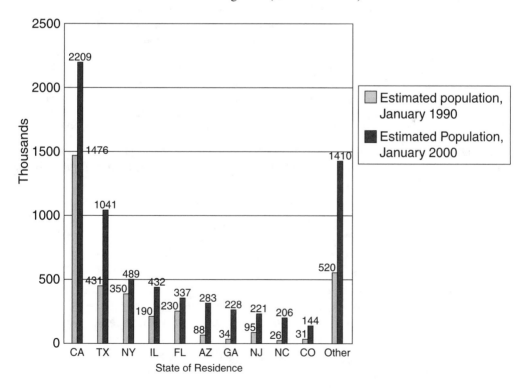

Exhibit 1.7   Estimates of the Unauthorized Immigrant Population in the Top Ten States: January 1990 to January 2002.
Source: U.S. Immigration and Naturalization Services, Office of Policy and Planning, January, 2003.

majority of them, with 4.8 million or 69 percent of the national total. Over 100,000 unauthorized persons came from El Salvador, Guatemala, Colombia, Honduras, China, and Ecuador (INS, 2003).

Immigrant Women: Victims of Domestic Violence and Fear of Deportation

In a 2003 report to a Congressional Subcommittee on Immigration, Leslye E. Orloff, director of the Immigrant Women's Program (National Organization of Women's Legal Defense and Education Fund), presented a full account of problems that continue to face battered immigrant women. Even though the frequency of domestic violence is consistent across socioeconomic classes, racial groups, and geographic areas, according to Orloff, immigrant women still face additional challenges in seeking help from their communities.

> [The] Violence Against Women Act (VAWA) passed by Congress in 1994 and improved in 2000, set out to reform the manner in which officers responded to domestic violence calls for help. Although significant improvement following the passage of VAWA has been noted, the response continues to be lacking. Some police officers' personal attitudes regarding domestic violence (i.e., it is a private problem) and how it should be handled (through mediation rather than arrest or formal charges) in essence, marginalizes victims of domestic violence. In extreme cases, victims' requests for help are disregarded. The lack of appropriate response to domestic violence from the police are further compounded when the battered woman is an immigrant. The police often do not have the capacity to communicate effectively with the immigrant victim in her own language. The police may use her abuser or her children to translate for her, and/or police may credit the statements of her citizen spouse or boyfriend over her statements to the police due to gender, race or cultural bias. (Orloff, 2000)

Jang and colleagues (1994) offer the following explanations for the high rate of domestic violence experienced by immigrant women. This appears to be as relevant now as it was when this statement was made:

1. Immigrant women may suffer higher rates of battering than U.S. citizens because they come from cultures that accept domestic violence, or because they have less access to legal and social services than U.S. citizens. In addition, immigrant batterers and victims may believe that the penalties and protections of the U.S. legal system do not apply to them.

2. A battered woman who is not a legal resident, or whose immigration status depends on her partner, is isolated by cultural dynamics that may prevent her from leaving her husband or seeking assistance from the legal system. These factors contribute to the higher incidence of abuse among immigrant women.

3. Some obstacles faced by battered immigrant women include a distrust of the legal system arising from their experiences with the system in their native countries, cultural and language barriers, and fear of deportation.

4. A battered immigrant woman may not understand that she can personally tell her story in court, or that a judge will believe her. Based on her experience in her native country, she may believe that only those who are wealthy or have

ties to the government will prevail in court. Batterers often manipulate these beliefs by convincing the victim he will prevail in court because he is a male, a citizen, or that he has more money. (p. 313)

Orloff (2003) told the house subcommittee that a survey of battered immigrant women revealed that only 27 percent of respondents were willing to call the police for help in a domestic violence incident. Specifically, concerning women who were physically and/or sexually abused versus emotionally abused, 31 percent said they called the police for help. Orloff compared these numbers to a 1998 Department of Justice survey where 53 percent of domestic violence victims said they reported the crime to police.

The phenomenon of new immigrants, women or men, legal or illegal, presents challenges to law enforcement officers working the streets. Immigrants must learn a great deal about U.S. laws, the law enforcement system in general, and the role of police officers. Many immigrants fear the police because in their native countries police engaged in arbitrary acts of brutality in support of repressive governments (e.g., in Central America). In other countries, citizens disrespect police because they are poorly educated, inefficient, and corrupt and have a very low occupational status (e.g., in Iran). The barriers immigrants bring to the relationship with police suggest that American officers have to double their efforts to communicate and to educate. A further challenge for law enforcement is that for the reasons mentioned, new immigrants often become victims of violent crimes. In part, the acculturation and success of immigrants in this society depend on how they are treated while they are still ignorant of the social norms and laws. Those who have contact with new Americans will need extraordinary patience at times. Adaptation to a new country can be a long and arduous process.

INTERPLAY BETWEEN POLICE INCIDENTS AND CULTURE

With community changes have come shifts in the concerns of law enforcement and criminal justice, as well as the nature of some crime and reactions to police tactics. Without knowledge of citizens' cultural and national backgrounds, law enforcement officers in today's society are likely to experience baffling incidents and to observe citizens' surprising reactions to police tactics.

Expert in cultural diversity and the law, Alison Renteln (a University of Southern California political science professor), was cited in the following case, in an article entitled "Cultural Sensitivity on the Beat" from the *Los Angeles Times*.

The City of Spokane, Washington, paid a Gypsy family $1.43 million in 1997 to settle a civil rights suit over an illegal police search. The most controversial element of the case was the body search of the 13 family members, male and female, including a number of people who were not targets of the investigation. The family claimed that the unmarried girls who were searched were now considered defiled and unclean in the Gypsy culture. As a result, they could never marry another Gypsy. In fact, the entire household was considered contaminated, a family patriarch testified, and was soon after ostracized and unwelcome at weddings and funerals. (Los p. A12)

A Danish woman was jailed in 1997 for leaving her baby in a stroller outside a Manhattan restaurant—a case that focused international attention on New York City Police Tactics. . . . The woman and the baby's father were charged with endangering a child and were jailed for two nights. The

14-month-old baby girl was placed in foster care for four days before she was returned to her mother. The incident precipitated a war of words between Danish newspapers and city administrators. Copenhagen columnists called New York police "Rambo cops." Pictures wired from Denmark showed numerous strollers [with babies] parked outside cafes in view of their parents. (p. A12)

An understanding of accepted social practices and cultural traditions in citizens' countries of origin can provide officers with the insight needed to understand and even predict some of the reactions and difficulties new immigrants will have in America. However, some customs are simply unacceptable in the United States, and arrests must be made in spite of the cultural background. Regardless of the circumstances, immigrant suspects need to be treated with respect; officers and all others in the criminal justice system must understand the innocent state of mind the citizen was in when committing the "crime." For example, female circumcision is illegal under all circumstances in the United States but is still practiced in certain African countries. The Hmong, mountain people of Southeast Asia, and particularly Laos, have a tradition considered to be an acceptable form of eloping. "Marriage by capture" translates into kidnap and rape in the United States. This Hmong tradition allows a male to capture and take away a female for marriage; even if she resists, he is allowed to take her to his home, and it is mandated that he consummate the union. Perpetrators of such crimes in the United States must be arrested.

In interviews with a deputy public defender and a deputy district attorney, a legal journal posed the following question: Should our legal system recognize a "cultural" defense when it comes to crimes? The deputy district attorney's response was, "No. You're treading on shaky ground when you decide something based on culture, because our society is made up of so many different cultures. It is very hard to draw the line somewhere, but [diverse cultural groups] are living in our country, and people have to abide by [one set of] laws or else you have anarchy." The deputy public defender's response to the question was: "Yes. I'm not asking that the [various cultural groups] be judged differently, just that their actions be understood according to their own history and culture" (Sherman, 1986, p. 33).

If law enforcement's function is to protect and serve citizens from all cultural backgrounds, it becomes vital to understand the cultural dimensions of crimes. Obviously, behaviors or actions that may be excused in another culture must not go unpunished if they are considered crimes in this country (e.g., spouse abuse). Nevertheless, there are circumstances in which law enforcement officials at all levels of the criminal justice system would benefit by understanding the cultural context in which a crime or other incident occurred. Law enforcement professionals must use standard operating procedures in response to specific situations, and the majority of these procedures cannot be altered for different groups based on ethnicity. In a multicultural society, however, an officer can modify the way he or she treats a suspect, witness, or victim given knowledge of what is considered "normal" in that person's culture. When officers suspect that an aspect of cultural background is a factor in a particular incident, they may earn the respect of—and therefore, cooperation from—ethnic communities if they are willing to evaluate their arrests in lesser crimes. (See the section "Police Knowledge of Cultural Groups" later in this chapter.)

Many officers say that their job is to uphold the law, but it is not up to them to make judgments. Yet discretion, to not take a citizen into custody, in lesser crimes may be appropriate. When officers understand the cultural context for a crime, the crime will and should be perceived somewhat differently. Consider the Sikh religion (a strict religious tradition followed by a minority of people from northern India), which requires that its followers wear a ceremonial dagger, a sacred symbol, at all times, even during sleep. Consider Pacific Islanders having barbecues in their garages, where they roast whole pigs. And consider a Vietnamese family who eats dog. When officers understand the cultural context within which a "crime" takes place, then it is much easier to understand a citizen's intent. Understanding the cultural dimensions of a crime may result, for example, in not taking a citizen into custody. With lesser crimes, this may be the appropriate course of action and can result in the preservation of good police–community relations. Before looking at specific case studies of incidents and crimes involving cultural components, we present the concept of culture and its tremendous impact on the individual.

All people (except for very young children) carry "cultural do's and don't's," which some might also refer to as "cultural baggage." The degree of this "baggage" is determined by their own conscious and unconscious identification with their group and their relative attachment to their cultural group's traditional values. Being influenced by cultural baggage is a natural human phenomenon. Much of who we are is sanctioned and reinforced by the society in which we have been raised. According to some experts, culture has a far greater influence on people's behavior than any other variable such as age, gender, race, and socioeconomic status (Hall, 1959), and often this influence is unconscious. It is virtually impossible to lose one's culture completely when interacting in a new environment, yet change will inevitably take place.

The Definition of Culture

Although there are many facets of culture, the term is defined as beliefs, values, patterns of thinking, behavior, and everyday customs that have been passed on from generation to generation. Culture is learned rather than inherited and is manifested in largely unconscious and subtle behavior. With this definition in mind, consider that most children have acquired a general cultural orientation by the time they are 5 or 6 years old. For this reason, it is difficult to change behavior to accommodate a new culture. Many layers of cultural behavior and beliefs are subconscious. Additionally, many people assume that what they take for granted is taken for granted by all people ("all human beings are the same"), and they do not even recognize their own culturally influenced behavior. Anthropologist Edward T. Hall (1959) said, "Culture hides much more than it reveals and, strangely enough, what it hides, it hides most effectively from its own participants." In other words, people are blind to their own deeply embedded cultural behavior.

To further understand the hidden nature of culture, picture an iceberg (Ruhly, 1976). The only visible part of the iceberg is the tip, which typically constitutes only about 10 percent of the mass. Like most of culture's influences, the remainder of the iceberg is submerged beneath the surface. What this means for law enforcement is that there will be a natural tendency to interpret behavior, motivations, and criminal activity from the officer's cultural point of view. This tendency is due largely to an inability to understand behavior from alternative perspectives and because of the inclination toward ethnocentrism (i.e., an attitude of seeing and judging all other cultures from the perspective of one's own culture). In other words, an ethnocentric person would say that there is only one way of being "normal" and that is the way of his or her own culture. When it comes to law enforcement, there is only one set of laws to which all citizens must adhere, whether native-born or not. However, the following case studies will illustrate that culture does affect interpretations, meaning, and intention.

MINI CASE STUDIES: CULTURE AND CRIME

The following mini case studies involve descriptions of crimes or offenses with a cultural component. If the crime is a murder or something similarly heinous, most people will not be particularly sympathetic, even with an understanding of the cultural factors involved. However, consider that understanding other cultural patterns gives one the ability to see and react in a different way. The ability to withhold judgment and to interpret a person's intention from a different cultural perspective is a skill that will ultimately enable a person to identify his or her own cultural blinders. Each case study describes an increasingly serious crime—from driving under the influence to child abuse to murder.

Mini Case Study 1: Driving under the Influence?

The following case, among others, was the subject of discussion in an officers' course in ethnic understanding in a San Francisco Bay Area police department ("Officers Being Trained," 2000).

> A Tongan man living in [the Bay Area] was arrested on Highway 101 on the Peninsula in August 1999 for driving under the influence of kava, a relaxing elixir popular with Pacific Islanders. But a hung jury effectively acquitted [this man] in October. The jury determined, in part, that police didn't fully understand the effect and the importance of the drink. Tongans, Samoans, and Fijians say the kava ritual is an integral part of life, a way to share information and reinforce traditions. And they say it doesn't affect their ability to drive any more than soda pop.

Mini Case Study 2: A Tragic Case of Cross-Cultural Misinterpretation*

In parts of Asia, there are medical practices unfamiliar to many law enforcement officials (as well as medical practitioners) in the West. A number of these practices result in marks on the skin that can easily be misinterpreted as abuse by people who have no knowledge of these culturally based medical treatments. The practices include rubbing the skin with a coin ("coining," "coin rubbing," or "wind rubbing"), pinching the skin, touching the skin with burning incense, or applying a

---

*Chapter 5, "Law Enforcement Contact with Asian/Pacific Americans," includes several other examples regarding the involvement of police and child protective services and coining cases. Please note that, regarding the case above ("A Tragic Case of Cross-Cultural Misinterpretation"), we have no further facts about the case regarding what the police officers knew.

heated cup to the skin ("cupping"). Each practice leaves highly visible marks, such as bruises and even burns. The following is an account of a serious misreading of some very common Southeast Asian methods of traditional folk healing on the part of U.S. school authorities and law enforcement officials.

> A young Vietnamese boy had been absent from school for a few days with a serious respiratory infection. His father, believing that "coining" would help cure him, rubbed heated coins on specific sections of his back and neck. The boy's condition seemed to improve and he was able to return to school. Upon noticing heavy bruising on the boy's neck, the teacher immediately informed the school principal, who promptly reported the "abuse" to the police (who then notified Child Protective Services). When the police were notified, they went to the child's home to investigate. The father was very cooperative when questioned by the police and admitted, in broken English, that he had caused the bruising on his son's neck. The man was arrested and incarcerated. While the father was in jail, his son, who was under someone else's custody, apparently relapsed and died of his original illness. Upon hearing the news, the father committed suicide in his jail cell. Of course, it is not known whether the father would have committed suicide as a response to his son's death alone. The tragic misinterpretation on the part of the authorities involved, including the teacher, the principal, and the arresting police officers, provides an extreme case of what can happen when people attribute meaning from their own cultural perspective.
>
> Cultural understanding would not have cured the young boy, but informed interaction with the father could have prevented the second tragedy. All of the authorities were interpreting what they saw with "cultural filters" based on their own belief systems. Ironically, the interpretation of the bruises (i.e., child abuse) was almost the opposite of the intended meaning of the act (i.e., healing). Even after some of the parties involved learned about this very common Southeast Asian practice, they still did not accept that it existed as an established practice and they could not fathom how others could believe that "coining" might actually cure illness. Their own conception of medical healing did not encompass what they perceived as such "primitive treatment."
>
> Ethnocentrism is a barrier to accepting that there is another way, another belief, another communication style, another custom, or another value that can lead to culturally different behavior. Ethnocentrism often causes a person to assign a potentially incorrect meaning or attribute an incorrect motivation to a given act. Consider how the outcome could have differed if only one person in the chain of authorities had viewed the bruises as something other than abuse. The tragic outcome of serious cultural misunderstandings might have been averted. (personal communication with social worker, 1992, who wishes to remain anonymous)

Mini Case Study 3: Latino Values as a Factor in Sentencing

In a court of law, a cultural explanation or rationalization (i.e., a cultural defense) rarely affects a guilty or not-guilty verdict. Nevertheless, culture may affect sentencing. Consider the following case, in which, according to Judge Lawrence Katz, cultural considerations lessened the severity of the sentence.

A Mexican woman living in the United States became involved in an extramarital affair. Her husband became outraged when the wife bragged about her extramarital activities at a picnic at which many extended family members were present. At the same time, the wife also made comments about her husband's lack of ability to satisfy her and how, in comparison, her lover was far superior. Upon hearing his wife gloat about her affair, the husband left the picnic and drove 5 miles to purchase a gun. Two hours later, he shot and killed his wife. In a case such as this, the minimum charge required in California would be second-degree murder. However, because the jury took into consideration the cultural background of this couple, the husband received a mitigated sentence and was found guilty of manslaughter. It was argued that his wife's boasting about her lover and her explicit comments made specifically to emasculate him created a passion and emotion that completely undermined his machismo, masculine pride, and honor. To understand the severity of her offense, the law enforcement officer and the prosecutor had to understand what it means to be humiliated in such a manner in front of one's family, in the context of Latino culture. (Katz, 2003)

The purpose of these three mini case studies is not to discuss the "rightness" or "wrongness" of any group's values, customs, or beliefs but to illustrate that the point of contact between law enforcement and citizens' backgrounds must not be ignored. Officers must be encouraged to consider culture when investigating and presenting evidence regarding an alleged crime or incident involving people from diverse backgrounds. This consideration does not mean that standard operating procedures should be changed, nor does it imply that heinous crimes such as murder or rape should be excused on cultural grounds. However, as a matter of course, officers need to include culture as a variable in understanding, assessing, and reporting certain kinds of incidents and crimes.

POLICE KNOWLEDGE OF CULTURAL GROUPS

Law enforcement representatives have the ultimate authority to arrest or admonish someone suspected of a crime. According to Judge Katz, "Discretion based on cultural knowledge at the police level is much more significant than what happens at the next level in the criminal justice system (i.e., the courts)." Individual police officers have the possibility of creating positive public relations if they demonstrate cultural sensitivity and respect toward members of an ethnic community. Judge Katz cited the example of police contact with the San Francisco Bay Area Samoan community, in which barbecues and parties can include a fair amount of drinking, sometimes resulting in fights. In Judge Katz's opinion,

The police, responding to neighbors' complaints, could come in with a show of force and the fighting would cool down quickly. However, word would spread that the police officers had no cultural understanding or respect for the people involved. This would widen the gap that already exists between police and many Pacific Islander and other Asian groups and would not be a way to foster trust in the Samoan community. Alternatively, the police could locate the leader, or the "chief," of this group and let that person deal with the problem in the way that he would have handled the conflict in Samoa. There is no question about the chief's ability to handle the problem. He has a prominent role to play and can serve as a bridge between the police and the community. The matai is also a resource; he is an elder who has earned the respect of the community.

The heads of Samoan communities are traditionally in full control of members' behavior, although this is changing somewhat in the United States. Furthermore, according to traditional Samoan values, if a family member assaults a member of another family, the head of the family is required to ensure punishment. Given the power entrusted to the chiefs, it is reasonable to encourage officers first to go through the community and elicit assistance in solving enforcement problems. This recommendation does not imply, in any way, that groups should be left to police themselves; instead, understanding and working with the leadership of a community represents a spirit of partnership.

The awareness of and sensitivity to such issues can have a significant impact on the criminal justice system, in which police have the power to either inflame or calm the people involved in a particular incident. According to Judge Katz, "Many cases, especially those involving lesser offenses, can stay out of court." He asks, "Do you always need a show of force? Or can you counsel and admonish instead?" In certain types of situations, such as the one described earlier, officers can rethink traditional police methods in order to be as effective as possible. This involves knowledge of ethnic communities and a desire to establish a positive and trustworthy image in those communities (Katz, 2003).

PREJUDICE IN LAW ENFORCEMENT

The following questions were asked of police officers participating in a cultural diversity program:

"Raise your hand if you are a racist." Not a single officer raised a hand.

"Raise your hand if you think that prejudice and racism exist outside this agency." Most officers raised their hands.

The instructor then asked with humor: "Then where were you recruited from?" (Berry, 2003).

When discussing the implications of multicultural diversity for police officers, it is not enough simply to present the need to understand cultural background. Whenever two groups are from entirely different ethnic or racial backgrounds, there is the possibility that prejudice exists (because of fear, lack of contact, ignorance, and stereotypes). To deny the existence of prejudice or racism in any given law enforcement agency would be to deny that it exists outside the agency.

What Is Prejudice?

Prejudice is a judgment or opinion formed before facts are known, usually involving negative or unfavorable thoughts about groups of people. Discrimination is action based on prejudiced thought. It is not possible to force people to abandon their own prejudices in the law enforcement workplace or when working in the community. Because prejudice is thought, it is private and does not violate any law. However, because it is private, a person may not be aware when his or her judgments and decisions are based on prejudice. In law enforcement, the expression of prejudice as bias discrimination and racism is illegal and can have tragic consequences. All police must consider the implications of prejudice in their day-to-day work as it relates to equal enforcement and professionalism.

It is not uncommon to hear in diversity or cross-cultural workshops for officers sentiments such as the following: "We've already had this training (i.e., on prejudice). Why do we need to go over it again and again?" As with other training areas in law enforcement, such as self-defense and tactics, the area of prejudice needs to be reviewed on a regular basis. One only has to read the headlines periodically to see that the problem of prejudice and racism in law enforcement is not yet solved. For example, in November 2000, the New York Times reported that racial profiling was routine in a large agency in the Eastern part of the U.S. It is not our intention to single out any particular department but to state directly that prejudice has not yet disappeared from law enforcement. Although police chiefs cannot mandate that their officers banish prejudicial thoughts, this subject should be dealt with seriously. While some police officers say they have every right to believe what they want, the chiefs of all departments must be able to guarantee, with as much certainty as possible, that no officer will ever act on his or her prejudices. All officers must understand where the line is between prejudice and discrimination, whether in the law enforcement agency with coworkers or with citizens. It becomes eminently clear that prejudice in the law enforcement agency must be addressed before it turns into racism and discrimination. Indeed, an agency cannot be expected to treat its multicultural population fairly if people within the agency are likely to act on their prejudiced thoughts.

HOW PREJUDICE INFLUENCES PEOPLE

Prejudice is encouraged by stereotyping, which is a shorthand way of thinking about people who are different. The stereotypes that form the basis of a person's prejudice can be so fixed that he or she easily justifies his or her racism, sexism, or other bias and even makes such claims as, "I'm not prejudiced, but let me tell you about those __ I had to deal with today." Coffey et al. (1982) discuss the relationship between selective memory and prejudice:

A prejudiced person will almost certainly claim to have sufficient cause for his or her views, telling of bitter experiences with refugees, Koreans, Catholics, Jews, Blacks, Mexicans and Puerto Ricans, or If you are normal, you have cultural blind spots which will give you an unbalanced view of people who are different from you. Officers must look at themselves first before getting into situations in which they act upon their biases (Berry, 2003).

Police prejudice received a great deal of attention in the latter half of the 1990s—so much so that it was addressed as a topic of concern in the President's Initiative on Race:

Racial disparities and prejudices affect the way in which minorities are treated by the criminal system. Examples of this phenomenon can be found in the use of racial profiling in law enforcement and in the differences in the rates of arrest, conviction, and sentencing between whites and minorities and people of color (Advisory Board to the President's Initiative on Race, 1998).

Law enforcement professionals have recognized, especially as they enter the 21st century, that prejudices unchecked and acted on can result in not only citizen humiliation, lawsuits, loss of jobs, and long-term damage to police–community relations but in personal tragedy as well. Sometimes, training can be successful in changing behavior and possibly attitudes. Consider the example of firing warning shots. Most officers have retrained themselves to refrain from this action because they have been mandated to do so. They have gone through a process of "unfreezing" normative behavior (i.e., what is customary) and have incorporated desired behavior. Thus explicit instruction and clear directives from the top can result in profound changes of police actions. The success of mandated change is supported by Fletcher Blanchard (1991), a social psychologist at Smith College, who conducted and published research findings on fighting acts of bigotry. His contention is that clear policies that unequivocally condemn racist acts or forms of speech will prevent most manifestations of prejudice. Asking a citizen, "What are you doing here?" just because he or she is of a different background than those of a particular neighborhood is not acceptable. Officers will listen to these specific and unambivalent directives coming from the top, even if their personal biases do not change. As Blanchard explains: "A few outspoken people (e.g., in an organization/agency) who are vigorously anti-racist can establish the kind of social climate that discourages racist acts. It may be difficult to rid an officer of his or her stereotypes, but not acting upon prejudices become[s] the mandate of the department."

Peer Relationships and Prejudice

Expressions of prejudice in police departments may go unchallenged because of the need to conform or to fit into the group. Police officers do not make themselves popular by questioning peers or challenging their attitudes. It takes a leader to voice an objection or to avoid going along with group norms. Some studies have shown that peer behavior in groups reinforces acts of racial bias. For example, when someone in a group makes ethnic slurs, others in the group may begin to express the same hostile attitudes more freely. This behavior is particularly relevant in law enforcement agencies given the nature of the police subculture and the strong influence of peer pressure. Thus law enforcement leaders must not be ambiguous when directing their subordinates to control their expressions of prejudice, even among peers. Furthermore, according to some social scientists, the strong condemnation of any manifestations of prejudice can at times affect a person's feelings: Using pressure from authorities or peers to keep people who are prejudiced from acting on those biases can, in the long run, weaken the prejudice itself, especially if the prejudice is not virulent. People conform; that is, people will behave differently, even if they still hold the same prejudicial thoughts. Even if they are still prejudiced, they will be reticent to show it. National authorities have become much more vocal about dealing directly with racism and prejudice in law enforcement as an institution, especially in light of the quantity of allegations of racial profiling in police departments across the country.

A process of socialization takes place when change has been mandated by top management and a person is forced to adopt a new standard of behavior. When a mistake is made and the expression of prejudice occurs, a police department will pay the price (in adverse media attention, lawsuits, citizen complaints, human relations commissions involvement, or dismissal of the chief or other management). Government officials' public expressions are subject to a great deal of scrutiny. Alison Berry-Wilkinson, a lawyer and expert on harassment issues, cited the case of a prosecutor who was publicly reprimanded for a hallway comment to another lawyer during a murder trial: "I don't believe either of those chili-eating bastards." The court stated: "Lawyers, especially . . . public officials, [must] avoid statements as well as deeds . . . indicating that their actions are motivated to any extent by racial prejudice" (*People v. Sharpe,* 789 p.2d 659 [1989], Colorado, in Berry-Wilkinson, 1993, p. 2d). Berry-Wilkinson's concluding statement following the reporting of this case reads: "What once may have been acceptable is now definitely not and may bring discipline and monetary sanctions. While public employees may be free to think whatever they like, they are not free to say whatever they think. A public employee's right to free speech is not absolute" (p. 2d).

When officers in a police department are not in control of their prejudices (in either their speech or in their behavior), the negative publicity affects the reputation of all police officers (by reinforcing the popular stereotype that police are racists or bigots). Yet because of publicized instances of discrimination, officers become increasingly aware of correct and incorrect behavior toward ethnic minorities.

Beginning in 1990, a California police department was besieged by the press and outraged citizens for over 2 years because six police officers had exchanged racist messages on their patrol car computers, using the word *nigger* and making references to the Ku Klux Klan. The citizens of the town in which the incident took place ended up conducting an investigation of the department to assess the degree of racism in the institution. In their report, the committee members wrote that the disclosure of the racial slurs was "an embarrassment and a crushing blow" to the image and credibility of the city and police department. In addition, citizens demanded the chief's resignation. In a cultural diversity workshop (April 13, 1993) some of the officers said they believed that the entire incident was overblown and that there was no "victim." These officers failed to understand that the use of derogatory terms alone is offensive to citizens. Officers who do not grasp the seriousness of the matter may not realize that citizens feel unprotected knowing that those entrusted with their safety and protection are capable of using such hateful language. While the language is offensive, the problem is more with the attitudes it conveys. Such incidents are extremely costly from all points of view; it may take years for a department to recover from one incident connected to an officer's prejudice or racism.

Officers need to be aware that anything they say or do with citizens of different backgrounds that even hints at prejudice automatically creates the potential for an explosive reaction. Here the experience of the minority and the nonminority do not even begin to approach each other. An officer can make an unguarded casual remark and not realize it is offensive. For example, an officer can offend a group member by saying "You people" (accentuating a we–they division) or by implying that if a member of a minority group does not fit a stereotype, he or she is exceptional (e.g., "She's Hispanic, but she works hard" or "He's African American, but very responsible").

Members of culturally diverse groups are up against the weight of history and tradition in law enforcement. Ethnic groups have not traditionally been represented in police work (especially in top management), nor have citizens of some ethnic groups had reasons to trust the police. The prejudice that might linger among officers must be bat-tled constantly if they are to increase trust with ethnic communities. The perception of many ethnic group members is that police will treat them more roughly, question them unnecessarily, and arrest them more often than they arrest whites. Awareness of this perception is not enough, though. The next step is to try harder with ethnic groups to overcome these barriers. African American psychiatrist Wendell Lipscomb (1993), who himself experienced biased treatment from officers in his younger years, advises officers to go out of their way to show extra respect to those citizens who least expect it. He suggests "disarming" the citizen who has traditionally been the object of police prejudice and who expects rude or uncivil behavior from the officer (Lipscomb, 1993).

Beyond eliminating the prejudice manifested in speech, police management can teach officers how to reduce or eliminate acts of bias and discrimination. A large met-ropolitan police department hired several human relations consultants to help assess community–police problems. The chief insisted that they ride in a police car for four weekends so that they would "appreciate the problems of law officers working in the black ghetto." Every Friday through Sunday night, the consultants rode along with the highway patrol, a unit other officers designated as the "Gestapo police." When the month ended and the chief asked what the consultants had learned, they replied, "If we were black, we would hate the police." The chief, somewhat bewildered, asked why. "Because we have personally witnessed black citizens experiencing a series of unjust, unwarranted intimidations, searches, and series of harassments by unprofessional po-lice." Fortunately, that chief, to his credit, accepted the feedback and introduced a suc-cessful course in human relations skills. After this training, the officers demonstrated greater professionalism in their interactions with members of the black community.

When it comes to expressions of prejudice, people are not powerless. No one has to accept sweeping stereotypes (e.g., "You can't trust an Indian," "All whites are racists," "Chinese are shifty," and so on). To eliminate manifestations of prejudice, people have to begin to interrupt biased and discriminatory behavior at all levels. Offi-cers have to be willing to remind their peers that ethnic slurs and offensive language, as well as differential treatment of certain groups of people, is neither ethical nor profes-sional. Officers need to change the aspect of police culture that discourages speaking out against acts or speech motivated by prejudice. An officer or civilian employee who does nothing in the presence of racist or other discriminatory behavior by his or her peers becomes a silent accomplice. Law enforcement organizations across the country have used community-based policing to help overcome cultural barriers between offi-cers and the different groups with whom they come into contact.

COMMUNITY-BASED POLICING

> We need to open up dialogue with officers—we need a dialogue of critique. Let's look at what is working and what needs improvement. We need to work together to create a blueprint of cooperation. (Pastor R. Griffin, Detroit-based clergyman and African American community leader, 2003)

Today's officers are increasingly comfortable with contemporary community-based policing described as a problem-solving approach. Community-based policing enables officers to work with civilians outside the conventional channels by meeting with com-munity groups and learning of their concerns. It also allows community members to understand the "culture" of law enforcement and to help them grasp the reasons for which officers make the decisions they do. It encourages unconventional and creative ways of dealing with crime and peacekeeping at the neighborhood level, and allows for a change of image of the traditional officer. This is especially true in certain immigrant neighborhoods or ethnic conclaves where citizens have traditionally feared the police.

Community-based policing has, for the majority of local police departments around the country, become a fact of life. As of June 30, 2000, "Two-thirds of all local police departments and 62 percent of sheriffs' offices had full-time sworn personnel engaged in community policing activities. Local police departments had an estimated 102,598 full-time sworn personnel serving as community policing officers or otherwise regularly engaged in community policing activities, and sheriffs' offices had 16,545 full-time sworn so assigned" (U.S. Department of Justice, 2000).

According to Sergeant Aaron T. Olson (Oregon State Police), "If the police take the initiative to reach out into the community—it could be to a minority group, or any neighborhood—the community appreciates it, but the relationship has got to be ongoing" (Olson, 2003). The "storefront office," for example, which is not a new concept, whereby police work at a desk in an office in a neighborhood location during day or swing shifts, serves this purpose. In Sergeant Olson's experience, the officer will show up to that facility (school, business, or apartment complex) and park their patrol vehicle where it is visible to the public. Inside, the officer will complete reports, return telephone calls, or visit with the facility's staff or occupants. This way, people in the community see the police on a frequent basis. This creates more positive and personal interaction. According to Olson, this has worked quite well with such a "storefront office" at a particular elementary school. At the school, Olson and other troopers have personally provided intervention for problem students, resources for counselors, and classes to students and neighborhood organizations. According to Olson, "It's extremely productive."

Community-based policing is one of several terms that police agencies across the nation use to refer to working partnerships with communities. A few of the more commonly used terms are problem-oriented policing (POP), community policing (CP), and community-oriented policing (COP). The concept of and practices associated with community-based or community-oriented policing are central to any discussion on minority groups and immigrant populations. The legislative basis of what became known as Community Oriented Policing Services (COPS, Title 1 of the Violent Crime Control and Law Enforcement Act of 1994) listed four specific goals intended to change the level and practice of policing in the United States. The first two goals link directly to our discussion of police interaction and professionalism with community members, including those from diverse racial, cultural, ethnic, religious, and lifestyle backgrounds. These two goals are as follows (National Institute of Justice, 2000): (1) To increase the number of officers deployed in American communities and (2) To foster problem solving and interaction with communities by police officers.

A great deal of literature is available to law enforcement agencies on community-based policing. Community-based policing depends on a strong partnership with the various communities that make up a city or jurisdiction. The partnership ensures dialogue and provides the mechanism by which a police department is aware of current relevant issues in the community. The following description of a police department without a community-based approach, while dated, is a graphic example of how world events and the influx of refugees have to be monitored in a community-based partnership format.

This dramatic example involves the case of a medium-sized police department in southern California that exemplifies the problems associated with not using community-based policing. Neither the management of the department nor the city was aware that the ethnic community had been changing significantly. Only 2 years after dramatic events began to take place did patrol officers start to pay attention to the changes, most of which had occurred suddenly following the fall of Saigon in 1975. After the withdrawal of American forces from Vietnam, the United States changed its immigration policy to relocate peoples in jeopardy from Southeast Asia. Police officers were performing their "crime fighter" role, but because there was no partnership with the community, there was no reason or incentive to monitor and report the changes they were noticing. This particular community, therefore, was not prepared for the increase in racial disputes and violence on the streets and in the schools, nor was it prepared for increasing needs in government, infrastructures, and social services. Former Captain Stan Knee of the Garden Grove Police Department, in a 1987 interview, observed that officers spent five times longer answering calls involving Vietnamese citizens than those in the Anglo community because of language and cultural differences. Officer and management frustrations resulted. Community-based policing would have had a plan in place for that neighborhood transition. Why? Because the department, including all local government institutions, and the neighborhoods would have been working together closely.

Community-based policing allows for collaboration with the community. As Deputy Chief Ondra Berry (2003) says, "We don't know the community as well as the community does." (Berry, 2003) Community-based policing represents a more democratic style of policing. It allows for openness and dialogue. The police department is not cut off or insulated from the community (Skolnick, 1999). It has proven to be a contributing factor to the decrease in crime in certain areas. Deputy Chief Berry shared the following firsthand account of how the implementation of community-based policing in his community (Reno, Nevada) was the definitive factor in the decrease in gang-related activities, including homicide.

Deputy Chief Berry spoke of the alarming homicide rates in Reno, Nevada, in 1992, which included the deaths of two Hispanic children—a 13-year-old girl killed at a soccer game and a 3-year-old boy, both victims of Hispanic gang-related shootings. The dissension between the community and the police department was growing rapidly. The police department had no choice but to address the homicide rate in the community from an enforcement point of view; the community's needs were to address basic issues of survival and quality of life. Deputy Chief Berry's dedication to the community resulted in the ultimate collaborative effort in community-based policing. Berry, with the help of the ethnic communities as well as the community at large, brought together representatives from the police department (and especially the gang task units), officials from the school districts, government, and nonprofit sectors of the community, and business representatives. Together they devised a plan for combating gang activity in Reno. The community had a strong voice; the police department valued and listened to community members' input. As a result of the collaboration, the police–community partnership created the Gang Alternative Partnership Center, which includes (1) gyms open until 1:00 A.M., (2) officers helping to coach basketball teams consisting of gang members, (3) drill teams and after-school programs, (4) community assistance to youth in the finding of jobs, and (5) organized tattoo removal available to gang members. In addition, the community and the police directed nonprofit organizations (such as the United Way) in the channeling of funds to provide programs for youth. The police department also increased its gang units.

According to Deputy Chief Berry, because of the successful collaboration of police department and community, lives have been saved. Since 1995 there have been one or two gang-related shootings. Drive-by shootings went down from an average of 140 shots-fired calls a month to an average of 20 calls per month. Gangs are still present in the city, but activity has decreased in Reno.

The Police Executive Research Forum (PERF) looked for commonalities among various community-policing programs across the country, and conducted thorough research in the subject. The researchers outlined five different perspectives on community policing within agencies throughout the United States. Though this report was published in 1992, these principles are not any less applicable today.

1. Deployment perspective: Placing officers in closer proximity to members of the community and thereby improve their knowledge of the area in which they work.

2. Community revitalization perspective: Focusing on preventing deterioration of neighborhoods by police paying closer attention to fear-inducing characteristics of neighborhoods.

3. Problem-solving perspective: Maintaining that the most critical element of community policing is the problem-solving efforts in which the police and community (residents, other government agencies, and private businesses) participate.

4. Customer perspective: Developing proactive mechanisms for determining the needs of the public relative to the police function; the approach uses routine surveys of citizen and advisory groups to accomplish this goal.

5. Legitimacy perspective: Attempting, via community policing, for officers to be more equitable in their relationships with the minority community.

Such perspectives require opening a dialogue between the police and diverse community groups so that groups can identify their peacekeeping concerns and the police can respond to them. Departments typically mix varieties of community policing perspectives; however, the common thread within all approaches is that the police assist the community in policing and protecting itself. To do so, the police must engage the community in the task of policing. The police are actually dependent on a relationship and partnership (some call it "building bridges") with the community to perform these tasks. The community identifies problems with the encouragement, direction, and participation of the police.

SUMMARY

Dramatic changes in the ethnic and racial makeup of the population have created new challenges at all levels of police work. Willingness to gain cultural information about the new communities that they serve will ultimately benefit officers in their interactions with people of different backgrounds. Officers' knowledge of cultural differences, coupled with an ability to demonstrate respect for those differences, can result in increased rapport and effective communication with people from various ethnic and racial backgrounds. Trust in many ethnic communities has to be earned because of the cultural "baggage" that community members bring to their relationships with the police. Members of the law enforcement profession have to examine their words, behaviors, and actions to evaluate whether they are conveying professionalism and respect to all people, regardless of their race, culture, religion, or ethnic background. Law enforcement agencies must be free of all expressions of prejudice on the part of their officers and civilian employees. Finally, law enforcement agencies in partnership and collaboration with communities are likely to experience decreased crime rates and increased trust and cooperation with citizens of all backgrounds.

EIGHT TIPS FOR IMPROVING LAW ENFORCEMENT IN MULTICULTURAL COMMUNITIES*

- Make positive contact with community group members from diverse backgrounds. Don't let them see you only when something negative has happened.

- Allow the public to see you as much as possible in a nonenforcement role.

- Make a conscious effort in your mind, en route to every situation, to treat all segments of society objectively and fairly.

- Remember that all groups have some bad, some average, and some good people within them.

- Go out of your way to be personable and friendly with minority-group members. Remember, many don't expect it.

- Don't appear uncomfortable with or avoid discussing racial and ethnic issues with other officers and citizens.

- Take responsibility for patiently educating citizens and the public about the role of the officer and about standard operating procedures in law enforcement. Remember that citizens often do not understand "police culture."

- Don't be afraid to be a change agent in your organization when it comes to improving cross-cultural relations within your department and between police and community. It may not be a popular thing to do, but it is the right thing to do.

"Remember the history of law enforcement with all groups and ask yourself the question, Am I part of the past, or a part of the future?"

DISCUSSION QUESTIONS AND ISSUES*

1. ***Views on the Multicultural Society.*** The following viewpoints regarding our increasingly multicultural population reflect varying levels of tolerance, understanding, and acceptance. Discuss these points of view and their implications for law enforcement:

---

*Tips and quotes are from Deputy Chief Ondra Berry, Reno Police Department, 2003

*See the Instructor's Manual accompanying this text for additional activities, role-play activities, questionnaires, and projects related to the content of this chapter.

- Diversity is acceptable if there is not too much of it, but the way things are going today, it is hard to absorb and it just may result in our destruction.
- They are here now and they need to do things our way.
- To advance in our diverse society, we need to accept and respect our differences rather than maintaining the myth of the melting pot.

2. *Police Work and Ethnicity.* In a 1988 study entitled *Policing Multi-Ethnic Neighborhoods,* Alpert and Dunham say that ethnicity complicates every police procedure. In your experience, do race, culture, and ethnicity complicate police procedures and interactions? Explain why or why not.

3. *Dealing with Illegal Immigrants.* Does the police department in which you work have a policy regarding undocumented immigrants? Are officers instructed not to inquire into their status unless a crime has been committed? How do you think police officers should deal with illegal immigrants?

4. *Mini Case Study 1.* Reread, then discuss.

   Driving under the Influence?

   a. Has this issue (kava drink and its use among Pacific Islanders) been identified as an issue or problem in your jurisdiction? If so, what has the prosecuting attorney said about dealing with these cases?

   b. What would the officer's liability be if he released the driver and the erratic driving continued?

5. *Mini Case Study 2.* Reread, then discuss.

   A Tragic Case of Cross-Cultural Misinterpretation

   a. Do you think this case would have proceeded differently if all the authorities involved understood the cultural tradition of the medical practice ("coin rubbing") that caused the bruising? Explain your answer.

   b. Discuss whether you think Southeast Asian refugees should give up this medical practice, because it can be misinterpreted.

6. *Mini Case Study 3.* Reread, then discuss.

   Latino Values as a Factor in Sentencing

   a. Discuss whether culture should play any part in influencing the sentencing of a criminal convicted of violent crimes such as murder and rape. Was the lighter verdict in this case justified? Explain your answer.

   b. According to Superior Court Judge Katz, culture influenced the sentencing in this case. In your opinion, if the husband involved were not Latino, would the sentence have been the same?

7. *Prejudice and Discrimination in Police Work.* In your own words, define prejudice and discrimination. Give examples of (a) discrimination in society in general, (b) discrimination against police officers, and (c) discrimination toward minorities by police officers.

8. *Community-Based Policing.* Why is community-based policing in minority, ethnic, and immigrant communities especially crucial to the success of law enforcement in any given city? Discuss the two cases presented in this section of

the chapter (i.e., the case of the police department without community policing in place [at the time of the fall of Saigon] and the case of the police department whose community policing efforts resulted in a dramatic decline of the homicide rate in the city). What lessons can you extract from these two examples that may be applicable to your jurisdiction?

WEBSITE RESOURCES

Visit these websites for additional information related to the content of Chapter 1.

The Community Policing Consortium: www.communitypolicing.org

The website presents a consortium of organizations that work to improve community-based law enforcement; the site has a wealth of materials and links related to the topic.

Vera Institute of Justice: http://www.vera.org

The Vera Institute of Justice works closely with leaders in government and civil society to improve the services people rely on for safety and justice. It creates innovative programs, studies social problems, and provides practical advice and assistance to government officials around the world. The Vera Institute has publications on many topics of interest to law enforcement.

The International Association of Chiefs of Police: http://www.theiacp.org

This comprehensive website provides a wide variety of information on police-related topics. It includes research, publications, and such topics as leadership and training. It also contains selected publications on community policing from the viewpoints of Chiefs of Police.

U.S. Census Bureau: http://www.census.gov

This website provides comprehensive information about changing demographics in the United States.

REFERENCES

Alpert, G. P., and R. G. Dunham. (1988). *Policing Multi-Ethnic Neighborhoods: The Miami Study and Findings for Law Enforcement in the United States.* Westport, Conn.: Greenwood Press.

Barlow, H. D. (2000). *Criminal Justice in America.* Upper Saddle River, N.J.: Prentice-Hall.

Berry, Ondra. (2003, December 8). Deputy Chief, Reno, Nevada, Police Department, personal communication.

Berry-Wilkinson, Alison. (1993). "Be Careful What You Say When . . .," *Labor Beat,* 5(1), 16.

Blanchard, Fletcher. (1991, September 16). New York Times, pp. C-1, C-8.

Coffey, Alan, Edward Eldefonson, and Walter Hartinger. (1982). *Human Relations: Law Enforcement in a Changing Community,* 3rd ed. Englewood Cliffs, N.J.: Prentice-Hall. *The Convention on the Elimination of all Forms of Racial Discrimi-*

nation: Initial Report of the United States of America to the United Nations Committee on the Elimination of Racial Discrimination, September 2000. Available:
http://www.state.gov/www/global/human_rights/cerd_report/cerd_intro.html

Council of Economic Advisors for the President's Initiative on Race. (1998, September). "Indicators of Social and Economic Well-Being by Race and Hispanic Origin," in *Changing America: Crime and Criminal Justice* (Chapter 7). Available:
http://www.whitehouse.gov/Initiatives/OneAmerica/cevent.html

Cross, T., Bazron, B. J., Dennis, K. W., and Isaacs, M. R. (1989). *Toward a Culturally
Competent System of Care.* Volume 1: Monograph on Effective Services for Minor-
ity Children who are Severely Emotionally Disturbed. Washington, DC: CASSP
Technical Assistance Center, Georgetown University Child Development Center.

Cultural sensitivity on the beat. (2000, January 10). *Los Angeles Times,* p. A12.

Fernandez, Donya. (2000, December 20). Language Rights attorney for the Language
Rights Project, Employment Law Center/Legal Aid Society, San Francisco, California, personal communication.

Griffin, Ronald Pastor (2003), Detroit-based Pastor and Community Leader, personal
communication, OCTOBER, 2003).

Hall, Edward T. (1959). *The Silent Language.* Greenwich, Conn.: Fawcett.

Handlin, Oscar. (1975). *Out of Many: A Study Guide to Cultural Pluralism in the
United States.* Anti-Defamation League of B'nai B'rith, published through Brown
& Williamson Tobacco Corporation.

Harris, P. R. (1994). *High Performance Leadership: HRD Strategies for the New Work
Culture.* Amherst, Mass.: Human Resource Development Press.

Hunter, R. D., P. D. Mayhall, and T. Barker. (2000). *Police Community Relations and
the Administration of Justice.* Upper Saddle River, N.J.: Prentice-Hall.

Immigration and Naturalization Service. (2003). Yearbook of Immigration Statistics:
"Estimates of the Unauthorized Immigrant Population Residing in the United
States: 1990 to 2000." Washington, D.C.: U.S. Government Printing Office. Avail-
able: http://www.immigration.gov/graphics/shared/aboutus/statistics/Illegals.htm

Jang, D.L. (1994). Caught in a Web: Immigrant Women and Domestic Violence, national clearing house (Special Issue 1994)

Katz, Lawrence. (2003, December 15). Residing judge, Juvenile Court of Contra Costa
(California) County, personal communication.

Kennedy, John F. (1986). *A Nation of Immigrants.* New York: Harper & Row.

Lewis, Robert. (2000, December). Sergeant, San Diego, California, Police Department,
personal communication.

Multiracial data in census adds categories and controversies. (2000, December 10).
San Francisco Chronicle, p. A-14.

Miller, Char. (2003, December). Professor of History, Trinity College, San Antonio,
Texas, personal communication.

National Institute of Justice. (2000, August). *The COPS Program after 4 Years: National Evaluation,* by Jeffrey A. Roth and Joseph F. Ryan. Washington, D.C.: U.S.
Department of Justice.

National Office of Samoan Affairs. (1984). *Samoan Family Care, Child Abuse, and Neglect Prevention: A Service Provider Handbook.* Grant 90CA923-01. San Francisco: National Center on Child Abuse and Neglect.

Officers being trained in ethnic understanding. (2000, November 29). *San Jose Mercury News,* p. A3.

Oliver, W. M. (2001). *Community Oriented Policing: A Systematic Approach to Policing.* Upper Saddle River, N.J.: Prentice-Hall.

Olson, Sergeant Aaron T. (2003). Sergeant and patrol supervisor with Oregon State Police; Instructor at Oregon's Public Safety Standards and Training for Regional and Academy students; and police liaison with IRCO (Immigrant Refugee Community Organization) in Portland area, personal communication (July, 2003).

One America in the 21st Century: Forging a New Future, Executive Summary, Advisory Board to the President's Initiative on Race, September 1998. Available: http//www.whitehouse.gov/Initiatives/OneAmerica/cevent.html

Orloff, Leslye. (2003, February 27). Testifying as the director of the Immigrant Women Program, NOW Legal Defense and Education Fund, before the Subcommittee on Immigration, Border Security, and Claims House Judiciary Committee.

Peak, K. J., and R. W. Glensor. (1997). *Community Policing and Problem Solving: Strategies and Practices.* Upper Saddle River, N.J.: Prentice-Hall.

Police Executive Research Forum (PERF). (1992). *Revisiting Community Policing: A New Typology.* Washington, D.C.: Author.

Prewitt, Kenneth. (2001, Fall). "Beyond Census 2000: As a Nation, We are the World." *The Carnegie Reporter,* 1(3), p. 1.

Public Policy Institute. (2000, July). "Research Brief." *Ethnicity, Neighborhoods, and California Politics,* 38.

Rawlins, Gary H. (1992, October 8). "Africans Came 200 Years Earlier," *USA Today,* p. 2a.

Redefining race in America. (2000, September 18). *Newsweek,* p. 38.

Ruhly, Sharon. (1976). *Orientations to Intercultural Communication: Modules in Speech Communication.* Chicago: Science Research Associates.

Sherman, Spencer. (1986). "When Cultures Collide." *California Lawyer,* 6(1), 33.

Skolnick, Jerome H. (1999). *On Democratic Policing.* Washington, D.C.: Police Foundation.

Stevens, D. J. (2001). *Case Studies in Community Policing.* Upper Saddle River, N.J.: Prentice-Hall.

Trojanowicz, Robert, and Bonnie Bucqueroux. (1990). *Community Policing: A Contemporary Perspective.* Lansing: Michigan State University, Cincinnati, Ohio: Anderson Publishing.

Trojanowicz, Robert, and David Carter. (1990). "The Changing Face of America." *FBI Law Enforcement Bulletin, 59,* 6–12.

U.S. Census Bureau. (2002) "The Foreign Born Population in the United States," the U.S. Census Bureau Current Population Survey, March 2002.

U.S. Census Bureau. (2003). Current Population Survey: "The Foreign Born Population in the United States: March 2002." Washington, D.C.: U.S. Government Printing Office.

U.S. department of justice. (2000). Office of Justice Programs, Bureau of Justice Statistics: "Community Policing." Available: http://www.ojp.usdoj.gov/bjs/sandlle.htm#policing

Zangwill, Israel. (1908). *The Melting Pot: Drama in Four Acts.* New York: Macmillan.

Chapter 2

The Changing Law Enforcement Agency: A Microcosm of Society

OVERVIEW

The ethnic, racial, gender, and lifestyle composition of law enforcement agencies is changing in the United States. In this chapter we address the increasingly pluralistic workforce and provide examples of racism and cultural insensitivity within the law enforcement agency. We present suggestions for defusing racially and culturally rooted conflicts and address issues related to women, gay men, and lesbians in law enforcement. The chapter ends with recommendations for all employees who work within a diverse workforce and particularly emphasizes the role of the chief executive.

COMMENTARY

The changing law enforcement environment, both internal and external, is strikingly evident in today's diverse society:

It would be naïve to say women have finished the gender battle in law enforcement. Women make up a scant 13 percent of major police agencies nationwide, according to the National Center for Women and Policing, a division of the Feminist Majority Foundation. Women do face some unique challenges, including the attitudes of society and of some of their male co-workers and bosses. ("Women Still Underrepresented," 2003, p. A32)

In what is described as the most comprehensive analysis of women in policing, authorities say women remain grossly under-represented in the ranks; they are routine targets of gender bias and sexual harassment; and they have largely been unable to punch through a virtually bullet-proof glass ceiling. ("Female Cops," 1998, p. 1)

Last week they celebrated gay pride day at the CIA. The most stuffy and insular of all government institutions, the intelligence community routed out gay employees in the 1950s on the theory that they could easily be blackmailed and therefore pose a security risk. But last week, gay Central Intelligence Agency employees and a busload of employees from the National Security Agency gathered at CIA headquarters in Virginia for the gay pride event, and even the director of the CIA showed up. ("America Accepting Gays Easier," p. A27)

Eight current or former Secret Service agents who are black charged . . . that top officials are dragging their feet on ridding the agency of deep-rooted racial discrimination, which they said has also infected Vice President Al Gore's protective detail. ("8 Agents," 2000, p. A22)

INTRODUCTION

In Chapter 1, we presented the evolution of multicultural communities and the demographic changes that the United States has experienced in recent decades. The most notable demographic changes mentioned involve the increases in racial, ethnic, and immigrant populations in our country. Diversity is becoming so commonplace in communities that terms such as "majority group" and "minority group" are almost obsolete. There has been a negative reaction to the term "minority," which critics find not just outmoded, but offensive. The term leaves nonwhites feeling diminished—almost second-class. The word carries overtones of inferiority and inequity. The word, technically, is used to describe numerical designations, but over the years, it has come to have much larger implications.

The range of reactions to these changes by society as a whole is no different from the range within law enforcement agencies. Members of police communities across the country have demonstrated both tolerance of and resistance to the changing society and workforce. Some officers dislike the multicultural workforce and the involvement of women in policing, although the latter is becoming a nonissue in law enforcement. They may resent diversity because of their own prejudices or biases. This resentment is due in part to perceived or actual advantages others receive when competing for law enforcement positions, either entry level or promotional. In addition, because of past inept affirmative action hiring (i.e., management rushed to fill quotas but did not focus on competence), some officers perceive that affirmative action (where still being used) means the lowering of standards. Indeed, where standards have been lowered, everyone suffers, especially less-qualified employees hired because of affirmative action. (This issue is discussed further in Chapter 3.)

Leading positively and valuing the diversity within an agency are the keys to meeting the challenge of policing multicultural communities. As discussed in Chapter 1, racial and ethnic tensions still exist in the law enforcement community. Agency personnel must first address the conflicts in their own organizations before dealing with community racial and ethnic problems. For example, in the "Commentary" section of this chapter there is a reference to accusations of discrimination by eight black Secret Service agents. In the article quoted, the journalist continued: "But the Secret Service is in complete denial and [it is] stonewalling us." Some agents reported racial harassment and a hostile work environment. Others said they were "routinely denied" the opportunity to take management training courses that were necessary for promotion. These allegations must be addressed on a timely basis or they fester and result in lawsuits, court injunctions, and unhappy employees who do not remain with the organization.

The action or inaction of police departments determine whether social problems that manifest themselves in law enforcement agencies are resolved. Across the United States the national press has reported numerous cases in which police departments did nothing or took the wrong action. Whether they like it or not, police officers are primary role models for citizens and are judged by a higher standard of behavior than are others. While supervision of police officers is important to ensure that a higher standard of behavior is maintained, no supervision of officers working with the public, no matter how thorough and conscientious, will prevent some officers from violating policies; there simply are too many police officers and too few supervisors. Thus, it is important that police officers have integrity and a stable set of core moral virtues. These virtues must include the ability to remain professional in protecting and serving a diverse public.

As stated in Chapter 1, those concerned with peacekeeping and enforcement must accept the realities of a diverse society, as well as the heterogeneity in their workforce. The irony is that the peacekeepers sworn to uphold laws pertaining to acts of bias sometimes themselves become perpetrators, even with their own peers. If police departments are to be representative of the populations served, police executives must effect changes. These changes have to do with the treatment of peers as well as recruitment, selection, and promotion of employees who have traditionally been underrepresented in law enforcement. The argument (Chapter 1) that the United States has never really been a melting pot applies also to the law enforcement community. In some cases relationships within the law enforcement workplace, especially as diversity increases, are characterized by disrespect and tension. Although many in the police subculture would argue that membership implies brotherhood (and therefore belonging), this membership has traditionally excluded certain groups in both subtle and obvious ways.

CHANGING WORKFORCE

As microcosms of their communities, law enforcement agencies increasingly include among their personnel more women, ethnic and racial minorities, and gays and lesbians. Although such groups are far from achieving parity in most agencies in the United States, advances have been made (see Chapter 3). In many regions of the country, today's law enforcement workforce differs greatly from those of the past; the profound shift in demographics has resulted in notable changes in law enforcement.

Law Enforcement Diversity: A Microcosm of Society

According to a Bureau of Justice Statistics (BJS) report, as of June 2000, local police, sheriffs' offices and State governments in the United States operated 17,784 full-time law enforcement agencies. The total included 12,666 general-purpose local police departments, 3,070 sheriffs' offices, the 49 primary State law enforcement agencies, 1,376 State and local agencies with a special geographic jurisdiction or special enforcement responsibilities, and 623 constable offices in Texas. Overall, these State and local agencies employed 1,019,496 persons on a full-time basis. This total included 708,022 full-time sworn personnel (69 percent) and 311,474 nonsworn (or civilian) personnel (31 percent) (BJS Report, October 2002). The same report established the overall percentage of racial and ethnic minority-group representation among full-time sworn personnel nationwide as of June 2000. The percentage of change in minority representation between 1990 and 2000 was as follows:

- Among local police officers, minority representation increased from 14.5 percent to 22.7 percent.

- Among sheriffs' offices, minority representation increased from 13.4 percent to 17.1 percent.

With increases came a corresponding reduction in the number of white officers and deputies in law enforcement workforces. Exhibits 2.1 and 2.2 provide more details on the percentages by ethnic and racial groups in local police and sheriffs' departments.

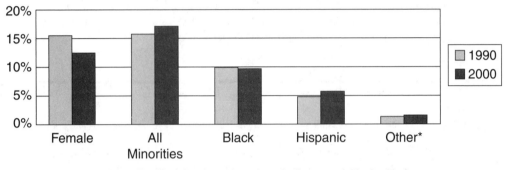

*includes Asians, Pacific Islanders, American Indians, and Alaska Natives

Exhibit 2.1   Female and minority officers in sheriff's offices, 1990–2000

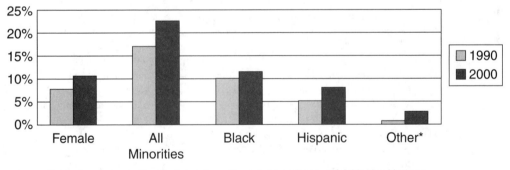

*includes Asians, Pacific Islanders, American Indians, and Alaska Natives

Exhibit 2.2   Female and minority local police officers, 1990–2000

Some major law enforcement agencies have achieved parity in terms of the percentage of diverse groups in their workforce compared to the percentage in the community; most have not, but the numbers are improving. For example, using a ratio based on the percentage of sworn personnel in local police departments who were members of a racial or ethnic minority relative to the percentage of city residents who were members of that minority group indicates that, on average, police departments in large cities were slightly more representative of the cities they served in 2000 than in 1990. From 1990 to 2000, the average ratio increased from .59 to .63 for minorities overall. This means that, on average, police departments in large cities had 63 minority police officers per every 100 minority residents in 2000, compared to 59 for every 100 in 1990. For blacks or African Americans, the average ratio increased from .64 in 1990 to .74 in 2000, for Hispanics or Latinos from .54 to .56, and for other minority groups (such as Asians and American Indians) from .26 to .37 (BJS, 2002). Law enforcement is still a predominantly white male occupation, and there must be an expansion of efforts in the recruitment, hiring, and promotion of women and people of other races and ethnicities nationwide. This issue is discussed further in Chapter 3.

Measuring Responsiveness to Diversity

A manual produced by the Canadian Association of Chiefs of Police includes a 10-question checklist and scoring method for law enforcement organizations to determine how responsive they are in adapting to diversity. It is reproduced here (Exhibit 2.3) for use in rating your own agency.

Circle and count the number of initiatives that your police service has undertaken. See how you rate.

( )   1. Are members of ethnic/cultural communities participating in your community and crime prevention programs?

( )   2. Do your programs provide for community input into the development and implementation of local policing programs?

( )   3. Does your organization have a race relations policy that is integrated into your overall mission?

( )   4. Do your patrol officers use foot patrols in areas of high concentrations of ethnic minorities?

( )   5. Do you use translators or interpreters from within your police department or from local immigrant service agencies or ethnic community organizations in your contacts with linguistic minorities?

( )   6. Are your ads and brochures multilingual, and do they depict a multicultural community?

( )   7. Do you have a recruitment campaign that actively targets ethnic and visible minorities?

( )   8. Have your hiring and promotional practices been evaluated to see if they recognize and value knowledge and skills related to community policing, especially with ethnic/cultural communities?

( )   9. Have your in-service training programs dealt with the issue of diversity?

( ) 10. Have your officers participated in programs in multicultural or race relations training for trainers?

Scoring:

0–3,   Don't panic. The fact that you did the checklist shows that you are interested. Start small, but start today!

4–6,   Good start. You are part of a community-based policing movement. You are beginning to tackle some of the issues that face police services in a multicultural environment.

7–9,   Well done. It is obvious that you understand and value the benefits of ethnoculturally sensitive and community-based policing. You're on the right track, keep up the good work!

10,   Congratulations. Your challenge is to maintain the momentum and evaluate the effectiveness of your initiatives.

Source: Canadian Association of Chiefs of Police. (1992). *Police Race Relations: Raising Your Effectiveness in Today's Diverse Neighborhoods through Community Policing.* Place de Ville, Tower B, 112 Kent St., Suite 1908, Ottawa, Ontario KIP 5P2, Canada.

Exhibit 2.3   How responsive is your organization?

ETHNIC AND RACIAL ISSUES WITHIN THE WORKFORCE

Racism

Racism within law enforcement agencies has been documented for decades. An African American history display at the New York Police Academy contains the following written account of the experiences of one of the first black officers in the New York Police Department:

> Seven years before the adoption of the charter creating New York City, Brooklyn, then an independent city, hired the first black policeman. Wiley G. Overton was sworn in March 6, 1891. . . . His first tour of duty was spent in civilian clothing because fellow officers breaking with tradition refused to furnish him with a temporary uniform. . . . Officers in his section refused to sleep in the same room with him. . . . The officers in the precinct ignored him and spoke only if it was necessary in the line of duty.

The New York Police Department is not alone. Racism can occur in police departments regardless of size or region. The Dallas police strike in 1992, with its racial overtones, polarized the department—cop versus cop. The *New York Daily News* in 1993 had bold headlines: "Racism on the Job: Black N.J. Troopers Charge Harassment, Bias, and Discrimination" (p. C3). In May 2000, the federal government concluded that there was sufficient evidence of civil rights violations within the Los Angeles Police Department (LAPD) to file a so-called pattern and practice discrimination suit. The LAPD faced the possibility of intervention by the federal government. The department was warned to make changes in police training and procedures to avoid a lawsuit. Similar accusations could be heard in other communities and state patrols across the nation in reaction to accusations of racial profiling in traffic stops (see Chapter 14) and police brutality directed toward persons of color. Unfortunately, racism has been an issue for decades. In 2003, the highest-ranking Arab American agent in the FBI filed a discrimination lawsuit against the bureau alleging that he was excluded from the investigation into the September 11 attacks and denied promotion because of his ethnicity. As long as racism exists in society, the potential exists for police agencies to reflect these attitudes.

We spoke with several officers from different states about racism in their departments. Those interviewed requested that their names not be included, because they felt they might face repercussions. One African American officer recalled almost coming to blows with a white officer who used a racial slur against him; the use of such slurs was commonplace for the white officer and his friends. A Cuban American officer recounted the story of a nonresistant Latino suspect who was caught in the commission of a minor crime and beaten by the white arresting officers, who used racial epithets. One major city in Massachusetts suspended a deputy superintendent of police for using the word "nigger" directed toward one of his own officers. An African American officer in a large city in Florida was fired after using racial epithets against other blacks in violation of a strict citywide policy. In this particular case, the African American officer's conduct was reported by another officer at the scene. In yet another city, an African American officer was overheard telling a white prisoner, "Wait until you get to central booking and the niggers get a hold of you."

Defusing Racially and Culturally Rooted Conflicts

Racism exists within our law enforcement organizations; police are not immune to social ills. One of the greatest challenges for police officers is dealing with their own racism. The first step in addressing the problem is for police department personnel, on all levels, to admit that racism exists rather than denying it. One reads an account, for example, of an African American police officer, off duty or on plainclothes assignments who is an instant suspect in the eyes of some white officers. If this occurs in one city or county, it can occur in another. Police researcher David Shipler, after 2 years of interviews across the country, maintained that he encountered very few black officers who had not been "hassled by white cops." He was quick to point out, however, that not every white police officer is a bigot and not every police force a bastion of racism; in fact, some agencies have made great strides in improving race relations.

Shipler recommends that law enforcement should combat and defuse racism by using the U.S. Army model developed during a time of extreme racial tension in the military in the early 1970s ("Report Recommends Using Military Model," 1992, p. A17). Obviously, no model of training will bring guaranteed success and alleviate all acts of prejudice and racism. However, professional groups can build on each other's attempts, especially when these have proven to be fairly successful. Shipler recognizes that police officers are not identical to soldiers, because the former have constant contact with the public (where they see the worst) and must use personal judgment in dangerous and ambiguous situations. Nevertheless, he suggests that some military approaches are adaptable to law enforcement. According to Shipler, the basic framework for combating and defusing racism in the military has been:

- *Command commitment:* The person at the top sets the tone all the way down to the bottom. Performance reports document any bigoted or discriminatory behavior. A record of racial slurs and discriminatory acts can derail a military career.

- *Training of advisers:* Military personnel are trained at the Defense Equal Opportunity Management Institute in Florida as equal opportunity advisers. The advisers are assigned to military units with direct access to commanders. They conduct local courses to train all members of the unit on race relations.

- *Complaints and monitoring:* The advisers provide one channel for specific complaints of racial and gender discrimination, but they also drop in on units unannounced and sound out the troops on their attitudes. Surveys are conducted and informal discussions are held to lessen racial tensions.

Sondra Thiederman (1991), cultural diversity consultant and author, provides nine tips that will help organizational managers or leaders identify and resolve conflicts that arise because of cultural (not only racial) differences in the workplace. She says that the following guidelines are applicable no matter what cultures, races, religions, or lifestyles are involved:

1. Give each party the opportunity to voice his or her concerns without interruption.

2. Attempt to obtain agreement on what the problem is by asking questions of each party to find out specifically what is upsetting each person.

3. During this process, stay in control and keep employees on the subject of the central issue.

4. Establish whether the issue is indeed rooted in cultural differences by determining:

    a. If the parties are from different cultures or subcultures.

    b. If the key issue represents an important value in each person's culture.

    c. How each person is expected to behave in his or her culture as it pertains to this issue.

    d. If the issue is emotionally charged for one or both of the parties.

    e. If similar conflicts arise repeatedly and in different contexts.

5. Summarize the cultural (racial, religious, or lifestyle) differences that you uncover.

6. State the negative outcomes that will result if the situation is not resolved (be specific).

7. State the positive outcomes that will result if the situation is resolved (be specific).

8. Negotiate terms by allowing those involved to come up with the solutions.

9. Provide positive reinforcement as soon as the situation improves.

Thiederman's approach is based on conflict resolution and crisis intervention techniques training that many police and correctional officers receive in either their academy or in-service training. Police department command must encourage the use of conflict resolution techniques by officers of all backgrounds as a way of handling issues prior to their becoming flash points. With professionalism and patience, the use of conflict resolution techniques to reduce racial and ethnic problems will work within both the workforce and neighborhoods.

John Sullivan and Henry DeGeneste, in a July 1997 article for *Fresh Perspectives* (a Police Executive Research Forum publication), wrote:

> Police play a pivotal role in the life of communities. As the most visible branch of civil government, police agencies are called on to mitigate and resolve conflict among both groups and individuals. This intimate relationship with conflict resolution and management is a natural extension of the primary police duty to preserve the public peace and prevent crime. The recent focus on community policing and problem solving strengthens these traditional police roles, highlighting the importance of police interaction with the diverse communities they serve. Communities, however, are not static collections of people. Rather, communities are dynamic and constantly changing. The ethnic, social and class composition of nations and individual communities shifts over time.

As a result of allegations of racism against it, the Alameda, California, Police Department developed a series of general orders as one approach to remedy the problem. Violation of the department general orders (DGOs) carries progressive disciplinary ramifications up to and including termination. The general orders deal with control of prejudicial conduct based on race, religion, ethnicity, disability, sex, age, or sexual orientation and are as follows:

1. *Code of ethics:* Commits to personal suppression of prejudice, animosities, malice, and ill will, as well as respect for the constitutional rights of all persons.

2. *DGO 80-1:* Specifically addresses discrimination and racial remarks and requires courtesy and respect for all persons. It states: "Discrimination or racism in any form shall never be tolerated."

3. *DGO 80-1:* Requires impartiality toward all persons and guarantees equal protection under the law. Prohibits exhibition of partiality due to race, creed, or influence.

4. *DGO 90-3:* Deals with harassment in the workplace based on race, religion, color, national origin, ancestry, disability, marital status, sex, age, or sexual preference. (Chief R. Shields, 1993.)

The Alameda Police Department also produced the following as an in-service training guide and a posted announcement within the agency:

Alameda Police Department Mortal Sins

1. Racism, racial slurs, racial discrimination.

2. Sexism, offensive sexual remarks, sexual harassment, sexual discrimination.

3. Discrimination or harassment for sexual orientation.

4. Religious discrimination.

5. Untruthfulness and falsifications.

6. Unnecessary or excessive force.

7. Use of illegal drugs.

8. Violations of the law.

This department sent a clear message to its employees that its leaders will not tolerate discriminatory behavior. The same department adapted a San Diego Police Department attitude assessment survey instrument on perceptions regarding contact with the multicultural community and workforce. The survey instrument is reproduced in Appendix A.

Police Fraternal Organizations

Police fraternal, religious, and ethnic organizations offer members social activities, fellowship, counseling, career development, resources, and networking opportunities with persons of common heritage, background, or experience. The New York Police Department, for example, has many clubs, societies, and associations to address the needs of its pluralistic organization. The Irish are represented by the Emerald Society, African Americans by the Guardians Association, Christian officers by Police Officers for Christ, those of Asian or Pacific Islander heritage (which includes Chinese, Japanese, Korean, Filipino, and Asian Indian officers) by the Asian Jade Society, Italian officers by the Columbia Association, and so on. The police subculture can be a stressful environment, so it is only natural that persons different from the majority workforce members seek emotional comfort zones with those of similar background. Membership in these groups provides emotional sanctuary from the stereotypes, hostility, indifference, ignorance, or naïveté that members encounter within their organizations and communities.

Occasionally, one hears of criticism within a department or by the public that such organizations actually highlight the differences between groups of people. At a National Organization of Black Law Enforcement Executives (NOBLE) conference, a white female (nonattendee) asked the meaning of the acronym NOBLE. When given the answer, she asked: "Is it ethical for blacks to have their own organization? Could whites have an organization called the 'National Organization of White Law Enforcement Executives' without being referred to as racists? Why can't the multicultural, social, and professional organizations that already exist satisfy the needs of everyone?"

The woman's concern was brought up directly with one of the conference participants, Sergeant Thomas Hall, an African American, who at the time was a Virginia state trooper. Sergeant Hall explained:

> In America, we need independent black institutions . . . to foster cultural pride, and have a place where we can go and feel comfortable. We cannot express ourselves in society. We cannot assimilate in society. We cannot even assimilate like some Hispanic groups can because of their complexions. I can't assimilate on a bus. As soon as I step on the bus, you are going to realize there is a black guy on the bus. I can't assimilate in a police organization . . . so without these black institutions, I cannot survive. We all have survival mechanisms. I have cultural needs and I have to be around people that share my needs and frustrations. I cannot do that in organizations that are predominantly white. The whites don't suffer from the racial pressures and tensions that I suffer from. So how can they [mostly white organizations] meet my interests and needs? It is impossible. (Hall, 1992)

Hall stressed that African American law enforcement organizations provide him with a network of persons with similar interests, concerns, and backgrounds.

The racial, ethnic, religious, and lifestyle organizations within law enforcement are not meant to divide but, rather, to give support to groups that traditionally were not accepted in law enforcement fully and had no power in the organization. Yet the sentiment expressed by the white female who inquired into the meaning of NOBLE is a common sentiment among some police officers. Police command officers and supervisors must not ignore this debate (whether expressed or not). They must address the issues underlying the need for the support groups within the department. They must also foster dialogue and shared activities between all formalized groups within the organization. All officers must hear from the officers of different ethnic, racial, and lifestyle perspectives what benefit they receive from membership in the groups. Officers must be willing to discuss ways to guard against divisiveness, either real or perceived, within their agencies.

Assignments Based on Diversity

There has been limited research on the assumption that an increase in the proportion of any underrepresented group in a police agency would have a positive effect in the community. Some believe that an increase in Hispanic, African American, or Asian officers in a neighborhood of the same race or ethnicity would improve police–community relations. The same argument could be made regarding gay and lesbian officers. One can speculate that there would be a more sensitive response of "like folks" who are aware of needs and issues of "their kind." In fact, historically, immigrants (Irish, Italians, and Germans) were hired by police departments because they could communicate and operate more effectively than could nonimmigrant officers in neighborhoods with immigrants.

Although citizens appreciate having officers of their own color or national origin work their area, this deployment strategy may result in unfairness. Studies have concluded that this practice can result in a career path for minorities that may be a very different path than that of white officers in agencies that follow this practice (Benson, 1992; Ross, Snortum, & Beyers, 1982; Wells, 1987). For example, instead of receiving specialized assignments in traffic, investigations, Special Weapons and Tactics (SWAT) team, and so on, the minority officer who is working effectively in the minority community may have an extended tour of duty in that function. In addition, the area to which this officer is assigned is often a tougher, high-crime area, which means that he or she is exposed more frequently to violence.

Officers of the same background as the predominant ethnicity or race in the neighborhood do not necessarily make the best crime fighters or problem solvers there. Not all racially or ethnically diverse officers may have the skills or desire to work with their own cultural or racial group. Assignments based on diversity alone, therefore, are generally unfair and may be a disservice to both the officer and the neighborhood. Officers should not be restricted to work in specific areas based on the notion that police–community relations will improve automatically. In addition, it cannot be assumed that an officer of the same background as the citizens will always show sensitivity to their particular needs.

Ron Hampton, a Washington, D.C., peace officer and executive director of the National Black Police Officers Association, illustrated this point at a 1992 NOBLE conference when he discussed the reasons why a new African American recruit wanted to work the black areas of Washington, D.C. The recruit said that he could tell people of his own race what to do and could not always do so in predominantly white neighborhoods. Hampton noted that the young recruit "called people from his neighborhood 'maggots.' " Hampton made the point that supervisors must hold subordinates accountable for their conduct, and the chief executive must make it known that inappropriate behavior will be disciplined no matter what the neighborhood. We present this example here also to illustrate how some officers may have internalized the hatred society has directed toward them and, consequently, are not automatically the most effective officers in certain neighborhoods.

When Chief Robert Burgreen was the top executive of the San Diego Police Department, he, like many other law enforcement managers, did not deploy officers according to color or ethnicity. Deployment was based on the best fit for the neighborhood and was related to an officer's competence and capabilities. However, Chief Burgreen had four community relations sergeants, one acting as a liaison for each major group in the city: Hispanic, African American, Asian, and gays and lesbians. He describes these sergeants as his "eyes and ears" for what is going on in the various communities. Some cities use cultural affairs committees made up of people from diverse groups in the community and the officers who provide them service.

WOMEN IN LAW ENFORCEMENT

Historically, women have always been part of the general workforce in American society, although usually in jobs that fulfilled traditional female employment roles, such as nurses, secretaries, schoolteachers, waitresses, and flight attendants. In 1845 New York City hired its first police "matron." In 1888 Massachusetts and New York passed legislation requiring communities with a population over 20,000 to hire police matrons to care for female prisoners. According to More (1992), during the first half of the 19th century a number of police practices were challenged, thus allowing for the initial entry of women into the police field. In 1922 the International Association of Chiefs of Police passed a resolution supporting the use of policewomen. The first major movement of women into the general workforce occurred during World War II. With men off to war, women entered the workforce in large numbers and successfully occupied many nontraditional employment roles. After the war, 30 percent of all women continued working outside the home (*History of Woman in Workforce,* 1991, p. 112). By 1990 almost 55 percent of women in the United States worked outside the home.

Barriers to female entry into the police field, however, included separate entrance requirements, limits on the number of women who could be employed, and lower pay (More, 1992). Women police officers were given duties that did not allow or require them to work street patrol. Assignments and roles were limited to positions such as juvenile delinquency and truancy prevention, child abuse, crimes against women, and custodial functions (Bell, 1982). It was not until 1968 that the Indianapolis Police Department made history by assigning the first two female officers to patrol on an equal basis with their male colleagues (Schulz, 1995). This delay was due, in part, to role perceptions. The predominant belief is that law enforcement agencies function to exercise authority and use force is accompanied by the idea that women are not capable of performing the necessary functions.

In 1972 the passage of the Equal Employment Opportunity (EEO) Act applied to state and local governments the provisions of Title VII of the Civil Rights Act of 1964. The EEO Act prohibited employment discrimination on the basis of race, color, religion, sex, or national origin. Selection procedures, criteria, and standards were changed or eliminated and/or made "job related." The law played an important role in opening up police departments to women. Adoption of affirmative action policies, now illegal in many states, along with court orders and injunctions, also played a role in bringing more women into law enforcement.

Considering how long organized police departments have existed in the United States, women entered relatively late into sworn law enforcement positions within them. A 1986 Police Foundation study reported the following findings: "In those agencies under court order to increase the representation of women and minorities, women made up 10.1 percent of the sworn personnel in 1986; in those with voluntary affirmative action policies, women made up 8.3 percent of the personnel; and, in those without affirmative action plans, women constituted only 6.1 percent of the personnel" (Martin, 1990, p. 1).

The number of women in law enforcement remains small and is increasing very slowly. The most recent research shows that nationally only 14.3% of sworn personnel are female, with an annual increase of only 0.5% over the last several years (National Center for Women and Policing, 2001). At this rate, women will not achieve parity within the police profession for at least another 70 years, and many have cautioned that time alone is not sufficient to substantially affect this rate (Garrison, 1998). Researchers in the late 1980s had made various predictions of the numbers of women expected to be in law enforcement professions by the turn of the 21st century, ranging from 47 to 55 percent of the workforce, but those predictions never materialized. The Law Enforcement Management and Administrative Statistics (LEMAS) report, issued by the U.S. Department of Justice in 2001, established the overall percentage change of sworn women in local and sheriffs' departments nationwide for the 10 year period from 1990 to 2000 (see Exhibits 2.1 and 2.2) as follows:

- Local women police officers increased from 8.1 percent to 10.6 percent.
- Women sheriffs' deputies decreased from 15.4 percent to 12.5 percent.

The reason for the decrease (1,200 women officers, or 5.5 percent) in the number of women sheriffs' deputies has not been explained by any research known to the authors, but hypotheses are suggested in Chapter 3.

McCoy (1992) conducted enlightening research that is still useful to law enforcement executives today. His study concluded that, at the time of his research, the organizational structure of most police departments did not support a positive work environment for policewomen. He recommended that police executives create an organizational culture that values the diversity of women within law enforcement, one that recognizes the complex role and competing interests that policewomen face in society and in the workplace. Such an environment would not view women as an intrusion into the male-dominated profession of law enforcement, but instead would appreciate that the personal traits that women bring to law enforcement will foster a more service-oriented approach to the organization and a more flexible approach to the policing ranks. His recommendations included the creation of support programs for women in policing to assist in family responsibilities, including child care, the development of mentoring and network programs, and specific programs designed to reduce stress created by gender-related issues.

In November 1998 the International Association of Chiefs of Police (IACP) released the results of a study it had commissioned entitled "The Future of Women in Policing." The stated purpose of the survey was to query IACP members on their perspectives and opinions about the following issues:

- Status and roles of women in policing.
- Recruitment and selection of women officers.
- Supporting and mentoring women officers.
- Training and supervision as correlates of tenure, success, and promotion of women officers.
- Attrition and resignation of women officers.
- Gender discrimination and sexual harassment.
- Whether a glass ceiling exists as a barrier to promotions.
- Future directions for women in policing.

The study confirmed that although the number of women in law enforcement is growing and women are progressing through the ranks, the following are also true:

- There are fewer women than men in policing.

- Women officers still face bias from male officers.

- Many departments lack strategies for recruiting women.

- Women officers may face gender discrimination and a glass ceiling that inhibits promotion.

- Sexual harassment still occurs in many departments.

- Although the need is great, there are very few mentoring programs for women officers.

According to research conducted both in the United States and internationally, studies:

> . . . demonstrate that women police officers rely on a style of policing that uses less physical force. They are better at defusing and de-escalating potentially violent confrontations with citizens and less likely to become involved in problems with use of excessive force. Additionally, women officers often possess better communication skills than their male counterparts and are better able to facilitate the cooperation and trust required to implement a community-policing model. In an era of costly litigation, hiring and retaining more women in law enforcement is likely to be an effective means of addressing the problems of excessive force and citizen complaints. As an additional benefit, female officers often respond more effectively to incidents of violence against women—crimes that represent one of the largest categories of calls to police departments. Increasing the representation of women on the force is also likely to address another costly problem for police administrators—the pervasive problem of sex discrimination and sexual harassment—by changing the climate of modern law enforcement agencies. Because women frequently have different life experiences than men, they approach policing with a different perspective, and the very presence of women in the field will often bring about changes in policies and procedures that benefit both male and female officers. All of these factors can work to the advantage of those in the police profession and the communities they serve. (National Center for Women & Policing, 2001)

The integration of women into policing has led many chief executives to grapple with gender issues within their departments.

Gender Issues

Research on gender issues confronting women in law enforcement focus on discrimination and sexual harassment, role barriers, the "brotherhood," a double standard, differential treatment, and career versus family.

Discrimination and Sexual Harassment. Although sexual harassment exists in both private and public sectors, we believe it is particularly problematic in law enforcement—an occupation that is still mostly male. The predominantly male makeup and macho image of law enforcement lead to problems of sexual harassment in the workplace. Harassment on the basis of sex is a violation of Section 703 of Title VII of the Civil Rights Act (29CFR Section 1604.11[a][1]) and is defined as unwelcome or unsolicited sexual advances, requests for sexual favors, and other verbal or physical conduct of a sexual nature when:

- Submission to such conduct is made either explicitly, or implicitly, a term or condition of an individual's employment; or

- Submission to, or rejection of, such conduct by an individual is used as the basis for employment decisions affecting such individual; or

- Such conduct has the purpose, or effect of unreasonably interfering with an individual's work performance or creating an intimidating, hostile, or offensive working environment

The majority of women officers interviewed for this book (who requested that their names not be used) said they had been sexually harassed in the workplace. Few of the recent national studies on sexual harassment have examined sexual harassment in police agencies, but those that have done so indicate that the problem is pervasive. In a 1995 survey of female officers in a medium-sized department, 68 percent responded "yes" to the question, "Have you ever been sexually harassed while on duty by a member of your agency?" (Nichols, 1995). Most of the women indicated that when they were exposed to offensive behavior by male officers, they remained quiet for fear of negative male backlash. Those interviewed revealed that sexual harassment occurs at all levels of an organization and is not limited to male harassment of women. Women, too, can be offenders when they initiate sexual jokes or innuendoes and use provocative language with men. This kind of behavior usually results in men countering in a similar fashion, which contributes to and escalates the problem. In these instances, women must be held accountable. The questions of what is offensive and where the line should be drawn are frequently the central issues and must be addressed. Rather than simply stating, "We don't have a harassment problem here," command officers must first model acceptable behavior and then set very clear guidelines for what constitutes acceptable behavior.

Department executives must institute a zero-tolerance sexual harassment policy and send that message throughout the department. Police-specific training must also be provided on sexual harassment and its prevention. Some departments have revised their promotional exam to include questions on the department's sexual harassment policies and procedures. The Albuquerque, New Mexico, Police Department went so far as to move the investigation of sexual harassment complaints from within the department to an external city agency with expert Equal Employment Opportunity investigators on staff. According to Albuquerque PD, this approach tends to speed up the process, ensure impartiality, and increase confidence in the procedures. Officers who make a complaint do not have to go through the chain of command. Also of value, the Institute for Women in Trades, Technology and Science (IWITTS) developed an 8-hour police-specific training course for sworn supervisors on preventing sexual harassment. It is presented in a case-study format that analyzes police legal cases, and has been highly rated by those who have attended. IWITTS can be found on their website, listed in the "Website Resources" section of this chapter.

When harassment takes place, the results can be devastating in terms of the involved employees' careers, the internal environment of the organization, and the department's public image. The importance of training all law enforcement employees (sworn and nonsworn) on the issues of sexual harassment cannot be stressed enough. With policies and procedures as well as training, sexual harassment is expected to decrease in the law enforcement workforce as the once male-dominated occupation makes its transition to mixed-gender, multiethnic, and multilifestyle organizations—a microcosm of the society served. Discrimination and sexual harassment training should deal not only with legal and liability issues but also with deep-seated attitudes about differences based on sex.

Role Barriers. Barriers based on gender have diminished, both in the general population and within law enforcement. For example, ideas about protection differ by gender—who protects whom? In American society, women may protect children, but it has been more socially acceptable and traditional for men to protect women. In the act of protecting, the protectors become dominant and the protected become subordinate. Although this gender-role perception has not completely broken down, especially in the law enforcement and corrections workforce, it is subsiding due to the number of women and young male officers in law enforcement today. There are now fewer veteran male officers who have never worked with women. Many veteran police and correctional officers initially had difficulty with the transition as women came into the dangerous, male-dominated occupations that men felt required "male" strength and abilities. The result has been described as a clash between cultures—the once male-dominated workforce versus the new one in which women are integral parts of the organizational environment. The veteran male police or correctional officers, socially conditioned to protect women, often feel that in addition to working with inmates or violent persons on the streets, they have the added responsibility of protecting the women officers with whom they work. These feelings, attitudes, and perceptions can make men and women in law enforcement positions uncomfortable with each other. Women sometimes feel patronized, overprotected, or merely tolerated rather than appreciated and respected for their work. Again, these attitudes and perceptions are diminishing as many in the new generation of male officers are more willing to accept women in law enforcement. In our numerous interviews with veteran officers we found that, with few exceptions, women were generally accepted by men, but the acceptance was related to how well a specific woman performed her duties. Those who favored women in law enforcement recognized that even some men were not suited for such an occupation.

The Christopher Commission, assigned to investigate the LAPD in the wake of the Rodney King beating, observed that although female officers in the department were performing effectively, they were still not fully accepted as part of the workforce on an equal basis (Independent Commission on the Los Angeles Police Department, 1991). Another one of its conclusions was that women officers are better equipped to peacefully resolve situations of potential violence. None of the 120 LAPD officers who were most frequently charged with excessive use of force were women. Women's advocacy groups and law enforcement administrators also say that female officers get involved in fewer physical confrontations than male officers. Women officers tend to be good communicators, which is a prized attribute in any police employee because of the current emphasis on community policing. In this regard, women prove themselves to be as effective as male officers.

The Brotherhood. Women who are accepted into the "brotherhood" of police or correctional officers have generally had to become "one of the guys." (Refer to Chapter 4 for more information on how language used in the brotherhood excludes women.) However, a woman who tries to act like one of the guys on the street or in a jail or

prison is considered too hard, too coldhearted, or too unemotional and may be criticized by peers and supervisors. Karen Kimball, the women's coordinator in the LAPD,
says that she has seen some " 'Jane Waynes' in the department who swagger, spit and
are so aggressive they make many testosterone-charged men seem tame" ("Jane
Waynes in Law Enforcement," 1993, p. A12). If she is too feminine or not sufficiently
aggressive, men will not take her seriously and she will not do well in either police or
correctional work. Women are confronted with a dilemma: They must be aggressive
enough to do the job but feminine enough to be acceptable to male peers, and they
must also be able to take different approaches to problems. Pat Ellis, a police officer
with the Lothian and Borders Police, headquartered in Edinburgh, Scotland, was a 26-
year veteran of the force as of September 2000. Noting that attitudes toward women in
policing are the same in Great Britain as in the United States, she described her experience on the force:

> I had to work hard at being as good or better than my male counterparts on a
> daily basis. I also made sure I maintained my feminine side by always looking
> feminine. Hair done, makeup, perfume. I know a lot of males are really put off
> by women who not only act like men, but look like them (Ellis, 2000).

When women feel compelled to behave like men in the workplace, the results can
be counterproductive and can even result in disciplinary action. To succeed, women
have to stay within narrow bands of acceptable behavior and exhibit only certain traditionally masculine and feminine qualities. Walking this fine line is difficult. This phenomenon is not unique to law enforcement. An article on a woman ironworker reported
that "today's female ironworkers are still pioneers. . . . [N]o matter how skilled she becomes, she's got to prove herself over and over again. 'What it is, is attitude,' [one
woman ironworker] says. 'I know that I'm on male-dominated home turf' " ("Male
Dominated Occupation" 2000, p. A3).

Sue Jones, Chief of Police of the Healdsburg, California, Police Department, says
that the term "brotherhood" still exists along with the associated behaviors. She hopes
that one day there will be just the "family of law enforcement" (Jones, 2003).

A Double Standard. Interviews with women officers for the first (1995) and second
(2002) editions of this book showed clearly that the majority felt they had to perform
better than male officers just to be considered equal—a double standard. These women
spoke of how they imposed pressures on themselves to perform up to or exceed the expectations of their male peers. (Note that minority employees often express the same
sentiment.) One woman officer explained that many women were using a community
policing philosophy long before it became the practice of their agency. She mentioned
that when she tried to do problem solving, she was criticized in her evaluations. Her
supervisor rated her negatively for "trying too hard to find solutions to complainants'
problems" and said she "spends too much time on calls explaining procedures" and
"gets too involved" (Jones, 1993). Today, however, women police officers report that
the double standard is less common because of the emphasis that law enforcement
places on Community-Oriented Policing. Now this approach is seen as the norm and is
expected of all officers (Jones, 2003).

Differential Treatment. Many women in law enforcement have indicated that they are
treated differently by staff members than are men and they are frequently held back

from promotions or special assignments in areas like Special Weapons and Tactics, homicide investigations, and motorcycles because of the perception that these are "male" jobs. They report feeling that they were also held back from training for these assignments and are not promoted at the same rate as men. A 2002 Census Bureau report indicated that in private corporations, "Women hold nearly half the executive and managerial jobs in the United States, up from only about a third in 1983" ("Women land more top jobs," 2003, p. A16). This is far from the case in law enforcement.

Police executives must determine if their female officers are receiving opportunities for assignments and training that will provide the groundwork and preparation for their eventual promotion. They need to determine if female officers are applying for promotions in numbers proportionate to their representation in the department. If not, perhaps women officers need encouragement from their supervisors. It is also possible that the promotion process disproportionately screens out female officers. Research show that the more subjective the process is, the less likely women are to be promoted. The use of assessment center, "hands-on" testing is said to offer some safeguards against the potential for the perception of bias against women. Utilizing structured interviews and selecting interview board members who represent different races and both sexes can also minimize this risk. Many departments are now training interview board members on interviewing techniques. The Institute for Women in Trades, Technology and Science has developed a well-received half-day training session for supervisors, "Creating a Supportive Work Environment," to address issues of integration and retention of women.

Career versus Family. Women in law enforcement are faced with another dilemma—trying to raise a family and have a successful career, two goals that are difficult to combine. Women, especially single parents, who had children when they entered law enforcement frequently find that they have difficulty balancing their commitments to family and work. If they had children after entering the occupation, they may be confronted with inadequate maternity-leave policies. In both cases, women often have a sense of guilt, stress, and frustration in trying to both do well in a job and maintain a family. As an International Association of Chiefs of Police 1998 study indicated, this is one of the top reasons for women leaving the profession. Progressive criminal law enforcement organizations have innovative work schedules, modified duty assignments during pregnancy, child care programs, mentoring and support groups, and a positive work atmosphere for women. Such programs benefit all employees within the organization. Today, men are taking a more active role in parenting and family; therefore, child care, creative work schedules, and even maternity leave should be of importance to them as well.

Mentor and Support Programs

A national study of women in law enforcement concluded that policewomen have a significantly higher rate of divorce than do male officers and have a lower rate of marriage as a group than the national female rate (Pogrebin, 1986). Research also revealed that although both male and female officers were affected by burnout, females experienced higher levels of emotional burnout, while males showed higher levels of depersonalizing citizens (Johnson, 1991). As already mentioned, issues of child care, maternity leave, family responsibilities, flexible work schedules, job sharing, mentoring and support programs, and promotional opportunities are all important to women peace officers and must be addressed adequately by law enforcement agencies. If not, frustration and stress result. Many of these issues are seen as barriers to women and their ability to work and advance in law enforcement. Women's performance and attitudes can be enhanced if they have access to support and mentoring programs.

Why are mentors important? Marrujo and Kleiner (1992) found that "women who had one or more mentors reported greater job success and job satisfaction than women who did not have a mentor" (p. 13). A mentor is described as an experienced, productive supervisor or manager (usually 8 to 10 years older than the employee) who relates well to a less experienced employee and facilitates his or her personal development for the benefit of both the individual and the organization. Usually, mentoring occurs in a one-on-one coaching context over a period of time through suggestions, advice, and support on the job. Several associations provide an organized voice for the interests of women in policing: the International Association of Women Police (IAWP), the National Association of Women Law Enforcement Executives (NAWLEE), and the National Center for Women and Policing (NCWP). The NAWLEE focuses on helping women to strengthen their leadership roles in policing, while the NCWP focuses on growth and leadership. However, these organizations cannot take the place of departmental, in-house mentoring programs for women. A report ("Advancing Asian Women in the Workplace") released in 2003 by Catalyst, a nonprofit group that studies women and business trends, stated that Asian-American women face difficult challenges in the workplace. "Many have trouble finding mentors or feel their managers don't understand their culture" ("Obstacles hinder minority women," 2003, p. C1). The report mirrors one released earlier in 2003 about Latinas in business. Latinas and Asian American women are among the fastest-growing groups in the U.S. labor force.

> In the study, 413 women of Asian decent were broken into two groups—those who grew up in the United States and those who immigrated as adults. Regardless of their acculturation, many said their Asian cultural values are frequently at odds with their ability to successfully navigate the corporate landscape. "We are taught in our culture to let good work speak for itself and that it's not becoming to bring attention to yourself or your work," said Quinn Tran. (p. C1)

In both Catalyst surveys, Latinas and Asian American women said they encounter stereotypes in the workplace. Asian women said they often feel overlooked by their companies' diversity programs, in part, because they are labeled "overachievers" who don't require specific diversity efforts. Both reports suggest managers should encourage more experienced Asian American women and Latinas to serve as mentors for younger women and make more of an attempt to understand the cultural background of their diverse workforce.

The Transition

A survey containing 43 questions was administered by Seklecki and Allen of the University of Minot randomly to 2,000 female police officers across the United States in 2003. The questions were designed to collect information about employment motivations, experiences and attitudes of women who became law enforcement officers. The response rate to the scientifically designed survey was approximately 27%. The summary of their findings were:

> Our research indicates that female law enforcement officers have made a promising transition from their professional status some thirty years ago. While still a minority, they view themselves quite often as equally, if not more capable than their male peers and upon completion of training, the overwhelming majority of women officers are intent to stay on their present career path. In addition, we must note the perception of working conditions has clearly improved as agencies have become more harassment conscious, while remaining undeniably male influenced. The study respondents confirm the continued presence of the traditional "male behaviors"; however most female officers, surprisingly, do not take great exception to them. This suggests the female officers entered the profession expecting to encounter these behaviors and consider such behavior normal to the work setting." (2004, p. 39) "A National Survey of Female Police Officers: On Overview of Findings," A paper presented at the Academy of Criminal Justice Sciences Conference in Las Vegas, Nevada, March 2004. Presented by Dr. Richard Seklecki and Dr. Rebecca Allen, Associate Professors, Criminal Justice Department, Minot State University, ND

GAY MEN AND LESBIANS IN LAW ENFORCEMENT

For the purposes of this discussion, the terms lesbian, homosexual, gay, bisexual, and transgender will be used to describe the sexual orientation of underrepresented groups in law enforcement agencies. These terms are defined here as follows: gay: a male homosexual; homosexual: characterized by sexual attraction to those of the same sex as oneself; lesbian: a homosexual woman; bisexual: the ability to be sexually attracted to both men and women. The term transgender covers a range of people, including heterosexual cross-dressers, homosexual drag queens, and transsexuals who believe they were born in the wrong body. There are also those who consider themselves to be both male and female, or intersexed, and those who take hormones and believe that is enough to complete their gender identity without a sex change.

Most authors and police administrators group "gay" and "lesbian" together as if the experiences of the two genders are synonymous. However, nowhere is the dichotomy more visible than within law enforcement. Stemming from persistent sexism, many officers assume that "macho" women are lesbians, and that stereotypically "feminine" women are heterosexual, although such mapping of gender roles onto sexual orientation is frequently erroneous. This is discussed later in this chapter.

Policy versus Practice

As the issue of sexual orientation has come of age in the public consciousness, due in part to movies and television shows (such as *Will & Grace* and HBO's *Six Feet Under,* which featured a gay police officer), so have gay and lesbian individuals become more willing to stand up against discrimination. Fearful of litigation and negative publicity, most police agencies have removed discriminatory language from their hiring criteria. However, most law enforcement administrators have maintained the ban on hiring gay men and lesbians, some covertly. Consider the following:

The Dallas, Texas, Police Department, which was sued for refusing to hire a qualified woman who was a lesbian, continues to ask applicants if they have ever had sex in a public place. While this question is lawful, the follow-up is a query where male applicants are asked if the "girl" they had sex with was at least 18 years of age. (Grobeson, 2003)

The Los Angeles Police Department, which was repeatedly sued for antigay discrimination between 1988 and 1996, continued throughout 2000 to ask male applicants about drugs that were specifically used within the gay community (inhalant "poppers" with names such as "locker room"). The LAPD also asked "the nature of the relationship" with roommates who were of the same gender. (Grobeson, 2000)

Many law enforcement agencies give the public impression of nondiscrimination, but in fact discriminate by disqualifying lesbian, gay, bisexual, and transgender applicants. (Grobeson, 2003)

The past decade has seen the removal of the explicit ban against the hiring of gay men and lesbians by most law enforcement agencies. Despite this apparent dramatic paradigm shift, the reality remains that the vast majority of law enforcement agencies, including those within many urban areas with large, openly gay populations, find ways to surreptitiously avoid hiring openly gay men. To a lesser extent, this includes openly lesbian individuals. Some law enforcement agencies have used sodomy laws to disqualify applicants for being individuals with a "propensity" to violate the law. On June 26, 2003, the United States Supreme Court issued a ruling regarding the 1998 arrests by Houston police officers of two men engaged in consensual sexual activity in the privacy of their own bedroom. The ruling overturned the sodomy laws of the 13 states that still had such laws on the books, stating that they violated the constitutional right to privacy.

The rejection of homosexuals in law enforcement by some agencies continues despite recent studies that have shown that the presence of openly lesbian, gay, bisexual, and transgender personnel enhanced service, and did not negatively impact morale or unit cohesion, in integrated police departments (e.g., San Diego Police Department; Belkin & McNichol, 2002) and armed forces (e.g., Israel, Britain, and Australia; Belkin & McNichol, 2002).

Public Relations versus Recruitment

According to Grobeson, many urban law enforcement agencies engage in public relations campaigns as substitutes for actual recruitment efforts. His observation is that many city or county personnel departments place recruitment advertisements in the gay and lesbian media or assign officers to attend gay and lesbian events such as gay pride festivals. However, he believes that these agencies are only providing "lip service" while avoiding actual recruitment. Law enforcement administrators seeking to have a workforce on parity with their community need to be cognizant of artificial barriers. To ensure equal opportunity, it is important to conduct applicant tracking, in which applicant information is taken at an event, and contact with the applicant is maintained to determine if the applicant is hired or where in the process he or she is disqualified. If a disproportionate number of these applicants are failing during a specific part of the hiring process, such as oral interviews, background investigations, or polygraph exams, then administrators must be able to capture this information starting from the original point of contact. Further, this approach can help determine if funding for these events or advertisements is an effective use of resources.

Other areas to monitor to determine if a department provides equal opportunity are the number of openly gay officers who voluntarily participate in events with the lesbian, gay, bisexual, and transgender communities and the number who are willing to be named when interviewed by the mainstream media. Department personnel who cite numbers of gays and lesbians on a police force are usually viewed skeptically by lesbian, gay, bisexual, and transgender community organizations.

The Controversy

Some police officers view openly gay and lesbian individuals as extremist militant types who publicly display their sexuality in offensive or socially unacceptable ways. This is a stereotype; the majority of heterosexuals do not draw attention to their sexual preference, and neither do most homosexuals. Concerns about homosexuals in the military or in law enforcement include beliefs that gay soldiers or police officers will walk hand in hand, dance together at clubs, make passes at nongay colleagues, and display aspects of their private lives (as well as seek benefits for gay marriages). These arguments for bans are not based in reality, however, since the majority of gays in the military and the criminal justice system are as work-oriented as their heterosexual colleagues. They do not wish to provoke anyone in the system; rather, like the majority of other officers, homosexual officers want to accomplish their missions, work special assignments, promote and avoid confrontation. In fact, gay and lesbian officers and military personnel are much less likely than their heterosexual counterparts to engage in even such mundane acts as putting a picture of their partner on their desk or posted inside their locker. Gay and lesbian officers are no different from others in wanting to support the disciplinary processes, and they believe that any inappropriate conduct should be handled with proper discipline. Research on the subject of homosexuals in the military and in law enforcement at the beginning of the 21st century concluded that the presence of gays and lesbians has not caused morale to drop in either setting. The research also determined that there were no negative consequences in urban police departments that adopt nondiscrimination statutes and actively recruit and hire homosexual officers. One comprehensive study of gays and lesbians in a large police agency was designed to discover whether the integration of open gay and lesbian officers has undermined the organizational effectiveness of the San Diego Police Department (SDPD).

> Based on an analysis of prior research and a 3-day site visit, our findings are that a quiet process of normalization has reduced much of the emotional charge that heterosexual officers originally anticipated. Although integration has proceeded largely uneventfully, subtle forms of discrimination do persist, and gay officers who do not already enjoy respect may face challenges. Despite these uneven effects, integration has enhanced cohesion as well as the SDPD's standing with the communities it serves. (Belkin & McNichol, 2002, p. 63)

The report indicates that the integration of gay men and lesbians into law enforcement has been similar to the earlier experiences of women and minorities: Initial reactions among officers within the organization and some prominent community members were often negative, and longstanding work cultures were slow to change (Belkin & McNichol, 2002). Research on police culture through the early 1990s depicts a work environment that was seeking to reinforce traditional notions of masculinity and describes casual remarks ridiculing or stereotyping homosexuals as being commonplace in formal and informal settings (Belkin & McNichol, 2002, p. 64). The report's key finding is that

> . . . the increasing participation of self-disclosed homosexuals in the SDPD has not led to any overall negative consequences for performance, effectiveness, recruiting, morale, or other measures of well-being. Even though incidents of harassment and discrimination continue and new internal tensions have arisen concerning the integration of homosexuals, self-disclosed gay personnel, their peers and commanders, and outside observers all agree that disruptive incidents continue to decline in frequency and are usually handled effectively through both informal and formal channels. (Belkin & McNichol, 2002, p. 65)

The researchers noted that complaints by gay and lesbian officers at the San Diego Police Department about harassment or discrimination are extremely low, resulting in underestimates of the actual number of occurrences. They hypothesize that the low number is related to the fact that closeted personnel fear being identified as gay and are reluctant to complain. The study also suggests, however, that another reason might be that, like most departments, the work culture of the SDPD strongly emphasizes the informal and discreet resolution of problems at the unit level. According to the study, the number of self-described gay and lesbian officers in the department has grown from about five in 1992 up to 50 out of 2,100 in 2003, scattered among patrol, investigations, the SWAT team, community relations, and training. The report concludes that

> . . . concern over working with openly gay men and lesbians has subsided as day-to-day interactions with gay colleagues become more commonplace. In many divisions, for straight and gay people alike, sexual orientation issues are relatively unimportant vis-à-vis the daily challenges of being a cop. Although isolated comments and misconduct may occur, the professional working environment and strong support for equal treatment from headquarters tend to diffuse their frequency and significance. . . . Virtually all respondents believe that the increasing, taken-for-grantedness [sic] of gay cops reflects in part the more tolerant values of new recruits coming into the department. Younger cohorts of recruits have brought with them more diverse views and greater comfort levels with gay issues than in years past, and EEO policies and training programs are allowing for more candid give-and-take as recruits wrestle with uncertainties over how to work with gay people. (Belkin & McNichol, 2002, p. 76)

Differences in Treatment of Gay versus Lesbian Officers

Many law enforcement professionals have voiced opinions that, because of the "macho" requirements of police work, a double standard exists with respect to the way gay and lesbian officers are viewed. The traditional male dominance of the profession has made it difficult for many male officers to accept that women or gay men are equally able to perform the same tasks they do. They view their work as an occupation for only the "strongest and the toughest." Male officers' self-esteem can be threatened by the ability of women and gay men to do "their" job. (This issue is discussed further in this chapter under "Women in Law Enforcement.")

According to Grobeson, there has been a trend of acceptance of "macho" lesbians into law enforcement. Many male officers are more accepting of lesbian officers, particularly those who are not openly homosexual, than they are of heterosexual women. It appears that male officers are more fearful that "feminine" women will not provide them with sufficient backup where physicality is required. They are more willing to rely on lesbian officers, whom they stereotype as being macho and athletic. Grobeson believes that there is still a great deal of discrimination directed toward women who break the cultural mores and choose to be open or apparent about their sexual orientation.

In addition, the pervasive stereotype of gay men as effeminate remains a factor in most officers' bias against the hiring of and working with gay men. Allowing openly gay men to serve as officers is perceived by many as threatening to the "macho" image of police work: if a gay man can successfully complete the necessary tasks, their job is therefore less "macho." Further, those officers whose self-image is based on their job, perceiving themselves as "John Wayne," are generally the most uncomfortable with the concept of working with gay officers.

Significantly, within those urban agencies that actively seek to hire gay men and lesbians, lesbians are frequently used to insulate management against accusations of discrimination and homophobia. When gay men are disqualified, their background investigations are often conducted by lesbian (or "butch" women perceived to be lesbian) officers. The same holds true for gay officers accused of misconduct; invariably a lesbian investigator, or if none are in the agency, then a woman, usually from a minority group, will be used to conduct or participate in the disciplinary process.

Grobeson asserts that gay men are relegated to the least desirable status of any minority group in terms of acceptance in police culture. Homophobic jokes and nicknames, for example, are still prevalent locker room banter, whereas racial epithets have been mostly eliminated. One stereotype characterizes effeminate men as unworthy of trust as partners, despite the fact that many gay officers are military combat veterans with awards and accolades for bravery, heroism, and service under fire. For example, many gay officers in New York and San Francisco have received medals for their valor ("Policeman with Pride," Cybersocket, 2000). Officers suspected of being gay are often teased, belittled, or openly harassed with little or no intervention from supervisors or managers. Some newly hired gay officers have reported that they believe it is important to stay "in the closet" until they have proven to their peers and supervisors that they are effective officers.

Gay officers often identify more readily with their fellow officers than they do with members of the gay community. Even as late as 2000, many gay men and lesbians viewed law enforcement as society's arm of social control. With many law enforcement officers still hostile toward gay men and lesbians, gay officers are forced to choose a side, particularly when it comes to the issue of vice enforcement. Therefore, gay and lesbian officers are often accepted neither by the gay community nor by their peers.

The Transition

Problems will inevitably surface within law enforcement agencies as gay and lesbian officers "come out of the closet." Many organizations and employees will be hesitant to welcome such a major change, and may resist it unless measures are taken to allay their fears. Officers thought to be or who are openly gay or lesbian may encounter discriminatory treatment and/or hostility because of other employees' negative stereotypes and attitudes. People without proper education on acquired immune deficiency syndrome (AIDS), for example, may be afraid of AIDS transmission. This and other fears may mean that gay men will have an even more difficult time in assimilating into departments than ethnic or racial minorities, heterosexual women, or lesbians.

Gay and lesbian officers are often placed in a position of having to prove themselves on the job. This may be through a physical confrontation with an arrestee or a test that includes confidential information regarding the personal conduct of patrol officers. As openly gay and lesbian officers are recruited and hired, however, the organizational comfort level will undoubtedly become more tolerant. Individual and group prejudices and assumptions, for example, will be challenged. Law enforcement agencies should have written policies to assist gay and lesbian officers' transition into the department as well as operational plans to promote employee acceptance of these officers.

Because of the small number of openly gay and lesbian officers in law enforcement, there are currently no policies dealing specifically with inappropriate displays of sexuality; obviously, discipline would have to be applied equally to both gay and lesbian and heterosexual officers who behave unprofessionally. Among gay and lesbian law enforcement officers, however, there is a strong desire to conform to the norms of the organization and to prove their worth as members of that organization. They seldom engage in behaviors that would challenge those norms or shock or offend fellow officers.

These new challenges confronting law enforcement must be addressed in a timely manner. Otherwise, agencies will be ill prepared to deal with the complex, controversial issues that are certain to arise, nor will they be able to address the negative attitudes of certain officers.

Policies against Discrimination and Harassment

Unfortunately, there have been many incidents in which gay and lesbian officers have been subjected to discrimination or harassment by fellow officers. A few examples follow:

> A gay Manhattan Beach, California police sergeant sued the city and police chief alleging that the chief told another senior officer, "Don't send that fag an application" when an openly gay man sought to join the force. The night after making a complaint against a fellow officer, someone threw three steaks laced with strychnine over the fence of the sergeant's home, poisoning his cocker spaniel. Then, the tires of his personal car were slashed while in the Police Department parking lot. ("Gay *MB* Police officer alleges harassment," 2002)

> In June 1999, a former Long Island, New York police officer was awarded $380,000 by a federal jury for antigay harassment. A superior had threatened the officer with a knife, telling him, "I kill queers. All faggots deserve to die." This verdict was perhaps the first time in the nation that a police agency was held liable for antigay harassment. ("Gay Officer Wins Harassment Suit," 1999)

> A New York police officer filed a suit accusing his fellow officers of placing posters throughout the city announcing his sexual orientation and also for at-

tacking him in the presence of supervisors, physically forcing him inside his locker. (*ABC News 20/20,* April 16, 1999)

The chief executive must establish departmental policies and regulations regarding gay and lesbian officers. These policies must clearly state that discrimination, harassment, or failure to assist fellow gay and lesbian officers are unacceptable and will result in severe discipline. The chief executive must obtain the support of his or her supervisors and managers to ensure that the intent of these rules, policies, and procedures is clear and that all employees adhere to these regulations. All employees must be held accountable, and those who do not support these antidiscrimination policies will not be promoted nor awarded special assignments. Evaluations of employees should reflect how supportive they are of departmental policy that protects gay and lesbian officers. Department executives must be aware that gay and lesbian officers might not report victimization by other employees. For example, an independent investigation conducted in late 2000 determined that within the LAPD, 64 percent of gay and lesbian employees interviewed stated they would fear retaliation if they made a departmental complaint against another officer for discrimination or harassment ("LAPD Confidential," 2000).

If the state does not have one, the city, county, or law enforcement agency should adopt an antidiscrimination policy with regard to gays and lesbians in the workplace. As of June 2003, 14 states have passed laws prohibiting discrimination based on sexual orientation. Four of these laws also prohibit gender identification–based discrimination. City or county officials must support and possibly even champion such legislation. The policy should establish that:

- Sexual orientation is not a hindrance in hiring, retention, or promotion.
- Hiring is based solely on merit as long as the individual meets objective standards of employment.
- Hiring is done on the basis of the identical job-related standards and criteria for all individuals.

Law enforcement managers and supervisors must routinely check to ensure that this policy is being carried out as intended.

Training on Gay, Lesbian, and Transgender Issues

Cultural awareness programs that train department personnel on diversity within communities and in the workforce must also educate employees on gay, lesbian, and transgender issues. The training should address and show the falsehoods of stereotypes and myths. It must cover legal rights, including a discussion of statutes and departmental policies on nondiscrimination and the penalties for violating them. These penalties include liability for acts of harassment and discrimination. Often, involving openly gay or lesbian officers (from other agencies, if necessary) in these training programs provides the best outcome. Ideally, this training will enable employees to know the gay or lesbian officers they work with as human beings, reduce personal prejudices and false assumptions, and thus change behavior. This type of training furthers the ideal of respect for all people. A secondary benefit of this training is the decreased likelihood of personnel complaints and lawsuits by gay or lesbian employees or community members against a city, county, or individual officer.

For a nondiscrimination policy to be implemented effectively, managers must provide regular and ongoing training at all levels of their department (see curricula in Instructor's Manual). This nondiscrimination policy must be articulated and communicated clearly and enforced consistently. Because homophobic attitudes are present among the rank and file, and because sensitivity training and similar programs usually provoke resentment rather than tolerance, the emphasis on training is most successful when it focuses on strict standards of professional conduct and behavior (RAND's National Defense Research Institute, 1993).

Cultural diversity training, which is much more confrontational than sensitivity training but is not abrasive, challenges officers' current attitudes without being condescending. In measuring officers' attitudes, beliefs, feelings, and knowledge, this type of training has been shown to have a positive impact. The training uses simulated situations in which officers deal with partners who are gay. Managers and supervisors are required to handle situations in which a fellow officer is being harassed for perceived homosexuality. Such presentations are most successful when conducted by gay or lesbian officers who are experienced diversity trainers, but this is not to suggest that trainers will be qualified or successful merely because of their sexual orientation.

It is recommended that the training include discussion panels made up of local gay and lesbian community members, business owners, service providers, and community groups, as well as gay youth and gay youth service providers. For supervisors and managers, additional panels comprising attorneys, including municipal attorneys who prosecute hate crimes and who specialize in defense work dealing with homosexual arrestees, HIV issues, and sexual orientation employment discrimination, should be provided.

Successful training programs about gay, lesbian, and transgender issues have been completed at the San Francisco, Alameda, and Sacramento Police Departments and the Santa Clara Sheriff's Department. The San Francisco Police Department is a good source of information about transgender people. San Francisco probably has the largest population of transgender residents with an estimated 15,000 to 18,000 people. The city has attracted transgender people from all over the world ("S.F.'s Transgender Gain Visibility," 2001, p. A33). (For more information on conducting diversity training, refer to the Instructor's Manual available for this textbook, which offers suggestions for a cultural diversity training program that includes gay, lesbian, bisexual, and transgender awareness.)

Police officers are the protectors of individuals in a diverse society that includes gay, lesbian, bisexual, and transgender people. Although we recognize that police officers are human and entitled to their own personal beliefs, they cannot display biased behavior or engage in discriminatory actions. Police officers who are prejudiced against gay, lesbian, bisexual, or transgender people must still uphold their rights. When prejudice or bias by an officer results in an overt discriminatory act, he or she must be appropriately punished for harassment. Officers also cannot remain silent if they witness a discriminatory act of homophobic crime committed by fellow employees. These same officers must maintain a good working relationship with peers who may be different than themselves. Police officers represent the entire community. Any act they commit while on duty (or off) can bring dishonor not only to them but also to their agency, the community they serve, and the entire profession of law enforcement. Repercussions of an act of discrimination could be the "shot heard 'round the world," as happened in the Rodney King case.

Many managers and supervisors need to change their leadership style to meet the challenges and requirements of a culturally diverse society and workforce. Management experts suggest that modern leaders must have two important traits: vision and the ability to communicate their visions and values to others within the workforce and the community who come from diverse backgrounds, including different ethnicity, race, religion, gender, and sexual orientation.

Support Groups for Lesbian, Gay, Bisexual, and Transgender Officers

Lesbian, gay, bisexual, and transgender (LGBT) officers benefit from support groups and peer counselors in their own or neighboring police agencies. In the early 1980s, openly gay and lesbian officers formed networks of support within the San Francisco Sheriff's Department. In the late 1980s, the San Francisco and New York City Police Departments, along with other agencies, assisted gay and lesbian officers in forming support groups. In the early 1990s, chapters of the Golden State Peace Officers Association (founded in San Francisco) and the Gay Officers Action League (founded in New York) were established in southern California to assist them. In addition to networking, the groups provide mentoring and support for their members. Heterosexual employees who support the rights of gay, lesbian, bisexual, and transgender personnel have also joined as members and associate members of these organizations.

The Need Remains

With notable exceptions such as the San Francisco Sheriff's Department, the San Francisco Police Department, and the New York Police Department, the presence of openly gay and lesbian officers within law enforcement is relatively new. As such, it is still critically important that agency officials establish openly gay and lesbian liaisons to the LGBT community. This assignment provides role models to qualified LGBT persons who may desire a career in law enforcement. Critically, with the increasing prevalence of hate crimes, it also gives an agency the ability to provide victims with LGBT officers, whose expertise and compassion will likely elicit both cooperation and information that could impact the outcome of the investigation. Police officials realized years ago the invaluable service of providing women rape victims the comfort of female officers in conducting the interview. That need is duplicated when it comes to LGBT hate crime victims. Moreover, with the reticence of LGBT crime victims to come forward due to the real or perceived bias of law enforcement personnel, the ability for them to approach an LGBT officer negates the fear of "double victimization." In the end, both the community as a whole, as well as the law enforcement agency, benefit from the presence of such forthright and honest personnel.

THE CHIEF EXECUTIVE

The chief law enforcement executive should follow specific guidelines to meet the challenge of policing a multicultural and multiracial community. As emphasized previously, he or she must first effectively manage the diversity within his or her own organization. Progressive law enforcement executives are aware that before employees can be asked to value diversity in the community, it must be clear that diversity within the organization is valued. Managing diversity in the law enforcement workplace is therefore of high priority.

Executive leadership and team building are crucial to managing a diverse workforce and establishing good minority–community relations. The chief executive must take the lead in this endeavor by:

- Demonstrating commitment
- Developing strategic, implementation, and transition management plans
- Managing organizational change
- Developing police–community partnerships (community-based policing)
- Providing new leadership models

Demonstrate Commitment

The organization must adopt and implement policies that demonstrate a commitment to policing a diverse society. These policies must be developed with input from all levels of the organization and community. Valuing diversity and treating all persons with respect must be the imperative first from the chief executive. His or her personal leadership and commitment are the keystones to implementing policies and awareness training within the organization and to successfully building bridges to the community. One of the first steps is the development of a "macro" mission statement for the organization that elaborates the philosophy, values, vision, and goals of the department to foster good relationships with a diverse workforce and community. All existing and new policies and practices of the department must be evaluated to see how they may affect women, members of diverse ethnic and racial groups, gays, lesbians, bisexuals, and transgender employees on the force. Recruitment, hiring, and promotional practices must be reviewed to ensure that there are no institutional barriers to different groups in an agency. The chief executive stresses, via mission and values statements, that the agency will not tolerate discrimination, abuse, or crimes motivated by hate against protected classes within the community or within the agency itself. The policy statements should also include references to discrimination or bias based on physical disability or age.

The executive must use every opportunity to speak out publicly on the value of diversity and to make certain that people inside and outside the organization know that upholding those ideals is a high priority. He or she must actively promote policies and programs designed to improve community relations and use marketing skills to sell these programs, both internally and externally. Internal marketing is accomplished by involving senior management and the police association in the development of the policies and action plans. The chief or sheriff can use this opportunity to gain support for the policies by demonstrating the value to the department's effectiveness and to officer safety of having community support. External marketing is accomplished by involving representatives of community-based organizations in the process.

Police leaders must institute policies that develop positive attitudes toward a multicultural workplace and community even as early as the selection process. During background interviews, polygraphs, and psychological exams, candidates for law enforcement employment must be carefully screened. The questions and processes can help determine candidates' attitudes and beliefs and, at the same time, make them aware of the agency's strong commitment to a multicultural workforce.

Develop Strategic, Implementation, and Transition Management Plans

Textbooks and courses that teach strategic, implementation, and transition management planning are available to law enforcement leaders. The techniques, although not difficult, are quite involved and are not the focus of this book. Such techniques and methodologies are planning tools, providing the road map that the organization uses to implement programs and to guide the agency through change. An essential component is the action plans that identify specific goals and objectives. Action plans include budgets and timetables and establish accountability—who is to accomplish what by when. Multiple action plans involving the improvement of police–community relations in a diverse society would be necessary to cover such varied components as policy and procedures changes; affirmative action recruitment (where legal), hiring, and promotions; cultural awareness training; and community involvement (i.e., community-based policing).

Manage Organizational Change

The department leadership is responsible for managing change processes and action plans. This is an integral part of implementation and transition management, as discussed previously. The chief executive must ensure that any new policies, procedures, and training result in increased employee responsiveness and awareness of the diversity in the community and within the organization's workforce. He or she must require that management staff continually monitor progress on all programs and strategies to improve police–community relations. Additionally, the chief must ensure that all employees are committed to those ideals. Managers and supervisors need to ensure application of these established philosophies and policies of the department, and they must lead by example. When intentional deviation from the system is discovered, retraining and discipline should be quick and effective. Employees (especially patrol officers) must be rewarded and recognized for their ability to work with and within a multicultural community. The reward systems for employees, especially first- and second-line supervisors, would recognize those who foster positive relations with individuals of different gender, ethnicity, race, or sexual orientation both within and outside the organization. As we have illustrated, the chief executive, management staff, and supervisors are role models and must set the tone for the sort of behavior and actions they expect of employees.

Develop Police–Community Partnerships

Progressive police organizations have adopted community-based policing as one response strategy to meet the needs and challenges of a pluralistic workforce and society. The establishment of community partnerships is a very important aspect of meeting the challenges. For example, a cultural awareness training component will not be as effective if police–community partnerships are not developed, utilized, and maintained. The chief executive establishes and maintains ongoing communications with all segments of the community. Open lines of communication are best established by community-based policing (discussed in detail in Chapter 1).

Provide New Leadership Models

In the past all methods or models of management and organizational behavior were based on implicit assumptions of a homogeneous, white male workforce. Even best-sellers such as *The One-Minute Manager* and *In Search of Excellence* that continue to be useful management tools are based on that traditional assumption. Managers must learn to value diversity and overcome personal and organizational barriers to effective leadership, such as stereotypes, myths, unwritten rules, and codes (one of those being that the organizational role model is a white male). New models of leadership must be incorporated into law enforcement organizations to manage the multicultural and multiracial workforce.

Jamieson and O'Mara (1991) address the topic of motivating and working with a diverse workforce, explaining that the leader must move beyond traditional management styles and approaches. They indicate that the modern manager must move from the traditional one-size-fits-all management style to a "flex-management" model. They describe flex management as not just another program or quick fix but one that is "based on the need to individualize the way we manage, accommodating differences and providing choices wherever possible" (p. 31). The flex-management model they envision involves three components:

1. *Policies:* Published rules that guide the organization.
2. *Systems:* Human resources tools, processes, and procedures.
3. *Practices:* Day-to-day activities.

The model is based on four strategies: matching people to jobs, managing and rewarding performance, informing and involving people, and supporting lifestyle and life needs. Five key management skills are required of the modern manager to use this model successfully:

1. Empowering others.
2. Valuing diversity.
3. Communicating responsibly.
4. Developing others.
5. Working for change.

Good leaders not only acknowledge their own ethnocentrism but also understand the cultural values and biases of the people with whom they work. Consequently, such leaders can empower, value, and communicate more effectively with all employees. Developing others involves mentoring and coaching skills, important tools for modern managers. To communicate responsibly leaders must understand the diverse workforce from a social and cultural context and flexibly utilize a variety of verbal and nonverbal communication strategies with employees. Modern leaders are also familiar with conflict mediation in cross-cultural disputes.

Jamieson and O'Mara (1991) explain that to establish a flex-management model, managers must follow a six-step plan of action that includes:

1. Defining the organization's diversity.

2. Understanding the organization's workforce values and needs.

3. Describing the desired future state.

4. Analyzing the present state.

5. Planning and managing transitions.

6. Evaluating results.

They contend that to be leaders in the new workforce, most managers will have to "unlearn practices rooted in old mindsets, change the way their organization operates, shift organizational culture, revamp policies, create new structures, and redesign human resource systems" (p. 25).

The vocabulary of the future involves leading employees rather than simply managing them. Hammond and Kleiner (1992) wrote about the distinction between the two:

> One of the first things companies must look at in multicultural environments is the leadership vs. management issue. Leadership, in contrast to management, deals with values, ethics, perspective, vision, creativity and common humanity. Leadership is a step beyond management; it is at the heart of any unit in any organization. Leadership lies with those who believe in the mission and through action, attitude, and attention pass this on to those who have to sustain the mission and accomplish the individual tasks. People want to be led, not managed; and the more diverse the working population becomes the more leadership is needed. (p. 3)

Hammond and Kleiner (1992) explain that in a multicultural and multiracial society and workforce, "the genius of leadership" is

1. Learning about and understanding the needs of the diverse people you want to serve—not boss, not control—but serve

2. Creating and articulating a corporate mission and vision that your workers can get excited about, participate in, and be a part of

3. Behaving in a manner that shows respect to and value for all individual workers and their unique contributions to the whole. Those you can't value, you can't lead. (p. 13)

This approach to leadership was echoed in the introduction to *Transcultural Leadership—Empowering the Diverse Workforce:*

Transcultural leadership addresses a new global reality. Today productivity must come from the collaboration of culturally diverse women and men. It insists that leaders change organizational culture to empower and develop people. This demands that employees be selected, evaluated, and promoted on the basis of *performance and competency,* regardless of sex, race, religion, or place of origin. Beyond that, leaders must learn the skills that enable men and women of all backgrounds to work together effectively (Simons, Vazquez, & Harris, 1993).

Management, to build positive relationships and show respect for a pluralistic workforce, needs to be aware of differences, treat all employees fairly (and not necessarily in identical ways), and lead. The differing needs and values of a diverse workforce require flexibility by organizations and their leaders. Modern leaders of organizations recognize not only that different employees have different needs but also that these needs change over time. The goal of law enforcement leaders is to bridge cultural and racial gaps within their organizations.

SUMMARY

Officers who traditionally worked in predominantly white male workforces must learn to work with increasing numbers of women, gay men and lesbians blacks, Hispanics, Asians, and others within our diverse society. In this chapter we have suggested that to be effective in this new environment, officers must have a knowledge of conflict resolution techniques to reduce racial and ethnic problems.

The chapter focused on concerns and issues of members of underrepresented ethnically and racially diverse groups as well as women and gay men and lesbians in law enforcement. The importance of support and mentoring programs for women and diverse groups was stressed. Such programs help them make transitions into organizations, cope with stress, and meet their workplace challenges more effectively.

In the chapter we provided suggestions for law enforcement executives whose jurisdictions are pluralistic and whose workforces are diverse. Law enforcement leaders must be committed to setting an organizational tone that does not permit bigoted or discriminatory acts and must act swiftly against those who violate these policies. They must monitor and deal quickly with complaints both within their workforce and from the public they serve.

DISCUSSION QUESTIONS AND ISSUES*

1. *Measuring Responsiveness to Diversity.* Using the check-off and scoring sheet (Exhibit 2.3), determine how responsive your police department has been to the diversity of the jurisdiction it serves. If you are not affiliated with an agency, choose a city or county police department and interview a command officer to determine the answers and arrive at a score. Discuss with the com-

*See the Instructor's Manual accompanying this text for additional activities, role-play activities, questionnaires, and projects related to the content of this chapter.

mand officer what initiatives his or her department intends to undertake to address the issues of community diversity.

2. ***Defusing Racially and Culturally Rooted Conflicts.*** What training does the police academy in your region provide on defusing racially and culturally rooted conflicts? What training of this type does your local city or county law enforcement agency provide to officers? What community (public and private) agencies are available as referrals or for mediation of such conflicts? Discuss what training should be provided to police officers to defuse, mediate, and resolve racially and culturally rooted conflicts. Discuss what approaches a law enforcement agency should utilize.

3. ***Women in Law Enforcement.*** How many women officers are there in your local city or county law enforcement agency? How many of those women are in supervisory or management positions? Are any of the women assigned to nontraditional roles such as special weapons and tactics teams, motorcycle enforcement, bomb units, hostage negotiations, or community relations? Have there been incidents of sexual harassment of women employees? If so, how were the cases resolved? Has the agency you are examining implemented any programs to increase the employment of women, such as flextime, child care, mentoring, awareness training, or career development? Has the agency been innovative in the recruitment efforts for women applicants? Discuss your findings in a group setting.

4. ***Diversity in Law Enforcement.*** Comment on the diversity in your local city or county law enforcement agency. What is the breakdown in your agency's hierarchy? For example, who holds supervisory or management positions? Have there been reported acts of discrimination against people of diverse backgrounds? Has the agency you are examining implemented any programs to increase the employment of minorities? Discuss your findings in a group setting.

WEBSITE RESOURCES

Visit these websites for additional information related to the content of Chapter 2.

International Association of Chiefs of Police: http://www.theiacp.org

An online resource for law enforcement issues publications including "Recruitment/Retention of Qualified Police Personnel: A Best Practices Guide," December 7, 2001.

International Association of Women Police (IAWP):   http://www.iawp.org

A website for information about training conferences, careers, jobs, publications, and research pertinent to women in law enforcement.

Institute for Women in Trades, Technology and Science (IWITTS):
http://www.womenpolice.com

This website features fact sheets, news articles, and publications for departments on women and policing, including a free women in policing e-newsletter, which provides best practice information.

National Center for Women and Policing (NCWP):   http://www.feminist.org

This website provides information concerning regional training seminars on recruiting and retaining women. It also is a resource for the latest research about women in policing and other critical issues. The organization has consultants to help agencies identify and remove obstacles to recruiting and retaining women.

National Association of Women Law Enforcement Executives (NAWLEE):
http://www.nawlee.com

The website contains resources, news, member directory, conference and training information, seminars, and an information exchange for women executives in law enforcement.

Vera Institute of Justice: http://www.vera.org

The Vera Institute of Justice works closely with leaders in government and civil society to improve the services people rely on for safety and justice. Vera develops innovative, affordable programs that often grow into self-sustaining organizations, studies social problems and current responses, and provides practical advice and assistance to government officials around the world. They have publications on many law enforcement subjects.

REFERENCES

America accepting gays easier. (2000, June 17). *Contra Costa Times,* p. A27.

Belkin, Aaron, and Jason McNichol. (2002, March). "Pink and Blue: Outcomes Associated with the Integration of Open Gay and Lesbian Personnel in the San Diego Police Department." *Police Quarterly, 5*(1), 63–96.

Bell, Daniel. (1982). "Policewomen: Myths and Reality." *Journal of Police Science and Administration, 10*(1), 112.

Benson, Katy. (1992, August). "Black and White on Blue." *Police,* p. 167.

Blanchard, Kenneth H., and Spencer Johnson. (1983). *The One-Minute Manager.* New York: Berkley.

Business Week. (1991, September 19). "History of Woman in Workforce."

Cordner, Gary, and Donna Hale (1992). "Women in Policing," in *What Works in Policing: Operations and Administration Examined.* Cincinnati, Ohio: Anderson Publishing, pp. 125–142.

DeGeneste, Henry I., and John Sullivan. (1997). "Policing a Multicultural Community," in *Fresh Perspectives: A Police Executive Research Forum Publication,* Washington D.C.

8 agents accuse Secret Service of racial bias. (2000, August 31). *Contra Costa Times,* p. A22.

Ellis, Patricia (2000 October). Officer, Lothian and Borders Police, Edinburgh, Scotland, personal communication.

Female cops: Nation's policewomen are facing a bullet-proof glass ceiling. (1998, November 24). *USA Today,* p. 1.

Gay officer wins harassment suit. (1999, July 15). *Daily Journal,* p. *1.*

Gay MB Police Officer Alleges Harassment, Sues City and Chief. (2002, August 22). *Daily Breeze,* p. A2 & A9.

Grobeson, Mitchell. (2000 and 2003). Sergeant-Retired, Los Angeles Police Department, California, personal communication, November, 2000 and July, 2003).

Hall, Thomas. (1992). Sergeant, Virginia State Troopers, personal communication, October, 1992.

Hammond, Teresa, and Brian Kleiner. (1992). "Managing Multicultural Work Environments." *Equal Opportunities International, 11*(2).

Hampton, Ron. (1992, September 27-29). "Unfinished Business: Racial and Ethnic Issues Facing Law Enforcement II." Paper presented at a conference sponsored by the National Organization of Black Law Enforcement Executives and the Police Executive Research Forum, Reno, Nevada.

Hartmann Report (2000, August). City of Los Angeles Police Department Study. Independent Commission on the Los Angeles Police Department (1991). Summary: Racism and Bias. Los Angeles: Independent Commission, pp.7–8.

International Association of Chiefs of Police. (1998). *The Future of Women in Policing: Mandates for Action.* Washington, D.C: Author.

Jamieson, David, and Julie O'Mara. (1991). *Managing Workforce 2000: Gaining the Diversity Advantage.* San Francisco: Jossey-Bass.

Johnson, L. (1991). "Job Strain among Police Officers: Gender Comparisons." *Police Studies, 14*(1), 12–16.

Jones, Susan (1993). Sergeant, Concord, California Police Department, personal communication. (2003, May) Chief of Police, Healdsburg, California Police Department, personal communication, February, 1993.

LAPD confidential anti-gay cover up. (2000, October 13). *fab! Newspaper,* p. *1.*

Marrujo, Robert, and Brian Kleiner (1992). "Why Women Fail to Get to the Top." *Equal Opportunities International, 11*(4), 1.

Martin, Susan (1990, September). *The Status of Women in Policing.* Washington, DC: Washington, D.C. Police Foundation.

McCoy, Daniel. (1992, June). "The Future Organizational Environment for Women in Law Enforcement." California Command College Class XIV, Peace Officer Standards and Training, Sacramento, Calif.

McMahon, Brook. (1990, June). "How Will the Role of Law Enforcement Change by the Year 2000 as it Deals with Suspected or Openly Gay Police Officers?" California Command College Class X, Peace Officer Standards and Training, Sacramento, Calif.

More, Harry. (1992). *Male-Dominated Police Culture: Reducing the Gender Gap.* Cincinnati, Ohio: Anderson Publishing, pp. 113–137.

Naisbitt, John, and Patricia Aburdene. (1986). *Re-inventing the Corporation.* New York: Warner Books, p. 243.

National Center for Women and Policing. (2001). *Equality Denied: The Status of Women in Policing.* Los Angeles: National Center for Women and Policing, pp. 1–17.

Nichols, D. (1995, Summer). "The Brotherhood: Sexual Harassment in Police Agencies." *Women Police,* pp. 10–12.

Obstacles hinder minority women. (2003, August 7). *Contra Costa Times,* p. C1.

Peters, Thomas J., and Robert H. Waterman. (1984). *In Search of Excellence.* New York: Warner Books.

Pogrebin, Mark. (1986, April–June). "The Changing Role of Women: Female Police Officers' Occupational Problems." *Police Journal, 59*(2), 131.

Police Chief (1998). "Utilization of Police Women," Carole G. Garrison, Nancy Grant and Kenneth McCormick, 32 (7).

Policemen with Pride. (2000, September/October). *Cybersocket,* p. 34.

Racism on the job: Black N. J. troopers charge harassment, bias, and discrimination. (1993, April 22). *New York Daily News,* p. C3.

RAND's National Defense Research Institute. (1993). *Sexual Orientation and U.S. Military Personnel. Policy, Options and Assessment.* Santa Monica, Calif.: RAND Institute.

Report recommends using military model to defuse racism in police departments. (1992, May 26). *New York Times,* p. A17.

Ross, Ruth, John Snortum, and John Beyers. (1982). "Public Priorities and Police Policy in a Bicultural Community." *Police Studies, 5*(1), 18–30.

Schulz, Dorothy M. (1995). *From Social Worker To Crime Fighter: Women in United States Municipal Policing.* Westport, Conn.: Praeger, p. 5.

S.F.'s transgender gain visibility, rights, a civil voice. (2001, February 25). *Contra Costa Times,* p. A33.

Simons, George, Carmen Vazquez, and Philip Harris (1993). *Transcultural Leadership—Empowering the Diverse Workforce.* Houston, Texas: Gulf Publishing.

Theiderman, Sondra. (1991). *Bridging Cultural Barriers for Corporate Success.* San Francisco: Jossey-Bass.

Sheilds, Robert (1993, February). Chief of Police, Alameda, California Police Department, personal communications. University of California at Santa Barbara (2000). Center for the Study of Sexual Minorities in the Military.

U.S. Department of Justice, Bureau of Justice Statistics: Census of State and Local Law Enforcement Agencies, 2000: October 2002, NCJ 194066. Washington D.C.

Watts, P. (1989). "Breaking into the Old-Boy Network." *Executive Female Magazine, 12*(32), 12–14.

Wells, James. (1987). "Crime and the Administration of Criminal Justice," in Gerald D. Jaynes and Robin M. Williams, eds., *A Common Destiny: Blacks and American Society,* Washington, DC: The National Academies Press, pp. 491–497.

Women land more top jobs, but not top pay. (2003, March 25). *Contra Costa Times,* p. A16.

Women still underrepresented in law enforcement. (2003, March 16). *Contra Costa Times,* p. A32.

Chapter 3

Multicultural Representation in Law Enforcement: Recruitment, Retention, and Promotion

OVERVIEW

In this chapter we discuss recruitment trends and the probability that recruitment of women and minorities will be an ongoing challenge for law enforcement agencies. A brief historical perspective of women and minorities in law enforcement is provided, including a profile of their numbers in state, county, and local agencies across the country. We discuss reasons for recruitment difficulties and offer strategies for success. The retention and promotion of minorities and women are addressed in the final section of the chapter.

COMMENTARY

The following quotes draw attention to the recruitment crisis for law enforcement occupations and illustrate the importance of recruitment, hiring, retention, and promotion of women and minorities.

> The law enforcement profession needs intelligent, not just educated, officers who can solve problems and accept racial and cultural diversity. In short, agencies prefer smarter over tougher. Law enforcement is moving away from the "big tough cops" in favor of candidates, regardless of size, who possess qualities that mirror the tenets of the COP (Community Oriented Policing) and POP (Problem Oriented Policing) philosophies. Also, more and more, communities want service-oriented people with interpersonal skills as their guardians of justice. (Vest, 2001, p. 13)

> Many police chiefs would like to increase the number of sworn women officers in their departments but find that there are few women in the applicant pool. This isn't surprising, since law enforcement remains a male-dominated profession. Even in the year 2002, most women don't think of policing as a viable career choice because there are still few female role models in their own communities that they can look to. (Milgram, 2002)

> One of the greatest challenges facing law enforcement organizations today is the successful recruitment and retention of highly qualified employees. Community safety can be compromised when substantial experience and training is lost through staff turnover and vacancy. It is imperative, then, to recruit, select

and retain the kind of personnel who will bring to the department and to the community a strong commitment to and talent for the job. (McKeever & Kranda, 2000)

According to Trojanowicz and Carter, "By 2010, more than one third of all American children will be black, Hispanic, or Asian." The Caucasian majority of today will become a minority within America in less than 100 years. Obviously, this change in society will have a tremendous impact on the recruiting process of the future. (Osborn, 1992, p. 21)

In the harsh battleground over jobs, college education and access to the promotion ladder, the issues of quotas and racial preferences can come to dominate, if not supersede, the national struggle to achieve equity in the workplace and on the college campus. Take, for example, the core of city government: the police and fire departments. In many communities well into the 1960's, these departments were white male enclaves, controlled by such European ethnic groups as Irish, Italian and Polish Americans. (Edsall, 1991)

INTRODUCTION

Our society is becoming more and more diverse. In California, demographers predict that by 2005 there will be no single racial or ethnic group constituting the majority. That trend is occurring in some major cities in other states as well. Some demographers say that in the future every group will be a minority.

To recruit and retain a representative staff and provide effective services, therefore, law enforcement executives must have a clear understanding of their community and their own workforce. The recruitment and retention of qualified employees, and especially of women, blacks, Asians, Hispanics, and other diverse groups, has become a concern and a priority of law enforcement agencies nationwide. Many agencies are having difficulty finding qualified applicants, resulting in a general recruitment crisis, and it appears this is the case regardless of the economic condition of state or local governments. The recruitment pool of eligible and qualified candidates is diminishing. The crisis is multidimensional and is discussed in detail in this chapter.

RECRUITMENT OF A DIVERSE WORKFORCE

The recruitment of women and members of diverse groups has been a concern and a priority of law enforcement agencies nationwide for a few decades. This is not a new issue in the history of U.S. law enforcement. A President's Crime Commission Report in 1967 recommended that more minorities be hired and that they receive opportunities for advancement. Soon after the Watts riot in Los Angeles, the 1968 Kerner Commission Report identified the underrepresentation of blacks in law enforcement as a serious problem. The report recommended improved hiring and promoting policies and procedures for minorities. The Warren Christopher Commission report on the Los Angeles Police Department, released soon after the 1992 riots following the first Rodney King trial, cited the problems of racism and bias within the LAPD. The commission recommended, among other things, improved hiring and promotions processes that would benefit all groups.

Profile of Federal Agents, Local Police, and County Sheriffs' Offices

The U.S. Department of Justice collects information from criminal justice organizations and produces a report every 3 years. One part of the report profiles the demographic makeup of law enforcement agencies in the United States. According to the Bureau of Justice Statistics report, as of June 2000:

- *Female officers and deputies:* The percentage of female officers ranged from 16.5 percent in departments serving a population of 500,000 or more to about 4 percent in jurisdictions with fewer than 2,500 residents. The estimated 46,659 female officers represented an increase of about 17,300, or 59 percent, from 1990. Females represented 10.6 percent of local police departments, up from 8.1 percent in 1990. Females comprised 12.5 percent of sheriffs' offices, down from 15.4 percent in 1990 (see Exhibits 2.1 and 2.2 in Chapter 2).

- *Racial and ethnic minority officers and deputies:* Racial and ethnic minorities in local departments comprised 22.7 percent, up from 17 percent in 1990. They comprised 17.1 percent of sheriffs' offices, up from 15.5 percent in 1990. From 1990 to 2000, the number of African American local police officers increased by 35 percent and the number of Hispanic officers increased by 93 percent. From 1990 to 2000, the number of African American officers in sheriffs' departments increased by 12 percent and Hispanic deputies increased by 51 percent (see Exhibits 2.1 and 2.2 in Chapter 2).

- *Federal agents:* Federal agencies (INS, FBI, U.S. Customs, etc.) employed 88,496 full-time agents as of June 2000, of which 14.4 percent were women and 30.5 percent were members of a racial or ethnic minority.

Recruitment Crisis

In 1990, Gordon Bowers, who teaches justice administration courses, said, "There is a crisis developing in recruitment that will change law enforcement as it is known today. For each year over the next decade, the number of new police officers needed and the minimum qualifications will be raised, but both the number and percentage of high school graduates in the normal age range of police applicants will decrease" (Bowers, 1990, p. 64).

The situation in 2000 confirmed Gordon Bowers's prediction of a shortage of applicants for police departments and a struggle for departments to maintain authorized strength. A number of factors contributed to the reduction of the once-substantial law enforcement applicant pool. One explanation is offered by the futurists Cetron, Rocha, and Luckins (1988). They predicted that "the percentage of the population between 16 and 24 years old [would] shrink from 30 percent of the labor force in 1985 to 16 percent in the year 2000" (p. 64) and that "during the next decade, white men will account for only one in four new workers" (p. 34). Therefore, the field of law enforcement is attempting to recruit from an applicant pool that is not only shrinking but also expected to be dominated by minorities and women. An additional reason that there are fewer applicants within the typical age range eligible for careers as peace officers is that millions of young people between the ages of 15 and 29 are arrested each year for crimes that disqualify them for police work.

For a period of time during the late 1990s and into 2000, the United States experienced the lowest unemployment rate in 30 years (3.9%) because of a robust economy. There were plenty of jobs, but the number of applicants for law enforcement positions was substantially lower than in the past. Due to the employees' market, those seeking jobs could be very selective. Many jobs in private industry, especially high-tech jobs, came with high salaries, stock options, signing bonuses, company cars, and year-end bonuses. Public-sector employers have difficulty competing with such incentives. Another factor in recruitment difficulties was court decisions (and pretrial settlements) against such companies as Coke, Texaco, and Wall Street's Smith Barney in race bias lawsuits. U.S. firms scrambled to recruit and promote talented women and minorities. Many large companies, aware that the populations within their recruitment areas were diversifying, knew that their employee demographics had to match those of the world outside or they, too, would be subject to lawsuits and/or criticism. This is particularly true of companies that sell products or services to the public. Their recruitment efforts, therefore, focused on women and members of diverse groups. The wide-open market also made for transitory employees, causing retention problems for employers, especially of trained employees. During this period, smaller law enforcement agencies lost their employees as larger agencies lured experienced officers away with promises of benefits. The effort was compared to the National Football League draft, in which everyone was competing for qualified candidates.

Compounding the law enforcement recruitment problem was the negative impact of highly publicized scandals involving police in major cities—New York, Los Angeles, and Philadelphia, to name a few. These scandals, it is suggested, "tarnished the image" of law enforcement work ("A Law Enforcement Shortage," 2000, p. A1). At the same time, departments were not fully staffed because many employees who had been hired in the police expansion wave of the 1960s and 1970s were retiring. Other reasons that young people are not applying for careers in law enforcement are related to the paramilitary organizational structure of most agencies. It has been suggested that the independent-minded youth of today are less tolerant of the rigid paramilitary hierarchy to which most police agencies still adhere. In addition, most young people do not like being micro-managed.

Serious budget shortfalls in most states, which started in 2002 and extended into 2003, forced cities and counties to reduce law enforcement personnel through layoffs, attrition, and not increasing department size. Some law enforcement agencies benefited because unemployed people turned to civil service jobs, including law enforcement, but most agencies did not. Whenever there is a recession causing layoffs, it creates a problem because cities and counties must lay off or fire those employees who were hired most recently. Women and people of diverse ethnic and racial groups, therefore, are usually the first to lose their jobs, thereby canceling any gains made in terms of a multicultural workforce, including women.

Recruitment Difficulties

Cultural Diversity at Work, a newsletter addressing multicultural issues, presented a list of the 10 most frequent causes of the failure to attract and retain high-level minority and female employees. The following is a brief synopsis, still valid today, of those most pertinent to law enforcement:

1. *Senior management is not sending the "diversity message" down the line.* Senior management does not always demonstrate commitment in the form of value statements and policies emphasizing the importance of a diverse workforce.

2. *Informal networking channels are closed to outsiders.* Women and minorities often experience discomfort within the traditional all-white, all-male informal career networks, including extracurricular activities. For example, some women police officers are uncomfortable participating in police association activities that involve recreational gambling, fishing, sports activities, or the roughhousing that can take place at meetings.

3. *In-house recruiters are looking in the wrong places.* Recruiters must use different methods and resources than those they have traditionally used to find diverse candidates.

4. *Differences in life experience are not taken into account.* Some applicants, both women and minorities, will have had life experiences that differ from those of the traditional job candidate. For example, the latter has typically had some college experience, with a high grade point average, and is often single (and thus does not have the many responsibilities associated with marriage and children). On the other hand, many minority job candidates have had to work through school and are married and may have children. Therefore, their grade point averages may have suffered.

5. *Negative judgments are made based on personality or communications differences.* Although not everybody's style reflects cultural, racial, or gender characteristics, there are distinct differences in communication style and personality between women and minorities and traditional white-male job applicants. Communication style differences are especially apparent when English is the applicant's second language. Generally speaking, women are not as assertive as men in communication. Sometimes these factors can affect the outcome of a pre-employment interview and become barriers to a job offer.

6. *The candidate is not introduced to people who are like him or her.* It is important that the candidate or new hire meet people of the same gender, race, or ethnicity within the agency. A mentor or support group may be crucial to a successful transition into the organization.

7. *Organizations are not able or willing to take the time to do a thorough search.* Recruitment specialists indicate that searches for qualified minority and women candidates take 4 to 6 weeks longer than others. These searches take commitment, resources, and time.

8. *Early identification is missing from the recruitment program.* Programs that move students into the proper fields of study early on and that provide the education required for the job are essential. Examples of these programs include internships, scholarships, and police programs (e.g., police athletic league) that bring future job candidates into contact with the organization (Micari, 1993).

The Police Executive Research Forum (PERF, 1987) created a nationwide task force to address the issue of decreasing numbers of qualified police applicants. Two of the findings of the task force are as follows:

1. *Identification of recruiting problems.* The problems most frequently reported were a decreasing number of qualified applicants; the inability to offer competitive compensation; and difficulty in recruiting Asians, blacks, Hispanics, and other minorities. Those responding to the survey who perceived a decline in the number of qualified applicants attributed it to a lack of education, the use of drugs, and limited life experience.

2. *Identification of tests on which candidates are likely to fail.* The top three in rank order were the written test, background investigation, and polygraph.

To address the latter, departments should perform a statistical analysis of the selection processes and tests they use by gender and ethnic or racial group to determine whether women or minorities are being disproportionately eliminated by these tests. The department should then evaluate whether those screening devices contain outdated or biased questions or questions that are no longer job-related. If the tests contain questions that have an adverse impact on targeted groups, then these obstacles must be studied further to determine if they can be removed.

Recruitment Strategies

To build a diverse workforce, recruitment strategies used in the past will no longer be sufficient and will not provide agencies with high-quality applicants. In fact, a study commissioned by the International Association of Chiefs of Police and completed in 1998, *The Future of Women in Policing: Mandates for Action,* concluded that "unfocused, random recruiting is unlikely to attract diversity. Targeted programs are more likely to do so." The study determined that approximately one in four departments (26 percent) have had policies and strategies in place to recruit women and that larger departments are about three times more likely to actively recruit female applicants than are smaller ones. According to Kim Lonsway, research director for the National Center for Women and Policing, women really need a special invitation to consider a career in law enforcement. In an article for the Center, she wrote that the message from agencies must be: "Yes, we want you, come apply" ("Woman Recruits Meet High Standard," 2003, p. A32). Agencies with the most success in recruiting women and minorities have had specific goals, objectives, and timetables in place; these policies must be established at the top level of the organization. At the same time, management must commit to not lowering standards for the sake of numbers and deadlines. The philosophy and procedures required are discussed in the following sections.

Commitment. Recruiting minority and women applicants, especially in highly competitive labor markets, requires commitment and effort. Police executives must communicate that commitment to their recruiting staff and devote the resources necessary to achieve recruitment goals. This genuine commitment must be demonstrated both inside and outside the organization. Internally, chief executives should develop policies and procedures that emphasize the importance of a diverse workforce. Affirmative action and/or programs that target certain applicants (where legal) will not work in a vacuum. Chief executives must integrate the values that promote diversity and affirmative action into every aspect of the agency, from its mission statement to its roll-call training. Externally, police executives should publicly delineate the specific hiring and promotion goals of the department to the community through both formal (e.g., media) and informal (e.g., community-based policing, networking with organizations representing the diverse groups) methods. While chief executives promote the philosophy, policies, and procedures, committed staff who are sensitive to the needs for affirmative hiring and promotions carry them out. Executives should also build partnerships with personnel officials so that decisions clearly reflect the hiring goals of the department. It is recommended that police executives audit the personnel selection process to ensure that neither the sequencing of the testing stages nor the length of the selection process is hindering the objective of hiring women and minorities (Fridell, 2001, p. 76).

Although chiefs may be genuine in their efforts to champion diversity and affirmative action hiring, care must be taken that their policies and procedures do not violate Title VII of the Civil Rights Act of 1964. Also, agencies in states that have enacted laws prohibiting affirmative action hiring programs and the targeting of "protected classes" (e.g., California's Proposition 209, passed in 1996, which is discussed later in this chapter) must adhere to these regulations. A knowledgeable personnel department or legal staff should review policies and procedures prior to implementation.

Planning. A recent study by the National Center for Women and Policing (NCWP), published in 2001 by the Bureau of Justice Assistance of the Department of Justice, offers recommendations for greatly increasing the pool of qualified female applicants. Among other suggestions, the study stressed the importance of making an assessment of your department's current recruitment practices and developing a strategic marketing plan. A strategic marketing plan would include the action steps that commit the objectives, goals, budget, accountability, and timetables for the recruitment campaign to paper. Demographic data should form one of the foundations for the plan, which must also take into account the current political, social, and economic conditions of the department and the community. To avoid losing qualified applicants to other agencies or private industry, the plan should provide for fast tracking the best candidates through the testing and screening processes. Fast tracking is an aggressive recruitment process wherein a preliminary, qualifying check quickly takes place concerning the driving, credit, and criminal history of the applicant before any other screening process occurs. Applicants who do not meet established standards are immediately notified. The remaining applicants are then interviewed by a trained, ranking officer or civilian holding the position for which he or she is applying. Applicants earning a passing score on the personal interview immediately receive a letter advising them that they passed, thereby giving them tangible evidence that the agency is seriously considering hiring them. The letter also informs them that they must pass additional qualifying steps, including a background investigation, which must be commenced immediately. The applicant must complete the final testing within 10 days, or the agency may withdraw the offer. To streamline the process, background investigators have established blocks of time for other testing such as polygraphs and psychological and medical evaluations.

> In today's labor market, the best-qualified candidates are not willing to wait months for your selection process to run its course. Public safety organizations must develop valid selection approaches that are also timely. Otherwise, by the time the selection process has run its course, the best-qualified candidates may have found other jobs. (Hulsey & Goodwin, 2001, p. 5)

The strategic recruitment plan should include an advertising campaign that targets:

- Colleges and universities
- Military bases and reserve units
- Churches, temples, synagogues, and other places of worship
- Gymnasiums, fitness and martial arts studios, athletic clubs, and the like

Participation of women and minority officers within the department in recruitment efforts is crucial (see "Recruiting Incentives"), as is the involvement of groups and organizations that represent the target groups. If within the community there are high-profile minorities and women, such as athletes and business executives, they should be enlisted to promote police work as a career through media releases and endorsements on flyers and brochures.

The Fulton, New York, Police Department offers one example of how such planning can be accomplished. For them, newspaper advertising proved the most significant medium from which candidates learned about their department's police test, followed closely by television advertising. The department went a step further, however. They learned that 45 percent of candidates obtained police test packages from the police station and 33 percent from the personnel office, so they made test packages available 24 hours a day, 7 days a week at the station because the personnel office is only open 8:00–5:00 Monday through Friday (Spawn, 2003).

Professor Bowers (1990) believes that law enforcement agencies will have to find alternatives to the traditional applicant pool to secure qualified candidates. He suggests that it is possible to develop a recruitment strategy that would target people not usually recruited (where such strategies are legal). Bowers defined the "alternative applicant pool" as those people who are qualified but who have no current intention of pursuing law enforcement as a career. An applicant's age is one criterion that law enforcement agencies need to reexamine. Older, physically fit applicants looking for a second career can bring wisdom, maturity, and other skills to the occupation, especially because police academies are now emphasizing moral decision making and minimizing physical factors. Also, despite history and tradition, applicants should not always have to start in patrol assignments. Agencies employing community policing could hire well-qualified personnel to perform specific types of police work that do not require them to be "crime fighters." Veteran police officers, however, may resent and reject this idea, and attitudes would have to change for this concept to be implemented (Bowers, 1990).

Resources. Adequate resources, including money, personnel, and equipment, must be made available to the recruitment effort. Financial constraints challenge almost every organization's recruitment campaign. The size or financial circumstances of an agency may necessitate less expensive—and perhaps more innovative—approaches. For example, many small law enforcement jurisdictions can combine to implement regional testing. One large county on the West Coast successfully formed a consortium of agencies and implemented regional testing three times per month for law enforcement candidates. To participate, each agency pays into an account based on the population of its jurisdiction. Alternatively, each agency can pay according to how many applicants it hired from the list. The pooled money is then used for recruitment advertising (e.g., billboards, radio, television, newspapers) and the initial testing processes (e.g., reading, writing, and agility tests, including proctors). The eligibility list is then provided to each of the participating agencies, which continue the screening process for applicants in whom they have an interest. Police agencies should not see other agencies as competitors with respect to recruiting. By combining their efforts, they may be able to:

- Save money (consolidate resources)
- Develop a larger pool of applicants
- Become more competitive with private industry and other public agencies
- Test more often
- Reduce the time it takes from application to hire

In terms of recruiting a diverse workforce, the second benefit listed—developing a larger pool of applicants—is central to reaching beyond the traditional applicant pool. Law enforcement agencies, in taking advantage of the Internet's global coverage, can post position openings in the effort to recruit individuals with a wide variety of backgrounds and skills. Agencies should also create their own websites describing their departments and offering information on recruitment and on how to obtain applications. Department websites have been found to be valuable recruiting tools when used to highlight the work of women and minorities within an agency.

Selection and Training of Recruiters. A recruiter is an ambassador for the department and must be selected carefully. Police recruiters should reflect the diversity within the community and include women. Full-time recruiters are a luxury most often found only in large agencies. The benefit of a full-time recruiter program is that usually the employees in this assignment have received some training in marketing techniques. They have no other responsibilities or assignments and can, therefore, focus on what they do and do it well. They develop the contacts, resources, and skills to be effective. Whether full-time, part-time, or assigned on an as-needed basis, however, the following criteria should be considered when selecting recruiters:

- Commitment to the goal of recruiting
- Belief in a philosophy that values diversity
- Ability to work well in a community policing environment
- Belief in and ability to market a product: law enforcement as a career
- Comfort with people of all backgrounds and ability to communicate this comfort
- Ability to discuss the importance of entire community representation in police work and the advantages to the department without sounding patronizing

Recruiters must be given resources (e.g., budget and equipment) and must have established guidelines. They must be highly trained with respect to their role, market research methods, public relations, and cultural awareness. They must also understand, appreciate, and be dedicated to organizational values and ethics. They must be aware and in control of any biases they might have toward individuals or groups of people who might be different from themselves.

The California Commission on Peace Officer Standards and Training (POST) developed a 24-hour course entitled "Techniques and Methods of Recruitment." For information about this course, contact California POST at (916) 227-4820. Other state POST commissions have also developed such courses. Large, progressive agencies (or a consortium of agencies) could develop an in-house program patterned after these model courses. The Institute for Women in Trades, Technology and Science (IWITTS) is an organization with resources and training programs on recruiting and retaining women. The organization conducts national workshops and also provides technical assistance to departments via personal contact or via the Internet. Their materials include an environmental assessment tool (LEEAT) involving institutional checklists and data collection methods to help determine the best recruiting strategies for a particular law enforcement agency.

Recruiting incentives. It is recommended that police executives consider using financial and other incentives to recruit women and minorities where such programs are lawful (monetary incentive programs may be adversely affected by Fair Labor Standards Act considerations). Financial and other incentive programs are especially useful to agencies that cannot afford the luxury of full-time recruiters. They are used to encourage officers to recruit bilingual whites, women, and ethnically and racially diverse candidates, informally, while on or off duty. One possible program would give officers overtime credit for each person they recruit in those categories who makes the eligibility list, additional credit if the same applicant is hired, and additional credit for each stage the new officer passes until the probation period ends. There are departments that offer officers (not assigned to recruiting) up to 20 hours compensatory time for recruiting a lateral police officer. Department members can also receive an additional 40 hours of compensatory time for recruiting a lateral who is bilingual or from a protected class. The department defines a member of a protected class as African American, Asian, Hispanic, Native American, Filipino, or female. The time is awarded in increments at a straight-time rate based on phases of employment (San Jose, California, Police Department).

Another agency awards $250 to employees who recruit applicants (of any racial or ethnic group) who are hired, complete all phases of the background process, and start the academy. The same department awards $250 to employees who recruit lateral police officer candidates once they complete all phases of the background process, are hired, and report for duty. When these recruits make it through probation, the employee who recruited them receives $250 as an additional incentive. The Boise, Idaho, Police Department developed a unique incentive program that rewards officers for bringing in a recruit who is qualified to perform the duties of a community law enforcement officer. Encouraging all department members to be involved in the recruitment effort, including the promotion of law enforcement as a career, is usually effective. To be competitive in recruiting employees, especially minorities and women, agencies must offer incentives just as corporations do.

Community Involvement. A pluralistic community must have some involvement early in the recruitment effort of candidates for police work. Representatives from different ethnic and racial backgrounds should be involved in initial meetings to plan a recruitment campaign. They can assist in determining the best marketing methods for the groups they represent and can help by personally contacting potential candidates. They should be provided with recruitment information (e.g., brochures and posters) that they can disseminate at religious institutions, civic and social organizations, schools, and cultural events. Community-based policing also offers the best opportunity for officers to put messages out regarding agency recruiting.

Community leaders representing the diversity of the community should also be involved in the selection process, including sitting on oral boards for applicants. The San Francisco Police Department utilizes community leaders in all the processes mentioned. Many progressive agencies have encouraged their officers to join community-based organizations, in which they interact with community members and are able to involve the group in recruitment efforts for the department.

High School Police Academy. Another innovative recruitment tool (or grow-your-own-cop program) was launched in San Jose, California, in 2002. Called the San Jose, California, High School Police Academy, it is a year-long academy program that helps both students and law enforcement by preparing students for careers and giving recruiters a larger pool of candidates. The program is offered to about 60 students at a time from six school districts in Santa Clara County, California. The students spend half of each day at the academy and the other half at their own schools. Students, who wear uniforms, learn all the steps of policing, from identifying evidence and collecting clues at crime scenes to arresting suspects and writing reports. They learn defensive moves, simulate weapons handling, and learn how to make traffic stops. The class also focuses on lessons for sheriff's deputies, corrections officers, and dispatchers ("High School Police Academy," 2003, p. A37). For more information about career academies, contact the National Career Academy Coalition, Bakersfield, California, at (661) 664-7667 or see their e-mail and website addresses at the end of this chapter.

Adopt-a-Cop Program. In the city of Clever, Missouri, the community, schools, and businesses can adopt an officer in training. They help the officer with training and equipment costs, making it possible for the trainee and/or the department to afford the costs involved (Newton, 2002, p. 12).

SELECTION PROCESSES

Prior to initiating any selection processes, law enforcement agencies must assess the satisfaction level of current employees and the workplace environment of the department.

Satisfaction Level for Employees

The first step before outreach recruitment can take place is for the department to look inward. Are any members, sworn or nonsworn, experiencing emotional pain or suffering because of their race, ethnicity, nationality, gender, or sexual orientation? A department seeking to hire applicants from these groups cannot have internal problems, either real or perceived, related to racism, discrimination, or hostility toward female or gay or lesbian officers. A department with a high turnover rate or a reputation for not promoting women, minorities, or gays and lesbians will also deter good people from applying. The department must resolve any internal problems before meaningful recruitment can occur. To determine the nature and extent of any such problems, law enforcement agencies can perform an assessment of all their employees through anonymous surveys about their work environment. There should be a review of policies and procedures (especially those related to sexual harassment) and an examination of statistical information, such as the number of officers leaving the department and their reasons for doing so, and which employees are promoted. The goal is not only to evaluate the workplace environment for women and minorities, but also to determine what steps need to be taken to dissolve barriers confronting them. See Appendix A for a sample survey that can be used for this purpose.

Supervisors and managers must talk with all members of their workforce on a regular basis to find out if any issues are disturbing them. They must then demonstrate that they are taking steps to alleviate the source of discomfort, whether this involves modifying practices or simply discussing behavior with other employees.

The field-training program for new recruits should also be reviewed and evaluated to ensure that new officers are not being arbitrarily eliminated or subjected to prejudice or discrimination. By the time a recruit has reached this stage of training, much has been invested in the new officer; every effort should be made to see that he or she completes the program successfully. Negligent retention, however, is a liability to an organization. When it is well documented that a trainee is not suitable for retention, release from employment is usually the best recourse regardless of race, ethnicity, lifestyle, or gender.

Role models and mentoring programs should be established to give recruits and junior officers the opportunity to receive support and important information from senior officers of the same race, ethnicity, gender, or sexual orientation. However, many successful programs include role models of different backgrounds than the recruits.

Applicant Screening

Law enforcement agencies must assess applicants along a range of dimensions that include, but are not limited to:

- Basic qualifications such as education, requisite licenses, and citizenship
- Intelligence and problem-solving capacity
- Psychological fitness
- Physical fitness and ability
- Current and past illegal drug use
- Character as revealed by criminal record, driving record, work history, military record, credit history, reputation, and polygraph examination
- Aptitude and ability to serve others
- Racial, ethnic, gender, sexual orientation, and cultural biases

The last dimension, testing for biases, deserves particular attention. An agency whose hiring procedures screen for unacceptable biases demonstrates to the community that it seeks police officers who will carry out their duties with fairness, integrity, diligence, and impartiality, officers who will respect the civil rights and dignity of the people they serve and work with. Such screening should include not only the use of psychometric testing instruments developed to measure attitudes and bias, but also careful background investigation of the candidate by personnel staff. The investigation should consider the applicant's own statements about racial issues, as well as interviews with references who provide clues about how the applicant feels about and treats members of other racial, ethnic, gender, and sexual-orientation groups. These interviews would include questions on:

- How the applicant has interacted with other groups
- What people of diverse groups say about the applicant
- Whether the applicant has ever experienced conflict or tension with members of diverse groups or individuals and how he or she handled the experience

Because of the emphasis on community-oriented policing, law enforcement recruiters must also seek applicants who demonstrate the mentality and ability to serve others (not just fight crime). Recruiters therefore are looking for candidates who are adaptable, analytical, communicative, compassionate, courageous (both physically and morally), culturally sensitive, decisive, disciplined, ethical, goal-oriented, incorruptible, mature, responsible, and self-motivated. Agencies also expect officers to have good interpersonal and communication skills, as well as sales and marketing abilities, so applicants should be screened for these attributes, and for their desire for continued learning and ability to work in a rapidly evolving environment.

> As communities face the transient issues of globalization, immigration, and language barriers, law enforcement officers increasingly will see more diverse opinions from within the community as this globalization spreads. Language and generation barriers continue to challenge law enforcement. Agencies must develop methods of bridging trust among the diverse groups that they will serve in the future. Law enforcement agencies may need to employ bilingual officers, interpreters, and computer translation programs to communicate along with recruiting immigrants. Officers also must learn about cultural issues, such as ethnic holidays, traditions, and customs. (Vest, 2001)

The search for recruits should focus on those who demonstrate an ability to take ownership of problems and work with others toward solutions. These potential officers must remain open to people who disagree or have different opinions from themselves. Law enforcement agencies should make their goals and their expectations clear to candidates for employment, recognizing that some will not match the department's vision, mission, and values and therefore should be screened out at the beginning of the process.

Robert Jones, professor of psychology at Southwest Missouri State University, says that recruiters can get a clear appraisal of applicants in service-related jobs, such as law enforcement, by applying the five basic traits of human behavior. The traits are: (1) emotional stability, (2) extroversion versus introversion, (3) openness to experience, (4) agreeableness versus toughness, and (5) conscientiousness. Today, effective law enforcement agents work closely with neighborhood groups, social welfare agencies, housing code officials, and a host of others in partnerships to control crime and improve quality of life. Law enforcement agents must be eager to understand a task, draw up a plan, and follow it through to completion in concert with others. Without an agreeable nature, officers and deputies faced with today's changing attitude toward crime fighting would not have a chance (Newton, 2003, p. 7).

It is in the best interest of law enforcement agencies, before implementing tests, to complete a job analysis. Although a time-consuming process, the final result is a clear description of the job for which applicants are applying and being screened. Utilizing the job analysis data, tests and job performance criteria can be developed and become part of the screening process. Applicants, when provided a copy of the job analysis, can decide in advance if they fit the criteria.

A study by the National Center for Women and Policing (NCWP) produced a self-assessment guide to assist agencies seeking to recruit and retain more women in sworn law enforcement positions. The resulting publication, *Recruiting and Retaining Women: A Self-Assessment Guide for Law Enforcement,* provides assistance to federal, state, and local law enforcement agencies on examining their policies and procedures to identify and remove obstacles to hiring and retaining women at all levels of the organization. The guide also provides a list of resources for agencies to use when they plan or implement changes to their current policies and procedures. "The guide promotes increasing the number of women at all ranks of law enforcement as a strategy to strengthen community policing, reduce police use of force, enhance police response to domestic violence, and provide balance to the workforce" (Bureau of Justice Statistics, 2001). It is also recommended that chiefs of police, police recruiters, and city and county personnel department employees review *Recruitment and Retention of Qualified Police Personnel—A Best Practices Guide,* published by the International Association of Chiefs of Police (McKeever & Kranda, 2000).

Examples of Successful Recruiting Programs

Successful recruitment programs vary by community. If recruitment efforts result in a large enough pool of qualified applicants, the pool will contain individuals of all backgrounds. The following agencies have had success in recruiting female and minority applicants, and might be contacted to determine the strategies they used:

- *Portland, Oregon:* The department had hired a professional recruiter from outside the department for a period of time, and this yielded some positive results. A reduced budget, however, eliminated the position. As of November 2003, the department consisted of 161 women (16 percent of the agency) and a total sworn workforce of 994. The percentage of women is higher than many other agencies its size nationwide. Portland requires entry-level candidates with no previous law enforcement experience to have a 2-year college degree. Lateral applicants are required to have an associate of arts degree or its equivalent number of units. In 2003, the department had 46 Asian, 37 African American, 23 Hispanic, 8 Native American, and 880 Caucasian officers.

- *Madison, Wisconsin:* As of September 2003, the department had 382 sworn personnel of whom 116 were female, or 30 percent, well above the national averages for agencies their size. The race/ethnicity breakdown of the sworn workforce was 36 African American (9 percent), 21 Hispanic (5.5 percent), 7 Asian (1.8 percent), 6 Native American (1.6 percent), and the balance Caucasian officers.

- *Pittsburgh, Pennsylvania:* One of the nation's most diverse police departments, with women making up 25 percent of the force.

- *Albuquerque, New Mexico:* Police executives point to Albuquerque as a potential model for other departments regarding recruitment. Between 1995 and 2002, female recruits increased from 8 percent in academy classes to 33 percent. Also, women are retained at rates comparable to those for men.

- **Tucson, Arizona:** Tucson had a population of 490,000 and police department with 1,000 sworn in 2003. Due to a New Workplace for Women Project and its recommendations, the department was able to recruit many more women. The number of women recruits increased from 10 to 29 percent in two classes and minority recruits increased to 47 percent of the first class following the project.

The Albuquerque and Tucson police departments held career fairs and obtained free publicity about them in major newspapers and on television and radio. The departments designed flyers and posters advertising the career fairs and posted them in places where physically fit women were likely to be, such as gyms, martial arts schools, and outdoor sporting stores. Notices were also placed at supermarkets, laundromats, and shopping malls. The first career fair held by the Tucson Police Department drew 450 women. Career fairs feature panels of female role models who describe their jobs and talk about working in a male-dominated occupation. The fairs include information about the job, the academy, the application process, the physical conditioning designed for women, and organizations for women in policing (Polisar & Milgram, 1998).

To assist law enforcement agencies that wish to increase the number of women employees in their workforce, the National Center for Women and Policing offers the following services:

- A regional training seminar on recruiting and retaining women. This two-day seminar helps law enforcement agencies develop effective recruiting programs to increase the number of female employees.

- Online updates to the self-assessment guide. New programs in law enforcement agencies across the country are described on the website, where readers can gain access to the latest research about women in policing and other critical issues. See "Website Resources" at the end of this chapter.

- Onsite consulting by a team of professional law enforcement experts to help agencies identify and remove obstacles to recruiting and retaining women.

For additional information on these services, contact the National Center for Women and Policing at (323) 651-2532, or see their e-mail address at the end of this chapter.

Legal Issues and Affirmative Action

The authors acknowledge that there may be some controversial and even legal aspects, in some states or jurisdictions, to recruitment efforts that target women, as well as ethnically and racially diverse candidates for law enforcement jobs. Federal law prohibits programs that require meeting specific hiring goals for any particular group except when necessary to remedy discrimination.

In California, Proposition 209, which outlawed governmental discrimination and preferences based on race, sex, color, ethnicity, or national origin, was passed in 1996. In September 2000 justices of the California Supreme Court affirmed that the proposition was legal. The justices, in their decision, placed strict limits on employers regarding the types of outreach programs they can legally use to recruit employees; any outreach program that gives minorities and women a competitive advantage is a violation of Proposition 209. Many other states followed California's example by enacting similar legislation. Agencies need to research what strategies are legal and appropriate within their state and jurisdiction.

In 2003, however, the Supreme Court of the United States ruled that the University of Michigan's Law School admissions policy, which uses race as a factor, was not in violation of the Constitution's 14th Amendment. The court actually issued two rulings. One, a 5-4 decision, was that race can be considered in the admissions process to the School of Law. The other, a 6-3 decision, was that the University of Michigan's undergraduate admissions policy, which used a point system to give minority students a considerable edge, was unconstitutional. The court ruled that the University could not use "rigid systems that seem like quotas, and must adopt race-neutral admissions policies as soon as practical." Only time will tell what impact, if any, this decision will have nationwide and, therefore, what impact it will have upon the recruitment of a diverse law enforcement workforce.

The practice of tracking race, ethnicity, and gender via questionnaires is considered controversial. Ward Connerly, an African American who championed the end of affirmative action in California, argues that the practice is divisive, especially in California where no single race holds a majority and where people increasingly consider themselves multiracial ("Connerly Starts Push," 2001, pp. A1, A12). Opponents of this view contend that collecting such data is crucial to preventing discrimination and allocating state resources. "Racial and ethnic data are essential to health care, law enforcement and criminal justice policy, social scientists said discussing a ballot initiative that would bar California from collecting such information" ("Sociologists oppose ballot measure," 2003, p. C3).

Affirmative action and consent decrees have been only moderately successful in achieving parity in the hiring of women and individuals from ethnically diverse backgrounds. There has been even less success with promotions of these groups to command ranks. In fact, studies have found that affirmative action has produced uneven results by race, gender, and occupation across the nation.

An unfortunate problem that can be associated with the promotion of women and nonwhites is that doubts are raised about their qualifications: "Are they qualified for the job or are they products of affirmative action?" Peers may subtly or even explicitly express to each other that the promotion was not the result of competence, and the promoted candidate may feel that his or her success is not based entirely on qualifications. Consequently, employees may experience strained relationships and lowered morale. There is no denying the potential for a strong negative internal reaction in an organization when court orders have mandated promotions. Some white employees feel anger or frustration with consent decrees or affirmative action-based promotions. Clearly, preventive work must be done to avoid these problems.

Mini-Case Study: What Would You Do?

You are the new personnel sergeant responsible for a department with 50 sworn officers. The department has one African American man, two Hispanic men, and two women officers. There has never been a large number of minority or women candidates applying for sworn positions in the department, and your agency does not reflect the demographics of the city. Your city has an affirmative action program, but to date, no outreach programs have been initiated to recruit women and minorities. Your chief has asked that you provide a proposal on what strategies you would suggest to recruit women and minorities. Develop a list of what you would propose. Make a list of what other departmental processes should take place prior to applicant testing.

RETENTION AND PROMOTION OF A DIVERSE WORKFORCE

Recruiting officers who reflect the gender, racial, ethnic, and sexual orientation demographics of the community is one important challenge of law enforcement agencies. Retention and promotion are equally important. Retention of any employee is usually the result of good work on the part of the employee and a positive environment wherein all employees are treated with dignity and respect. A high rate of retention is most likely in organizations that meet the basic needs of employees and offer reasonable opportunities for career development. In fact, once an agency earns a reputation for fairness, talented men and women of all ethnicities and races will seek out that agency and will remain longer.

The lack of promotions of protected classes and women to supervisor and command ranks has been cited as a severe problem in policing for at least three decades by scholars and police researchers. Authors and advocates for the promotion of women have used the term "glass ceiling" to describe an unacknowledged barrier that inhibits those officers from reaching ranks above entry level. The Glass Ceiling Commission, a federal bipartisan group studying diversity in the workplace (1994–1995), discovered that the glass ceiling has not been broken to any significant extent in most organizations, including law enforcement agencies.

Within organizations, women and others of diverse backgrounds are frustrated when promotional opportunities seem more available to white males than to them. The disenchantment that often accompanies frustration frequently leads to low productivity and morale, early burnout, and resignation because opportunities appear better elsewhere. Lack of attention to equal opportunity promoting practices at some law enforcement agencies has resulted in court-ordered promotions. These have a negative impact on a department's operations and relationships, both internally and externally, and often lead to distrust and dissatisfaction.

In 1998, the International Association of Chiefs of Police published a comprehensive analysis of women in policing. The study, which involved surveys of 800 police departments, highlighted the following major points regarding promotions: first, that women remain grossly underrepresented in the ranks; and second, that they have largely been unable to punch through a virtually "bulletproof glass ceiling." The study also found that:

- Approximately 91 percent of departments reported having no women in policymaking positions.
- Of the nation's 17,000 police departments, only 123 had female police chiefs or top executives.

- Nearly 10 percent of the departments listed gender bias among the reasons that women were not promoted.

A 2001 report by the National Center for Women and Policing established the following:

- In departments with over 100 sworn officers, women hold 7.3 percent of top command positions and 9.6 percent of supervisory positions. Women of color hold 1.6 percent of top command positions and 3.1 percent of supervisory positions.
- In departments with under 100 sworn officers, women hold 3.4 percent of top command positions and 4.6 percent of supervisory positions. Women of color hold fewer than 1 percent of top command positions and 0.4 percent of supervisory positions. (Moore, 2003)

Although women are making gains, they still constitute only a small proportion of police supervisors and managers. Police executives and city or county managers cannot afford to minimize the consequences of poor retention and inadequate promotional opportunities for women and diverse groups within their organizations. Some departments have done very well in recruiting and hiring women, but, for reasons that have yet to be studied, women have left departments more quickly than men. "You can imagine that there is a level of frustration here," says Susan Riseling, president of the National Association of Women Law Enforcement Executives. "Until we figure out what drives women away from this business, we're not going to see any progress" ("Female Cops," 1998). A 1998 study by the International Association of Chiefs of Police found that about 60 percent of the women who leave law enforcement occupations do so between their second and fifth year on the job. The reasons vary, but family pressures are the most frequently cited cause. The report recommended fairer screening procedures, tougher sexual harassment policies, and sustained drives designed to attract women and keep them on the job.

Chief executives need to determine if female officers are applying for promotions in numbers that are proportional to their numbers in the department. If not, perhaps female officers need encouragement from their supervisors. It is also possible that the promotional process disproportionately screens out female officers. Research shows that the more subjective the process is, the less likely women are to pass it. Some safeguards against bias include weighting the process toward "hands-on" tasks (e.g., assessment center testing), conducting structured interviews, selecting board members who represent different races and both sexes, and training the board members on interviewing techniques.

Failure to promote qualified candidates representative of the diverse populations agencies serve, including women, can result in continued distrust of the police by the communities. Underrepresentation within police departments also aggravates tensions between the police and the community. Some scholars and criminal justice experts argue that underrepresentation at all levels within law enforcement agencies hurts the image of the department in the eyes of the community (Walker, 1989).

Penny Harrington, a former Portland, Oregon, police chief and past executive director of the National Center for Women and Policing in Los Angeles, said, however, "I don't think things are getting worse, I think they're getting better." She also commented, "This younger generation is more apt to speak out about it than the first groups of women who were just interested in surviving" ("Bias Still Handcuffing," 1998, p. A1). Unfortunately, too often when they do speak out, and especially if they sue the department, women face retaliation. Women who have complained or sued have reported retaliatory verbal abuse, petty reprimands from supervisors and managers, dead-end assignments, and, in some cases, no backup on patrol.

Mini-Case Study: How Would You Handle It?

You are a male lieutenant in charge of the special weapons and tactics unit. The first female officer will be assigned to your specialized unit shortly. The special weapons and tactics team members are voicing negative opinions about a female officer being assigned to the unit. They are complaining that there will be a lowering of standards in the unit because women are not as physically fit as men for this assignment. When you have overheard these conversations, or when they have been addressed to you directly, you have refuted them by pointing to the women in the department who are in outstanding physical shape. This strategy has not been effective, as the squad members continue to complain that women officers can't do the job and that their personal safety might be in jeopardy.

SUMMARY

Recruiting, hiring, retaining, and promoting a diverse workforce will remain important issues in law enforcement for a long time. Too many of the issues of equity and diversity have not been resolved in the law enforcement workplace, by the courts, or even in the legislative and executive branches of the U.S. government. The number of people available and qualified for entry-level jobs will continue to decrease; more employers, both public and private, will be vying for the best candidates. This seems to be true regardless of the economic condition of federal, state, or local government.

Hiring and promoting women and minorities for law enforcement careers are achievable goals when agencies use strategies outlined in this chapter. As more and more departments move toward community policing, the need to recruit and retain female and minority officers is becoming critical.

With changes in the hiring, screening, and promotional policies and practices of law enforcement agencies comes an unprecedented opportunity to build a future in which differences are valued and respected in our communities and our workforces. Progressive law enforcement executives must strive to secure the most qualified employees to serve the public. To do so, they must not only be committed to the challenges of affirmative hiring (where legal) but also be capable of educating and selling their workforce on the legitimate reasons, both legal and ethical, for such efforts. Law enforcement agencies, to be competitive in the market for qualified employees, must develop new ways to recruit targeted people or risk losing highly skilled potential employees to other occupations.

In this chapter we presented effective strategies and successful programs for implementing changes in recruitment and promotion of a diverse workforce. Law enforcement will have to use innovative and sophisticated marketing techniques and advertising campaigns to reach the population of desired potential applicants, and must develop fast-track processes for hiring these candidates.

A transition is taking place as police continue to move from the aggressive, male-dominated (and predominantly white) police departments and culture of the past. Most law enforcement observers agree that with the shift to community policing, women can thrive. Law enforcement agencies must overcome the common perception that policing is a male-oriented profession that requires only physical strength. Departments are looking for people who are community-oriented and who have good interpersonal skills, and they are finding increasingly that women meet these qualifications. Law enforcement executives should seek minority employees for the same reasons.

Although it contributes to better police–community relations, improvement in protected class representation in law enforcement and other criminal justice professions will not alone resolve misunderstandings. Increased numbers of diverse staff members provide only the potential for improved dialogue, cooperation, and problem solving within both the organization and the community the organization serves. Community and law enforcement officials should remember that serving multicultural and multiracial neighborhoods can never be the sole responsibility of workforce members from diverse ethnic and racial groups. In most jurisdictions, their limited numbers make this level of responsibility unrealistic. All staff should be prepared to understand and relate to diverse groups in a professional and sensitive manner, whether the people contacted are perpetrators, victims, or witnesses.

DISCUSSION QUESTIONS AND ISSUES*

1. *Institutional Racism in Law Enforcement.* Law enforcement agencies typically operate under the pretense that all their members are one color and that the uniform or job makes everyone brothers or sisters. Many members of diverse ethnic and racial groups, particularly African American, do not agree that they are consistently treated with respect and believe that there is institutional racism in law enforcement. Caucasians clearly dominate the command ranks of law enforcement agencies. Discuss with other students in your class whether you believe that this disparity is the result of subtle forms of institutional racism or actual conscious efforts on the part of the persons empowered to make decisions. Consider whether tests and promotional processes give unfair advantage to white applicants and whether they discriminate against department employees of other races and ethnicities. Do officers from diverse groups discriminate against members of other, different cultures?

2. *Employment of a Diverse Workforce and Police Practices.* How has the employment of a diverse workforce affected police practices in your city or county? Is there evidence that significant changes in the ethnic or racial composition of the department alter official police policy? Can the same be said of gay and lesbian employment? Does employment of protected classes have any

---

*See the Instructor's Manual accompanying this text for additional activities, role-play activities, questionnaires, and projects related to the content of this chapter.

significant effect on the informal police subculture and, in turn, police performance? Provide examples to support your conclusions.

WEBSITE RESOURCES

Visit these websites for additional information about recruitment and related issues:

Bureau of Justice Statistics (BJS): http://www.ojp.us.doj.bjs

A resource of crime statistics collected and analyzed by the Federal Bureau of Investigation

International Association of Chiefs of Police: http://www.theiacp.org

An online resource for law enforcement issues and publications including "Recruitment/Retention of Qualified Police Personnel: A Best Practices Guide."

International Association of Women Police (IAWP): http://www.iawp.org

A website for information about training conferences, careers, jobs, publications, and research pertinent to women in law enforcement.

Institute for Women in Trades, Technology and Science (IWITTS): http://www.womenpolice.com

This website features fact sheets, news articles, and publications for departments on women and policing, including a free women-in-policing e-newsletter, which provides best practice information.

National Career Academy Coalition (NCAC): http://www.ncacinc.org

A website for information concerning career academies.

National Center for Women and Policing (NCWP): http://www.feminist.org

This website provides information concerning regional training seminars on recruiting and retaining women. It also is a resource for the latest research about women in policing and other critical issues. The organization has consultants to help agencies identify and remove obstacles to recruiting and retaining women.

National Association of Women Law Enforcement Executives (NAWLEE): http://www.nawlee.com

The website contains resources, news, member directory, conference and training information, seminars, and an information exchange for women executives in law enforcement.

REFERENCES

Bias still handcuffing female police officers. (1998, April 18). *Contra Costa Times*, p. A1.

Bowers, Gordon A. (1990). "Avoiding the Recruitment Crisis." *Journal of California Law Enforcement, 24*(2), 64.

Bureau of Justice Statistics. (2001). *Recruiting and Retaining Women: A Self-Assessment Guide for Law Enforcement*. Washington, DC: United States Department of Justice.

Cetron, Marvin J., Wanda Rocha, and Rebecca Luckins. (1988, July–August). "Into the 21st Century: Long-Term Trends Affecting the United States." *The Futurist,* p. 64.

Connerly starts push to end tracking race. (2001, March 27). *Contra Costa Times,* pp. A1, A2.

Dettweiler, Josh. (1993, September). "Women and Minorities in Professional Training Programs: The Ins and Outs of Higher Education." *Cultural Diversity at Work,* 6(1), 3.

Edsall, Thomas B. (1991, January 15). "Racial Preferences Produce Change, Controversy." *The Washington Post.* p. A3.

Female cops, nation's policewomen are facing a bullet-proof glass ceiling. Survey: Women muscled out by bias, harassment. (1998, November 24). *USA Today,* p. A10.

Francis, Stephanie B. (2001, March). "Ideal Candidates." *Community Links, Newsletter of the Community Policing Consortium,* Phase VIII, Issue 1, 2–4.

Fridell, Lorie, Robert Lunney, Drew Diamond, and Bruce Kubu. (2001). *Racially Biased Policing: A Principled Response,* A Police Executive Research Forum Publication.

Goldstein, Herman. (1977). *Policing a Free Society.* Washington, D.C: U.S. Department of Justice Law Enforcement Assistance Administration.

Guyot, Dorothy. (1977). "Bending Granite: Attempts to Change the Rank Structure of American Police Departments." *Journal of Police Science and Administration, 3,* 253–284.

High school police academy. (2003, January 5). *Contra Costa Times,* p. A37.

International Association of Chiefs of Police. (1998). *The Future of Women in Policing: Mandates for Action.* Washington, D.C: Author.

Hulsey, Floyd, and Maureen Goodwin. (2001, June). "Fast Track Application Process Speeds Hiring." *FBI Law Enforcement Bulletin,* pp. 5–8.

A law enforcement shortage. Area agencies scramble for recruits. (2000, May 1). *Contra Costa Times,* p. A1.

Lonsway, Kim. (2003, March 16). *"Women Recruits Meet High Standard," Contra Costa Times,* p. A32.

Marrujo, Robert, and Brian Kleiner. (1992). "Why Women Fail to Get to the Top." *Equal Opportunities International,* II(4), pp. 13–16.

McKeever, Jack, and April Kranda. (2000). "Recruitment and Retention of Qualified Police Personnel—A Best Practices Guide." *Big Ideas for Smaller Departments,* International Association of Chiefs of Police, 1(2), 1–15.

Micari, Marina. (1993, September). "Recruiters of Minorities and Women Speak Out: Why Companies Lose Candidates," *Cultural Diversity at Work,* 6(1), 1.

Milgram, Donna. (2002, April). "Recruiting Women to Policing: Practical Strategies That Work." *The Police Chief Magazine,* pp. 7–10.

Morrison, Ann M. (1987). *The New Leaders: Leadership Diversity in America.* San Francisco: Jossey-Bass.

Newton, Steven J. (2002, November). "Tips for Filing the Roster." *Community Links— Magazine, The Community Policing Consortium,* pp. 1–2.

Oborn, Ralph (1992, June). "Police Recruitment: Today's Standard—Tomorrow's Challenge." *FBI Law Enforcement Bulletin 21,* Washington, D.C.

Polisar, Joseph and Donna Milgram. (1998, October). "Recruiting, Integrating and Retaining Women Police Officers: Strategies That Work by the Institute for Women in Trades, Technology & Science." *The Police Chief Magazine,* pp. 42, 44, 46, 48–50.

Sociologists oppose ballet measure, say ethnic data is vital. (2003, May 29). *San Diego Union,* p. C3.

Spawn, Mark. (2003, March). "Recruitment Strategies—A Case Study in Police Recruitment." *FBI Law Enforcement Bulletin,* p. 2.

U.S. Department of Labor. (1994–5). *Glass Ceiling Commission Reports,* Washington, D.C.

Vest, Gary. (2001, November). "Closing the Recruitment Gap—A Symposium's Findings." *FBI Law Enforcement Bulletin,* pp. 13–17.

Walker, Samuel J. (1989). "Employment of Black and Hispanic Police Officers 1983–1988: A Follow-Up Study." Occasional paper 89-1, Center for Applied Urban Research, University of Nebraska, Omaha.

Watts, P. (1989). "Breaking Into the Old-Boy Network." *Executive Female, 12* (32).

Chapter 4

Cross-Cultural Communication for Law Enforcement

OVERVIEW

This chapter begins with a discussion of language barriers and their implications for law enforcement, and gives examples of police departments' efforts to work with limited English-speaking populations. We discuss commonly held attitudes about non-native English speakers and explain the challenges involved in second-language acquisition. The section on language barriers and law enforcement ends with a list of tips for communicating in situations in which English is an individual's second language. Next, the chapter provides an overview of specific issues that law enforcement professionals face with regard to communication in a diverse environment. We discuss several common reactions that people have when communicating with people from different backgrounds, including defensiveness, overidentification, denial of biases, and the creation of "we–they" attitudes. In addition, we discuss responses to citizens' accusations of racial profiling as well as communication post-9/11. We then present information on key issues and skills required for interviewing and gathering data, particularly across cultures. The next section covers cross-cultural nonverbal differences, emphasizing areas of contrast of which officers should be aware. The final section presents male–female communication issues, particularly within law enforcement agencies.

COMMENTARY

The challenge of communication across cultures for law enforcement personnel is multifaceted. Officers not only have to consider how communicating with speakers of other languages affects their day-to-day work, but also have to deal with the changing culture within their agencies and the sensitivities required in a multicultural workforce.

> In many parts of Asia, Africa, and the Middle East, people often show respect by not making eye contact. Some officers think this behavior as defiant, but first-generation refugees or immigrants from these parts of the world are communicating respect. These officers totally miss the intended meaning behind this behavior. In addition, if the citizen has a certain tone of speech or is talking loudly, an officer may assume him to be out of control or aggressive. I often hear my fellow officers making judgments about citizens by the way they talk. The tone, the accent, the pace of speaking is not supposed to be the same as ours. This is their second language. This is ethnocentrism on the part of an

officer, and just a lack of awareness. (personal communication with Arab American police officer,* Cultural Awareness Session, 2003)

It is important not to assess a person's speech patterns based solely on what you are hearing . . . one can easily misunderstand when a speaker is not fluent in English. One should have several indicators for interpreting correctly what the citizen intends to say. (Olson, 2003)

For the first few months of being here, I was always tired from speaking the language. I had to strain my ears all day long and all my nerves were bothered. It was hard work to make people understand my broken English and to listen to them. Sometimes, I just could not anymore and I just stopped speaking English. Sometimes I had to pretend I understood what they said and why they were laughing. But inside I felt very depressed. I am an adult and my language sounded worse than a child's. Sometimes it was better not to say anything at all. (Personal communication with Vietnamese police officer,*2003).

Language barriers can lead to serious problems for non-English speakers. . . . In one case, a man was in jail for agreeing that he molested his daughter. It turned out that the man had agreed that his drinking bothered his daughters. In Spanish, the word for bother, or annoy, is "molestar." After this was explained [by the court interpreter], the man was released. ("Helping People," 1999, p. A32)

LANGUAGE BARRIERS AND LAW ENFORCEMENT

Nationwide, changing demographics have resulted in the need for law enforcement to deal increasingly with a multicultural population who are speakers of other languages, and do not have the equivalent skills with English. From citizens who report crimes in limited English to crime suspects and victims, there are no absolute assurances that officers will understand them. Officers are justifiably frustrated by language barriers and find it difficult to do their jobs the way they have been trained to do them. On a "good day," some officers make a point to modify their English so that they will be better understood; on a stressful day, many officers are frustrated at having to slow down and listen more patiently. Some law enforcement officers are noticeably impatient when they deal with non-native English speakers. Citizens who do not speak English know when police are not listening to their side of the story. As a result, a citizen with a language barrier is not successful at communicating even the minimum amount of necessary information. Perhaps most difficult is the situation in which a person with limited English skills is traumatized, further affecting the victim's ability to speak English. Officers need to be aware of the potential for inadvertent discrimination based on a citizen's language background, which could fall under "language and national origin discrimination" (Fernandez, 2000).

Clearly, the more bilingual officers a department has, the more efficient and effective the contact. Many agencies subsidize foreign-language training for their personnel or seek recruits with multiple-language skills. When the resources are not available for such programs, however, there can be serious and sometimes tragic consequences. Non-English-speaking citizens may not understand why they are being arrested or searched. They may not know their rights if they are unfamiliar with the legal system,

*Officer wishes to remain anonymous

as is the case with many recently arrived immigrants and refugees. Using the wrong translator can mislead officers, so much so that a victim and his or her translator may give two completely different versions of a story—for example, using the friend of a suspected child abuser to translate the allegations of the child who has been abused.

In some cases there is no sensitivity when it comes to language obstacles. For example, within a largely Spanish-speaking area in Los Angeles, a deputy, according to witnesses, asked a Hispanic male to get out of his car. The man answered in Spanish, "I'm handicapped," and he reached down to pull his left leg out of the car. The deputy apparently believed that the man was reaching for a weapon and, consequently, "struck him on the head with the butt of his gun" ("The Troubled LA County Sheriff's Department," 1992, p. A18).

Insensitivity to language differences was also involved in the case of an officer who had been called to the scene of an accident in which a third-grade girl had died almost immediately after having been struck by a car that leaped a curb and hurled the girl 60 feet through the air. When the police investigator arrived, he tried to ascertain what had happened: "[The police officer] shouted out if anyone had seen what had occurred. No one responded because they had not actually been witnesses. The officer in apparent disgust and derision then remarked, 'Why don't any of you speak English?'" (Ogawa, 1990).

Sensitivity to the difficulties of those who do not speak English is in order, but that is only a partial solution to the problem. In attempting to cope with the problem of non-English-speaking citizens, suspects, and criminals, many departments have not only increased the number of bilingual officers in their forces but have also begun to utilize translation services, some of which provide translation in over 150 languages 24 hours a day. The 911 emergency line has interpreters 24 hours a day for some languages. Having access to translation services and referrals is a first step in addressing the challenge of communication with those who speak no or limited English, but this is not a long-term solution. Having bilingual officers or nonsworn personnel, however, constitutes a more direct method of addressing the problem. Many departments across the country offer language classes on the job with tuition reimbursement for classes and extra pay for second-language proficiency. Police department training personnel are encouraged to look for classes specially designed for law enforcement. If they do not exist, a few selected officers and language educators should form a partnership so that officers can guide language teachers in the development of police-specific second-language curricula (i.e., to meet the specialized needs of officers on the street). In *Policing a Multicultural Community*, DeGeneste and Sullivan (1997) write:

> Since a degree of ethnic or racial distrust is undoubtedly the result of frustration stemming from language and communication difficulties, enhanced language training during initial entry-level police academies, with subsequent refresher courses throughout an officer's career, should be strongly considered. [And, on a practical level,] developing language skills for a police agency can be a costly undertaking. Initial training would extend the length of academy training, leading to additional costs for instructors, training space and course development. Agencies in large urban areas would need to craft curricula for multiple languages (for example, Spanish, Mandarin, Cantonese, etc.). Refresher training would require replacing officers while they receive updated, or perhaps even initial instruction in a new language if demographic shifts warrant. Limiting

these costs requires close monitoring of demographic trends to match language skills with community needs.

Increasing bilingual hires is the most practical direction in which to go; in addition, these officers often have a better understanding of the communities they serve. Some community-based police programs use trained community volunteers to assist them in situations in which English is not spoken. When translation is not available, officers have no choice but to rely on English. In doing so, the tips listed in Exhibit 4.1 on modifying one's language will be helpful.

ATTITUDES TOWARD NON-ENGLISH OR LIMITED ENGLISH SPEAKERS

Most officers are aware that a citizen with few or no English skills is not necessarily an illegal immigrant. However, sometimes officers have seen English difficulties as a sign that a person is an illegal immigrant and the consequences have been unfortunate. Donya Fernandez (2000), a language rights attorney, cited the case of a Spanish speaker with extremely limited English skills whom police turned over to the Immigration and Naturalization Services (INS). The INS held him for 48 hours, despite the fact that the man was a U.S. citizen who was born in the United States but had spent most of his life in Mexico.

---

1. Speak slowly and enunciate clearly.
2. Face the person and speak directly even when using a translator.
3. Avoid concentrated eye contact if the other speaker is not making direct eye contact.
4. Do not use jargon, slang, idioms, or reduced forms (e.g., "gonna," "gotta," "wanna," "couldja").
5. Avoid complex verb tenses (e.g., "If I would have known, I might have been able to provide assistance.").
6. Repeat key issues and questions in different ways.
7. Avoid asking questions that can be answered by "yes" or "no"; rather, ask questions so that the answer can show understanding.
8. Use short, simple sentences; pause between sentences.
9. Use visual cues such as gestures, demonstrations, and brief written phrases.
10. Use active rather than passive verbs (e.g., "I expect your attention" [active] rather than "Your attention is expected" [passive].
11. Have materials duplicated in bilingual format.
12. Pause frequently and give breaks. Monitor your speed when you speak.
13. Use only one idea per sentence.
14. Respect the silence that non-native English speakers need to formulate their sentences and translate them in their minds.
15. Check comprehension by having the other speaker repeat material or instructions, and summarize frequently.
16. Encourage and provide positive feedback on the person's ability to communicate.
17. Listen even more attentively than you do when communicating with a native speaker of English.
18. Be patient. Every first generation of immigrants struggles with the acquisition of English.
19. Do not speak louder; it will not help.

Exhibit 4.1 Tips for communicating when English is a second language.

Citizens' constant use of a second language and the accompanying frustrations for officers can be overwhelming. In general, whether the society at large (or police as a microcosm of society) is concerned about a particular group's use of their native language seems to be directly related to the population size of that group. For example, when large groups of Cubans or Puerto Ricans speak Spanish, there is often a higher level of anxiety among the dominant white population than when a few Armenians speak their native language. Virtually every immigrant group is said to resist learning English, yet the pattern of language acquisition among the generations of immigrants follows a predictable course. Members of the second and third generations of an immigrant family almost always become fluent in English, while many of the first-generation immigrants (the grandparents and the parents) struggle, sometimes partly learning English and sometimes not learning it at all. Many immigrants, however, are extremely motivated to learn English and become productive members of society. In urban areas, access to English classes is often limited (e.g., there have been known to be 4- and 5-year waiting lists for English programs at Los Angeles community colleges). Newcomers are fully aware that without English, they will never be able to integrate into society.

Nevertheless, some people, including established immigrants, have a tendency to overgeneralize their observations about newcomers. It is true that some people do not want to learn English, and even some middle-class U.S.-born Americans do not make efforts to improve their language abilities. How often does one hear that high school graduates who are native English speakers have not learned to write or speak well? Here laziness or lack of high-quality education (or both) may have contributed to this aspect of illiteracy. In fairness, all groups have a percentage of lazy people, but sometimes people tend to stereotype others. Although not all first-generation immigrants learn English, there is a great deal of mythology around the "masses" of immigrants who hold on to their native language.

The native language for an immigrant family is the language of communication for that family. It is not uncommon to hear comments such as, "They'll never learn English if they insist on speaking their native tongues at home." Imagine having been away from your family all day and coming home and interacting in a foreign language. Is it reasonable to expect that one could express affection, resolve conflicts, show anger, and simply relax in another language? Language is an integral part of a person's identity. During the initial months and even years of communicating in a second language, a person does not truly feel like him- or herself. Initially, one often has a feeling of play acting or taking on another identity when communicating in a second language.

From a physiological point of view, speaking a foreign language can be fatiguing. As a child, when speaking one's own native language, one uses a set of muscles to articulate the sounds of a given language. Changing to another language, particularly as an adult, requires the use of an entirely new set of muscles. This causes mental strain and facial tension, which can result in a person "shutting down"—the result being an inability to communicate in English (or whatever the new language is). It is no wonder that in the multicultural workforce, clusters of people from different ethnic groups can be seen having lunch together, taking breaks together, and so on. Simply put, it is more relaxing to be able to speak one's own language than to struggle with a new one all day.

Sometimes police officers say, "I know they speak English because they speak it among themselves [i.e., when the group is culturally mixed]. The minute I'm on the scene, it's 'No speak English.' Why do they have to play dumb? What do they think I am—stupid?" It would be naive to say that this situation does not occur. There will always be some people who try to deceive others and use or not use English to their own advantage. However, there may be other reasons that people "feign" not knowing English. Several factors affect an immigrant's ability to use English at any given moment. A few of these, in particular, are of special significance to law enforcement officers. Generally speaking, an immigrant's ability to express him- or herself in English is best when that person is comfortable with the officer. So the more intimidating an officer is, the higher the likelihood that anxiety will affect the speaker's ability in English. Language breakdown is one of the first signs that a person is ill at ease and stressed to the point of not being able to cooperate and communicate. It is in the officer's best interest to increase the comfort level of the citizen, whether a victim, a suspect, or simply a person requiring help. Language breakdown in a person who is otherwise fairly conversationally competent in English can also occur as a result of illness, intoxication, fatigue, and trauma.

Finally, officers must realize that their attitudes about immigrants and non-native English speakers, whether positive or negative, may very well affect their interaction with them. This is especially true when an officer is under pressure and negative attitudes are more likely to surface in communication.

CROSS-CULTURAL COMMUNICATION IN THE LAW ENFORCEMENT CONTEXT

To understand the need for skillful communication with members of culturally and ethnically diverse groups, including women, officers should recognize some of the special characteristics of cross-cultural communication in the law enforcement context (Exhibit 4.2). To best protect and serve communities made up of individuals from many different racial and cultural backgrounds, officers as peacekeepers, crime fighters, and law enforcement representatives need to look beyond the "mechanics" of policing and examine what takes place in the process of cross-cultural communication. Communication,

---

- Officers have traditionally used styles of communication and language that at one time were considered acceptable. Now, because of diverse groups within the police agency and within our cities, the unspoken rules about appropriate and inappropriate communication are changing.
- For officers, communication can be tense in crises and culturally unfamiliar environments.
- Officers' perceptions of a cultural group may be skewed by the populations they encounter.
- Officers' communication will be enhanced when they are aware of
  1. Perceptions
  2. Cultural filters
  3. "High- and low-context" communication (see explanation in text)
  4. Possible biases and stereotypes
- Through communication, officers have tremendous power to influence the behavior and responses of the citizens they contact. A lack of knowledge of the dynamics of cross-cultural communication will diminish this power.
- Improved communication with all citizens will also result in safer interactions for officers

---

Exhibit 4.2   Key cross-cultural areas in communication for officers to consider.

in general, is a challenge because it is "both hero and villain—it transfers information, meets people's needs, and gets things done, but far too often it also distorts messages, develops frustration, and renders people and organizations ineffective" (Harris & Moran, 1991). Why does communication pose this much of a challenge? Talking to others, making one's points, and giving explanations should not be so difficult.

Every communication act involves a message, a sender, and a receiver; given that any two human beings are fundamentally different, there will always be a psychological distance between the two involved (even if they have the same cultural background). Professional police officers have learned ways of bridging the gap, or psychological distance, between the two very different worlds of sender and receiver. In instances of cross-cultural communication, including cross-racial and cross-ethnic interactions, in which the sender and receiver are from different cultures, officers have an even greater gap to try to bridge. In Exhibit 4.2, the reader will find a summary of key factors that can potentially contribute to cross-cultural and cross-racial communication challenges. Psychological distance exists between any two human beings because every individual is "wired" differently from the next. Styles of communication that differ across culture can contribute to perceptions or misperceptions and incorrect filtering of communication "data."

High- and Low-Context Communication

Edward Hall, author of two dated, but seminal books in the field of cross-cultural communication (*The Silent Language* and *The Hidden Dimension*) coined terms to describe very different frameworks of communication across cultures and individual styles. An understanding of the continuum of "high- and low-context communication" will contribute to officers' understanding of direct and indirect communication (or explicit and implicit communication). People or cultural groups who tend toward the high-context end of this communication continuum may exhibit the following characteristics, to varying degree, in communication:

Higher context communication tendencies

- Tendency to avoid saying "no"

- Tendency to avoid conflict

- Difficulty answering "yes" and "no" and either/or type questions; usually not "binary thinkers"—awareness of shades of gray and broad context or scope

- Concerned about saving face (theirs and others)

- Preference for harmonious communication; avoidance of disagreement

- Focus on "wide context" of interaction—past events, tone, nonverbal communication, relationship, and status of speakers, good readers of implicit communication

- Preference for getting to the point slowly and or indirectly

- Appearance of "beating around the bush" (i.e., this is a low-context communicator's perception and filter of the higher context style); beating around the bush in high-context communication is seen as a polite style of communication, and the "right" way to communicate

Lower context communication tendencies

- "Yes" equals "yes" and "no" equals "no"
- Ease with direct communication and responding directly to conflict
- Saving face (theirs and others) not as important as saying the truth
- Focus more on words and what is verbalized than what is not communicated implicitly—less focus on tone, nonverbal, relationship, status, past events, implicit communication)
- Preference for getting right to the point; "beating around the bush" seen as negative

As officers know, rapport-building with all citizens is key in building trust, which is preliminary to their opening up. This is especially true when communicating with people who have higher context communication styles. Typically, these styles are more characteristic of cultural groups coming from Asian and Latin American cultures, and there are gender differences even in lower context cultures as well (i.e., women tend to have a higher context style than men). Chapter 5 provides several examples of higher context communication in the law enforcement context, and makes recommendations for responding effectively to this style (see chapter entitled Law Enforcement Contact with Asian/Pacific Americans, section on "Verbal and Nonverbal Styles").

One of the key tools for building rapport in law enforcement is Neuro-Linguistic Programming (NLP), a communication model and a set of techniques for establishing rapport. Officers have successfully used this communication tool, for example, in building rapport in interviews with witnesses and victims of crimes. The basis for the techniques involved have to do with a fundamental principle in interpersonal relationships, which is the need to create harmony with others in order to establish rapport. As such, the type of communication one uses with NLP is that of "matching" nonverbal and verbal behavior with a witness, victim, or interviewee (for example). This may prove to be especially challenging, but useful, with people from different cultural backgrounds as a way to minimize the cultural gap between the officer's style and that of the citizen with whom he or she is interacting. It is beyond the scope of this chapter to detail the theory behind and steps involved in NLP. However, we have included in the website section of this chapter a link that will take the reader to an informative FBI publication entitled, "Subtle Skills for Building Rapport," by Sandoval and Adams (2001).

CROSS-CULTURAL COMMUNICATION ATTEMPTS

It can sometimes be less challenging to interact with people from one's own background than with those from a different group. Communication can be strained and unnatural when there is no apparent common ground. The "people are people everywhere" argument and "just treat everyone with respect" advice both fall short when one learns that there can be basic differences in the areas of behavior and communication across cultures. Some police officers feel that an understanding of cross-cultural communication is unnecessary if respect is shown to every person. Yet, if officers have had limited contact with people from diverse backgrounds, they may inadvertently communicate their lack of familiarity. In the next few sections we exemplify typical ways people attempt to accommodate or react to cultural or racial differences and how they may cover up their discomfort in communication across cultures.

Using Language or Language Style to Become Just Like One of "Them"

Black officer to a white officer: Hey, what kind of arrest did you have?

White officer: Brotha-man was trying to front me . . .

Lieutenant Darryl McAllister from the Hayward, California, Police Department uses the preceding example to illustrate how obviously uncomfortable some non-African Americans are when communicating cross-racially. One of his pet peeves is hearing other officers trying to imitate him in speech and trying to act like a "brother." He explained that this type of imitative language is insincere and phony. The artificiality makes him feel as if people are going overboard to show just how comfortable they are (when, in fact, they may not be). He explained that he does not feel that this style of imitation is necessarily racist, but that it conveys others' discomfort with his "blackness" (McAllister, 2003).

Similarly, officers attempting to establish rapport with citizens should not pretend to have too much familiarity with the language and culture or use words selectively to demonstrate how "cool" they are (e.g., using "señor" with Spanish-speaking people, calling an African American "my man," or referring to a Native American as "chief"). People of one cultural background may find themselves in situations in which an entire crowd or family is using a particular dialect or slang. If the officer lapses into the manner of speaking of the group, he or she will likely appear to be mocking that style. Ultimately, the officer should be sincere and natural. "Faking" another style of communication can have extremely negative results.

Walking on Eggshells

When in the presence of people from different cultural backgrounds, some find that they have a tendency to work hard not to offend. Consequently, they are not able to be themselves or do what they would normally do. In a cultural diversity training workshop for employees of a city government, one white participant explained that he normally has no problem being direct when solicitors come to the door trying to sell something or ask for a donation to a cause. His normal response would be to say, "I'm not interested," and then he would promptly shut the door. He explained, however, that when a black solicitor comes to the door, he almost never rudely cuts him or her off, and most of the time he ends up making a donation to whatever cause is being promoted. His inability to be himself and communicate directly stems from his concern about appearing to be racist. It is not within the scope of this subsection to analyze this behavior in depth but simply to bring into awareness some typical patterns of reactions in cross-cultural and cross-racial encounters. A person must attempt to recognize his or her tendencies to reach the goal of communicating in a sincere and authentic manner with people of all backgrounds (Exhibit 4.3).

- Self-awareness about one's early life experiences that helped to shape perceptions, filters, and assumptions about people.
- Self-awareness about how one feels toward someone who is "different."
- Management of assumptions and discomfort in dealing with people who are different (e.g., do we try to deny that differences exist and laugh differences away, or imitate "them" in order to appear comfortable?).
- Ability to be authentic in communication with others while modifying communication style, when necessary.

Exhibit 4.3   Key areas for officers to consider: self-awareness.

"Some of My Best Friends Are . . ."

In an attempt to show how tolerant and experienced they are with members of minority groups, many people often feel the need to demonstrate their tolerance strongly by saying things such as "I'm not prejudiced" or "I have friends who are members of your group" or "I know people . . . ," or, worse, "I once knew someone who was also [for example] Jewish/Asian/African American." Although the intention may be to break down barriers and establish rapport, these types of statements often sound patronizing. To a member of a culturally or racially different group, this type of comment comes across as extremely naive. In fact, many people would understand such a comment as signifying that the speaker actually does have prejudices toward a particular group. Minority-group members would question a nonmember's need to make a reference to others of the same background when there is no context for doing so. These types of remarks indicate that the speaker is probably isolated from members of the particular group. Yet the person making a statement such as, "I know someone who is [for example] Asian" is trying to establish something in common with the other person and may even go into detail about the other person he or she knows. As one Jewish woman reported in a cross-cultural awareness session, "Just because a person I meet is uncomfortable meeting Jews or has very little experience with Jews doesn't mean that I want to hear about the one Jewish person he met 10 years ago while traveling on a plane to New York!"

"You People," or the We–They Distinction

Some may say "I'd like to get to know you people better" or "You people have made some amazing contributions." The usage of "You people" may be another signal of prejudice or divisiveness in one's mind. When someone decides that a particular group is unlike his or her own group (i.e., not part of "my people"), that person makes a simplistic division of all people into two groups: "we" and "they." Often accompanying this division is the attribution of positive traits to "us" and negative traits to "them." Members of the "other group" (the out-group) are described in negative and stereotypical terms (e.g., "They are lazy," "They are criminals," "They are aggressive") rather than neutral terms that describe cultural or ethnic generalities (e.g., "They have a tradition of valuing education" or "They have a communication style that is more formal than that of most Americans"). The phenomenon of stereotyping makes it very difficult for people to communicate with each other effectively because they do not perceive others accurately. By attributing negative qualities to another group, a person creates myths about the superiority of his or her own group. Cultural and racial put-downs are often attempts to make people feel better about themselves.

"You Stopped Me Because I'm . . . ," or Accusations of Racial Profiling

There are three recurring situations in which an officer may hear the accusation: "You stopped me because I'm [black, Arab, and so forth]." The first situation is when citizens from a neighborhood with people predominantly from one culture are suspicious of any person in their neighborhood from another background. Thus they may call 911, reporting a "suspicious character," and maybe even adding such statements as "I think he has a gun" when there is no basis for such an accusation. In this situation the police officer must understand the extreme humiliation and anger citizens feel when they are the object of racist perceptions. Once the officer determines that there is no reason to arrest the citizen, it is most appropriate for the officer to apologize for having made the stop and to explain that department policy requires that officers are obliged to investigate all calls.

Indeed, there are many incidents all over the country in which citizens call a police department to report a "suspicious character" just because he or she does not happen to fit the description of the majority of the residents in that area. Since there is a history of stopping minorities for reasons that are less than legitimate, the officer must go out of his or her way to show respect to the innocent citizen who does not know why he or she has been stopped and is caught totally off guard. Many people reported to be "suspicious" for merely being of a different race would appreciate an officer's making a final comment, such as "I hope this kind of racism ends soon within our community" or "It's too bad there are still people in our community who are so ignorant." Comments such as these, said with sincerity, may very well get back to the community and contribute to improved future interactions with members of the police department. Of course, some people who are stopped will not appreciate any attempt that the officer makes to explain why the stop was made. Nevertheless, many citizens will react favorably to an officer's understanding of their feelings.

A second situation in which an officer may hear, "You stopped me because I'm . . ." may occur not because of any racist intentions of the officer but rather as a "reflex response" of the citizen (in other words, it has no bearing on reality). Many people have been stopped without reason in the past or know people who have; they carry this baggage into each encounter with an officer. One police officer explained: "I don't consider myself prejudiced. I consider myself a fair person, but let me tell you what happens almost every time I stop a black in City X. The first words I hear from them are 'You stopped me because I'm black.' That's bugging the hell out of me because that's not why I stopped them. I stopped them because they violated the traffic code. It's really bothering me and I'm about to explode."

Officers accused of racially or ethnically motivated stops truly need to remain professional and not escalate a potential conflict or create a confrontation. Law enforcement officials should not only try to communicate their professionalism, both verbally and nonverbally, but also try to strengthen their self-control. The best way to deal with these types of remarks from citizens is to work on your own reactions and stress level. One could potentially receive such remarks on a daily basis. People react to officers as symbols, and are using the officer to vent their frustration.

This response assumes no racial profiling has taken place.

Let's assume that the officer did not stop a person because of his or her ethnicity or race and that the officer is therefore not abusing his or her power. George Thompson, founder and president of the Verbal Judo Institute, Inc., believes that in these situations, people bring up race and ethnicity to throw the officer off guard. According to Thompson (who is white and a former English professor and police officer), the more professional an officer is, the less likely he or she will let this type of statement become a problem. Newer officers, especially, can be thrown off by such allegations of racism when, in fact, they are simply upholding the law and keeping the peace as they have been trained to do. Thompson advocates using "verbal deflectors" when citizens make such remarks as "You stopped me because I'm . . ." He recommends responses such as "I appreciate that, but . . . [e.g., you were going 55 miles in a 25-mile zone]," or "I hear what you're saying, but . . . you just broke the law." The characteristics of "verbal deflectors" are (1) they are readily available to the lips, (2) they are nonjudgmental, and (3) they can be said quickly. Contrary to what Martin advocates, Thompson believes that statements from citizens should not be ignored because silence or no response can make people even more furious than they already are (because they were stopped).

> Pay attention to what citizens say, but deflect their anger. You are not paid to argue with citizens. You are paid to keep the peace. If you use tactical language and focus every word you say so that it relates to your purpose, then you will sound more professional. The minute you start using words as defensive weapons, you lose power and endanger your safety. If you "springboard" over their arguments, and remain calm, controlled, and nonjudgmental, you will gain voluntary compliance most of the time. The results of this professional communication are that (1) you feel good, (2) you disarm the citizen, and (3) you control them in the streets (and in courts and in the media). Never take anything personally. (Thompson, 2003)

The third and final situation in which an officer may hear "You stopped me because I'm [black, Arab, and so forth]" is when the citizen is correct and, indeed, racial profiling is taking place. Police department personnel are not immune from the racism that still exists in our society. Reflecting biased attitudes outside the law enforcement agency, some officers use their positions of power to assert authority in ways that cannot be tolerated. Here we are not only referring to the white officer who subjugates citizens from different backgrounds but also, for example, to an African American officer who has internalized the racism of the dominant society and may actually treat fellow group members unjustly. Alternatively, this abuse of power could take place between, for example, a black or Latino officer and a white citizen. (See Chapter 14 for a detailed description of racial profiling.)

Officers must consider the reasons a citizen may say, "You stopped me because I'm . . ." and respond accordingly. The situations described call for different responses* on the part of the officer (i.e., citizens call in because of racist perceptions and the "suspicious character" is innocent; the citizen stopped is simply "hassling" the officer, and may or may not have been unjustly stopped in the past; and the citizen making the accusation toward the officer is correct). The officer would do well, in all three situations, to remember the quote included in the final section of Chapter 1: "Remember the history of law enforcement with all groups and ask yourself the question, Am I part of the past, or a part of the future?" (Berry, 2003).

Communication Considerations—Post-9/11

Many Arab Americans, in particular, feel that they are automatic suspects when approached by law enforcement representatives. Since 9/11, and particularly the first few months following the terrorist acts (and continuing), there has been what Lobna Ismail, an Arab American cross-cultural specialist, characterizes as collateral damage to the entire Arab American community. They may hesitate to call the police when they are victims of crimes, and fear being treated as suspects rather than victims of a crime (Ismail, 2003). For this reason, it is especially important to consider the importance of building trust, rapport, and relationship with Arab Americans and people from the Middle East. According to Dr. James Zogby, President of the Arab American Institute Foundation in Washington D.C., the more a community policing mindset has developed in a particular locale, the more easily do communication barriers come down between law enforcement and Arab Americans. Despite initiatives from the Department of Justice to call up several thousand Arab Americans (and, consequently, widespread resentment and fear among Arab American community members), where police and community leaders held advisory meetings together, where police officers visited mosques and attended community events, effective communication, along with trust, ensued. "We have found that when FBI and police department leadership, for example, are willing to sit down and dialogue with community leaders, then it is much more likely that citizens will be willing to share information, provide tips because officers have gone out of their way to build trust" (Ibid).

Regarding communication with Arab Americans (and this applies to communication with other cultural groups as well), officers should not try too hard, and in an unnatural way, to demonstrate cultural sensitivity. An officer should understand differences in communication style where they exist, but should not act stiff or uncomfortable in an attempt to get it right. With cultural groups that may appear very different from one's own, or where sensitivities may be high as with members of the Arab American community, law enforcement representatives need to think about approaching others in a way that will increase their comfort level. This means being natural, and not beginning with the assumption that they are foreign and strange, and not being able to communicate with them unless you know their ways (Ibid). In the end, it is the spirit of respect toward fellow human beings, with some knowledge of cultural detail, that will lead to effective communication.

---

*Brookline Police Department in Massachusetts uses an interactive simulation training exercise that creates a variety of scenarios, including those related to racial profiling. In responding to scenarios, officers have to focus on their own behavior and response in order to effectively control the situation. ("Brookline," 2003, p. 8)

INTERVIEWING AND DATA-GATHERING SKILLS

Interviewing and data-gathering skills form the basic techniques for communication and intervention work with multicultural populations. For the officer, the key issues in any interviewing and data-gathering situation are as follows:

- Establishing interpersonal relationships with the parties involved to gain trust and rapport for continual work

- Bringing structure and control to the immediate situation

- Gaining information about the problems and situations that require the presence of the law enforcement officer

- Giving information about the workings of the law enforcement guidelines, resources, and assistance available

- Providing action and interventions, as needed

- Bolstering and supporting the different parties' abilities and skills to solve current and future problems on their own

Listed in Exhibit 4.4 are helpful guidelines for providing and receiving better information in a multicultural context.

In the area of data gathering and interviewing, the officer in a multicultural law enforcement and peacekeeping situation cannot assume that his or her key motivators and values are the same as those of the other parties involved. Recognizing such differences in motivation and values will result in greater effectiveness. For example, the values of saving face and preserving one's own honor as well as the honor of one's

---

1. Be knowledgeable about who is likely to have information. Ask questions to identify the head of a family or respected community leaders.

2. Consider that some cultural groups have more of a need than others for rapport and trust building before they are willing to share information. Do not consider the time it takes to establish rapport a waste of time. For some, this may be a necessary step.

3. Provide background and context for your questions, information, and requests. Cultural minorities differ in their need for "contextual information" (i.e., background information) before getting down to the issues or business at hand. Remain patient with those who want to go into more detail than you think is necessary.

4. Expect answers to be formulated and expressed in culturally different ways. Some people tend to be linear in their answers (i.e., giving one point of information at a time in a chronological order), some present information in a zigzag fashion (i.e., they digress frequently), and others tend to present information in a circular style (i.e., they may appear to be talking in circles). And, of course, there are individual differences in ways of presenting information, as well as cultural differences.

5. It is important to speak simply, but do not make the mistake of using simple or "pigeon" English. Remember, people's comprehension skills are usually better than their speaking skills.

6. "Yes" does not always mean "yes"; do not mistake a courteous answer for the facts or the truth.

7. Remember that maintaining a good rapport is just as important as coming to the point and getting work done quickly. Slow down!

8. Silence is a form of speech; do not interrupt it. Give people time to express themselves by respecting their silence.

Exhibit 4.4   Interviewing and data gathering in a multicultural context.

family are extremely strong motivators and values for many people from Asian, Latin American, and Mediterranean cultures. An Asian gang expert from the Oakland, California, Police Department illustrated this value system with the case of a niece who had been chosen by the police to translate for her aunt, who had been raped. The values of honor and face-saving prevented the aunt from telling the police all the details of the crime of which she was the victim. Her initial story, told to the police through her niece's translation, contained very few of the facts or details of the crime. Later, through a second translator who was not a family member, the rape victim gave all the necessary information. Precious time had been lost, but the victim explained that she could not have revealed the true story in front of her niece because she would have shamed her family.

Exhibit 4.5 lists key values or motivators for police officers. In any given situation, these values may be at odds with what motivates the victim, suspect, or ordinary citizen of any background. However, when the officer and citizen are from totally different backgrounds, additional cultural or racial variables may also be in conflict.

Finally, when interviewing and data gathering in the area of hate incidents and crimes (as well as threats [e.g., phone calls, letters] targeted at individuals of particular backgrounds), the officer's need for control and structure may have to encompass possible hysterical or at least highly emotional reactions from other people of the same background. In the officer's attempt to be in control of the situation, he or she must consider that there will also be a community needing reassurance. For example, an officer will need to be willing to respond sensitively to heightened anxiety on the part of group members and not downplay their fears. Interviewing and data gathering may therefore last much longer when the officer is required to deal with multiple community members and widespread fears.

NONVERBAL COMMUNICATION

Up until this point in the chapter we have discussed verbal communication across cultures and its relevance to the law enforcement context. Nonverbal communication, including tone of voice, play a key role in the dynamics between any two people. Dr. Albert Mehrabian of the University of California at Los Angeles, described in the well-known book *Silent Messages* (1971) the general impact between two or three people when a person's verbal and nonverbal messages contradict each other. In this scenario,

---

1. Survival or injury avoidance
2. Control and structure
3. Respect and authority
4. Use of professional skills
5. Upholding laws and principles
6. Avoiding conflict and tensions
7. Harmony and peacekeeping
8. Conflict resolution and problem solving
9. Self-respect and self-esteem

Exhibit 4.5   Key values or motivators in law enforcement.

it is almost always tone of voice and body language, including facial expressions, that convey an individual's true feeling. Of course, officers have to attend to citizens' words; however, tone of voice and body language can reveal much more. In addition, across cultures, there are additional considerations that relate directly to the interpretation of meaning.

Consider the following examples of reactions to nonverbal differences across cultures and their implications for day-to-day police work:

> He didn't look at me once. I know he's guilty. Never trust a person who doesn't look you in the eye.—American police officer

> Americans seem cold. They seem to get upset when you stand close to them.—Jordanian teacher

In the first example, if an officer uses norms of eye contact as understood by most Americans, he or she could make an incorrect judgment about someone who avoids eye contact. In the second example, an officer's comfortable distance for safety might be violated because of a cultural standard defining acceptable conversational distance. The comments demonstrate how people can misinterpret nonverbal communication when it is culturally different from their own. Misinterpretation can happen with two people from the same background, but it is more likely when there are cultural differences. Universal emotions such as happiness, fear, and sadness are expressed in similar nonverbal ways throughout the world. However, nonverbal variations across cultures can cause confusion.

Take the example of the way people express sadness and grief. In many cultures, such as Arabic and Iranian cultures, people express grief openly and out loud. In contrast, in other parts of the world (e.g., in China and Japan), people are generally more subdued or even silent in their expressions of grief. In Asian cultures, the general belief is that it is unacceptable to show emotion openly (whether sadness, happiness, or pain). Without this cultural knowledge, in observing a person who did not openly express grief, for example, one might come to the conclusion that he or she is not in emotional distress. This would be an incorrect and ethnocentric interpretation based on one's own culture.

The expression of friendship is another example of how cultural groups differ in their nonverbal behavior. Feelings of friendship exist everywhere, but their expression varies. It is acceptable for men to embrace and kiss each other (in Saudi Arabia and Russia, for example) and for women to hold hands (in China, Korea, Egypt, and other countries). Russian gymnasts of the same sex have been seen on television kissing each other on the lips; this is apparently an acceptable gesture in their culture and does not imply that they are gay or lesbian. What is considered "normal" behavior in one culture may be viewed as "abnormal" or unusual in another.

The following areas of nonverbal communication have variations across cultures; the degree to which a person displays the nonverbal differences depends on how Westernized the person has become. Note that some people who are very Westernized in their thinking may still display traditional forms of nonverbal communication simply because they are unaware that the differences exist.

1. ***Gestures:*** A few American gestures are offensive in other cultures. For example, the OK gesture is obscene in Latin America, the good luck gesture is

offensive in parts of Vietnam, and the "come here" gesture (beckoning people to come with the palm up) is very insulting in most of Asia and Latin America (Levine & Adelman, 1992).

2. **Body position:** A police sergeant relaxing at his desk with his feet up, baring the soles of his shoes, would most likely offend a Thai or Saudi Arabian (and other groups as well) coming into the office. To show one's foot in many cultures is insulting because the foot is considered the dirtiest part of the body. (Another example of this was the intended insult toward Saddam Hussein when Iraqis hit a statue of him with their shoes.) Officers need to be mindful of this taboo with respect to the foot, and should refrain, whenever possible, from making physical contact with the foot when, for example, someone is lying on the ground.

3. **Facial expressions:** Not all facial expressions mean the same thing across cultures. A smile is a great source of confusion for many people in law enforcement when they encounter people from Asian, especially Southeast Asian, cultures. A smile or giggle can cover up pain, humiliation, and embarrassment. Some women (e.g., Japanese, Vietnamese) cover up their mouths when they smile or giggle. Upon hearing something sad, a Vietnamese person may smile. Similarly, an officer may need to communicate something that causes a loss of face to a person, resulting in the person smiling. This smile does not mean that the person is trying to be a "smart aleck"; it is simply a culturally conditioned response.

4. **Facial expressiveness:** People in law enforcement have to be able to "read faces" in certain situations to be able to assess situations correctly. The degree to which people show emotions on their faces depends, in large part, on their cultural background. Whereas Latin Americans, Mediterraneans, Arabs, Israelis, and African Americans tend to show emotions facially, other groups, such as many of the Asian cultural groups, tend to be less facially expressive and less emotive. An officer may thus incorrectly assume that a person is not being cooperative or would not make a good witness.

5. **Eye contact:** In many parts of the world, eye contact is avoided with authority figures. In parts of India, for example, a father would discipline his child by saying, "Don't look me in the eye when I'm speaking to you"; an American parent would say, "Look me in the eye when I'm speaking to you." To maintain direct eye contact with a police officer in some cultures would be disrespectful. Direct eye contact with some citizens can also be perceived as threatening to that citizen. A security officer in a large store in San Jose, California, offered the example of officers looking directly at Latino/Hispanic young people suspected of stealing items from the store. On a number of occasions, the officers' direct eye contact was met with a physical reaction (i.e., the young person attempting to punch the officer). He explained that the Latino/Hispanic individual mistook the eye contact as confrontation and a challenge for a fight.

6. **Physical or conversational distance:** All people unconsciously keep a comfortable distance around them when communicating with others, resulting in

invisible walls that keep people far enough away. (This subcategory of nonverbal communication is called "proxemics.") Police officers are perhaps more aware than others of the distance they keep from people in order to remain safe. When someone violates this space, a person often feels threatened and backs away or, in the case of an officer, begins to think about protective measures. Although personality and context also determine interpersonal distance, cultural background comes into play. In general, Latin Americans and Middle Easterners are more comfortable at closer distances than are northern Europeans, Asians, or the majority of Americans. An officer should not necessarily feel threatened, for example, if approached by an Iranian or a Greek in a manner that feels uncomfortably close. While maintaining a safe distance, the officer should also consider cultural background. Consider the example of a Middle Eastern suspect (for example) who ignores an officers' command to "step back." The social distance for interacting in the Middle East (as in other areas of the world) is much closer than it is in the United States. For officers, where safety is paramount, this could easily lead to misinterpretation. Generally, Americans are comfortable at a little more than an arm's distance from each other.

For the law enforcement professional, nonverbal communication constitutes a major role in all aspects of peacekeeping and enforcement. For multicultural populations, it is even more important that the officer be aware of the variety of nuances and differences that may exist from one group to another. Clearly, studies show that a large percentage of interpersonal communication is understood because of the nonverbal "body language" aspects of the speaker. Moreover, in many cultures, as is true for many ethnic minorities in the United States, greater weight and belief are placed on the visual and nonverbal aspects of communication (Exhibits 4.6 and 4.7).

Officers must be authentic in their communication with people from various backgrounds. When learning about both verbal and nonverbal characteristics across cultures,

---

1. Body language and nonverbal messages can override an officer's verbal content in high-stress and crisis situations. For example, the officer's statement that he or she is there to help may be contradicted by a body posture of discomfort and uncertainty in culturally unfamiliar households.

2. For people of different ethnic backgrounds, stress, confusion, and uncertainty can also communicate unintended messages. For example, an Asian may remain silent and look nervous and anxious at the scene of a crime. He or she may appear to many as being "uncooperative" when in fact this person may have every intention of helping the officer.

3. For people with limited English skills, the nonverbal aspects of communication become even more important. Correct gestures and nonverbal cues help the non-native English speaker in understanding the verbal messages.

4. It is important for officers to learn about and avoid offensive gestures and cultural taboos. However, immigrants and international visitors are quick to forgive and to overlook gestures and actions made out of forgetfulness and ignorance. Officers should realize, too, that in time, newcomers usually learn many of the nonverbal mannerisms with which officers are more familiar. Nevertheless, learning about offensive gestures can help officers avoid interpersonal offenses.

Note: Each of the culture-specific chapters (Chapters 5 through 9) contains information about nonverbal characteristics of particular groups.

Exhibit 4.6   Nonverbal communication: key points for law enforcement.

- When is touch appropriate and inappropriate?
- What is the comfortable physical distance between people in interactions?
- What is considered proper eye contact? What do eye contact and lack of eye contact mean to the people involved?
- What cultural variety is there in facial expressions? For example, does nodding and smiling mean the same in all cultures? If someone appears to be expressionless, does that mean he or she is uncooperative?
- What are appropriate and inappropriate gestures for a particular cultural group?
- Is the person in transition from one culture to another and unaware of culturally different norms of communication?

Exhibit 4.7   Key questions concerning nonverbal communication across cultures.

officers do not need to feel that they must communicate differently each time they are in contact with someone of a different background. However, understanding that there are variations in communication style will help the officer interpret people's motives and attitudes more accurately and, overall, assess situations without a cultural bias.

MALE–FEMALE COMMUNICATION IN LAW ENFORCEMENT

> You have to go along with the kind of kidding and ribbing that the guys partici-
> pate in; otherwise, you are not one of them. If you say that you are offended by
> their crass jokes and vulgar speech, then you are ostracized from the group. I
> have often felt that in the squad room men have purposely controlled them-
> selves because of my presence, because I have spoken up. But what I've done
> to them is make them act one way because of my presence as a woman. Then
> they call me a prude or spread the word that I'm keeping track of all their re-
> marks for the basis of a sexual harassment suit down the road. I have no interest
> in doing that. I simply want to be a competent police officer in a professional
> working environment. (comments by a woman police officer* made at a
> Women's Peace Officer Association Conference [WPOA])

With the changing workforce, including increasing numbers of women in traditionally male professions, many new challenges in the area of male–female communication are presenting themselves. Within law enforcement, in particular, a strong camaraderie characterizes the relationships mainly among the male members of a police force, al-though, in some cases, women are part of this camaraderie. Women allowed into what has been termed the "brotherhood" have generally had to become "one of the guys" to gain acceptance into a historically male-dominated profession.

Camaraderie results when a group is united because of a common goal or purpose; the glue cementing the camaraderie is the easy communication among its members. The extracurricular interests of the members of the group, the topics selected for con-versation, and the jokes that people tell all contribute to the cohesion or tightness of police department members. In some departments, women find that they or other women are the object of jokes about sexual topics or that there are simply numerous references to sex. Because certain departments within cities have consisted mostly of

*Wishes to remain anonymous

men, they have not had to consider the inclusion of women on an equal basis and have not had to examine their own communication with each other.

Young women who are new to a department feel that they must tolerate certain behaviors to be accepted. A female sheriff participating in a WPOA conference said that on a daily basis she confronts vulgar language and sexual references in the jail where she works. Her list was long: "I am extremely bothered about the communication of the men where I work. Without mincing words, I'll tell you—at the county jail, officers are very degrading to women. . . . They sometimes make fun of rape victims, they are rude and lewd to female inmates, and they are constantly trying to get me to join into the 'fun.' A woman is referred to as a 'dyke,' a 'cunt,' a 'douche bag,' a 'whore,' a 'hooker,' a 'bitch,' and I'm sure I could come up with more. The guys don't call me those names, but they use them all the time referring to other women." This sheriff also noted that she did not experience the disrespectful verbal behavior in one-to-one situations with male deputies, only when they were in a group. She wondered out loud, "What happens to men when they group with each other? Why the change?"

It is not only the male grouping phenomenon that produces this type of rough, vulgar, and sexist language. One study of a large urban police department conducted for California Law Enforcement Command College documented inappropriate communications from patrol cars' two-way radios and computers. The language on the official system was often unprofessional—rough, vulgar, offensive, racist, and sexist. Obviously, both discipline and training were needed in this agency.

Certainly, not all men behave and talk in offensive ways, but the phenomenon is frequent enough that women in traditionally male work environments mention this issue repeatedly. Some women join in conversations that make them uneasy, but they do not let on that their working environment is uncomfortable and actually affecting their morale and productivity. Other women seem to be comfortable with the sexual comments of their male counterparts and may not object to the use of certain terms that other women find patronizing (e.g., "honey," "doll," "babe"). However, the percentage of women who fall into this category may very well be decreasing. Through sexual harassment policies, both women and men have learned that, for some, sexual innuendoes and patronizing terms can contribute to a hostile working environment.

In male-dominated institutions, vocations, and professions, women find that speaking out against this type of talk and joking creates discomfort for them and puts them in a double bind. A female police officer at a workshop on discrimination in the workplace said she felt that women's choices regarding communication with fellow male officers were limited. She explained that when a woman objects or speaks up, she risks earning a reputation or label that is hard to shed. If she remains quiet, she must tolerate a lot of verbal abuse and compromise her professionalism. This particular police officer decided to speak up in her own department, and, indeed, she earned a reputation as a troublemaker. In fact, she had no interest in going any further than complaining to her supervisor, but nevertheless was accused of preparing for a lawsuit. She explained that a lawsuit was the farthest thing from her mind and that all she wanted was professional respect.

Some women who have objected to certain mannerisms of their male counterparts' communication say that when they come into a room or office, the men stop talking. The result is that the communication that normally functions to hold a group together is strained and tense. The ultimate result is that the workplace becomes segregated by gender. When shut out from a conversation, many women feel excluded and unempowered; in turn, many men feel resentful about having to modify their style of communication.

Women in traditionally male work environments such as police and fire departments find that they are sometimes put in a position of having to trade their professional identity for their personal one. A woman officer who proudly tells her sergeant about the arrest she made may be stunned when he, totally out of context, compliments the way she has been keeping in shape and tells her how good she looks in her uniform. This is not to say that compliments are never acceptable. But in this context, the woman is relating as a professional and desires reciprocal professional treatment. Men and women often ask, "Where do I draw the line? When does a comment become harassment?" In terms of the legal definition of sexual harassment, when the perpetrators are made aware that their comments are uninvited and unwelcome, then they must be reasonable enough to stop making them. It is not within the scope of this chapter to detail sexual harassment and all its legal implications; however, it should be noted that everyone has his or her own limits. What is harassment to one may be appreciated by another. When communicating across genders, each party must be sensitive to what the other party considers acceptable or insulting (see Exhibit 4.8). It is also the responsibility of the individual who has been offended, whether male or female, to make it clear that certain types of remarks are offensive.

SUMMARY

In cross-cultural communication in law enforcement, officers' own filters and perceptions influence the assessment of each situation and the reactions the officers choose to exhibit. Each officer has unique "blind spots" and emotional "buttons" that may negatively affect the communication. To explore one's own skills in this regard, the reader is urged to undertake a self-evaluation by filling out the Communications Inventory in Appendix D.

Officers must keep in mind that rapport building is related to trust for many persons of different backgrounds. The more trust officers earn with members of ethnic

---

- Use terms that are inclusive rather than exclusive.
  Examples: "police officer," "chairperson," "commendations" (instead of the informal "atta boys")
- Avoid using terms or words that many women feel diminish their professional status. Examples: "chick," "babe"
- Avoid using terms or words that devalue groups of women or stereotype them.
  Example: Referring to women officers as "dykes"
- Avoid sexist jokes, even if you think they are not offensive. (Someone is bound to be offended; the same applies to racist jokes.)
- Avoid using terms that negatively spotlight or set women apart from men.
  Examples: "For a woman cop, she did a good job" (implying that this is the exception rather than the rule) (also applies to references about other cultural groups: "He's Latino, but he works hard." "He's black, but he's really skilled.")

Exhibit 4.8   Inclusive workplace communication.

communities, the more helpful these group members will be when officers need cooperation and information. To improve communication across cultures, it is essential that people in law enforcement understand the overall style of communication of different groups, including the special challenges facing men and women in the profession, and utilize multicultural communication skills.

Finally, we would like to reiterate two points made earlier in this chapter regarding police officer communication:

- Officers have traditionally used styles of communication and language that at one time were considered acceptable, not only within the police agency but with citizens as well. Because of cultural diversity in the population and the accompanying need to respect all individuals, the unspoken rules about what is appropriate have changed dramatically.

- Through communication, officers have tremendous power to influence the behavior and responses of the citizens with whom they contact. This is true of all citizens, regardless of background. A lack of knowledge of the cross-cultural aspects of communication will diminish that power with people whose backgrounds differ from that of the officer.

DISCUSSION QUESTIONS AND ISSUES*

1. ***The Origins of Stereotypes.*** In this chapter, we argue that officers need to recognize how their early experiences in life and later adult experiences shape their perceptions and "filters" about people from groups different from their own. What do you remember learning about various ethnic and racial groups when you were young? Did you grow up in an environment of tolerance or did you hear statements such as "That's the way they are . . ." or "You've got to be careful with those people . . ." or "They are lazy [or dishonest, etc.]? Also discuss your experiences as an adult with different groups and how those experiences may be affecting your perceptions.

2. ***Police Officer Interaction with Speakers of Other Languages.*** The following dialogue illustrates a typical interaction between a police officer and a non-native speaker of English, in this case a Vietnamese man. Judging from the English that the Vietnamese is speaking, how would you rate the officer's use of English? Analyze this interaction by being specific as to how the officer can improve.

Situation: An officer pulls a car over, gets out of the car, and approaches the driver. The driver, who is Vietnamese, says, in poor English, "What happen? Why you stop me?"

Officer: I pulled you over because you ran a red light.

Citizen: (*No response*)

Officer: This is a traffic violation. (*Receives no feedback.*) Do you understand?

*See the Instructor's Manual accompanying this text for additional activities, role-play activities, questionnaires, and projects related to the content of this chapter.

Citizen: (*Nodding*) Yeh, I understand.

Officer: I'm going to have to issue you a traffic citation.

Citizen: (*Staring at officer*)

Officer: Where's your driver's license?

Citizen: License? Just a minute. (*Leans over to open glove compartment, but finds nothing. He gets out of car and goes to trunk.*)

Officer: (*Irritated and slightly nervous*) Hey! (*in a loud voice*) What's going on here? I asked to see your driver's license. Are you the registered owner of this car?

Citizen: Yeh. I go get my license.

Officer: (*Speaking much louder*) Wait a minute. Don't you understand? Are you not the owner of this car? Do you even have a license?

Citizen: Wait. (*Finds license in trunk and produces it for officer*)

Officer: OK. Would you mind getting back into the car now?

Citizen: (*Does nothing*) Yeah, I understand.

Officer: (*Pointing to the front seat*) Back into the car!

Citizen: (*Does as told*)

Note: The officer could make improvements in at least four areas: (1) choice of words, (2) manner of asking questions, (3) use of idioms (there are at least two or three that could be changed to simple English), and (4) tone and attitude.

3. **Police Officers' "Hot Buttons."** Discuss how citizens (e.g., suspects, victims, complainants) affect your reactions in communication. Specifically, what words and attitudes do they use that break down your attempts to be professional? What emotionally laden language "sets you off"?

4. **Professional Communication with Citizens.** After you have discussed what affects your communication negatively (question 3), role-play with fellow officers situations in which you respond professionally to abuses you hear. (Refer back to the section on verbal judo if you need suggestions.)

5. **Racially Derogatory Remarks.** In late 1992, Marge Schott, the 61-year-old owner of the Cincinnati Reds, was accused of making racist remarks over a period of years; she was accused of allegedly calling two Reds outfielders her "million dollar niggers" and admitted to keeping a swastika armband in her desk drawer. She also told the *New York Times* that Hitler was "good" but that he went too far. One of the issues related to her racially and culturally insensitive remarks was that her comments were made in front of other people, but that no one said anything to her or objected. Some felt that she should have been confronted.

   Answer the following questions as accurately as you can. If you were with friends in a social gathering and one friend made an off-color remark similar to those of Mrs. Schott, what would you do? If you think that you would say something, what would it be? If you know that you would not say anything, does this mean that you condone the behavior? Would things change if the re-marks were made in the law enforcement agency or you overheard officers on the streets making such remarks? Explain your answer.

6. ***Cultural Observations.*** Make a list of your observations for each of the cultural groups with which you have had a substantial amount of contact. After you make your list, try to find someone from that culture with whom you can discuss your observations.

   a. Display of emotions and expressions of feelings

   b. Communication style: loud, soft, direct, indirect

   c. Expressions of appreciation; conventions of courtesy (i.e., forms of politeness)

   d. Need (or lack thereof) for privacy

   e. Gestures, facial expressions, and body movements

   f. Eye contact

   g. Touching

   h. Interpersonal space (conversational distance)

   i. Taboo topics in conversation

   j. Response to authority

7. ***Discomfort with Unfamiliar Groups.*** Try to recall a situation in which you found yourself in a culturally unfamiliar environment (e.g., responding to a call in an ethnically different household or being the only minority person of your background among a group of people from another cultural or ethnic group). How much discomfort, if any, did you experience? If the situation was uncomfortable, did it affect your communication effectiveness or professionalism?

8. ***Accusations of Racially or Ethnically Motivated Stops.*** Have you encountered, "You stopped me because I'm [any ethnic group]?" If so, how did you handle the situation? How effectively do you think you responded?

WEBSITE RESOURCES

Visit these websites for additional information about cross-cultural and general communication applicable to law enforcement.

Verbal Judo Institute: http://www.verbaljudo.com

This website centers around "Verbal Judo," a tactical form of communication used as a tool to generate voluntary compliance from citizens under difficult situations. It lists various types of Verbal Judo courses available as well as books and articles on the subject. There is a link explaining the applicable Verbal Judo to police officers.

United States Department of Justice, Federal Bureau of Investigation:
http://www.fbi.gov/publications/leb/2001/aug01leb.htm

This FBI website makes available an excellent article on neurolinguistic programming entitled, "Subtle Skills for Building Rapport," by Vincent A. Sandoval and Susan H. Adams.

Royal Canadian Mounted Police: http://www.rcmp-learning.org/vietnam/
module_a.htm

This is the website for the Royal Canadian Mounted Police (RCMP) and their
Cross Cultural Communications Series—"The Vietnamese" is the second in a new
series of Individualized Instruction Modules that have been developed to educate
and sensitize employees of the RCMP.

International Association of Campus Law Enforcement Agencies (IACLEA):
http://www.iaclea.org/pubs/

This is the website for the IACLEA, which has many publications, specifically, "If
I Look Confused and Lost, It's Probably Because I Am . . ." This is a Video Workshop on Cross-Cultural Communications with a Focus on Foreign Students. Created and conducted by Dr. Jennifer Lund, Director of International Student
Services at Georgia State University, this 57-minute videotape is intended for use
in training campus staff to deal positively with foreign students, and comes with a
discussion guide. The video covers our perceptions of foreign students and their
perceptions of us, behavioral and attitudinal differences, and the 12 "shoulds" to
improve communication.

REFERENCES

Berry, Ondra. (2003). Deputy Chief, Reno, Nevada, Police Department, personal communication. November, 2003.

Brookline: This cop show aims to reach, and educate officers. (2003, August 3). *Boston
Globe,* p. 8.

Degeneste, Henry I., and John D. Sullivan. (1997, July). "Policing a Multicultural
Community." *Fresh Perspectives: A Police Executive Research Forum Publication,* p. 7.

Fernandez, Donya. (2000). Language Rights attorney for the Language Rights Project,
Employment Law Center/Legal Aid Society, San Francisco, Calif., personal communication, December, 2000.

Hall, Edward. (1959). *The Silent Language.* Garden City, N.Y.: Doubleday, 1959.

Hall Edward. (1966). *The Hidden Dimension.* Garden City, N.Y.: Doubleday, 1966.

Harris, Philip R. (1989). *High Performance Leadership.* Carmel, Ind.: Scott Foresman.

Harris, Philip R., and Robert T. Moran. (1991). *Managing Cultural Differences: High
Performance Strategies for a New World of Business.* Houston, Texas: Gulf.

Helping people who lack English. (1999, September 19). *Contra Costa Times,* p. A32.

Ismail, Lobna. (2003). President of Connecting Cultures, a training and consulting
organization specializing in Arab American culture, personal Communication,
October 2003.

Levine, Deena and Mara Adelman. (1992). *Beyond Language:* Cross-cultural communication. Englewood Cliffs, NJ: Prentice Hall.

Mehrabian, Albert, Dr. (1971). *Silent Messages.* Wadsworth Publishing Belmont, Calif.

Miller, Scott. (1996, July). "Communicating Effectively with Non-English Speaking
Customer Populations in Mid-Size California Cities by the Year 2005." California
Command College Class XXII, Peace Officer Standards and Training, Sacra-
mento, Calif.

Ogawa, Brian. (1990). *Color of Justice: Culturally Sensitive Treatment of Minority Crime Victims* Sacramento, Calif.: Office of Criminal Justice Planning.

Olson, Sergeant Aaron T. (2003). Sergeant and patrol supervisor with Oregon State Police; Instructor at Oregon's Public Safety Standards and Training for Regional and Academy students; and police liaison with IRCO (Immigrant Refugee Community Organization) in Portland area, personal communication (July, 2003).

Sandoval, V.A., and Susan H. Adams, S.H. (2001, August). "Subtle Skills for Building Rapport." *FBI Law Enforcement Bulletin, 70* (8), 1–9. Available: http://www.fbi .gov/publications/leb/2001/aug01leb.htm

Thompson, George. (2003). President of Verbal Judo Institute, Yucca Valley, California, personal communication, November, 2003.

Thompson, George. (2004). *Verbal Judo: The Gentle Art of Persuasion.* Yucca Valley, Calif., Verbal Judo Institute, Inc.

The troubled LA County Sheriff's Department. (1992, July 21). *Los Angeles Times,* p. A18.

Weaver, Gary. (1992, September). "Law Enforcement in a Culturally Diverse Society." *FBI Law Enforcement Bulletin,* 4.

Part 2

CULTURAL SPECIFICS FOR LAW ENFORCEMENT

Part Two presents information on Asian/Pacific, African American, Latino/Hispanic, Middle Eastern, and Native American cultural backgrounds with regard to the needs of law enforcement and criminal justice representatives. We have selected these groups, as opposed to other groups not described in this book, for one or more of the following reasons: (1) the group is a relatively large ethnic or racial group in the United States, (2) the traditional culture of the group differs widely from that of mainstream American culture, and/or (3) typically or historically there have been problems between the particular group and law enforcement officials.

In these culture-specific chapters, general information is presented on the following areas: historical background, demographics, and diversity within the cultural group. Following the introductory information, we present specific details relevant to law enforcement and criminal justice in the following areas: communication styles (both verbal and nonverbal), group identification terms, offensive labels, stereotypes, and family structure. Each chapter ends with key concerns for officers related to the particular cultural group, a summary of recommendations for law enforcement officials, and resources for additional information about the cultural group.

Important note: In this section's presentation of specific cultural and racial groups, we would like to reference the section "The Overlap of Race and Ethnicity" in Chapter 1.

This is to remind readers that individuals in our multicultural population do not always easily fall into neat categories of only one race or culture. There can be an overlap of race and ethnicity, as in the example of a black Latino. Our categorization of different groups is a convenient way of presenting information; we do not wish to imply that there can be no overlap among the group categories.

Chapter 5

Law Enforcement Contact with Asian/Pacific Americans

OVERVIEW

This chapter provides specific ethnic and cultural information on Asian Americans and Pacific Islanders. The label Asian Americans/Pacific Islanders encompasses over 40 different ethnic and cultural groups. For ease of use, we will use the shortened version Asian/Pacific Americans to refer to members of these ethnic groupings. We first define this very diverse group and then present a historical overview, focusing on the relationship between law enforcement and other criminal justice personnel and citizens. We present demographics and elements of diversity among Asian/Pacific Americans as well as issues related to ethnic and cultural identity. Aspects of the Asian/Pacific American family are discussed including myths and stereotypes, assimilation and acculturation processes, the extended family and community, gender roles, generational differences, and adolescent and youth issues. The section "Cultural Influences on Communication" discusses the subtle aspects of nonverbal and indirect communications that peace officers (and others in similar public service roles like firefighters, emergency medical technicians, 911 personnel, probation staff) often find troublesome. The closing section presents several key issues for law enforcement: underreporting of crimes, differential treatment, increasing Asian/Pacific American community police services, increasing the number of Asian/Pacific peace officers, and the rise in crimes within the Asian/Pacific community. Finally, we review recommendations for improved communication and relationships between law enforcement personnel and Asian/Pacific American communities.

COMMENTARY

For many Asian/Pacific American groups, especially those who have recently immigrated into the United States, the law enforcement system is somewhat of a mystery. As such, Asian/Pacific Americans may find it difficult to cooperate and to participate fully with law enforcement officers.

> To the Vietnamese immigrant, our law enforcement system doesn't seem to serve his community well. In Vietnam, if you are arrested, then the work of the attorney is to prove that you are innocent. You remain locked up in jail until your innocence is proven. In the United States, a suspect who is arrested is

released upon posting bail, usually within 24 hours. To the Vietnamese immigrant, it would seem that if you have the money, you can buy your way out of jail! (Vietnamese community advocate's comments about a local merchant's reluctance to cooperate with the police)

Many law enforcement officers have difficulty understanding the diversity of customs, activities, behaviors, and values within the different Asian/Pacific American groups. They do not know where to go to get such cultural information without the fear of offending. Yet this cultural knowledge is vital to understanding and to effective peacekeeping in any Asian/Pacific American community.

For some of the Asian groups, you just hear things that you're not sure about, but there's no one you can turn to ask sometimes. For example, in our work, we hear that Sikhs always carry a sword or knife on their person (which they carry as a religious object), so is it insensitive to confiscate it? We also hear that if it is drawn, they must also draw blood—true or false? Moreover, what is the thing to do with their turbans? Would it be an insult to pat-search a turban while it's on the person's head? (police officer's comments in a cultural awareness training session)

With the increased emphasis and attention on the war on terrorism and on homeland security, law enforcement officers have heightened responsibilities and challenges in understanding and protecting emerging Asian/Pacific American communities. For example, various South Asian community members have been targets of hate crimes as well since 9/11. In the Detroit area, there is a sizeable South Asian community from Bangladesh (the people are called Bengalis). These citizens are Muslim and dark-skinned, and are often mistaken for Arabs. Immediately following 9/11, the media reported incident after incident whereby the identities of citizens were confused with those of people from Arab backgrounds:

Attacks on Asian-Americans, particularly Pakistani and Indian immigrants, increased greatly in the United States in the weeks after Sept. 11, a report by an advocacy group says. . . . Immigrants from South Asia appear to have been the subjects of attacks and other racially motivated incidents because they were perceived, often incorrectly, to be Arab or Muslim, . . . Sikhs, for example, a religious group with many members of South Asian descent, were victimized because the men wear turbans and long beards, the report said. About one out of five attacks was violent, mainly aggravated assault, the report said. But two people were killed. On Sept. 15, Balbir Singh Sodhi, 49, a Sikh from Mesa, Ariz., was fatally shot while working at a gasoline station. When the police arrested a man in the killing, the report said, he screamed, "I am a patriot." Waqar Hasan, 46, a Pakistani, was killed in September while working at a grocery store in Pleasant Grove, Tex. There was no indication of a robbery, the report said, and the Federal Bureau of Investigation is investigating the incident as a hate crime. ("A Nation Challenged," 2002, p. A12)

INTRODUCTION

For the past four decades, the Asian/Pacific American population has experienced the largest proportional increases of any ethnic minority population in the United States (over 100 percent growth for the decades from 1960 to 1990 and 76 percent growth for the decade from 1990 to 2000). The population growth can be attributed to (1) higher immigration from the Pacific Rim countries, (2) greater longevity, (3) higher birth rates, (4) immigrants admitted for special skills and expertise for work in high-technology industries in the United States, and (5) existing ethnic groups added to this population category (including the Asian/Pacific Americans who consider themselves "multiracial"). Growth in major urban areas has been particularly striking, as is seen in New York City, Los Angeles, San Jose (CA), San Francisco, Honolulu, San Diego, Chicago, Houston, Seattle, Fremont (CA), Fairfax (VA), and Quincy (MA). Growth in the population as a whole is most dramatically reflected in terms of increased numbers of Asian/Pacific Americans in politics, community leadership, business, education, and public service areas. Law enforcement contact with Asian/Pacific people has increased because of their greater presence in communities. Asian/Pacific Americans have one of the highest citizenship rates among all foreign-born groups; in 2000, 47 percent of the immigrants from Asian/Pacific countries were naturalized citizens (U.S. Bureau of the Census, 2002).

ASIAN/PACIFIC AMERICAN DEFINED

The term Asian/Pacific Americans is actually a contraction of two terms, Asian Americans and Pacific Islander peoples. Although used throughout this chapter, Asian/Pacific Americans is, in fact, a convenient summary label for a very heterogeneous group. There certainly is not universal acceptance of this labeling convention, but for practical purposes it has been adopted frequently, with occasional variations (e.g., Asian and Pacific Americans, Asian Americans/Pacific Islanders, Asians and Pacific Islanders). It represents the self-designation preferred by many Asian and Pacific people in the United States, particularly in preference to the more dated (and, to some, offensive) term Orientals. The U.S. government and other governmental jurisdictions usually use "Asian Americans/Pacific Islanders" to refer to members within any of the 40 or more groups comprising this category.

At least 40 distinct ethnic and cultural groups might meaningfully be listed under this designation: (1) Bangladeshi, (2) Belauan (formerly Palauan), (3) Bhutanese, (4) Bruneian, (5) Cambodian, (6) Chamorro (Guamanian), (7) Chinese, (8) Fijian, (9) Hawaiian (or Native Hawaiian), (10) Hmong, (11) Indian (Asian, South Asian, or East Indian), (12) Indonesian, (13) Japanese, (14) Kiribati, (15) Korean, (16) Laotian, (17) Malaysian, (18) Maldivian, (19) Marshallese (of the Marshall Islands, to include Majuro, Ebeye, and Kwajalein), (20) Micronesia (to include Kosrae, Ponape, Truk, and Yap), (21) Mongolian, (22) Myanmarese (formerly Burmese), (23) Nauruan, (24) Nepalese, (25) Ni-Vanuatu, (26) Okinawan, (27) Pakistani, (28) Pilipino (preferred spelling of Filipino), (29) Saipan Carolinian (or Carolinian, from the Commonwealth of the Northern Marianas), (30) Samoan, (31) Singaporian, (32) Solomon Islander, (33) Sri Lankan (formerly Ceylonese), (34) Tahitian, (35) Taiwanese, (36) Tibetan, (37) Tongan, (38) Thai, (39) Tuvaluan, and (40) Vietnamese. Although there are marked differences between the 40 groups listed, individuals within any of the 40 groups may also differ in a vast number of ways.

From the viewpoint of law enforcement, it is important to recognize some of the differences that may cut across or be common to all Asian/Pacific ethnic groups. For example:

1. Area of residence in the United States

2. Comfort with and competence in English

3. Generational status in the United States (first, second, third generation, and so forth)

4. Degree of acculturation and assimilation

5. Education (number of years outside and inside the United States)

6. Native and other languages spoken and/or written

7. Age (what is documented on paper and what may be the real age)

8. Degree of identification with the home country and/or region of self or parents' origin

9. Family composition and extent of family dispersion in the United States and globally

10. Extent of identification with local, national, and global Asian/Pacific sociopolitical issues

11. Participation and degree to which the individual is embedded in the ethnic community network

12. Religious beliefs and cultural value orientation

13. Economic status and financial standing

14. Sensitivity to ethnic and cultural experiences and perceptions as an Asian/Pacific person in the United States

15. Identification with issues, concerns, and problems shared by other ethnic-racial groups (e.g., racial profiling and other discrimination issues voiced by African American, Latino/Hispanic Americans, and Middle Eastern and Arab Americans)

It should be noted that the definition itself of the Asian/Pacific group points to and embodies an ever-emerging ethnic mosaic of diverse constituencies. Groups are added and removed based on self-definition and needs for self-choice. In our definition, we have not added immigrants or refugees from the more recently formed Central Asian nations of Kazakhstan, Kyrgyzstan, Tajikistan, Turkmenistan, and Uzbekistan (all were republics of the Soviet Union before that country dissolved at the end of 1991) because of the self-choice issue. As more immigrants from Central Asia settle in the United States, these groups may (or may not) be added to the definition of Asian/Pacific Americans. Clearly, the pooling of separate Asian and Pacific Islander groups under the label of Asian/Pacific Americans emerged, in part, out of the necessity to have a larger collective whole when a greater numerical count may make a difference (especially in political and community issue areas). Merging these 40 ethnic groups into a collective entity allowed for sufficiently large numbers for meaningful representation in communities and other arenas.

Although one may focus upon "nationality" or "nation of origin" as the basis of identifying Asian/Pacific American groupings (e.g., "Korean" for those whose ancestry is from Korea, "Vietnamese" for those whose ancestry is from Vietnam), there may be other demographic variables of greater importance than that of "nationality." For example, whether one is from the Central Asian nation of Uzbekistan, the Southeast Asian nation of Vietnam, or the Pacific Island nation of Micronesia, the demographic variable of ethnicity, if one were Chinese, may be a more important identifier than that of "national origin" for some persons or groups. As another example, one's "religion" may be a more important "group" identifier than either ethnicity and/or nationality as might be seen with Muslim (i.e., people who practice Islam). Given that the four largest countries with Muslim populations are in South Asia, that is, Indonesia, Pakistan, Bangladesh, and India (Glasse & Smith, 2003), Asian/Pacific American people who practice Islam might see "religion" as a more important identifier than ethnicity and nationality.

Other Key Definitions

Since a large proportion of Asian/Pacific Americans whom law enforcement officers may encounter are born outside the United States, it is important to understand some of the key differences that relate to immigration status. One key difference is that of Asian/Pacific Americans who are considered refugees and those who are considered immigrants at the time that they enter the United States. Some of the between-group hostilities (within the Asian/Pacific community and among other ethnic minority communities) have been a result of not understanding how refugee status differs from immigrant status in the United States.

Refugees are sponsored into the United States under the authority of the U.S. government. Although many ethnic groups have come in under the sponsorship of the federal government with refugee or emigre status, the largest numbers have come from Southeast Asia as a result of the past upheaval brought on by the Vietnam War. Refugees, since they are sponsored into the United States by the government, are expected to utilize public support services fully (welfare, English as a Second Language [ESL] programs, educational tuition, job training programs, and case management). Since it is part of being a "good refugee" to participate fully, case managers are often assigned refugee families to ensure that family members are fully utilizing all of the services provided. Such participation in public programs may also create dependency and learned helplessness that can result from having others help or interfere with what many could have done for themselves.

Immigrants enter into the United States under the direct sponsorship of individuals' families. The federal government establishes that immigrants are allowed to enter the United States only if their families can completely support or establish work for the individual. In fact, one criterion for being able to attain permanent residence status (a "green card") is that the immigrant will not become a burden to the government, which means that participation in any publicly funded program may jeopardize that individual's chances for attaining permanent residence status. (Thus, immigrants try very hard to avoid getting involved in public or community programs and services.) In contrast to the refugee, being a "good immigrant" means avoiding any participation in public service programs.

TYPOLOGY OF ASIAN/PACIFIC AMERICANS

As we look at Asian/Pacific American individuals, families, and communities, we have developed a seven-part typology that will be useful in understanding and in summarizing some of the differences between individuals within this group (see Exhibit 5.1).

Type I	Asian/Pacific recently arrived immigrant or refugee (less than 5 years in the United States, with major life experiences in Asia or the Pacific Islands)
Type II	Asian/Pacific immigrant or refugee (5 or more years in the United States, with major life experiences in Asia or the Pacific Islands)
Type III	Asian/Pacific American (second generation; offspring of immigrant or refugee)
Type IV	Asian/Pacific Immigrant (major life experiences in the United States)
Type V	Asian/Pacific American (third or later generations in the United States)
Type VI	Asian/Pacific national (anticipates return to Asia or to the Pacific Islands, to include visitors and tourists)
Type VII	Asian/Pacific national (global workplace and residency)

Exhibit 5.1   Typology of Asian/Pacific Americans.

Our typology suggests that as law enforcement and public safety organizations prepare and train their personnel to work with Asian/Pacific American communities, a focus on the key differences within each of the typological groups would be most effective. We will come back to this typology in a later section to discuss how the motivational components within each of the groupings can affect the way Asian/Pacific American persons may respond in law enforcement situations.

HISTORICAL INFORMATION

The first Asians to arrive in the United States in sizable numbers were the Chinese in the 1840s to work on the plantations in Hawaii. Then, in the 1850s, they immigrated to work in the gold mines in California and later on the transcontinental railroad. Of course, the native populations of the Pacific Island areas (e.g., Samoans, Hawaiians, Guamanians, Fijians) were there before the establishment of the 13 colonies of the United States. The Chinese were followed in the late 1800s and early 1900s by the Japanese and the Pilipinos (and in smaller numbers by the Koreans and South Asian Indians). Large numbers of Asian Indians (nearly 500,000) entered the United States as a result of Congressional action in 1946 for "persons of races indigenous to India" to have the right of naturalization. Most immigrants in these earlier years were men, and most worked as laborers and at other domestic and menial jobs. Until the change of the immigration laws in 1965, the number of Asian and Pacific Islander peoples immigrating into the United States was severely restricted (families often had to wait over a decade or more before members of a family could be reunited). With the change in the immigration laws, large numbers of immigrants from the Pacific Rim came to the United States from Hong Kong, Taiwan, China, Japan, Korea, South Asia (e.g., India, Ceylon, Bangladesh), the Philippines, and Southeast Asia (e.g., Vietnam, Thailand, Singapore, Cambodia, Malaysia). After the Vietnam War, large numbers of Southeast Asian refugees were admitted in the late 1970s and early 1980s. The need for engineering and scientific expertise and skills by "high-tech" and Internet companies resulted in many Asian/Pacific immigrants (under special work visas) immigrating to the United States in the late 1990s and early 2000s.

Law Enforcement Interactions with Asian/Pacific Americans: Law Enforcement as Not User-Friendly

Asian/Pacific Americans have found the passage and enforcement of "anti-Asian" federal, state, and local laws to be more hostile and discriminatory than some of the racially motivated community incidents they have experienced. Early experiences of Asians and Pacific Islanders were characterized by the majority population's wanting to keep them out of the United States and putting tremendous barriers in the way of those who were already here. It was the role of law enforcement and criminal justice agencies and officers to be the vehicle to carry out these laws against Asian/Pacific American immigrants. From the beginning, the interactions of Asian/Pacific Americans with law enforcement officials were fraught with conflicts, difficulties, and mixed messages.

Anti-Asian Federal, State, and Local Laws

Almost all of our federal immigration laws were written such that their enforcement made Asian newcomers feel neither welcomed or wanted. Following the large influx of Chinese in the 1850s to work in the gold mines and on the railroad, many Americans were resentful of the Chinese for their willingness to work long hours for low wages. With mounting public pressure, the Chinese Exclusion Act of 1882 banned the immigration of Chinese laborers for 10 years, and subsequent amendments extended this ban indefinitely. Because of this ban and because the Chinese population in the United States was primarily male, the Chinese population in the United States dropped from 105,465 in 1880 to 61,639 in 1920 (Takaki, 1989a). Since the Chinese Exclusion Act only applied to Chinese, Japanese immigration started around 1870 to Hawaii, with larger numbers to the mainland in the 1890s to work as laborers and in domestic jobs on farms on the West Coast. Similar to the Chinese, public pressure to restrict Japanese immigration ensued. In the case of the Japanese, the Japanese Government did not want a "loss of face" or of international prestige through having its people "banned" from immigrating to the United States. Rather, the "Gentleman's Agreement" was negotiated with President Theodore Roosevelt in 1907, which resulted in the Japanese Government voluntarily restricting the immigration of Japanese laborers to the United States. Family members of Japanese already in the United States, however, were allowed to enter. Under the Gentleman's Agreement, large numbers of "picture brides" began entering into the United States, resulting in a large increase in Japanese American populations—25,000 in 1900 to 127,000 in 1940 (Daniels, 1988). Subsequent laws banned or prevented immigration from the Asiatic countries: The Immigration Act of 1917 banned immigration from all counties in the Pacific Rim except for the Philippines (a U.S. territory). The Immigration Act of 1924 restricted migration from all countries to 2 percent of the countries' national origin population living in the United States in 1890. This "2 percent" restriction was not changed until 1965. Moreover, it was not until 1952 that most Asian immigrants were eligible to become naturalized citizens of the United States, and therefore, have the right to vote (African Americans and American Indians were able to become citizens long before Asian/Pacific Americans were given the same rights).

While Pilipinos* have been immigrating to the United States since the early 1900s (primarily for "practical training" as selected, sponsored, and funded by the United

*Preferred spelling for Filipino

States government), large numbers of Pilipino laborers began entering in the 1920s because of the need for unskilled laborers (and due in part to the unavailability of Chinese and Japanese immigrants who were restricted entry by law). Similar to previous Asian groups, Pilipino immigration was soon to be limited to a quota of 50 immigrants per year with the passage of the Tydings-McDuffie Act of 1934. Moreover, Congressional resolutions in 1935 reflected clear anti-Pilipino sentiment by providing free, one-way passage for Pilipinos to return to the Philippines with the agreement that they not return to the United States.

Anti-Asian immigration laws were finally repealed starting with the removal of the Chinese Exclusion Act in 1943. Other laws were repealed to allow immigration of Asians and Pacific Islanders, but the process was slow. It was not until 1965 when amendments to the McCarran-Walter Act opened the way for Asian immigrants to enter in larger numbers (a fixed quota of 20,000 per country, as opposed to 2 percent of the country's national origin population living in the United States in 1890). The 1965 amendment also established the "fifth preference" category, which allowed highly skilled workers needed by the United States to enter this country. Because of the preference for highly skilled workers, a second major wave of immigrants from Hong Kong, Taiwan, India, Korea, the Philippines, Japan, Singapore, and other Asiatic countries entered in the mid-1960s. The earlier wave of South Asian immigrants (from India, Pakistan, and Sri Lanka) with expertise to help with America's space race against the Soviets resulted in large numbers of professional and highly educated South Asians immigrating into the United States under the "fifth preference" after 1965. For example, as part of this second wave of immigration, 83 percent of the Asian Indians who immigrated under the category of professional and technical workers between 1966 and 1977 were scientists with PhDs (about 20,000) and engineers (about 40,000) (Prashad, 2001). With the upheaval in Southeast Asia and the Vietnam War, the third major wave of close to 1 million refugees and immigrants arrived in the United States from these affected Southeast Asian countries starting in the mid-1970s and lasting to the early 1980s (Special Services for Groups, 1983). Most recently, the need for expertise and scientific skills as well as the opportunities present in high-technology, engineering, computer, software, and Internet industries have led to an additional influx of immigrants from India, Pakistan, Singapore, Korea, China (including Hong Kong), Taiwan, and other Asiatic countries in the mid-1990s and early 2000s. Even today, in some state and local jurisdictions, anti-Asian laws continue to be changed and removed:

> War and terrorism have hardened American attitudes toward immigration, but some legislators are pushing ahead with plans for a ballot measure asking voters to eliminate a little-known clause in the Florida Constitution that one lawmaker calls a "clearly racist Jim Crow provision." The provision allows the state to prohibit property ownership by "aliens ineligible for citizenship." It was added to the Constitution in 1926, aimed chiefly at Asians, who by federal decree were ineligible for U.S. citizenship at the time and were turning to farming in the United States. "It is an outdated, clearly racist Jim Crow provision," state Rep. Phillip Brutus, D-North Miami, told members of the Senate Committee on Home Defense, Public Security and Ports. "It's a stain on our Constitution." (Stockfisch, 2003, p. 1)

Although many immigrant groups (e.g., Italians, Jews, Poles) have been the target of discrimination, bigotry, and prejudice, Asian/Pacific Americans, like African Americans, have experienced extensive legal discrimination, hindering their ability to participate fully as Americans. This discrimination has gravely affected their well-being and quality of life. Some states had laws that prohibited intermarriage between Asians and whites. State and local laws imposed restrictive conditions and taxes specifically on Asian businesses and individuals. State courts were equally biased; for example, in the case of People v. Hall heard in the California Supreme Court in 1854, Hall, a white defendant, had been convicted of murdering a Chinese man on the basis of testimony provided by one white and three Chinese witnesses. The California Supreme Court threw out Hall's conviction on the basis that state law prohibited blacks, mulattos, or Indians from testifying in favor of or against whites in court. The court's decision read:

> Indian as commonly used refers only to the North American Indian, yet in the days of Columbus all shores washed by Chinese waters were called the Indies. In the second place the word "white" necessarily excludes all other races than Caucasian; and in the third place, even if this were not so, I would decide against the testimony of Chinese on the grounds of public policy. (California Supreme Court: *People v. George W. Hall,* October 1854)

This section of anti-Asian/Pacific American laws and sentiments cannot close without noting that Japanese Americans are the only immigrant group of Americans in the history of the American people who have been routed out of their homes and interned without due process. President Roosevelt's Executive Order 9066 resulted in the evacuation and incarceration of 100,000 Japanese Americans in 1942. For Asian/Pacific Americans, the internment of Japanese Americans represents how quickly anti-Asian sentiments can result in incarceration and punishment by law, even if no one was convicted of a crime. Moreover, stereotypes and bigotry against Asian/Pacific Americans are not only issues of the past, as is illustrated in the following:

> Bruce Yamashita, a Japanese American born in Hawaii, had decided to join the U.S. Marine Corp after earning his law degree from Georgetown University. Prior to entering law school, Yamashita had many accomplishments including serving as his high school's student body president and as an elected delegate to the Hawaii State Constitution Convention. Bruce Yamashita was admitted to the Marine Corp's Officer Candidate School (OCS), and throughout his 10 weeks of training, was the target of steady, vicious, and stereotypic ethnic and racial harassment with remarks like "kamikaze man" and "go back to your country." Upon his completion of the 10-week OCS and passing all of his written examinations, Bruce Yamashita was discharged for "leadership failure" and was not allowed to serve in the United States Marine Corp. (Schmitt, 1992, p. A8)

DEMOGRAPHICS: DIVERSITY AMONG ASIAN/PACIFIC AMERICANS

As we noted in the section defining Asian/Pacific Americans, this is an extremely heterogeneous population comprised of many different ethnic and cultural groups with generational differences within the United States, educational and socioeconomic diversity, and many other background and life experience differences. Asian/Pacific Americans currently number about 12.8 million and represent approximately 4.5 percent of the U.S. population. As stated, the Asian/Pacific American population more than doubled with each census from 1970 to 1990 (1.5 million in 1970, 3.5 million in 1980, and 7.3 million in 1990) and increased by 76 percent from 1990 to 2000 (12.8 million in 2000). While greater longevity and higher birth rates contribute to this population increase, the major contributor to the growth of the Asian/Pacific American population is immigration from the Pacific Rim countries. Since the 1970s, Asian/Pacific American immigration has made up over 40 percent of all immigration to the United States (U.S. Bureau of the Census, 2002). As is evident in Exhibit 5.2, Chinese are the largest group, with 23.0 percent of the total Asian/Pacific American population. Pilipinos are close behind, with 19.9 percent of this population; in the next decade, Pilipinos will be the largest Asian/Pacific American group in the United States. Asian Indians are the fastest growing among the Asian and Pacific American population, with 16.0 percent. Vietnamese and Koreans each comprise approximately 10.3 percent of the Asian/Pacific American population. The Japanese American population was the third largest in 1990 and dropped to sixth place in 2000, with 9.7 percent, in part because of the lower immigration from Japan. All other Asian/Pacific American groups account for 10.8 percent of this population.

For law enforcement officers, the key Asian/Pacific American groups to understand would be the six largest groups: Chinese, Pilipino, Asian Indian, Vietnamese, Korean, and Japanese (considering, in addition, local community trends and unique qualities of the community's populations). Knowledge of the growing trends among this Asian/Pacific American population would also be important for officer recruitment and other human resource considerations. Current Asian/Pacific Americans involved in professional law enforcement and criminal justice careers are largely Japanese, Chinese, and Korean Americans. To plan for the changing Asian/Pacific American population base, it is critical to recruit and develop officers from the Pilipino, Vietnamese, and Asian Indian communities.

Asian/Pacific American Groups	Percentage of Total
Chinese	23.0
Pilipino	19.9
Asian Indian	16.0
Vietnamese	10.3
Korean	10.3
Japanese	9.7
Cambodian	1.7
Pakistani	1.7
Laotian	1.7
Hmong	1.6
Thai	1.3
Taiwanese	1.2
All other groups	—
All Asian/Pacific Americans	100.0

Exhibit 5.2   Asian/Pacific American population by groups.
Source: Blake & Bennett (2002). The Asian Population: 2000. U.S. Bureau of the Census. Table 4.

Country of Birth	Number Foreign-Born
China	1,391,000
Philippines	1,222,000
India	1,007,000
Vietnamese	863,000
Korean	701,000

Exhibit 5.3   Asian/Pacific American Top Countries of Birth of Foreign-Born.
Source: Bennett (2002). A Profile of the Nation's Foreign-Born Population from Asia (2000 Update), U.S. Bureau of the Census. P23-206.

More than half of all Asian/Pacific Americans are foreign-born (7.2 million) and comprise 26% of the foreign-born population in the United States (Bennett, 2002). Five countries contributed the largest numbers of foreign-born Asian/Pacific Americans, as seen in Exhibit 5.3.

Foreign-born Asian/Pacific Americans have the second highest percentage of becoming naturalized citizens at 47% (only those born in Europe had a higher rate at 52%) (Bennett, 2002).

As further illustrated in Exhibit 5.4, the vast majority of all Asian/Pacific Americans are not born in the United States. Most of the Japanese, Pilipinos, Cambodians, and Indonesians reside in the western states. Chinese, Koreans, Vietnamese, Laotians, and Thais are fairly widely distributed in the large urban areas of the United States. Most of the Asian Indians and Pakistanis live in the eastern states. The state of Minnesota and Fresno, California, have the largest Hmong populations in the country.

Asian/Pacific American Group	Percentage Not U.S.-Born	Percentage who Do Not Speak English Well	Percentage in the West
Chinese	63.3	23.0	52.7
Pilipino	64.7	6.0	68.8
Japanese	28.4	9.0	80.3
Asian Indian	70.4	5.0	19.2
Korean	81.9	24.0	42.9
Vietnamese	90.5	38.0	46.2
Laotian	93.7	69.0	45.7
Thai	82.1	12.0	43.0
Cambodian	93.9	59.0	55.6
Hmong	90.5	63.0	37.4
Pakistani	85.1	10.0	23.5
Indonesian	83.4	6.0	56.2
All Asian/Pacific Americans	62.1	15.0	56.4

Exhibit 5.4   Asian/Pacific American population by three key demographic characteristics.
Source: U.S. Commission on Civil Rights, 1992.

Proficiency in the English language varies within groups: groups that have immigrated most recently (Southeast Asians) have the largest percentage of those not able to speak English well.

Law enforcement and peace officers, depending on their jurisdictions, can use Exhibit 5.4 to determine what additional languages and skills training might be appropriate in their work with Asian/Pacific American communities.

Asian/Pacific Americans' Key Motivating Perspectives

Earlier in this chapter, we provided a typology for viewing Asian/Pacific Americans. We provide in Exhibit 5.5 the same typology and have appended to it the key motivating perspectives for members in each group. By understanding some of these key motivating perspectives, law enforcement officers might be better able to understand the behaviors exhibited by citizens from these groupings.

For example, the key to understanding the behavior of the most recent immigrants and refugee group (Asian/Pacific Refugee Type I) is to recall that members are in a survival mode (see Exhibit 5.5). Many members from this category may remember that law enforcement and police officers in their country of origin were corrupt, aligned with a repressive government and the military, and subjected to bribes by those who were more affluent. All activities tend to be guided by this perspective to survive, to get through. This perspective also makes sense in terms of the traumatic ordeals faced by refugees (as revealed by their past memories) in their journeys to the United States. Encounters with law enforcement personnel by these people usually involve saying and doing anything to discontinue the contact because of possible fears of personal harm (e.g., not speaking English, not having any identification, "Yes, I will cooperate!").

> Mr. Pok and Mr. Nguyen came in as part of the "boat people" in 1979. Although both of them are in their early thirties, because of their size and informal dress, they look much younger. Both worked as building maintenance personnel for one of the high-technology companies on the West Coast. One evening as they were driving home following their work at approximately 1:30 A.M., Mr. Pok and Mr. Nguyen found themselves pulled over by two police cars. Two officers approached their car and requested that they step outside. The officers were responding to a call about two young Asian males, driving a

Surviving	Asian/Pacific most recent immigrant or refugee (less than 5 years in the United States with major life experiences in Asia or the Pacific Islands)
Preserving	Asian/Pacific immigrant or refugee (5 or more years in the United States with major life experiences in Asia or the Pacific Islands)
Adjusting	Asian/Pacific American (second generation; offspring of immigrant or refugee)
Changing	Asian/Pacific immigrant (major life experiences in the United States)
Choosing	Asian/Pacific American (third or later generations in the United States)
Maintaining	Asian/Pacific national (anticipates return to Asia or to the Pacific Islands)
Expanding	Asian/Pacific national (global workplace and residency)

Exhibit 5.5   Key motivating perspectives in understanding Asian/Pacific American groups.

light-colored car, involved in an armed robbery of a nearby convenience store. Mr. Pok's and Mr. Nguyen's car was light-colored. When the officers asked both individuals to take a kneeling position while the officers conducted a search and verified DMV information, Mr. Pok fell to the ground and pleaded at the feet of one of the officers, "Please don't kill me!" It was Mr. Nguyen who finally explained that the kneeling position is the "execution position," and Mr. Pok saw many individuals executed that way in his escape from Cambodia. (Example cited by community organizer, Center for Southeast Asian Refugees Resettlement [CSEARR], San Francisco, California)

With regard to Asian/Pacific immigrants (Type II), understanding their behaviors should focus on preserving their home culture as the motivating perspective. Since the majority of their life experiences occurred in Asia or the Pacific Islands, members are trying to preserve much of the values and traditions of their culture as it was alive and operating. Many Asian businesspersons and investors in the United States are included in this category. Much intergenerational conflict between grandparents or parents and youths occurs within this group. Members are inclined to keep to their ethnic communities (e.g., Little Saigons, Chinatowns, Koreatowns, Japantowns, Manilatowns) and have as little to do with law enforcement as possible. Many remember that the police have not served them well in the past (e.g., immigration laws, Japanese internment).

Police officers in a West Coast city were confused and wondered if a local "private bar" frequented by Japanese and Korean businessmen was a front for prostitution. They noticed that the bar had many Asian female "hostesses" and that companies paid hundreds of dollars per bottle for the liquor served to guests (when the off-the-shelf price of these liquors was one-fifth of what the bar charged). Only after much exchange between members of the local Asian/Pacific American community and the community relations police officers was the understanding made that these "private bars" allowed many immigrant businesspersons to feel at home in this culture. Among their own peers and in keeping with their own customs and cultural practices, they were comfortable, and no prostitution nor any other illegal activities were involved. (police officer's anecdote in a cultural awareness training session)

Asian/Pacific Americans (second generation, Type III) tend to be who we picture when we hear the term Asian American. Those of the second generation work very hard at being assimilated into the mainstream, adjusting and changing to be a part of mainstream America. Oftentimes, the expectations of second-generation parents are high; parents will sacrifice so that their offsprings will "make it" in their lifetime. Members may interact primarily with non-Asians and take on many of the values and norms of the mainstream society. This group may be considered "marginal" by some in that, try as each person may to become like the mainstream ("become white"), others may still consider them Asian. Many from this group try to minimize their contact with law enforcement personnel and agencies primarily because of the immigration and other experiences relayed to them by their parents' generation. Individuals of the second generation were born in the United States before the mid-1960s and may have had relatives (or parents) who entered the United States by using false papers. Fears of disclosure of such illegal entries have prevented many Asian/Pacific Americans from cooperating with peace officers and with other human and social service agencies and programs. With the emphasis on homeland security in the United States, many from this group have taken extra efforts to not be misidentified about their ethnicity (e.g., South Asians with darker skin tones being mistaken for Middle Easterners) or stereotyped because of their religion (e.g., Asian/Pacific Americans who are moderate Muslims, not fundamentalists).

The Asian/Pacific immigrant (Type IV), whose major life experience is in the United States, focuses much of the member's energies on changes (through assimilation or acculturation) that have to be made in order to succeed. Although these individuals have tended to continue to value the cultural and ethnic elements of their former homeland, most know that changes are necessary. Members of this group reflect the socioeconomic standings of the different waves on each entered into the United States. For example, individuals who entered as part of the first wave of laborers and domestic workers (primarily Chinese and Japanese, with some Pilipinos, Koreans, and Asian Indians) represent one grouping. Others entered more as part of the second wave of immigration as foreign students and/or under the "fifth preference" as professional skilled workers. Asian/Pacific immigrants (Type IV) who are designated as entering the United States under "fifth preference" are those who checked the fifth category on the Immigration and Nationalization Service form. This category indicates that the reason for immigration into the United States was because the person has a professional skill in short supply in the United States and it would be in the best interest of the United States to allow that person to enter. This group consists of educated, professional individuals (e.g., the largest numbers of foreign-trained medical doctors and psychiatrists in the United States are from India, the Philippines, and Korea [President's Commission on Mental Health, 1978]). Since the fall of Saigon in 1975 and the beginning of the immigration of Southeast Asians into the United States, this third wave has included over 1 million Asian/Pacific immigrants who suffered great trauma in their escape; many are young adults today. For members of this group, reactions to law enforcement officials vary depending on their time of immigration and socioeconomic experiences. For law enforcement officers, it is critical to understand the differences among the immigrant groups (i.e., do not confuse the professional Asian/Pacific immigrant with one of the other groups).

The Asian/Pacific American (third or later generation, Type V) category includes individuals who are more able to choose which aspects of the old culture to keep and which of the new culture to accept. The focus is on choosing activities, values, norms, and lifestyles that blend the best of Asian/Pacific and American cultures. The importance of being bicultural is a unique aspect of this group. Many may no longer have as much skill with their native language and may rely on English as their primary or only language (thus an individual can be bicultural and not bilingual). Contact by members of this group with law enforcement personnel may not be any different than contact by any other Americans.

For the last two categories, Asian/Pacific nationals, we make a key distinction between those who plan to return to their own country following a work assignment in the United States (Type VI) and those whose work is truly global, in that individuals may have several residences in different parts of the world (Type VII). Those in the former category (Type VI, on a work assignment in the United States that may last 5–7 years) maintain their home-base cultural orientation and experiences knowing that when the work assignment is over, they will go back to their home country again. Because they mean to maintain their native cultures, many individuals of this group may be inadequately prepared to understand many of the laws and practices of the United States. For members of this group, being able to stay in the United States to complete their assignments is of key importance. Oftentimes, individuals may not be aware of the differences between "minor" violations (e.g., minor traffic violations, small claims) and "major" violations and crimes. Let's look at the following example:

> Mr. Sato is a manager assigned to oversee a technical department in a joint United States–Japan automobile plant in the Midwest. One evening, while driving home from a late night at the plant, Mr. Sato did not see a stop sign and went right through it on a nonbusy intersection. A police officer in a patrol car saw the violation and pulled Mr. Sato over. The interaction puzzled the police officer, since Mr. Sato seemed very cooperative but kept asking the officer "to forgive him and to please let him go!" After much discussion and explanation, it was discovered that Mr. Sato thought that the officer would have to confiscate his passport because of the stop-sign violation (something that is done in many Asiatic countries) and that he might be "kicked out" of the country and, thus, be unable to complete his work assignment. Upon clearing up this misconception, Mr. Sato accepted the traffic citation "with appreciation." (police officer's anecdote in a cultural awareness training session)

For the second group of Asian/Pacific nationals (Type VII), the key focus of these individuals is their ability to "expand" their actions and behaviors effectively into different global environments. These individuals see themselves as being able to adapt to life in a variety of global environments; many may speak three or more languages (including English). Individuals within this group pride themselves in knowing about the different laws, norms, values, and practices of the countries they encounter. Law enforcement personnel would find this group equally able to understand and to follow the laws and practices of a given community as well.

LABELS AND TERMS

As we noted earlier, the term Asian/Pacific Americans is a convenient summarizing label used to refer to a heterogeneous group of people. Which particular terms are used is based on the principle of self-designation and self-preference. Asian and Pacific Islander people are sensitive about the issue because up until the 1960 census the population was relegated to the "Other" category. With the ethnic pride movement and ethnic minority studies movement in the late 1960s, people of Asian and Pacific Islands descent began to designate self-preferred terms for group reference. The terms were chosen over the previous term Oriental, which many Asian/Pacific Americans consider to be offensive. Oriental is considered offensive because it symbolizes to many the past references, injustices, and stereotypes of Asian and Pacific people. It was also a term designated by those in the West (i.e., the Occident, the Western Hemisphere) for Asian people and reminds many Asian/Pacific Americans of the colonial mentality of foreign policies and its effects on the Pacific Rim countries.

In federal and other governmental designations (e.g., the Small Business Administration), the label used is "Asian American/Pacific Islanders." Although very few Asian/Pacific Americans refer to themselves as such, the governmental designation is used in laws and regulations and in most reports and publications. For individuals within any of the groups, often the more specific names for the groups are preferred (e.g., Chinese, Japanese, Vietnamese, Pakistani, Hawaiian). Some individuals may prefer that the term American be part of their designation (e.g., Korean American, Pilipino American). For law enforcement officers, the best term to refer to an individual is the term he or she prefers to be called. It is perfectly acceptable to ask an individual what ethnic or cultural group(s) he or she identifies with and what he or she prefers to be called.

The use of slurs such as "Jap," "Chink," "Gook," "Chinaman," "Flip," "Babas," and other derogatory ethnic slang terms is never acceptable in crime-fighting and peacekeeping, no matter how provoked an officer may be. The use of other stereotypic terms, including "Chinese fire drill," "DWO (Driving While Oriental)," "Fu Man Chu mustache," "Kamikaze kid," "yellow cur," "yellow peril," "Bruce Lee Kung Fu type," "slant-eyed," "Turban man," "Vietnamese bar girl," and "dragon lady" does not convey the kinds of professionalism and respect for community diversity important to law enforcement and peacekeeping and needs to be avoided in law enforcement work. Officers hearing these words used in their own departments (or with peers or citizens) should provide immediate helpful feedback about such terms to those who use them. Officers who may out of habit routinely use these terms may find themselves (or their superiors) in the embarrassing situation (on the 6:00 news) of explaining to offended citizens and communities why these terms were used and that they had intended no prejudice.

MYTHS AND STEREOTYPES

Knowledge of and sensitivity to Asian/Pacific Americans' concerns, diversity, historical background, and life experiences will facilitate the crime-fighting and peacekeeping missions of peace officers. It is important to have an understanding about some of the myths, environmental messages, and stereotypes of Asian/Pacific Americans that contribute to the prejudice, discrimination, and bias they encounter. Many Americans do not have much experience with the diversity of Asian/Pacific American groups and learn about these groups only through stereotypes, often perpetuated by movies and the media. The effect of this is to reduce Asian/Pacific Americans to simplistic, one-dimensional characters that many people lump into one stereotypic group. Oftentimes, the complexities of the diverse Asian/Pacific American groups in terms of language, history, customs, cultures, religions, and life experiences become confusing and threatening, and it is easier to deal with stereotypes of these groups. Nonetheless, it is important for law enforcement officers to be aware of the different stereotypes of Asian/Pacific Americans. The key to effectiveness with any ethnic or racial group is not the complete elimination of myths and stereotypes about these groups, but rather, awareness of these stereotypes and management of our behaviors when the stereotypes are not true of the person with whom we are dealing.

Some of the stereotypes that have affected Asian/Pacific Americans in law enforcement include the following:

1. *Viewing Asian/Pacific Americans as "all alike."* That is, because there are many similarities in names, physical features, and behaviors, many law enforcement officers may make comments about their inability to tell people apart, or they may deal with them in stereotypic group fashion (e.g., they are all "inscrutable,"

involved in gangs). Cultural awareness training and sensitivity would allow the officer the skills and knowledge to avoid a mistake like the following:

> The City Council of Des Moines avoided a lawsuit by agreeing to pay $7,500 to each of nine Asian-American men who were handcuffed and forced to kneel in the street outside a cafe in June. The men were hand-cuffed on June 24 as police searched for an armed assault suspect they believed to have gone to the cafe. The suspect was never identified and even the victim disappeared shortly after the incident, police said. Police have said the incident was mishandled and say they will change their policies. One of the nine men said he met with Police Chief William Moulder and one of the officers involved about a month ago. "We told the police chief how we felt about that day. We worked it out," said Cuong Nguyen. After hearing the police explanation of the incident, Nguyen said he does not feel it was a result of racial profiling. He also said $7,500 was fair compensation. ("Des Moines to Pay $7,500," 2001)

2. ***Viewing Asian/Pacific Americans as successful, "model minorities" or worse yet, as a "super minority."*** Some hold the stereotype that Asian/Pacific Americans are "all" successful, and this stereotype is further reinforced by the media (Lee, 1996). Such stereotypes have resulted in intergroup hostilities and hate crimes directed toward Asian/Pacific Americans and have served to mask true differences and diversity among the various Asian and Pacific Islander groups. Some Asian/Pacific American groups have had to highlight the incorrect perceptions of the "model minority" stereotype:

> Four outlaws gathered at a Decatur coffeehouse to talk over their crimes. One had married an African-American man. Another chose the wrong career. One is openly gay. The fourth, well, she just isn't sub-missive enough. The group looked like a caramel-colored version of the cast of "Friends": four attractive, well-educated Indian-Americans brimming with confidence and laughter. But each has become an out-law of sorts in Atlanta's South Asian community—people from India, Pakistan, Sri Lanka, Bangladesh and Nepal—because they've broken the rules for being a good South Asian, sometimes considered a "model minority" in America. . . . More than 70,000 South Asians now live in the Atlanta metro area, with the Indian-American population alone having recorded a 230 percent increase in Georgia from 1990 to 2000. Indians are also estimated to own nearly half the roadside hotels and motels in the state. None of those numbers reflects the escalating divi-sions within the South Asian community, many of whose younger members say they're tired of being viewed as the "good minority": hardworking, submissive overachievers. They say this image has be-come an ethnic straitjacket that stifles individuality—and is often used to demean African-Americans by comparison. (Blake, 2002, p. M1)

Clearly no groups of people are "all successful" or "all criminals." Nonethe-less, the "success" and the "model minority" stereotypes have affected Asian/ Pacific Americans negatively. For example, because of their implied success, law enforcement organizations may not spend the time to recruit Asian/Pacific American individuals for law enforcement careers (assuming that they are more interested in other areas such as education and business pursuits). This stereotype also hides the existence of real discrimination for those who are successful, as seen in glass ceilings in promotional and developmental opportunities, for example. The success stereotype has resulted in violence and crimes against Asian/Pacific persons:

> The murder of Vincent Chin, and the subsequent inability of the court system to bring the murderers to justice, is now a well-known case among Asian/Pacific American communities. The perpetrators in this case, Ronald Ebens and Michael Nitz, were two white automobile factory workers who blamed Vincent Chin (a Chinese American) for the success of the Japanese automobile industry that was, in turn, blamed for taking away American jobs in the automobile factory. (Takaki, 1989b)

> Hate-motivated killings have claimed eight Asian American lives in the past two years. In the latest incident, three Asian Americans, a Jewish American and an African American were killed in Pittsburgh on April 28. These hate-motivated killings have had a devastating effect on a broad cross-section of Asian Americans across the U.S., in part because the ethnic backgrounds of the victims have been so diverse, including South Asian, Filipino, Japanese, Korean, Vietnamese and Chinese. This horrible loss of life was for no other apparent reason than the color of the victims' skin and often their perceived immigrant status. It is an unprecedented number of hate killings of Asians since monitoring of such incidents began in the 1980s by the National Asian Pacific American Legal Consortium.

> Further, the government's concerted campaign against Los Alamos National Laboratory scientist Wen Ho Lee has especially stirred the Chinese American community. While his guilt or innocence is certainly open to inquiry, community leaders are united in the view that Lee has not received due process, may not receive a fair trial and that his incarceration in solitary confinement and without bail is an abuse of human rights. ("Asians Battle Rights Abuses-in the U.S.," *Los Angeles Times,* May 28, 2000, p. M8)

3. ***Viewing some Asian/Pacific Americans as possible "foreign" terrorists because of their religious affiliation and cultural dress.*** Many Asian/Pacific Americans immigrate from countries with very large populations that practice Islam (e.g., Indonesia, Pakistan, Bangladesh, India, and China) and the majority of these Muslims are from the more moderate wing of Sunni Islam (and not from the more fundamentalist branch). However, it is highly possible for the unfamiliar to group Asian/Pacific Americans who are Muslims into a collective group associated with "fundamentalism" and "terrorism." Moreover, for many immigrants who may stay close to their cultural traditions and cultural dress (e.g., Sikhs who wear turbans and have beards), it is easy to misidentify cultural dress and nuances and come to stereotypic conclusions about who might be a "foreign" terrorist. Two examples: (1) One of the first suspects detained for questioning on September 11, 2001 (as seen on the national television news), was the misidentification of a Sikh who was wearing a turban as being an Afghanistan Taliban (who also wear a head covering that is called a "turban"), and (2) South Asians (e.g., Bangladeshis) with darker skin tones in the Midwest

were often misidentified as Arabs and were detained for questioning on home-land security issues. Roland Paris, an assistant professor of political science at the University of Colorado in Boulder, notes that moderate Muslims still out-number the radicals, and this belief is shared by Prince Hisham bin Abdullah al-Aloui of Morocco, a cousin of King Hassan and second-in-line to the throne:

> "Freedom-loving Muslims," he wrote in an editorial for al-Quds al-Arabi, "need to take a stand against the fundamentalists' bid to establish a monopoly on interpreting Islam and the Quran, and their attempt to in-timidate us. We need to adopt a tolerant Islam, one with which we can live in confidence in the contemporary world. We shall fail if we show tolerance toward those who kill and hijack, and who continue to try to exploit the convincing cover of charitable social initiatives. The perpe-trators of these attacks have presented us Muslims with a provocation which we cannot afford to ignore." (Jensen, 2001, p. A21)

> Asian Americans have long borne the stereotype of the perpetual for-eigner—the unwelcome immigrant or the disloyal or distrusted foreign agent. Japanese Americans bore the brunt of this during World War II as 120,000 were interned. Filipino World War II veterans have never received proper recognition and benefits for fighting bravely under U.S. command. When the 1996 campaign finance scandal implicated a handful of Asian Americans, thousands were investigated or stigma-tized without cause. The recent hate crime wave and treatment of sci-entists are reminders of this ugly past. (Kwoh, 2000, p. M8)

From a law enforcement perspective, many hate crimes against Asian/Pa-cific Americans are related to the stereotype of the group as "foreigners" and not as "Americans."

4. *Misunderstanding Asian/Pacific cultural differences and practices and view-ing differences stereotypically as a threat to other Americans.* The more than 40 Asian/Pacific American groups encompass great differences in life experi-ences, languages, backgrounds, and cultures. It is easy to make mistakes and draw incorrect conclusions because of such cultural differences. Certainly, when one lacks information about any group, it is natural to draw conclusions based on our own filtering system, stereotypes, and assumptions. Most of the time, these incorrect assumptions and stereotypes are corrected by favorable contact and actual interpersonal relationships with Asian/Pacific American people. From a law enforcement perspective, the thrust of community polic-ing, as well as cultural awareness training, is to provide the opportunities to modify stereotypes and to provide opportunities to learn about ethnic commu-nities. Law enforcement agencies, however, have to intervene in situations in which individuals and/or groups view Asian/Pacific American cultural differ-ences as perceived "threats" to themselves. For the Asian/Pacific American communities, violent incidents like that of Patrick Edward Purdy stand out in their minds. On January 17, 1989, Purdy entered the school yard at Cleveland Elementary School in Stockton, California, firing an AK47 assault rifle. In the ensuing few minutes of fire, Purdy had killed five Southeast Asian children and wounded 30 other children. He then turned the rifle on himself and killed

himself. More than 60% of the children at this school were Southeast Asians. The California Attorney General's Report noted that, "It appears highly probable that Purdy deliberately chose Cleveland Elementary School as the location for his murderous assault in substantial part because it was heavily populated by Southeast Asian children. His frequent resentful comments about Southeast Asians indicated a particular animosity against them" (Mathews & Lait, 1989). Stereotypic and racially biased views of Asian/Pacific Americans as "threats" require the ongoing attention of law enforcement agencies:

> In a case that invoked the Vietnam War, America's promise of freedom and the tragedy of Sept. 11, a 23-year-old Manitowoc man who helped burn a house down was sentenced Tuesday to nearly 19 years in prison. . . . Franz, a two-time burglar who has served prison time, had pleaded guilty in October to two hate crimes and a gun charge in the Hmong case. He said at the time that the 1998 arson, as well as an unfulfilled murder plot, were meant to "send a message" that Asians in the Manitowoc area should leave him and his friends alone. . . . Like other victims in the case, Lee and her family had resettled in the Manitowoc area from their native Laos after the war in Vietnam. Many Hmong fought with Americans and faced almost certain death had they remained in their homeland after the Communists took over. . . . One who saw combat with the CIA in Vietnam was Humphrey Chang, 57, who was wounded twice during the war. Three days before the Lee fire, Franz and two of his co-defendants, armed with shotguns, had gone to Two Rivers intending to shoot Asians. They ignited an explosive outside Chang's home, hoping it would flush people out, but no one fled and no shots were fired. "America is a country where freedom began," Chang said. Americans cannot allow such racial terrorism, "the act of killing innocent life for the only reason of hate," he said. (Kertscher, 2002, p. B1)

The misunderstanding of cultural differences that leads to "erroneous" conclusions about Asian/Pacific American behaviors has resulted in law enforcement involvement with the full range of the criminal justice system (e.g., courts, district attorneys, police, child protective services) as seen in the following case:

> Seng Chang and Kaying Lor were glad to learn Monday afternoon that their family's journey through the courts was over. Police took away the couple's four children on April 30 after employees at Sherman Elementary School noticed marks on the youngsters' bodies. The marks had been produced by a traditional Asian healing technique commonly called coining. The children were returned to their parents on May 3 but officially remained in state custody. Prosecutors Monday dropped the case against Chang and Lor after medical experts reviewed the case and determined that there was no evidence of child abuse. "We feel like everything can be like it was before," Lor said Monday. "We feel relieved." The family is Hmong, an ethnic group from the hills of Laos. Lor said he and his wife will continue using the coining remedy when their children are sick. The technique involves rubbing ointment into the skin with a coin or a spoon. He said he hopes those who investigate abuse allegations have learned a lesson and will listen more carefully to what parents are saying before removing children from their homes. Six other children were taken from a Vietnamese couple in a separate

but similar case. Prosecutors dismissed that case last week. (Morton, 2002, p. B1)

THE ASIAN/PACIFIC AMERICAN FAMILY

Obviously, with over 40 different cultural groups under the label of Asian/Pacific Americans, we find great differences in how families operate within the various subgroups. We would like to share some common characteristics to describe Asian/Pacific American families that might be of value in crime-fighting and community peacekeeping. Asian/Pacific American families generally exhibit very strong ties among extended family members. It is not unusual for three to four generations of the same family to live under one roof. Moreover, the extended family can even have an ongoing relationship network that spans great geographic distance. For example, family members (all of whom consider themselves as one family) can be engaged in extensive communications and activities with members in the same family in the United States, Canada, Hong Kong, and Vietnam, all simultaneously. It is not uncommon for an officer to come into contact with members of the extended Asian/Pacific American family in the course of servicing these communities. One key to the success of law enforcement officers in working with an extended family network is the knowledge of how best to contact an Asian/Pacific American family and which family member to speak to for information, help, and referral.

Culture Shock and the Asian/Pacific American Family

Because the traditional cultures of Asia and the Pacific Islands are so very different from that of the United States, many Asian/Pacific American families (whether refugees, immigrants, businesspersons, students, or tourists) experience some degree of culture shock when they enter and reside in the United States. Culture shock results not only from differences in values and traditions but also from differences in urbanization, industrialization, and modernization from technology that may be different from that in their homeland. Peace officers need to be aware that Asian/Pacific Americans may cope with their culture shock by becoming "clannish" (e.g., Chinatowns, Koreatowns). Other survival mechanisms include avoiding contact and interaction with those who are different (including police officers).

The Role of the Man and the Woman in an Asian/Pacific American Family

In most Asian/Pacific American families, relationship and communication patterns tend to be quite hierarchical, with the father as the identified head of the household. Although many decisions and activities may appear to be determined by the father, other individuals may come into the picture. Generally, if there are grandparents in the household, the father would still act as the spokesperson for the family, but he would consult the grandparents, his wife, and others regarding any major decision. As such, it may be important in any kind of law enforcement contact that requires a decision and/or choice to allow the parties time to discuss issues in, as much as feasible, a "private" manner. Self-control and keeping things within the family are key values for

Asian/Pacific Americans. Officers thus may find that there is more control in a situation by allowing the Asian/Pacific American to come to the same conclusion as he/she with respect to a situation and to exercise his or her own self-choice (which may be the same as what the officer would want the parties to do anyway). For example, the officer can explain an arrest situation to the father of a family member, and instead of saying directly to the family member to be arrested that he or she has to leave with the officer, the officer can allow the father to suggest to the family member that he or she leave with the officer. What may appear to be a minor consideration in this case can result in a higher degree of persuasion, control, and cooperation by all parties concerned.

Although there are no clear-cut rules as to whether one goes to the male head of the household or to the female head to make a law enforcement inquiry, the general rule of thumb is that one would not go too wrong by starting with the father. It should be noted that for most Asian/Pacific American families, the role of the mother in discipline and in decision making is very important. While the household may appear to be "ruled" by the father, the mother's role in finances, discipline, education, operations, and decision making is major.

Children, Adolescents, and Youths

Most Asian/Pacific American families involve at least two or more individuals within the same household working outside of the home. Thus, if young children are present, there is a high reliance on either family members or others to help care for them while the parents are at work. It is not uncommon for older children to care for younger children within a household. Moreover, latchkey children within an Asian/Pacific American home are common, especially for families that cannot afford external child care. In recent immigrant and refugee families, Asian/Pacific American children have a special role in being the intermediaries between parents and the external community because of the ability of the younger individuals to learn English and the American ways of doing things. Children often serve as translators and interpreters for peace officers in their communication and relations with Asian/Pacific American families involving recent immigrants and refugees. In such situations, it is suggested that the officer review the role expected of the youthful member of the family, and determine how sensitive an area the translated content is to the different family members and the consequences if the content is incorrectly translated. (For example, asking a juvenile to translate to his or her parents who speak no English that the juvenile had been involved in a sexual abuse situation at the school may result in significant omission and/or changed content because of the embarrassment caused to the juvenile and possibly to the parents.) In all cases, when a child is acting as a translator, the officer should direct all verbal and nonverbal communication to the parents (as one would normally do without a translator). Otherwise, the parents may view the officer's lack of attention to them as an insult.

Asian/Pacific American Family Violence

Given the Asian/Pacific American cultural values and norms to keep family issues within the family and to use self-help and personal effort strategies, reports of and research studies on family violence (e.g., spousal physical abuse, child abuse, sexual abuse) by Asian/Pacific Americans are, at best, incomplete. The few reported studies seem to indicate significant and emerging problems with family violence within the Asian/Pacific American community. Song (1996), in his interview of 150 Korean immigrant women from the Chicago area, found that 60 percent of those sampled reported being battered, with 37 percent of those battered at least once a month. Abraham (2000), in her survey of community-based women's service organizations, found that over 1,000 South Asian women sought help for abuse and family violence. Anecdotal reports for the Chinese (Chin, 1994), Pilipino (Cimmarusti, 1996), Cambodian (Frye & D'Avanzo, 1994), Vietnamese (Kibria, 1993), and other Asian/Pacific American groups indicate that family violence within these Asian/Pacific American communities has been underestimated and underreported. Song noted that most of the abused women used self-help efforts to keep the problem within the home (e.g., fought back physically and verbally, ignored the battering or did nothing, stared at the abusing person), and 70 percent of the battered women indicated that they did not know about community services that could have helped them. The role of peace officers in detecting, assessing, and intervening in family violence situations within Asian/Pacific American communities is a critical one given this emerging area of needs and problems. The sensitivity of the peace officer to the cultural influences and patterns of communication (as noted in the next section) will be significant in the effective gathering of initial information and subsequent referral and interventions with Asian/Pacific American families involved in domestic violence and other issues of abuse.

CULTURAL INFLUENCES ON COMMUNICATION: VERBAL AND NONVERBAL STYLES OF ASIAN/PACIFIC AMERICANS

We do not wish to create any kind of stereotypes, but there are key features of Asian/Pacific American verbal and nonverbal communication styles that necessitate explanation. Misunderstanding resulting from style differences can result in perceptions of poor community services from police agencies, conflicts resulting from such misunderstandings, and safety and control issues for peace officers.

1. It is important that officers take the time to get information from witnesses, victims, and suspects even if the individuals have limitations to their English speaking abilities. The use of officers who may speak different Asian/Pacific dialects or languages, translators, and language bank resources would greatly enhance this process. Often Asian/Pacific Americans have not been helped in crime-fighting and peacekeeping situations because officers could not or did not take information from individuals who could not speak English well.

> Language was the first barrier to investigating the slaying of 6-year-old Volith Long. Things kept getting lost in the translation. But a parent's grief is a universal language, and that grief has followed Rady Long like a family member from Cambodia to the United States. In 1985, most Austinites, police included, had never heard a word of Cambodian. Long had arrived in the United States two years earlier with only one of her three children. Two older children remained with in-laws in Cambodia. She just wanted to forget about life under the Khmer Rouge regime, which killed her husband. . . . For 15 years, Long has waited for answers in a case that was recently reopened along with other old cases. During that time, Austin's diverse Asian community, once invisible, has become

increasingly visible. Today, the police department has a liaison to the Asian American community. . . . Volith's body was found in a trash bin at the North Austin apartment complex where she and her mother lived with another family. She was wrapped in a curtain and stuffed into a large plastic bag. Police believe she was raped and strangled in an empty apartment at 615 W. St. Johns Ave., where many Southeast Asians lived. Long discovered her daughter was missing when she returned from work. . . . But language and cultural barriers complicated the investigation, according to earlier accounts of the case. "We had trouble questioning the victim's mother. We needed one interpreter to translate Vietnamese to English, and another to translate Cambodian to Vietnamese," a senior police sergeant told the American-Statesman in 1985. (Smith, 2000, p. B1)

2. Asian/Pacific Americans tend to hold a more "family" and/or "group" orientation. As such, the lack of the use of I statements and/or self-reference should not be evaluated as not being straightforward or as being evasive about oneself or one's relationships. The officer may be concerned because an Asian/Pacific American may wish to use the pronoun "we" when the situation may call for a personal observation involving an "I" statement. For example, in a traffic accident, the Asian/Pacific American may describe what he or she saw by saying "We saw . . . " Using such group statements to convey what the individual saw is consistent with the family and group orientation of Asian/Pacific Americans.

3. The officer must be aware that for many Asian/Pacific Americans, it is considered to be rude, impolite, and to involve a "loss of face" to directly say "no" to an authority figure such as a peace officer. Peace officers need to understand the following possibilities when an answer of "yes" is heard from an Asian/Pacific American. It can mean (1) "Yes, I heard what you said (but I may or may not agree with you)"; (2) "Yes, I understand what you said (but I may or may not do what I understand)"; (3) "Yes, I can see this is important for you (but I may not agree with you on this)"; or (4) "Yes, I agree (and will do what you said)." Because the context of the communication and the nonverbal aspects of the message are equally meaningful, it is vital for law enforcement officers to be sure of the "yes" answers received, as well as other language nuances from Asian/Pacific Americans. Two examples might be illustrative: (1) If an Asian/Pacific American says that he or she will "try his or her best to attend," this generally means that he or she will not be there, especially for more voluntary events and situations such as community neighborhood safety meetings. (2) If an Asian/Pacific national says in response to a question "It is possible," this generally means do not wait for the event to happen. Such communications, as noted previously, may be more applicable to some Asian/Pacific Americans than others, but sensitivity on the part of law enforcement officers to these language nuances will facilitate communication. Specific rules for interacting with each Asian/Pacific American group are not necessary, but officers should have a general understanding of language and cultural styles. In a communication situation in which the response of "yes" may be ambiguous, it is suggested that law enforcement officers rephrase the question so that the requested outcome in action and understanding are demonstrated in the verbal response.

Ambiguous Response

Officer:	"I need you to show up in court on Tuesday. Do you understand?"
Asian witness:	"Yes!"

Rephrasing of Questions to Show Understanding and Outcome

Officer:	"What are you going to do on Tuesday?"
Asian witness:	"I will be in court on Tuesday. I must go there."

4. Asian/Pacific Americans tend to be "high context" in communication style. This means that the officer needs to provide both interpersonal and situational contexts for effective communications. Context for Asian/Pacific Americans means that members of the community know the officers in the community. Community members may have had previous working relationships with the officer (e.g., crime prevention meetings, police athletic league). Moreover, other members of the community may help to provide information and context for police cooperation based on past relationships. Context also means providing explanations and education to members or groups within Asian/Pacific Americans about procedures and laws before asking them questions and/or requesting their participation in an activity. By providing background information and by establishing prior relationships with Asian/Pacific American communities, the Asian/Pacific American individual has a context for cooperating with law enforcement agencies and officers.

5. Be aware of nonverbal and other cultural nuances that may detract from the effective communication of the officer with a member of the Asian/Pacific American community. Many Asian/Pacific Americans find it uncomfortable and, sometimes, inappropriate to maintain eye contact with authority figures like police officers. It is considered in many Asian/Pacific American cultures to be disrespectful if there is eye contact with someone who is of higher status, position, importance, or authority. As such, many Asian/Pacific Americans may look down on the ground and/or avert their eyes from gazing at a police officer. The officer should not automatically read this nonverbal behavior as indicating a lack of trust or respect, or as a dishonest response. Likewise, for the police officer, he or she should be aware of possible nonverbal gestures and actions that may detract from his or her professional roles (e.g., gesturing with the curled index finger for a person to come forward in a manner that might be used only for servants in that person's home culture).

6. Asian/Pacific Americans may not display their emotionality in the same way that the officer expects. The central thesis guiding Asian/Pacific Americans is the Confucian notion of "walking the middle road." This means that extremes, too much or too little of anything, are not good. As such, Asian/Pacific Americans tend to moderate their display of positive and/or negative emotion. Often, in crisis situations, nonverbal displays of emotions are controlled to the point that the affect of the Asian/Pacific American appears "flat." Under such circumstances, the officer needs to correctly understand and interpret such displays of emotion appropriately. For example, just because the parent of a murder victim does not appear emotionally shaken by an officer's report does not mean that the person is not experiencing a severe emotional crisis.

KEY ISSUES IN LAW ENFORCEMENT

Underreporting of Crimes

Asian/Pacific Americans, because of their past experiences with some law enforcement agencies (e.g., anti-Asian immigration laws, health and sanitation code violations in restaurants, as well as perceived unresponsiveness by police), are reluctant to report crimes and may not seek police assistance and help. Many Asian/Pacific Americans remember how police in their home countries have brutalized and violated them and others (e.g., in Southeast Asian and other Asian countries). Crimes that occur within a family's home (e.g., home invasion, family violence) or within the confines of a small family business (e.g., robbery of a Chinese restaurant) often go unreported unless these crimes are connected to larger criminal activities, as in the example that follows:

> A grand jury has indicted three Chinese nationals accused of traveling to Western New York last month to burglarize the Lancaster home of a man whose family owns a local Chinese restaurant. Law enforcement officials said Wednesday they were investigating allegations that the three are part of an organized-crime outfit that has been targeting the operators of Chinese restaurants. . . . Lin's family owns a local Chinese restaurant, and law enforcement officials said they believe the robbery may be tied to other recent robberies targeting the owners of Chinese restaurants. (Herbeck, 2000)

Many immigrants and refugees are simply not knowledgeable about the legal system of the United States and therefore avoid any contact with law enforcement personnel. Outreach and community policing perspectives will enhance the contact and relationship with Asian/Pacific American communities, helping to correct the underreporting of crimes.

Differential Treatment

The U.S. Commission on Civil Rights (1992) highlighted several areas in which Asian/Pacific Americans may have received different treatment in police services as a result of their culture or ethnic heritage. Incidents reported included police misconduct and harassment. The commission reported the following case as an example:

> On June 1, 1991, a young Italian American man who had recently moved to Revere, Massachusetts was murdered. Witnesses said that he was brutally beaten and stabbed repeatedly by a group of Asian men. The Revere Police Department, which has no Asian American police officers and has no access to interpreters, was unable to solve the case and apprehend the murderers quickly and came under increasing criticism from the victim's family. On July 1, in an attempt to force information about the murder to the surface, a team of 40 Revere police officers, along with representatives of the Immigration and Naturalization Service, made a 2-hour sweep through a Cambodian neighborhood in search of persons with outstanding warrants and possible illegal aliens. "We wanted to break open the case," said one of the police officers involved in the sweep. The Cambodian Americans living in Revere were frightened and angered by the police sweep.

Positive Collaborative Asian/Pacific American Community and Law Enforcement Agencies

Increasingly, we see that when there are collaborative and cooperative efforts among the law enforcement, criminal justice, and community advocacy systems, the Asian and Pacific American communities will begin to gain greater trust and confidence resulting from effective multicultural and multidisciplinary law enforcement actions taken. The following case is a positive example of how police, prosecutors, courts, community advocates, and victims join together to ensure the conviction involving the rape cases for nine Asian women:

> Simply seeing the Mark Anthony Lewis rape case go to trial last week wasn't enough to satisfy Asian Americans in the Chicago area that police care about their fears. Just like it wasn't enough to see Lewis arrested almost two years ago in the Philippines, where he had traveled after the last of nine attacks against mostly Asian women that shocked the area from April to July 2000. . . . The rape on Chicago's North Side was the eighth of the nine assaults that prompted an unprecedented mobilization of police and community resources to catch the attacker. Police in Chicago, Mount Prospect, Arlington Heights, Skokie, Niles, Morton Grove and Cook County—where the attacks occurred—helped lead efforts. The guilty verdict in the first assault case to go to trial shows "it was worth it to bring out as many community advocates as we could at every step in this process," Dolar said. "It proves to the courts that Asians can step up and be active in stopping crime. It proves it to ourselves." Although prosecutors ultimately decided against trying Lewis on a hate crime charge, Asian community leaders say the prosecution has proved they understand the series of assaults two years ago had a racial maliciousness that struck the heart of their community. "Our focus was to get justice for the victim, so we understand if the state's attorney's office thought it was a stronger case to go on without it," said Jean M. Fujiu, executive director of the Japanese American Service Committee, of the hate crime charge. "We think the state's attorney's office has done a very good job acting on the evidence.". . . "I think this shows that there's not this need to have an assumed distrust of police or state's attorneys or the government or whoever that's outside the (Asian) community," Khan said of the guilty verdict. "I think they see that they're there to help us and help everyone in getting justice served." (Cliatt, 2002, p. 3)

Asian/Pacific American officers involved in community policing in their local neighborhoods have been seen as a viable model for cities with growing Asian/Pacific American populations:

> When Asian-Americans began moving into Quincy in the 1980s, there was not a single Asian-American police officer in the city. That lack of diversity, language barriers and a general fear of authority that developed in homelands thousands of miles away made many of the city's newest residents reluctant to turn to law enforcement for help. That reticence lingers today. To prove the point, Yee notes how several workers avert their eyes when the officers walk into Super 88 market under construction on Hancock Street. . . . But Yee and Mar—both Asian-American—say they are making progress. "Just being an Asian face to an Asian face seems to break some of those barriers down," Mar said. Both Yee and Mar speak Chinese dialects, enabling them to elicit information that

might normally be difficult to get. Just recently, they helped with a possible ab-
duction investigation. Through a series of interviews, they learned that the man
was picked up by federal immigration officers, something his family did not
know. (Eschbacher, 2003, p. 8)

James Chin (1987), an officer with the Los Angeles Police Department Airport Police Bureau, describes one of the first storefront outreach efforts that resulted in improved police–community relationships and better service benefits to the Asian/Pacific
American neighborhood in the Korean area of Los Angeles. Storefront outreach efforts
are now utilized in most urban cities with large Asian/Pacific American communities
like San Francisco, New York, Oakland, Chicago, Boston, and Seattle. (Chapter 1 discusses this in the section on community policing.)

> The Los Angeles Police Department has two storefronts serving Asian/Pacific
> Islander communities, one located in a Korean neighborhood; the other in a
> Chinese neighborhood. Both storefronts are the results of organized community
> demands for such operations and subsequent donations from individuals and
> organizations within the community who helped provide space and needed ma-
> terials. The storefronts are staffed by a police officer and a bilingual community
> person whose salary is paid by community donations and the police depart-
> ment. (Chin, 1987, pp. 52–60)

Another outreach approach is the use of Asian/Pacific American bilingual community service officers (CSOs), nonsworn officers with badges and uniforms who serve
the Southeast Asian communities in San Diego, California. The CSOs provide many of
the supportive services available from the police department by using bilingual
nonsworn personnel.

Increasing Asian/Pacific American Peace Officers

There is a noticeable underrepresentation of Asian/Pacific Americans in federal, state,
and local law enforcement and criminal justice positions, although the number of
Asian/Pacific Americans as peace officers and in law enforcement has increased in the
past decade. The small number of Asian/Pacific American officers has hampered many
departments in neighborhoods with large Asian/Pacific American populations in effectively serving those communities with appropriate role models and bicultural expertise.
A variety of reasons exist for such underrepresentation, including (1) history of law enforcement relationships with Asian/Pacific American communities, (2) interest of
Asian/Pacific Americans in law enforcement careers, (3) image of law enforcement
personnel in Asian/Pacific American communities, (4) lack of knowledge about the different careers and pathways in law enforcement, (5) concern with and fear of background checks, physical requirements, and the application process, and (6) limited
number of role models and advocates for law enforcement careers for Asian/Pacific
Americans. With the growing Asian/Pacific American populations in areas throughout
the United States, law enforcement agencies have emphasized the importance of "diversity" in their recruitment efforts:

> The Marathon County Sheriff's Department is set to hire its first Southeast
> Asian cadet, highlighting the call for a more diverse police force, officials said.
> "Diversity brings different attitudes and different aspects of life, different ways

of looking at things," said Wausau police officer Kay Hansen, one of five women in a 59-officer department. Law enforcement officials say having a diverse force with officers who can speak different languages can help in dealing with the public and in developing close ties to the community. The Wausau Police Department has two women detectives, and the Marathon County Sheriff's Department has one. Despite a growing Wausau-area Hmong population, Southeast Asian residents have only recently begun to enter law enforcement, including two on Wausau's police force. The Marathon County Sheriff's Department is set to receive federal grants to hire five bilingual cadets over the next five years, Capt. Tom Kujawa said. The department should recruit bilingual officers in part to help ease the transition for the area's Hmong residents, who often don't understand law enforcement, Wausau Minority Affairs Director Thomas Lee said. He said Hmong families would benefit from uniformed officers of similar backgrounds. A police department with officers that mirror a community's population can more easily develop mutual trust with area residents, said Chris Ahmuty, executive director of the American Civil Liberties Union of Wisconsin. ("Wausau Wants More Diversity," 2001)

Crimes within Asian/Pacific American Communities

Many crimes committed in Asian/Pacific American communities are perpetrated by others within the same group, particularly among Asian/Pacific refugee and Asian/Pacific immigrant groups. Law enforcement officials have often found it difficult to get cooperation from refugee and immigrant victims of extortion, home robbery, burglary, theft, blackmail, and other crimes against persons. In part, the lack of cooperation stems from a fear of retaliation by the criminal, who is within the Asian/Pacific American community. Other concerns of Asian/Pacific American victims include (1) the perceived level of responsiveness of the peacekeeping officers and agencies, (2) lack of familiarity with and trust in police services, (3) perceived level of effectiveness of law enforcement agencies, and (4) prior stereotypes and images of law enforcement agencies as discriminatory (e.g., immigration laws) and unresponsive to crimes against Asian/Pacific Americans. Recent Asian/Pacific American refugees and immigrants are often prime targets, in part because of their distrust of most institutions (e.g., banks, police departments, hospitals). As a result, they are more inclined to hide and store cash and other valuables in the home. A key challenge for police agencies is to educate this group and to work cooperatively with Asian/Pacific Americans to reduce the crimes within these communities.

SUMMARY OF RECOMMENDATIONS FOR LAW ENFORCEMENT

As a result of the early immigration laws and other discriminatory treatment received by Asian/Pacific Americans in the United States, the experiences of Asian/Pacific Americans with law enforcement officials has been fraught with conflicts, difficulties, and mixed messages. Officers should realize that some Asian/Pacific Americans may still remember this history and carry with them stereotypes of police services as something to be feared and avoided. Law enforcement officials may need to go out of their way to establish trust and to win cooperation in order to effectively accomplish their goals to serve and protect Asian/Pacific Americans.

As noted earlier, the label Asian Americans/Pacific Islanders encompasses over 40 very diverse ethnic and cultural groups. Law enforcement officials need to be aware that great differences exist between the 40 diverse ethnic groups (e.g., different cultural and language groups) as well as the differences that may result from the individual life experiences of members within any one of the 40 groups (e.g., generational differences). Since a key stereotype of much concern to Asian/Pacific Americans is that they are regarded by mainstream Americans as very much alike, it is important that peace officers not make such errors in their interactions with Asian/Pacific Americans.

There is tremendous diversity among Asian/Pacific Americans, and one way to understand individuals within these communities is to look at some of the motivating forces that might affect decisions by Asian/Pacific American citizens. Earlier in this chapter we provided a seven-part typology that will assist officers in viewing some of these motivational bases.

Although there are many ethnicities, cultures, and languages among the 40 or more groups within Asian/Pacific American communities, one way to understand the impact of their immigration and life experiences is by learning the motivational determinants of individuals within different generational and immigrant groups.

The self-preferred term for referring to Asian/Pacific Americans varies with contexts, groups, and experiences of the individual. Law enforcement officials need to be aware of terms that are unacceptable and derogatory and terms that are currently used. When in doubt, officers have to learn to become comfortable in asking Asian/Pacific Americans which terms they prefer. Officers are advised to provide helpful feedback to their peers when offensive terms, labels, and/or actions are used with Asian/Pacific Americans. Such feedback will help reduce the risk of misunderstanding and improve the working relationships between officers and Asian/Pacific American communities. Moreover, it will help enhance the professional image of the department for those communities.

Many Asian/Pacific Americans are concerned with their ability to communicate clearly, and this is of particular concern among Asian/Pacific Americans who are immigrants and refugees. Peace officers need to take the time and be aware that bilingual individuals and non-native English speakers want to communicate effectively with them. Maintaining contact, providing extra time, using translators, and being patient with speakers will allow Asian/Pacific Americans to communicate their concerns.

Cultural differences in verbal and nonverbal communication often result in misinterpretation of the message and of behaviors. Officers need to be aware of nonverbal aspects of Asian/Pacific Americans in their communication styles, including eye contact, touch, gestures, and affect (show of emotions). Verbal aspects such as accent, limited vocabulary, and incorrect grammar may give officers the impression that an Asian/Pacific American individual is not understanding what is communicated. It is important to remember that the English listening and comprehension skills of Asian/Pacific American immigrants and refugees are usually better than their speaking skills.

Asian/Pacific Americans, because of their past experiences with law enforcement agencies, along with their own concerns about privacy, self-help, and other factors, are reluctant to report crimes and may not seek police assistance and help. Law enforcement departments and officials need to build relationships and working partnerships with representative groups from the Asian/Pacific American communities. Relationship building is often helped by outreach efforts such as community storefront offices, bilingual officers, and participation of officers in community activities.

DISCUSSION QUESTIONS AND ISSUES*

1. *Law Enforcement as Not User-Friendly.* Under the historical information section of this chapter, we noted that many anti-Asian/Pacific American laws and events may leave Asian/Pacific Americans with the view that law enforcement agencies are not user-friendly. What are the implications of this view for law enforcement? What are ways to improve such possible negative points of view?

2. *Diversity among Asian/Pacific Americans.* As noted earlier in this chapter, the Asian/Pacific American category comprises over 40 diverse ethnic and cultural groups. Which groups are you most likely to encounter in crime-fighting and peacekeeping in your work? Which groups do you anticipate encountering in your future work?

3. *How Asian/Pacific American Groups Differ.* A typology for understanding motives for some of the behaviors of Asian/Pacific American people (in terms of their generational and immigration status in the United States) was provided. How might you apply this typology to better understand an Asian/Pacific American refugee involved in a traffic moving violation? An Asian/Pacific American immigrant involved as a victim of a house robbery? An Asian/Pacific national involved as a victim of a burglary? Southeast Asian youths involved in possible gang activities?

4. *Choice of Terms.* The term Asian Americans and Pacific Islanders is used in many publications and by many people to refer to members of the more than 40 diverse groups included in this category. How might you find out which is the best term to use in reference to an individual if ethnic and cultural information of this kind is necessary?

5. *Offensive Terms and Labels.* We strongly urge that offensive terms such as Chinks, Gooks, and Flips not be used in law enforcement work at any time. Give three practical reasons for this perspective.

6. *Effects of Myths and Stereotypes.* Myths and stereotypes about Asian/Pacific Americans have greatly affected this group. What are some of the Asian/Pacific American stereotypes that you have heard of or have encountered? What effects would these stereotypes have on Asian/Pacific Americans? What are ways to manage these stereotypes in law enforcement? How might your awareness of Asian/Pacific American stereotypes be helpful in an interview with an Asian/Pacific American about homeland security issues?

7. *Verbal and Nonverbal Variations among Cultures.* How do you think that the information in this chapter about verbal and nonverbal communication styles can help officers in their approach to Asian/Pacific American citizens? When you can understand the cultural components of the styles and behaviors, does this help you to become more sensitive and objective about your reactions? Provide some examples of rephrasing questions in such a way that they elicit

*See the Instructor's Manual accompanying this text for additional activities, role-play activities, questionnaires, and projects related to the content of this chapter.

responses that show understanding and the intended actions on the part of Asian/Pacific Americans.

8. ***Self-Monitoring and Avoidance of Law Enforcement.*** Why do you think many Asian/Pacific Americans keep to their own communities and express the desire for self-monitoring and within-community resolution of their problems? When are such efforts desirable? When are they ineffective? How can police agencies be of greater service to Asian/Pacific American communities in this regard?

WEBSITE RESOURCES

Visit these websites for additional information about law enforcement contact with Asian/Pacific Americans, as well as for information about Asian/Pacific American community organizations:

Asian American Legal Defense and Education Fund (AALDEF): http://www.aaldef.org

This website provides information about civil rights issues with Asian/Pacific Americans and highlights issues of immigration, family law, government benefits, anti-Asian violence and police misconduct, employment discrimination, labor rights, and workplace issues.

Asian American Network: http://www.asianamerican.net

This website provides a national listing of many of the networks of Asian/Pacific American community-based organizations in the United States (as well as some in Asia).

National Asian Pacific American Legal Consortium: http://www.napalc.org

This website provides a national network of information about legal and civil rights issues affecting Asian/Pacific Americans in terms of litigation, advocacy, public education, and public policy.

National Asian Peace Officers Association: http://www.napoa.org/

This website provides information to promote the interests of Asian American peace officers on community issues, career development and opportunities, education and workshops, and awareness about the Asian culture.

REFERENCES

Abraham, M. (2000). *Speaking the Unspeakable: Marital Violence against South Asian Immigrant Women in the United States.* New Brunswick, N.J.: Rutgers University Press.

Ancheta, A. N. (1998). *Race, Rights, and the Asian American Experience.* New Brunswick, N.J.: Rutgers University Press.

Barkan, E. R. (1992). *Asian and Pacific Islander Migration to the United States: A Model of New Global Patterns.* Westport, Conn.: Greenwood Press.

Barnes, J. S., and Bennett, C. E. (2002). *The Asian Population: 2000.* Washington, DC: U.S. Census Bureau.

Bennett, C. E. (2002). *A Profile of the Nation's Foreign-Born Population from Asia (2000 Update).* Washington, DC: U.S. Census Bureau.

Blake, J. (2002, February 3). "Ethnic Straitjacket: South Asians Confront Stereotype as 'Model Minority.'" *Atlanta Journal and Constitution,* p. M1.

Chang, R. S. (1999). *Disoriented: Asian Americans, Law, and the Nation-State.* New York: New York University Press.

Chin, J. (1987). "Crime and the Asian American Community: The Los Angeles Response to Koreatown." *Journal of California Law Enforcement, 19,* 52–60.

Chin, K. (1994). "Out-of-Town Brides: International Marriage and Wife Abuse among Chinese Immigrants." *Journal of Comparative Family Studies, 25,* 53–69.

Cimmarusti, R. A. (1996). "Exploring Aspects of Filipino-American Families." *Journal of Marital and Family Therapy, 22,* 205–217.

Cliatt, C. (2002, May 5). "Rape Case Rallies Asian Community: Fear of Police, Fierce Protection Gives Way to Doing What It Takes to Convict." *Chicago Daily Herald,* p. 3.

Daniels, R. (1988). *Asian America: Chinese and Japanese in the United States since 1850.* Seattle: University of Washington Press.

"Des Moines to Pay $7,500 to Men Who Were Handcuffed at Cafe." (2001, September 26). Associated Press.

Du, P. L. (1996). *The Dream Shattered: Vietnamese Gangs in America.* Boston: Northeastern University Press.

Effron, S. (1989, September). "Racial Slaying Prompts Fear, Anger in Raleigh." *Greensboro News and Record.*

Eschbacher, K. (2003, August) "Two Asian-American Officers Make Inroads in Neighborhoods." *Patriot Ledger,* Special Report, p. 8.

Frye, B. A., and C. D. D'Avanzo. (1994). "Cultural Themes in Family Stress and Violence among Cambodian Refugee Women in the Inner City." *Advances in Nursing Science, 16,* 64–77.

Glasse, C., and Smith, H. (2003). *The New Encyclopedia of Islam* (Revised). Walnut Creek, Calif.: AltaMira Press.

Goldstein, L. (1990, May 8). "Split between Blacks, Koreans Widens in N.Y. Court." *Washington Post.*

Herbeck, D. (2000, July 6). "Asian Organized-Crime Ties Eyed in Lancaster Robbery." *Buffalo News.*

Kalavar, J. M. (1998). *The Asian Indian Elderly in America.* New York: Garland.

Kandel, B. (1991, January 4). "Tensions Ease Year after NYC Grocery Boycott." *USA Today,* p. A8.

Kempsky, N. (1989, October). "A Report to Attorney General John K. Van de Kamp on Patrick Edward Purdy and the Cleveland School Killings." Sacramento: State of California Attorney General's Office.

Kertscher, T. (2002, February 13). "Arsonist Sentenced for Hate Crimes; Hmong Family Tells of Fleeing Burning Home." *Milwaukee Journal Sentinel,* p. B1.

Kibria, N. (1993). *Family Tightrope: The Changing Lives of Vietnamese Americans.* Princeton, N.J.: Princeton University Press.

Kwoh, S. (2000, May 28). "Asians Battle Rights Abuses—in the U.S." *Los Angeles Times,* p. M8.

Jensen, H. (2001, October 9). "Winning Over Muslims a Must." *Rocky Mountain News,* p. A21.

Lee, L. C., and Zane, N. W. S. (1998). *Handbook of Asian American Psychology.* Thousand Oaks, Calif.: Sage.

Lee, S. J. (1996). *Unraveling the "Model Minority" Stereotype: Listening to Asian American Youths.* New York: Teachers College Press.

Mathews, J., and M. Lait. (1989, January 18). "Rifleman Slays Five at School: 19 Pupils, Teacher Shot in California; Assailant Kills Self." *Washington Post,* p. A1.

Morton, J. (2002, May 14). "Second Coining Case is Dropped: Asian Dad Hopes Case Helps Others." *Omaha World Herald,* p. B1.

"A Nation Challenged: The Immigrants; More Insulted and Attacked After September 11." (2002, March 11). *New York Times,* p. A12.

Ng, F. (1998a). *Asian American Family Life and Community.* New York: Garland.

Ng, F. (1998b). *The History and Immigration of Asian Americans.* New York: Garland.

Prashad, V. (2001). *The Karma of Brown Folk.* Minneapolis: University of Minnesota Press.

President's Commission on Mental Health. (1978). *Report of the Special Population Subpanel on Mental Health of Asian/Pacific Americans, Vol. 3.* Washington, D.C.: U.S. Government Printing Office.

Schmitt, E. (1992, November 20). "Marines Find Racial Disparity in Officer Programs." *New York Times,* p. A8.

Smith, S. (2000, May 20). "Grief after Girl's Death is Unspeakable." *Austin American-Statesman,* p. B1.

Song, Y. I. (1996). *Battered Women in Korean Immigrant Families.* New York: Garland.

Special Services for Groups. (1983). *Bridging Cultures: Southeast Asian Refugees in America.* Los Angeles: Author.

Stockfisch, J. R. (2003, April 1). "Lawmakers Want End of 'Racist' Clause." *Tampa Tribune,* p. 1.

Takaki, R. (1989a). *Strangers from a Different Shore: A History of Asian Americans.* Boston: Little, Brown.

Takaki, R. (1989b). "Who Killed Vincent Chin?" in G. Yun (ed.), *A Look Beyond the Model Minority Image: Critical Issues in Asian America.* New York: Minority Rights Group, pp. 23–29.

Tuan, M. (1998). *Forever Foreigners or Honorary White? The Asian Ethnic Experience Today.* New Brunswick, N.J.: Rutgers University Press.

U.S. Bureau of the Census. (2002). *Census 2000 Brief Reports.* Washington, D.C.: U.S. Government Printing Office.

U.S. Commission on Civil Rights. (1992). *Civil Rights Issues Facing Asian Americans in the 1990s.* Washington, D.C.: U.S. Government Printing Office.

"Wausau Wants More Diversity among Area Law Enforcement Officers." (2001, November 18). Associated Press.

Woo, D. (2000). *Glass Ceiling and Asian Americans: The New Face of Workplace Barriers.* Walnut Creek, Calif.: AltaMira Press.

Chapter 6

Law Enforcement Contact with African Americans

OVERVIEW

This chapter provides specific cultural and historical information on African Americans that both directly and indirectly affect the relationship between law enforcement officials and citizens. It presents information about demographics and diversity among African Americans as well as issues related to cultural and racial identity. Following the background information is a section on group identification terms and a discussion of myths and stereotypes. Aspects of the family are discussed, including the extended family, the roles of men and women, single-mother families, and adolescents. A section on cultural influences on communication deals with Ebonics (also known as Black English Vernacular), nonverbal and verbal communication, including emotionalism, and fighting words, threats, and aggressive behavior. The closing section presents several key concerns for law enforcement, including information on differential treatment, racial profiling, perceptions of and reactions to legal authority, excessive force and brutality, police interaction in poor urban communities, the needs of the inner city, and issues related to women. The summary of the chapter reviews recommendations for improved communication and relationships between law enforcement officials and African Americans.

COMMENTARY

The history of intimidation of African Americans by police continues to affect the dynamics of law enforcement in some black communities today.

> There is no point in telling blacks to observe the law. . . . It has almost always been used against them.
>
> *(Senator Robert Kennedy after visiting the scene of the Watts Riot, 1965)*

> We must learn to live together as brothers or perish together as fools.
>
> *(Martin Luther King, 1964).*

> If . . . inclusion of African Americans and other minorities in policing and in the broader society are continued, then community policing might finally realize a vision of police departments as organizations that protect the lives, property, and rights of all citizens in a fair and effective way.
>
> *(Williams & Murphy, 1990)*

159

> Law enforcement should move away from thinking only about the inner-city when "African American" comes to mind. African Americans are more sophisticated [than 10 and 20 years ago]; they understand societal rules and community resources, including complaint procedures when it comes to law enforcement actions. Their expectations for law enforcement professionalism have risen significantly.
>
> *(Berry, 2003)*

African Americans today enjoy equal protection under the law, and have higher expectations of law enforcement than they did in the past. Community leaders expect to become involved with law enforcement agencies in community-based policing formats. In Chapter 1, we presented an example of the San Diego Police Department whose leaders collaborated with African Americans and other community members (Latinos, Asians) to interpret racial profiling data and to deal jointly with the problem. While this example is not intended to gloss over the reality that law enforcement still has much progress to make with respect to relations with the African American community, it illustrates that a shift is beginning to take place between law enforcement and some segments of the African American population.

AFRICAN AMERICAN CULTURE

The overwhelming problems associated with the racial aspects of black–white relations sometimes overshadow the cultural differences between white and black Americans. The effects that slavery and discrimination have had on the black experience in America are not to be downplayed, but in addition, African American culture must also be considered. African American culture is in part influenced by African culture and is significantly different from white culture. Many police executives have come to recognize that when there is an influx of immigrants from a particular part of the world, their officers are better equipped to establish trust, good communication, and mutual cooperation if they have some basic understanding of the group's cultural background. However, past history has shown when it comes to African Americans, cultural differences are seldom considered, even though they can cause serious communication problems between citizens and police officers. Failing to recognize the distinctiveness of black culture, language, and communication patterns can lead to misunderstandings, conflict, and even confrontation. In addition, understanding the history of African Americans (which is related to the culture) is especially important for law enforcement officials as they work toward improving relations and changing individual and community perceptions.

HISTORICAL INFORMATION

The majority of African Americans or blacks (the terms will be used interchangeably) in the United States trace their roots to West Africa. They were torn from their cultures of origin between the 17th and 19th centuries when they were brought here as slaves. Blacks represent the only migrants to come to the Americas, North and South, against their will. Blacks from Africa were literally kidnap victims, kidnapped by Europeans, as well as purchased as captives by Yankee traders. This has made African Americans, as a group, very different from immigrants, who chose to come to the United States to better their lives, and different from refugees, who fled their homelands to escape religious or political persecution.

The very word *slave* carries the connotation of an "inferior" being; slaves were counted as three-fifths of a person during census-taking. Slave owners inwardly understood that treating people as animals to be owned, worked, and sold was immoral, but they wanted to think of themselves as good religious, moral people. Hence they had to convince themselves that their slaves were not really human, but a lower form of life. They focused on racial differences (skin color, hair texture, etc.) as "proof" that black people were not really people after all. Racism began, then, as an airtight alibi for a horrifying injustice. The notion of the slave (and by extension, any African American) as less than human has created great psychological and social problems for succeeding generations of both black and white citizens. Slavery lead to a system of inferior housing, schools, health care, and jobs for black people, which persists to this day.

The institution of slavery formally ended in 1863, but the racist ideas born of slavery have persisted. These ideas continue even now to leave deep scars on many African Americans. Today, particularly in the lower-socioeconomic classes, many blacks continue to suffer from the psychological heritage of slavery, as well as from active, current discrimination that still prevents them from equal opportunity in many realms of life.

Until recently, the "public" history that many Americans learned presented a distorted, incomplete picture of black family life (emphasizing breakdown) during the slave era, which had crippling effects on families for generations to come. This version of history never examined the moral strength of the slaves or the community solidarity and family loyalty that arose after emancipation. There is no doubt that these strengths have positively affected the rebuilding of the African American community.

> According to almost all witnesses, the roads of the South were clogged in 1865 [after emancipation] with Black men and women searching for long-lost wives, husbands, children, brothers and sisters. The in-gathering continued for several years and began in most communities with mass marriage ceremonies that legalized the slave vows. This was a voluntary process for husbands and wives who were free to renounce slave vows and search for new mates. Significantly, most freedmen, some of them 80 and 90 years old, decided to remain with their old mates, thereby giving irrefutable testimony on the meaning of their love. (Bennett, 1989)

Despite slave owners' attempts to destroy black family life, some slaves did manage to form lasting families headed by a mother and a father, and many slave couples enjoyed long marriages. Although white slave masters would often do everything possible to pull families apart (including the forced "breeding" and the selling of slaves), there is evidence that slaves maintained their family connections as best as they could and produced stable units with admirable values. According to U.S. Historian Char Miller, "Despite the fact that slavery tore apart many families, blacks maintained links, loves, and relationships just as anyone else would under these circumstances" (personal communication, November 2003).

The more accurate version of history counters the impression that all slave families were so helpless that they were always torn apart and could never reestablish themselves, or that their social relationships were chaotic and amoral. The resolve of large numbers of blacks to rebuild their families and communities as soon as they were freed represents an impressive determination in a people who survived one of the most brutal forms of servitude that history has seen. African American survival, and consequently, African American contributions to American society, deserve a high level of respect and testify to a people's great strength. It is not within the scope of this chapter to discuss African American contributions to society, but suffice it to say that frequently the perceptions of some people in law enforcement are often conditioned by their exposure to the black underclass, for whom crime is a way of life.

Law Enforcement Interaction with African Americans: Historical Baggage

> Many of the police and African-American problems in our communities today go way back and stem from history. Some of the issues can be traced directly from the Civil War reconstruction era, in slavery days, when police and the army were required to return runaway slaves. (G. Perry, 2003)

In the United States during the late 17th and 18th centuries, following slave uprisings in a number of colonies, the colonists created strict laws to contain the slaves. Even minor offenses were punished harshly. This set the negative tone between law enforcement and blacks. American police were called on to form "slave patrols" and to enforce racially biased laws (Williams & Murphy, 1990). In many areas of the country, police were expected to continue enforcing deeply biased, discriminatory laws (including those setting curfews for blacks, and barring blacks from many facilities and activities). Today, segments of the African American population continue to struggle with interaction with the police. "The fact that the legal order not only countenanced but sustained slavery, segregation and discrimination for most of our Nation's history—and the fact that the police were bound to uphold that order—set a pattern for police behavior and attitudes toward black communities that has persisted until the present day. That pattern includes the idea that blacks have fewer civil rights, that the task of the police is to keep them under control, and that the police have little responsibility for protecting them from crime within their communities" (Williams & Murphy, 1990).

Most police officers have had some exposure to the historical precedents of poor relationships between police and minority communities. The damages of the past give us no choice but to make a greater effort, today, with groups such as African Americans, for whom contact with law enforcement has long been problematic.

DEMOGRAPHICS: DIVERSITY AMONG AFRICAN AMERICANS*

Currently, blacks comprise approximately 35 million people, or about 13 percent of the population of the United States (U.S. Bureau of the Census, 2000). Until the last few decades, the vast majority lived in the south. Between 1940 and 1970, over 1.5 million blacks migrated initially to the north and then to the west coast, largely seeking better job opportunities. Historically, over 50 percent of the black population has lived in urban areas. Since 1980, that number has decreased slightly, to where 12.5 percent live in nonmetropolitan areas and 36 percent live in suburban areas, up from 21.2 percent in

---

*Refer back to Chapter 1, "The Overlap of Race, Culture and Ethnicity," for information about individuals who do not "neatly" fit into one demographic category such as black.

1980 (Frey, 1998). The rural black population has decreased and the shifting flow has contributed to the increase in numbers in suburban areas (some rural blacks may migrate directly into the inner city while others may move to more suburban areas; the flow is not actually known). In any case, urban cores experience cycles of repopulation, mainly by blacks, Hispanics, and various new immigrant groups. The most vivid example is the city of Detroit, where approximately 85 percent of the population is black, while most whites and immigrant groups have settled in outlying areas. Similarly, other cities, such as Washington D.C., St. Louis, Chicago, and Cleveland, are populated mainly by blacks and new immigrants, creating layers of tension where diverse groups with conflicting values and customs suddenly find themselves crowded into the same urban neighborhoods.

Between 1970 and 1980, 3.5 million blacks and Hispanics moved to cities that had been abandoned by more than 3 million white residents (Lohman, 1977). These population shifts have created "two Americas." One America is the world of the suburbs, where schools, recreational facilities, and community resources are far better. The other is the inner city, where many African Americans (as well as Latinos and other diverse groups) have much poorer access to educational and job opportunities and where living conditions are often closer to those of cities in the ravaged developing world than to those of America's comfortable suburban environment.

Although many African Americans belong to the lower socioeconomic classes, blacks are represented in all the classes, from the extremely poor to the extremely affluent, and have moved increasingly into the middle classes. As with all ethnic groups, there are significant class-related differences among blacks, affecting values and behavior. It is no more true to say that a poor black has a great deal in common with an affluent black than to say that poor and rich whites are the same. (Later in this chapter we discuss stereotyping of all blacks based on the black underclass.) However, color, more so than class, often determines how the larger society reacts to and treats blacks. Therefore, the racial (as opposed to cultural) experience of many African Americans in the United States is similar, regardless of an individual's level of prosperity or education.

The cultural diversity that exists among African Americans is related to a variety of factors. Over the last 400 years, black families have come from many different countries (e.g., Jamaica, Trinidad, Belize, Haiti, Puerto Rico). By far, the largest group's forefathers came directly to the United States from Africa. In addition, there are cultural differences among African Americans related to the region of the country from which they came. As with whites, there are "southern" and "northern" characteristics as well as urban and rural characteristics.

Religious backgrounds vary, but the majority of American-born blacks are Protestant, and many are specifically Baptist. The first black-run, black-controlled denomination in the country was the African Methodist Episcopal church (which was created because churches in the north and south either banned blacks or required them to sit apart from whites). In addition, a percentage of blacks belong to the Black Muslim religion, including the "Nation of Islam" and "American Muslim Mission." (The term Black Muslim is often used but is rejected by some members of the religion.) There are also sizable and fast-growing black populations among members of the Seventh-Day Adventists, Jehovah's Witnesses, Pentecostals (especially among Spanish-speaking blacks), and especially among blacks of Caribbean origin, Santeria, Candomble, Voudun, and similar sects blending Catholic and West African (mainly Yoruba) beliefs and rituals. Rastafarianism has spread far beyond its native Jamaica to become an influential religious movement among immigrants from many other English-speaking Caribbean nations.

ISSUES OF IDENTITY

In the 1960s and 1970s the civil rights and Black Pride movements marked a new direction in black identity. The civil rights movement opened many barriers to educational and employment opportunities and to active political involvement. Some adults marched in the civil rights movement knowing that they themselves might never benefit directly from civil rights' advances: They hoped that their efforts in the struggle would improve the lives of their children. The middle-class youths who attended community churches and black colleges became the leaders in the movement for equal rights (McAdoo, 1992).

Many blacks (both American-born and Caribbean-born), inspired by a growing sense of community identification and increased pride in racial identity, have determined to learn more about Africa. Despite the great differences in culture between African Americans and Africans, blacks throughout this hemisphere are discovering that they can take pride in the richness of their African heritage, including its high ethical values and community cohesiveness. Examples of African culture that have influenced American black culture or are held in high esteem by many African Americans are (Walker, 1982):

- Cooperative interdependence among and between people (contrasted with Western individualism)
- Partnership with nature and with the spirit world reflected in the approach to ecology and in communication with the spirit world (closer to Native American beliefs)
- Balance and harmony among all living things, reflected in the placing of human relations as a priority value (contrasted with the Western view of achievement and "doing" as taking priority over the nurturing of human relations)
- Joy and celebration in life itself
- Time as a spiral, focused on "now" (contrasted with the Western view of time as "money," and time running away from us)
- Focus on the group and not on the individual
- Giving of self to community
- Renewed interest in respecting elders

The combination of the Black Pride movement of the 1960s and 1970s and the more current focus on cultural roots has freed many African Americans from the "slave mentality" that continued to haunt the African American culture long after emancipation. A new pride in race and heritage has, for some, replaced the sense of inferiority fostered by white racial supremacist attitudes.

GROUP IDENTIFICATION TERMS

Several ethnic groups, in a positive evolution of their identity and pride, have initiated name changes for their group, including African Americans. This is not confusion (although it can be confusing), but rather represents, on the part of group members, growth and a desire to name themselves rather than be named by the dominant society. Until approximately the early 1990s, the most widely accepted term was "black," this term having replaced "Negro" (which, in turn, replaced "colored people"). "Negro" has been out of use for at least two decades, although some older blacks still use the term (as do some younger African Americans among themselves). To many, the term Negro symbolizes what the African American became under slavery. The replacement of "Negro" with "black" came to symbolize racial pride. (The exception to the use of "Negro" and "colored" is in titles like "United Negro College" and "National Association of Colored People [NAACP].") African American, a term preferred by many, focuses on positive historical and cultural roots rather than race or skin color.

In the 1990s, the usage of the term "African American" grew in popularity. (It is the equivalent of, for example, Italian American or Polish American.) Many feel that the word "black" is no more appropriate in describing skin color than is "white." (Yet, some Americans who are black do not identify with "African American," as it does not fully represent their background, which may be Caribbean or Haitian; they may not identify with the "African" part at all.) Since the 1980s and early 1990s, the term "people of color" has sometimes been used, but this catch-all phrase has limited use for police officers, as it is used to describe anyone who is not white and can include Asian/Pacific Americans, Latino/Hispanic Americans, and Native Americans. Indeed, there is much controversy and history associated with broad, collective terms that attempt to too quickly categorize people.

The use of the words "nigger," "boy," or "coon" are never acceptable at any time and especially in crime-fighting and peacekeeping, no matter how provoked an officer may be. (Although you may hear black youths using "nigger" to refer to each other, the word is absolutely taboo for outsiders—especially outsiders wearing badges.) Police who do not like to be called "pigs" can certainly relate to a person's feelings about being called "gorilla." Officers hearing these types of labels used in their own departments, even when they are not being used to address somebody directly, should remind their peers of the lack of professionalism and prejudice that those terms convey. Officers who fall into the habit of using these words in what they think are harmless situations may find that they are unable to control themselves during more volatile situations with citizens.

MYTHS AND STEREOTYPES

Many of the impressions that people in the society (and consequently, in law enforcement) form about African Americans come from their exposure to messages and images in the media about African Americans. Here the phenomenon of stereotyping is as much at work as it is when citizens see all police officers as repressive and capable of brutality. Police officers know that they will all take a beating nationwide when there is publicity about an instance of police brutality against blacks or reports of racial profiling.

The white majority's view of blacks reflects the same problem. Those who are bent toward prejudice may feel that their racism is justified whenever a crime involving an African American makes the evening news. A suburban African American mother addressing a community forum on racism pointed out: "Every time I hear that there has been a murder or a rape, I pray that it is not a black who committed the crime. The minute the media reports that a black person is responsible for a crime, all of us suffer.

When something negative happens, I am no longer seen as an individual with the same values and hopes as my white neighbors. I become a symbol, and more so my husband and sons, become feared. People treat us with caution and politeness, but inside we know that their stereotypes of the worst, criminal element of blacks have become activated" (personal communication, source wishes to remain anonymous).

Even the fact of a crime rate that is disproportionately high among young black males does not justify sweeping statements about all African Americans. Certainly, 36 million African Americans cannot be judged by a statistic about the criminal element. Unfortunately for the vast majority of the African American population, some whites do base their image of all blacks largely on the actions, including criminal behavior, of the black members of America's "underclass." It is well known that women clutch their purses harder when they see a black man approaching. Similarly, officers have been known to stop blacks and question them simply for not "looking like they belong to a certain neighborhood." (This is discussed and illustrated further in this chapter as well as in Chapter 14.) Many people, including whites and Asians, often harbor unreasonable fears about black people. Having never had a black friend or acquaintance, they feed such fears, instead of reaching out to meet or get to know people who look different from themselves.

African Americans have to contend with many myths and stereotypes that are central to a prejudiced person's thinking. For example, one myth, related to "raw and uncontrolled sex," leads people to believe that blacks have no morals, easily surrender to their "instincts," and can't practice self-restraint (Bennett, 1989). This type of thinking gives some people a sense of moral superiority over blacks for what they perceive to be black sexual habits. In a nationwide survey on sex practices of married couples, including adultery, it was found that blacks are no more likely (or, expressed differently, precisely as likely) as whites to commit adultery. White sexuality never became a racial issue during the interlude of highly publicized "wife swapping" among middle- and upper-class suburbanites, nor did white sexuality become an issue during the 1960s and 1970s when many young people (e.g., white "hippies" in the 1960s and whites on the singles-bar scene a few years later) engaged in widespread sexual promiscuity. Although these practices were often criticized, the white racial element was ignored.

For African Americans race has historically been connected to sexuality in ways that it would never occur to people to do with whites. This is another legacy of slavery and of the self-justifying racist thinking that arose from that institution. Many slave owners routinely and brutally raped their female slaves (often even before puberty), as well as forced their healthiest slaves to couple and breed regardless of the slaves' own attachments and preferences. (The fact that many African American's genetic background is part Caucasian is testimony to the slave owners' "tendencies" to violate slave girls and women.) While using slaves to indulge their desires, white slave owners convinced themselves that Africans had no morals and would couple indiscriminately like animals if left to do so. Like the myth of black inferiority, the white view of black sexuality was shaped by the need of slave owners to find an excuse for their cruel and unjust behavior.

CROSS-RACIAL PERCEPTIONS IN LAW ENFORCEMENT

Prejudice, lack of contact, and ignorance lend themselves to groups' developing perceptions about the other that are often based on biased beliefs. Unfortunately, perceptions are reality for the individuals and groups who hold them. Perceptions are seen as

BLACK MALE	WHITE MALE
Arrogant	Confident
Chip on shoulder	Self-assured
Aggressive	Assertive
Dominant personality	Natural leader
Violence prone	Wayward
Naturally gifted	Smart
Sexual prowess	Sexual experimentation

Exhibit 6.1   Are People Viewed in Equal Terms?

the truth, whether or not they are the truth. Exhibit 6.1 illustrates differing perceptions that some members of the dominant society have toward black and white males. In this case, the media and popular literature have contributed to the differing perceptions.

How about perceptions that African Americans have developed of police officers' actions? Because of a past history of prejudice and discrimination toward blacks, police officers have used techniques that indeed continue to create perceptions among many African Americans. In other words, while some officers no longer exhibit racist actions, the perceptions remain. The description of perceptions as listed in Exhibit 6.2 were presented to northern California police officers in the early 1990s by then vice president of the Alameda, California, NAACP chapter (the late Al Dewitt). When Dewitt presented these perceptions to police officers, he explained that, over time, African

POLICE ACTION	BLACK PERCEPTION
Being stopped or expelled from so-called "white neighborhoods."	Whites want blacks to "stay in their place."
Immediately suspecting and reacting to blacks without distinction between dope dealer and plainclothes police officer.	Police view black skin itself as probable cause.
Using unreasonable force, beatings, adding charges.	When stopped, blacks must be submissive or else.
Negative attitudes, jokes, body language, talking down to people.	Officers are racists.
Quick trigger, take-downs, accidental shootings.	Bad attitudes will come out under stress.
Slow response, low priority, low apprehension rate.	Black-on-black crime not important.
Techniques of enforcing local restrictions and white political interests.	Police are the strong arm for the status quo.
Police stick together, right or wrong.	We-against-them mentality; they stick together . . . we have to stick together

Exhibit 6.2   Perceptions of Police Officers' Actions by Some Blacks

Americans formed perceptions about police behavior that lead to a lack of trust, riots, and race problems. According to Glenn Perry, the perceptions listed in Exhibit 6.2 are still entirely valid today. However, due to increased educational requirements and professional standards for police officers, the perceptions, fortunately, do not exist equally everywhere, and vary by jurisdiction. Improving and preventing racial misperceptions will take time and effort on the part of the officer, but will inevitably benefit him or her by way of increased cooperation and officer safety.

THE AFRICAN AMERICAN FAMILY

African American families generally enjoy very strong ties among extended family members, especially among women. Female relatives will often substitute for each other in filling family roles; for example, a grandmother or aunt may raise a child if the mother is unable to do so. Sometimes several different family groups may share one house. When there is a problem (i.e., an incident that has brought an officer to the house), extended family members are likely to be present and to want to help. An officer may observe a number of uncles, aunts, brothers, sisters, sweethearts, and friends who are loosely attached to the black household. Enlisting the aid of any of these household members (no matter what the relationship) can be beneficial.

The Role of the Man and the Woman

A widespread myth holds that African American culture is a matriarchy, with one or more women heading the typical household. Historically, it is true that women did play a crucial role in the family, because of repeated attempts to break down "black manhood" (Bennett, 1989). However, in a true matriarchy (female-ruled society), women control property and economic activities. This is not generally true of black America, but outsiders often assume that African American women are always the heads of the household. In the 1960s and 1970s, for instance, the media stereotyped the black mother as loud and domineering, clearly the boss. In addition, African American women have, in a sense, been considered less of a threat to the status quo than the African American male, and consequently have been able to be more assertive in public. Historically, in contacts with law enforcement, an African American man may feel that, unlike a woman, he risks arrest or at least mistreatment if he "talks back."

African American fathers, regardless of income, usually view themselves as heads of the household (Hines & Boyd-Franklin, 1982), and thus any major decisions regarding the family should include the father's participation. It is insulting to the father when, with both parents present, officers automatically focus on the mother. An assertive mother does not mean that the father is passive or indifferent, and a father's silence does not necessarily indicate agreement. It is always worthwhile to get his view of the situation.

The Single Mother

Feeding the stereotype of the female-headed black household is the fact that in many urban African American homes, no father is present. In 1965, about 25 percent of African American families nationally were headed by women. Between 1970 and

1997, births to single African American women increased by 93 percent, resulting in 68.4 percent of black births being to single women in 2001. Police observed that in some urban core areas (particularly in housing projects) in 2000, it was not uncommon to find nearly 90 percent of African American women living alone with children.

The single mother, particularly in the inner city, does not always receive the respect that she is due; outsiders may be critical of the way she lives—or the way they think she lives. She is often stereotyped by officers who doubt their own effectiveness in the urban black community. For instance, an unmarried welfare mother who has just had a fight with her boyfriend should receive the same professional courtesy that a married suburban mother is likely to receive from an officer of the same background. In practice, this is not always the case. Some officers may mistakenly speak to the single African American mother as if she were a slut, or treat her callously as though "She's seen it all and done it all; therefore, it does not matter how I [the officer] treat her." (A complaint frequently heard in the African American community by women is that white men, in particular, treat the African American woman poorly. This means that they feel comfortable using profanity in the woman's presence and treat them with little respect.)

Deputy Chief Ondre Berry offers advice regarding relations between the peace officer and the single African American mother. He advises officers to go out of their way to establish rapport and trust. Following are his suggestions for assisting the single mother:

- Offer extra assistance to low-income mothers.

- Proactively engage youth and encourage them to participate in organized social activities.

- Show warmth to the children (e.g., touch them,) as one would to any traumatized child.

- Offer the children something special, such as toy badges or other police souvenirs.

- Give your business card to the mothers to show that you are available for further contact.

- Make follow-up visits when there are not problems so that the mother and the children can associate the officer with good times.

- Carefully explain to the mother her rights.

- Use the same discretion you might use with another minor's first petty offense (e.g., shoplifting), simply by bringing the child home and talking with the mother and child, rather than sending the child immediately to juvenile hall.

All of these actions will build a perception on the part of the African American single mother (and her children) that you can be trusted and that you are there to help. "Since you are dealing with history, you have to knock down barriers and work harder with this group than with any other group" (Berry, 2003).

Children/Adolescents/Youth

Since there are so many homes, especially in the inner city, in which the father is absent, young boys in their middle childhood years (7 to 11) are at real risk and school is often where serious behavior problems show up. According to Berry, many single mothers unwittingly place their young sons in the position of "father," giving them the message that they have to take care of the family. These young children can get the mistaken impression that they are the heads of the household, and in school situations, they may try to control the teacher—who is often female and often white. Berry observed that many young boys are placed in special education programs because they have been belligerent and domineering with the teacher. What these boys lack is an older male role model who can help them to grow into the appropriate behavior. An officer who refers these children to agencies that can provide such role models (even if only on a limited-time basis) will gain the family's and community's trust and respect. Eventually, he or she will win more cooperation from community members.

Among older African American male children, especially in inner cities, statistics indicate a disproportionately high crime rate, stemming from the difficult economic conditions of their lives. Officers have to remind themselves that the majority of African American teenagers, regardless of economic condition, are law-abiding citizens. Perfectly responsible African American teens and young adults report being stopped on a regular basis by officers when they are in predominantly "white neighborhoods" (including those where they happen to live). A 19-year-old African American male living in an upper-middle-class suburban neighborhood in Fremont, California, reported that he was stopped and questioned four times in two weeks by different officers. On one occasion, the conversation went this way:

Officer: "What are you doing here?"

Teen: "I'm jogging, sir."

Officer: "Why are you in this neighborhood?"

Teen: "I live here, sir."

Officer: "Where?"

Teen: "Over there, in that big house on the hill."

Officer: "Can you prove that? Show me your I.D."

On another occasion, when he was jogging, a different officer stopped him and asked (referring to the very expensive jogging shoes he was wearing), "Where did you get those shoes?" When the boy answered that he had bought them, the next question was, "Where do you live?" When the teen answered, "In that large house on the hill," the officer apologized and went on his way. (Racial profiling is discussed further in this chapter, and in Chapter 14.)

LANGUAGE AND COMMUNICATION

Racial conflicts between African Americans and non–African American citizens can cover up cultural differences, which until recently, have been largely ignored or minimized. Yet many would acknowledge that cultural differences between, for example, a white officer and a Vietnamese citizen could potentially affect their respective communication as well as their perceptions of each other. Similarly, culture comes into play when looking at patterns of language and communication among many African Americans.

"Ebonics" or African American Vernacular English

"The use of [what has been called] black language does not represent any pathology in blacks. . . . The beginning of racial understanding is the acceptance that difference is just what it is: different, not inferior. And equality does not mean sameness" (Weber, 1991).

There are many varieties of English that are not "substandard," "deficient," or "impoverished" versions of the language. Instead, they often have a complete and consistent set of grammatical rules and may represent the rich cultures of the groups that use them. For example, Asian Indians speak a variety of English somewhat unfamiliar to Americans, while the British speak numerous dialects of British English, each of them containing distinctive grammatical structures and vocabulary not used by Americans. Similarly, some African Americans speak a variety of English that historically has been labeled as substandard because of a lack of understanding of its origins.

Many African Americans use (or have used at least some of the time) what has been called "black English," African American Vernacular English, or Ebonics. While some African Americans speak this variety of English, many enjoy the flexibility and expressiveness of speaking Ebonics among peers, and switching to "standard English" when the situation calls for it (e.g., at work, in interviews, with white friends).

Most language and dialect researchers accept the notion that Ebonics is a dialect with its own rules of grammar and structure (Labov, 1972). To many white people, Ebonics merely sounds "southern." However, the fact that some of the same grammatical structures—spoken in a wholly different accent—are found throughout the English-speaking Caribbean (as far south as Trinidad, 8 miles north of Venezuela) points to an earlier, African origin for the grammar. Linguists have done years of research on the origins of Ebonics and now believe that it developed from the grammatical structures common to several West African tribal languages. For example:

Ebonics:	You lookin' good.
Standard English:	You look good right now.
Ebonics:	You be looking good.
Standard English:	You usually look good.

That is, the presence of the word "be" indicates a general condition and not something related only to the present. Apparently, some West African languages have grammatical structures expressing these same concepts of time. Nonetheless, many people cling to an unscientific (and racist) view of language varieties of African Americans.

One [view] says that there was African influence in the development of the language and the other that says there was not. Those who reject African influence believe that the African arrived in the United States and tried to speak English. And [according to this first view,] because he lacked certain intellectual and physical attributes, he failed. This hypothesis makes no attempt to examine the . . . structures of West African languages to see if there are any similarities. . . . When the German said zis instead of this, America understood. But, when the African said dis [instead of this], no one considered the fact that [the sound] *th* may not exist in African languages. (Weber, 1991)

Slaves developed black English to overcome the differences in their tribal languages and communicate with one another and with their English-speaking slave masters. They also developed a type of "code language" so that they could speak and not be understood by their slave owners.

Many people still assume that Ebonics is "bad" English, and they display their contempt nonverbally, either facially or through an impatient tone of voice. They may interrupt and finish the speaker's sentences for him or her, as though that person were unable to speak for him- or herself. Acceptance of another person's variety of English can go a long way toward establishing rapport. People interacting with blacks who do not use standard English should realize that blacks are not making random "mistakes" when they speak and that they are not necessarily speaking badly. In fact, verbal skill is a highly prized value in most African-based cultures.

Finally, attempting to establish trust and rebuild relations with a people who historically have not been able to trust the police, white officers should not try to imitate black accents, dialects, and styles of speaking. Imitation can be very insulting and may give blacks the impression that they are being ridiculed—or that the officer is seriously uncomfortable with them. (This was elaborated on in Chapter 5.) Officers should not try to fake a style that is culturally different from their own. Being authentic and sincere when communicating with all people, while remaining aware and accepting of differences, is key to beginning to build better relationships with people.

Nonverbal Communication: Style and Stance

Black social scientists have been studying aspects of black nonverbal communication, which have been often misunderstood by people in positions of authority. Psychologist Richard Majors at the University of Wisconsin termed a certain stance and posturing as the "cool pose," which is demonstrated by many young black men from the inner city. "While the cool pose is often misread by teachers, principals and police officers as an attitude of defiance, psychologists who have studied it say it is a way for black youths to maintain a sense of integrity and suppress rage at being blocked from usual routes to esteem and success" (Goleman, 1992).

Majors explains that while the "cool pose" is not found among the majority of black men, it is commonly seen among inner-city youth as a "tactic for . . . survival to cope with such rejections as storekeepers who refuse to buzz them into a locked shop." The goal of the pose is to give the appearance of being in control. However, a storekeeper, a passerby, or a police officer may perceive this stance as threatening, so a negative dynamic enters the interaction (e.g., the officer seeing the "cool pose" feels threatened, and then becomes more authoritarian in response). This form of nonverbal communication may include certain movements and postures designed to emphasize the youth's masculinity. The pose involves a certain way of walking, standing, talking, and remaining aloof facially. The pose, writes Majors, is a way of saying, "[I'm] strong and proud, despite [my] status in American society" (Goleman, 1992).

A Harvard Medical School psychiatrist, Dr. Alvin Poussaint (1992), points out that because so many inner-city male youths have no male role models in their families, they feel a need to display their manliness. Problems occur when others read their nonverbal language as a sign of irresponsibility, apathy, defiance, and/or laziness. With the knowledge that for some black youths, the "cool pose" is not intended to be a personal threat, officers should be less on the defensive (and, consequently, less on the offensive) when observing this style.

In a *20/20* broadcast entitled "Presumed Guilty" (ABC News, 1992), the mother of an African American pre-med student referred to style and communication: "They don't have to be doing anything but being who they are, and that's young black men, with a rhythm in their walk and an attitude about who they are, and expressing their pride and culture by the clothes they choose to wear." This young man had been stopped on numerous occasions for no apparent reason. (This subject is discussed in the section "Differential Treatment" later in this chapter.)

Verbal Expressiveness and Emotionalism

> The ebonics vernacular style of speech emphasizes emotional response—being "real" is the term. This means it is OK to express one's indignation, to be emotional and to express to someone how you feel. Many African Americans perceive that the mainstream culture is taught to shut down and control their emotions. This is a cultural difference that can be misunderstood by law enforcement. (Perry, 2003)

Linguist and sociologist Thomas Kochman has devoted his professional life to studying differences in black and white culture that contribute to misunderstandings and misperceptions. Chicago's African American mayor Harold Washington passed out copies of Kochman's book *Black and White Styles in Conflict* (1981) to the city hall press corps because he believed that he was seriously misunderstood by the whites of the city. According to Kochman, "If a person doesn't know the difference in cultures, that's ignorance. But if a person knows the difference and still says that mainstream culture is best, that 'white is right,' then you've got racism."

Kochman (1981) explains in *Black and White Styles in Conflict* (which is still used widely) that blacks and whites have different perspectives and approaches to many issues, including conversation, public speaking, and power. This notion is supported in the following advice to police officers: "Don't get nuts when you encounter an African American who is louder and more emotional than you are. Watch the voice patterns and the tone. Blacks can sound militant [even when they are not]. Blacks have been taught (i.e., socialized) to be outwardly and openly emotional. Sometimes we are emotional first and then calm down and become more rationale" (Berry, December, 2003). Berry went on to say that often whites are rational at first but express more emotion as they lose control. This cultural difference has obvious implications for overall communication, including how to approach and react to angry citizens.

Kochman (1981) explains that many "whites [are] able practitioners of self-restraint [and that] this practice has an inhibiting effect on their ability to be spontaneously self-assertive." He continues to explain that "the level of energy and spiritual intensity that blacks generate is one that they can manage comfortably but whites can only manage with effort." The problems in interaction come about because neither race understands that there is a cultural difference between them. Kochman states: "Blacks do not initially see this relative mismatch, because they believe that their normal animated style is not disabling to whites. . . . Whites are worried that blacks cannot sustain such intense levels of interaction without losing self-control [because that degree of 'letting go' of emotions for a white would signify a lack of control]." In other words, a white person or an Asian, for that matter, unaware of the acceptability in black culture of expressing intense emotion (including rage) may not be able to imagine that he, himself, could express such intense emotion without losing control. He may feel threatened, convinced that the ventilation of such hostility will surely lead to a physical confrontation.

While racism may also be a factor for some in communication breakdowns, differing conventions of speech do contribute in ways that are not always apparent. In several cultural awareness training sessions, police officers have reported that neighbors (non-African Americans), upon hearing highly emotional discussions (among African Americans), called to report fights. When the police arrived on the scene of the "fight," the so-called guilty ones responded that they were not fighting, just talking. While continuing to respond to all calls, officers can still be aware of different perceptions of what constitutes a fight. Although you can never make any automatic assumptions, an awareness of style can affect the way you approach the citizen.

Berry illustrated how a white police officer can let his own cultural interpretations of black anger and emotionalism influence judgment. He spoke of a fellow officer who made the statement: "Once they [i.e., blacks] took me on, I wanted to take control." This officer, working in a predominantly black area for a 3-month period, made 120 stops and 42 arrests (mainly petty offenses such as prowling and failure to identify). He then worked in a predominantly white area for the same period of time, making 122 stops and only six arrests. The officer went on to say, "One group will do what I ask; the other will ask questions and challenge me." His need to "take control" over people whom he perceived to be out of control was so extreme, it resulted in his getting sued (Berry, 2003). His perception of the level of threat involved was much higher in the black community than in the white community. One of the factors involved was, undoubtedly, this officer's inability to deal with being "taken on." If he had used communication skills to defuse citizens' anger rather than to escalate it, he might have been able to work situations around to his advantage rather than creating confrontations. Listening professionally, instead of engaging in shouting matches with citizens of other backgrounds, can require a great deal of self-control, but it will usually bring better results. (Once again, George Thompson of the Verbal Judo Institute reminds officers, "You are not paid to argue." See Chapter 4.)

Threats and Aggressive Behavior

Kochman, who has conducted cultural awareness training nationwide (for police departments as well as corporations) asks the question, "When does a fight begin?" Many whites, he notes, believe that "fighting" has already begun when it is "obvious" that there will be violence ("when violence is imminent"). Therefore, to whites, a fight begins as soon as the shouting starts. According to whites, then, the fight has begun whenever a certain intensity of anger is shown, along with an exchange of insults. If threats are also spoken, many whites would agree that violence is surely on its way.

Kochman explains that while the situation described above (verbal confrontation, threats) may indeed be a prelude to a fight for blacks, many blacks have a clear boundary between their fighting words and their physical actions. Kochman includes a quote to show how fighting does not begin until one person does something physically provocative: "If two guys are talking loudly and then one or the other starts to reduce the distance between them, that's a sign, because it's important to get in the first blow. Or if a guy puts his hand in his pocket, and that's not a movement he usually makes, then you watch for that—he might be reaching for a knife. But if they're just talking— it doesn't matter how loud it gets—then you got nothing to worry about" (Allen Harris, quoted in Kochman, 1981).

Of course, officers who are trained to think about officer safety might have a problem accepting this dismissal ("then you got nothing to worry about"). Similarly, a threat in today's society, where anyone may be carrying semiautomatic weapons, may be just that—a very real threat that will be carried out. A threat must always be taken seriously by officers. However, there can be instances when cultural differences are at work and extreme anger can be expressed without accompanying physical violence. When this is the case, an officer can actually escalate hostilities with an approach and communication style that demonstrates no understanding toward culturally/racially different modes of expression.

KEY ISSUES IN LAW ENFORCEMENT

Differential Treatment

The results of a national survey, entitled *Police Attitudes Toward Abuse of Authority*, showed race to be a divisive issue for American police. In particular, black and non-black officers had significantly different views about the effect of a citizen's race and socioeconomic status on the likelihood of police abuse of authority. (Weisburd & Greenspan, 2000).

"I am not prejudiced. I treat all citizens fairly." This type of statement can be heard by police officers around the country. Inevitably, this statement holds true for some officers (although explicit utterance of this type of statement usually signals prejudice). In the wake of many publicized allegations of differential treatment toward African Americans (and other groups), officers who do hold prejudices have to face them and recognize when the prejudices result in action:

> My partner and I several years ago went to an all-white night club. He found cocaine on this white couple. He poured it out and didn't make an arrest. Later we were at an all-black nightclub. He found marijuana on one individual and arrested him. I was shocked, but I didn't say anything at the time because I was fairly new to the department. He had told me on two occasions that he "enjoyed" working with black officers and "has no difficulty" with the black community. (African American police officer)

In an ABC *20/20* television segment entitled "Presumed Guilty," an undercover investigation set out to answer the question "Are black men being singled out by police, pulled over even when they're doing nothing wrong?" (This program was made in 1992 before the term "racial profiling" came into existence.) Many officers will deny that they are doing this, and register the counterpart complaint (heard repeatedly in cultural awareness training sessions), "They're always saying that I'm stopping them because they're black when, in fact, I've pulled them over because they have violated the law." African American parents continue to complain that their teenage and young adult children are pulled over or stopped as pedestrians and questioned when there has been no violation. How are these two viewpoints reconciled? How can perceptions be so far apart?

The truth most likely lies between the categorical denial of some police officers and the statement, "We're always being stopped only because we're black." Undoubtedly, there are police procedures of which citizens are unaware, and they do not see all the other people an officer stops in a typical day. However, the citizen is not getting paid to be professional, truthful, or even reasonable with the officer. We know that some officers feel that they are doing "good policing" when they stop citizens whom they feel will be guilty of a crime. However, this "feeling" for who may be guilty can actually be a reflection of a bias or assumption that substitutes for real "data." Observing and selecting "guilty-looking" motorists can be the result of unconscious biased thinking. (Refer to Chapter 14 for an explanation of the "Ladder of Inference" with respect to racial profiling.)

In a discussion of drug arrests among blacks, a high-ranking African American officer in a Southern California department made the following statement:

> When officers go out to make arrests, they'll go immediately into the inner city where they can find the "lowest hanging fruit." What I mean is . . . blacks are easy to identify, in the inner city they're standing out on the street and it's natural for officers to be suspicious and try to do their drug arrests there. But we all know that alcohol abuse is rampant among white kids and if we go to just about any campus, we'll find drugs. But that's not where officers first gravitate to. Whites don't stand on street corners, but they're still using drugs and alcohol pretty heavily . . .

Racial Profiling in the African American Community

> An ordinary commuter turns the key in the ignition, glances in the rear view mirror, and pulls away from the curb. Rounding the corner, his slightly worn tires slip on a fresh layer of light rain. He executes a perfect "California rolling stop" at an intersection and enters the freeway, accelerating to a comfortable 70 mph for the cruise into downtown. Our commuter just violated the traffic code at least four times, just as we all do each time we get behind the wheel. But if our commuter is a person of color, there's a good chance he won't make it to work without being pulled over for "driving while black or brown." (Opinion page, *San Diego Union*, October 2000)

> From: Beyond the Mythology of Racial Profiling by Linda Hills, Executive Director, ACLU of San Diego and Imperial Counties, Randa Trapp, President of NAACP of San Diego

Although "Presumed Guilty" (on the ABC news program *20/20*) was made in 1992, we know that the phenomenon of racial profiling (a term that was not used when the program was made) has always existed throughout America's history. In the program, the reporters cite the case of Al Joyner, Olympic track and field athlete, who at the time of that piece said that he "refused to drive the streets of L.A. for fear of the police." He was stopped because it was believed that he was driving a stolen car. Joyner was asked to walk with his hands behind his head when he noticed about five or six police cars "out there, and all of them in their gun position with their guns out on me." Joyner was instructed to get on his knees while his license plate was being checked. When the police discovered that the car was registered in his wife's name (Griffith-Joyner), the officers realized their mistake and let Joyner go. Joyner then drove less than two blocks before he was stopped again by the same group of officers. This time he was told that he was a suspect in a hit and run: The officers were looking for "a burgundy RX7; a black man with a baseball cap." Joyner explained to the *20/20* reporters: "I didn't have an RX7, but I am black with a baseball cap." This was one of the earlier, widely publicized cases of racial profiling.

Officers in cultural awareness training have said they have been surprised when suburban middle-class African Americans express as much anger and outrage about differential treatment, including racial profiling, as do poorer blacks in inner-city areas. Many middle- and upper-class parents whose children have experienced the types of stops described above are likely to be even less forgiving: Stops like these are painful indications, despite much hard-won social and economic success, that race prevails for some as the defining characteristic.

Racial profiling is not limited to police officers and stops of motorists or bicyclists. The case of Yvette Bradley at Newark International Airport in April 1999 is a widely publicized example in the context of searches and U.S. customs. Upon returning from Jamaica with her sister, Yvette Bradley, an African American advertising professional with SpikeDDB (a partnership between Spike Lee and DDB), was singled out to be strip-searched for no reason immediately apparent to her. Prior to the search, Ms. Bradley had observed "that during the search selection process, a disproportionately large percentage of black women were singled out for searches, while nearly all the white passengers, were allowed to continue on their way" (Bradley, 1999). Ms. Bradley filed a complaint with the customs officer in charge; the investigation revealed that she indeed was strip searched (by a female officer); the reason that was given had to do with the designer hat she was wearing (i.e., drugs could have been hidden in it). The search was a degrading and highly invasive physical probe, which did not yield any drugs or contrabands. Despite the reason given for the search, according to Ms. Bradley's testimony, none of the officers involved ever asked her to remove her hat nor did they examine it. Her sister, who was wearing a baseball hat, was also sent through to the secondary search area. But, apparently, the group of white college-age men nearby (all wearing baseball caps) were not asked to be searched. In Ms. Bradley's words:

> I felt completely degraded, and worst of all, helpless. My pride, self-respect and dignity were trampled on. I think that if I had been a blonde, blue-eyed white woman under the same circumstances this would not have happened to me. . . . My body and my civil liberties were violated because I am a black woman.

According to Hills and Trapp (2000), the U.S. Custom Service's own figures show that the "hit rates" for drugs and contrabands searches for people of color were actually lower than for whites, despite figures showing that over 43% of those searched were from minority groups. According to the Policy News and Information Services, Representative John Lewis (Georgia) formally petitioned the Treasury Department to investigate alleged racial and gender biases by U.S. Customs' officers at airports in the United States. Specifically, the petition comes as "lawsuits related to the filing of strip search allegations, including a class action law suit in Chicago by close to 100 women."

Law enforcement agents throughout the criminal justice system need to recognize that racial profiling is a reality. While recognizing that many stops are justified (and the citizen may be unaware of the reasons involved), stops or searches reflecting racial profiling represent one of the most persistent legacies of institutional and individual racism. (See Chapter 14 for a full treatment of the subject.)

Reactions to and Perceptions of Authority

As a response to a series of racial events (in California) that received national and international attention in the 1990s, including the beating of black motorist Rodney King in 1991, the riots in Los Angeles in 1992, and the trial of O.J Simpson in 1995, the Public Policy Institute of California asked two social scientists to begin a study in which ethnic reactions to legal authority were studied (Huo & Tyler, 2000). Following are three of the major findings of the study:*

- Compared to whites, African Americans (and Latinos) report lower levels of satisfaction with interactions with legal authorities. They also report less willingness than whites to comply with the directives of the authorities they deal with. This pattern of difference between minorities and whites was especially apparent among those who reported interactions with the police compared to those who reported interactions with authorities in court.

- Much of the difference between minorities and whites in their reactions to legal authorities can be accounted for by differences in their perceptions of how fairly or unfairly they were treated. When asked whether the legal authorities involved in their encounters used fair procedures to make decisions, African Americans (and Latinos) reported experiencing less procedural fairness than did whites.

- The perception of fair treatment and positive outcomes was the most important factor in forming reactions to encounters with the police and courts. It was more important than the concerns about the outcomes people received from legal authorities. This pattern held up across different situations and ethnic groups.

African Americans (and Latinos) are still reporting more negative treatment from legal authorities than whites. These perceptions, on the part of minorities, are significant in that they directly relate to compliance rates with authority among members of minority groups (Huo & Tyler, 2000). The study indicated that all groups were equally satisfied with their experiences in court, and that, as a result, there was compliance with court directives. However, African Americans (and Latinos) were less willing to comply with directives from police. The findings in this study were similar to results found from the Milwaukee Domestic Violence Experiment, conducted in 1997. In that study, African Americans (and Latinos) perceived that "legal authorities treated them with less procedural fairness than they do whites" (Paternoster, Bachman, Brame, & Sherman, 1997). The results of both these studies suggest that "group differences in perceived procedural fairness may lead to group differences in compliance with legal directives" (Huo & Tyler, 2000).

> Even as opinion polls across the country reflect the perception among both blacks and whites that race relations are improving, according to a 2003 ABC/*Washington Post* poll, only 28% of blacks think that they "receive equal treatments as whites from police," as opposed to 66% of whites, who believe that both groups are treated equally. The poll found that within the black

*1,500 residents of L.A. and Oakland, California, were questioned.

population, 65% of the men surveyed reported being stopped "just because of your race," as opposed to 22% of black women; from that, 61% of the women and 79% of the men said that blacks don't get the same treatment as whites from the police in their communities. (ABC NEWS/Washington Post Poll)

Excessive Force and Brutality

Patrolling the mean streets can be a dangerous and dehumanizing task for police officers. Drawing the line between necessary force and deliberate brutality is perhaps the toughest part of the job. . . . A career of confronting the vicious, conscienceless criminal-enemy frays the nerves. (Morrow, 1991)

The year 1992, with the case of Rodney King, brought public attention to the fact that excessive force and brutality were serious problems in America. The existence of brutality has been a problem that blacks and other racial and ethnic groups have asserted, but until the early 1990s (i.e., with several highly publicized cases), many whites either did not believe or closed their eyes to this reality. Nearly a decade after the Rodney King event, in 1999, Americans and citizens worldwide witnessed another incident of brutality against a black American, Abner Louima, a Haitian immigrant. The majority of officers around the nation do not use excessive force. Nevertheless, we know that police brutality is not yet a thing of the past.

Controlling racist behavior based on biases and prejudices must be a priority training issue in all departments across the country. (Chapter 1 deals with prejudices and biases.) Police departments need to recognize that reducing an officer's buildup of stress has to be addressed as frequently and seriously as, for example, self-defense. Finally, the individual officer must remember that even though abusive behavior from citizens constitutes one of the worst aspects of the job, it is not the citizens who have to behave like professionals.

Law Enforcement Interaction with Poor, Urban African American Communities

Many police officers feel that they are putting their lives in danger when going into certain communities, particularly those in urban areas where poverty and crime go hand in hand. As a result, some segments of the African American community feel police are not protecting them, and are extremely fearful of "black-on-black" crime. The increase in citizens' weapons in urban areas, including increased self-protective weaponry, contributes to defensive reactions among both the police and the citizens. There is a vicious cycle that escalates and reinforces hostilities. Police are often expected to solve the social ills of society, but have neither the resources nor the training to deal with problems that are rooted in historical, social, political, and economic factors. African Americans and police officers are often frustrated with each other and barriers seem insurmountable. While the following quote comes from a source in the early 1970s, the dynamic described below is still operative:

Many policemen find themselves on the alert for the slightest sign of disrespect. One author has shown [McNamara] that the police [officer] is often prepared to coerce respect and will use force if he feels his position is being challenged. Likewise, the attitudes and emotions of the black citizen may be similar when

> confronted with a police [officer]. Intervention by police is often seen as an infringement on the blacks' rights and as oppression by the white population. Consequently many blacks are on the alert for the slightest sign of disrespect that might be displayed by the police [officer]. (Cross & Renner, 1974)

Cross and Renner go on to explain that fear of belittlement and fear of danger operate for both the African American citizen and the officer, and these fears cause both sides to misinterpret what might otherwise be nonthreatening behavior. The problem often arises not from the reality of the situation but from the results of mutual fears. In some parts of the country, this is as true now as it was in the mid-1970s when the article cited above was written.

Social scientists have been studying the problems of inner-city young men, in particular, since this group is most endangered. Consider the following statistics:

> Authors of the National Urban League's report, the "State of Black America 2003," found that although "blacks make up about 12% of the nation's population, they account for nearly half of the people in prison." The authors said that the "incarceration disparities have been fueled by drug enforcement policies that have harsher effects on blacks . . . [who] account for 13% of the nation's drug users, but 35% of drug arrests and 53% of drug convictions." (Source: The National Urban League: The State of Black America 2003.) In 2000, blacks were 6 times more likely than whites to be murdered, and were 7 times more likely than whites to commit murder. The vast majority of murders for both blacks and whites were intra-racial. (Bureau of Justice Statistics, 2001)

> Homicide victimization rates for blacks have been at least five times those of whites for the last half century, sometimes reaching more than ten times the white rate. In 1996, blacks had the highest victimization rates at 29.8% per 100,000, compared to homicide rates of Hispanics (12.4%), American Indians (9.8%), non Hispanic whites and Asians (3.5% and 4.6%). (Council of Economic Advisors, 1998)

> Additionally, Clinton's Council of Economic Advisors found that "Discriminatory behavior on the part of police and elsewhere in the criminal justice system may contribute to blacks' high representation in arrests, convictions, and prison admissions." (Council of Economic Advisors, 1998)

African American Women and Police

It is beyond the scope of this book to delve into depth into the specific issues and attitudes of African American women toward police and authority. However, one area, in particular, is worthy of attention. There is a perception and, in some cases, the reality, that the rape of an African American woman has not always been considered as serious by law enforcement as the rape of a white woman either legally or psychologically (Wriggens, 1983; Wyatt, 1992). Some African American women perceive that their assailants are less likely to be tried and convicted. Perceptions by African American women are indeed supported by research (Wriggens, 1983; Wyatt, 1992).

Law enforcement officials alone cannot solve social ills but should realize that African Americans in disadvantaged communities desperately need excellent police protection. The perception that whites in middle-class communities are better served by the police forces naturally reinforces existing antipolice attitudes among the lower class.

Addressing the Needs of the Inner City

"Black-on-black crime seems to be tolerated and even accepted as inevitable" (1991). This statement, made by an African American chief of police in 1991, is as true today as it was then. African Americans and other racial and ethnic groups have criticized law enforcement for underpolicing in the inner city, however, progress has been made to improve relations between police and community members. There are currently more African American officers and police executives who are influencing and changing policy that directly affects police–black relations. Many departments (although by no means all) have put into writing strict rules regarding the use of excessive force, discourtesy, racial slurs, and aggressive patrol techniques. Police management in some locales is beginning to understand why many people in urban black communities believe they receive unequal police services.

Efforts Toward a Positive Relationship between Police and the Community

Communities and police departments differ widely in the way that they build positive relationships with each other. On the one hand, "consent decrees" have forced a change of inappropriate (prejudicial or unjust) behavior or actions. A consent decree is an-out-of court settlement whereby the accused party (i.e., accused of inappropriate behavior or actions) agrees to modify or change behavior rather than plead guilty or go through a hearing on charges brought to court (CSIS, 2003). It is beyond the scope of this chapter to delve into the details and the controversy surrounding consent decrees, however, there have been many in appropriate police actions within African American communities that have resulted in the implementation of consent decrees. Some police leaders believe that a consent decree is not a symbol of a positive relationship; at the same time, many community leaders have supported them. "One leader mentioned that the . . . decree had given the community greater confidence in the police. Another leader commented that the consent decree 'gave people an opportunity to feel as though they had a voice.' One community leader felt that some white and black officers were working better together and that they were responding more quickly to calls for service from the African American community. 'It seems they are trying to ask more questions and there is more respect for the community,' she said" (Davis, 2002).

While there is controversy around consent decrees, and some officers complain that they add too much paperwork and bureaucracy to their already demanding jobs, they serve a purpose. They are an attempt, on the part of the federal government, local and state police departments, and communities, to try to improve community–police interaction in a quick and dramatic manner. Some outcomes can be influenced informally and others by consent decrees. The key to improved relationships deeply rests upon all of the following:

- Leadership
- Vision
- Respect
- Goals

- Strategies
- Mutual benefits for police and community
- Effective communication and practices of both law enforcement agencies and the community

Added to all of the above, community members, leaders, and police officers need to rely upon private means . . . one-on-one and face-to-face interaction, as well as good-will, to improve relations. The following words are those of Detroit-based pastor and prominent leader in the African American community Ronald Griffin:

> Face-to-face contact opens up dialogue. We as human beings really say we lis-ten, but we often don't, and instead we come prepared to respond. So some-times we put up our defenses and get into attack mode. We're already predisposed and most of us, then, are willing and ready for battle. This leads to a lot of pointless negative action even if both sides have a lot in common. We have had executive officers come to church activities to encourage the mem-bers, and to help the members see officers in another light. So we're building on this, and learning to trust each other. There's nothing I can't ask of the precinct, and the same from them for me. (Griffin, 2003)

SUMMARY OF RECOMMENDATIONS FOR LAW ENFORCEMENT

1. The experience of slavery and racism as well as cultural differences have shaped African American culture.
   - Patterns of culture and communication among black Americans differ from those of white Americans. In face-to-face communication, officers should not ignore or downplay these differences.
2. For many African Americans, particularly those in the lower socioeconomic rungs of society, the history of slavery and later discrimination continues to leave its psychological scars.
   - Law enforcement officials, in particular, represent a system that has oppressed African Americans and other minorities. To protect and serve in many African American communities across the nation necessarily means that officers will need to go out of their way to establish trust and win cooperation.
3. The changing terms that African Americans have used to refer to themselves reflect stages of racial and cultural growth, as well as empowerment.
   - Respect the terms that African Americans prefer to use. "Negro" and "col-ored" are no longer used and have been replaced by "black" for the purposes of many police communications. However, in speech, many people prefer the term "African American." Officers can learn to become comfortable ask-ing a citizen which term he or she prefers if there is a need to refer to ethnic-ity in the conversation.
   - Officers are advised to stop each other when they hear offensive terms being used. Not only does this contribute to the first step of making a department free of overt prejudices, it will also help the individual officer to practice

control when he or she is faced with volatile citizens. An officer in the habit of using offensive terms may not be able to restrain him- or herself in public situations. Therefore, officers monitoring each other will ultimately be of benefit to the department.

4. African Americans react as negatively to stereotypes that they hear about themselves as officers do when they hear such statements as, "Police officers are biased against blacks" or "All police officers are capable of brutality."

- Many of the stereotypes about African Americans stem from ignorance as well as an impression people receive from the criminal element. Law enforcement officers, in particular, must be sensitive to how their own perceptions of African Americans are formed. The disproportionately high crime rate among African American males does not justify sweeping statements about the majority of African Americans, who are law-abiding citizens.

5. The predominance of households headed by women, particularly in the inner city, coupled with the myth of woman as the head of the household, has created situations where officers have dismissed the importance of the father.

- Despite common myths and stereotypes regarding the woman, officers should always approach the father to get his version of the story and to consider his opinions in decision making. If the father is ignored or not given much attention, he is certain to be offended.

6. Young African American males, in particular, and their parents (of all socioeconomic levels) feel a sense of outrage and injustice when officers stop them for no apparent reason.

- You will destroy any possibility of establishing trust (and later winning cooperation) for stopping people because it "looks like they don't belong in a given neighborhood." Every time an instance of this nature occurs, police–community and police–youth relations suffer.

7. The use of African American varieties of English does not represent any pathology or deficiency and is not a combination of random errors, but rather reflects patterns of grammar from some West African languages.

- Many people have strong biases against this variety of spoken English. Do not convey a lack of acceptance through disapproving facial expressions, a negative tone of voice, or a tendency to interrupt or finish the sentences for the other person.
- When it comes to "black English" or an accent, do not fake it in order to be accepted by the group. People will immediately pick up on your lack of sincerity; this, in and of itself, can create hostility.

8. People in positions of authority have often misunderstood aspects of black nonverbal communication, including what as been termed the "cool pose."

- Police officers may interpret certain ways of standing, walking, and dressing as defiant. This can create defensive reactions on the part of the police officer. In many cases, the police officer need not take this behavior personally or feel threatened.

9. Cultural differences in verbal communication can result in complete misinterpretation:
   - Do not necessarily equate an African American's expression of rage and verbal threats with a loss of control that leads automatically to violence. Within the cultural norms, it can be acceptable to be very expressive and emotional in speech. This is in contrast to an unspoken white mainstream norm, which discourages the open and free expression of emotion, especially anger.

10. The existence of racial profiling, excessive force, and brutality is still a reality in policing in the United States. When acts of bias, brutality, and injustice occur, everyone suffers, including officers and entire police departments.
    - Every officer should be on the lookout for unchecked biases within themselves and others that could result in inappropriate language or force with citizens of all backgrounds. This also involves awareness of one's own level of stress and frustration and having the means and support to release tension before it breaks loose in the streets.

11. A dynamic exists between some officers and African Americans, particularly in poor urban areas, whereby both the officer and the citizen are on the "alert" for the slightest sign of disrespect.
    - The fear that both the citizen and the officer experience can interfere with what may actually be a nonthreatening situation.
    - The police officer can be the one to break the cycle of fear by softening his or her verbal and nonverbal approach.

12. In areas populated by African Americans and other racial and immigrant groups all over the United States, there is a need for increased and more effective police protection.
    - Bridging the gap that has separated police from African Americans involves radical changes in attitudes toward police–community relations. Together with changes in management, even the individual officer can help by making greater efforts to have positive contact with African Americans.
    - The task of establishing rapport with African Americans at all levels of society is challenging because of what the officer represents in terms of past discrimination. Turning this image around involves a commitment on the part of the officer to break with deeply embedded stereotypes and to have as a goal, respect and professionalism in every encounter.

DISCUSSION QUESTIONS AND ISSUES*

1. *Racism: Effects on Blacks and Whites.* Under "Historical Information" in this chapter, the authors state that the fact of African Americans having been slaves in this country has created great psychological and social problems for blacks

*See Instructor's Manual accompanying this text for additional activities, role-plays, questionnaires and projects related to the content of this chapter.

and whites for generations to come. How is this true for both races? What are the implications for law enforcement?

2. ***Offensive Terms.*** The authors advise refraining from using such offensive terms as "nigger" at all times, even where there are no African Americans present. Give two practical reasons for this.

3. ***"Cool Pose" and the Use of Threats.*** How do you think the information in this chapter about threats, emotional expression (including rage), and the "cool pose" can help officers in their approach to citizens? Describe or role-play how an officer would communicate if he or she did not feel threatened by such behavior. Describe or role-play how an officer might approach and interact with the citizen if he or she was threatened by the behavior.

4. ***Inner Cities: Officers and Citizens' Reactions.*** Toward the end of the chapter, the authors mention the vicious cycle that is created in urban areas, especially where citizens have become increasingly armed (with highly sophisticated weapons) and officers, consequently, have to take more self-protective measures. Each views the other with fear and animosity and approaches the other with extreme defensiveness. Obviously, there is no simple answer to this widely occurring phenomenon, and police cannot solve the ills of society. Discuss your observations of the way officers cope with the stresses of these potentially life-threatening situations and how the coping or lack thereof affects relations with African Americans and other minorities. What type of support do police officers need to handle this aspect of their job? Do you think police departments are doing their job in providing the support needed?

5. ***When Officers Try to Make a Difference.*** Many young African American children, especially in housing projects in inner cities, live without a father in the household. This means that they do not have a second authority figure as a role model and are, consequently, deprived of an important source of adult support. No one can take the place of a missing parent, but there are small and large things a police officer can do to at least make an impression in the life of a child. Compile a list of actions officers can take to demonstrate their caring of children in these environments. Include in your first list every gesture, no matter how small; your second list can include a realistic list of what action can be taken given resources available. Select someone to compile both sets of suggestions (i.e., the realistic and ideal suggestions). Post these lists as reminders of how officers can attempt to make a difference in their communities not only with African American children but with other children as well.

6. Every criminal justice, policy academy student, and law enforcement representative needs to look closely at instances of racial profiling, study them, and learn from previous officers' mistakes. Discuss the following incident of racial profiling, using the questions below as guidelines for your discussion.

   A student from Liberia attending college in North Carolina was driving along I-95 in Maryland when he was pulled over by state police who said he wasn't wearing a seatbelt. The officers detained him and his two passengers for two hours they searched the car for illegal drugs, weapons, or other contraband. Finding nothing, they proceeded to dismantle the car and removed part of the door panel, a seat panel and part of the sunroof. Again finding nothing, the officers in the end handed the man a screwdriver as they left the scene saying, "You're going to need this. (Rice, 1999)

Questions to discuss: First, describe, in detail, all the potential negative consequences from this police incident.

What else do we need to know about this incident to reach a decision as to whether the stop was legitimate or related to racial profiling. For example, would we want to know the following?

- Time of day (could the trooper have seen that he wasn't wearing a seat belt)?
- Does the state police administration encourage stops on I-95 of individuals and vehicles that fit the profile of drug runners?
- What other information would you want to know?

Officers usually ask for permission or consent to search a vehicle they stop when probable cause does not exist for a search. Do you think the officer(s) requested a voluntary consent to search this vehicle?

Was the length of the detention reasonable? Was it disrespectful and unwarranted to leave the student to replace his vehicle parts? If you are a police officer, could you justify this sort of traffic stop to your supervisor, department or community, or in your own conscience?

WEBSITE RESOURCES

American Civil Liberties Union (ACLU):   http://www.aclu.org

This website contains multiple locations for information about many issues including racial profiling.

National Organization of Black Law Enforcement (NOBLE)   http://www.noble natl.org

This website provides information on the public-service organization itself, and its involvement in issues of interest and concern to law enforcement and the black community. It is the source of information on many procedures. It provides information on NOBLE activities such as community outreach and professional development. The goal of NOBLE is to be recognized as a highly competent public service organization that is at the forefront of providing solutions to law enforcement issues and concerns, as well as to the changing needs of communities.

Police Executive Research Forum (PERF):   http://www.policeforum.org/racial.html

This website has an abundance of information about racial profiling and model programs. PERF produced a free video and guide to facilitate police–citizen discussions on racially biased policing. They also produced a helpful guide, titled *Racially Biased Policing: A Principled Response.*

National Association of Black Criminal Justice (NABCJ):　http://www.nabcj.org

This website provides information on the organization itself (e.g., member chapters and events) as well as on issues toward improving law enforcement. NABCJ seeks to focus attention on relevant legislation, law enforcement, prosecution, and defense-related needs and practices, with emphasis on the courts, corrections, and the prevention of crime. Among its chief concerns is the general welfare and increased influence of African Americans and people of color as it relates to the administration of justice.

VERA Institute of Justice:　http://www.vera.org

The website provides information on the research projects and activities of the VERA Institute of Justice. This organization works closely with leaders in government and civil society to improve the services people rely on for safety and justice. Vera develops innovative, affordable programs that often grow into self-sustaining organizations, studies social problems and current responses, and provides practical advice and assistance to government officials in New York and around the world.

African American Web Connection　http://www.aawc.com/aawc.html

This website is devoted to providing the African American community with valuable resources on the Web. It includes such topics as arts and poetry, businesses, churches, organizations, and topics of concern, to name a few.

REFERENCES

ABC News. (1992, November 6). *20/20* ABC News Report, "Presumed Guilty," Transcript 1247.

ABC NEWS/*Washington Post* Poll: Race Relations—1/20/03: "Despite a Chasm in Perceptions of Racism, Public Views of Race Relations Improve."

Bennett, Lerone Jr. (1989, November). "The 10 Biggest Myths about the Black Family." *Ebony.* pp. 1, 2.

Berry, Ondre. (2000). Deputy Chief, Reno, Nevada Police Department. Interview, December 8, 2003.

Bradley, Yvette. (1999). Statement of Yvette Bradley, Victim of Racial Profiling at Newark Airport, ACLU Freedom Network News. Available: http://www.moncriefassociates.com/programs.html

Council of Economic Advisors. (1998).

Cross, Stan, and Edward Renner. (1974). "An Interaction Analysis of Police–Black Relations." *Journal of Police Science Administration, 2* (1).

CSIS. (2003). Consumer Services Information Systems Project—Glossary. Available: http://csisweb.aers.psu.edu

Davis, Robert C., et al. (2002). "Turning Necessity Into Virtue: Pittsburgh's Experience with a Federal Consent Decree," Vera Institute of Justice. Available: http://www.cops.usdoj.gov/Default.asp?Item=565)

Fillmore, Charles J. (1997). *A Linguist Looks at the Ebonics Debate.* Washington, D.C. Center for Applied Linguistics.

Frey, William H. (1998). New Demographic Divide in the US: Immigrant and Domestic "Migrant Magnets." *The Public Perspective, 9* (4).

Getman, K. (1984) Sexual Control in the Slaveholding South: The Implementation and Maintenance of a Racial Caste System. *Harvard Women's Law Review, 7.* pp. 5–7.

Goleman, Daniel. (1992, April 21). "Black Scientists Study the 'Pose' of the Inner City." *New York Times.*

Griffin, Ronald Pastor. (2003), Detroit-based Pastor and Community Leader. (Personal Communication, October, 2003).

Hines, Paulette Moore, and Nancy-Boyd Franklin. (1982). "Black families," *in Ethnicity and Family Therapy,* M. McGoldrick et al., eds. New York: Guilford Press.

Huo, Yuen J., and Tom R. Tyler. (2000) *How Different Ethnic Groups React to Legal Authority.* Public Policy Institute of California. San Francisco, California.

Kochman, T. (1981). Black and White Styles in Conflict Labor, William. Chicago: Univ. of Chicago Press, 121.

Lohman, D. L. (1977). "Race Tension and Conflict," in *Police and the Changing Community,* N.A. Watson, ed. Washington D.C.: International Association of Chiefs of Police.

McAdoo, Harriet Pipes. (1992). "Upward Mobility and Parenting in Middle Income Families," in *African American Psychology.* Newbury Park, Calif.: Sage.

Miller, Char (2003). U.S. Historian and Professor Trinity College, San Antonio, Texas, Personal Communication, December 2000.

Morrow, Lance. (1991, April 1). "Rough Justice." *Time,* pp. 16, 17.

National Center for Health Statistics, Series 21, Number 53, 1995, report of Final Natality Statistics, 1996, Monthly Vital Statistics Report, Vol. 46, No. 11, National Center for Health Statistics, 1998 and National Vital Statistics Report, June 25, 2003 (http://www.childtrendsdatabank.org/figures/75-Figure-1.gif)

The National Urban League. (2003). *The State of Black America 2003.* Available: http://www.nul.org/

Paternoster, R., R. Bachman, R. Brame, and L.W. Sherman. (1997). "Do Fair Procedures Matter. The Effect of Procedural Justice on Spouse Assault." *Law and Society Review.* pp. 163–204

Perry, Glenn. (2003). Youth Opportunity Case manager with the Immigrant and Refugee Community Organization (IRCO) in Portland, Oregon, and Community-policing outreach volunteer with the Oregon state police. (Personal Communication, October, 2003).

Poussaint, Alvin. (1992). Raising Black Children. New York, New York. Penguin Group

Rice, George. (1999). *People and Possibilities, Racial Profiling: Prejudice or Protocol?*

Shusta, Robert. (1986). *Cultural Issues Manual.* Concord, Calif.: Concord Police Department.

Thompson, George. (2003). President of Verbal Judo Institute, Yucca Valley, California. Personal communication, November, 2003.

Thompson, George. (2004). *Verbal Judo: The Gentle Art of Persuasion.* Yucca Valley, CA., Verbal Judo Institute, Inc.

Thornton, Jeanne, and David Whitman, with Dorian Friedman. (1992, November 9). "Whites myths about blacks." *U.S. News & World Report,* pp. 41–44.

Tyler, T. R., R. J. Boeckmann, H. J. Smith, and Y.J. Huo. (1997). Social Justice in a Diverse Society. Boulder Colo.: Westview Press.

U.S. Census Bureau, Current Population Reports. (2003, April). "The Black Population in the United States: March 2002."

U. S. Department of Justice: Bureau of Justice Statistics: Homicide trends in the U.S. http://www.ojp.usdoj.gov/bjs/homicide/race.htm

USA Today, "Black on Black Crime," April 24, 1991.

Walker, Anna. (1982). "Black American Cultures," in *California Cultural Awareness Resource Guide.* San Francisco: Chinatown Resources Development Center.

Walker, Samuel. (1992). *The Police in America.* New York: McGraw-Hill.

Weber, Shirley N. (1991). "The need to be: The socio-cultural significance of black language," in *Intercultural Communication: A Reader,* 6th ed., Larry Samovar and Richard Porter, eds. Belmont, Calif.: Wadsworth Press.

Weisburd, David, and Rosann Greenspan. (2000, May). Police Attitudes toward Abuse of Authority: Findings from a National Study," National Institute of Justice Research in Brief.

Williams, H, and P. V. Murphy. (1990). The Evolving Strategy of Police: A Minority View. Washington D.C.: The National Institute of Justice, U.S. Department of Justice.

Wriggens, J. (1983). Rape, Racism, and the Law. *Harvard Women's Law Journal, 6,* 103–141.

Wyatt, G. E. (1992). The Sociocultural Context of African American and White Women's Rape. *Journal of Social Issues, 48,* 77–91.

Chapter 7

Law Enforcement Contact
with Latino/Hispanic Americans

OVERVIEW

This chapter provides specific ethnic and cultural information on Latino/Hispanic Americans. The label Latino/Hispanic Americans encompasses over 25 different ethnic and cultural groups from Central and South America and the Caribbean. For ease of use, we will use the term Latino/Hispanic Americans to refer to members of these ethnic groupings. We first define this highly diverse group and then provide a historical overview that will contribute to readers' understanding of the relationship between law enforcement personnel and citizens. We present demographics and elements of diversity among Latino/Hispanic Americans, as well as issues related to ethnic and cultural identity: myths and stereotypes, the extended family and community, gender roles, generational differences, and adolescent and youth issues. The section "Cultural Influences on Communication" introduces the subtle aspects of nonverbal and indirect communications that law enforcement and other related personnel (e.g., 911 dispatchers, emergency medical technicians, criminal justice staff) often find challenging in their interactions with Latino/Hispanic Americans. We present, in the closing section, several key issues for law enforcement: underreporting of crimes, victimization, differential treatment, racial profiling of Latino/Hispanic Americans, attitudes toward crime and safety, exposure to environmental risks and job hazards, and increasing police services to the Latino/Hispanic American community. Finally, we review recommendations for improved communication and relationships between law enforcement personnel and members of Latino/Hispanic American communities.

COMMENTARY

In this chapter, we refer to Latino/Hispanic Americans more in terms of the similarities shared across groups rather than the differences. Certainly, there are great differences with respect to culture, values, and behaviors among the various groups that comprise the broad categorization "Latino/Hispanic Americans." Labeling groups, especially, when describing a high level of diversity is a challenge; ethnic and minority group members, themselves, can be sensitive to the way others refer to them. Accordingly, a first concern by many law enforcement officers is how to refer to the different groups comprising Latino/Hispanic Americans.

The term Hispanic means so many different things to so many different people. To the typical American, stereotypes of poverty, illegal aliens, laborers, and the uneducated come to mind. For those who are part of the so-called Hispanic group, there is really no agreement as to what we want to be called: Is it Latino, Hispanic, or the people from the specific countries of origin like Mexican, Puerto Rican, Cuban, Salvadorian, Colombian, Dominican, Nicaraguan, Chilean, Argentinean, Brazilian, and other South and Central Americans? (Latino/Hispanic American community organizer)

Law enforcement officers are called to respond to concerns or complaints by community members against Latino/Hispanic Americans. Often, such complaints are made by individuals who do not understand the Latino/Hispanic American community. At the same time, law enforcement officers are asked to serve and protect the Latino/Hispanic community. Moreover, law enforcement officers, in response to community members' concerns and complaints, may see only one side of a diverse group of people. The Latino/Hispanic American community reflects the full range of economic, educational, and cultural diversity, as is illustrated by the examples in the following quotes:

Every day, we get complaints from parents, merchants, and commuters wanting the police to do something about the "Mexicans" and other "Latino/Hispanic" types waiting to be picked up for a job around the freeway on-ramps. They stand there for hours waiting for a patron, a boss, to drive up and employ them for a day, a week, or a few hours. It's a community issue, yet the police are expected to solve it. We can ask them to disband and move on, but all that would do is to have them move around the corner. (police officer's anecdote told at a cultural awareness training session)

It's unfortunate that for the average American, the stereotypes of Latino/Hispanic Americans include the characteristics of poor, uneducated immigrants, and perhaps those of illegal status. What's missing from the picture are the vast numbers of us who are successful in business, university-educated, community leaders, and active in shaping the political future of our country. (business owner's comment at a Hispanic Chambers of Commerce Conference in Denver, Colorado)

INTRODUCTION

Latino/Hispanic Americans are the fastest growing cultural group in the United States in terms of numbers of people. Between the 1990 and 2000 censuses, the population increased by more than 50 percent, from 22.4 million in 1990 to 32.8 million in 2000. Growth in all urban and rural areas of the United States has been striking, with half of all Latino/Hispanic Americans living in two states in the United States: California and Texas. The population growth can be attributed to (1) higher birthrates; (2) higher immigration from Mexico, Central and South America, and the Caribbean; (3) greater longevity, since this is a relatively young population; and (4) larger numbers of subgroups being incorporated into the Latino/Hispanic American grouping.

LATINO/HISPANIC AMERICANS DEFINED

Hispanic is a generic term referring to all Spanish-surname and Spanish-speaking people who reside in the United States and in Puerto Rico (a Commonwealth). Latino is generally the preferred label on the West Coast, parts of the East Coast, and the

Southeast. The term "Latino" is a Spanish word indicating a person of Latin American origin, and it reflects the gender-specific nature of its Spanish language derivation: Latino, for men, and Latina, for women. Hispanic is generally preferred on the East Coast, primarily by the Puerto Rican, Dominican, and Cuban communities (although individual members within each of these communities may prefer the specific term referring to their country of heritage). Objections to the use of the term Hispanic include the following: (1) Hispanic is not derived from any culture or place (i.e., there is no such place as "Hispania") and (2) the term was primarily invented for use by the U.S. Census Bureau. Sometimes, the term Spanish speaking/Spanish surnamed may be used to recognize the fact that one may have a Spanish surname, but may not speak Spanish (which is the case for a large number of Latino/Hispanic Americans). La Raza is another term used, primarily on the West Coast and in the Southwest, to refer to all peoples of the Western Hemisphere who share a cultural, historical, political, and social legacy of the Spanish and Portuguese colonists and the Native Indian and African people; it has its origins within the political struggles of this region and the mixing of the races, *el mestizaje.*

Like La Raza, Chicano is another term that grew out of the ethnic pride and ethnic studies movement in the late 1960s. "Chicano" refers specifically to Mexican Americans, and it is used primarily on the West Coast, in the Southwest, and in the Midwest. It is also commonly used in college communities across the United States that provide an ethnic studies curriculum.

In 1976, Congress passed Public Law 94-311, called the Roybal Resolution, which required the inclusion of a self-identification question on Spanish origin or descent in government surveys and censuses. As such, "Hispanic" is the official term used in federal, state, and local governmental writings and for demographic references. Federal standards implemented in 2003 allow the terms "Latino" and "Hispanic" to be used interchangeably (Office of Management and Budget, 1997).

The definition of Latino/Hispanic is considered by many to be associated with stereotypical perceptions to be a "mega-label" that does not represent well all members within this group. These views are illustrated in the following two examples:

> One version of this objection argues against all existing ethnic names, and particularly "Hispanic" or "Latinos/Latinas," because these labels have had connotations among the general population. They create a negative perception of those named and tend to perpetuate their disadvantageous situation in society. To call someone Hispanic or Latino/Latina, like calling someone negro or colored, carries with it all sorts of negative baggage, demeaning the person and harming him or her in diverse ways. (Gracia, 2000)

> Younger people in some cities, especially, find Hispanic archaic, if not downright offensive, much as "Negro" displeased a previous generation of blacks and African-Americans. They say it recalls the colonization by Spain and Portugal and ignores the Indian and African roots of many people it describes. Yet others, including business and political leaders, dismiss "Latino" as a fad. Still others use the terms Hispanic and Latino interchangeably. (Gonzalez, 1992, p. 6)

As the Latino/Hispanic American communities grow and develop in the United States, the preferred and specific terms to be used will evolve and change by the members of these communities.

HISTORICAL INFORMATION

The historical background of Latino/Hispanic Americans contains key factors that affect their interactions with and understanding of law enforcement and peacekeeping personnel. Clearly, this brief historical and sociopolitical overview can only highlight some of the commonalities and diverse cultural experiences of Latino/Hispanic Americans. Our historical review will focus primarily on the larger Latino/Hispanic communities in the United States (those with Mexican, Puerto Rican, and Cuban ethnic and historical roots).

In the 1800s, under the declaration of Manifest Destiny, the United States began the expansionist policy of annexing vast territories to the south, north, and west. As Lopez y Rivas (1973) noted, the United States viewed itself as a people chosen by "Providence" to form a larger union through conquest, purchase, and annexation. With the purchase (or annexation) of the Louisiana Territories in 1803, Florida in 1819, Texas in 1845, and the Northwest Territories (Oregon, Washington, Idaho, Wyoming, and Montana) in 1846, it seemed nearly inevitable that conflict would occur with Mexico. The resulting Mexican-American War ended in 1848 with the signing of the Treaty of Guadalupe Hidalgo, in which Mexico received $15 million from the United States for the land that is now Texas, New Mexico, Arizona, and California, with more than 100,000 Mexican people living in those areas. As is obvious from this portion of history, it makes little sense for many Mexican Americans to be stereotyped as "illegal aliens," especially since more than a million Mexican Americans (some of whom are U.S. citizens and some of whom are not) can trace their ancestry back to families living in the southwestern United States in the mid-1800s (Fernandex, 1970). Moreover, for Latino/Hispanic Americans (especially Mexican Americans), the boundaries between the United States and Mexico are seen as artificial. "The geographic, ecological, and cultural blending of the Southwest with Mexico is perceived as a continuing unity of people whose claim to the Southwest is rooted in the land itself. (Montiel, 1978)

While one-third of Mexican Americans can trace their ancestry to families living in the United States in the mid-1800s, the majority of this group migrated into the United States after 1910 because of the economic and political changes that occurred as a result of the Mexican Revolution.

Puerto Rico, on the other hand, was under the domination of Spain until 1897, at which time it was allowed the establishment of a local government. The United States invaded Puerto Rico and annexed it as part of the Spanish-American War (along with Cuba, the Philippines, and Guam) in 1898. Although Cuba (in 1902) and the Philippines (in 1949) were given their independence, Puerto Rico remained a territory of the United States. In 1900 the U.S. Congress passed the Foraker Act, which allowed the President to appoint a governor; to provide an Executive Council consisting of 11 presidential appointees (of which only five had to be Puerto Rican); and to elect locally a 35-member Chamber of Delegates. In reality, the territory was run by the President-appointed governor and the Executive Council. The Jones Act of 1917 made Puerto Ricans citizens of the United States. It was not until 1948 that Puerto Rico elected its first governor, Luis Munoz Marin. In 1952 Puerto Rico was given Commonwealth status, and Spanish was allowed to be the language of instruction in the schools again (with English taught as the second language).

Following World War II, large numbers of Puerto Ricans began migrating into the United States. With citizenship status, Puerto Ricans could travel easily and settled in areas on the East Coast, primarily New York City (in part because of the availability of jobs and affordable apartments). The estimated number of Puerto Ricans in the United States is 2 million on the mainland and 3.8 million on the island (Therrien & Ramirez, 2000).

Cubans immigrated into the United States in three waves. The first wave occurred between 1959 and 1965 and consisted of primarily white, middle-class, or upper-class Cubans who were relatively well educated and had business and financial resources. The federal government's Cuban Refugee Program, Cuban Student Loan Program, and Cuban Small Business Administration Loan Program were established to help this first wave of Cuban immigrants achieve a successful settlement (Bernal & Estrada, 1985). The second wave of Cuban immigrants occurred between 1965 and 1973. This wave resulted from the opening of the Port of Camarioca, allowing all who wished to leave Cuba to exit. Those who left as part of the second wave were more often of the working class and lower middle class, primarily white adult men and women. The third wave of immigrants leaving Cuba from Mariel occurred from the summer of 1980 to early 1982. This third wave was the largest (about 125,000 were boat-lifted to the United States) and consisted primarily of working-class persons, more reflective of the Cuban population as a whole than previous waves. Most immigrated into the United States with hopes for better economic opportunities. Within this group of *Marielito* were many antisocial, criminal, and mentally ill persons released by Fidel Castro and included in the boat lift (Gavzer, 1993).

In addition to the three major groups that have immigrated to the United States from Mexico, Puerto Rico, and Cuba are immigrants from 21 countries of South and Central America, as well as the Caribbean. Arrival of these immigrants for political, economic, and social reasons began in the early 1980s and has added to the diversity of Latino/Hispanic American communities in the United States. The total numbers of some groups, such as the Dominicans (a rapidly growing group on the East Coast), are difficult to determine because of their undocumented entry status in the United States.

DEMOGRAPHICS: DIVERSITY AMONG LATINO/HISPANIC AMERICANS

The historical background above illustrates the heterogeneity of Latino/Hispanic Americans. Composed of many different cultural groups, this broad label encompasses significant generational, educational, and socioeconomic differences, varying relocation experiences, and many other varieties of life experience. Although the Spanish language may provide a common thread among most Latino/Hispanic Americans, there are cultural and national differences in terms and expressions used, including nonverbal nuances. Moreover, the language of Brazil is Portuguese, not Spanish, and thus the language connection for Brazilian Latino/Hispanic Americans is unique. The Latino/Hispanic American population numbers about 32.8 million and represents 12 percent of the U.S. population (not including the 3.9 million people who live in Puerto Rico). About 85 percent of Latino/Hispanic Americans trace their roots to Mexico, Puerto Rico, and Cuba, while the remaining 15 percent are from the other countries of Central and South America, the Caribbean, and Spain. The numerical growth of the Latino/Hispanic American population is the fastest of all American ethnic groups, with more than 10 million people added to the U.S. population between the 1990 and 2000 censuses (Therrien & Ramirez, 2002).

Latino/Hispanic Americans are concentrated in five states: California (31.1 percent), Texas (18.9 percent), New York (8.1 percent), Florida (7.6 percent), and Illinois (4.3 percent). Some of the key demographics information about this population includes the following (the implications of the demographic information that follows are presented in the "Key Issues in Law Enforcement" section):

1. *Age:* The Latino/Hispanic American population tends to be younger than the general U.S. population. The median age is 25.9 years, in contrast to 35.3 for the rest of America.

2. *Size of household:* The average Latino/Hispanic household consists of 3.5 people, which is nearly one person more for every Latino/Hispanic household than that for other U.S. households, which average 2.6 persons per household.

3. *Birthrate:* Latino/Hispanic Americans have a higher birthrate than the general U.S. population. The Latino/Hispanic American birthrate per 1,000 is 104.8, in comparison to 65.4 for the rest of America.

4. *Purchasing power:* The estimated purchasing power of Latino/Hispanic Americans in the United States is $383 billion (Rodriguez, 2000).

5. *Urban households:* About 88 percent of all Latino/Hispanic Americans live in metropolitan areas, making this group the most highly urbanized population in the United States. For example, Latino/Hispanic Americans constitute notable percentages of the population for the following large cities: El Paso (74 percent), Corpus Christi (57 percent), San Antonio (52 percent), Fresno (41 percent), Seattle-Tacoma (40 percent), Los Angeles (38 percent), Albuquerque (38 percent), Miami-Ft. Lauderdale (37 percent), Tucson (27 percent), San Diego (25 percent), Austin (24 percent), and San Francisco/ Oakland (19 percent) (Hornor, 1999).

6. *Language:* Latino/Hispanic American self-identification is most strongly demonstrated in the use and knowledge of Spanish. The Spanish language is oftentimes the single most important cultural aspect retained by Latino/Hispanic Americans. The Hispanic Monitor, based on research by Yankelovich Clancy Shulman and Market Development, Inc., summarized its findings relative to Spanish spoken at home in Latino/Hispanic American households (see Exhibit 7.1).

As might be expected, with the large number of Latino/Hispanic Americans born in the United States, English may soon be the dominant language as this population moves into successive future generations.

	Total	Born in the U.S.	Born outside the U.S.
Language Spoken at Home	(%)	(%)	(%)
Spanish dominant	56	18	78
Spanish and English equally	23	35	16
English dominant	21	47	6

Exhibit 7.1   Language spoken at home by Latino/Hispanic Americans.

LABELS AND TERMS

As noted earlier, the term Latino/Hispanic American is a convenient summarizing label to achieve some degree of agreement in referring to a very heterogeneous group of people. Similar to the case of Asian/Pacific Americans, the key to understanding which terms to use is based on the principle of self-preference. As Cisneros noted in Gonzalez (1992):

> "To say Latino is to say you come to my culture in a manner of respect," said Sandra Cisneros, the author of "Women Hollering Creek: And Other Stories," who refuses to have her writing included in any anthology that uses the word Hispanic. "To say Hispanic means you're so colonized you don't even know for yourself or someone who named you never bothered to ask what you call yourself. It's a repulsive slave name." (p. 6)

Although many Latino/Hispanic Americans may not hold as strong a point of view as Cisneros, sensitivity is warranted in use of the term Hispanic with the Latino/Hispanic American community. For those who have origins in the Caribbean (e.g., Puerto Rican, Cuban, Dominican), the term Latino may be equally problematic for self-designation and self-identification.

Until 2003, Federal and other governmental designations used only "Hispanic"; Latino and Hispanic are now used interchangeably. The governmental designations are used in laws, programs, and regulations and in most reports and publications. For individuals within any of the groups, often the more specific names for the groups are preferred (e.g., Mexican, Puerto Rican, Cuban, Dominican, Argentinean, Salvadorian). Some individuals may prefer that the term American be part of their designation (e.g., Mexican American). For law enforcement officers, the best term to use in referring to individuals is the term that they prefer to be called. It is perfectly acceptable to ask individuals what they prefer to be called.

The use of slurs like "wetback," "Mex," "Spic," "Greaser," or other derogatory ethnic slang terms are never acceptable for use by law enforcement officers, no matter how provoked an officer may be. Other stereotypic terms like "Illegal," "New York Rican," "Macho man," "Latin lover," "Lupe the Virgin," and "Low Rider" do not convey the kinds of professionalism and respect for community diversity important to law enforcement and peacekeeping, and need to be avoided in law enforcement work. Officers hearing these or other similar words used in their own departments (or with peers or citizens) should provide immediate feedback about the inappropriateness of the use of such. Officers who may, out of habit, routinely use these terms may find themselves or their superiors in the embarrassing situation of explaining to offended citizens and communities why they used the term and how they intended no bias, stereotype, or prejudice.

TYPOLOGY OF LATINO/HISPANIC AMERICANS

Similar to our typology for Asian/Pacific American individuals, families, and communities, we have developed a seven-part typology that may be useful in understanding and in summarizing some of the differences between individuals within this Latino/Hispanic American group (see Exhibit 7.2).

Our typology suggests that as law enforcement, criminal justice, and public safety organizations prepare and train their personnel to work with Latino/Hispanic American

Type I	Latino/Hispanic Recently Arrived Immigrant or Refugee
	(Less than 3 Years in the U.S. with Major Life Experiences in Mexico, the Caribbean, or South and Central America)
Type II	Latino/Hispanic Immigrant and Refugee (3 or More Years in the U.S. with Major Life Experiences in Mexico, the Caribbean, or South and Central America)
Type III	Latino/Hispanic American (Second-Generation Offspring of Immigrant or Refugee)
Type IV	Latino/Hispanic Immigrant (Major Life Experiences in the U.S.)
Type V	Latino/Hispanic American (Third-Generation or Longer in the U.S.)
Type VI	Latino/Hispanic National (Anticipates Return to Mexico, the Caribbean, or South and Central America, to include Visitors and Tourists)
Type VII	Latino/Hispanic multinational (Global Workplace and Residency)

Exhibit 7.2   Typology of Latino/Hispanic Americans.

communities, a focus on the key differences within each of the typological groups would be most effective. Please refer to Chapter 5 for examples with Asian and Pacific Americans on the use of this typology. It is a convenient framework for discussing how the motivational components within each of the groupings may affect the way people respond in a law enforcement situation (in the case for those of Latino/Hispanic descent).

MYTHS AND STEREOTYPES

Knowledge of and sensitivity to Latino/Hispanic Americans' concerns, diversity, historical background, and life experiences will facilitate the crime-fighting and peace-keeping mission of law enforcement officers. It is important to have an understanding about some of the myths and stereotypes of Latino/Hispanic Americans that contribute to the prejudice, discrimination, and bias this population encounters. Many law enforcement officers do not have much experience with the diversity of Latino/Hispanic American groups and learn about these groups only through stereotypes (often perpetuated by movies) and through the very limited contact involved in their law enforcement duties. Stereotypic views of Latino/Hispanic Americans reduce individuals within this group to simplistic, one-dimensional characters and have led many Americans to lump members of these diverse groups into one stereotypic group, "Mexicans." It is important for law enforcement officers to be aware of the different stereotypes of Latino/Hispanic Americans. The key to effectiveness with any ethnic or racial group is not that we completely eliminate myths and stereotypes about these groups, but that we are aware of these stereotypes and can monitor our thinking and our behaviors when the stereotypes are not true of those persons with whom we are interacting.

Some of the stereotypes that have affected Latino/Hispanic Americans in law enforcement include the following:

1. ***Viewing Latino/Hispanic Americans as "illegal aliens."*** Although many may argue over the number of Latino/Hispanic illegal and undocumented immigrants (see Ferriss, 1993), the vast majority of Latino/Hispanic Americans do not fall into this stereotype (i.e., the vast majority of Latino/Hispanic Americans

in the United States are U.S. citizens or legal residents). The issues of illegal aliens and undocumented immigrants are complex ones (see Chapter 1), but cultural awareness and sensitivity will allow officers the knowledge to avoid an offensive situation by acting on the stereotype of Latino/Hispanic Americans as illegal immigrants. The following illustrates this point:

> Juan Vasquez worked in the maintenance department of one of the larger downtown hotels in southern California. While at work on his day shift, all "immigrant members" of his maintenance department were asked to go to personnel. When he had arrived, he found himself (and others) questioned by several officers of the Immigration and National-ization Services (INS), asking for identification and "papers." Juan was asked if he was an illegal and undocumented alien. He explained that he was a fourth-generation Mexican American, that he was born and grew up in Arizona, and that his family had lived for several generations in Arizona and Colorado. When Juan was asked for proof of citizenship and/or permanent residency, he told the officers that he had a driver's li-cense and car insurance papers. He further explained that he had grown children in college and one was even pursuing a master's degree. While the INS officers were finally satisfied with his explanations, Juan felt very insulted and offended by the assumption made that he was an ille-gal alien and not a United States citizen. (anonymous)

2. *Viewing Latino/Hispanic Americans as lazy and as poor workers.* This is a stereotype that has been perpetuated in the workplace. Moreover, this stereo-type of Latino/Hispanic Americans is often extended to include being a "party people." A workplace law enforcement example illustrates this stereotype:

> A flyer was sent out through interdepartmental mail announcing the re-tirement party for Sergeant Juan Gomez. The flyer showed a man (with sergeant's stripes) dressed in traditional Mexican garb (sombrero, serape, sandals) sleeping under a large shade tree. While Sergeant Gomez did not appear offended by the stereotype, a Latina nonsworn departmental employee was deeply offended by this flyer and requested that it not be used to announce a party by the organization. The people planning the event said that she was being "overly sensitive" and ignored her request. (police officer's anecdote told at a cultural awareness training session)

It is difficult to understand why some continue to hold this stereotype or what factors continue to perpetuate it given what we know about the Latino/ Hispanic American workforce in the United States and globally. Harbrecht, Smith, and Baker (1993) noted that the Mexican workers in Mexico comprise a smart, motivated, and highly productive workforce and "a potent new eco-nomic force to be reckoned with." Latino/Hispanic American community ad-vocates make the argument that it is difficult to imagine anyone being labeled as "lazy" or "poor workers" if they are willing to work as laborers from dawn to dusk in the migrant farm fields, day in and day out, year after year. More-over, comparisons of the labor force participation rate for all persons 16 years old and over showed virtually no differences between Latino/Hispanic Ameri-cans (67.9 percent) and all other ethnic and racial groups (67.1 percent) work-ing into today's labor force (Hornor, 1999).

Yrma Rico embraces both her farm work past in Orange Cove and her prosperous present, evident from her media corporation, her new co-ownership of Weber BMW in Fresno and the 15-carat diamond on her ring finger. In fact, the expected lifetime earnings of her entire family as she worked and grew up in the fields would not come close to buying the bauble on that finger. Rico describes her success with a joy of achievement but without arrogance or bragging. She is a founder of Entravision Communications Corp, a Spanish-language media company traded on the New York Stock Exchange. Its Web site says it reaches 80% of Hispanic households in the United States plus border markets in Mexico. Entravision, with corporate offices in Santa Monica, owns 32 television stations, 60 radio stations and 11,000 billboards. Its market value is $425 million. Rico also is vice president and general manager of a Univision network affiliate in Denver. These lofty business positions grew logically from her beginnings in the dirt. Rico decided early on that farm labor would not be her ultimate career destination. "But I never saw it as an obstacle," she says. Instead, she considered farm work a platform, and she began climbing from it without ever attending college. . .

Far from seeing farm labor as a dead end, Rico considers it an opportunity, something she built on. (Steinberg, 2001, p. C1)

3. ***Perceiving Latino/Hispanic Americans as uneducated and uninterested in educational pursuits.*** Prior to 1948 many Latino/Hispanic American children were denied access to the educational system available to others and instead were relegated to "Mexican" schools. A challenge in the U.S. courts on segregated schools allowed Latino/Hispanic children access to the "regular" school system (see *Mendez v. Westminster School District,* 1945, and *Delgado v. Bastrop Independent School District,* 1948). This stereotype of "uneducated" relates to how Latino/Hispanic officers may be inappropriately stereotyped and seen in terms of their ability to learn and to achieve in law enforcement and other professional peacekeeping training.

George I. Sanchez High School, a charter school operated by the Association for the Advancement of Mexican Americans, has become so popular that AAMA officials have begun offering additional services to students and their families to improve academic achievement even more. . . . "The school is so popular among area Hispanic families that we're starting to see third-generation students," . . . Moreno said. "Our programs that emphasize success on the TAAS are helping students jump three or four grade levels on the test. "Remember, we may have had a student only eight or nine months at the time they take the TAAS as a sophomore. Given this fact, our test scores speak for themselves." TAAS scores in math jumped 28 points in 2000, according to Moreno, and sophomores at Sanchez tested in the 80th percentile while juniors tested in the 90th percentile. (Evans, 2001, p. 1)

4. ***Viewing Latino/Hispanic Americans as dishonest and untrustworthy.*** Clearly, this stereotype would affect professionals in law enforcement and peacekeeping. Cultural understanding would allow the following shopkeeper (and peace officers as well) to avoid insulting situations such as the following:

Angel Llano, a New York native of Hispanic descent who works for the State of California and lives in a Northern California city, wrote in complaining about a local video store that fingerprints only male Latinos among its new customers. (A subsequent review of 200 membership cards found 11 with fingerprints—all those of men with Hispanic surnames.) (Mandel, 1993)

5. *Seeing Latino/Hispanic American young males as gang members and drug dealers.* Some hold the stereotype, especially among young males in inner cities, that Latino/Hispanic Americans are commonly involved in gangs and the illegal drug trade. Latino/Hispanic cultures are group oriented, and people from young to old tend to congregate as groups rather than as individuals or couples. "Hanging out" as a group tends to be the preferred mode of socialization. However, given the stereotype of Latino/Hispanic American young males as being gang members, it is easy to perceive five young Latino/Hispanic males walking together as constituting a "gang." Such stereotypes have resulted in suspicion, hostility, and prejudice toward Latino/Hispanic Americans and have served to justify improper treatment (e.g., routine traffic stops) and poor services (e.g., in restaurants and stores). Such stereotypes can be perpetuated by the television media (as illustrated in the following account) and can lead law enforcement officers to associate Latino/Hispanic Americans with criminal activity.

A "Law & Order" episode about violence during New York's Puerto Rican Day parade provoked angry complaints from Hispanic groups and a promise from NBC never to air the hour again. The episode that aired depicted a parade day rampage by Puerto Rican youths in which women are molested and one is killed. A Brazilian youth is shown convicted in the death. NBC made the decision after a meeting in New York with Hispanic representatives, including Manuel Mirabal, head of the National Puerto Rican Coalition, and Maria Roman, parade president. . . . Mirabal said the drama distorted a real occurrence on parade day last year in which groups of men sexually assaulted women in Central Park. The attacks occurred after, not during, the parade and the majority of those arrested were not Latino, Mirabal said. "Every Puerto Rican shown in that show was portrayed negatively as a criminal, as a delinquent, as someone who abuses women," he said in a telephone interview from New York. Such depictions reflect negatively on all Hispanics because many viewers fail to distinguish between different groups, he said. (Elber, 2001)

6. *Assuming that all Latino/Hispanic Americans speak Spanish.* As noted earlier in the chapter, 21 percent of Latino/Hispanic Americans reported that their families speak predominately English in the home. Many Latino/Hispanic Americans have been in the United States for six generations or more and English is the only language that they speak and write. George Perez is a Latino/Hispanic American cultural awareness trainer for many law enforcement, emergency service, and other public service organizations. As one of the outstanding trainers in his field, he is not surprised by the frequently heard stereotypic comment of, "You speak English so well, without an accent. How

did you do it?" His reply would usually be, "It's the only language I know! I'm a fifth-generation Latino/Hispanic American. I grew up in northern California and received my bachelor's and master's degree in the field that I teach."

THE LATINO/HISPANIC AMERICAN FAMILY

Understanding the importance of family for Latino/Hispanic Americans might be of significant value in community peacekeeping and crime-fighting. Obviously, with over 25 different cultural groups that make up the Latino/Hispanic American category, many differences exist among the groups in this collective in their family experiences. We would like to address some family characteristics that many of the different cultural groups share. *La familia* is perhaps one of the most significant considerations in working and communicating with Latino/Hispanic Americans. (In places where we use the Spanish term, we have done so to indicate the additional cultural meanings encompassed in a term such as *La familia* that is not captured in the English term "family.") The Latino/Hispanic American family is most clearly characterized by bonds of interdependence, unity, and loyalty and includes nuclear and extended family members, as well as networks of neighbors, friends, and community members. Primary importance is given to the history of the family, which is firmly rooted in the set of obligations tied to both the past and the future. In considering the different loyalty bonds, the parent–child relationship emerges as primary, with all children owing *respecto* to parents (*respecto* connotes additional cultural meanings than in the English term "respect"). Traditionally, the role of the father has been that of the disciplinarian, decision-maker, and head of the household. The father's word is the law, and he is not to be questioned. The father will tend to focus his attention on the economic and well-being issues of the family and less on the social and emotional issues. The mother, on the other hand, is seen as balancing the father's role through her role in providing for the emotional and expressive issues of the family. Extended family members such as grandmothers, aunts and uncles, and godparents (*compadrazgo*) may supplement the mother's emotional support. In the Latino/Hispanic American family, the older son is traditionally the secondary decision-maker to the father and the principal inheritor (*primogenito*) of the family. Because of the central nature of the Latino/Hispanic American family, it is common for police officers to come into contact with members of nuclear and extended families in the course of working with the Latino/Hispanic American community. One key to the success of law enforcement officers in working with the Latino/Hispanic American extended network is the knowledge of how best to communicate within the family context and an understanding of with whom to speak for information, observations, and questions.

THE ROLE OF THE MAN AND THE WOMAN IN A LATINO/HISPANIC AMERICAN FAMILY

In many Latino/Hispanic American families, the relationship and communication patterns are hierarchical with the father as the identified head of the household who is held in high respect. When it comes to family well-being, economic issues, and discipline, the father may appear to be the decision-maker; however, many other individuals may come into the picture. Generally, if there are grandparents in the household, the father may consult them, as well as his wife, on major decisions. In the case of law enforcement matters, it may be of great importance for officers to provide the father and the family with some privacy, as much as possible, to discuss key issues and situations. With central values like *respecto* (respect) and *machismo* (see below) in the Latino/ Hispanic American culture, it is critical for the father and other family members to demonstrate control in family situations. In this way, law enforcement officers may find that there is more control in a situation by allowing the citizen to think through a decision, come to the same conclusion as that of the officer, and exercise self-control in behaving in the best interests of all parties concerned. In the training videotape *Common Ground,* by the Orange County Sheriff's Department (1990), some examples are provided:

1. In a vignette in which the father of the family had to be arrested, the officers responded to the father's concern about being handcuffed in the presence of his children. The arresting officers were willing to wait until the father had left the house and gotten into the car before handcuffing the father (provided that he was willing to go peacefully).

2. In the scenario in which neighbors had complained about the noise of a wedding party and officers were dispatched to disband the party, the officer in charge allowed the father to tell everyone that the party was over and to bid his guests farewell (instead of the officers closing down the party).

Within the Latino/Hispanic American family, the sex roles are clearly defined; boys and girls are taught from childhood two different codes of behavior (Comas-Diaz & Griffith, 1988). Traditional sex roles can be discussed in the context of the two codes of gender-related behaviors: *machismo* and *marianismo. Machismo* literally means maleness, manliness, and virility. Within the Latino/Hispanic American cultural context, *machismo* means that the male is responsible for the well-being and honor of the family and is in the provider role. *Machismo* is also associated with having power over women, as well as responsibility for guarding and protecting them. Boys are seen as strong by nature and do not need the protection that is required by girls, who are seen as weak by nature.

Women are socialized into the role of *marianismo,* based on the beliefs about the Virgin Mary, in which women are considered spiritually superior to men and therefore able to endure all suffering inflicted by men (Stevens, 1973). Women are expected to be self-sacrificing in favor of their husbands and children. Within the context of the Latino/Hispanic American family, the role of the woman is as homemaker and caretaker of the children. In the current U.S. context, the traditional gender roles of women and men in the Latino/Hispanic American community have undergone much change and this has resulted in key conflicts. Since women have begun to work, earn money, and have some of the financial independence men have (e.g., they can go out and socialize with others outside of the family), they have pursued many experiences inconsistent with the traditional Latino/Hispanic female role. Although there are no clear-cut rules as to whether officers should go to the male head of the household or to the female family member, law enforcement officers would probably be more correct to address the father first in law enforcement inquiries. Consistent with the cultural values of *machismo* and *marianismo,* the Latino/Hispanic American household appears to be run by the father; however, in actual practice, the mother's role in discipline, education, finance, and decision making is also central.

Children, Adolescents, and Youth

Within the Latino/Hispanic American family, the ideal child is obedient and respectful of his or her parents and other elders. Adults may at times talk in front of the children as if they are not present and as if the children cannot understand the adults' conversations. Children are taught *respecto* (respect), which dictates the appropriate behavior toward all authority figures, older people, parents, relatives, and others. If children are disrespectful, they are punished and scolded. In many traditional families, it is considered appropriate for parents (and for relatives) to discipline a disrespectful and misbehaving child physically.

In Latino/Hispanic American households, there is a high reliance on family members (older children and other adults) to help care for younger children. Both parents within a Latino/Hispanic American family often work. As such, it is not uncommon for Latino/Hispanic American families to have latchkey children or have children cared for by older children in the neighborhood. As in other communities in which English is the second language, Latino/Hispanic American children have a special role in being the intermediaries for their parents on external community matters because of the ability of the younger individuals to learn English and the American ways of doing things. Children often serve as translators and interpreters for peace officers in their communication and relations with Latino/Hispanic American families involved in legal matters, immigration concerns, and community resources. Although the use of children and family members as translators is viewed as professionally and culturally inappropriate, oftentimes it is the only means available to the law enforcement officer. In such situations, it is suggested that the officer review what role is expected of the youthful member of the family. The officer needs to see how sensitive a topic might be for different family members. Moreover, the consequence of an incorrect translation needs to be evaluated (e.g., asking a juvenile to translate [to his or her parents who speak no English] that the juvenile has been involved in drinking and riding in a stolen vehicle may result in significantly changed content). Because of the embarrassment and fear of punishment by the juvenile and possibly a sense of shame or embarrassment to the parents, the message may be altered to avoid negative ramifications by the child. In all cases, when a child is acting as a translator for parents, the officer should direct all verbal and nonverbal communication to the parents. Otherwise, the parents may view the officer's lack of attention to them as an insult. Such sensitivity by the peace officer is particularly important for Latino/Hispanic Americans because of the cultural value of *personalismo,* which emphasizes the importance of the personal quality of any interaction. This cultural concept implies that relationships occur between particular individuals as persons, not as representatives of institutions (e.g., law enforcement) or merely as individuals performing a role (e.g., as a person who enforces the law).

Cross-National Family Issues

In Exhibit 8.2, we provide a typology of the Latino/Hispanic American to identify the different immigration and migration patterns within Latino/Hispanic American communities. This typology can also be used to understand the family, personal, and political issues involved in the interactions of Latino/Hispanic Americans crossing several types. For example, the Latino/Hispanic American (third generation or later; Type V) category consists of individuals who desire to choose which aspects of the old culture to keep and which of the new culture to accept. The focus is on choosing activities, values, norms, and lifestyles that blend the best of that which is Latino/Hispanic and the best of that which is American. The importance of being bicultural is a unique aspect of this group. However, much conflict may occur when there are family conflicts that involve cross-national value differences between being American and being bicultural, as was illustrated in the custody case of 9-year-old Elian Gonzalez (Lewis, 2000). In this particular case, Elian Gonzalez had escaped from Cuba with his mother, and, because of the hazardous trip, the mother died at sea. Elian's relatives in Miami took the boy into their home; however, Elian's father, a Cuban national, fought to regain legal custody of his son and to return him to Cuba. As illustrated by the case, today's law enforcement personnel may often have to intervene in such family and domestic disputes as well as in cross-national political situations involved in community peacekeeping assignments.

CULTURAL INFLUENCES ON COMMUNICATION: VERBAL AND NONVERBAL STYLES OF LATINO/HISPANIC AMERICANS

Although we do not wish to create stereotypes of any kind, key features of Latino/Hispanic American verbal and nonverbal communication styles necessitate explanation. Misunderstanding resulting from style differences can result in perceptions of poor community services from police agencies, conflicts resulting from such misunderstandings, and safety and control issues for the peace officer.

1. Latino/Hispanic Americans' high cultural value for *la familia* results in a very strong family and group orientation. As such, officers should not view the frequently seen behavior of "eye checking" with other family members before answering and the lack of the use of "I" statements and/or self-reference as Latino/Hispanic Americans not being straightforward about themselves or their relationships. The officer may be concerned because a Latino/Hispanic American witness may wish to use the pronoun "we" when the situation may call for a personal observation involving an "I" statement. For example, a Latino/Hispanic American family member who witnessed a store robbery may first nonverbally check with other family members before talking and then describing what he or she saw. Such verbal and nonverbal behavior is consistent with the family and group orientation of Latino/Hispanic Americans.

2. Speaking Spanish to others in the presence of a law enforcement officer, even though the officer had requested responses in English, should not automatically be interpreted as an insult or as attempts to hide information from the officer. In times of stress, those who speak English as a second language will automatically revert to their first and native language. In a law enforcement situation, many individuals may find themselves under stress and may speak Spanish, which is the more accessible and comfortable language for them. Moreover, speaking Spanish gives the individual a greater range of expression (to discuss and clarify complex issues with other speakers and family members), thus yielding more useful and clearer information to law enforcement personnel about critical events.

3. It is important for officers to take the time to get information from witnesses, victims, and suspects even if the individuals have limited skills in speaking English (the use of officers who speak Spanish, translators, and language bank resources will help). Often Latino/Hispanic Americans have not been helped in crime-fighting and peacekeeping situations because officers could not or did not take information from non-native English speakers.

> One incident involving officer Luis Franco shows why it helps to have officers who can communicate with non-English speakers. Franco recalled a domestic dispute where he found a middle-aged Hispanic man wouldn't cooperate with other officers. The man spoke no English and aggressively resisted the investigation of the dispute between him and his wife. Franco immediately told him to calm down and asked—in Spanish—what the problem was. The man turned toward Franco and answered quickly.
>
> The man said he expected the police to beat him up, then take him downtown. We don't do that here, Franco explained. Sit down and tell us your side of the story and we'll work it out. The man calmed and agreed. Afterward, he went downtown anyway, but the arrest stayed peaceful as Franco explained each step. ("Wanted in Wichita," 2001)

4. Although Latino/Hispanic Americans may show respect to law enforcement officers because of police authority, they do not necessarily trust the officers or the organization. *Respecto* is extended to elders and those who are in authority. This respect is denoted in the Spanish language, by the use of *Usted* (the formal you) rather than *tu* (the informal you). Showing respect, however, does not ensure trust. The cultural value of *confianza* (or trust) takes some time to develop. Like many from ethnic minority communities, Latino/Hispanic Americans have experienced some degree of prejudice and discrimination from the majority community, and citizens with such experiences need time to develop trust with law enforcement officers, who are identified as being a part of the majority community.

5. The cultural value of *personalismo* emphasizes the importance of the person involved in any interaction. Latino/Hispanic Americans take into strong consideration not only the content of any communication, but also the context and relationship of the communicator. This means that it is important for the officer to provide information about why questions are asked, who is the person asking the question (i.e., information about the officer), and how the information will be used in the context for effective communications. Additionally, context for Latino/Hispanic Americans means taking some time to find out, as well as to self-disclose, some background information (e.g., living in the same neighborhood, having similar concerns about crime). Additional contextual elements, such as providing explanations and information to Latino/Hispanic Americans about procedures, laws, and so forth before asking them questions or requesting their help, will ease the work of the officer. By providing background information and establishing prior relationships with community members, law enforcement agencies and officers build a context for cooperation with Latino/Hispanic American individuals.

6. Officers should be cognizant of nonverbal and other cultural nuances that may detract from effective communication. Many Latino/Hispanic Americans, especially younger individuals, find it uncomfortable and sometimes inappropriate to maintain eye contact with authority figures such as police officers. Strong eye contact with someone who is of higher position, importance, or authority is considered a lack of *respecto* in Latin/Hispanic American cultures. As such, many citizens from this background may deflect their eyes from gazing at police officers. It is important that officers not automatically read this nonverbal behavior as indicative of a lack of trust or as a dishonest response.

7. Latino/Hispanic Americans may exhibit behaviors that appear to be evasive, such as claiming not to have any identification or by saying that they do not speak English. In some of the native countries from which many Latino/Hispanic Americans have emigrated, the police and law enforcement agencies are aligned with a politically repressive government. The work of the police and of law enforcement in those countries is not one of public service. Therefore, many Latino/Hispanic Americans may have similar "fear" reactions to law enforcement officers in the United States. It is suggested that officers take the time to explain the need for identification and cooperation, and that they acknowledge the importance of comprehension on the part of the Latino/Hispanic American individual(s) involved.

> Carlos and his family had escaped from one of the South American countries where he saw the police serving as part of the politically repressive force upon his community. He was aware of the role of some of the police as members of the "death squad." He and his family were admitted to the United States and given political asylum and lived in southern California. Although he speaks fluent English and Spanish and has been in the United States for over 5 years, he relates how on one occasion when he was pulled over by the police (for a broken taillight) he automatically had this fear reaction and had the thought of saying to the officer, "No habla English" in the hope of avoiding any further contact. (Latino/Hispanic American trainer's anecdote told in a police cultural awareness training course)

KEY ISSUES IN LAW ENFORCEMENT

Underreporting of Crimes

Latino/Hispanic Americans, because of their past experiences with some of the law enforcement agencies in their countries of origin (e.g., repressive military force in their native country, as well as perceived "unresponsiveness" by police), are reluctant to report crimes and may not seek police assistance or help. Many people bring with them memories of how police in their home countries have brutalized and violated them and others (e.g., as members of the "death squad"). Many immigrants and refugees are just not knowledgeable about the legal system of the United States and may try to avoid any contact with law enforcement personnel. Outreach and community policing perspectives will enhance the contact and relationship with Latino/Hispanic American communities and may help alleviate the underreporting of crimes.

Investigators have broken a crime ring and charged five men with robbery and assault for attacks in which Hispanic immigrants were singled out as victims, authorities said Thursday. District Attorney Bill Gibbons said the attackers apparently believed the immigrants would hesitate reporting the crimes to police. He thanked the victims who stepped forward to help police identify the suspects and urged all immigrants, and other citizens alike, to report crimes. Some Hispanic residents are reluctant to do that because of language barriers and "fears they may have had in their native countries about government," Gibbons said. ("Five Robbers Charged," 2003)

Victimization

The Bureau of Justice Statistics published a report, "Criminal Victimization in the United States, 1997." Following are some key conclusions from the ongoing study of persons of age 12 or older, interviewed twice a year in about 50,000 households:

1. Latino/Hispanic Americans experienced higher rates of victimization from violent crime than all other populations. For every 1,000 Latino/Hispanic Americans age 12 and over, there were 16.2 aggravated assaults and 7.3 robberies (as compared to 11.6 aggravated assaults and 4.3 robberies for all other populations).

2. Latino/Hispanic Americans suffered a higher rate of household crimes (e.g., burglary, household larceny, motor vehicle theft) than all other populations. In the 1994 Bureau of Justice Statistics study, there was an annual average of 425.5 household victimizations per 1,000 households headed by a Latino/Hispanic American, as compared to 307.6 crimes per 1,000 households for all other populations.

> Hispanic day laborers in Forest Park are the latest metro Atlanta Latinos to become victims of armed robberies. . . . Some Latinos simply don't trust banking institutions, preferring to leave their money at home where they can see it, observers say. . . . The problem is not isolated to Forest Park, where police estimate 75 percent of robberies involve this type of Hispanic victim.
>
> Observers say it is a common offense in counties where there's a concentration of immigrants. Over a nine-month period ending in 1999 there were 34 robberies of Hispanic victims in one Atlanta apartment complex alone. In 1998, DeKalb County detectives charged two men with more than 50 home invasion robberies stretching from Buford Highway to Marietta. Their victims were all Hispanic families. At the time, police said it was the longest string of robbery cases in DeKalb County history. In Cobb County, Marietta police say about 95 percent of person-to-person robberies in the last two years in the southeastern part of the city, where there's a concentration of Latinos, have been against Hispanic immigrants. Smyrna police say the majority of person-to-person robberies and home invasion robberies in the last three years have involved Hispanic victims. (Bruner, 2001, p. B1)

3. The street was the most common place for violent crimes to occur: 45 percent of the robberies of Latino/Hispanic Americans occurred on city streets (Bastian, 1990). As such, the higher victimization rate can be partly explained by some of

the individual and environmental characteristics of Latino/Hispanic Americans; that is, a younger, poorer population concentrated in large urban areas.

4. Latino/Hispanic American victims of violent crime were more likely to be accosted by a stranger (65 percent) than were African American victims (54 percent) or Caucasian (white) victims (58 percent). Latino/Hispanic American and African American victims were more likely to face an offender with a weapon (57 percent for each group) than were Caucasian victims (43 percent) (Bastian, 1990).

> A teenager covered with 18 tattoos, including swastikas and white supremacist symbols, has confessed that he left his Queens home before 5 on a Sunday morning and traveled 50 miles to a Long Island town to attack two day laborers because they were Mexican, the police said today. The teenager, Ryan Wagner, a 19-year-old construction worker who lives with his parents in Maspeth, was arraigned today in Islip on two counts of attempted murder and two counts of aggravated harassment in the Sept. 17 attack, in which the police say he used a knife. He was held without bail at the Suffolk County jail in Riverhead. The two laborers said that two white men, posing as contractors promising work, had picked them up in a car in Farmingville and driven them to an abandoned factory in Shirley, where they were attacked but managed to escape. . . . In a confession on Tuesday, the police said, Mr. Wagner said he was simply doing what the other suspect wanted him to do. "What we gather from his confession was, the motive was in fact to go out and attack Mexicans," said Detective Sgt. Robert Reecks, commanding officer of the bias crimes unit. "We cannot say they are tied to any organization, or they were hired by anybody, or they were prompted to do this by any particular group." (Kelley, 2000, p. B5)

Differential Treatment

In Bastian's (1990) study, Latino/Hispanic Americans gave as one of the reasons for not reporting victimizations to the police that "the police would not do anything." Among nonreporting Latino/Hispanic American and African American victims of robbery, personal theft, and household crimes, similar percentages in each group said that they did not call the police or other law enforcement agencies because they felt that the police would think the incident unimportant or would do little to respond. Clearly, outreach and community efforts are needed to change this stereotype. Many of the crimes within Latino/Hispanic American communities are perpetrated by others within the same group; however, for this community, as noted earlier, a greater number of violent crimes are committed by strangers (65 percent). Law enforcement officials have often found it difficult to get cooperation from Latino/Hispanic American crime victims. To some degree, the fear on the part of the Latino/Hispanic American person in these cases relates to the retaliatory possibilities of the criminal within his or her own community. Other concerns of the Latino/Hispanic American victim include (1) the perceived nonresponsiveness of the peacekeeping officers and agencies, (2) lack of familiarity with and trust in police services, (3) perceived lack of effectiveness of the law enforcement agencies, and (4) stereotypes and images of law enforcement agencies as discriminatory. A key challenge for police agencies is to educate this group and to work cooperatively with the communities to reduce crime.

Racial Profiling of Latino/Hispanic Americans

The issue of racial profiling, as discussed in Chapter 14, is a major problem and concern, in particular for African Americans and Arab Americans, and is also a problem for Latino/Hispanic Americans. They believe that the determining factor in whether peace officers exercise their discretion in stopping a vehicle driven by a Latino/Hispanic American has to do with the driver's race and ethnicity. To many Latino/Hispanic Americans, racial profiling may even be "encouraged," as noted in the following example:

> Jose Pineda says he wasn't breaking any traffic law in January 1999 when a Mount Prospect police officer pulled him over and ticketed him for driving without insurance. Hiram Romero claims he was pulled over in Mount Prospect in May 1999 and ticketed for a defective front license plate—even though the officer could not see the front of Romero's car when he signaled him to stop. And Silvia Meyers, stopped by an officer in July 1999 while driving a Mercedes-Benz, says she was asked if she really owned the car. The three people—all Hispanic—filed a class-action lawsuit against the village contending police singled them out because of their race. On Wednesday, a federal judge set the stage for them to be awarded $3,000 each. As many as 3,200 other Hispanic drivers ticketed in Mount Prospect between Feb. 11, 1998, and Feb. 11, 2000, will each be eligible for $75 to $225 under a legal settlement recently agreed to by village officials. . . . In March 2000, Mount Prospect paid $900,000 to settle three lawsuits from three of its police officers who claimed they were encouraged to pull over Hispanic drivers. Mount Prospect admitted no wrongdoing in those settlements, a position it also took in the class-action case. (Fusco, 2002, p. 5)

According to Hills and Trapp (2000), "Every study of racial profiling shows that, contrary to popular belief, people of color are not more likely to carry drugs or other contraband in their vehicles than whites. In Maryland, the percentage of black and white drivers carrying contraband was statistically identical. The U.S. Customs Service's own figures show that while over 43 percent of those searched were minorities, the 'hit rates' for these searches were actually lower for people of color than for whites." In a study by the San Diego Police Department (Hills & Trapp, 2000), African Americans and Latino/Hispanic Americans were stopped more often than would be expected given their numbers in the local population; that is, 40 percent of those stopped and 60 percent of those searched were African Americans and Latino/Hispanic Americans, whereas both groups together only represent 28 percent of the driving population. The following New Jersey racial profiling case illustrates the issues for Latino/Hispanic Americans:

> The *Star-Ledger* of Newark reported that the state was close to agreeing to a nearly $13 million settlement with the four black and Hispanic men from New York City whose van was stopped on the turnpike in April 1998 by Troopers John Hogan and James Kenna. . . . The state is engaged in a complicated and contentious criminal case it filed against Troopers Kenna and Hogan, and the state's lawyers have expressed an eagerness to want the civil case out of the

way before the outcome of the criminal case is known. . . . [A] New Jersey appeals court reinstated the criminal charges against the two troopers, overruling a lower-court judge who had dismissed the charges. Mr. Kenna is now charged with attempted murder and aggravated assault and Mr. Hogan with aggravated assault. (Peterson, 2001, p. B5)

Attitudes toward Crime and Safety

The National Opinion Survey on Crime and Justice, conducted in 1996 (Hornor, 1999), provided some key differences on attitudes toward crime and safety by Latino/Hispanic American respondents when compared to all other respondents:

1. Approximately 32.5 percent of Latino/Hispanic Americans worried "very frequently" about getting murdered as compared to 10.6 percent of all other race and ethnic groups.

2. About 29.5 percent of Latino/Hispanic Americans worried "very frequently" about getting beaten up, knifed, or shot as compared to 12.5 percent of all other race and ethnic groups.

> When dusk comes, the streets empty and the esquineros hurry to the homes they share with 15, 20 and sometimes 30 others to drink beer and eat supper. The esquineros—the men of the corner—used to walk home alone from the corners where they gather each morning to be hired out for yardwork or other day jobs. Now they walk in groups. At one house, where the Guatemalans live, the door is punctured with bullet holes; a white man recently drove by and unloaded a pistol. . . . The people taunt each other. Some Americans picket the Latinos every Saturday as they stand on the corners waiting for work. The esquineros have become schooled in the ways of America. They picket back. And after the ambush of the two workers, more than 500 of the illegal immigrants took to the streets demanding their civil rights. (LeDuff, 2000, p. 1)

3. Approximately 40 percent of Latino/Hispanic Americans worried "very frequently" about oneself or someone in one's family getting sexually assaulted as compared to 18.1 percent of all other race and ethnic groups.

4. About 47.4 percent of Latino/Hispanic Americans worried "very frequently" about their home being burglarized as compared to 20.4 percent of all other race and ethnic groups.

As noted, a key challenge for police agencies is to educate this group, work cooperatively with the communities, and provide police services to reduce crime and the fears associated with crime victimization within these communities. Unfortunately, some Latino/Hispanic Americans may fear the police as much as they fear crime and criminals:

> Latino New Yorkers are almost as fearful of the police as they are of becoming crime victims, according to an annual poll released yesterday by the Hispanic Federation. While seven in 10 Hispanics worry about becoming crime victims, nearly six in 10 also fear becoming victims of police brutality, the poll found.

"It's a very interesting finding," said Doug Muzzio, a Baruch College pollster who assisted in the eighth annual survey by the federation, an alliance of 60 nonprofit health and human service agencies. "It's a very nuanced view. It's not simplistic." Muzzio said some of the negative view Hispanics have of cops has been influenced by media coverage of such recent cases as the police shooting deaths of Amadou Diallo and Patrick Dorismond and the torture of Abner Louima. But also contributing to Hispanics' dim view of cops is "direct experience" with brutal or disrespectful officers, Muzzio said. "They are experiencing these stops and searches," he said. (Lombardi, 2000, p. 8)

Another key challenge to effective cooperation with the Latino/Hispanic American community is to help allay the fears and concerns expressed by community members with regard to their multiple interactions with law enforcement officers inquiring about violent crimes, homeland security, immigration, health, and drug abuse:

At the outset of the investigation, initial lookout reports mentioned possible "Hispanic" suspects or someone with "olive" skin. . . . Mrs. Garcia said she understands that police have to search, but she stood firm in her belief that the searches were "not equal." "When they stop the white guy, they just look and let him go, but the Latino they put there on the ground and put the face to the gun and then take away," she says, demonstratively recreating the scene she's seen played out several times on television. Not only did they believe that Latinos were being stopped more frequently by the police and detained longer, their bigger concern was with their being turned over to the Immigration and Naturalization Service when they have done nothing wrong. (Washington, 2002, p. B2)

Exposure to Environmental Risk and Job Hazards

The Environmental Protection Agency (2001) confirms in its Toxic Release Inventory (TRI) emissions research studies what Morales and Bonilla (1993) documented in the state of California that Latino/Hispanic Americans live in some of the most polluted neighborhoods and work in many of the most hazardous jobs. For example, in Oakland, California, 24 percent of whites and 69 percent of Latino/Hispanic Americans live in communities with hazardous waste sites; in Los Angeles, the percentages are 35 percent for whites and 60 percent for Latino/ Hispanic Americans. In addition to Latino/Hispanic American community members' concern regarding crime and violence are the concerns for the environmental safety of their homes and fears over their exposures to environmental hazards and risks. Such concerns add to the role of law enforcement and peace officers within Latino/Hispanic American communities. In addition, as is illustrated in the following case, some job risks are related to stereotypic and oppressive actions of the employer:

W. R. Grace & Company said yesterday that it would pay $850,000 to settle a lawsuit in which the United States Equal Employment Opportunity Commission charged managers at a Maryland food-processing plant with egregious sexual harassment of 22 female workers from Central America. The Commission said four plant managers and two non-supervisors had engaged in systematic harassment that included exposing themselves, demanding oral sex and touching workers' breasts, buttocks and genital areas. Commission officials said that the harassment had lasted four years and that there had been one case of rape. "This stuff was pretty bad, and it seemed to be pervasive, all over this large plant," said Regina Andrew, one of the lawyers at the Commission's Baltimore office who handled what became a class-action lawsuit. "This was one of the worst sexual harassment cases we've seen." The Commission said numerous women at the plant in Laurel, MD, were given menial or difficult work assignments after they rejected the managers' sexual demands. (Greenhouse, 2000, p. A12)

Law enforcement professionals need to be alert to environmental risks including workplace exploitation of Latino/Hispanic Americans and to be particularly sensitive to the fear many immigrants have in reporting crimes to the police.

Increasing Police Services to the Latino/Hispanic American Community

The Police Neighborhood Resource Center model, started in 1991 in the largely Hispanic community of Rolling Meadows, Illinois, has shown the positive cooperative results of the police department, the Latino/Hispanic American community, and the local and regional businesses (Claitt, 2001):

> In 1991, police opened a substation called the Police Neighborhood Resource Center on the south side, nestled among a troubled cluster of apartment complexes. . . . "I believe that because we faced up to a high problem area and looked for ways to resolve that, we became problem solvers as compared to just trying to push a problem away," Menzel said. Other communities might have tried to push a troubled immigrant population out of town, but Rolling Meadows set a national standard for finding a way to assimilate its Hispanic residents. Police departments in West Chicago, Mundelein and Riverdale soon followed Rolling Meadows' example. More recently, resource centers opened in Hoffman Estates, Palatine, Des Plaines and even Cleveland, Ohio. (Cliatt, 2001, p. 1)

The outreach approach of using bilingual community service officers (CSOs) who are nonsworn officers (i.e., they hold badges and wear uniforms) to serve the ethnic communities in San Diego, California, provides yet another viable model for the Latino/Hispanic American community as a whole. The CSOs provide many of the informational, referral, educational, and crime-reporting services available through the police department. The use of bilingual CSOs increases the effectiveness of law enforcement in Spanish-speaking communities. The use of Latino/Hispanic American Police Outreach Coordinators is similar to the CSO approach:

> The police department has hired its first Latino outreach coordinator to combat many Latinos' distrust of police officers and overcome the language barrier. . . . As a civilian member of the police department, Sanchiz will oversee the dozen part-time translators for the department, serve as a translator himself and organize outreach efforts in Burlington's Latino neighborhoods. He has already reached an agreement with Burlington's lone Catholic parish, Blessed Sacrament, to speak to its Latino parishioners at Saturday's Mass. Sanchiz will immediately help the police, Lt. Steve Smith said. "In the past, we've sometimes had trouble getting cooperation from Latino witnesses because of distrust or language barriers," Smith said. "I can see Juan going out to a crime scene with our detectives and helping overcome those difficulties." "Latino people come

from countries where police are often abusive," Sanchiz said. "They come here and think, 'It's going to be the same.' " (Frago, 2001, p. B1)

To bridge the service gap and to reinforce the Latino/Hispanic American community with local and statewide law enforcement and public safety agencies, cities like Durham, North Carolina, have experimented with the Spanish Police Academy ("Durham Civilian Police Academy," 2003). The classes meet twice each week and mirror the regular Citizens' Police Academy, with the major difference being the use of translators. Another way to bridge the gap is to have officers learn Spanish, and some officers will attest that even "survival" Spanish-language training and "crash courses" in minority community relations (Taylor, 2000) have some degree of effectiveness.

The willingness of law enforcement officers to use Spanish phrases in their interactions with Latino/Hispanic Americans is very useful even if the officers have not attained Spanish-language fluency. The use of everyday greetings and courteous phrases in Spanish indicates officers' respect and positive attitude and is seen favorably by members of the Latino/Hispanic American community. (See Chapter 4 for a discussion of language training in police departments.)

Increasing the Number of Latino/Hispanic American Police Officers

Latino/Hispanic Americans are significantly underrepresented in federal, state, and local law enforcement positions. Police departments' attempts to effectively serve states, cities, and community neighborhoods with large Latino/Hispanic American populations have been hampered by the small number of Latino/ Hispanic American officers. A variety of reasons exist for such underrepresentation, including (1) history of law enforcement stereotypes and relationships with Latino/Hispanic American communities; (2) interests of Latino/Hispanic Americans with respect to law enforcement careers; (3) image of law enforcement personnel in Latino/Hispanic American communities; (4) lack of knowledge about the different careers and pathways in law enforcement; (5) concern with and fear of background checks and immigration status, physical requirements, and the application process; (6) ineffective and misdirected law enforcement recruitment and outreach efforts in the Latino/Hispanic American community; and (7) lack of role models and advocates for law enforcement careers for Latino/ Hispanic Americans.

> When John Garcia, a senior law enforcement executive, was traveling through some of the Latino/Hispanic American neighborhoods to do some research on how law enforcement agencies might better serve the community, he was constantly receiving comments from Latino/Hispanic American community residents like, "You must be very rich to be a police chief." "You must have been very famous to be a police captain." "Are you really a police chief? I've never seen anyone like you before." (Latino/Hispanic American law enforcement executive's anecdote in a cultural awareness seminar in southern California)

Clearly, role models are needed to help clarify to the community what is required for a career in law enforcement. Law enforcement agencies have clearly seen the need for increasing their ability to serve the Latino/Hispanic American community with more bilingual/bicultural personnel. The following examples have been used in a variety of agencies (a) to increase understanding of the law enforcement and criminal justice agencies, (b) to create more favorable recruitment possibilities, and (c) to increase understanding between law enforcement and public safety agencies and the Latino/Hispanic American community:

1. ***Red Carpet Mystery:*** Latino/Hispanic American families are invited to solve "crime scene" mysteries staged by the police agency and other local organizations:

> Waukesha—A 37-year-old man is found dead on an apartment floor. Evidence of excessive drug and alcohol use is in plain view. Clearly, the death is due to an overdose. Or is it? Other clues indicate a possible violent end. In a first-of-its-kind program, the mock mystery will be solved not by police but by 30 Hispanic families who have recently immigrated to Waukesha. . . . Avila said the effort is important, because about 100 Hispanic immigrant families move to Waukesha annually and need to feel safe while adjusting to the community. "They need to learn that here police can be friends," she said. UW Extension staff, along with police and the medical examiner's office, have created a five-part series called "The Red Carpet Mystery," financed with a $191,000 federal grant aimed at stemming domestic violence. (Enriquez, 2003, p. B4)

2. ***Establishing Recruitment Opportunities at Community Festivals and Events:*** The Jacksonville Sheriff's Department and other local and regional law enforcement agencies have used large-size community events as a venue for passing out recruitment brochures and scanning the crowd for potential candidates (Andino, 2002). Events, like the World of Nations Festival, which represents more than 40 countries and attracts about 70,000 people across cultural, racial, and ethnic lines, provide opportunities for recruitment. 'It's such a wide, diverse group that you might not otherwise get all together in one place,' said Wendy Raymond Hacker, a spokeswoman for the city's special events office. Law enforcement agencies see events like this as excellent opportunities for meeting possible candidates to serve the growing Latino/Hispanic American communities.

SUMMARY OF RECOMMENDATIONS FOR LAW ENFORCEMENT

The experience of Latino/Hispanic Americans with law enforcement officers in the United States has been complicated (1) by the perceptions of Latino/Hispanic Americans regarding the enforcement of immigration laws against illegal aliens and by the discriminatory treatment received by Latino/Hispanic Americans in the United States and (2) by community conflicts as well as perceptions of police ineffectiveness and unresponsiveness. Officers should realize that some citizens may still remember this history and carry with them stereotypes of police services as something to be feared and avoided. Law enforcement officials need to go out of their way to establish trust, to provide outreach efforts, and to win cooperation in order to effectively accomplish their goals to serve and protect Latino/Hispanic Americans. Building partnerships focused on community collaboration in the fight against crime is important.

The label Latino/Hispanic American encompasses over 25 very diverse ethnic, cultural, and regional groups from North, Central, and South America. Law enforcement officials need to be aware of the differences between the diverse groups (e.g., nationality, native cultural and regional differences and perceptions, and language dialects), as well as the within-group differences that may result from individual life experiences (e.g., sociopolitical turmoil). Since key stereotypes of Latino/Hispanic Americans by mainstream Americans are regarded as more negative than positive, it is important that peace officers make a special effort to extend respect and dignity to this community of very proud people with a culturally rich heritage.

The preferred term for referring to Latino/Hispanic Americans varies with the contexts, groups, and experiences of Latino/Hispanic American individuals. Law enforcement officials need to be aware of terms that are unacceptable and derogatory and terms that are currently used. When in doubt, officers have to learn to become comfortable in asking citizens which terms they prefer. Officers are advised to provide helpful feedback to their peers whenever offensive terms, slurs, labels, and/or actions are used with Latino/Hispanic Americans. Such feedback will help reduce the risk of misunderstanding and improve the working relationships of officers within the Latino/Hispanic American communities. Additionally, it will help enhance the professional image of the department for those communities.

Many Latino/Hispanic Americans are concerned with their ability to communicate clearly and about possible reprisal from the police, as associated with the role of law enforcement in more politically repressive countries. Peace officers need to take the time needed to understand communications and need to be aware that bilingual and non-native English speakers want to communicate effectively with them. Maintaining contact, providing extra time, using translators, and being patient with speakers encourage citizens to communicate their concerns. Cultural differences in verbal and nonverbal communication often result in misinterpretation of the message and of behaviors. Officers need to be aware of the nonverbal aspects of some Latino/Hispanic Americans' communication styles, such as eye contact, touch, gestures, and emotionality. Verbal aspects such as accent, mixing English with Spanish, limited vocabulary, and incorrect grammar may give the officer the impression that the individual does not understand what is communicated. As in all cases when English is the second language, it is important to remember that listening and comprehension skills with English are usually better than speaking skills.

Latino/Hispanic Americans, because of their past experiences with law enforcement agencies, along with their own concerns about privacy, self-help, and other factors, are reluctant to report crimes and may not seek police assistance and help. It is important for law enforcement departments and officials to build relationships and working partnerships with Latino/Hispanic American communities. This is helped by outreach efforts such as community offices, bilingual officers, and participation of officers in community activities.

Latino/Hispanic Americans tend to hold a severe, punishment-oriented perception of law enforcement and corrections. That is, citizens have strong authoritarian views and an equally strong sense of "rightness" and of punishing the criminal. Because of this perspective, members from this community may view law enforcement as more severe than it really is. It is important for law enforcement departments and officials to be aware of this and to approach Latino/Hispanic Americans with knowledge that they may perceive law enforcement as more punitive than it is in actuality.

DISCUSSION QUESTIONS*

1. ***Latino/Hispanic Americans Viewing Law Enforcement as Not Sensitive.*** In the historical information section of this chapter, we noted many associations made about immigration law enforcement and events that may leave Latino/Hispanic Americans with the view that law enforcement agencies are not "sensitive, effective, and responsive." What are ways to improve such possible negative points of view?

2. ***Diversity among Latino/Hispanic Americans.*** Latino/Hispanic Americans consist of over 25 diverse regional, national, ethnic, and cultural groups. Which groups are you most likely to encounter in crime-fighting and peacekeeping in your work? Which groups do you anticipate encountering in your future work?

3. ***Choice of Terms.*** Use of the terms Latino, Hispanic, Chicano, Mexican, La Raza, Puerto Rican, and so forth is confusing for many people. How might you find out which term to use when referring to an individual if ethnic and cultural information of this kind is necessary? What would you do if the term you use seems to engender a negative reaction?

4. ***Offensive Terms and Labels.*** Offensive terms such as "Wetbacks," "Illegals," and "Spics" should not be used in law enforcement work at any time. Give three practical reasons for this perspective. How would you go about helping other officers who use these terms in the course of their work to become aware of their offensiveness?

5. ***Effects of Myths and Stereotypes.*** Myths and stereotypes about Latino/Hispanic Americans have affected this group greatly. What are some of the Latino/Hispanic American stereotypes that you have heard of or have encountered? What effect might these stereotypes have on Latino/Hispanic Americans? What are ways to manage these stereotypes in law enforcement? In what ways can you help an officer who uses stereotypes about Latino/ Hispanic Americans to become aware of the effects of these stereotypes?

6. ***Verbal and Nonverbal Variations among Cultures.*** How do you think that the information in this chapter about verbal and nonverbal communication styles can help officers in their approach to Latino/Hispanic American citizens? When you can understand the cultural components of the style and behaviors, does this help you to become more sensitive and objective about your reactions? In what ways might you use your understanding about Latino/Hispanic American family dynamics in law enforcement?

7. ***Avoidance of Law Enforcement and Underreporting of Crimes.*** Why do you think that many Latino/Hispanic Americans keep to their own communities and underreport crimes of violence? When are such efforts desirable? When are they ineffective? How can police agencies be of greater service to Latino/Hispanic American communities in this regard?

---

*See the Instructor's Manual accompanying this text for additional activities, role-play activities, questionnaires, and projects related to the content of this chapter.

8. ***The Future of Latino/Hispanic Americans and Law Enforcement.*** The Latino/Hispanic American population is the fastest growing segment in the U.S. population. What implications do you see for law enforcement in terms of services, language, recruitment, and training?

WEBSITE RESOURCES

Visit these websites for additional information about law enforcement contact with Latino/Hispanic Americans and related community organizations:

National Council of La Raza (NCLR)   http://www.latino.sscnet.ucla.edu /community/nclr.html

This website provides information about capacity-building assistance to support and strengthen Hispanic community-based programs and information regarding applied research, policy analysis, and advocacy for Latino/Hispanic Americans.

League of United Latin American Citizens (LULAC)   http://www.lulac.org

This website provides information on education, training, scholarships, and services to underprivileged and unrepresented Latino/Hispanic Americans. LULAC is the largest and oldest Latino/Hispanic organization in the United States, with over 115,000 members.

Hispanic American Police Command Officers Association (HAPCOA) http://www.hapcoa.com/

This website provides information to promote the interests of Hispanic American peace officers for recruitment, career development, promotion, and retention of qualified Hispanic police command officers.

Latin American Law Enforcement Association (LA LEY)   http://www.laley.org/

This website provides law enforcement links important to the Latino/Hispanic American community in the areas of advocacy, education, and leadership, and identification of key organizations.

REFERENCES

Andino, A. T. (2002, April 26). "Police to Scan Ethnic Fest for Potential New Recruits." *Florida Times-Union* (Jacksonville, FL), p. B1.

Barnhardt, L. (2003, July 31). "Latino Activists in County Urge Police Training Aids in Spanish: Fatal Shooting of Honduran Highlights Need, They Say." *Baltimore Sun,* p. B3.

Bastian, L. D. (1990). Hispanic victims (NCJ-120507). Washington, D.C.: Bureau of Justice Statistics, U.S. Department of Justice.

Bernal, G., and A. Estrada. (1985). "Cuban Refugee and Minority Experiences: A Book Review." *Hispanic Journal of Behavioral Sciences, 7,* 105–128.

Bernal, G., and M. Gutierrez. (1988). "Cubans," in L. Comas-Diaz and E. E. H. Griffith, eds., *Cross-Cultural Mental Health.* New York: Wiley, pp. 233–261.

Bruner, T. K. (2001, October 15). "International Atlanta: Cash in hand makes Latinos robbery targets; Police, banks try to build trust." *Atlanta Journal and Constitution,* Metro News, p. B1.

Cliatt, C. (2001, September 6). "How Small Steps Healed Town: Innovative Police Outpost Plays Key to Cutting Crime." *Chicago Daily Herald,* p. 1.

Comas-Diaz, L., and E. E. H. Griffith (Eds.). (1988). *Cross-Cultural Mental Health.* New York: Wiley.

"Durham Civilian Police Academy Caters to Hispanics." (2003, June 9). Associated Press.

Elber, L. (2001, January 25). "NBC Apologizes for 'Law & Order' Episode That Offended Some Hispanics." Associated Press.

Enriquez, D. (2003, April 10). "Mystery Program Offers Clue About Culture: Waukesha Hispanic Families Get Lessons on Criminal Justice System." *Milwaukee Journal Sentinel,* p. B4.

Environmental Protection Agency. (2001). "Comprehensive Environmental Response, Compensation, and Liability Act Overview." Washington, DC: Author, Available: <http://www.epa.gov/superfund/action/law/cercla.htm>

Evans, B. (2002, September 18). "Violence against Latinos gets city's attention: Top administrators discuss ways to aid, protect immigrants." *Herald-Sun* (Durham, N.C.), p. A1.

Evans, M. (2001, September 20). "From Success Comes Growth at Sanchez." *Houston Chronicle,* This Week, p. 1.

Fernandex, L. F. (1970). *A Forgotten American.* New York: B'nai B'rith.

Ferriss, S. (1993, March 21). "Racists or Realists? All over California, forces are being mustered against undocumented immigrants." *San Francisco Examiner.*

"Five Robbers Charged with Targeting Hispanics." (2003, May 1). Associated Press.

Frago, C. (2001, September 24). "Police Bridge Gap with Latinos: New Outreach Coordinator Juan Sanchiz Will Help Build Trust Between the Burlington Department and Spanish-Speaking Residents." *News & Record* (Greensboro, NC), p. B1.

Fusco, C. (2002, November 14). "Suburb settles in profiling suit: Up to 3,200 Hispanic motorists may get as much as $225 each." *Chicago Sun-Times,* p. 5.

Gavzer, G. (1993, March 21). "Held without Hope." *Parade.*

Gonzalez, D. (1992, November 15). "What's the Problem with 'Hispanic'? Just Ask a 'Latino.'" *New York Times,* Section 4, p. 6.

Gracia, J. J. E. (2000). *Hispanic/Latino Identity: A Philosophical Perspective.* Malden, Mass: Blackwell.

Greenhouse, S. (2000, June 2). "Companies Pay $1 Million in Harassment Suit." *New York Times,* p. A12.

Harbrecht, D., G. Smith, and S. Baker. (1993, April 19). "The Mexican Worker." *Business Week,* p. 84.

Hill, L., and R. Trapp. (2000, October 29). "African Americans and Latinos in a San Diego Study." *San Diego Union-Tribune,* p. B11.

Hispanic Monitor. (1991). *Segmenting the Hispanic Market.* New York: Yankelovich, Clancy Shulman and Market Development, Inc.

Hornor, L. L. (Ed.). (1999). *Hispanic Americans: A Statistical Sourcebook—1999 Edition.* Palo Alto, CA: Information Publications.

Kelley, T. (2000, October 12). "Suspect Admits Attacking Immigrant." *New York Times,* p. B5.

LeDuff, C. (2000, September 24). "For Migrants, Hard Work in Hostile Suburbs." *New York Times,* p. 1.

Lewis, A. (2000, April 29). "Abroad at Home: Elian and the Law." *New York Times,* p. A13.

Lombardi, F. (2000, June 24). "Most Hispanics Fear Cops: Poll Finds Concern about NYPD Brutality and Bigotry." *New York Daily News,* p. 8.

Lopez y Rivas, G. (1973). *The Chicanos.* New York: Monthly Review Press.

Mandel, B. (1993, January 24). "Black man's ad is the talk of the town." *San Francisco Examiner.*

Martinez, C., Jr. (1988). "Mexican-Americans," in L. Comas-Diaz and E. E. H. Griffith, eds., *Cross- Cultural Mental Health.* New York: Wiley, pp. 182–203.

Montiel, M. (1978). *Hispanic Families: Critical Issues for Policy and Programs in Human Services.* Washington, D.C.: Coalition of Spanish Speaking Mental Health Organizations.

Morales, R., and F. Bonilla (Eds.). (1993). *Latinos in a Changing U.S. Economy.* Newbury Park, CA: Sage.

Office of Management and Budget. (1997, October 30). "Revisions to the Standards for the Classification of Federal Data on Race and Ethnicity." *Federal Register,* 62(280), 58,782–85,790.

Orange County Sheriff's Department. (1990). *Common Ground* [videotape by the Orange County Sheriff's Department]. Santa Ana, CA: Author.

Peterson, I. (2001, January 26). "Settlement Is Said to Be Near in Case of Turnpike Shooting." *New York Times,* p. B5.

Rodriguez, C. E. (2000). *Changing Race: Latinos, the Census, and the History of Ethnicity in the United States.* New York: New York University Press.

Steinberg, J. (2001, October 13). "Fielding Prosperity: Ex-farm worker sees her past as a start to success." *Fresno Bee,* p. C1.

Stevens, E. (1973). "Machismo and Marianismo." *Transaction-Society, 10*(6), 57–63.

Taylor, L. G. (2000, March 1). "Police Get Crash Course in Minority Relations." *Pittsburgh Post-Gazette,* p. B4.

Therrien, M., and Ramirez, R. R. (2000). "The Hispanic Population in the United States." (Current Population Reports, P20-535). Washington, DC: U.S. Census Bureau.

"Wanted in Wichita: Bilingual Police Officers." (2001, October 8). Associated Press.

Washington, A. T. (2002, October 25). "Some Hispanics Feeling Singled Out in Sniper Furor." *Washington Times,* p. B2.

Chapter 8

Law Enforcement Contact with Arab Americans and Other Middle Eastern Groups

OVERVIEW

This chapter provides specific cultural information on the largest group of Middle Easterners to settle in the United States, Arab Americans. We begin with an explanation of the scope of the term Middle Easterner as it is used in this chapter and provide information briefly on non-Arab Middle Eastern groups. This is followed by a summary of the two major waves of Arab immigration to the United States. The chapter presents demographics and the diversity among Arab Americans as well as information on basic Arab values and beliefs. The background information leads into a discussion of commonly held stereotypes of Arabs as well as how those stereotypes contributed to anti-Arab incidents or backlash after September 11, 2001. A brief presentation of some aspects of the Islamic religion is included in the chapter, as well as a summary of the commonalities between Islam, Christianity, and Judaism. Elements of family life are presented, including a discussion of the role of the head of the household and issues related to children and "Americanization."

The next section presents various cultural practices and characteristics, including greetings, approach, touching, hospitality, verbal and nonverbal communication, gestures, emotional expressiveness, and general points about English language usage. The final section describes several key concerns for law enforcement, with information on perceptions of police, women and modesty, Arab store owners in urban areas, and hate crimes against Arab Americans, especially those that occurred after the September 11 terrorist attacks. In the chapter summary, readers will find recommendations for improved communication and relationships between law enforcement personnel and Arab American communities.

COMMENTARY

Middle Easterners come to the United States for numerous reasons: to gain an education and begin a career, to escape an unstable political situation in their country of origin, and to invest in commercial enterprises with the goal of gaining legal entry into the country. People in law enforcement continue to have contact with Middle Easterners from a number of different countries. Officers would benefit from having a rudimentary knowledge about past and present world events related to Middle Easterners and should be aware of stereotypes that others hold of them. Attitudes toward Middle

Easterners in this country as well as geopolitical events in the Middle East can have implications for law enforcement.

Established Americans of Arab origin are sometimes treated as if they had just come from the Middle East and may be potential terrorists. This perception increased significantly after the terrorist attacks of September 11, 2001. Stereotypes, which have long been imprinted in people's minds, can and do significantly affect people's perceptions of Arab Americans, whether they are second or third generation or recent refugees. (See "The Terrorist Stereotype and Post-9/11 Backlash" and "Hate Crimes against Arab Americans" in this chapter.)

MIDDLE EASTERNERS AND RELATED TERMINOLOGY DEFINED

Among the general population there is considerable confusion as to who Middle Easterners are and, specifically, who Arabs are. Although commonly thought of as Arabs, Iranians and Turks are not Arabs. Many people assume that all Muslims are Arabs, and vice versa. In fact, many Arabs are also Christians, and the world's Muslim population is actually comprised of dozens of ethnic groups. (The largest Muslim population is in Asia, and not the Middle East.) Nevertheless, the predominant religion among Arabs is Islam, and its followers are called Muslims. They are also referred to as Moslems, but Muslims is the preferred term as it is closer to the Arabic pronunciation. People sometimes confuse the words Arab, Arabic, and Arabian.

The following excerpt is from *100 Questions You Have Always Wanted to Ask about Arab Americans* (Detroit Free Press, 2001); it clears up common confusion around terminology related to Arab Americans.

Should I say Arab, Arabic or Arabian?

Arab is a noun for a person, and is used as an adjective as in "Arab country." Arabic is the name of the language and generally is not used as an adjective. Arabian is an adjective that refers to Saudia Arabia, the Arabian Peninsula, or as in Arabian horse. When ethnicity or nationality are relevant, it is more precise and accurate to specify the country by using Lebanese, Yemeni or whatever is appropriate.

What all Arabs have in common is the Arabic language, even though spoken Arabic differs from country to country (e.g., Algerian Arabic is different from Jordanian Arabic). The following countries constitute the Middle East and are all Arab countries with the exception of three:

- Aden
- Bahrain
- Egypt
- Iran (non-Arab country)
- Iraq
- Israel (non-Arab country)
- Jordan
- Kuwait
- Lebanon

- Oman

- Palestinian Authority

- Qatar

- Saudi Arabia

- Syria

- Turkey (non-Arab country)

- United Arab Emirates

- Yemen

There are other Arab countries that are not in the Middle East (e.g., Algeria, Tunisia, Morocco, Libya) in which the majority population shares a common language and religion (Islam) with people in the Arabic countries of the Middle East. In this chapter, we cover primarily information on refugees and immigrants from Arab countries in the Middle East, as they constitute the majority of Middle Eastern newcomers who bring cultural differences and special issues requiring clarification for law enforcement. We only briefly mention issues related to the established Arab American community (i.e., the people who began arriving in the United States in the late 19th century). Following is a brief description of the population from the three non-Arab countries.

Iranians and Turks

Iranians use the Arabic script in their writing, but for the most part speak mainly Farsi (Persian), not Arabic. Turks speak Turkish, although there are minority groups in Turkey who speak Kurdish, Arabic, and Greek. More than 99.8 percent of Iranians and Turks are Muslim, Islam being the most common religion among people in many other Middle Eastern countries (Central Intelligence World Fact Book, 2003). However, many Iranians in the United States are Jewish and Bahai, both of which groups are minorities in Iran. Of the Muslim population in Iran, the majority belong to the Shi'ah sect of Islam, the Shi'ah version of Islam being the state religion. Persians are the largest ethnic group in Iran, making up about 50 percent of the population (Central Intelligence World Fact Book, 2003), but there are other ethnic populations, including Kurds, Arabs, Turkmen, Armenians, and Assyrians (among others), most of whom can be found in the United States. During the Iranian hostage crisis in 1979, many Iranians in the United States were targets of hate crimes and anti-Iranian sentiment: the same attitudes prevailed against other Middle Easterners (Arabs) and South Asians (Indians from India) who were mistakenly labeled as Iranian. Iranians and Turks are not Arabs, but some of the cultural values related to the extended family with respect to pride, dignity, and honor are similar to those in the traditional Arab world. Many Iranian Americans and Turkish Americans came to the United States in the 1970s and were from upper-class, professional groups such as doctors, lawyers, and engineers. Many of the Jewish Iranians in the United States left Iran after the fall of the Shah. In the United States, there are large Iranian Jewish populations in the San Francisco Bay Area, Los Angeles, and New York. Also, one can find populations of Muslim Iranians in major U.S. cities, such as New York, Chicago, and Los Angeles.

Israelis

Israel is the only country in the Middle East in which the majority of the population is not Muslim. Approximately 20 percent of the population in Israel is made up of Arabs (both Christian and Muslim). Eighty percent of the Israeli population is Jewish (Central Intelligence World Fact Book, 2003), with the Jewish population divided into two main groups: Ashkenazim and Sephardim. The Ashkenazim are descended from members of the Jewish communities of Central and Eastern Europe. The majority of American Jews are Ashkenazi, while currently the majority of Israeli Jews are Sephardim, having come originally from Spain, other Mediterranean countries, and the Arabic countries of the Middle East. Israeli immigrants in the United States may be either Ashkenazi or Sephardic and their physical appearance will not indicate to an officer what their ethnicity is. An Israeli may look like an American Jew, a Christian, or a Muslim Arab (or none of these).

Most of the Israeli Arabs who live within the borders of Israel are Palestinians whose families stayed in Israel after the Arab–Israeli war in 1948, following the birth of Israel as a nation. The Six-Day War in 1967 resulted in Israel occupying lands that formerly belonged to Egypt, Syria, and Jordan, but where the majority of the population was Palestinian. Thus, until the signing of the Oslo 1993 peace accord between Israel and the Palestine Liberation Organization (PLO), Israel occupied territories with a population of approximately 1 million Palestinians. The Palestinian–Israeli situation in the Middle East has created a great deal of hostility on both sides. In the fall of 2000, failure to reach a negotiated settlement agreement required by the Oslo peace accords of 1993 resulted in a period of increased hostilities. The tension continues (as this book goes into press) and can have implications for law enforcement officials in the United States, especially in communities where there are large populations of Jews and Arabs, or where Israelis and Palestinians reside in large numbers (e.g., Los Angeles, New York, Chicago). Police should also know whether individuals and groups with extremist views operate out of their cities.

Public events such as Israeli Independence Day celebrations and Israeli or Palestinian political rallies have the potential for confrontation, although the majority of these events have been peaceful. Police presence is required at such events, but as with other situations, excessive police presence can escalate hostilities. Law enforcement officials need to be well informed about current events in the Middle East, as conflicts there often have a ripple effect across the world. The monitoring of world events and community trends (discussed in Chapter 11) will help police officers take a preventive posture that can ultimately help to avoid confrontation between various Middle Eastern ethnic groups in this country.

HISTORICAL INFORMATION

Although many recent Middle Eastern immigrants and refugees in the United States have come for political reasons, not all Arab Americans left their country of origin because of these. There have been two major waves of Arab immigrants to the United States. The first wave came between 1880 and World War I and were largely from Syria and what is known today as Lebanon (at the time these areas were part of the Turkish Ottoman Empire). Of the immigrants who settled during this wave, approximately 90 percent were Christian. Many people came to further themselves economically (thus these were immigrants and not refugees forced to leave their countries), but in addition, many of the young men wanted to avoid the military in the Ottoman Empire (A. Naff, personal communication, January 25, 1993). A substantial percentage of these immigrants were farmers and artisans and became involved in the business of peddling their goods to farmers and moved from town to town.

Middle Eastern social and political historian Alixa Naff has recorded several conversations with older immigrants in which they have recounted their early experiences with and perceptions of American police at the time they were newly arrived immigrants. She explains that because the Arabs competed with local, native-born merchants, there were calls to the police requesting that the Arab peddlers be sent away. Naff has several accounts whereby Arab immigrants reported that they had positive views toward the American police. One immigrant from Syria said that he appreciated the way police treated him in the United States and that in his own country, the police (i.e., the Turkish military police) would have beaten him; there was no civilian police force at the time. This immigrant was impressed with the hospitality of the police—a police officer actually let him sleep in the jail! (Naff, 1993). In the way of crime statistics, not much is reported, partly due to the fact that in the Arab immigrant community, people took care of their own. When there was a crime, the tendency would have been to cover it up.

In sharp contrast to the characteristics and motivation of the first wave of immigrants, the second wave of Arabic immigrants to the United States, beginning after World War II, came in large part as students and professionals because of economic instability and political unrest. As a result, these groups brought a "political consciousness unknown to earlier immigrants" (John Zogby 2003). The largest group of second-wave immigrants is made up of Palestinians, many of whom came around 1948, the time of the partition of Palestine, which resulted in Israel's independence. In the 1970s, after the Six-Day War between Israel and Egypt, Syria, and Jordan, another large influx of Palestinians came to the United States. In the 1980s a large group of Lebanese came as a result of the civil war in Lebanon. Yemenis (from Yemen) have continued to come throughout the century; Syrians and Iraqis have made the United States their home since the 1950s and 1960s because of political instability in their countries (John Zogby, 2003). Thus these second-wave immigrants came largely because of political turmoil and have been instrumental in changing the nature of the Arab American community in the United States.

The most dramatic example of how Arab immigration has affected a U.S. city is the Detroit area in Michigan. There Arabs began to arrive in the late 19th century, but the first huge influx was between 1900 and 1924, when the auto industry attracted immigrants from all over the world (Woodruff, 1991). The Detroit–Dearborn area has the largest Arab community in the United States, with Arab Americans constituting about one-fourth of the population in Dearborn. A large percentage of the Detroit area's Middle Eastern population is Chaldean, Christian Iraqis who speak the Chaldean language. While they are from the heart of the Middle East, most do not identify themselves to be Iraqi, and some are deeply offended if referred to as Arab (Haddad, 2003). This is particularly true in the Detroit area as well as in other large urban concentrations, but may be less applicable to Chaldeans in other areas (Samhan, 2003).

DEMOGRAPHICS

Immigrants from all over the Arabic world continue to settle in the United States. For example, in 2000 approximately 12,000 visas (combined total) were issued to immigrants coming to the United States from Bahrain, Egypt, Iraq, Jordan, Kuwait, Lebanon, Qatar, Saudi Arabia, Syria, the United Arab Emirates, and Yemen (Samhan, 2003).

There are approximately 3.5 million Americans of Arabic ancestry in the United States, but this figure does not include those who have not declared their ancestry to census officials (John Zogby, 2003). The communities with the largest Arab American populations are in Los Angeles/Orange County, Detroit, the greater New York area, Chicago, and Washington D.C. California has the largest "cluster" of Arab American communities (Samhan, 2003).

After the September 11 attacks, immigration to the United States declined significantly, given the increased security and background checks given to people wishing to come to America ("Immigration down," 2003, p. A3).

DIFFERENCES AND SIMILARITIES

There is great diversity among Arab American groups. Understanding this diversity will assist officers in not categorizing Arabs as one homogeneous group and will encourage people to move away from stereotypical thinking. Arabs from the Middle East come from at least 13 different countries, many of which are vastly different from each other. The governments of the Arabic countries also differ, ranging from monarchies to theocracies to military governments to socialist republics (Central Intelligence World Fact Book, 2003). Arab visitors such as foreign students, tourists, businesspeople, and diplomats to the United States from the Gulf states (e.g., Saudi Arabia, Qatar, Oman, Bahrain, United Arab Emirates) are typically wealthy, but their Jordanian, Lebanese, and Palestinian brethren do not generally bring wealth to the United States, and in fact, many are extremely poor. Another area in which one finds differences is clothing. In the Middle East in a number of countries, many older men wear headdresses, but it is less common among men who are younger and who have more education. Similarly, younger women in the Middle East may choose not to wear the head covering and long dress that covers them from head to toe.

The younger generation of Arabs, much to the disappointment of the parents and grandparents, may display entirely different behavior from what is expected of them (as is typical in most immigrant and refugee groups). In addition, as with other immigrant groups, there are Arab Americans who have been in the United States for generations who are completely assimilated into the American culture. They may not identify with their roots. Others, although they have also been in the United States for generations, consciously try to keep their Arabic traditions alive and pass them on to their children. Officers should not treat established Arab Americans as if they were newcomers.

There are broad differences among Arab American groups associated with social class and economic status. Although many Arab Americans who come to the United States are educated professionals, there is a percentage who come from rural areas (e.g., peasants from southern Lebanon, West Bank Palestinians, Yemenis) who differ in outlook and receptiveness to modernization. On the other hand, despite traditional values, many newcomers are modern in outlook. Many people have a stereotypical image of the Arab woman, yet the following description certainly illustrates that not all women of Arabic descent adhere to the image. For example, John Zogby, president of Zogby International, describes many modern Arab women who defy the stereotype: "Among the upper-class, educated Palestinian population here, you can find many women who are vocal and outspoken. You might see the young husbands wheeling the babies around in strollers while the women are discussing world events" (John Zogby, 2003).

On the other hand, certain Arab governments (e.g., Saudi Arabia) place restrictions on women mandating that they do not mix with men, that a woman must always be veiled, and that she not travel alone or drive a car. Women, then, from less-restrictive Arab countries (e.g., Egypt and Jordan) might exhibit very different behavior from those whose governments grant them fewer freedoms. Nevertheless, women in traditional Muslim families from any country typically have limited contact with men outside their family and wear traditional dress. Some implications of these traditions as they relate to Arab women and male police officers in the United States are discussed further in this chapter.

It is important to look at people's motivation for coming to the United States to help avoid stereotypical thinking. Arab American police Corporal Mohamed Berro of the Dearborn, Michigan, Police Department makes a distinction between immigrants (who have "few problems adjusting to the United States") and refugees. He explains that refugees, having been forced to leave their country of origin, believe that they are here temporarily because they are waiting for a conflict to end. As a result, they may be more hesitant to change and relationship building may take more time.

Similarities

Despite most differences, whether apparent in socioeconomic status, levels of traditionalism, or motivation for coming to the United States, there are values and beliefs associated with Arab culture that law enforcement officials should understand in order to establish rapport and trust. Officers will recognize that some of the information listed below does not apply only to Arab culture. At the same time, the following explains deeply held beliefs that many Arab Americans would agree are key to understanding traditional Arab culture.

Basic Arab Values

1. Traditional Arab society upholds honor; the degree to which an Arab can lose face and be shamed publicly is foreign to the average Westerner. Officers recognize that dignity and respect should be shown to all individuals, but citizens from cultures emphasizing shame, loss of face, and honor (e.g., Middle Eastern, Asian, Latin American) may react even more severely to loss of dignity and respect than do other individuals. People will go so far to avoid shame that they will not report crimes. "It is often difficult to get members of Arab communities to be full-fledged complainants, because they either don't complain in the first place, or do not follow through. Therefore, because of their primary concern to save face, avoid shame, and maintain harmony, it becomes more difficult to gain successful prosecution." (Haddad, 2003). (Keep in mind that

"shame" cultures have sanctioned extreme punishments for loss of face and honor, e.g., death if a woman loses her virginity before marriage.)

2. Loyalty to one's family takes precedence over other personal needs. A person is completely intertwined with his or her family; protection and privacy in a traditional Arab family often overrides relationships with other people. Members of Arab families tend to avoid disagreements and disputes in front of others, much preferring to resolve issues themselves (Haddad, 2003).

3. Communication should be courteous and hospitable. Harmony between individuals is emphasized. Too much directness and candor can be interpreted as extremely impolite. From a traditional Arab view, it may not be appropriate for a person to give totally honest responses if they result in a loss of face, especially for self or family members (this may not apply to many established Arab Americans). From this perspective, the higher goals of honor and face-saving are operative. This aspect of cross-cultural communication is not easily understood by most Westerners (and is often criticized). Certainly, officers will not accept anything but the whole truth, despite arguments rationalized by cultural ideals having to do with face and shame. However, it may lead an officer nowhere to explicitly draw attention to a face-saving style. The officer would be well advised to work around the issue of the indirect communication rather than insinuating that the citizen may not be honest.

STEREOTYPES

The Arab world has long been perceived in the West in terms of negative stereotypes, which have been transferred to Americans of Arab descent. . . . Briefly put, Arabs are nearly universally portrayed as ruthless terrorists, greedy rich sheiks, religious fanatics, belly dancers or in other simplistic and negative images. When these stereotypes are coupled with the growing centrality of the Middle East in world politics and the increased political visibility of Arab-Americans, one result is that our community becomes more susceptible to hate crimes. (American-Arab Anti-Discrimination Committee, 1992)

The above characterization of discrimination against Arabs still holds true today, over a decade after the publication of the report. The Western media have been continually responsible for representing Arabs in a less than accurate way. When one hears the word "Arab," several images come to mind: (1) wealthy sheik (despite the class distinctions in the Middle East [as elsewhere] between a wealthy Gulf Arab sheik and a poor Palestinian or Lebanese); (2) violent terrorist (the majority of Arabs worldwide want peace and do not see terrorism as an acceptable means for achieving peace); (3) sensuous harem owner; man with many wives ("harems" are rare and for the most part, polygamy, or having more than one wife, has been abolished in the Arab world); and (4) ignorant, illiterate, and backward (Arab contributions to civilization have been great in the areas of mathematics, astronomy, medicine, architecture, geography, and language, among others, but this is not widely known in the West) (Macron, 1989). Despite these stereotypes, there are high-profile Arab Americans in all sectors of the professional world. Since the first edition of this book in 1995, sizeable percentages of Arab Americans have moved out of marginal urban areas and into the suburbs (James

Zogby, 2003). There are over 600 Arab Americans who are members of the National Arab American Medical Association, and the Michigan Arab American legal society has a highly respected and substantial membership as well (Haddad 2003).

As with all distorted information of ethnic groups, it is important to understand how stereotypes interfere with a true understanding of a people. Laurence Michalak, cultural anthropologist and former director of the Center for Middle Eastern Studies at the University of California, Berkeley, points out: "When we consider the Western image of the Arab—Ali Baba, Sinbad the Sailor, the thief of Baghdad, the slave merchant, the harem dancer, and so on—we have to admit that, at least in the case of Arabs, fiction is stranger than truth. . . . The Arab stereotype, while it teaches us very little about the Arabs, teaches us a good deal about ourselves and about mechanisms of prejudice" (Michalak, 1988).

Movies and Television

Perhaps the most offensive type of Arab stereotypes comes from the media; programs and movies routinely portray Arabs as evil womanizers, wealthy oil sheiks who wear turbans, thieves, and terrorists. Even films and programs aimed at children propagate this stereotype of the Arab as a villain. The original lyrics of the opening song of Disney's *Aladdin,* "Arabian Nights," are sung by an Arab who has been portrayed as a stereotype: "Oh I come from a land, from a faraway place/ Where the caravan camels roam/ Where they cut off your ear if they don't like your face/ It's barbaric, but hey, it's home" (Shaheen, 2001, p. 51).

A 1997 poll asked Americans how they viewed recent immigrant groups and how they felt these groups were portrayed in the media. Nearly one-third of those polled gave unfavorable opinions of Middle Easterners and nearly half of the same group thought that Middle Easterners were negatively portrayed in TV shows, movies, and books. (The two other groups rated more negatively were Cubans and Mexicans.) (Knight-Ridder poll by Princeton Survey Research of 1,314 adults, May 1997). A similar opinion poll (without questions regarding the media) conducted within 4 days of the terrorist attacks found that 35 percent of Americans said they had even less trust in Arabs living in the United States post-9/11 (CNN/USA Today/Gallup poll, September 14 and 15, 2001, from DiversityInc.com).

Because many Americans do not know Arabs personally, media images become embedded in people's minds. Jack Shaheen, author of *Reel Bad Arabs: How Hollywood Vilifies a People* (2001), writes, "By depicting Arabs solely as slimy, shifty, violent creeps, Hollywood has been not only misrepresenting the Arab world, but also creating a climate for hate." For example, the film *The Siege,* released in 1998, continues to receive extremely negative reactions from Islamic groups. The film, about Palestinian terrorists, was said to have linked Islam to terrorism and showed Muslim-Americans being rounded up and placed in internment camps (Shaheen, 2001, pp. 430–433). "Whenever Hollywood productions and TV series portray terrorism or violence, it always has to be an Arab. They seem to think it is our monopoly" (comment by the president of the American-Arab Anti-Discrimination Committee, as reported in "Film's Portrayal of Muslims," 1998).

Shaheen argues that the atmosphere created by Hollywood helped contribute to the recorded 326 hate crimes against Arab Americans in the first month alone following the terrorist attacks. Though military retaliations after the attacks were labeled "anti-terrorist" rather than "anti-Islamic," the movie industry has continued the negative stereotyping of Arabs and Muslims. In Shaheen's view, "There certainly should be movies based on what happened, but if [images of Arabs as terrorists] are the only images we see from now on, if we continue to vilify all Muslims and all Arabs as terrorists instead of making clear this is a lunatic fringe, what are we accomplishing?" (Shaheen, 430–433). He adds that the more a people is defamed, the easier it is to "deny them civil rights and no one will say anything. Look at all the hate crimes since [9/11]. Could it be that stereotypes in part played a role?" (p. 37)

The "Terrorist" Stereotype and Post-9/11 Backlash

Images of those responsible for the horrific September 11 carnage were eerily similar to the terrorist image described above. The backlash that ensued against Arab Americans, Muslim Americans, or those thought to be of Middle Eastern origin was predicted by many organizations and individuals, including critics of the media's stereotyped image of a Middle Easterner as a terrorist. Even prior to the September 11, 2001, attacks, Arabs were labeled as terrorists. A most convincing example of the persistence of discrimination against Arabs occurred after the Oklahoma City bombing in April 1995. Immediately following the bombing, many journalists and political leaders said that the tragedy appeared to be the work of Muslim terrorists. This was the initial conclusion without any supporting evidence; the arrest and conviction of Timothy J. McVeigh proved them wrong. The paranoia that led to the conclusion of Arab involvement in the bombing gave way to Arab-bashing, including many hate calls to Arabs. The scapegoating against Arabs spread pervasively across the country.

The justifiable rage that ensued after September 11, 2001, turned into general Arab- and Muslim-bashing, thus the predictions made by representatives of Arab American and Muslim American organizations became a reality. Within the first 9 weeks following the attacks, there were more than 700 reported violent crimes against Arab Americans and Muslim Americans, or those who were perceived to be. Even Sikhs, who may be dark-skinned and wear turbans, but are neither Muslim nor of Middle Eastern descent, were targets and victims of hate crimes in the aftermath of the attacks. (See Chapter 5.)

Post-September 11, the government instituted new emergency legislation aimed at avenging the terrorist attacks and also at preventing future ones. Such measures allowed law enforcement officials to search homes without a warrant and to detain suspects without due cause. Other measures included a more stringent tracking of international students in the United States, registration of foreign nationals (non-U.S. citizens), and "Operation TIPS (Terrorist Information and Prevention System)," which many viewed as encouragement of low-level espionage. The Attorney General also requested "voluntary" interviews with thousands of young Arab men (none of which, as of 2003, have provided evidence linked to the attacks). From the Arab American community's perspective, these were acts of organized racial profiling by government officials, who appeared to define young Arab men as inherently dangerous.

In addition to feeling targeted by the government, a November/December 2001 poll by Zogby International found that 57% of American Muslims felt that the attitude of Americans toward Muslims or Arabs after September 11 was somewhat or very unfavorable, compared to 37% who felt somewhat or very favorable attitudes from Americans. Zogby International reports that the majority of reported discrimination was against young immigrants, with a large proportion of incidents against young women. A Zogby International poll showed that one-third of all Arab Americans and upward of 40% of all Muslim Americans have experienced discrimination since September 11 (John Zogby, 2003). Indeed, CNN/USA Today/Gallup poll conducted immediately following the attacks found that 60% of Americans believed there should be more intensive security checks for Arab Americans wishing to fly on American planes, and 50% of Americans believed that *all* Arab Americans should be required to carry a special form of identification (cited in "Who are Arab Americans? Doug Flutie, Paula Abdul, Ralph Nader," on DiversityInc.com, October 18, 2001). The terrorist stereotype seemed to overpower the words denouncing the attacks by Muslim American and Arab American leaders. In fact, the Zogby International Poll also found that Muslim Americans gave President George W. Bush a 58% approval rating for handling the attacks and 41% of those interviewed felt more patriotic after the attacks (compared to 5% who felt less patriotic and 56% who felt the same). "I know I speak for millions of Muslims in this country," writes freelance writer Mona Elahawy, "when I say I feel a disconnect between what our beliefs and lives are actually like and what we hear they are like in government statements and news reports" ("All Muslims Not In on Terrorist Plot," 2003, p. 9).

The hundreds of violent crimes against Arab Americans, or those thought to be Arab American, Arab, or Muslim, that occurred after the attacks did include recorded FBI and police misconduct. However, as news of the anti-Arab and anti-Muslim backlash spread, collaboration of federal, state, and local law enforcement with community members helped to curb the growing violence. In a report from the Arab-American Anti-Discrimination Committee (ADC), organization leaders praise the work of local law enforcement after the attacks. "Overall, the ADC is grateful and pleased with police response to the enormous increase in bias crimes following September 11." The report cites quick responses to the new challenge as well as extra enforcement sent to protect mosques, Arab businesses, and organizations (ADC Report, 2002). (See section on "Hate Crimes" in this chapter, as well as in Chapter 12.)

ISLAMIC RELIGION

Misunderstanding between Americans and Arabs or Arab Americans can often be traced, in part, to religious differences and a lack of tolerance of these differences. Islam is practiced by the majority of Middle Eastern newcomers to the United States, as well as by many African Americans. Many Arab Americans (especially those from the first wave of Arab immigration) are Christian, however, and prefer that others do not assume they are Muslim simply because they are Arabs.

Remember that Muslims are the people who practice the religion, which is called Islam. By and large, most Americans do not understand what Islam is and, because of stereotyping, wrongly associate Muslims with terrorists or fanatics. Many, but by no means all, Arab Muslims in the United States are religious and have held on to the traditional aspects of their religion, which are also intertwined with their way of life. Islam means submission to the will of God and for traditional, religious Muslims, the will of God (or fate) is a central concept. The religion has been called "Mohammedanism," which is an incorrect name for the religion because it suggests that Muslims worship

Mohammed* rather than God (Allah). It is believed that God's final message to man was revealed to the prophet Mohammed. "Allah" is the shortened Arabic word for the God of Abraham, and it is used by both Arab Muslims and Arab Christians.

The Qur'an (Koran) and the Pillars of Islam

The Qur'an is the holy text for Muslims, and is regarded as the word of God (Allah). There are five "Pillars of Islam," or central guidelines that form the framework of the religion:

1. Profession of faith in Allah (God)
2. Prayer five times daily
3. Alms giving (concern for the needy)
4. Fasting during the month of Ramadan (sunrise to sunset)
5. Pilgrimage to Mecca (in Saudi Arabia) at least once in each person's lifetime

There are several points where law enforcement officials can respect a Muslim's need to practice his or her religion. The need to express one's faith in God and to be respected for it is one area. Normally, people pray together as congregations in mosques, the Islamic equivalent of a church or synagogue. People, however, can pray individually if a congregation is not present. Religious Muslims in jails, for example, will continue to pray five times a day and should not be ridiculed or prevented from doing so. Remember that prayer, five times a day, is a "pillar" of Islam and that strict Muslims will want to uphold this "command" no matter where they are. Call to prayer takes place at the following times:

- One hour before sunrise
- At noon
- Mid-afternoon
- Sunset
- Ninety minutes after sunset

Taboos in the Mosque

A police officer will convey respect to a Muslim community if he or she can avoid entering a mosque and interrupting prayers (emergencies may occasionally make this impossible). Religion is so vital in Arab life that law enforcement officials should always show respect for Islamic customs and beliefs. Thus, other than in emergency situations, officers are advised to:

- Avoid entering a mosque, or certainly the prayer room of a mosque, during prayers.
- Never step on a prayer mat or rug with your shoes on.

*An alternate spelling is Muhammad, which is closer to the Arabic pronunciation of the name.

- Never place the Qur'an on the floor or put anything on top of it.
- Avoid walking in front of people who are praying.
- Speak softly while people are praying.
- Dress conservatively (both men and women are required to dress conservatively; shorts are not appropriate).
- Invite people out of a prayer area to talk to them.

Proper protocol in a mosque (also referred to as a masjid) requires that people remove their shoes before entering, but this must be left to the officer's discretion. Officer safety, of course, comes before consideration of differences.

Ramadan: The Holy Month

One of the holiest periods in the Islamic religion is the celebration of Ramadan, which lasts for one month. There is no fixed date because, like the Jewish and Chinese calendars, the Islamic calendar is based on the lunar cycle (related to the phases of the moon) and dates vary from year to year. During the month of Ramadan, Muslims do not eat, drink, or smoke from sunrise to sunset. The purpose of fasting during Ramadan is to "train one in self-discipline, subdue the passions, and give [people]. . . . a sense of unity with all Moslems" (Devine & Braganti, 1991, p. 28). On the 29th night of Ramadan, when there is a new moon, the holiday is officially over. The final fast is broken and for up to 3 days, people celebrate with a feast and other activities. Throughout the month of Ramadan, Muslim families tend to pray more often in the mosque than during other parts of the year.

For Muslims, Ramadan is as important and holy as Christmas; this fact is appreciated when others, who are not Muslim, recognize the holiday's importance. One city with a sizable Arab American population puts up festive lights in its business district during Ramadan as a gesture of acceptance and appreciation of the diversity that the Arab Americans bring to the city. The Arab American community reacted favorably to this symbolic gesture. Meanwhile, in the same city, at the end of Ramadan, while many families were in the mosque, police ticketed hundreds of cars that were parked in store parking lots across from the mosque, even though, according to some Arab American citizens, the stores were closed. When people came out of the mosque and saw all the tickets, the mood of the holiday naturally was spoiled. The perception from the Arab American citizens was that "They don't want to understand us . . . they don't know how we feel . . . they don't know what's important to us." (Readers can analyze this situation from an enforcement and community relations' point of view and discuss whether the situation could have been prevented. See question 1 in the discussion section at the end of the chapter.)

Knowledge of Religious Practices

Knowledge of religious practices, including what is considered holy, will help officers avoid creating problems and conflicts. A belief in the Islamic religion that may occasionally arise in the course of police work will illustrate this point. In a suburb of San Francisco, California, a group of police officers and Muslims (from Tunisia, an Arab country in North Africa) were close to violence when, in a morgue, police entered to try to get a hair sample from a person who had just been killed in a car accident. Apparently, the body had already been blessed by an "Iman" (a religious leader) and, according to the religion, any further contact would have been a defilement of the body since the body had already been sanctified and was ready for burial. The police officers were merely doing what they needed to do to complete their investigation and were unaware of this taboo. This, together with a language barrier, created an extremely confusing and confrontational situation in which officers lost necessary control. In this case they needed to explain what had to be done and communicate their needs in the form of a request for permission to handle a body that had already been sanctified. If the citizens had not granted permission, the police would then have had to decide how to proceed. Most members of the Arab American community would comply with the wishes of police officers. As in many other situations involving police–citizen communication, the initial approach sets the tone for the entire interaction.

Similarities between Christianity, Judaism, and Islam

In reading the above tenets of the Muslim faith, notice that there are certain practices and aspects of Islam also found in Christianity and Judaism. All three religions are monotheistic, that is, each has a belief in one God. Followers of the religions believe that God is the origin of all, and is all-knowing as well as all-powerful. Because God is merciful, it is possible for believers to be absolved of their sins, though the practices for obtaining absolution vary in the different ideologies. All three religions have a Holy Book central to the faith: Judaism has the Torah (the first five books of the Old Testament), Christianity the Bible, and Islam has the Qur'an (Koran). All three religions regard their texts to be either the direct word of God, or inspired by the word of God. There are similarities between the three books. For example, the concept of the Ten Commandments is present in each. All three contain stories about many of the same people, such as Adam, Noah, Abraham, Moses, David, and Solomon. The bible and Qur'an also both contain stories about Mary, Jesus, and John the Baptist. The oral reading or recitation of each book constitutes part of regular worship. Prophets exist in each tradition, and are revered as those who transmit the word of God to the people. Chronologically, Judaism became a religion first, followed by Christianity and then Islam. Islam builds upon the foundations of the previous ones, and believes in the authenticity of the prophets of earlier books. For example, Islamic belief sees both Moses and Jesus as rightful prophets, and as precursors to Mohammed, who is believed to be the final prophet of God. As there are different interpretations of Christianity and Judaism, so too followers of Islam interpret the religion in different ways. Differing readings of the Qur'an can lead to more or less tolerance within the religion. Lastly, both the Islamic and Judeo-Christian traditions are said to stem from the same lineage; Abraham was father to both Isaac, whose progeny became the people of Israel, and Ishmael, who started the Arabic lineage.

FAMILY STRUCTURE

Arab Americans typically have close-knit families in which family members have a strong sense of loyalty and fulfill obligations to all members, including extended family (aunts, uncles, cousins, grandparents). Traditionally minded families also believe strongly in the family's honor, and members try to avoid any behavior that will bring shame or disgrace to the family. The operating unit for Arab Americans (and this may be less true for people who have been in the United States for generations) is not the individual but the family. Thus if a person behaves inappropriately, the entire family is disgraced. Similarly, if a family member is assaulted (in the Arab world), there would be some type of retribution. For the police officer, three characteristics of the Arabic family will affect his or her interaction with family members:

- Extended family members are often as close as the "nuclear family" (mother, father, children) and are not seen as secondary family members. If there is a police issue, officers can expect that many members of the family will become involved in the matter. Although officers might perceive this as interference, from an Arabic cultural perspective, it is merely involvement and concern. The numbers of people involved are not meant to overwhelm an officer.

- Family loyalty and protection is seen as one of the highest values of family life. Therefore, shaming, ridiculing, insulting, or criticizing family members, especially in public, can have serious consequences.

- Newer Arab American refugees or immigrants may be reluctant to accept police assistance. Because families are tightly knit, they can also be closed "units" whereby members prefer to keep private matters or conflicts to themselves. As a result, officers will have to work harder at establishing rapport if they want to gain cooperation.

There is an important point of contact between all three of these characteristics and law enforcement interaction with members of Arab American families. Berro explains: "When we respond to a call at a home, the police car is like a magnet. Every family member comes out of the house and everyone wants to talk at once. It can be an overwhelming sensation for an officer who doesn't understand this background" (Berro, 2003).

A police officer who is not trained in understanding and responding appropriately and professionally to cultural differences could alienate the family by (1) not respecting the interest and involvement of the family members, and (2) attempting to gain control of the communication in an authoritarian and offensive manner. The consequences may be that he or she would have difficulty establishing the rapport needed to gain information about the conflict at hand and would then not be trusted or respected. To do the job effectively, law enforcement officials must respect Arab family values, along with communication style differences (the latter will be discussed shortly).

Head of the Household

As in most cultures with a traditional family structure, the man in the Arab home is overtly the head of the household and his role and influence are strong. The wife has a great deal of influence, too, but it can often be more "behind the scenes." An Arab woman does not always defer to her husband in private as she would in public (Nydell, 1987). However, as mentioned earlier in the chapter, there are many women who have broken out of the traditional mold and tend to be more vocal, outspoken, and assertive than their mothers or grandmothers. Traditionally, in many Arab countries, some fathers maintain their status by being strict disciplinarians and demanding absolute respect, thus creating some degree of fear among children and even among wives. Once again, Arab Americans born and raised in this country have, for the most part, adopted middle-class "American" styles of child-raising whereby children participate in some of the decision making, and are treated in an egalitarian manner just as an adult would be. In addition, as with changing roles among all kinds of families in the United States, the father as traditional head of the household and the mother as having "second-class" status is not prevalent among established Arab Americans in the United States. Wife abuse and child abuse are not considered respectable practices by educated Arab Americans, but the practice still occurs, just as it does in mainstream American society (particularly, but not exclusively, among people on the lower- socioeconomic levels).

In traditional Arab society, men exert influence and power publicly. This power may be seen by Westerners in a negative light, but it is important to caution against misinterpreting a husband's or father's behavior as merely control. (Shabbas, 1984). He, and other male figures of importance, can be employed in securing the compliance of the family in important matters. The husband or father can be a natural ally of authorities. Officers would be well advised to work with both the father and the mother, for example, in matters where children are involved. On family matters the woman frequently is the authority, even if she seems to defer to her husband. Communicating with the woman, even if indirectly, while still respecting the father's need to maintain his public status, will win respect from both the man and the woman.

Children and "Americanization"

"Americanization," the process of becoming "American" in behavior, attitudes, and beliefs, has always been an issue with refugees/immigrants and their children. Typically, children are better able than their parents to learn a language and pick up the nuances of a culture. In addition, peer influence and pressure in American society begin to overshadow parental control, especially beginning the pre-teen years. Arab children, who are cherished by their parents, face an extremely difficult cultural gap with their parents if they reach a stage where they are more "American" than "Arab." Children in Arabic families are taught to be respectful in front of parents and to be conscious of family honor. Parents do not consider certain aspects of "Americanized" behavior, in general, to be respectful or worthy of pride. When children exhibit certain behaviors that bring shame to the family, discipline can indeed be harsh.

In extreme and infrequent cases, shame to the family can result in crimes against the children, involving violence. A police officer in a Midwest police department described a case whereby a father shot his daughter because she had a boyfriend (Arab women are not allowed to associate freely with men before marriage and are expected to remain virgins). This case does not suggest that violent crime, in the Arab cultural context, is an appropriate response. Mental problems or drugs and alcohol accompany most violent acts. However, when a child's (and especially a girl's) behavior involves what is seen as sexual misconduct, the family's "face" is ruined. When this happens, *all* members of the family suffer. Culturally, when a crime is committed by a family member, there is great shame that colors the reputation of the entire family (Ismail, 2003).

There is very little an officer can do to change the attitudes of parents who oppose their children's behavior. However, if an officer responds to calls where he or she notices that the family has become dysfunctional because of children's behavior, it would be a service to the family to initiate some sort of social service intervention or make a referral. If a family is already at the point of needing police assistance in problems involving children and their parents, then, more likely than not, they need other types of assistance as well. At the same time, newer immigrants and refugees will not necessarily be open to social service interventions, especially if the social workers do not speak Arabic. On the other hand, according to Lobna Ismail, President of Connecting Cultures, a training and consulting company, some individuals may end up revealing more information to people outside the community even if it means having to speak in English. This is because the refugee or immigrant may be concerned about a loss of face or shame on the family if something were revealed to fellow community members. (Ismail, 2003).

CULTURAL PRACTICES

As with all other immigrant groups, the degree to which people preserve their cultural practices varies. The following descriptions of everyday behavior will not apply equally to all Arab Americans, but they do not necessarily apply only to recent newcomers. Immigrants may preserve traditions and practices long after they come to a new country by conscious choice or sometimes because they are unaware of their cultural behavior (i.e., it is not in their conscious awareness).

Greetings/Approach/Touching

Most recent Arab American newcomers expect to be addressed with a title and their last name (Mr. _____; Miss _____), although in many Arab countries people are addressed formally by Mr./Mrs., followed by their first name. Most Arab women do not change their names after they are married or divorced. They, therefore, may not understand the distinction between a "maiden" name and a "married" name. The usual practice is to keep their father's last name for life (Boller, 1992).

Many Arab Americans who have retained their traditional customs shake hands and then place their right hand on their chest near the heart. This is a sign of sincerity and warmth. In the Middle East, Americans are advised to do the same if they observe this gesture (Devine & Braganti, 1991). Officers can decide whether they are comfortable using this gesture—most people would not expect it from an officer, but some might appreciate the gesture as long as the officer was able to convey sincerity. Generally, when Arabs from the Middle East shake hands, they do not shake hands briefly and firmly. (The expression, "He shakes hands like a dead fish" does not apply to other cultural groups!) Arabs (i.e., not assimilated Arab Americans) tend to hold hands longer than other Americans and shake hands more lightly. Older children are taught to shake hands with adults as a sign of respect. Many Arabs would appreciate an officer shaking hands with their older children. With a recent immigrant or refugee Arab woman, it is generally not appropriate to shake hands unless she extends her hand first. This would definitely apply to women who wear head coverings.

Many Arabs of the same sex greet each other by kissing on the cheek. Two Saudi Arabian men, for example, may greet each other by kissing on both cheeks a number of times. This does not suggest homosexuality, but rather is a common form of greeting. Public touching of the opposite sex is forbidden in the traditional Arabic world and officers should make every effort not to touch Arabic women, even casually (discussed further under "Key Issues in Law Enforcement").

Police officers should be aware that some Arab American citizens (e.g., Lebanese) who are new to the United States may react to a police officer's approach in an unexpected way. For example, an officer who has just asked a person to give his driver's license may find that this person will then get out of his car in order to be able to talk to the officer. From the person's perspective, he or she is simply trying to be courteous (since this is done in the home country). An officer, always conscious of safety issues, may simply have to explain that in the United States, officers require citizens to remain in their cars.

Hospitality

"Hospitality is a byword among [Arabs], whatever their station in life. As a guest in their homes you will be treated to the kindest and most lavish consideration. When they say, as they often do, "My home is your home," they mean it (Salah Said, as quoted in Nydell, 1987, p. 58). Hospitality in the Arab culture is not an option; it is more an obligation or duty. In some parts of the Arab world, if you thank someone for their hospitality, they may answer with a common expression meaning, "Don't thank me. It's my duty." (Here the word "duty" has a more positive than negative connotation.) Officers need to understand how deeply ingrained the need to be hospitable is and not to misinterpret this behavior for something that it is not. Whether entering a home or a business owner's shop or office, an Arab American may very well offer coffee and something to eat. This is not to be mistaken for a bribe and, from the Arab perspective, carries no negative connotations. According to Berro, most people would be offended if you did not accept their offers of hospitality. However, given police regulations, you may have to decline. If this is the case, Berro advises that officers decline graciously. On the other hand, if the decision to accept the Arab American's hospitality depends on the officer's discretion, accepting can also be good for police–citizen relations. The period of time spent socializing and extending one's hospitality gives the person a chance to get to know and see if he or she can trust the other person. Business is not usually conducted among strangers. Obviously, on an emergency call, there is no time for such hospitality. However, with the move toward increasing community-based police organizations, officers may find that they are involved in more situations where they may decide to accept small gestures of hospitality, if within departmental policy.

Verbal and Nonverbal Communication

Arabs in general are very warm and expressive people, both verbally and nonverbally, and appreciate it when others extend warmth to them. There are some areas in the realm of nonverbal communication where Americans, without cultural knowledge, have misinterpreted the behavior of Arab Americans simply because of their own ethnocentrism (i.e., the tendency to judge others by one's own cultural standards and norms).

Conversational distance. What is acceptable conversational distance between two people is often related to cultural influences. Officers are very aware of safety issues and keep a certain distance from people when communicating with them. Generally, officers like to stand about an arm's length or farther from citizens to avoid possible assaults on their person. This distance is similar to how far apart "mainstream Americans" stand when in conversation. Cultures subtly influence the permissible distance between two people. When the distance is "violated," a person can feel threatened (either consciously or unconsciously). Many but not all Arabs, especially if they are new to the country, tend to have a closer acceptable conversational distance with each other than do other Americans. In Arab culture, it is not considered offensive to "feel a person's breath." Yet many Americans, unfamiliar with this intimacy in regular conversation, have misinterpreted the closeness. While still conscious of safety, the law enforcement officer can keep in mind that the closer than "normal" behavior (i.e., "normal" for the officer) does not necessarily constitute a threat.

Devine and Braganti (1991) give the following advice to American travelers in the Middle East. There is application for police officers in the United States, especially in conjunction with communication with recent immigrants and refugees. "Don't back away when an Arab stands very close while speaking to you. He won't be more than two feet away. Arabs constantly stare into other people's eyes, watching the pupils for an indication of the other person's response [i.e., dilated pupils mean a positive response]. However, foreign men should never stare directly into a woman's eyes, either in speaking to her or passing her on the street. He should avert his eyes or keep his eyes on the ground."

Gestures. There are gestures that Arabs from some countries use that are distinctly different from those familiar to non-Arab Americans. In a section entitled "Customs and Manners in the Arab World," Devine and Braganti (1991, p. 13) describe some commonly used gestures among Arabs:

- "What does it mean? or What are you saying? Hold up the right hand and twist it as if you were screwing in a light bulb one turn.
- Wait a minute. Hold all fingers and thumb touching with the palm up.
- No. This can be signaled in one of three ways: moving the head back slightly and raising the eyebrows, moving the head back and raising the chin, or moving the head back and clicking with the tongue.
- Go away. Hold the right hand out with the palm down, and move it as if pushing something away from you.
- Never. A forceful never is signaled by holding the right forefinger up and moving it from left to right quickly and repeatedly."

As with many other cultural groups, pointing a finger directly at someone is considered rude.

Emotional expressiveness

When I came to my brother's house to see what the problem was [i.e., with the police], I asked, "What the hell is going on?" I held my hands out and talked with my hands as I always do. I repeated myself and continued to gesture with my hands. Later (i.e., at a trial) the police officer said that the Arab woman was yelling and screaming and acting wild, waving her arms and inciting observers to riot by her actions.*

*The names of individuals and departments have been omitted even though permission has been granted to quote. The purpose of including these incidents is not to put undue attention on any one department or individual, but rather to provide education on police professionalism in interethnic relations.

The Arab American involved in the above situation explained that Arab women, in particular, are very emotional and that police sometimes see this emotionalism as a threat. She explained that upon seeing a family member in trouble, it would be most usual and natural for a woman to put her hands to her face and say something like, "Oh, my God" frequently and in a loud voice. While other Americans can react this same way, it is worth pointing out that in mainstream American culture, there is a tendency to subdue one's emotions and not to go "out of control." What some Americans consider to be "out of control," Arabs (like Mexicans, Greeks, Israelis, and Iranians, among other groups) consider to be perfectly "normal" behavior. In fact, the lack of emotionalism that Arabs observe among mainstream Americans can be misinterpreted as lack of interest or involvement.

Although a communication-style characteristic never applies to all people in one cultural group (and we have seen that there is a great deal of diversity among Arab Americans), there are group traits that apply to many people. Arabs, especially the first generation of relatively recent newcomers, tend to display emotions when talking. Unlike many people in Asian cultures (e.g., Japanese and Korean), Arabs have not been "taught" that the expression of emotion is a sign of immaturity or a lack of control. Arabs, as other Mediterranean groups, such as Israelis or Greeks, tend to shout when they are excited or angry and are very animated in their communication. They may repeatedly insert expressions into their speech such as "I swear by God." This is simply a cultural mannerism.

Westerners, however, tend to judge this "style" negatively. To a Westerner, the emotionalism, repetition, and emphasis on certain statements can give the impression that the person is not telling the truth or is exaggerating for effect. An officer unfamiliar with these cultural mannerisms may feel overwhelmed, especially when involved with an entire group of people. It would be well worth it for the officer to determine the spokesperson for the group, but to refrain from showing impatience or irritation at this culturally different style. The following comment was made by an Arab American community member (who prefers not to be identified) about police reactions to Arab Americans:

> Police see Arab emotionalism as a threat. They see the involvement of our large families in police incidents as a threat. They don't need to feel overwhelmed by us and try to contain our reactions. We will cooperate with them, but they need to show us that they don't view us as backward and ignorant people who are inferior just because we are different and because we express ourselves in a more emotional way than they do. . . . (Arab American community member)

Swearing, the use of obscenities and insults. Officers working in Arab American communities should know that for Arabs, words are extremely powerful. Whether consciously or unconsciously, some believe that words can affect the course of events and can bring misfortune (Nydell, 1987). If an officer displays a lack of professionalism by swearing at an Arab (even words like "damn"), it will be nearly impossible to repair the damage.

In one case of documented police harassment of several Arab Americans (names have been omitted in order not to single out this department), witnesses attest to officers' saying, "Mother-f _____ Arabs, we're going to teach you. Go back home!" One of the Arab American citizens involved in the case reported that officers treated him like an animal and were very insulting by asking questions in a demeaning tone such as, "Do you speak English? Do you read English?" (The man was a highly educated professional who had been in the United States for several years.) In asking him about his place of employment (he worked at an Arab American organization), the man reported that they referred to his place of employment as " . . . the Arab Islamic shit or crap? What is that?"

Officers who understand professionalism are aware that this type of language and interaction is insulting to all persons. The choice to use obscenities and insults, especially in conjunction with one's ethnic background, however, means that officers risk never being able to establish trust within the ethnic community. This can translate into not being able to secure cooperation when needed. Even a few officers exhibiting this type of behavior can damage the reputation of an entire department for a long period of time.

English language problems. If time allows, before asking the question "Do you speak English?" officers should try and assess whether the Arab American is a recent arrival or an established citizen who might react negatively to the question. A heavy accent does not necessarily mean that a person is unable to speak English (although that can be the case). There are specific communication skills that can be used with limited-English-speaking persons (see Chapter 5) that should be applied with Arab Americans. Officers should proceed slowly and nonaggressively with questioning and wherever possible, ask open-ended questions. An officer's patience and willingness to take extra time will be beneficial in the long run.

KEY ISSUES IN LAW ENFORCEMENT

Perceptions of and Relationships and Interactions with Police

It is not possible to generalize about how all Arab Americans perceive the police. As mentioned earlier, the Arab immigrants who came in the late 19th century through World War II had the Turkish military police with whom to compare to the American police. Their experiences, then, in the United States were largely positive and they were cooperative with police. Since the majority of Arab Americans today are from that wave of immigrants, it is fair to say that a large part of the Arab American community does respect the police. On the other hand, some of the immigrants, such as Jordanians and Palestinians, do not understand the American system and have an ingrained fear of police because of political problems in their own region of the world (Dr. James Zogby, 2003). Since they distrust government, they are more likely to reject help from the police and this puts them at a decided disadvantage in that they can more easily become victims. Their fear, in combination with the interdependence and helpfulness that characterizes the extended family, results in families not wanting assistance from the police. Thus police will encounter some families who would prefer to handle conflict themselves even though police intervention is clearly needed. Some of the newer immigrants and refugees feel that it is dishonorable to have to go outside the family (e.g., to police and social service providers) to get help, and if given a choice, they would choose not to embarrass themselves and their families in this manner.

In the Arab world of the Middle East, there are major differences in the institution of policing and the manner in which citizens are required to behave with police. In 2000, a new wave of violence, known as the *intifada,* broke out in the occupied territories. Especially since the start of this intifada, Palestinians have a deep distrust and fear of the law enforcement institution because of they way that they (the Palestinians) are treated by their occupiers. Law enforcement officials in the United States, then, must assure Palestinian immigrants that "they are not an occupier and not against them" (James Zogby, 2003). Immigrants from Iraq, for example, have complained that "Saddam's enforcers robbed them of their jewelry, even if it meant cutting off their fingers to get it" (Haddad 2003). Similarly, in Saudi Arabia there is more of a fear of police than in some other countries because the punishments are stricter. For example, if a person is caught stealing, he or she will have a hand removed if a repeat offender. A Saudi Arabian woman caught shoplifting in a San Francisco Bay Area "7-11" store begged a police officer on her knees not to make the arrest because she feared being sent back to Saudi Arabia and did not know what would happen to her there. As it turned out, the officer did let her go since this was her first offense. He felt that he had some discretion in this case and decided to consider the woman's cultural background and circumstances. When it comes to interpreting cultural influences on police incidents and crimes, especially those of a lesser nature, each officer has to decide for him- or herself. (This aspect of law enforcement is discussed in Chapter 1.)

Women and Modesty

In the traditional Muslim world, women do not socialize freely with men and are required to dress modestly. However, the everyday practices in the various Arabic countries differ greatly. In some countries, such as Lebanon, Jordan, and Egypt, women dress more in the manner of people in the West, whereas in countries like Saudi Arabia, strict rules are maintained (e.g., the "morals police" tap women on the ankles with a long stick if their dresses are too short).

There is a great deal of diversity in the United States as to how people interpret the religious preference for dressing modestly (Ismail, 2003). The practice a woman chooses differs from family to family. Some traditional families, even in the United States, may encourage their daughters and wives to dress modestly. In some cases, young women themselves choose to dress more modestly than their parents may expect. For example, in the United States, some young women may choose to wear the head covering even if their mothers do not (Ibid.) (In the Middle East, women may wear head coverings or not; this depends on multiple factors such as their family, their age, personal preference, and background.)

Modesty for a traditional Arab Muslim woman may include the need to cover her head so that men will not see her hair. In some traditional Islamic societies, a man must not see a woman's hair, and officers should understand that asking a woman to remove a head covering (e.g., for the purpose of searching her or getting a photo identification) is analogous to asking her to expose a private part of her body. Arab American (Corporal) Berro advises officers to approach this matter sensitively: "Don't overpower the woman, intimidate her, or grab her head cover. Ask her to go into a private room and have her remove it or get a female officer to help with the procedure" (Berro, 2003).

American officers may have difficulty understanding the violation that a traditional Arab woman feels when her head covering is taken away forcibly. Even if a woman is arrested for something like disorderly conduct, she will be offended by any aggressive move on the part of the officer to remove her head cover. When police procedures require that a head cover be removed, the officers should explain the procedure and offer some kind of an apology to show empathy. Having dealt with this same issue, the Immigration and Naturalization Service (INS) modified its regulations in the following way: "Every applicant . . . shall clearly show a three-quarter profile view of the features of the applicant with the head bare (unless the applicant is wearing a headdress as required by a religious order of which he or she is a member)" (INS Regulation 8 C.F.R. 331.1(a), 1992). Thus, INS officials photograph Muslim women with their head coverings on. Because police departments deal with safety issues (such as concealed weapons), they may not have the liberty to accommodate this particular cultural difference in the same way as the INS was able to do. The matter of women and head coverings must be handled with extreme sensitivity. Lobna Ismail advises that, if a woman has to remove her head covering (whether for a photo or a search), a female photographer and/or female officer must be in the room with her rather than a male. (Ismail, 2003)

Arab Small Business Owners

Racial and ethnic tensions exist between Arab grocers and liquor store-owners in low-income areas (such as Detroit and Cleveland) and members of other minority groups. The dynamics between Arab store-owners and African Americans are similar to those between Koreans and African Americans in inner cities. The non-Arab often views the Arab as having money and exploiting the local residents for economic gain. Dr. James Zogby explains that this perception is reinforced because, in some locales, one rarely sees a non-Arab working in an Arab-owned store. The local resident, according to Dr. Zogby, does not understand that the Arabs, for the most part, are political refugees (e.g., Palestinians) and have come to the United States for a better life. Despite stereotypes that these store owners have connections to "Arab money" (i.e., oil money), when they first arrive, the only work that they can do is operate small "marginal" businesses. Most of the small Arab-run grocery stores, liquor stores, and gas stations are family-operated businesses where two brothers or a father and two sons, for example, are managing the operation. It would not be economically possible for them to hire outside their family (the situation is similar to Korean family-run businesses) (James Zogby, 2003). Police officers, in the midst of the conflicts between the store-owners and the residents, can attempt to explain the position of the refugees, but of course, the explanation by itself cannot take care of the problem. Many poor American-born citizens harbor a great deal of animosity toward immigrants and refugees because of scarce resources.

Alcohol is forbidden in the Muslim religion, yet Arab liquor store-owners sell it to their customers. There has been a debate in the Arab American community as to whether Muslim immigrants and refugees should go into this type of business. For the majority of newcomers, however, the choices are very limited. Members of other ethnic groups have also owned many of the mom-and-pop stores throughout the years.

Finally, there is another dimension to the problem of Arab store-owners in inner cities. Many inner-city residents (Arab Americans and African Americans included) do not feel that law enforcement officials take the needs of the inner city as seriously as they do elsewhere. A pattern in the Arab American community has emerged whereby Arab American store owners feel that they, themselves, have to take on problems of crime in their stores (John Zogby, 2003). If an Arab store-owner is robbed and is treated in a nonsupportive or harsh way by the police, he feels that he has to defend himself and his store alone. In some cases, Arab store-owners have assaulted shoplifters in their stores, potentially risking becoming the victims themselves. Like other minority-group members, some Arab shop owners in the inner city have given up on the police. Police officers cannot solve the social ills that plague the inner city, but at a minimum need to instill the confidence that they will be as supportive as possible when dealing with the crimes that immigrant/refugee store-owners experience. Additionally, Arab shop or gas station owners will assist their more recently arrived relatives in opening a similar business. Many of these recent immigrants do not know the system or all the regulations for running a business. There have been instances of store-owners being chastised for running "illegal" businesses, when in fact they were not familiar with the complete process required for proper licensing (Haddad, 2003).

Hate Crimes against Arab Americans

Hate crimes are discussed fully in Chapter 12. The following explanation deals mainly with the stereotyping and scapegoating of Arabs that often takes place when a crisis in the Arab world involves Americans, or when significant events in America are linked to Arabs. Arab Americans also have a special need for protection during times of political tensions in the Middle East. As discussed in the section in this chapter entitled "Terrorist Stereotype and Post-9/11 Backlash," the weeks and months following the attacks were accompanied by a huge spike in hate crimes directed at Arab Americans, Muslim Americans, and those thought to be of the same background. There were more than 700 violent crimes against Arab Americans reported within the first 9 weeks after the tragedy of September 11, and 165 reported hate crimes from January 1, 2002, through October 11, 2002, a figure higher than most years in the previous 10 years (ADC Report, 2002). However, the ADC emphasized the fact that this did not represent the actual total number of hate crimes; victims feared additional violence against them, thus many cases were not made public. Senior Deputy Chief Ronald Haddad points out that fear is a universally human emotion when one is victimized, and this fear factor plays an important role as to why many hate crimes go unreported. However, in explaining the lack of reporting incidents to police, it is also important to recognize the Arab value of saving face and maintaining harmony whenever possible (Haddad 2003).

Prior to the terrorist attacks of 9/11, "single-bias" hate crimes (with a single motivation) against people from one ethnic or national group were the second *least* reported hate crimes. According to the FBI's recorded hate crimes of 2000, of 8,144 single-bias incidents against people (as opposed to property or society), 11.3 percent of those were based on an ethnic or national origin bias, whereas more hate crimes were motivated by racial bias, religious bias, or a prejudice against sexual orientation. In 2001, the total number of single-bias hate crimes rose to 9,730, representing a 19 percent increase. (see Exhibit 8.1). Of those, 21.6 percent were the results of a bias against an ethnicity or national origin. In 2000, there were 36 victims of anti-Islamic hate crimes. In 2001, that number rose to 554 victims, more than a 1,500 percent increase (see Exhibit 8.2). Referencing the Hate Crime Statistics of 2001, the FBI states, "Hate crimes touch not only the individual victim, but they also affect the entire group associated with the particular bias motivation. Unfair and inaccurate stereotyping can make victims of all who share the same race, religion, ethnicity or national origin, sexual orientation, or disability" (see Exhibits 8.1– 8.2).

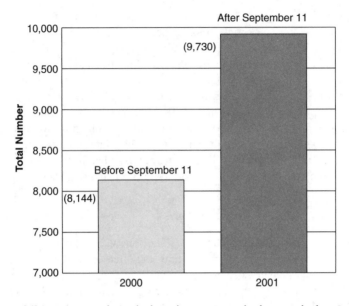

Exhibit 8.1   Total single-bias hate crimes before and after September 11, 2001, FBI Hate Crime Statistics

The initial spike in post-9/11 hate crimes declined significantly as community members and law enforcement officers worked together to curb the number of incidents. Just weeks before the war with Iraq, however, the FBI warned of a potentially similar surge in hate crimes. Top FBI officials met with Arab and Muslim leaders in the United States to assure them of the FBI's priority to prevent and investigate hate

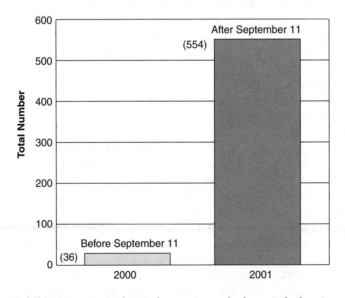

Exhibit 8.2   Anti-Islamic hate crimes, before and after September 11, 2001, FBI Hate Crime Statistics

crimes. This was a step that they had *not* initially taken in the aftermath of September 11. The targeted interviews of thousands of Iraqis living in the United States were also organized in part to reassure the Iraqi community that law enforcement officials would not tolerate any ethnic backlash in the case of a war ("FBI: War Could Trigger Hate Crimes," March 12, 2003, CBSNews.com). At the time that this book went into press, there were no official figures available for hate crimes statistics during and after the 2003 American intervention in Iraq. However, many Arab American agencies reported an increase in discriminatory incidents, though a less dramatic increase than that which followed the terrorist attacks. Continual positive work of government and local leaders to eliminate ethnic backlash is evidenced by the May 2003 unanimously approved Senate resolution written by Senator Dick Durban (D-IL) condemning violence and bigotry against Arab Americans, Muslim Americans, South Asian Americans, and Sikh Americans.

According to the *San Jose Mercury News,* local police reports showed a total of 1,659 hate crimes in 2002, down 27 percent from 2001, 199 of those against Middle Easterners or Arab Americans, down 54 percent, as of mid-July 2003. However, a report from the Council on American–Islamic Relations (CAIR) showed hate crimes against Muslim Americans up 64 percent. This large discrepancy shows the hesitation of Muslim Americans or Arab Americans to report crimes out of a fear that law enforcement officials will see them as potential terrorist suspects, and not as victims. ("Hate Crimes Hit Low in 2003," July 15, 2003. There has been significant progress made by local law enforcement agencies to work with Arab American or Muslim American communities. In recent years, Detroit-area gas station owners (primarily Arab, Middle Eastern, and Chaldean) have voluntarily established the "Metropolitan Detroit Service Station Association." Members, who meet regularly, have resolved to keep their stations crime-free zones, where narcotics paraphernalia and the sale of stolen goods is explicitly forbidden. What is more, members of the association have committed to be the "eyes and ears" of the local community, reporting suspicious and dangerous behavior to police (Haddad, 2003). Continued sensitivity to members of this group is of paramount importance, and especially the elimination of stereotyping and profiling, while encouraging all victims to report hate crimes.

Sensitivity to New Legislation

New homeland security measures (see Chapter 11) will require that many local and federal law enforcement officers be in constant and close contact with Arab American or Muslim American communities. It is necessary to proceed with caution in enforcing required alien registration or "voluntary" interviews by integrating sensitivity and techniques to avoid implicitly labeling people as threats to the nation. Following are both positive and negative examples of different communities and techniques, as well as recommendations from the ADC as to how to overcome this new challenge in law enforcement.

Following the attacks, the Attorney General demanded that FBI agents interview over 5,000 Arab and Muslim men. An ADC representative said these plans, along with later plans to interview 3,000 more, "smacks of racial profiling" (ADC Fact Sheet, 2002). Some law enforcement experts and officials, including polices chiefs, also deemed these interviews to be an "unacceptable form of racial profiling and unwise use of time," that led increasingly to more distrust. Many agencies did not participate in these interviews (ADC Report, 2002). When approached regarding how to enforce this legislation in his precinct, Senior Deputy Chief Haddad of Detroit suggested involving community leaders and members, such as Imams of the local mosques. Personal communication in such instances is of utmost importance for fostering and maintaining trust and cooperation. However, in some cases, police officers arrived unannounced at business or private homes to request that the residents or employees sign up for these interviews. Patterns of this could lead to deteriorating relationships between communities and law enforcement officials. Dr. Zogby stressed the importance of increasing the comfort level of those approached for interviewing. Law enforcement officials must remember that they are not interacting with hardened criminals in this instance, but with immigrants, many of whom are recent arrivals to the United States. For many of them, an unannounced visit from police officers is inherently humiliating, because of baggage from the "old country." Police officers must win the trust of the people they wish to interview before they can expect cooperation (James Zogby, 2003).

One month following the attacks of September 11, in attempts to strengthen security in their communities, police officers felt unable to target potential suspects because the FBI had "cut them [officers] out of almost every aspect of the probe and refused to share vital intelligence about possible terrorist suspects in their communities ("They're not Sharing Anything," 2001, p. 6). Local police reported lists too general to suspect someone, and could only chance upon a suspect during a routine check. A November 2001 *Boston Globe* article reported that while interrogating a Sikh man (Sikhs are of Indian descent and are not Muslim), officers strip-searched the man while deriding him with such comments as "How is Osama bin Laden?" (ADC Report, 2002). While this example does not represent the vast majority of police actions, it is essential to avoid emotional reactivity in situations such as this one. Heightened cultural awareness can also contribute to necessary sensitivity.

To build further trust, the ADC recommends that law enforcement agencies and Arab Americans work closely with one another especially to foster a safe environment where citizens feel comfortable reporting hate crimes. This is supported by Chief Haddad's example, illustrating that working with community members, more often than not, results in positive interactions. The ADC recommends that law enforcement officials avoid stereotyping those involved in lawful political and religious activities as suspects, with the reminder that racial profiling is neither effective nor acceptable (ADC Report, 2002). Dr. James Zogby emphasizes the benefits of positive interactions with community leaders and members. He cites an example of Arab American community leaders in the Washington, D.C., area who invited both law enforcement officials and community members to meet on a human level and build rapport. (James Zogby, 2003).

SUMMARY OF RECOMMENDATIONS FOR LAW ENFORCEMENT

1. There are several basic Arab cultural values that officers should keep in mind when interacting with Arab American citizens:

   - "A person's dignity, honor, and reputation are of paramount importance and no effort should be spared to protect them, especially one's honor" (Nydell, 1987).

- "Loyalty to one's family takes precedence over [other needs; thus an individual is completely intertwined with his family]" (Nydell, 1987).
- Communication should be courteous and hospitable; honor and face-saving govern interpersonal interactions and relationships.

2. Arab Americans have been wrongly characterized and stereotyped by the media, and as with all stereotypes, this has affected people's thinking on Arab Americans. Officers should be aware of stereotypes that may influence their judgments. Common stereotypes of Arabs include:

- Illiterate and backward
- Passive, uneducated women
- Thief
- Terrorist

3. Officers can demonstrate to Muslim Arabs a respect for their culture and religion by:

- Respecting the times when people pray (five times a day)
- Maintaining courteous behavior in mosques, such as not stepping on prayer mats, not walking in front of people praying, and speaking softly
- Working out solutions with community members regarding religious celebrations (e.g., parking problems, noise)

4. The basic unit for Arab Americans, especially recent arrivals and traditional families, is not the individual but the family (including the extended family).

- If a family member is involved in a police incident, officers should expect that other family members will become actively involved.
- Officers should not automatically assume that this involvement is an attempt to interfere with police affairs.
- The traditional Arabic family is used to working out their conflicts themselves; this is further reason for all members to become involved.

5. Traditionally and outwardly, the father is the head of the household and much of the conversation should be directed toward him. Officers should, however, keep in mind the following:

- Many Arab women are outspoken and vocal. Do not dismiss their input because men may appear to be, at least publicly, the ones with the power.
- Traditional Arab women who do not freely communicate with men may have difficulty expressing themselves to a male police officer. In their own families, however, they are often the real decision-makers. Consider various ways of getting information (e.g., the use of a female translator, female police officer, and indirect and open-ended questions).

6. There are a number of specific cultural practices and taboos that officers should consider when communicating with Arab Americans who have preserved a traditional lifestyle (i.e., this does not apply to the majority of Arab Americans who have been in the United States for generations).

- Avoid even the casual touching of women. Be respectful of the need that some Arab women have to be modest.
- Never point the sole of one's shoes or feet at a person.
- Expect people to extend hospitality by offering coffee or food (this is not a bribe, from their cultural perspective).
- Arab Americans may stand closer to each other than other Americans do when talking. This is not meant to be threatening; it is largely unconscious and reflects a cultural preference for closer interpersonal interaction.

7. There are cultural differences in communication style that can affect officers' judgments and reactions:

- Becoming highly emotional (verbally and nonverbally) and speaking loudly is not looked down upon in the Arab world. Officers who may have a different manner of communication should not express irritation at this culturally different style. Nor should they necessarily determine that the people involved are being disrespectful. Developing patience with culturally different styles of communication is a key cross-cultural skill.
- When a person speaks with an accent, it does not necessarily mean that he or she is not fluent in English or is illiterate. Many highly educated Arab Americans speak English fluently but with an accent, and would be insulted if they were treated as if they were not educated.

8. In areas where there are Arab American grocery, liquor store, and gas station owners as well as poor residents, there is great potential for conflict.

- Arab American grocery, liquor store, and gas station owners need to be able to depend on local police services. Many do not feel that they have the protection they need.
- Police officers may be in positions to explain to other residents why Arab American store-owners are usually not in positions to hire people from the community. This will not solve the conflicts, but at least officers can attempt to make some people understand the economic realities of life for refugees and immigrants.

9. During times of crises in the Middle East, Arab Americans become targets of prejudice and racism.

- Police departments need to monitor communities and keep informed of world events so that Arab American communities have more protection during times when they may be vulnerable to hate crimes.

10. As community members desire to be involved in decision-making processes that affect their lives, law enforcement officials are strongly urged to communicate personally with Arab American leaders. If police chiefs reach out to communities, showing their desire to foster good relations, they are more likely to have positive interactions with the community, while at the same time increasing the willingness of the community to provide tips crucial to keeping the peace. Police chiefs are also encouraged to develop a community policing model to help enforce new federal mandates in a more culturally sensitive manner.

DISCUSSION QUESTIONS AND ISSUES*

1. ***Police–Ethnic Community Relations.*** In the section entitled "Islamic Religion," the authors mention an incident that took place at the end of the holy month of "Ramadan" whereby officers ticketed many cars parked across the street from a mosque. According to community people, the stores adjacent to the parking lots were closed and although parking was technically for customers only, the Arab Americans did not anticipate that there would be a problem utilizing the parking lot after hours. From a community relations point of view, the mass ticketing created some very negative feelings and a collective perception that "They (meaning the police) don't respect us; they don't want to understand us." What is your opinion regarding the way things were handled? Do you have any suggestions as to how this situation could have been prevented? Comment on both what the community and the police could have done to prevent the problem.

2. ***Who Is the Head of the Household?*** The stated head of the household in most traditional Arab families is the father, although the mother actually has a great deal of power within the family. Although in public many Arab women will defer decision making to their husbands, a police officer should not totally discount what the woman might have to offer in various police-related situations. How can the police officer, while respecting the status of the father, still acknowledge the mother as well as get input from her?

3. ***Nonverbal Variations across Cultures.*** When Arab Americans greet each other, they sometimes shake hands and then place their right hand on their chest near their heart. This is a sign of sincerity. In your opinion, should officers greet Arab Americans using this gesture if a person greets them in this way? What would be the pros and cons of doing this?

4. ***Hospitality toward Officers: A Cultural Gesture.*** Hospitality is a virtue in Arab culture and also functions to help people get to know (and see if they can trust) others with whom they are interacting. Given this cultural emphasis on being hospitable, what should an officer do if offered a cup of coffee and something to eat? If an officer has to decline the hospitality, how should it be done politely? Should department policy regarding the acceptance of hospitality be reexamined in light of this cultural tendency? Would your answer be different for departments that have adopted a community-based policing philosophy?

5. ***"But It's the Custom in My Country."*** In January 1991, the Associated Press reported that a Stockton, California, man originally from Jordan was arrested for investigation of "selling his daughter into slavery" because he allegedly accepted $25,000 for her arranged marriage. After police officers had taken the girl to a shelter, a police lieutenant reported that the father protested that "he

---

*See Instructor's Manual accompanying this text for additional activities, role-plays, questionnaires, and projects related to the content of this chapter.

was within his rights to arrange his daughter's marriage for a price." The father contacted us and quite upset, explained it was the custom in his country and is perfectly acceptable. Of course, we explained that you can't do that in this country. "It is slavery. . . ." The father then went to the shelter [where the daughter was] and was arrested after creating a disturbance." If you were investigating this case, how would you proceed? How might you assess the validity of what the father was saying? If you found out that the act was indeed, "perfectly acceptable in his country," how would you explain practices in the United States? Comment on the statement that the lieutenant made ("It is slavery."). From the perspective of needing cooperation from this man, what type of approach should be taken?

6. ***Officer Discretion: To Let Her Go?*** In the section on the perceptions of police, the authors mention an incident involving a Saudi Arabian woman who was caught shoplifting in a "7–11." She begged the officer to let her go because she feared being sent home and there she would receive a harsh punishment (typically, in Saudi Arabia, a person's hand is cut off if he or she steals). The officer decided that since this was her first offense, he would let her go. What is your reaction to the officer's decision? What would you have done?

WEBSITE RESOURCES

Visit these websites for additional information about law enforcement contact with Arab Americans and Middle Easterners in the United States.

American-Arab Anti-Discrimination Committee (ADC):   http://www.adc.org

This website provides information about the ADC's civil rights efforts and useful summary data about cases and complaints regarding discrimination and hate crimes involving Arab Americans.

Arab American Institute Foundation (AAI):   http://www.aaiusa.org

This website is dedicated toward the civic and political empowerment of Americans of Arab descent. AAI provides policy, research, and public affairs services to support a broad range of community activities. In addition, the AAI also is a census information center on demographics of Arab Americans. On the website, you can access a PDF file entitled, *Healing the Nation: The Arab-American Experience After September 11.*

Connecting Cultures: http://www.connecting-cultures.net

This website introduces Connecting Cultures, a consulting organization that designs and implements workshops and seminars on diversity, religion, and cross-cultural communication. It provides resources for understanding how culture and religion impact the way we communicate and work with one another. Connecting Cultures' specialty is Arab and Muslim Americans, as well as Arab culture, the Middle East, and the Muslim world.

FBI website: http://www.fbi.gov

This website provides hate crime statistics as a <u>key feature</u>.

Zogby International: http://www.zogby.com

This website provides statistics from the latest international public opinion polls covering a variety of issues, including those related to attitudes toward Arab Americans post-9/11. On the website, go to: http://www.zogby.com/news/ReadNews .dbm?ID=629 *What Arabs Think: Values, Beliefs and Concerns Landmark Study of Arab Values and Political Concerns,* which contains the views of 3,800 Arab adults polled by Zogby International.

REFERENCES

"All muslims not in on terrorist plot." (2003, March 2). *Contra Costa Times,* p. 9.

American-Arab Anti-Discrimination Committee. (1992). *1991 Report on Anti-Arab Hate Crimes: Political and Hate Violence Against Arab-Americans.* Washington, D.C.: ADC Research Institute.

American-Arab Anti-Discrimination Committee. (2002). *Report on Hate Crimes and Discrimination against Arab Americans: The Post-September 11 Backlash, tracking crimes from September 11, 2001 through October 11, 2002.* Available: http://www.adc.org.

American-Arab Anti-Discrimination Committee. (2002). *ADC Fact Sheet, Condition of Arab Americans post-9/11.* Washington, D.C.: ADC Research Institute.

Arab American Institute. (2000). *Arab-Americans: Issues, Attitudes, Views,* Zogby International/Arab American Institute study.

Boller, Philip J., Jr. (1992, March). "A name is just a name—or is it?" *FBI Law Enforcement Bulletin,* p. 6.

Central Intelligence Agency, World Fact Book, 2003

Detroit Free Press. (2001). *100 Questions and Answers about Arab Americans: A Journalist's Guide.* Detroit, Mich.: Author.

Devine, Elizabeth, and Nancy L. Braganti. (1991). *The Traveler's Guide to the Middle Eastern and North African Customs and Manners.* New York: St. Martin's Press.

"Film's portrayal of muslims troubling to Islamic groups." (1998, November 8). *Boston Globe.*

"Immigration down in U.S. after 9/11." (2003, May 5). *Contra Costa Times,* p. A3.

Jabara, Abdeen (n.d.). "Time for a change," in *The Arab Image in American Film and Television. Cineaste,* 17 (1; Suppl.).

Macron, Mary. (1989). *Arab Contributions to Civilization, American–Arab Anti-Discrimination Committee,* ADC Issue 6. Washington, D.C.: American-Arab Anti-Discrimination Committee.

Michalak, Laurence. (1988). *Cruel and Unusual: Negative Images of Arabs in American Popular Culture,* ADC Issue 15. Washington, D.C.: American-Arab Anti-Discrimination Committee.

Nydell, Margaret K. (1987). *Understanding Arabs: A Guide for Westerners.* Yarmouth, Maine: Intercultural Press.

Shabbas, Audrey. (1984). *Cultural Clues for Social Service Case Workers and Special Educators.* Unpublished monograph, Arab World and Islamic Resources and School Services, Berkeley, Calif.

Shaheen, Jack G. Reel Bad Arabs: How Hollywoood Villifies A People, Olive Branch Press, New York, 2001. (p. 51 [song from Alladin])

Shaheen, Jack G. (2001). *Reel Bad Arabs: How Hollywoood Villifies A People.* New York: Olive Branch Press.

Smith, Houston. (1991). *The World's Greatest Religions.* San Francisco: HarperCollins.

San Jose Mercury News, "Hate Crimes Hit Low in 2003, July 15, 2003.

Suleiman, Michale W. (Ed.). (2000). *Arabs in America: Building a New Future.* Philadelphia: Temple University Press.

"They're not sharing anything." (2001, October 15). *Newsweek,* p. 6.

Woodruff, David. (1991, February 4). "Letter from Detroit: where the Mid-east meets the Midwest—uneasily." *Business Week,* p. 30A.

Zogby International Study. (2000). *Arab Americans: Protecting Rights at Home and Promoting a Just Peace Abroad.*

Chapter 9

Law Enforcement Contact with Native Americans

OVERVIEW

This chapter provides specific cultural information on Native Americans, including aspects of their history that can both directly and indirectly affect the relationship with law enforcement officials. It presents information about Native American identity, and group identification terms as well as explains briefly the tribal system, reservations, Native American mobility, and family structure. Chapter 9 addresses the diversity that exists among Native American groups, and includes a description of cultural differences and similarities found among various Indian groups. We include labels, terms, and stereotypical statements that are offensive to Native Americans. The final section outlines several key concerns for law enforcement, including information on perception of police, Native American victimization rates, police jurisdiction problems, peyote, medicine bags, trespassing, violation of Indian sacred places, casinos and Indian gaming, and problems related to fishing rights. In the summary of the chapter, we provide a review of recommendations for improved communication and relationships between law enforcement personnel and members of Native American communities.

COMMENTARY

"It's just a bunch of Indians—let them go!"

This quote is excerpted from a 1992 interview with retired Chief Jim Cox, a Comanche Indian and former chief of police at the Midwest City Police Department, Oklahoma. Chief Cox discussed the subject of officers' biased and prejudicial treatment of Indians. He described an incident during his youth in Oklahoma when he was riding with other American Indian teenagers in an old Nash automobile. Police officers stopped the car and discovered that the teens had been drinking. Instead of taking the appropriate action, which would have been to arrest the young people or at least to call the parents to pick up the kids, the officers let them go. Former Chief Cox recalls to this day having heard one of the officers tell the other (in the words quoted above) that Indians were not worth the time or bother: Cox interpreted this statement to mean that if they killed themselves, it did not matter because they were just Indians. This impression remained with him even after he became a police officer almost 35 years ago.

When an officer contacts an Indian person, there is often 500 years of frustration built up. . . . Officers should be aware of the "baggage" that they bring to the encounter.

—Jose Rivera, retired Native American California state peace officer

What treaty that the whites have kept has the red man broken? Not one. What treaty that the white man ever made with us have they kept? Not one. When I was a boy the Sioux owned the world; the sun rose and set on their land; they sent ten thousand men to battle. Who slew [the warriors]? Where are our lands? Who owns them? What white man can say I ever stole his land. . .? Yet, they say I am a thief. What white woman, however lonely, was ever captive or insulted by me? Yet they say I am a bad Indian. What white man has ever seen me drunk? Who has ever seen me . . . abuse my children? What law have I broken? Is it wicked for me because my skin is red? (Sitting Bull [Lakota], in Matthiessen, 1992)

(In this chapter, the authors use the terms Native American, American Indian, and Indian interchangeably. Native American is often preferred as the generic name, however, government agencies often break down this overly broad category into American Indian and Alaska Native.)

HISTORICAL INFORMATION AND BACKGROUND

Recorded history disputes the origins of the first "Indians" in America. Some researchers claim that they arrived from Asia more than 40,000 years ago; others claim that they did not arrive from anywhere else. In either case, despite their long history in North America and the fact that they were the first "Americans," traditional U.S. history books did not recognize their existence until the European conquests, beginning with Christopher Columbus in 1492. The subject of the native peoples as either nonexistent or simply as insignificant reflect an ethnocentric (in this case, a Eurocentric) view of history. Even the word "Indian" is not a term that native Americans originally used to designate their tribes or communities. Because Columbus did not know that North and South America existed, he thought he had reached the Indies, which then included India, China, the East Indies, and Japan. In fact, he arrived in what is now called the West Indies (in the Caribbean) and he called the people he met "Indians" (Los Indios). Eventually, this became the name for all the indigenous peoples in the Americas. However, before the white settlers came to North and South America, almost every "Indian" tribe had its own name, and despite some shared cultural values, native Americans did not see themselves as one collective group or call themselves "Indians." Most tribes refer to themselves in their own languages as "The People," "The Allies," or "The Friends." Some of the terms that whites use for various tribes are not even authentic names for that tribe. For example, the label Sioux, which means enemy or snake, was originally a term given to that group by an enemy tribe and then adopted by French traders. In many cases, a tribe's real name is not necessarily the name commonly used.

Today in public schools across the country, some educators are only beginning to discuss the nature of much of the contact with Native Americans in early American history. Traditionally, rather than being presented as part of the American people's common legacy, Native American cultural heritage is often presented as bits of colorful "exotica." Genocide, or the killing of entire tribes, is not a chapter in U.S. history on which people have wanted to focus. The reality is that Euro-American and Indian relations have been characterized by hostility, contempt, and brutality. The native peoples have generally been treated by Euro-Americans as less than human or as "savages," and the rich Native American cultures have been ignored or crushed. For this reason, many culturally identifying American Indians do not share in the celebrations of Thanksgiving or the Columbus Day parade. To say that Columbus discovered America implies that Native Americans were not considered "human enough" to be of significance. Ignoring the existence of the Native Americans before 1492 constitutes only one aspect of ethnocentrism. American Indians' experience with the "white man" has largely been one of exploitation, violence, and forced relocation. It is this historical background that has shaped many Native American views of Euro-Americans and their culture. While the majority of people in the United States have a sense that Native Americans were not treated with dignity in U.S. history, many are not aware of the extent of the current abuse toward them. This may be due to the fact that this group is a small and traditionally "forgotten minority" in the United States, constituting approximately 1.5 percent of the overall population.*

It would not be accurate to say that no progress at all has been made in the United States with respect to the awareness and rights of our nation's first Americans. On November 6, 2000, President Bill Clinton renewed his commitment to tribal sovereignty by issuing an Executive Order on consultation with tribal governments. The purpose of the Order was "to establish meaningful consultation and collaboration with tribal officials in the development of federal policies having tribal implications, to strengthen the administration's government-to-government relationship to tribes, and to reduce the imposition of unfounded mandates by ensuring that all executive departments and agencies consult with tribes and respect tribal sovereignty as they develop policies on issues that impact Indian communities" (Legix Social and General Update, November 9, 2000).

President George W. Bush, in 2002, announced the following in a proclamation in honor of National American Indian Heritage Month:

> My administration is working to increase employment and expand economic opportunity for all Native Americans. Several federal agencies recently participated in the National Summit on Emerging Tribal Economies to accomplish this goal. In order to build upon this effort, my Administration will work to promote cooperation and coordination among Federal agencies for the purpose of fostering greater economic development of tribal communities. By working together on important economic initiatives, we will strengthen America . . . with hope and promise for all Native Americans. (White House Government News Release, November 2002).

Despite progress that has been made on the records in Washington, D.C., many Native Americans do not see that the spirit behind the foregoing sentiments have actually changed their lives. Indians have among the highest school dropout rates and unemployment rates of all the ethnic and racial groups. As for protection from the federal government, American Indians continue to fight legal battles over the retention of

---

*This includes Alaska Natives. Source: Census 2000.

Indian lands and other rights previously guaranteed by U.S. treaties. They still feel abused by a system of government that has committed many treaty violations against tribes and individuals. The U.S. government has often not acted in good faith toward its Native American citizens by seriously and repeatedly disregarding Indian rights that have been guaranteed in the form of binding treaties.

Consequently, individuals and tribes are reluctant to trust the words of the government or people representing "the system" because of the breach of many treaties. Whether they are aware of it or not, law enforcement agents are perceived this way, and carry this "baggage" into encounters with Native Americans. Historically, the police officer from outside the reservation has been a symbol of rigid and authoritarian governmental control that has affected nearly every aspect of an Indian's life, especially on reservations. Often, officers (like most citizens) have only a limited understanding of how the government, including the criminal justice system, caused massive suffering by not allowing Indians to preserve their cultures, identities, languages, sacred sites, rituals, and lands. Because of this history, officers have a responsibility to educate themselves about the history of the treatment of Indian peoples in order to relate to them effectively and fairly today. Law enforcement officers must understand Indian communities, and put forth extra efforts to establish rapport. This will increase the possibility of success at winning cooperation and respect from people who never before had any reason to trust any representative of government.

For some American Indians, an additional phenomenon aggravates the repeated breach of trust by the federal government. There is a very proud tradition of American Indians serving in the military. For more than 200 years, they have participated with distinction in United States military actions. American military leaders, beginning with George Washington in 1778, recognized American Indians to be courageous, determined, and as having a "fighting spirit" (CEHIP, 1996). American Indians had already contributed to the military in the 1800s, and contributed on an even larger scale beginning in the 1900s. In World War I, it is estimated that 12,000 American Indians served in the military.

> More than 44,000 American Indians, out of a total Native American population of less than 350,000, served with distinction between 1941 and 1945 in both European and Pacific theaters of war. Native American men and women on the home front also showed an intense desire to serve their country, and were an integral part of the war effort. More than 40,000 Indian people left their reservations to work in ordinance depots, factories, and other war industries. American Indians also invested more than $50 million in war bonds, and contributed generously to the Red Cross and the Army and Navy Relief societies. . . . The Native American's strong sense of patriotism and courage emerged once again during the Vietnam era. More than 42,000 Native Americans, more than 90 percent of them volunteers, fought in Vietnam. (CEHIP, 1996)

THE QUESTION OF NATIVE AMERICAN IDENTITY

Law enforcement officials may find themselves confused as to who is an American Indian. Individuals may claim to have "Indian blood," but tribes have their own criteria for determining tribal membership. Because the determination of tribal membership is a fundamental attribute of tribal sovereignty, the federal government generally defers to tribes' own determinations when establishing eligibility criteria under special Indian entitlement programs. However, there are a number of Indian tribes that, for historical and political reasons, are not currently "federally recognized" tribes. Members of such tribes, although Indian, are not necessarily eligible for special benefits under federal Indian programs. On the other hand, fraud in this area is quite rampant, whereby people falsely claim Indian ancestry to take unfair advantage of governmental benefits and other perceived opportunities.

Officers may find themselves in situations where an individual claims to be Indian when he or she is not. If officers have any doubt, they should inquire as to what tribe the person belongs and then contact the tribal headquarters to verify that person's identity. Every tribe has its own administration and authority, the members of which will be able to answer questions of this nature. By verifying information with tribal authorities rather than making personal determinations of "Indianness," officers will help create a good rapport between tribal members and law enforcement officials (Rivera, 2003).

According to Census 2000, there were approximately 2.5 million (or 0.9 percent of the entire U.S. population) who identified themselves as American Indian or Alaska Native (U.S. Bureau of the Census, 2002). However, there is a great deal of numerical misinformation because of the lack of a method for verifying the accuracy of people's claims to be Native American. The term Native American came into popularity in the 1960s and referred to groups served by the Bureau of Indian Affairs (BIA), including American Indians and natives of Alaska. Later, the term under certain federal legislation began to include natives from Hawaii. "Native American," however, has rarely been accepted by all Indian groups and is seldom used on reservations. Alaska natives, such as Eskimos and Aleuts, are separate groups and prefer the term Alaska Native. To know by what terms individuals or tribes prefer to be called, officers should listen to the names they use for themselves rather than try to guess which one is "correct."

In the area of mislabeling, some Native Americans have Spanish first or last names (because of intermarriage) and may "look" Hispanic or Latino (e.g., the Hopis). Identification can be difficult for the officers so they should not assume that the person is Latino just because of their name or appearance. Many Native Americans do not want to be grouped with Latinos because: (1) they are not Latinos; (2) they may resent the fact that some Latinos deny their Indian ancestry and, instead, only identify with the Spanish part of their heritage; and (3) many tribes have a history of warfare with the "mestizo" populations of Mexico. As an aside, the majority population in Mexico, Central America, and South America is of "Indian" ancestry. However, they adopted or were given Spanish names by the "Conquistadores" (conquerors). Many Hispanics in U.S. border communities are really of Indian, not Spanish, heritage, or they may be a mixture of the two.

NATIVE AMERICAN POPULATIONS, TRIBES, AND RESERVATIONS

Census 2000 revealed that of all cities in the United States with a population of 100,000 or more, New York and Los Angeles had the largest American Indian populations. In general, the West has the largest population (43 percent of Native American population), the South has 31 percent, 17 percent lived in the Midwest, and 9 percent in the Northeast (U.S. Bureau of the Census, 2002). Cherokee, Navajo, and Latin American Indians comprised the most populated tribal groupings (U.S. Bureau of the Census, 2002). See Exhibit 9.1 for a listing of Native American tribes and the corresponding regions in which they live in North America.

Northeast

Abenaki, Algonkin, Beothuk, Delaware, Erie, Fox, Huron, Illinois, Iroquois, Kickapoo, Mahican, Mascouten, Massachuset, Mattabesic, Menominee, Metoac, Miami, Micmac, Mohegan, Montagnais, Narragansett, Nauset, Neutrals, Niantic, Nipissing, Nipmuc, Ojibwe, Ottawa, Pennacook, Pequot, Pocumtuck, Potawatomi, Sauk, Shawnee, Susquehannock, Tionontati, Wampanoag, Wappinger, Wenro, Winnebago.

Southeast

Acolapissa, Asis, Alibamu, Apalachee, Atakapa, Bayougoula, Biloxi, Calusa, Catawba, Chakchiuma, Cherokee, Chesapeake Algonquin, Chickasaw, Chitamacha, Choctaw, Coushatta, Creek, Cusabo, Gaucata, Guale, Hitchiti, Houma, Jeags, Karankawa, Lumbee, Miccosukee, Mobile, Napochi, Nappissa, Natchez, Ofo, Powhatan, Quapaw, Seminole, Southeastern Siouan, Tekesta, Tidewater Algonquin, Timucua, Tunica, Tuscarora, Yamasee, Yuchi.

Plains

Arapaho, Arikara, Assiniboine, Bidai, Blackfoot, Caddo, Cheyenne, Comanche, Cree, Crow, Dakota (Sioux), Gros Ventre, Hidatsa, Iowa, Kansa, Kiowa, Kiowa-Apache, Kitsai, Lakota (Sioux), Mandan, Metis, Missouri, Nakota (Sioux), Omaha, Osage, Otoe, Pawnee, Ponca, Sarsi, Sutai, Tonkawa, Wichita.

Great Basin

Bannock, Paiute (Northern), Paiute (Southern), Sheepeater, Shoshone (Northern), Shoshone (Western), Ute, Washo.

Plateau

Carrier, Cayuse, Coeur D'Alene, Colville, Dock-Spus, Eneeshur, Flathead, Kalispel, Kawachkin, Kittitas, Klamath, Klickitat, Kosith, Kutenai, Lakes, Lillooet, Methow, Modac, Nez Perce, Okanogan, Palouse, Sanpoil, Shushwap, Sinkiuse, Spokane, Tenino, Thompson, Tyigh, Umatilla, Wallawalla, Wasco, Wauyukma, Wenatchee, Wishram, Wyampum, Yakima.

Southwest

Apache (Eastern), Apache (Western), Chemehuevi, Coahuiltec, Hopi, Jano, Manso, Maricopa, Mohave, Navaho, Pai, Papago, Pima, Pueblo, Yaqui, Yavapai, Yuman, Zuni. Pueblo could potentially be defined further: Acoma, Cochiti, Isleta, Jemez, Laguna, Nambe, Picuris, Pojoaque, Sandia, San Felipe, San Ildefonso, San Juan, Santa Ana, Santa Clara, Santo Domingo, Taos, Tesuque, Zia.

Northwest

Calapuya, Cathlamet, Chehalis, Chemakum, Chetco, Chilluckkittequaw, Chinook, Clackamas, Clatskani, Clatsop, Cowich, Cowlitz, Haida, Hoh, Klallam, Kwalhioqua, Lushootseed, Makah, Molala, Multomah, Oynut, Ozette, Queets, Quileute, Quinault, Rogue River, Siletz, Taidhapam, Tillamook, Tutuni, Yakonan.

California

Achomawi, Atsugewi, Cahuilla, Chimariko, Chumash, Costanoan, Esselen, Hupa, Karuk, Kawaiisu, Maidu, Mission Indians, Miwok, Mono, Patwin, Pomo, Serrano, Shasta, Tolowa, Tubatulabal, Wailaki, Wintu, Wiyot, Yaha, Yokuts, Yuki, Yuman (California).

Exhibit 9.1   Tribal Groupings and Corresponding Regions in North America
(Source: Saltzman, 2003)

According to Bureau of Indian Affairs (BIA) figures in 2003, there were over 562 "federally recognized" tribal governments in the United States (the word "tribe" and "nation" may also be used), and these include native groups of Alaskans such as Aleuts. Each of the federally recognized tribes have a distinct history and culture and often a separate language. Federal recognition means that a legal relationship exists between the tribe and the federal government. There are still many tribes that do not benefit from federally recognized status. Some may be state recognized and/or in the process of seeking federal recognition, while others may not seek recognition at all.

The issue of the increasing rivalry among some Indian groups seeking recognition is reflected in the sentiment that some Indian tribes are pitted against each other over government benefits and resources.

An Indian reservation is land that a tribe has reserved for its exclusive use through the course of treaty-making. It may be on ancestral lands, or simply the only land available when tribes were forced to give up their own territories through federal treaties. A reservation is also land that the federal government holds in trust for the use of an Indian tribe. The BIA administers and manages 55.7 million acres of land that, as of 2003, was held in trust for American Indians, Indian tribes, and Alaska natives. The 2003 estimate held that about 1.2 million Indians (BIA, 2003) were living on reservations and that there were approximately 300 reservations (exact figures are difficult to obtain). The largest of the reservations is the Navajo reservation and trust lands, which extends into three states. Since reservations are self-governing, most have tribal police, and there are issues of jurisdiction (discussed later in this chapter). Indians are not forced to stay on reservations, but many who leave have a strong desire to remain in touch with and be nourished by their culture on the reservations. For this reason and because of culture shock experienced in urban life, many return to reservations.

In general, the Indian population is characterized by constant movement between the reservation and the city, and sometimes relocation from city to city. In urban areas, when officers contact an Indian, they will not necessarily know how acculturated to city life that individual is. In rural areas it is easier for officers to get to know the culture of a particular tribe. In the city, the tribal background may be less important than the fact that the person is an American Indian.

Since the early 1980s, more than half of the population of Native Americans have been living outside of reservation communities; many have left to pursue educational and employment opportunities, as life on some of the reservations can be very bleak. Although a large number return home to the reservations to participate in family activities and tribal ceremonies, many attempt to remake their lives in urban areas. A percentage of Indians do make adjustments to mainstream educational and occupational life, but the numbers are still disproportionately low.

DIFFERENCES AND SIMILARITIES AMONG NATIVE AMERICANS

As with other culturally or ethnically defined categories of people (e.g., Asian, African American) it would be a mistake to lump all Native Americans together and to assume that they are homogeneous. For example, in Arizona alone, one finds a number of different tribes with varying traditions: There are Hopis in the Northeast, Pimas and Papagos in the South, Apache in the North Central region, and Yuman groups in the West. All of these descend from people who came to what is now called Arizona. The relative "newcomers" are the Navajos and Apaches, who arrived about 1,000 years ago. These six tribes represent differences in culture, with each group having its own history and life experiences.

Broadly speaking, in the United States, one finds distinct cultural groups among Native Americans in Alaska, Arizona, California, the Central Plains (Kansas and Nebraska), the Dakotas, the Eastern Seaboard, the Great Lakes area, the Gulf Coast states (Florida, Alabama, Mississippi, Louisiana, Texas), the Lower Plateau (Nevada, Utah, Colorado), Montana, Wyoming, New Mexico, North Carolina, Oklahoma, and the

Northwest (Washington, Oregon, and Idaho). Every tribe has evolved its own sets of traditions and beliefs and each sees itself as distinct from other tribes, despite some significant broad similarities. It is beyond the scope of this book to delve deeply into differences among tribes; however, Exhibit 9.1 lists many of the tribes in North America (Saltzman, 2003). The list itself will impress upon the reader the variety and number of tribes, each sharing similarities and differences with other tribes.

Similarities among Native Americans

It is possible to talk about general characteristics of Native American groups without negating the fact of their diversity. The cultural characteristics that are described in the following section will not apply to all such Americans, but rather to many who are traditionally "Indian" in their orientation to life. While being aware of tribal differences, the law enforcement officer should also understand that there is a strong cultural link between the many worlds and tribes of Native Americans and their Indian counterparts throughout the American continent.

Philosophy toward the Earth and the Universe

"The most striking difference between . . . Indian and Western man is the manner in which each views his role in the universe. The prevailing non-Indian view is that man is superior to all other forms of life and that the universe is his to be used as he sees fit . . . an attitude justified as the mastery of nature for the benefit of man [characterizes Western man's philosophy]" (Bahti, 1982). Through this contrast with Western philosophy (i.e., that people have the capacity to alter nature) the reader can gain insight into the values and philosophies common to virtually all *identifying* Native Americans. While acknowledging the character of each Indian tribe or "nation," there is a common set of values and beliefs involving the earth and the universe, resulting in a deep respect for nature and "mother earth." According to American Indian philosophy, the earth is sacred and is a living entity. By spiritual involvement with the earth, nature, and the universe, individuals bind themselves to their environment. Indians do not see themselves as superior to all else (e.g., animals, plants, etc.), but rather as part of all of creation. Through religious ceremonies and rituals, the Indian is able to transcend himself such that he is in harmony with the universe connected to nature.

The inclination of some people who do not understand this philosophy would be to dismiss it as primitive and even backward. The costumes, the rituals, the ceremonies, and the dances are often thought of as colorful, but strange. Yet from an Indian perspective, "It is a tragedy indeed that Western man in his headlong quest for Holy Progress could not have paused long enough to learn this basic truth—one which he is now being forced to recognize (with the spoilage of the earth), much to his surprise and dismay. Ever anxious to teach 'backward' people, he is ever reluctant to learn from them" (Bahti, 1982). Many non-Indians now embrace certain Native American beliefs regarding the environment; what people once thought of as "primitive" now see as essential in the preservation of our environment.

An Indian prayer:
Oh our Mother the earth, Oh our Father the sky,

Your children are we, and with tired backs
We bring you the gifts you love.
Then weave for us a garment of brightness. . .
May the fringes be the falling rain.
May the border be the standing rainbow.
That we may walk fittingly where birds sing . . . and where grass is
green, Oh our mother earth, Oh our father sky. (author unknown)

When law enforcement officers make contact with people who are in the midst of celebrating or praying whether on reservations or in communities, it is vitally important to be as respectful as possible. They must refrain from conveying an air of superiority and ethnocentrism, conveying an attitude that "those rituals" are primitive. Native American prayers, rituals, and ceremonies represent ancient beliefs and philosophies, many of which have to do with the preservation of and harmony with the earth. An officer should, at all costs, try to avoid interrupting prayers and sacred ceremonies, just as one would want to avoid interrupting church services. (As an aside, officers should also be aware that taking photographs during ceremonies would constitute an interruption and is forbidden. In general, officers should seek permission before taking photos of Indians; this is true for many of the Indian tribes. Visitors to some reservations may be told that their cameras will be confiscated if they take pictures.)

Acculturation to Mainstream Society

Significant differences exist among the cultures, languages, history, and socioeconomic status of Native American tribes, communities, and individuals. Nevertheless, in studies on suicide and ethnicity in the United States, much has been written about patterns of what can be described as self-destructive behavior that has been generalized to many Indian groups. According to the Friends Committee on National Legislation (FCNL, 2001), the suicide rate for American Indians and Alaska Natives is 72 percent greater then the rate for all races in the United States. The suicide rate for males between the ages of 15 and 34 is double that of the national average.

Mortality rates attributed to alcohol consumption are nearly seven times as many for American Indians and Alaska Natives as for other races (FCNL, 2001). Alcoholism is the leading health and social problem of American Indians; 75 percent of the deaths for people under 45 years of age most often follow alcohol use (e.g., unintentional injury) (Demographics and Health Risk Indicator, 2000). However, it cannot be stressed enough that the origins of the psychosocial problems that some Indians experience in mainstream society are not as a result of their own weaknesses or deficiencies. The cause of the problems date back to the way government has handled and regulated Indian life. The dominant society in no way affirmed the cultural identity of Indians; thus many Indians have internalized the oppression that they experienced from the outside world. Furthermore, many young people feel the stresses of living between two cultural worlds. They are not fully part of the traditional Indian world as celebrated on the reservation or in a community that honors traditions; they are not fully adapted to the dominant American culture. People who are caught between two cultures and are successful in neither run the risk of contributing to family breakdown, often becoming depressed, alcoholic, and suicidal, as noted above. Comparing the suicide rate between white youths and Native Americans, the most recent statistics from the Pan American Health Organization indicate that, again, for Indian males, 15–24 years, it was one-third higher. Interestingly, according to the Committee on Cultural Psychiatry (1989), Indian groups that have remained tightly identified with their culture because of isolation from the mainstream society and because of remaining on indigenous lands, do not exhibit the type of behavior described above. At least at the time of the Committee's study, tribes exemplifying healthier attitudes toward their identities and a lower suicide rate include the southwestern Pueblos and the Navajo.

Despite the persistence of many social problems, progress has been made with respect to education and political participation. Law enforcement officials must not hold on to the stereotype of American Indians as being uneducated. There is a growing population attending colleges and rising to high positions in education, entertainment, sports, and industry. Many people are now working on revitalizing Native American culture rather than letting it die. This has resulted in the movement of "pan-Indianism," in which Native Americans across the United States are celebrating their cultural heritage, while organizing politically. For example, the National Congress of American Indians (NCAI) specifically deals with political and social issues that arise among Native Americans nationally. The NCAI made the following statement in 2003 on the issue of cultural affiliation, promoting the unity of Native Americans, as well as the education of the rest of society to become more aware of Native American issues and people:

> Whereas, we, the members of the National Congress of American Indians of the United States, invoking the divine blessing of the Creator upon our efforts and purposes, in order to preserve for ourselves and our descendents the inherent sovereign rights of our Indian nations, and all other rights and benefits to which we are entitled under the laws and Constitution of the United States, to enlighten the public toward a better understanding of the Indian people and their way of life, to preserve Indian cultural values, and otherwise promote the health, safety and welfare of the Indian people, do hereby establish and submit the following resolutions . . .

The NCAI is the oldest, largest, and most representative Indian organization devoted to promoting and protecting the rights of American Indian and Alaska Natives as a whole group. As an example of a specific organizational action, in 1999, the NCAI condemned the use of sports team "mascots" using Native American and native cultural terms (e.g., "Redskins").

An American Indian culture has been developing nationally, where members of tribes or communities with very different traditions are identifying as a group by following certain practices that are associated with Indians (D. Brown, personal communication, August 13, 1992): for example, (1) males wearing long hair (long hair is a sign of a free man, not a slave); (2) the use of the sacred pipe (i.e., the pipestone pipe, sometimes referred to as the "peace pipe"); and (3) participation in sweat lodges, purification rituals, and the sacred sun dance for purification. All the tribes have these elements in their traditions, but tribes practice them to varying degrees, and will gravitate more toward the one tradition over another (Rivera, 2003).

These rituals are not practiced by every tribe but are becoming symbols of a growing movement reflecting American Indian pride. It should be noted, however, that the pan-Indian movement is not necessarily viewed positively by all Indians, as some believe that there is a strong possibility of misusing a tradition or diluting the meaning of a ritual. In *A Short History of Pan-Indianism,* (Flattery, 1997) a brief synopsis of the movement is provided:

> Pan-Indianism involves the process of synthesizing the collective spiritual reality and traditional wisdom of more than one Native American Nation: [It] is a non-violent liberation philosophy with roots in Native American [philosophies]. The Pan-Indian movement serves to stabilize Indian youth . . . and to provide a way of practicing Native American spirituality [in order to] . . . stimulate the next generation to remain Indian. . . . [It] is open to all peoples. . .

Organizers of the Pan-Indian movement are devoted to helping educate and bring Native Americans back to their roots. Many younger people feel alienated when it comes to their native identity. Following is a quote from a Native American officer in a Southern California police department: "I know very little about my roots. My mother and grandmother were denied the opportunity to learn about their culture [forced assimilation] and nothing was passed on. I feel empty and have intense anger toward those who held the power to decide that certain traditions were not worth preserving. Forced denial of our ethnicity has resulted in extremely high alcohol and suicide rates as a collective response."

LANGUAGE AND COMMUNICATION

It is possible to make some generalizations about the way a group of people communicate, even when there is great diversity within the group. The following contains information about nonverbal and verbal aspects of communication as well as tips for the law enforcement officer interacting with Native Americans. The paragraphs that follow describe patterns of communication and behavior as exhibited by some American Indians who are traditional in their outlook. No description of communication traits, however, would ever apply to everyone within a group, especially one that is so diverse.

Openness and Self-Disclosure

Many Native Americans, in early encounters, will approach people and respond with caution. Too much openness is to be avoided, as is disclosing personal and family problems. This often means that the officer has to work harder at establishing rapport and gaining trust. In the American mainstream culture, appearing friendly and open is highly valued, especially in certain regions such as the West Coast and the South. Because different modes of behavior are expected and accepted, the non-Indian may view the Indian as aloof and reserved. The Indian perception can be that the Euro-American person, because of excessive openness, is superficial and thus untrustworthy. Mainstream American culture encourages speaking out and open expression of opinions, while American Indian culture does not.

Silence and Interruptions

The ability to remain quiet, to be still, and to observe is highly valued in Native American culture; consequently, silence is truly a virtue. (In mainstream American culture, it is said that "silence is golden," but this is probably more of an expression of an ideal than a description of a fact.) Indians are taught to study and assess situations and only act or participate when one is properly prepared. Indians tend not to act impulsively for fear of appearing foolish or bringing shame to themselves or to their family. When law enforcement officials contact Native Americans, they may mistake this reticence to talk as sullenness or lack of cooperation. The behavior must not be misinterpreted or taken personally. A cultural trait must be understood as just that (i.e., a behavior, action, or attitude that is not intended to be a personal insult). The officer must also consider that interrupting an Indian when he or she is speaking is seen as very aggressive and should be avoided whenever possible.

Talking and Questions

Talking just to fill the silence is not seen as important. The small talk that one observes in mainstream society ("Hi. How are you? How was your weekend?" and so on) is traditionally not required by Native Americans. Words are considered powerful and are therefore chosen carefully. This may result in a situation where Native Americans retreat and appear to be withdrawn if someone is dominating the conversation. When law enforcement officials question Native Americans who exhibit these tendencies (i.e., not being prone to talkativeness), the officer should not press aggressively for answers. Aggressive behavior, both verbal and physical, is traditionally looked down upon. Questions should be open-ended, with the officer being willing to respect the silence and time it may take to find out the needed information.

Nonverbal Communication: Eye Contact/Touching

With respect to American Indian cultures, people often make the statement that Indians avoid making direct eye contact. Although this is true for some tribes, it does not hold true for all. To know whether this applies or not, an officer can simply watch for this signal (i.e., avoidance of eye contact) and follow the lead of the citizen. In this section we explain the phenomenon of avoidance of eye contact from the perspective of groups who do adhere to this behavior. Some Indian tribes do have the belief that looking directly into one's eyes for a prolonged period of time is disrespectful just as pointing at someone is considered impolite. Lakota tribe members, for example, generally believe that direct eye contact is an affront or an invasion of privacy (Mehl, 1990). Navajo tribe members have a tendency to stare at each other when they want to direct their anger at someone. An Indian who adheres to the unspoken rules about eye contact may appear to be shifty and evasive. Officers and other law enforcement officials must not automatically judge a person as guilty or suspicious simply because that person is not maintaining direct eye contact. To put a person at ease, the officer can decrease eye contact if it appears to be inhibiting the Native American citizen. Avoidance of eye contact with the officer can also convey the message that the officer is using an approach that is too forceful and demanding. Where such norms about eye-contact avoidance apply, and if an officer has to look at a person's eyes, it would help to forewarn the person (i.e., "I'm going to have to check your eyes").

With regard to their sense of space, most Native Americans are not comfortable being touched by strangers, whether a pat on the back or an arm around the shoulder. Either no touching is appropriate or it should be limited to a brief handshake. Married couples do not tend to show affection in public. Additionally, people should avoid crowding or standing too close. Keep in mind that many Indian relations with strangers are more formal than those of the mainstream culture; therefore, an officer might be viewed as overly aggressive if he or she does not maintain a proper distance. Officers, therefore, who are going to pat down or search a Native American should first explain the process.

Language

Some Native Americans speak one or more Indian languages. English, for many, is a second language. Those who do not speak English well may be inhibited from speaking for fear of "losing face" because of their lack of language ability. In addition, because of a tendency to speak quietly and nonforcefully, law enforcement agents will need patience and extra time; interaction must not be rushed. The Native American who is not strong in English needs to spend more time translating from his or her own language to English when formulating a response (this is true of all second-language speakers who are not yet fluent). As with all other languages, English words or concepts do not always translate exactly into the various Indian languages. Indian languages are rich and express concepts reflecting views of the world. It is mandatory that the utmost respect be shown when Native Americans speak their own language. Remember that the Indians have a long history of forced assimilation into the Anglo society, in which, among other things, many were denied the right to speak their native languages.

Offensive Terms, Labels, and Stereotypes

In the interview mentioned in the opening of this chapter, retired chief of police Jim Cox, a Comanche Indian, described situations in which insensitive police officers told Indian jokes or used derogatory terms in his presence. He stated that he is proud of his heritage and is offended by commonly held stereotypes. Use of racial slurs toward any group are never acceptable in crime-fighting and peacekeeping, no matter how provoked an officer may be. Officers hearing disrespectful terms and stereotypes about Native Americans should educate fellow officers as to the lack of professionalism and respect for community diversity that such terms convey.

There are a number of words that are offensive to Native Americans: chief (a leader who has reached this rank is highly honored), squaw (extremely offensive), buck, redskin, Indian "brave," and skins (some young Indians may refer to themselves using "skins" but would be offended by others using the term). In addition, the use of Indian tribal names or references as mascots for sports teams has been highly objectionable.

Other terms used to refer to Native Americans are "apple" (a slightly dated term referring to a highly assimilated Indian, meaning "red" on the outside, "white" on the inside) and "the people" (more commonly used by some groups of Indians to refer to themselves). In some regions of the country, a reservation is called a "rez" by Indians; for example, in Oklahoma (where there is only one reservation), the term "reservation" is negative and the term "community" is used (Brown, 1992). It is also patronizing when non-Indians use certain kinship terms, such as "grandfather" when talking to an older man, even though other Indians may be using that term themselves.

Other terms that can be offensive and are used commonly include "sitting Indian style" to refer to sitting in a cross-leg position on the floor; "Indian giver" to characterize someone who takes back a present or an offer; children acting like "wild Indians"; having a "pow wow," meaning a discussion; "bottom of the totem pole," meaning lowest ranking; and he is on the "warpath." In addition, it is worth noting that some American Indians deliberately choose not to reveal their ethnic identity in the workplace because of concerns about stereotypes about Indians. Coworkers may make comments about Indians or use offensive expressions because they do not "see one in the room." People can be deeply offended and hurt by "unintentional" references to American Indians.

Many people growing up in the United States can remember the stereotypical picture of an Indian as a wild, savage, and primitive person. In older textbooks, including history books, recounting Native American history, Indians were said to "massacre" whites, whereas whites simply "fought" or "battled" the Indians (Harris & Moran, 1991). Other common stereotypes or stereotypical statements that are highly resented are: "All Indians are drunks" (despite the fact that there are a large percentage of alcohol-related arrests, not all Indians have a problem with liquor). Furthermore, the argument has been put forth that the white man introduced "fire water" or alcohol to the Indian as a means of weakening him. "You can't trust an Indian," "Those damn Indians" (as if they are simply a nuisance), and "The only good Indian is a dead one" (a remark that can be traced back to a statement made by a U.S. general in 1869). (Harris, 1991).

Indians find it offensive when non-Indians make claims that may or may not be true about their Indian ancestry: for example, "I'm part Indian—my great-grandfather was Cherokee." Although this may be an attempt to establish rapport, it rings of "Some of my best friends are Indians . . ." (i.e., to "prove" that one does not have any prejudice).

> [People] should not assume affinity [with American Indians] based on novels, movies, a vacation trip, or an interest in silver jewelry. These are among the most offensive, commonly made errors when non-Indians first encounter an American Indian person or family. Another is a confidential revelation that there is an Indian "Princess" in the family tree—tribe unknown, identity unclear, but a bit of glamour in the family myths. The intent may be to show positive bonding . . . , but to the Indian they reveal stereotypical thinking. (Attneave, 1982)

FAMILY-RELATED ISSUES

Respect for Elders

"Nothing will anger an Indian more than them seeing their grandmother or grandfather being spoken to belligerently or being ordered around with disrespect. [If that happens], that's a fire cracker situation right there" (Rivera, 2003). Unlike mainstream American culture, Indians value aging because of the respect they have for wisdom and experience. People do not feel that they have to cover up signs of aging, as this phase of life is highly revered. The elders of a tribe or the older people in Native American communities must be shown the utmost respect by people in law enforcement. This includes acknowledging their presence in a home visit, even if they are not directly related in the police matter at hand. In some tribes (e.g., the Cherokee) the grandmother often has the most power in the household and is the primary decision-maker. It is advisable for people in law enforcement to include the elders in discussions where they can give their advice or perspective on a situation. The elders are generally respected for their ability to enforce good behavior within the family and tribe.

It should also be noted, however, that because of assimilation or personal preference among some Native Americans, the elders in any given household may tend to avoid interfering with a married couple's problems. And although the elders are respected to a higher degree than in mainstream culture, they may withdraw in some situations where there is police contact, letting the younger family members deal with the problem. If in doubt, it is advisable to begin the contact more formally, deferring to the elders initially. Then officers can observe how the elders participate and if the younger family members include them.

Extended Family and Kinship Ties

In mainstream society, people usually think of and see themselves first as individuals and after that, they may or may not identify with their families or various communities and groups with which they are affiliated. In traditional Native American culture, a person's primary identity is related to his or her family and tribe. Some law enforcement agents may be in positions to make referrals when there is a problem with an individual (e.g., an adolescent) in a family. A referral for counseling for that person only may be culturally alienating. Individual Western-style counseling or therapy is a foreign way to treat problems. Additionally, Native American culture is highly group oriented.

Today, some family and tribal cohesiveness has lessened because of forced assimilation, extreme levels of poverty, and lack of education and employment. However, for many Native Americans, there are still large networks of relatives who are in close proximity with each other. It is not uncommon for children to be raised by someone other than their father or mother (e.g., grandmother, aunts). When law enforcement officials enter an Indian's home and, for example, ask to speak to the parents of a child, they may actually end up talking to someone who is not the biological mother or father. Officers must understand that various other relatives can function exactly as a mother or father would in mainstream culture. This does not mean that Indian "natural" parents are necessarily being lazy about their childrearing duties, even when the child is physically living with another relative (and may be raised by several relatives throughout childhood). The intensely close family and tribal bonds allow for this type of childraising. The officer must not assume that something is abnormal with this type of arrangement or that the parents are neglecting their children.

Children and Separation from Parents

It is crucial that police officers understand the importance of not separating children from family members, if at all possible. Many families in urban areas and on reservations have memories of or have heard stories from elder family members that involved the federal government's systematic removal of Indian children from their homes; in many cases, children were placed in boarding schools that were often hundreds of miles away. This phenomenon, including education for the children that stripped them of their language and culture, began in the late 19th century. Reports exist that say: "Until 1974, the Bureau of Indian Affairs (BIA) was operating 75 boarding schools with more than 30,000 children enrolled" (Ogawa, 1990).

Although for many families, the severe trauma of children being forcibly separated from parents took place years ago, the after-effects still linger. (Rivera, 2003). In the early 20th century there was a famous case in which Hopi Indian fathers were sentenced to years in high-security prisons and were subject to the fullest persecution. Their crime was hiding their children from BIA officials because they did not want the children to be taken by the BIA boarding schools. By hiding the children, the Hopi fathers violated federal law. This case is still talked about today. The memory of a "uniform coming to take away a child" is an image that can be conjured up easily by some Indians. It is this "baggage" that the law enforcement officer today brings into encounters; he or she may be totally unaware of the power of Native Americans' memories of these deplorable actions.

Since Native American parents can be very protective of their children, an officer would be well advised to let the parents know about any action that needs to be taken with regard to the child. Law enforcement officials can establish a good rapport with Indian families if they treat the children well.

KEY ISSUES IN LAW ENFORCEMENT

Perception of Police

The general distrust of police by Native Americans stems from a history of negative relations with "the system," which can refer to federal, state, and local governments. In their view, officers represent a system that has not supported Indian rights and their tribes or communities. Most of their contact with the police has been negative. Thus, many Native Americans often have not had a chance to build a relationship of trust and cooperation with people in law enforcement.

Victimization Rates/Comparisons with Several Other Groups

According to the Bureau of Justice Statistics (BJS) on American Indians and Crime, the rate of violent victimization of Native Americans far exceeds that of other racial or ethnic groups in the United States, and is more than double that of the national average. These rates affect American Indians of all age groups, geographies, economic status levels, and (both) genders.

American Indians were victims of violent crime at double the rate of blacks, whites, or Asians during 1998. American Indians comprised one-half of 1 percent of the U.S. population, but 1.3 percent of all violent crime victims (see Exhibit 9.2).

In addition, Native American women were victimized by an intimate partner at rates higher than others—23 per 1,000 American Indian females, 11 per 1,000 black

	PERCENT OF POPULATION	*PERCENT OF VIOLENCE VICTIMS*
Whites	84.2%	82.2%
Blacks	12.1%	14.7%
American Indians	0.5%	1.3%
Asians/Pacif. Island.	3.2%	1.8%

Exhibit 9.2   Percent of population: Violent victimizations

females, 8 per 1,000 white females, and 2 per 1,000 Asian females between 1993 and 1998. Approximately half of the American Indian female population who were victimized said that the reason for not reporting the violence was because it was a "private or personal matter" or the victim "feared reprisal," this fear being shared among other racial and ethnic groups as well (Bureau of Justice Statistics, 1993–1998).

Jurisdiction

Jurisdiction on tribal lands can cause a great deal of friction between tribal and civilian law enforcement, and particularly on reservations where the lines of jurisdiction are not clear. Jurisdiction of the tribal police may be limited, but the non-Indian is not always subject to Indian tribal law. Some tribes have taken to decriminalize their codes and take on civil codes of law (e.g., for basic misdemeanors, civil fines may go to the tribal court), yet still conduct a trial of the non-Indian in a tribal court. Who has authority and who has responsibility can be an ambiguous area in tribal and civilian law enforcement (Setter, 2000). Police officers are put into an unusual situation when it comes to enforcing the law among Indians. They may make an arrest on an area that is considered to be "Indian land" (on which tribal police have jurisdiction). The land may be adjacent to non-Indian land, sometimes forming "checkerboard" patterns of jurisdiction. In the case of an Indian reservation (on which tribal police may have authority), civil law enforcement agencies are challenged to know where their jurisdiction begins and where it ends. With the multijurisdictional agreements that many tribes have signed with local and state officials, civil police officers may have the right to enter reservations to continue business. For example, a criminal can be apprehended by a civil police officer on a reservation (Brown, 1992).

It is expected and desired (because it does not always happen) that civil law enforcement agents inform tribal police or tribal authorities when entering a reservation. Going onto reservation land without prior notice and contacting a suspect or witness directly is an insult to the authority of the tribal police (Willie, 1992). In other words, civil police should see themselves as partners with tribal police. Obviously, in dangerous or emergency situations, time may prevent civil authorities from conferring with the tribal police. Where possible, it is essential that the authority of the reservation be respected. As we mentioned, on some reservations, it may not be clear who has jurisdiction and it becomes all the more necessary to establish trusting relations. When on the reservation, the police officer must refrain from using abusive language or mannerisms. Officers need to know when and how federal laws apply to reservations.

Levels of cooperation and attitudes toward civil and tribal law enforcement partnerships differ from area to area. The Sac and Fox Nation, originally from the Midwest, is an example of a tribe that initiated a relationship with civil law enforcement resulting in a cooperative approach to law enforcement. The cross-deputization that resulted from the Sac and Fox Nation's efforts enabled both sets of officers (i.e., from the tribal and civil police) to make arrests in each other's jurisdiction without being sued. Similarly, certain police departments, Albuquerque, New Mexico, being one of them, have gone out of their way to work out relationships with local Indian tribes. If there is a will to work cooperatively, police departments and Indian tribal departments can be of tremendous benefit to each other. Initiating this type of effort means, for both Indians and non-Indians, putting aside history and transcending stereotypes. Furthermore, individual officers should be sensitive to their own potentially condescending attitudes toward tribal police and tribal law.

> American Indians have struggled to retain as much of their own culture and tradition within tribal police operations as possible. Within the very limited jurisdiction in which tribal police have been allowed to exercise their tribal police powers, American Indians have struggled to incorporate tribal laws and procedures. Dominant white authorities are reluctant to allow Indian police agencies to have power over their own when whites do not control the law and procedures of that agency. (Barlow, 2000)

According to Deloria and Lytle, *American Indians, American Justice* (quoted in Barlow, 2000):

> The tribal police continue to play an important role in resolving criminal cases on reservations. They are usually the ones who discover the crime, conduct initial interviews, know the personalities and circumstances involved, and provide continued assistance throughout the case. Their recommendations are well respected by the federal government.

Police Stops

When groups of Native Americans drive large, poorly maintained cars, there is the potential that they will be stopped simply because they are perceived as suspicious and because negative stereotypes are operating. We know that the phenomenon of profiling exists with other racial and ethnic groups. Similarly, negative biases against Native Americans are strong and have persisted for generations. A group of Indians in an old, run-down car should not signal anything but what it really is (i.e., a group of friends driving around together). When there is not a legitimate reason to stop a car, the next step is for officers to check their stereotypes of who they think a criminal is. Like members of other groups, Indians have repeatedly reported being stopped for no reason, and this obviously adds to their distrust of police.

Peyote

Many states in the United States have specific laws exempting the traditional, religious use of peyote by American Indians from those states' drug enforcement laws. Following is a definition of peyote:

> Peyote is a small turnip-shaped, spineless cactus [containing] nine alkaloid substances, part of which, mainly mescaline, are hallucinogenic in nature; that is, they induce dreams or visions. Reactions to peyote seem to vary with the social situation which it is used. In some it may merely cause nausea; believers may experience optic, olfactory and auditory sensations. Under ideal conditions color visions may be experienced and peyote may be "heard" singing or speaking. The effects wear off within twenty-four hours and leave no ill after effects. Peyote is non-habit forming. (Bahti, 1982)

There have been a variety of uses associated with peyote: (1) as a charm for hunting, (2) as medicine, (3) as an aid to predict weather, (4) as an object to help find things that are lost (the belief being that peyote can reveal the location of the lost object through peyote-induced visions; peyote was even used to help locate the enemy in warfare), and (5) as an object to be carried for protection. People have faith in peyote as a powerful symbol and revere its presence.

Peyote is carried in small bags or pouches and these can be "ruined" if touched.* Police officers may need to confiscate peyote, but can do it in a way that will cause the least amount of upset. It is far better to ask the Native American politely to remove the bag in which the peyote is contained rather than forcing it away from him or her.

In a 1990 freedom of religion case, the Supreme Court dealt a severe blow to traditional American Indians when the Court ruled that state governments could have greater leeway in outlawing certain religious practices. The ruling involved ritual use of peyote by some American Indians who follow the practices of the Native American Church (NAC). Until that time, the U.S. government allowed for the religious use of peyote among Native Americans based on the Bill of Right's "Free Exercise of Religion" guarantee; in other words, peyote use was generally illegal, except in connection with bonafide American Indian religious rituals.

From a law enforcement perspective, if drugs are illegal, no group should be exempt, and indeed, officers have to uphold the law. From a civil rights perspective, religious freedom applies to all groups and no group should be singled out for disproportionately burdensome treatment. The historical legal and illegal status of peyote is complex. There have been many attempts to prohibit the use of peyote on the federal level, and many states passed laws outlawing its use. However, several states modified such prohibitions to allow traditional American Indians to continue using peyote as a sacrament. Moreover, in some states, such as Arizona, anti-peyote laws have been declared unconstitutional by state courts insofar as they burden the religious practice of American Indians. The following is an example of how one state, Arizona, revised its statutes with respect to the use of peyote (see B below):

Arizona Revised Statutes State Law 13-3402(**B**). Possession and sale of peyote; classification

A. A person who knowingly possesses, sells, transfers or offers to sell or transfer peyote is guilty of a class 6 felony.

B. In a prosecution for violation of this section, it is a defense that the peyote is being used or is intended for use: 1. In connection with the bona fide practice of a religious belief, and 2. As an integral part of a religious exercise, and 3. In a manner not dangerous to public health, safety or morals.

This historic ambiguity on the state level, together with the 1990 ruling on the federal level, causes confusion and resentment on the part of many Native Americans. In 1993, Congress passed legislation preempting state law that would protect numerous Indian ceremonies and ritual practices, including the traditional use of peyote by Amer-

---

*Native Americans from many tribes across the country wear small bags referred to as medicine bags; these are considered to be extremely sacred. The medicine bags do not carry drugs or peyote, but hold symbols from nature (e.g., corn pollen, cedar, sage, bark of a tree), and they are believed to have certain powers. Law enforcement officers should handle these (if it becomes necessary) as they would handle any sacred symbol from their own religion. Ripping into the bags would be an act of desecration. The powerful medicine contained in the bags is often blessed and therefore must be treated in a respectful manner.

ican Indians in bonafide religious ceremonies, that is Native American Free Exercise of Religion Act of 1993. (Officers are advised to become familiar with the Native American Free Exercise of Religion Act of 1993, including 1994 amendments.) The Act was passed based on the following findings (partial list—Section 201.Findings):

> Some Indian people have used the peyote cactus in religious ceremonies for sacramental and healing purposes for many generations, and such uses have been significant in perpetuating Indian tribes and culture by promoting and strengthening the unique cultural cohesiveness of Indian tribes;
>
> While numerous states have enacted a variety of laws which protect the ceremonial use of peyote by Indians, many others have not, and this lack of uniformity has created hardships for Indian people who participate in such ceremonies;
>
> The traditional ceremonial use by Indians of the peyote cactus is integral to a way of life that plays a significant role in combating the scourge of alcohol and drug abuse among some Indian people;
>
> The United States has a unique and special historic trust responsibility for the protection and preservation of Indian tribes and cultures, and the duty to protect the continuing cultural cohesiveness and integrity of Indian tribes and cultures;
>
> Existing Federal and State laws, regulations and judicial decisions are inadequate to fully protect the ongoing traditional uses of the peyote cactus in Indian ceremonies. [Note: "Existing refers to laws (etc. prior to the passing of this Act.]
>
> (Title II—Traditional Use of Peyote; Sec. 201 Findings)

The use of peyote outside the Native American Church (NAC, established in 1918) is forbidden and regarded by church members as sacrilegious. If individuals are using peyote under the guise of religion, however, they are breaking the law. Within the NAC, there are very specific rules and rituals pertaining to its sacramental use. Establishing respectful communication with the leaders of the NAC would assist officers in determining whether peyote was being abused in certain circumstances.

This revised statute was referenced in the highly publicized case of the removal and confiscation of 11,323 plants from the home of Leonard Mercado in Pinal County, Arizona (press release, January 1999), an active member of the Native American Church. For bona fide members of the Native American Church, this type of act (which had happened earlier in 1995 with the removal of 700 plants) is an act of religious desecration.

Law enforcement officials should understand the importance and place of peyote in the culture from a Native American point of view. It is not the intent of the authors to recommend a particular course of action with regard to enforcement or lack thereof. If the use of peyote is understood from an Indian perspective, officers will communicate an attitude that shows respect for an ancient ritual that some researchers say dates back 10,000 years ago. When police officers come in suddenly to a meeting or ceremony where peyote is being used (often along with prayers and drumming) and they aggressively make arrests, it will be very difficult to establish trust and rapport with the community. When peyote is an issue, officers must recognize their own ethnocentrism (i.e., unconsciously viewing other cultures or cultural practices as primitive, abnormal, or inferior). Appreciating the fact that cultures are acquired (i.e., they are not passed on through the genes) includes the realization that, "If I had been born in (any other culture), I would be doing things similar to those being done by the majority of other people in the culture." With this attitude in mind, it is easier to remain respectful of differences. Law enforcement personnel working in communities where peyote use is an issue should anticipate the problems that will occur and should discuss it with members of the Indian community. The officer must also understand the law and his or her agency policy on enforcement.

Historically, the federal government actively tried to suppress and change Native American cultures, from condemning traditional marriage practices as being "loose and barbaric" to condemning Indians' "long-time tendency . . . to give too much time to dances, powwows, celebrations, and general festive occasions" (1992 Report of the Commissioner of Indian Affairs). The commissioner wrote in 1923: "To correct this practice a letter was widely circulated among the Indians . . . that they shorten somewhat the length of these gatherings and omit from them use of harmful drugs [peyote], intoxicants, gambling and degrading ceremonials." This explanation is given to illustrate to people in law enforcement that their peyote arrests symbolize official acts of condemning cultural practices. The banning of peyote was and has been viewed by Native American groups as a failure of the Bill of Rights to truly guarantee the freedom to practice one's own religion.

Trespassing and Sacred Lands

In a number of states, traditional Indian harvest areas or sacred burial and religious sites are now on federal, state, and especially private, lands. Indians continue to go to these areas just as their ancestors did to collect resources or to pray. The point of concern for law enforcement involves conflicts occurring between the ranchers, farmers, and homeowners on what Indians consider their holy ground. How the officer reacts to Indians' allegations of trespassing determines whether there will be an escalated confrontation (Rivera, 2003). When there is a dispute, the officer will alienate Indians by choosing an authoritarian and aggressive method of handling the problem (e.g., "You're going to get off this land right now"). Alternatively, he or she could show some empathy and the Native American may very well be more supportive of the officer's efforts to resolve the immediate conflict. If there is no immediate resolution, the officer can, at a minimum, prevent an escalation of hostilities.

Since police officers cannot solve this complex and very old problem, the only tool available is the ability to communicate sensitively and listen well. "The officer is put between a rock and a hard place. If the officer is sensitive, he could try to speak to the landowner and describe the situation, although often the landowners don't care about the history (claiming, "It's my land now"). However, there have been some people who have been sensitive to the needs of the Native Americans and who have worked out agreements" (Rivera, 2003).

Native American Sites—Use of, Desecration, and Looting

The Native American Free Exercise of Religion Act of 1993 (Senate Bill 1021, introduced to the 103rd Congress), Title I—Protection of Sacred Sites gives tribal authority over Native American religious sites on Indian lands:

> **(a) Right of Tribe**—All Federal or federally assisted undertakings on Indian lands which may result in changes in the character or use of a Native American religious site or which may have an impact on access to a Native American religious site shall, unless requested otherwise by the Indian tribe on whose lands

the undertakings will take place, be conducted in conformance with the laws or customs of the tribe.

(b) Protection by Tribes—Indian tribes may regulate and protect Native American religious sites located on Indian lands.

Beyond use or undertaking of religious sites by the federal government or any governmental agency is the history of desecration and looting of sacred sites and objects. Most often, the looting has been done to make a profit on Native American articles and artifacts. Native Americans witness vandalism on their archeological sites, but often without any criminal prosecution. In 1996, President Bill Clinton signed an Executive Order (13007) protecting Indian sacred lands from anything affecting their physical integrity and preserving Indian religious practices on those sites. At the time of the writing of this edition of this book, U.S. Representative Nick Rahall made the following statement:

> Across the country, sites of religious importance are in danger of becoming casualties of the current Administration's push to open federal lands to development. Despite several laws in place aiming to protect the religious freedom of Native Americans, and the historic and cultural value of their lands, there is no comprehensive or approachable law to protect sacred lands from energy development, and other potentially harmful activities. (Rahall, 2003)

Even more degrading to Native Americans than the violation of sacred lands is the taking of human remains (skulls and bones) from Indian reservations and public lands. Officers in certain parts of the country may enter non-Indian homes and see such remains "displayed" as souvenirs of a trip into Indian country. The Native American Grave Protection and Repatriation Act (NAGPRA) passed by Congress and signed by President George H. W. Bush resulted as a response to such criminal acts. If an officer sees any human remains, he or she must investigate whether foul play might have been involved. Officers should contact state agencies established to enforce laws that protect Indian relics to determine how to proceed in such situations.

Indian Casinos and Gaming

Native American reservations in the United States are considered to be sovereign nations, and, as such, leaders are responsible for providing and securing financing in order to pay for basic infrastructure and services (as in any city). To date, the most successful industry on the reservations has been casinos and other types of "gaming" for profit. The legal wording on most documents referring to this industry uses the term "Indian gaming." In addition, there is the National Indian Gaming Association, thus "Indian gaming" is the most common term used in publications on the subject.

Legalized gambling on reservations dates back to a landmark case in 1976 in which it was ruled by the Supreme Court that states no longer could have regulatory jurisdiction over Indian tribes. Because of lawsuits that followed, it was later ruled that states did not have the right to prohibit Native American tribes from organizing and participating in for-profit legalized gambling. The "Indian Gaming Regulatory Act" became law in 1988. For the first time, Native Americans were given the right to regulate all gaming activities on their sovereign lands.

According to the National Bureau of Economic Research (NBER, 2000), there are over 310 gaming operations of various types in more than 200 of the 550-plus tribes in the United States. About 220 are casinos in the style of Las Vegas, and they include slot machines or, in some cases, table games (or both). There is great controversy around the Indian gaming industry. On the one hand, according to NBER, "four years after tribes open casinos, employment . . . increase[s] by 26 percent, and tribal population . . . increase[s] by about 12 percent [i.e., Native Americans return to the reservation because of the promise of work]. . . . The increase in economic activity appears to have some health benefits in that four or more years after a casino opens, mortality has fallen by 2 percent." On the other hand, according to the same 2002 NBER study, "bankruptcy rates, violent crime, auto thefts and larceny are up 10 percent in counties with a casino."

Fishing

> If you ever want to get into a fight, go into a local bar [e.g., in parts of Washington State] and start talking about fishing rights. The fishing issue is a totally hot issue (Rivera, 2003).

> The wording of the treaties [i.e., with regard to the fishing rights of Native Americans] is clear and unequivocal in English as well as in the language of the specific tribes concerned. For example, the treaty with Indians of the Northwest regarding fishing rights on the rivers gives these rights to the Indians "for as long as the rivers shall flow." The rivers in the Northwest are still flowing, and the Indians are still struggling with the state of Washington about the state's violations of the treaty's terms, even on Indian property. (Association of Social Workers, 1972)

In the year 2003, Indians continued to say, "We have treaties with the government allowing us to fish here." Commercial and sports fishermen, on the forefront of trying to prevent Native Americans from exercising their treaty rights, claim that Indians are destroying the industry. From the Native Americans' perspective, they are providing sustenance to their families and earn extra money for themselves or their tribes to make it throughout the year. (For 150 years, there has been no industry on many, if not most, of the reservations.) Once again, the officer on the front line will be unable to solve a problem that has been raging for generations. The front-line officer's actions, in part, depend on the sensitivity of his or her department's chief executive. Admittedly, the commander is in a difficult position. He or she is between the state fish and game industry and the people trying to enforce federal treaties. Nevertheless, he or she can communicate to officers the need for cultural sensitivity in their way of approaching and communicating with Native Americans. The alternative could be deadly, as has at least one situation illustrated when, in northern California, peace officers with flack jackets and automatic weapons resorted to pursuing Native Americans with shotguns up and down the river (Rivera, 2003).

There are many complex dimensions to cases involving Native Americans "breaking the law" when, in parallel, the federal government is not honoring its treaties with them. Native Americans are frustrated by what they see as blatant violations of their rights. The history of the government's lack of loyalty to its American Indian citizens has caused great pain for this cultural group. Clearly, sensitivity and understanding on the part of the officer are required. The officer has to have patience and tact, remembering that history has defined many aspects of the current relationships between law enforcement and American Indians. Being forceful and displaying anger will alienate Native Americans and will not result in the cooperation needed to solve issues that arise.

SUMMARY OF RECOMMENDATIONS FOR LAW ENFORCEMENT

1. Those who are entrusted with keeping the peace in rural areas, in cities, or on Native American reservations should exhibit respect and professionalism when interacting with peoples who have traditionally been disrespected by governmental authority. It is important to remember that the U.S. government has violated many treaties with American Indians and that their basic rights as Americans have repeatedly been denied.

   - Understand the initial resistance to your efforts to establish rapport and goodwill and do not take it personally.
   - Make an effort to get to know the community in your particular area. Make positive contact with American Indian organizations and individuals. This behavior on your part will be unexpected, and will result in more cooperation.

2. The younger, more environmentally conscious generation of Americans have adopted much valuable ideology from the culture of America's original peoples.

   - Convey a respect for Native American values. They are not alienating or "un-American," and many believe that those very values of preservation are necessary for our environmental survival.

3. Indians have been victims of forced assimilation whereby their languages, religions, and cultures have been suppressed. The negative effects have stayed with generations of Indians.

   - The point of contact between a law enforcement professional and an American Indian can often involve issues related to poor adjustment to urban life. While the law must be upheld, consider the conditions that led some Native Americans toward, for example, alcoholism and unemployment. Having empathy for the conditions that lead to a person's circumstance need not make one any less effective in his or her line of duty.

4. Preferred mainstream American ways of communication often run counter to American Indian styles of communication. Keep the following in mind when trying to build rapport with citizens who are Indians:

   - Do not take advantage of the American Indian just because he or she may be silent, appear passive, or not be fluent in English.
   - Do not interrupt Indian people when they are speaking; it is seen as aggressive and rude.

5. Many American Indians who favor traditional styles of communication will tend toward:

   - Closed behavior and slow rapport-building with strangers. (This does not mean that the person is aloof or hostile; rather, this can be a cultural trait.)
   - Silent and highly observant behavior. (This is not necessarily an indication that an individual does not want to cooperate.)
   - Withdrawal if the method of questioning is too aggressive. (Remember to use time, patience, and silence, which will assist you in getting the response you need.)

- Indirect eye contact for members of some tribes, but not all. (Your penetrating or intense eye contact may result in intimidating the person and, consequently, in his or her withdrawal.)

6. The terms "chief," "redskin," "buck," "squaw," "braves," and "skins" are offensive when used by a non-Indian (sometimes younger Indians may use some of the terms themselves [e.g., "skins"], but this does not make it acceptable for others to use the terms).

   - If you need to refer to the cultural group, ask the person with whom you are in contact whether he or she prefers the term Indian, Native American, or another tribal name. Your sensitivity to these labels can contribute to establishing a good rapport. If asking seems inappropriate, listen carefully to how the individuals refer to each other.

7. The extended family is close-knit and interdependent among Native American peoples. Keep in mind the following:

   - Be respectful and deferential to elders.
   - Elders should be asked for their opinion or even advice, where applicable, as they are often major decision-makers in the family.
   - If there are problems with a child, consider other adults, besides the mother and father, who may also be responsible for child-raising.
   - Whenever possible do not separate children from parents. This can bring back memories of times when children were forcibly taken from their parents and sent to Christian mission schools or government boarding schools far from their homes.

8. With regard to key issues of law enforcement and contact with American Indians, particularly sensitive areas include:

   - Use of peyote
   - Allegations of trespassing
   - Sacred sites violations
   - Fishing
   - Casinos; Indian "gaming"
   - Victimization rates
   - Jurisdiction

   These all involve matters in which Native Americans feel that they have been deprived of their rights: in the case of peyote, the right to religious expression; in the case of trespassing, the right to honor their ancestors (e.g., when visiting burial grounds); and in the case of fishing, the ability to exercise their rights as guaranteed by treaties made with the U.S. government.

9. From a Native American perspective, many people feel that they are abused by a system of government that is neither honest nor respectful of their culture. They believe that the government degrades the land upon which all people depend. To a large extent, Indian rights are still ignored because members of the dominant society do not always uphold the laws that were made to protect

Indians. This background makes it especially difficult for people in law enforcement vis-à-vis their relationships and interactions with Indians. For this reason, law enforcement officials need to go out of their way to demonstrate that they are fair, given the complexities of history and current law. In addition, chief executives and command staff of police departments have a special responsibility to provide an accurate education to officers on American Indian cultural groups, with an emphasis on government–tribal relations, and to address the special needs and concerns of the Indian peoples.

DISCUSSION QUESTIONS AND ISSUES*

1. *Popular Stereotypes.* What are some commonly held stereotypes of Native Americans? What is your personal experience with Native Americans that might counter these stereotypes? How have people in law enforcement been influenced by popular stereotypes of Native Americans?

2. *Recommendations for Effective Contact.* If you have had contact with Native Americans, what recommendations would you give others regarding effective communication, rapport-building, and cultural knowledge that would be beneficial for officers?

3. *The Government's Broken Promises to American Indians.* The famous Lakota chief, Sitting Bull, spoke on behalf of many Indians when he said of white Americans: "They made us many promises . . . but they never kept but one: They promised to take our land, and they took it." There was a time when many acres of land in what we now call the United States were sacred to Native American tribes. Therefore, today many of us are living on, building on, and in some cases, destroying the remains of Indian lands where people's roots run deep. Given this, how would you deal with the problem of an Indian "trespassing" on someone's land when he or she claims to be visiting an ancestral burial ground, for example? What could you say or do so as not to totally alienate the Native American and thereby risk losing trust and cooperation?

4. *Jurisdiction.* (A) What are law enforcement agents supposed to do in situations whereby the state law is in conflict with a federal law that has been based on treaties with Native Americans signed by the federal government? How can officers who are on the front lines win the respect and cooperation of Native Americans when they are asked to enforce something that goes against the treaty rights of the Indians?

   (B) A special unit in the early 1990s was established by the San Diego Sheriff's Department to patrol Native American reservations that were overrun from the outside by drugs and violence. Federal Public Law 280 transferred criminal jurisdiction and enforcement on reservations to some states. Research law enforcement jurisdiction issues and tribal lands in your region or state (if applicable); note where there are still unresolved areas or areas of dispute.

---

*See Instructor's Manual that accompanies this text for additional activities, role-plays, questionnaires, and projects related to the content of this chapter.

WEBSITE RESOURCES

Native American Support Group of New York City: http://graywolf94.tripod.com/

This website provides a wide variety of information on and for Native Americans in the New York City area, as well as information of general interest to those interested in Native American issues locally, regionally, and nationally.

Public Community Listing of Bay Area Native American Cultural Events:
http://groups.msn.com/bayareaindiancalendar

Focused on Native Americans in the San Francisco Bay Area, this website offers chat rooms, articles, calendars, and other features for the community to stay connected locally, regionally, and nationally.

Bureau of Indian Affairs (BIA):   http://www.doi.gov/bureau-indian-affairs.html

As of the final preparation of this book, this website was "temporarily shut down as part of the Cobell Litigation accusing the U.S. government of improperly managing Indian assets entrusted to it" (see http://www.washingtonpost.com/ac2/wp-dyn/A25625-2002Apr21?); the page still references a wide variety of links to governmental and nongovernmental organizations related to Native Americans.

Office of Tribal Justice (OTJ):   http://www.usdoj.gov/otj/

The information contained in this website pertains to the Department of Justice's involvement with Native American tribes and organizations. The office is the single point of contact within the department for meeting responsibilities to the tribes.

National Congress of American Indians (NCAI):   http://www.ncai.org

The website for the national organization contains information on issues, events, and other information relevant to the organization and to Native Americans.

REFERENCES

Association of Social Workers. (1972). *Ethnicity and Social Work, 17*(3).

Attneave, Carolyn. (1982). "American Indians and Alaska Native Families: Emigrants in Their Own Homeland," in *Ethnicity and Family Therapy,* M. McGoldrick et al., eds. New York: Guilford Press.

Bahti, Tom. (1982). *Southwestern Indian Ceremonials.* Las Vegas, Nev.: KC Publications.

Barlow, David. (2000). Criminal Justice in America. Upper Saddle River, N.J.: Prentice-Hall.

Brown, Donald. (Ed.). (1992). *Crossroads Oklahoma: The Ethnic Experience in Oklahoma.* Stillwater, Okla.: Crossroads Oklahoma Project.

Bureau of Justice Statistics. (2001). *Differences in Rates of Violent Crime Experienced by Whites and Black Narrow: American Indians are the most Victimized by Violence.* 1993–1998 Study. Washington, D.C.: Author.

Bureau of Indian Affairs. (2003). http://www.doi.gov/bureau-indian-affairs.html

Committee on Cultural Psychiatry, Group for the Advancement of Psychiatry. (1989). *Suicide and Ethnicity on the United States.* New York: Brunner/Mazel.

CEHIP. (1996). "20th Century Warriors: Native American Participation in the United States Military." Prepared for the United States Department of Defense in partnership with Native American advisors, Rodger Bucholz, William Fields, and Ursula P. Roach. Washington, D.C.: Department of Defense. Available: http://www.history.navy.mil/faqs/faq61-1.htm

Demographics and Health Risk Indicator, (2000).

Friends Committee on National Legislation (FCNL), (2001).

Flattery, Elaine. (1997). *A Short History of Pan-Indianism.* Available: http://www.nativenet.uthsca.edu

Harris, Philip R., and Robert T. Moran. (1991). *Managing Cultural Differences: High Performance Strategies for a New World of Business.* Houston, Texas: Gulf Publishing.

Locklear, Herbert H. (1972). "American Indian Myths," in Special Issue on Ethnicity and Social Work. *Journal of the National Association of Social Workers, 17*(3).

Matthiessen, Peter. (1992). *The Spirit of Crazy Horse.* New York: Penguin Books.

Mehl, Lewis. (1990). "Creativity and Madness." Presentation held in Santa Fe, New Mexico, sponsored by the American Institute of Medical Education.

Native American Free Exercise of Religion Act of 1993, Senate Bill 1021 introduced to 103rd Congress.

National Bureau of Economic Research. (2002). "The Social and Economic Impact of Native American Casinos." NBER Working Paper No. w9198.

National Congress of American Indians. (2003). http://www.ncai.org Resolution [#PHX-03-024] May 25, 1993 by Mr. Inouye (D-HI) (eventually passed as the American Indian Religious Freedom Act Amendments of 1994).

Ogawa, Brian. (1990). *Color of Justice: Culturally Sensitive Treatment of Minority Crime Victims.* Sacramento: Office of the Governor, State of California, Office of Criminal Justice Planning.

Saltzman, Lee. (2003). *Compact History Geographic Overview.* Available: http://www.dickshovel.com/up/html

U.S. Bureau of the Census. (2002). http://www.cwnsus.gov/prod/2002pubs/c2kbr11o1-15.pdf.

Part 3

MULTICULTURAL LAW ENFORCEMENT ELEMENTS IN TERRORISM AND HOMELAND SECURITY

Part Three provides information on working with multicultural communities in the emerging areas of domestic and international terrorism. Peacekeeping efforts of homeland security within our local, state, regional, national, and global multicultural communities are addressed. Research and documented findings indicate that acts of terrorism and efforts towards homeland security start with key elements that are "local" in prevention, response, and implementation (Howard & Sawyer, 2004; International Association of Chiefs of Police, 2001; Nance, 2003). Generally speaking, acts of terrorism in the United States usually involve local law enforcement agencies and other public safety personnel as first responders. Thus, specific strategies and practices regarding the role of law enforcement personnel as first responders are provided as critical background information. Part Three highlights law enforcement prevention, response, control, and reporting strategies related to the war on terrorism and homeland security within multicultural communities. The chapters that follow contain (1) overviews, background, and historical information with respect to law enforcement's emerging roles in the war on terrorism and in homeland security; (2) self-protection practices and procedures important to law enforcement personnel as first responders to terrorist attacks and incidents; (3) policies, procedures, and practices relevant to multicultural law enforcement in dealing with crimes of terrorism and homeland security; (4) key multicultural law enforcement communication issues in dealing with terrorism and homeland security; and (5) relationships and processes inherent in multijurisdictional efforts and responses related to terrorism and homeland security work. Each chapter ends with key concerns relevant to officers, and specific challenges involved in emerging roles and practices in dealing with terrorism and homeland security within multicultural communities.

Chapter 10

Multicultural Law Enforcement and Terrorism: Overview, Response Strategies, and Multijurisdictional Actions

OVERVIEW

This chapter provides specific information on the emerging and vital role that law enforcement holds in the war on terrorism within multicultural communities. Although crimes involving terrorism affect our nation as a whole (and thus are seen as national in scope), the immediate targets, outcomes, and results are local in effect. Local law enforcement personnel and agencies are called upon to respond, provide assistance, establish order, and protect the immediate and larger community from any additional harm and danger. Multicultural knowledge and the skill that is required to working within diverse communities provide key resources in preventing and dealing with the aftermath of terrorism, investigation of crimes, and required intelligence gathering. We first provide an overview of the importance of multicultural law enforcement knowledge and skills for handling terrorism. We then define the scope of the problem in dealing with terrorism involving multicultural populations and communities. The section, "Local Community Issues/National and Regional Issues" highlights the complexities in responding to and solving crimes involving terrorism. We have provided specific "Response Strategies" and "Key Issues for Law Enforcement" in terms of collaborative and partnership work in the war on terrorism with the variety of public safety agencies across diverse departmental levels of government. Finally, we close the chapter with specific recommendations for law enforcement officers and other emergency services personnel in actively responding to terrorism within multicultural communities.

COMMENTARY

In the entire history of crime-fighting and public safety, law enforcement has never before had a challenge of the scope and complexity that it faces today with terrorism. Today's terrorists respect neither law nor community-established practices; they honor neither law enforcement personnel nor humanitarian-serving professionals. Their sole goal and mission is to inflict maximum casualty, mass destruction, and public fear, as is highlighted by the following excerpt from an al-Qaida terrorist manual found in a police raid of a cell member's home in Manchester, England:

> Pledge, O Sister:
>   . . . to make their women widows and their children orphans.
>   . . . to make them desire death and hate appointments and prestige.
>   . . . to slaughter them like lambs and let the Nile, al-Asi, and Euphrates
>   flow with their blood.
>   . . . to be a pick of destruction for every godless and apostate regime.
>   . . . to retaliate for you against every dog who touches you with even a
>   bad word.

Although terrorists commit crimes to bring national and international attention to their causes and purposes, the response to terrorist attacks and the actions that might prevent them are, nevertheless, usually accomplished in local cities, neighborhoods, and communities.

> In panel after panel, the same hard truths were expressed repeatedly: With the events of 9/11, the nation entered a new and sobering era. 9/ll shocked the nation with the chilling realization that foreign enemies from both within and without are bent on destroying our institutions, our lives, our very civilization. Terrorist crime, though national in scope, is usually local in execution. In the war on terror, community police will therefore have to shoulder an increasingly heavy burden. (Bankson, 2003)

Law enforcement's knowledge of and sensitivity to local and regional issues will be central to the success in the war on terrorism. Relationships with multicultural local and regional community leaders will be an essential resource in the war on terrorism. Law enforcement personnel have the dual role of protecting: (1) the public from acts of terrorism by those terrorists who may be hiding in multicultural communities in the United States, and (2) the members of multicultural communities who may have no ties to terrorists or criminals but are stereotyped, harassed, or discriminated because of the biases and prejudices of others.

DEFINITIONS

For the purposes of this chapter, we use the general definitions of terrorism developed by the U.S. Department of Justice (1997):

> *Terrorism:* A violent act or an act dangerous to human life, in violation of the criminal laws of the United States or any segment to intimidate or coerce a government, the civilian population, or any segment thereof, in furtherance of political or social objectives.

The FBI (1996) further defines two types of terrorism that occur in the United States:

> *Domestic terrorism* involves groups or individuals whose terrorist activities are directed at elements of our government, organizations, or population without foreign direction.

> *International terrorism* involves groups or individuals whose terrorist activities are foreign-based and/or directed by countries or groups outside the United States or whose activities transcend national boundaries.

Both the U.S. Department of State and the Department of Defense have their respective definitions of terrorism, which we are providing for comparison and reference purposes as follows:

- "Premeditated, politically motivated violence perpetrated against non-combatant targets by sub-national groups or clandestine agents, usually intended to influence an audience" (U.S. Department of State, 1997).

- "The calculated use of violence or threat of violence to inculcate fear, intended to coerce or to intimidate governments or societies in the pursuit of goals that are generally political, religious or ideological" (U.S. Departments of the Army and the Air Force, 1990).

Weapons of Mass Destruction (WMD): Three types of weapons are most commonly categorized as "Weapons of Mass Destruction" (WMD): (1) Nuclear weapons, (2) Biological weapons, and (3) Chemical weapons. Under the sub-categories of WMD includes activities that may be labeled as "agro terrorism" which is to harm our food supply chain and "cyber terrorism" which is to harm our telecommunication, Internet, and computerized processes and transactions.

B-NICE Incident: An acronym for any terrorist incident involving Biological, Nuclear, Incendiary, Chemical and/or Explosive weapons of mass destruction.

The Department of Justice's (1997) definition of terrorism tends to be more specifically and narrowly defined for use by law enforcement and with respect to other criminal justice objectives. For the purposes of this textbook, our definition of terrorism will be broadened in scope to include all crimes involving terrorism, bombings, and weapons of mass destruction, whether domestic or international. It is clear that criminals who resort to terrorism and weapons of mass destruction, regardless of their motives, are usually not restricted by any definition and/or categories. Since the primary goal of law enforcement is to ensure public safety and security, terrorist threats alone are a public safety issue and can send a community into confusion and even chaos. Law enforcement is called upon to respond to both threats of terrorism, as well as to actual incidents and acts of terrorism. Law enforcement's knowledge, skills, resources, and sensitivity to multicultural community issues and concerns will facilitate the effectiveness of its response in the three stages of a terrorism incident: before, during, and after an act of terrorism.

HISTORICAL INFORMATION AND BACKGROUND

Terrorism has always been a part of organized society (Hoffman, 1998; Ahmad & Barsamian, 2001). From the earliest history of establishing order through the enforcement of laws and government, extremist groups and individuals have used property damage and violence against people to generate fear and compel "change" in society and organizations. The Department of Justice (1997), in its training manual, *Emergency Response to Terrorism: Basic Concepts,* highlights some of the following historical examples of terrorism over the past 300 years and current events provide additional contemporary examples:

18th Century
- Infected corpses were used by the Russians in areas held by Sweden.

- Organized violence against government taxation included Shay's Rebellion in 1786 and the Whiskey Rebellion in 1791.

- British officials provided blankets from smallpox patients to Native Americans.

19th Century

- Ku Klux Klan began acts of violence against African Americans.
- An unknown person threw a bomb into a peaceful labor rally at Haymarket Square in Chicago, killing seven and injuring many others.
- Catholic churches were burned in Boston, Philadelphia, and other cities.
- Labor activists used 3,000 pounds of dynamite to blow up the Hill and Sullivan Company mine in Idaho, along with other housing units.

20th Century to Current Times

- In 1954, Puerto Rican nationalists wounded five members of Congress by gunfire.
- In 1975, a bombing at New York City's LaGuardia Airport by Croatian nationalists killed 11 and injured 75.
- In 1983, two left-wing radicals detonated a bomb in the cloak room of the U.S. Senate in the Capitol Building.
- Numerous airline hijackings and bomb threats occurred in the latter half of the 20th century.
- The 1993 World Trade Center bombing in New York City killed 6 people.
- The 1995 Alfred P. Murrah Federal Building bombing in Oklahoma City killed 168 people.
- In 1996–97, multiple bombing incidents occurred in Atlanta, including one at the 1996 Summer Olympic Games.
- On September 11, 2001, 3,047 died and many more injuries occurred with the attacks on the World Trade Center buildings, the Pentagon, and a hijacked plane in Pennsylvania.

The targets and tactics of terrorists have changed over time (Hoffman, 1998). In the past, targets of terrorists were often more individually directed. The death of a unique, single individual like a head of state, president, and/or prime minister would produce the major disruption that the terrorist desired. In modern times, governments and organizations have become far more bureaucratic and decentralized. The targets of terrorists have included unique individuals, their surrounding networks, affiliated organizations and institutions, and any functions or processes associated with any targeted individual or groups. Today, terrorists attack not only prominent individuals and their organizations but also a wider range of targets that have been considered immune historically. For example, prior to modern times, terrorists have granted certain categories of people immunity from attack (e.g., women, children, elderly, disabled, and doctors). By not recognizing any category of people as excluded from attack, terrorists today have an unlimited number of targets for attack. The apparent randomness and unpredictability of terrorist attacks make the work of law enforcement and other public safety officers extremely challenging, and solutions require a high level of sophistication.

As a result of the greater range of potential victims and the demographic background of terrorists, multicultural knowledge, skills, and resources constitute critical elements in the (1) preparation of local communities for safety and security with regard to terrorism, (2) prevention of possible terrorists' crimes and incidents, (3) participation in emergency response to terrorism, (4) investigation and information-gathering involving terrorists, and (5) follow-up actions and prosecution of crimes involving and/or resulting from terrorism. The following case illustrates the broad range of multicultural people, communities, organizations, agencies, and countries involved in the prevention and criminal prosecution of one terrorism threat:

> Revealing the fruits of an elaborate, 18-month-long sting operated with agents of the Russian secret police, federal authorities on Wednesday unveiled criminal charges against three men who they say conspired to sell a shoulder-mounted missile and sought to acquire as many as 50 more. A government affidavit in the case, filed in U.S. District Court here, spins an eerie tale of the ready availability of the deadly weapons on world markets and of the shadowy cast of characters standing ready to supply arms to terrorists. . . . The smuggling plot never came close to being executed. Court documents made public Wednesday showed that U.S. and Russian authorities constructed a complex ruse to lure a British arms dealer into the transaction, including a "cooperating" federal witness who posed as the buyer of the Russian-made SA-18. The disarmed weapon had been shipped into the United States—under the control of Russian and U.S. authorities—as "medical equipment," according to the affidavit. . . . In addition to Lakhani, who was charged with attempting to provide material support to terrorists and attempting to sell arms without a license, the government filed charges against two men who they said had conspired to help transfer money to pay for the Russian missile and as many as 50 more. They were identified as Yehuda Abraham, 76, a New York City gem dealer and money remitter, and Moinuddeen Ahmed Hameed, 38, a Malaysian who arrived in Newark on Tuesday, expecting to negotiate more missile sales, the government said. ("Details of Sting," 2003, p. MN1)

LOCAL COMMUNITY ISSUES
AND GLOBAL/NATIONAL/REGIONAL ISSUES

The targets and methods of terrorists have become more diverse and more difficult to predict. The terrorists attacks on September 11, 2001, clearly demonstrate that the global issues involving the Unites States in other parts of the world can result in terrorism within our own borders and affect victims in our local cities and towns. As highlighted by the Department of Justice,

> Terrorists in the United States continued a general trend in which fewer attacks are occurring in the United States, but individual attacks are becoming more deadly. Extremists in the United States continued a chilling trend by demonstrating interest in—and experimenting with—unconventional weapons. Over the past ten years, a pattern of interest in biological agents by criminals and extremists has developed. America and Americans have also been a favorite choice of target for terrorists. Reprisals for U.S. legal actions against domestic and international terrorists increase the likelihood that America will be the target of terrorist attacks either in the United States or overseas. (Terrorism Research and Analytical Center, 1995)

Often, clues surrounding the terrorist incident and/or attack will reveal whether domestic or international terrorism was involved and will point toward possible motives and the perpetrators behind the incident. Clues that might be helpful surrounding a terrorist event include the following:

Timing of the Event: For many years to come, September 11 will be a day for which all United States facilities around the world will operate at a heightened state of security and awareness because of the al Qaida simultaneous terrorist attacks. Within the United States, April 19 will continue for some time to be a day of heightened alert since it is the anniversary of both the bombing of the Alfred P. Murrah Federal Building in Oklahoma City and the fire at the Branch Dividian compound in Waco, Texas. The more that law enforcement works with a community policing model to understand the makeup of a multicultural community, the greater the likelihood that officers will have the knowledge to predict potential terrorist targets within communities.

Occupancy, location, and/or purpose related to the target include the following types of elements:

- ***Controversial businesses*** are those that have a history of inviting the protest and dislike of recognized groups, which include one or more components of extremist elements. For example, controversial businesses would include abortion clinics, logging mills, nuclear facilities, and tuna fishing companies.

- ***Public buildings and venues with large numbers of people*** are seen by terrorist as opportunities for attention-getting with mass casualties and victims. For some terrorists, causing massive destruction and casualties in targeted public buildings or in venues containing large numbers of people would be linked to the identity of the operator/owner of the building or venue. Examples of these targets would include the World Trade Center, entertainment venues, athletic events, tourist destinations, shopping malls, and convention centers.

- ***Symbolic and historical targets*** are links that the terrorists make regarding the relationship of the target and the organization, event, and/or services that specifically offend extremists. Examples of symbolic and historical targets would include the offices of the Internal Revenue Service (IRS) for tax resisters, the offices of the Bureau of Alcohol, Tobacco and Firearms (ATF) for those who oppose any form of gun control, and African American churches and Jewish synagogues for those who are members of white supremacist groups.

- ***Infrastructure systems and services*** include those structures and operations that are vital for the continued functioning of our country. Throughout the United States, these targets would include communication companies, power grids, water treatment facilities, mass transit, telecommunication towers, and transportation hubs. Terrorists' attacks on any of these targets have the potential for disabling and disrupting massive areas and regions, resulting in chaos, especially with respect to huge numbers of injuries and fatalities across large geographical areas. Law enforcement officers' and agencies' knowledge of possible targets linked to occupancy, location, and/or purpose of an organization within the local, multicultural communities will enhance the ability to prevent and to prepare for a terrorist incident. For any of the above-noted indicators of a terrorist incident or attack, law enforcement officers would nearly always be among the first responders to the scene (International Association of Chiefs of Police, 2001).

THE FIRST-RESPONSE CHALLENGE FOR LAW ENFORCEMENT

Law enforcement officers as "first responders" to a terrorism attack confront tremendous challenge, risk, and responsibility. The terrorist attack or crime scene is complicated by the confusion, panic, and casualty of the attack as well as any residual effects if WMD have been used. Moreover, it has been quite typical for terrorists to deliberately target responders and rescue personnel at the crime scene. Terrorists have utilized "secondary devices" to target law enforcement and other public safety personnel responding to a terrorist's attack. For example, in the 1997 bomb attack at an Atlanta abortion clinic, a second bomb went off approximately one hour after the initial explosion and was very close to the command post established for the first bomb attack.

As in all hazardous law enforcement situations, *officer safety and self-protection* are top priorities. However, in some terrorists' attacks as in the September 11, 2001, multiple-site scenario, no amount of self-protection at the scene would have prevented the deaths of the 69 police, fire, and port officers from New York and New Jersey who were killed in the attack. Neither could the U.S. Secret Service agent, FBI agent, and the U.S. Fish and Wildlife Service agent aboard Flight 93 that crashed in rural Pennsylvania have protected themselves from becoming victims.

Law enforcement personnel, as first responders to terrorists' crimes, need to know that the forms of self-protection against WMD can be defined in terms of the principals of time, distance, and shielding. Law enforcement personnel need to have sufficient cross-cultural language skills to communicate the importance of these principles for effective action and response within multicultural communities during a WMD incident:

1. *Time* is used as a tool in a terrorist crime scene. Spend the shortest amount of time possible in the affected area or exposed to the hazard. The less time one spends in the hazard area, the less likely one will become injured. Minimizing time spent in the hazard area will also reduce the chances of contaminating the crime scene.

2. *Distance* from the affected terrorist area or hazardous situation should be maximized. The greater the distance from the affected area while performing one's functions, the less the exposure to the hazard. Maintaining distance from the hazard areas will also ease the evacuation of the injured, allow for other emergency personnel requiring immediate access, and facilitate crowd control by law enforcement officers.

3. *Shielding* can be used to address specific types of hazards. Shielding can be achieved through buildings, walls, vehicles, body armor, and personnel protective equipment including chemical protective clothing, fire protective clothing, and self-contained breathing apparatuses.

Law enforcement officers need to be able to understand the various types of danger and harm that may result from a terrorist situation not only for their own self-protection, but in order to understand the reactions of affected victims and to be able to provide effective assistance to those affected by terrorist activities as well. Law enforcement personnel need to be aware that the many people who form multicultural communities may have had prior experiences (or have heard of prior experiences) with WMD incidents within their home countries (e.g., Vietnamese Americans' experience with thermal harm during the napalm bombing of their villages, or Iraqi Americans' experience with chemical harm from mustard gas attacks within their communities). Harm can be categorized utilizing the acronym TRACEM (U.S. Department of Justice, 1997), which provides an easy way to remember the following:

- Thermal Harm—injuries resulting from exposure to extreme heat such as that in a burning building or to extreme cold from materials like liquid oxygen or nitrogen

- Radiological Harm—injuries resulting from exposure to alpha particles, beta particles, or gamma rays

- Asphyxiation Harm—injuries resulting from a lack of oxygen in the atmosphere often caused by a heavier-than-air gas such as argon, carbon dioxide, or chemical vapors in a confined space.

- Chemical Harm—injuries resulting from toxic or corrosive materials. Corrosive materials include acids such as sulfuric acid or caustic agents such as lye. Toxins include chemical agents such as cyanides and nerve agents such as sarin.

- Etiological Harm—injuries from disease-causing organisms such as viruses, bacteria, rikettsia, and/or toxins derived from living organisms.

- Mechanical Harm—injuries from any sort of physical trauma such as bomb fragments or shrapnel, gunshot wounds, and falling building parts, as well as trip, fall, and slip hazards.

Different types of terrorist acts and attacks would result in a variety of harm and injury within the TRACEM categories. Law enforcement officers who are first responders need to ensure self-protection against TRACEM injury and harm and be aware of any on-scene warning signs of the variety of TRACEM harms at a terrorism or suspected terrorism crime scene. Law enforcement officers need to be cognizant that some members of multicultural communities may have more knowledge and familiarity with some WMD than they do as a result of experiences within their home countries. Knowledge by law enforcement officers of these prior experiences and an awareness of possible cultural reactions and behaviors to WMD would allow faster, more effective, and accurate evaluation and decision making regarding effective courses of action to take in response to a terrorist situation.

If the incident is a suspected act of terrorism, it is also a *crime scene.* Simultaneous actions in dealing with the criminal investigative elements and the public safety aspects present unique challenges to law enforcement and other first-responder personnel. For example, community members who have had experiences as victims of terrorism in the Middle East, South Asia, and the Philippines may not understand why the response efforts of police and other emergency services are not centered entirely upon helping the victims. They may not realize that law enforcement personnel are also involved in preserving the crime scene and interviewing witnesses. Although crowd control and public safety considerations are paramount, emergency responders must also act quickly and accurately assess the incident area and the severity of the danger. Once the magnitude of the danger and the public safety risk have been established, efforts to isolate the danger and to bring control to the incident can begin.

Responding to a terrorist event presents unique law enforcement and public safety challenges. Four key activities need to be simultaneously implemented and coordinated: (1) Initial Considerations and Assessment, (2) Perimeter Control, (3) Public Protection and Safety Considerations, and (4) Crime Scene Security Considerations.

Initial Considerations

Law enforcement and other emergency first responders must accurately and efficiently evaluate the incident area and determine the severity of the danger. Upon establishing the magnitude of the terrorist incident, efforts to control and to isolate the danger can begin.

Knowledge of the multicultural communities, customs, and practices of people affected in an incident would facilitate establishing control zones to enhance public safety, security, and care for the casualties and victims. For example, many multicultural communities have members who live in very large, extended families within several households of the same community. Law enforcement officers who do not recognize this may wonder why an order to evacuate and to leave the area resulted in limited and very delayed movement. It is important for them to understand that some members of the extended family might be separated or missing and that family members may be involved in efforts to locate them. Prior multicultural knowledge of and community policing relationships with the affected communities and people would enhance the control and rescue efforts. For example, information about the most effective ways to communicate and to rapidly disseminate warnings based upon the multicultural communities involved might be obtained through community leaders who could assist in interpreting and leading an evacuation (i.e., by keeping the community intact and by assisting in establishing perimeter control), as well as in the identification of sacred and religious structures for safeguarding.

Clearly, law enforcement first responders, given the severity of the situation, must use any and all available resources in an efficient, effective, and humane manner to prepare the scene for ongoing operations and public safety. However, knowledge and sensitivity to some of the prior experiences as victims of terrorism among multicultural people within the community may help to enhance action and safety.

Perimeter Control

Law enforcement officers need to use their standard operating procedures for establishing and maintaining perimeter control for "stand-off" distances and for "work zones." The magnitude and complexity of the terrorist incident will determine the need for having "outer" and "inner" perimeters. The *outer perimeter* would be the most distant control boundary for the incident, and is used to restrict all public access to the incident. Outer perimeters can be quite large and restrictive; for example, the outer perimeter established after the bombing of the Alfred P. Murrah Federal Building in Oklahoma City included 20 square city blocks. Following any establishment of perimeters, law enforcement officers may need to communicate to the multicultural community the reasons for their exclusion from the area. This is especially important if an *outer perimeter* resulted in community members being excluded or prohibited from their key meeting structures for religious, family, group, and other supports. For example, in their prior home country, people may have been able to return to their homes and community shortly after a terrorist incident (without consideration for the crime-scene investigative elements). If such exclusion is necessary for investigative work or for the protection of the community, effective communication with community members in this regard would be critical.

Public Safety and Protection Considerations

The extent that law enforcement and other first responders are able to act quickly and accurately in conducting a hazard and risk assessment of the affected population of a terrorist incident will determine the approach to public safety and protection. The following three options are available:

1. Evacuation of all threatened and affected population

2. Protection-in-place for all

3. Combination of evacuation and protect-in-place by evacuating some population and protecting other in-place

Effective communication of information and explanation of public safety and protection procedures to members of multicultural communities may be key challenges for many law enforcement agencies. During a terrorist incident, there would not be time to locate bilingual personnel or interpreters for assistance in communicating with speakers of other languages, and the customary resources like the AT&T language bank would be ineffective or unavailable. Explaining why multicultural community residents have to evacuate their homes and familiar surroundings, even in the event of a terrorist incident, will require personnel with language skills.

Evacuating the public from the affected area is based upon a decision that indicates the public is at greater risk by remaining in or near the B-NICE incident area. The decision to evacuate is determined in part by the following elements:

1. ***Degree or severity*** of public dangers, harm, and threats as estimated by the hazards and risk assessment.

2. ***Number*** of individuals or the magnitude of the population area affected by the danger or threat.

3. ***Resources*** available to evacuate the affected population to include law enforcement, fire, emergency and other personnel, school buses, privately owned vehicles, and/or public mass transit.

4. ***Notification*** and instructional resources to provide information to the public before and during the evacuation. For multicultural communities, these may include the use of local community leaders as well as ethnic-group media such as radio/television, mobile public address systems, and door-to-door contact. For communities with residents who are primarily speakers of other languages, the need for interpreters and translators would be very important in ensuring timely communication and notification.

5. ***Route security*** is a key factor that law enforcement officers and agencies need to ascertain and to maintain so that evacuees are not subjected to further terrorist attacks.

6. ***Opportunity*** to implement the evacuation requires assessing ongoing risks and hazards such as airborne chemical contamination, unexploded bombs, and other unexpected terrorist activities.

7. ***Special needs*** of the evacuees are taken care of to include accurate information regarding the terrorist event and updated summaries of the recovery effort.

Protection-in-place allows the affected populations to remain within the confines of their own dwelling. Like evacuations, the decision for protection-in-place depends on the risk and hazard assessment of the terrorist incident. Basically, if the anticipated dangers and the presenting hazards to the public are made less by having the affected population remain in-place, the protection-in-place option is the better solution. Consideration needs to be made for multicultural communities in which there are large, multifamily residents within one household involving family members who are frail, elderly, and/or very young children. For some within multicultural communities, the preference for the entire extended family to be together may be paramount. In their home countries, if family members became separated or moved, this often meant having members "disappear" and never be seen again. Protection-in-place, if safe and possible, may be much more easily implemented than attempts to evacuate such families, especially in multicultural communities where there may be some language issues involved in receiving and providing specific instructions for an evacuation.

LAW ENFORCEMENT RESPONSE STRATEGIES

Crime Scene Security Considerations

The *Incident Commander* has responsibility for the overall entry and exit routes from the incident area. The police are usually the first responders to most catastrophes, including a terrorist attack. However, depending on the nature, severity, and circumstances of the terrorist attack, the on-scene *Incident Commander* who will oversee the incident command system may or may not be from the police force. The overall structure and line-of-authority for all responders to a terrorist attack should operate under an incident command system (as referenced in 29 CFR 1910.120), which is described in the forthcoming section (and detailed in a Federal Emergency Management Agency (1992) document entitled, *The Federal Response Plan for Public Law 93-288, as amended).* Clear communication within the command structure is central to the effective work of the on-scene incident management system, which may consist of personnel from many local public safety departments, as well as state, regional, and Federal agencies and personnel. Effective language skills supported by prior multicultural communications training would be a positive benefit in these multijurisdictional, diverse leadership style crisis command systems. For example, law enforcement officers and managers who are experienced in knowing that different multicultural groups have different norms, values, communication styles, languages, and practices could transfer those experiences to understanding and working with the differences found within multijurisdictional and multiagency personnel involved in a terrorist incident. The key role of the Incident Commander is to ensure coordination and collaboration of the responders to the terrorist incident.

Conventional law enforcement procedures and methods should be used for: (1) controlling the access points, (2) organizing evacuation or stay-in-place efforts, (3) isolating unstable conditions, (4) preserving crime scene evidence, (5) establishing contamination reduction corridors and areas, and (6) maintaining security and site control. Generally, the agency assigned or designated with site security responsibilities may vary depending on the hazards encountered and the nature of the first responders on-scene (usually police or fire in the early stages of a terrorist incident). Clearly, any time there is ongoing criminal activity potential or presence, law enforcement officials need to determine and direct the security measures for crime scene control. In time, control of the perimeter will be the responsibility of law enforcement, unless the terrorist incident is of the magnitude that response activities may continue for several weeks. In such prolonged periods for perimeter security and control, the use of military units may be advised based upon the decisions of the Incident Commander and the Incident Command System that is established for the incident.

Incident Command System for Coordination of Multiple Response Agencies

The responsibilities for responding to a terrorist incident or attack involving nuclear, biological, and chemical WMD materials are outlined in Presidential Decision Directive-39 (PDD-39)—details provided in FEMA (1997). PDD-39 identifies the Federal Bureau of Investigation (FBI) as the lead agency for crisis management during terrorist attacks and incidents involving nuclear, biological, and chemical materials. PDD-39 also identifies the Federal Emergency Management Agency (FEMA) as the lead agency for the consequence and recovery management during terrorist attacks and incidents involving nuclear, biological, and chemical materials. The Federal Response Plan (FRP) is used as the outline and vehicle for coordinating consequence management efforts under PDD-39. FRP directs *other* federal agencies to support the FBI and FEMA, as needed.

The FRP makes the following planning assumptions (from FEMA, 1997):

1. No single agency at the local, state, federal, or private levels possesses the authority and the expertise to act unilaterally on many difficult issues that may arise in response to threats or acts of terrorism, especially if nuclear, biological, and chemical WMD are involved.

2. An act of terrorism, particularly an act directed against a large population center within the United States involving nuclear, biological, and chemical WMD, may produce major consequences that would overwhelm the capabilities of many local and state governments almost immediately. Major consequences involving nuclear, biological, and chemical WMD may overwhelm existing federal capabilities, as well.

3. Local, state, and federal responders may define individual working perimeters, which may overlap to some degree. Perimeters may be used to control access to the area, target public information messages, assign operational sectors among responding organizations, and assess potential effects on the population and the environment. Control of these perimeters may be enforced by different authorities, which may impede the overall response if adequate coordination is

not established. It is one of the responsibilities of the local *Incident Commander* within the Incident Management System in place to ensure adequate control of the different perimeters in a terrorist incident.

4. If protective capabilities are not available, responders cannot be required to put their own lives at risk in order to enter a perimeter contaminated with nuclear, biological, and chemical WMD materials. It is possible that the perimeter will be closed until the effects of the nuclear, biological, and chemical WMD materials have degraded to levels that are safe for first responders.

5. The instructions, as provided in the FEMA (1997) document entitled "Terrorism Incident Annex," may be implemented in situations involving major consequences in a single state or in multiple states. The FBI will establish coordination relationships among FBI field offices and with federal agencies supporting crisis management, including FEMA, based upon the locations involved.

6. The "Terrorism Incident Annex" may be implemented in situations that involve consequences in neighboring nations (FEMA, 1997).

Crisis Management

PDD-39 and the FRP designate the FBI with the federal lead responsibility for crisis management in response to threats or acts of terrorism that take place within the United States territory or in international waters and that do not involve the flag vessel of a foreign country. During crisis management, the FBI coordinates closely with local law enforcement authorities to provide a successful law enforcement resolution to the terrorist incident. The FBI also coordinates with other federal agencies and authorities, including FEMA. The FBI field office responsible for the incident site modifies the Field Office Command Post to function as the Joint Operations Center (JOC). The JOC, in turn, has responsibility for coordinating the crisis management effort with the local Incident Commander and the local Incident Command System established for the terrorist incident.

Multijurisdictional Action

As noted above in the command structure for crisis management, a variety of diverse federal, state, and local agencies and organizations will be involved in multijurisdictional actions that are involved in a terrorist incident or attack. Some of the key elements ensuring success for law enforcement agencies and officers in such incidents include the following:

1. *Preparation and Planning* provide some of the best avenues for successful crisis management and subsequent recovery from a terrorist incident. The following planned steps have been determined to be critical:

   - Develop pertinent plans and policies for terrorist incidents and attacks
   - Establish multijurisdictional plans/protocols and mutual-aid agreements
   - Ensure availability of multicultural law enforcement personnel with language expertise

- Implement, as much as possible, preventive procedures and plans
- Train law enforcement personnel as first responders and as members of multijurisdictional teams involved in a terrorist incident
- Provide background information about the makeup of the different multicultural communities and their prior experiences as victims of terrorism
- Rehearse possible events and incidents
- Acquire the necessary protective and communication equipment
- Establish multidiscipline community service teams (and, again, where possible, provide for the range of language expertise required by the community)
- Establish a network of multicultural leaders and communities for communication, intelligence, and response implementation

2. ***Cost and Deployment*** of resources have been highlighted by most local governments with respect to the degree of burden and expenditure needed by local law enforcement and by other public safety agencies involved in possible terrorism incidents.

> The U.S. Conference of Mayors has complained about federal terrorism alerts, saying they add an estimated $70 million per week to the nation's municipal security costs. . . . The Omaha Police Department so far has been able to use current on-duty personnel to meet additional surveillance needs during the heightened alerts without incurring overtime, says Capt. Tony Infantino, who oversees the department's special operations, including security planning for the College World Series. The situation is the same for the Omaha Fire Department, says Craig Schneider, the department's public information officer. Local officials say they're glad that, after a period of delay and uncertainty, the federal government has come through with a reasonable flow of funds to help Omaha-area departments cover the costs of first-responder equipment and training. For the next 12 to 24 months, "there will be a nice flow of funds to take care of these things," says Steve Lee, director of emergency management for the Douglas County Emergency Management Agency. ("Burdens of security," 2003, p. B6)

Since local tax-based resources are insufficient to address the enormity of costs involved in the planning, prevention, and deployment of resources to address terrorism concerns and issues, one of the key concerns within multicultural communities is the diversion of funds from community-policing activities to the war on terrorism.

3. ***Access to Intelligence and Informational Databases*** provide the information necessary for the prevention of and response to terrorist threats. The best prevention against terrorist incidents and acts at the local community level is to ensure coordination with federal and state intelligence sources and access to ongoing intelligence-gathering capacity from the federal level. On the local level, it is important that law enforcement officers and agencies develop critical relationships and networks with the local multicultural communities. Developing such relationships requires both ongoing efforts and constant renewal of the relationships through clear communication and building of trust be-

tween law enforcement and community members. Some of the strategies and practices for enhancing multicultural communications, as provided in an earlier chapter, would help to alleviate the communication problems noted in the following example:

> American Muslims still feel the pressure, even though the flow of tips to police has slowed, said Dr. Salman Malik, a Manchester dentist who sits on the board of the Islamic Society of Greater Manchester. Because police feel obliged to check out each terror tip, Muslims hear the knock on the door a lot more than they did before 9/11, he said. "It's very unnerving when a 'Joe Shmoe' Muslim is sitting at home and the police knock on his door and start asking questions," he said. "They don't answer your questions. They just want their questions answered. We understand they have to do their job, and we don't resent them for it. But it's scary. A horrible thing has happened. And we feel helpless because we don't know how to unassociate ourselves from it. "I feel sorry for all the Muhammed's in the U.S. right now. They get labeled left and right." (Fahey, 2003, p. A1)

As noted in the International Association of Chiefs of Police (IACP) (2001), "A very practical tool to ensure that this is done is to keep a running log, 24 hours a day, of all unusual events. This way, even if the immediate staff handling the incident does not perceive its intelligence value, senior staffs' later review of the log may pick up the opportunity and justify further investigation."

4. ***Multi-jurisdictional Training and Rehearsal*** have been identified as critical elements in the successful implementation of terrorist incident management and recovery. Clearly, in multijurisdictional efforts, there would have been very few prior opportunities to develop the relationships, awareness, communication, and other processes necessary for a coordinated effort. As illustrated in the following example, the involvement of these multijurisdictional agencies and their personnel provides for valuable lessons learned for any possible terrorist incidence.

> A massive cloud of lethal gas, dozens of agonizing deaths by asphyxiation, an unknown number of hidden nuclear devices, executions, a ship full of hostages, and an enemy mine bobbing in the harbor: If any of it had been real, it would have been an absolutely horrible couple of days at the Port of Hueneme. Fortunately, the series of catastrophes was part of an anti-terrorism exercise, an elaborate two-day drama staged Tuesday and Wednesday with the help of the Navy, the Coast Guard, some 140 FBI agents, 81 officers from the Ventura County Sheriff's Department—in all, representatives from 18 military and law-enforcement agencies. . . . Along the way, the participating agencies picked up lessons they will use to streamline some of their procedures. "There won't be wholesale changes," said Banks, of the warfare center. "But even an hour saved could be a crucial hour." The Ventura County sheriff's SWAT team learned that storming a ship is a lengthier process than taking over a home, said department spokesman Eric Nishimoto. With the FBI taking the lead in the antiterrorist operations, officers also realized that dealing with a hierarchy of agents from all over the U.S.

was not equivalent to dealing with operatives from the local office. "It's a totally different dynamic," Nishimoto said. Simply communicating with other agencies was sometimes difficult. "Everyone's enmeshed in their own acronyms," said Tom Netzer, who coordinated the exercise for the Center for Asymmetric Warfare. "It helped when we got everyone to just speak English." (Chawkins, 2003, p. M1)

Training for terrorist incidents that are multijurisdictional in nature would allow for the rehearsal and practices necessary for effective overall terrorism response efforts. As in any simulated practice exercise, not all components of a terrorist incident can be anticipated or incorporated. Nonetheless, such training and rehearsal would allow for a timelier implementation of the response strategies important to a terrorist incident, as noted in the next section. Training in response to terrorism, to date, has included limited scenarios related to multicultural community elements. In time, emphases upon language expertise, bilingual communications, and interpreter participation need to be added to training exercises.

Community Assessment

Preventing, limiting, and reducing a community's vulnerability to attack requires a careful and ongoing community assessment to locate and to measure the risks involved in the particular community. Such assessments would involve reviewing and analyzing all the localities that are likely targets for terrorism and working to improve the security of these locations. Some law enforcement agencies have developed a rating system and have cataloged their possible problem areas into different priority levels. The following four Priority Level assessment categories could be used in a community assessment or to a particular law enforcement department or agency (U.S. Department of Justice, 1997):

1. *First Priority Level—Fatal:* These are processes and functions that if they fail would result in death, severe financial loss, massive legal liabilities, or catastrophic consequences. Such processes and functions would include all essential mission-critical elements such as electrical power, communications, information systems, and command and leadership functions.

2. *Second Priority Level—Critical:* These would be processes and functional units of the agency, department, or organization that are critical to its operations and would be difficult to do without for any long period of time. Some examples of "critical" functional units might include computer terminals, elevators, perimeter security lights, and heat/air conditioning in the building. Examples of critical processes might include building entry and exit security and two-way communication radio network.

3. *Third Priority Level—Important:* These would include those processes and functional units that are not critical to the department, agency, or organization such as facsimile, copier, videotape player, video camera, and tape recorders. Some examples of important processes would include files and record access, administrative training, and new-hire orientation.

4. ***Fourth Priority Level—Routine:*** These would include processes and functional units that are not strategically mission-important (although they may cause some inconvenience) to the agency, department, or organization like coffeemakers, microwave ovens, and room thermostats. Nonessential and routine processes might include providing parking lot stickers and duty list for staff personnel to providing information at the reception area.

Community assessments of functional units and processes should be ongoing and scheduled routinely so that information of possible terrorist targets could be updated on a regular basis.

Building Community Networks and Resources

In order to detect and to deter terrorist incidents and attacks, the development of strong community networks, relationships, and resources is critical. As we have noted earlier, the ability to obtain critical information from a community assessment depends on ongoing, positive, and trusted relationships within the multicultural communities. It is equally important to develop the internal networks and relationships within the different agencies and departments of the local and statewide public safety community, as illustrated by this example involving several agencies from New Jersey:

> About 2,000 police officers statewide have already been trained by a consortium of federal and state experts to assist the anti-terror effort. One of those most involved with the effort to share intelligence with the myriad of local, county, state, and federal agencies is Sidney J. Caspersen, the director of the state Office of Counter-Terrorism. Armed with an $8.6 million budget, the former FBI agent is directing the installation of a terrorism database that will be linked to computer terminals in every police station in the state. Caspersen also sends out intelligence bulletins to several hundred private industrial concerns ranging from the state's largest corporations to more modest businesses. His office also sends similar bulletins to local officials, alerting them to potential terrorist threats, suspicious incidents, and vulnerabilities in the state's infrastructure. "I believe we are the intelligence-gathering organization for the state," Caspersen said, adding that he has been hiring analysts who understand the culture that fosters terrorism and investigators who can develop a network of informants. "My goal is to detect and deter," he said. "I'm not really looking at taking people to court." (Maddux, 2003, p. A1)

Part Two, "Cultural Specifics for Law Enforcement," includes discussion of group-specific strategies that may be used to enhance communications, develop relationships, and widen the community network within the different multicultural communities to develop strategies for effective detection and deterrence within those communities.

Using Ethnic and Multicultural Media as a Resource

For any terrorist incident, law enforcement agencies must help to provide a constant flow of credible information to the local community. Clearly, if positive relationships have been formed with the diversity of residents and the multicultural community leaders, the law enforcement agency's credibility would not be suspect and/or in question. Media sources used for the release of information should include the ones used by most populations, as well as those used by specific multicultural groups, especially that broadcast or print in the language of the key multicultural groups of the community. Some public safety agencies may be concerned about not having their information already prepared and translated into the language of the diverse ethnic and cultural groups; however, given the nature and importance of the information, most ethnic media will do the translation in order to provide critical information to their "audience."

Policies, procedures, and mechanisms need to be in place for releasing information to enable the safety and security of all community residents. This means that the involvement of ethnic and multicultural media is critical; the readiness of translations and interpretations are key in ensuring appropriate responses, alleviating any unnecessary fears or concerns, and providing assurances that public safety agencies and officers are in control of the situation. The media has been shown to be the most efficient and reliable means to disseminate information rapidly to the community regarding a terrorist incident and to notify community residents of the subsequent response by the public safety agencies. Strategic media events should be held to continuously inform the public that the incident is well under control, the personnel are well prepared and trained to handle the incident, and the community's recovery is fully expected.

Whether one is dealing with a terrorist incident or an everyday event, the basis for effective communications with the community through the media is a strong partnership and established positive relationships with the media. Law enforcement agencies need to understand that whether in crisis management or in daily peacekeeping, the media has a dual role: to obtain information, stories, and perspectives on the incident for news reporting objectives, and to inform the community efficiently of impending dangers and threats stemming from the incident. Good media relations allow for the strategic communication of critical incident information to the communities served by the law enforcement agencies. To reach multicultural communities, police officers must go beyond the conventional and mainstream media sources, and must become familiar with all media, in English and in other languages, that will reach the broadest populations in the shortest amount of time.

Critical Incident Stress Debriefing (CISD)

In any terrorist incident or attack, it is easy to recognize that victims experience trauma, suffering, stress, and harm. It is less known that public safety and other emergency workers also suffer from traumatic incidents as well. The Report of the International Association of Chiefs of Police (2002) entitled *Project Response: The Oklahoma City Tragedy* suggests the following approaches:

1. *Pre-Critical Incident Inoculation Training:* These are training sessions held well in advance of any terrorism or other critical incidents to prepare law enforcement personnel for what might be encountered in a terrorism incident. Usually presentation and discussion regarding inoculation training is led by veteran officers who can share their experiences and reactions in terrorism-critical incidents.

2. ***On-Site Critical Incident Debriefing:*** On-scene commanders need to be aware of and provide the resources for public safety personnel's critical incident debriefing. Seymour (2000) suggests following cultural considerations when conducting on-site critical incident debriefings with multicultural personnel:

- Orient, educate, and explain the critical incident debriefing procedures and approach used to the recipient. Listen to their suggestions and reactions, and incorporate the points of view that will allow accomplishing the debriefing objectives, even if this is contrary to the provider's training and the standard protocol recommended for the debriefing.

- Know one's limitations, and obtain consultation, especially when there are multicultural differences involved in the debriefing process. Frequently, it is important to engage the client's family and community system to provide the needed support for the person being debriefed.

- Be aware of and sensitive to one's own perspectives, biases, and prejudices. One cannot be too vigilant about one's own assumptions and perceptions in the aftermath of a terrorist incident. These can lead to responses and suggestions to the debriefing recipient that border on dangerous stereotypes, assignment of fault, and/or mistaken recommendations for unnecessary removal or inappropriate quarantine from a terrorist event site, especially for recipients from culturally different backgrounds and perspectives.

- Respect flexible roles in communications since the objectives of the critical incident debriefing is "to remove the excess emotion from the memory of the event so as to integrate the traumatic event into the life stories of the victims/survivors by organizing and interpreting the cognitive process and to create meaningfulness from the experience" (Seymour, 2000). It is critically important that the communication process used does not result in the recipient having a sense that while being helped, he/she felt violated because of the cultural mode of communication used by the provider.

- Respect the belief systems, worldviews, and cultural expressions of others. For example, if the recipient of the debriefing wants to include other cultural healers in the helping process (e.g., a shaman, priest, monk), it may be more important to respond to the request than to hold firm to the notion that the debriefing should only be done with the event participants.

- Speak the language of the recipient. A person assigned to debrief a person whose language the provider does not speak must ask for help from someone who does speak that language.

- Ensure that the recipient of the critical incident debriefing has advocates to help that person navigate the system after the debriefing. Following a terrorist incident, most victims would find their normal negotiating skills, tools, and resources compromised; this is even more pronounced for people who come from culturally different backgrounds and experiences. Providing advocacy and follow-up actions to ensure that the recipient can navigate the system is a critical part of providing culturally competent critical incident debriefings.

KEY ISSUES IN LAW ENFORCEMENT

1. ***False Tips from Informants:*** As with any information-gathering and intelligence operations, there will always be the need to determine the validity, reliability, and trustworthiness of information received. Law enforcement agencies have always depended on informants for sources of critical information as part of any investigative process. In a terrorism incident, some of these informants would be very connected with the criminal and oftentimes most notorious elements within the community. In a terrorist incident, some of these informants may be keenly aware of what is "on the street," but may have ulterior or personal motives for providing information. Both standard interviewing and incident interview skills and tools need to be used to sort out false information and to confirm the credible sources important to the facts of a terrorist incident.

2. ***Training to Heighten Awareness:*** Until recently, issues of terrorism and weapons of mass destruction were primarily the domain of the federal law enforcement agencies, with minor involvement of local law enforcement personnel. The awareness of terrorism cues, situations, and warnings of possible acts are not part of the everyday experience of local law enforcement personnel and their agencies. Terrorist-related awareness training has been used as an approach to heighten the awareness and skill levels of local law enforcement officers:

    > Charles Anderson, a five-year detective with the Baltimore Police Department, said he's seen a lot more training—nearly all of it terrorist-related. Anderson teaches a class on informant training, he said. "It kind of makes you more aware of what's going on," said the 34-year-old, dressed in a navy-blue shirt with his department's name on it. "You are not as laid-back. More cautious, I should say." The feeling is shared by officers in less urban areas, who also see their communities as vulnerable. An example is St. Charles Parish, in southeast Louisiana. Detective Othello Carter, with the parish's Sheriff's Office, said he views as targets the nuclear power plant, chemical plants and oil refineries in his jurisdiction, about 25 miles west of New Orleans. "You used to give it a little glance," the 40-year-old Carter said, about checks of the facilities. "Now, you're vigilant about looking around more." He continued: "You can always say something like that wouldn't happen here. But you just look at places now, and imagine how easily you could get into them." (Lewis, 2003).

3. ***Extension of Community Policing Approaches:*** Community-based policing has been proven to be a valuable approach to working with multicultural community groups and to learning about their needs, concerns, and problems (Oliver, 2001). Chapter 1 discusses some of the key concepts, principals, and practices for community-oriented policing within multicultural communities. In this chapter, we highlight the importance of using these same community-policing concepts, tools, and practices for information-gathering as well as for information-disseminating following a terrorism incident. As noted in the next example, the process of community policing could provide the "eyes and ears" for our country in the war on terrorism:

Two national experts on terrorism were scheduled to speak at a closed-door conference for several dozen police chiefs from Rhode Island, Massachusetts and other Northeast states that began here yesterday afternoon. . . . Mayor David N. Cicilline opened the conference by pointing out that the world is very different than it was before 9/11. "Mayors and city governments are on the front lines of defense in the war on terrorism," Cicilline said. "We spend $70 million a week in response to terrorism." State police Col. Steven M. Pare told the chiefs: "We need to think differently today. We need to get our recruits on the street. They are the ears and the eyes of our country. If we're going to make a difference, we need everyone collectively improving communications." ("Region's police chiefs," 2003, p. B3)

SUMMARY

Law enforcement agencies today have an emerging and vital role in the war on terrorism that involves the critical step of building key relationships and networks with multicultural communities, including ethnic and multicultural media sources. Multicultural knowledge and skills of local law enforcement can contribute to uncovering key information, resources, and tools in dealing with the prevention of and criminal investigation of terrorism, including intelligence-gathering needs. The chapter covered problems in dealing with terrorism involving multicultural communities and the actions of law enforcement officers' possible bias, prejudice, and stereotyping of certain multicultural groups. The chapter closed with specific recommendations important to the emerging roles of law enforcement officers and other emergency services personnel in dealing with terrorism within multicultural communities.

DISCUSSION QUESTIONS AND ISSUES

1. ***Terrorist Targets in Your Local Community:*** The chapter provided a four priority-level approach to implementing a community assessment of possible terrorist targets. Review the possible terrorist targets in your community using the four priority-level categorization. List the special challenges involved in protecting the top two priority levels of possible terrorist targets in your community. List some of the unique challenges in working with multicultural communities in this regard (either within your community or in a nearby community with multicultural neighborhoods).

2. Select an area in your city or town that would have the greatest diversity of population (e.g., race, ethnicity, age, income, and other dimensions of diversity) for this next discussion question. How would you implement and coordinate the four key activities (i.e., Initial Considerations and Assessment, Perimeter Control, Public Protection and Safety Considerations, and Crime Scene Security Considerations) in responding to a possible chemical terrorist incident in the area that you have selected?

3. The authors identified media resources as an effective way to communicate and to disseminate information to community residents. What media resources might you use for communicating a terrorist incident involving B-NICE

materials in your city or town? Provide some examples of multicultural media resources that might be used in your area. What approaches might you use to develop positive and effective relationships between these media resources and your local law enforcement agency?

4. Critical Incident Stress Debriefing (CISD) has been recognized as an effective tool for use with law enforcement personnel after a traumatic incident. Using the suggested list of cultural considerations provided in the chapter, how might you organize and provide CISD to nonsworn, multicultural law enforcement personnel involved in a terrorist attack like the bombing of the Alfred P. Murrah Federal Building in Oklahoma City?

5. Select an area in your city or town that would have the greatest diversity of languages spoken. How would you plan for and ensure adequate bilingual personnel or other language resources to assist these community residents in the case of a terrorist incident?

WEBSITE RESOURCES

Visit these websites for additional information about multicultural law enforcement issues in dealing with terrorism.

Federal Bureau of Investigation, Explosive Unit, Bomb Data Center: http://www.fbi.gov/lab/bomsum/eubdc.htm

This website provides the latest annual report of bombing incidents in the United States.

Federal Emergency Management Agency   http://www.fema.gov/

This website provides a range of useful information related to the management of community, state, and national emergencies.

U.S. Army Chemical and Biological Defense Command (CBDCOM)   http://www.cbdcom.apgea.army.mil/cbdcom/

The website provides background and technical information on biological and chemical weapons that might be encountered in a terrorist attack.

U.S. Army Medical Research Institute of Chemical Defense   http://chemdef.apgea.army.mil/

This website provides both general as well as research-oriented information and findings on chemical weapons of mass destruction.

REFERENCES

Ahmad, E., and Barsamian, D. (2001). *Terrorism: Theirs and Ours.* New York: Seven Stories Press.

Bankson, R. (2003). *Terrorism: National in Scope, Local in Execution. Community Links.* Washington, DC: Community Policing Consortium.

"Burdens of security Omaha-area agencies are cooperating well in guarding against attacks by terrorists." *Omaha World Herald,* p. B6. (2003, June 16).

Department of Justice Office of Justice Programs. (1997). *Emergency Response to Terrorism: Basic Concepts.* Washington, DC: U.S. Department of Justice.

"Details of sting tell of wider threat." (2003, August 14). *Los Angeles Times,* p. MN1.

Chawkins, S. (2003, November 6). "Agencies Get a Taste of Terrorism in Action; Simulated attacks at the Port of Hueneme help build teamwork among emergency groups." *Los Angeles Times,* p. M1.

Echegaray, C. (2003, November 26). "More work awaits police if criminal alien bill passes." *Worcester Telegram and Gazette* (MA), p. A2.

Fahey, T. (2003, September 16). " Maine terror tip leads FBI to fishermen." *Union Leader* (Manchester NH), p. A1.

Federal Bureau of Investigation. (1996). *Terrorism in the United States 1995.* Washington, DC: Terrorist Research and Analytical Center, National Security Division, Federal Bureau of Investigation (FBI).

FBI Bomb Data Center. (1999). *1999 Bombing Incidents.* General Information Bulletin 99-1. Washington, DC: Federal Bureau of Investigation.

Federal Emergency Management Agency (FEMA). (1992). *The Federal Response Plan for Public Law 93-288, as amended.* Washington, DC: Author.

Federal Emergency Management Agency (FEMA). (1997). *The Federal Response Plan Notice of Change: Terrorism Incident Annex.* Washington, DC: Author.

Gunaratna, R. (2002). *Inside Al Qaeda: Global Network of Terror.* New York: Berkeley.

Hoffman, B. (1998). *Inside Terrorism.* New York: Columbia University Press.

Howard, D. R., and Sawyer, R. L. (Eds.). (2004), *Terrorism and Counterterrorism: Understanding the New Security Environment,* Guilford, CT: McGraw-Hill/Dushkin.

International Association of Chiefs of Police. (2001). *Leading from the Front: Project Response: Terrorism.* Alexandria, VA: Author.

International Association of Chiefs of Police. (2002). *Project Response: The Oklahoma City Tragedy.* Alexandria, VA: Author.

Lewis, R. C. (2003, August 4). " FBI director speaks of 'new era' of cooperation since attacks." *Associated Press.*

Litchblau, E. (2003, June 18). "Threats and Responses: Law Enforcement; Bush Issues Racial Profiling Ban But Exempts Security Inquiries." *New York Times,* p. A1.

Maddux, M. (2003, September 8). "Guarding against future acts of terror." *Bergen Record* (NJ), p. A1.

Mendell, R. L. (1994). Terrorist Attacks: A Cause for Concern. *Security Management: American Society for Industrial Security, 38* (12).

Moss, M. (2003, June 19). "Threats and Responses: Law Enforcement; False Terrorism Tips to F.B.I. Uproot the Lives of Suspects." *New York Times,* p. A1.

Nance, M. W. (2003). *The Terrorist Recognition Handbook.* Guilford, CT: Lyons Press.

National Security Division. (1994). *Terrorism in the United States.* Washington DC: U.S. Department of Justice.

Oliver, W. M. (2001). *Community-Oriented Policing.* Upper Saddle River, NJ: Prentice-Hall.

"Region's police chiefs hear terrorism experts." (2003, November 13). *Providence Journal-Bulletin* (RI), p. B3.

Roth, S. (2003, September 11). "Anti-Terror Laws Increasingly Used Against Ordinary Criminals." *Legal Intelligencer, 229* (51), p. 4.

Schmitt, R. B., Goldman, J. J., and Silverstein, K. (2003, August 14). "Details of Sting Tell of Wider Threat." *Los Angeles Times,* p. MN1.

Seymour, G. O. (2000). "Cultural considerations in critical incident debriefing in the aftermath of a terrorist incident involving weapons of mass destruction." *NMTP Newsletter, 4.*

Stern, J. (2003, December 21. When-bombers," *Oakland Tribune,* Opinion-Editorial Section.

Terrorist Research and Analytical Center. (1995). *Terrorism in the United States.* Washington, DC: U.S. Department of Justice.

U.S. Departments of the Army and the Air Force. (1990). *Military Operations in Low Intensity Conflict.* Washington, DC: Author.

U.S. Department of State. (1995). *Patterns of Global Terrorism.* Washington, DC: U.S. Department of State, Publication No. 10239.

U.S. Department of State. (1997). *Patterns of Global Terrorism. 1996.* Washington, DC: Office of the Coordinator for Counterterrorism, U.S. Department of State, Publication No. 10433.

Chapter 11

Multicultural Law Enforcement and Homeland Security

OVERVIEW

The President of the United States created the Department of Homeland Security (DHS) as a cabinet-level Department on November 25, 2002, with the main objective of protecting the United States from terrorism. With the development of the DHS, law enforcement officers and agencies face many new roles and responsibilities. These include detecting threats of terrorism, coordinating the security efforts against terrorism, developing and analyzing information regarding threats and vulnerabilities, and using information and intelligence provided in coordination with the DHS. The major goals of the Department of Homeland Security focus on:

1. Preventing attacks of terrorism

2. Reducing vulnerabilities for terrorist attacks

3. Analyzing threats of terrorism and issuing warnings accordingly

4. Providing security for our transportation systems and for the borders of the United States

5. Preparing for emergency readiness and response

6. Minimizing the damage from terrorism and facilitating recovery from terrorist attacks

This chapter highlights the roles and functions of law enforcement officers and agencies in their work in addressing the six goals of homeland security in multicultural communities. Clearly, criminal justice practices and procedures already define much of the homeland security work and activities within law enforcement agencies. The emphasis in this chapter is on the specific aspects of multicultural law enforcement that are applicable to homeland security issues in the context of our diverse communities.

COMMENTARY

Americans' sense of security with respect to terrorism was "shattered" following the September 11, 2001, attacks on American soil. In one concerted and orchestrated set of terrorist attacks, it was clear to all Americans that the security of our homeland was vulnerable.

> . . . with the grace of Allah, the battle has moved inside America. We will strive to keep it going—with Allah's permission—until victory is attained or until we meet Allah through martyrdom. (Osama bin Laden interview, October 21, 2001, quoted in Robbins, 2002)

The United States rallied quickly to institute measures for overcoming the fear and shock of the terrorists attacks. As noted by Donohue (2002), more than 97 percent of the business conducted by Congress between September 11, 2001, and January 11, 2002, was related to terrorism and more than 450 bills, amendments, and resolutions relating to counterterrorism were proposed. Clearly our reaction to the fear and vulnerability generated by terrorism was to move forward.

The nation advanced and created the Department of Homeland Security (DHS), which incorporated the roles and functions of 22 federal agencies with 170,000 employees (the largest reorganization of the federal government since the creation of the Department of Defense in 1947). The DHS, in turn, extended, created, and developed new roles and functions for law enforcement in the war against terrorism and in providing homeland security, which never before were within the central realm of work for the public safety and legal systems.

> Terrorism poses a fundamental challenge to the legal system. Terrorists often do nothing indictable until they commit the act. Ninety percent of the time sleepers are absolutely legal, so you can't do anything about them even if you know who they are. Terrorism challenges our categories of what is legal and what is illegal. (Ford, 2002, p. 1)

These emerging roles and functions for law enforcement presented new challenges for the day-to-day work within the criminal justice system and for the Federal Response Plan (FRP) against terrorism and for homeland security. Additionally, they stretched the resources and knowledge base necessary to implement these areas of work, especially within multicultural communities. The prior chapter presented the unique issues of multicultural law enforcement in responding to acts of terrorism and the follow-up actions necessary to such attacks and incidents. This chapter focuses on the challenges and opportunities presented to multicultural law enforcement agencies and officers in detecting and preventing terrorism and the actions necessary to address the goals of homeland security within our diverse communities.

HISTORICAL INFORMATION AND BACKGROUND

Homeland security, through the gathering, processing, and application of intelligence, provides our nation with a blanket of protection against attacks. As a result of the geographic isolation of the United States, most Americans in the past have felt secure about their "homeland" and did not perceive that attacks could be launched on U.S. shores. Both Mexico and Canada were seen as friendly neighbors, and not as sources of threat or danger to Americans' sense of homeland security.

Prior to September 11, 2001, many Americans (the person on the street to governmental leaders) perceived that enemies would need to surmount the tremendous burden of first having to cross vast expanses of oceans just to get their troops in our country for an attack. Pearl Harbor was seen as an "exception," and no troops had actually landed on American soil. Moreover, extensive logistics were thought to be necessary to sustain any kind of attack effort for replenishing supplies and troops even if enemy troops could land on our shores. As a result of the perceived advantage of the intervening oceans to the United States, much of the efforts and activities for homeland security, in the past, were located within the functions of the federal government (e.g., FBI, CIA, military, Department of State) to be implemented outside of the United States.

Local and state criminal justice agencies like the police, sheriff, probation, and prison departments had limited roles in homeland security. The lesser involvement of local law enforcement in homeland security was unlike most countries around the world in which local and regional law enforcement agencies work closely with national departments on issues of homeland security. The roles of local and regional law enforcement agencies in the United States with respect to homeland security have increased greatly in recent times, and will most likely begin to resemble many of their global counterparts in cities and states around the world.

Throughout the "Cold War" era with Russia and the communist bloc countries, and also in the Vietnam War era, there were many indications that homeland security encompassed much more than merely keeping enemy troops from marching on U.S. soil. Some examples for the need for greater homeland security efforts in the United States during this period were: (1) spies infiltrating into agencies of the United States government, (2) Soviet missiles based in Cuba that would lead to the Missile Crisis and the Bay of Pigs invasion of Cuba, (3) assassinations of President John F. Kennedy and Rev. Martin Luther King, Jr., and (4) violent riots and demonstrations against the Vietnam War. However, the notion of the security of our country continued to be viewed as less the work of local law enforcement, and more the work of the national agencies (e.g., CIA, National Security Agency [NSA], FBI, Defense Intelligence Agency [DIA]). Even for many of the college student demonstrations and riots related to the protest of the war in Vietnam, security efforts were conducted via the mobilization of national troops into the local regions (e.g., the use of the National Guard at Kent State University and at the University of California, Berkeley). In part, as a result of the student riots on campus and surrounding areas, law enforcement agencies began to develop procedures and acquire specialized tools for gathering intelligence and for securing local areas (e.g., Special Weapons and Tactics [SWAT] teams). The lines of operation continued to be clearly drawn: (1) Issues affecting the security of our nation (even though local in nature) continued to be handled by federal agencies like the Federal Bureau of Investigation (FBI) and Federal Emergency Management Agency (FEMA), and (2) issues related to the enforcement of local laws and regulations remained the jurisdiction of the public safety agencies of the respective areas.

Up through the attacks of September 11, 2001, almost all of the homeland security efforts were seen as national in direction, leadership, and scope. Our policies for counterterrorism were still centered on dealing with enemies and events primarily outside of the United States. For example, the United States policy regarding terrorism included:

1. Make no concessions and strike no deals.

2. Bring terrorists to justice for their crimes.

3. Isolate and bring pressure on countries that sponsor terrorism to force them to change their behaviors.

4. Develop the counterterrorism capabilities of those countries that work with the United States and that request assistance (Pillar, 2001; PDD-39).

Starting around the mid-1990s, national policies and procedures for dealing with terrorism and homeland security were enacted; however, the focus was still very much on leadership and direction on a national level with implementation by federal agencies (PDD-39; FEMA, 1997). Involvement of local and regional law enforcement agencies was minimal in the planning, policy development, and implementation of the federal response to terrorism and homeland security.

Subsequent inquiries following the terrorist attacks on September 11, 2001, made it very clear that the detection and prevention of terrorism, and the response to both foreign or domestic terrorists, would require the coordinated and collaborative efforts of local public safety agencies and officers with federal departments and organizations. The role of the Department of Homeland Security (DHS) is one of facilitating and developing the avenues of communication between these entities to ensure viable and effective leadership, policies, and procedures for homeland security in the United States.

RESPONSE STRATEGIES

Detecting and Preventing Attacks of Terrorism

Law enforcement officers spend years studying criminal behaviors in order to prevent crimes and to capture and prosecute criminals. Homeland security roles for law enforcement agencies now require the use of some of these same skills in identifying the criminal behaviors of potential terrorists. To date, most of the training in law enforcement for homeland security has been in the form of short briefings, readings, and/or from the television by way of the news media. As noted by Hoffman (1998) and others, the most difficult and critical component of homeland security is to recognize and prevent a terrorist attack. As such, criminal justice officers need to be competent in recognizing the Terrorist Attack Pre-incident Indicators (TAPIs), a term used by the intelligence community to describe actions and behaviors taken by terrorists before they carry out an attack (Nance, 2003). We have discussed one source of TAPIs in Chapter 14, which include the tools of "profiling" used in law enforcement today. For example, Secret Service officers are trained to watch for individual behaviors, compiled as a profile, which may serve as indicators for possible actions toward those whom the officers are protecting. El Al, the Israeli airline, has used very successfully a behavior-recognition profile to detect individuals who might be potential skyjackers of its airliners (Howard & Sawyer, 2004).

Law enforcement officers, with training in observing and working with cultural differences and diverse communities, would have additional benefits in applying their skills and training to recognizing TAPIs. As noted in Chapter 14, public safety officers must avoid a stereotype-based approach to detecting criminals; this holds equally true in detecting terrorists. Stereotypes do not help in the detection and prevention of terrorism regardless of whether they are based on race or on the notion of what constitutes a "terrorist." Stereotyping will blind law enforcement officers to the real dangers in providing for our homeland security. For example, several of the September 11, 2001, terrorists behaved in ways that threw off any surveillance based on cultural and religious stereotypes: More than one skyjacker was seen in nightclubs and strip bars. Such behaviors would be contrary to the American stereotype of devout Muslim fundamentalists who would be adverse to alcoholic beverages, nightclub exotic dancers, and overt sexual behaviors of men and women at bars. Although it is beyond the scope of this chapter to go into the details and training to develop law enforcement skills for TAPIs, it is critical to emphasize that the application of stereotyping, racial profiling, and biased perceptions will not lead to the detection and capturing of terrorists (see Nance, 2003) for additional information on developing skills and tools with TAPIs.

Myths and Stereotypes about Terrorists

Knowledge of various multicultural communities' concerns, diversity, historical backgrounds, and life experiences will facilitate the homeland security and peacekeeping mission of law enforcement officers. It is important to have an understanding about some of the myths and stereotypes that are held of groups associated with terrorism and how these stereotypes might contribute to prejudice, discrimination, and biased encounters with members of these populations. Stereotypic views of multicultural groups who might be potential terrorists reduce individuals within this group to simplistic, one-dimensional caricatures as either "incompetent cowards" who can't fight face-to-face or "suicidal bogey persons" who can't be stopped. It is important for law enforcement officers to be aware of the different stereotypes of potential terrorists. The key to effectiveness in multicultural law enforcement with any ethnic or racial group is not that we completely eliminate myths and stereotypes about these groups, but that we are aware of these stereotypes and can monitor our thinking and our behaviors when the stereotypes do not apply to those persons with whom we are interacting.

Some of the current stereotypes that might affect law enforcement officers' perceptions of terrorists include the following:

1. *Arab and Middle Eastern Nationality or Ethnic/Cultural Background:* As a result of the September 11, 2001, attacks by al-Qaida and our images of the terrorists involved, it is easy to stereotype terrorists as having Arab and Middle Eastern backgrounds. Terrorists can be foreign or domestic, and clearly, the majority of the domestic terrorist incidents and attacks in the United States have not come from groups or individuals of Arab and Middle Eastern backgrounds. For example, a review of the FBI Bomb Incidents Report with the most current data available (FBI, 1999) shows that the vast majority of the terrorist incidents in the United States are conducted by Americans against other Americans.

Foreign terrorist groups include (examples from Howard & Sawyer, 2004):
- Abu Nidal Organization (Libya)
- Aum Shinrikyo, Aleph (Japan)
- Harakat ul-Mujahidin (Pakistan)
- Sinn Fein (Ireland)
- Euzkadi Ta Askatasuna (Spain)
- Red Army Faction (Germany)
- Red Brigade (Italy)
- Popular Front for the Liberation of Palestine (PLO)
- Sendero Luminoso (Peru)
- Black Tigers (Sri Lanka)
- November-17 (Greece)

- Interahamwe (Africa)
- Abu Sayyaf (Philippines)
- AUC (Colombia)
- People's War (Nepal)
- Free Aceh (Indonesia)
- Cosican Army (France)

Any of the current terrorist organizations around the world could combine forces or utilize operatives from other organizations to "look different" than expected or stereotyped.

2. ***Insane and/or behave like automatons:*** Unlike the movie or video industry's portrayal of terrorists, these individuals are usually not insane, although their actions may appear insane or not rational (Dershowitz, 2002). According to Malcolm W. Nance, a 20-year veteran of the U.S. intelligence community's Combating Terrorism Program and author of *The Terrorist Recognition Handbook*, most terrorists are generally intelligent, rational, decisive, and clearthinking. In the heat of an attack, terrorists may focus and harness their energies to accomplish their mission with dedication, motivation, ruthlessness, and commitment that may appear to outsiders as "insane."

3. ***Not as skillful or professional as U.S. law enforcement officers and personnel:*** As would be obvious, terrorists are not all similar in skills, training, and background. They vary in terrorist-training background from foreign-government-trained professionals who make up the foreign intelligence agencies of countries like Libya, Cuba, Iran, and North Korea to the novice, untrained civilian militia, vigilante, and criminals. The training and experience of *some* of the terrorists render them as skillful in their craft as any law enforcement professional in the United States. On the other hand, others have skill levels similar to petty criminals on the street. The use of intelligence information (i.e., not assumptions or stereotypes) to assess the skill and ability levels of terrorists or terrorist groups is central to homeland security. The use of intelligence information (not assumptions or stereotypes) to determine the skill and ability levels of terrorists or terrorist groups would be central to homeland security.

Throughout this text, the authors have emphasized attitudes and skills required of law enforcement officials in a multicultural society: (1) respecting cultural behaviors that may be different from one's own, (2) observing and understanding behaviors important to diverse communities, and (3) analyzing and interpreting diverse behaviors for application within multicultural communities. Similarly, multicultural skills and knowledge are also elements that can contribute to detecting and predicting terrorist actions and activities for homeland security when coupled with an intelligence-based approach. Just as it is important to understand one's own biases and stereotypes about multicultural communities before one can effectively serve those communities, law enforcement officers need to change their perceptions of who the terrorists are before they can effectively detect terrorist activities.

1. ***Anyone could be a terrorist:*** Law enforcement officers who start to look at specific groups may be blinded and overlook a group or people who may actu-

ally be the real terrorists sought. For example, if one was going by Arab descent or nationality, one would have missed Richard C. Reid, the Shoe Bomber (i.e., who was of British citizenship), and Jose Padilla, the alleged plotter for releasing a "dirty bomb" in the United States (born in Chicago of U.S. citizenship and Puerto Rican descent). If one thought that terrorists were inferior and not intelligent, one would have missed apprehending Theodore Kaczynski, the Unibomber, who was a professor at several major universities. Moreover, as noted by Stern (2004), "The official profile of a typical terrorist—developed by the Department of Homeland Security to scrutinize visa applicants and resident aliens—applies only to men. That profile was developed before the advent of Islamist chat rooms recruiting operatives for a global jihad, before the war in Iraq increased anti-American sentiment worldwide, and before women started serving as suicide bombers for Islamist terrorist organizations. . . . Although women represent a fraction of terrorists worldwide, it is naïve to assume they're not recruited to violent extremist groups."

2. ***Learn to acknowledge the terrorist's motivation, skills, and capabilities:*** Because of the actions of terrorists, law enforcement officers may view terrorists with contempt along with other negative stereotypic descriptors like "crazies," "camel jockeys," "suicidal," "scums of the earth," and "rag heads." Such contempt and disdain for terrorists may indeed be the perspective that blinds law enforcement officers and others to the fact that terrorists must be acknowledged for what they are: motivated, ruthless human beings who use destruction, death, and deceit to meet their lethal goals. For example, prior to the bombing of the Alfred P. Murrah Federal Building in Oklahoma City, one law enforcement and intelligence stereotype held that U.S. domestic terrorists were not capable of mass destruction, but were merely a criminal nuisance element of society (Heymann, 2001).

3. ***Observe and interpret street-level behaviors:*** Law enforcement officers are trained to observe and interpret street-level criminal behaviors, and such skills are applicable to recognizing some of the behaviors of terrorists. Terrorists are not invisible "ghosts" (i.e., terrorists' behaviors and actions are usually visible to the trained observer); however, stereotypes based on race, ethnicity, gender, age, nationality, and other demographic dimensions may blind a law enforcement officer from observing and correctly interpreting TAPIs. Racial profiling would be one of the actions that could blind law enforcement efforts in detecting a terrorist's intent. The only time that one could appropriately use racial profiling alone to detect a terrorist is when one has already had specific intelligence on a specific person as the terrorist (Howard & Sawyer, 2004).

   Without proper intelligence, it is almost impossible to interpret effectively behaviors that one observes. For example, three of the September 11, 2001, terrorists were involved in traffic stops by the police for speeding on three separate occasions prior to the terrorists attacks:

   - Mohammed Atta, the al-Qaida 9/11 skyjacker who piloted the American Airlines Flight 77 into the North Tower of the World Trade Center, was stopped in July 2001 by the Florida State Police for driving with an invalid license. A bench warrant was issued for his arrest since he ignored the issued ticket. Atta was stopped a few weeks later in Delray Beach, Florida, for speeding, but the officer was unaware of the bench warrant and let him go with a warning (Kleinberg & Davies, 2001, p. A1).

- Zaid al-Jarrah, the al-Qaida 9/11 skyjacker who investigators believe was a pilot on United Airlines Flight 93, which crashed in Pennsylvania, was stopped and cited by the Maryland State Police on September 9, 2001, for driving 90 miles per hour in a 65 mph-zone near the Delaware state line (a $270 fine). Trooper Catalano, who made the stop, reported that he looked over the car several times, videotaped the entire transaction, and said that the stop was a "regular, routine traffic stop" ("A Nation Challenged," 2002, p. A12).

- Hani Hanjour, one of the al-Qaida 9/11 skyjackers aboard the plane that crashed into the Pentagon, was stopped for speeding within a few miles of the military headquarters 6 weeks before the attack and was ticketed by the Arlington, Virginia, police for going 50 miles per hour in a 35-mph zone. Hanjour surrendered his Florida driver's license to the police officer who stopped him, but was allowed to go on his way (Roig-Franzia & Davis, 2002, p. A13).

In the case of Timothy McVeigh, the Oklahoma City bomber, law enforcement officials properly interpreted information, and this led to his arrest at a traffic stop. McVeigh was stopped by Trooper Charles Hanger of the Oklahoma Highway Patrol about 90 minutes after the bombing of the Alfred P. Murrah Federal Building. Trooper Hanger was looking for suspicious vehicles headed his way given the approximate travel distance and time of the bombing to his location.

> Oklahoma Highway Patrol Trooper Charles Hanger pulled over McVeigh's yellow Mercury Marquis on I-35 about 63 miles north of Oklahoma City because his car was missing a rear license plate. Hanger told the jury he took shelter behind the door of his cruiser as McVeigh got out of the car and walked toward him. As McVeigh reached for his camouflage wallet, Hanger said he noticed a bulge under his light windbreaker. "I told him to take both hands and slowly pull back his jacket," Hanger said. "He said, 'I have a gun.' I pulled my weapon and stuck it to the back of his head." As Hanger searched and cuffed him, McVeigh told the trooper he was also carrying a knife and a spare clip of ammunition. In the chamber of the pistol, Hanger found a round of Black Talon ammunition, bullets designed to inflict maximum damage on a shooting victim. Hanger then arrested McVeigh for carrying a concealed pistol in a shoulder holster. Three days later, McVeigh was tied to the blast as he waited for a court hearing on the gun charge ("Trooper describes arrest," 1997, p. A2).

4. ***Analyze and utilize intelligence and other source information:*** Law enforcement officers are trained to gather and use sources of information in a criminal investigation. For homeland security, key sources of information include not only local, state, and federal intelligence sources, but also knowledge, relationships, and networks developed within the local multicultural communities. As noted by Nance (2003), "Terrorism against America can only be defeated through careful intelligence collection, surveillance, cooperative efforts among law enforcement and intelligence agencies, and resolving the root complaints of the terrorist-supporting population."

Developing and Analyzing Information Regarding Threats and Vulnerabilities

Since the establishment of the Department of Homeland Security, law enforcement agencies have been receiving a variety of intelligence information, advisories, warnings, and other pertinent communications regarding the efforts and activities to be implemented in local communities. Local law enforcement agencies and officers, because of their knowledge of the existing multicultural communities and networks, have been called upon to aid in the data gathering and development of useful intelligence regarding possible terrorists. Such efforts have often sparked a mixed reception by law enforcement agencies. Some have regarded such requests for cooperative efforts as putting a strain on the established relationships of community policing within multicultural communities. As we have noted in Chapter 10, public confidence and trust in law enforcement agencies are essential for the effective prevention of and response to terrorism and for homeland security. Residents in diverse communities representing different races, ethnic backgrounds, religions, and other aspects of diversity must be able to trust that they will be treated fairly and protected as part of homeland security. This is of particular importance when there might be some perceptions, assumptions, and/or stereotypes among community residents as to who might be a "terrorist amongst us." When local law enforcement agencies and officers are called upon to provide assistance, the tasks of information gathering and interviewing possible terrorist suspects within multicultural communities involve the following critical steps:

1. ***Contact with Community Leaders:*** Law enforcement officers need to work closely with community leaders to establish a cooperative plan for gathering the needed information. Often, announcements made by the community leaders to inform the multicultural communities of the reasons for information gathering and the processes involved can be very effective. Community leaders could, for example, work with law enforcement agencies' community relations offices to develop a communication plan for the effective dissemination of information.

2. ***Utilize a Communication Plan:*** It is essential to have a well-developed and pilot-tested communication plan to ensure that the proper messages are provided to the multicultural communities involved. This is particularly important when language translations and interpreting are necessary. A carefully pretested "core message" regarding data-gathering procedures and interviews will usually work better than on-the-spot messages subject to the momentary interpretation of those who first hear such information.

3. ***Clearly Define and Spell out the Implications for Participation in the Data-Gathering Process:*** When it comes to possible accusations of terrorism and/or fears related to homeland security, members from multicultural communities who might be stereotyped as "terrorists" or have experienced prejudice by others in this regard would naturally be quite cautious of any contact with law enforcement agencies and officers. Providing clearly defined procedures and information regarding how the data gathering and interviews would be used would be most important. Additionally, if there are federal-agency consequences (e.g., being reported to the INS for a visa violation), these elements

should be clearly stated to ensure an ongoing relationship of trust with members of the multicultural communities involved.

4. ***Utilize Law Enforcement Personnel and Translators/Interpreters from the Same or Similar Multicultural Communities:*** To the extent that it is possible, use of law enforcement personnel who are from the same or similar ethnic/cultural communities would add to sustaining the building of relationship and trust-building necessary in such information-gathering processes. Clearly, the availability of bilingual personnel will make a significant difference to speakers of other languages.

Law enforcement agencies need to be concerned about how they participate in homeland security data-gathering efforts in order to avoid possible negative effects on their relationships with multicultural communities. For example, the effort to hunt down potential terrorists shortly after September 11, 2001, resulted in much concern by law enforcement agencies regarding their relationships with the Arab American and Muslim communities. The FBI's request to local law enforcement agencies for locating and interviewing terrorist suspects received a variety of responses. Law enforcement agencies in cities such as Dearborn and Detroit in Michigan assisted by helping to locate interviewees and by observing interviews conducted by the FBI (although they did not participate in conducting any of the interviews). Law enforcement agencies in Madison, Wisconsin, decided not to have local law enforcement officers involved in any aspect of locating and interviewing terrorist suspects. Law enforcement agencies in Cleveland, Ohio, participated fully and even had assigned a police detective to the interview process (Smith & Reed, 2001, p. A18). According to most commentators on the subject, the entire DHS effort to register over 85,000 men resulted in very few gains in homeland security as is noted in the following news article:

> The Department of Homeland Security has decided to discontinue a controversial program that required thousands of Arab and Muslim men to register with immigration authorities in the aftermath of the Sept. 11 attacks, officials said on Friday. Hoping to hunt down terrorists, immigration officials fingerprinted, photographed and interviewed about 85,000 Muslim and Arab noncitizens between November 2002 and May 2003 under the program. The effort—the largest to register immigrants in decades—required annual registration. Men from Iran, Iraq, Syria, Libya and Sudan have already begun reporting to immigration offices for a second round of registrations this month. Officials have acknowledged that most of the Arab and Muslim immigrants who have complied with the registration requirements had no ties to terrorist groups. Of the 85,000 men who showed up at immigration offices earlier this year, and the tens of thousands more screened at airports and border crossings during that time period, 11 had links to terrorism, officials said. ("U.S. halts Arab registry effort," 2003, p. A8)

Using Information and Intelligence Provided

Law enforcement agencies are provided many intelligence and information sources for their work related to homeland security. Such information generally is packaged from the different United States intelligence agencies and distributed by the FBI. The FBI's

Strategic Information Operations Center (SIOC) is one of the key centers for homeland security and the war on terrorism. Agents from the FBI, CIA, Defense Department, Customs, ATF, Secret Service, and NSA work side-by-side to consolidate the interagency intelligence work.

The new Terrorist Threat Integration Center (TTIC), which opened in January 2003 functioning under the CIA's direction, will incorporate the intelligence from both foreign and domestic sources regarding terrorists identified by the Department of Homeland Security, the FBI's Counterterrorism Division, the CIA's Counterterrorism Center, and the Department of Defense.

Law enforcement agencies' and officers' use of intelligence to deter and prosecute terrorists may be more troublesome in practice than in concept. Most terrorists commit no crime until their act of terrorism. The extent that law enforcement agencies might be able to take action prior to a terrorist act or incident present legal and jurisdictional dilemmas. As noted by Norwitz (2002), because "the objective of a criminal investigation is successful prosecution, all law enforcement effort must withstand judicial scrutiny at trial. Provision of Articles IV, V, and VI of the U.S. Constitution, as well as the Bill of Rights, offer powerful protections against law enforcement excess, which, by extension, applies to international terrorists operating on our soil."

Moreover, law enforcement must continue to maintain positive police–community relationships in order to properly serve the diverse society and multicultural communities within its jurisdiction. Such services include protecting those who might be wrongly accused and/or incorrectly stereotyped as "terrorists." Clearly, the sentiment of members from multicultural communities, as well as those from the mainstream majority community, is one of protecting the civil rights of citizens.

> The federal government wants to take the war on terrorism to the grass-roots level by encouraging truckers, bus drivers, railroad conductors, mail carriers and local utility workers to call in tips about suspicious activity. . . . As the program gears up to begin as soon as August with up to 1 million volunteers recruited in 10 cities, Muslims and civil liberties groups say they fear that the war on terrorism is about to take a decidedly ominous turn. "The American Civil Liberties Union of Wisconsin is concerned that the TIPS proposal may not make us safer, but will turn millions of Americans into government informants," Wisconsin ACLU director Chris Ahmuty said last week. He fears tipsters might phone in false reports about a disliked neighbor, or fall prey to racial profiling or bias. Syed Ahsani, chairman of the Southwest region of the American Muslim Alliance and a resident of Arlington, Texas, said he envisions amateur sleuths spying on innocent Americans—particularly those of Middle Eastern descent—in truck stop breakrooms, along isolated rail lines and in their own neighborhoods. . . . The Justice Department would act as a clearinghouse for the tips. Postal Service won't do it. Workers across the nation, and in Madison, offered mixed reactions to Operation TIPS last week. ("Tipline or a Spy Force?," 2002, p. B1)

For now and certainly for the near future, the work of law enforcement agencies in homeland security and the war on terrorism will continue to be a "work in progress." This will be especially true in the collection and application of intelligence information related to homeland security. Ford (2002) has noted the need for a new paradigm for law enforcement's efforts on homeland security that does not exist at this time. It is clear that law enforcement agencies have roles in the Department of Homeland Security's fight against terrorism; however, what exists now in terms of coordination and collaboration remains untested and is often beset with many limitations for law enforcement agencies.

WORKING WITH MULTICULTURAL COMMUNITIES ON PREVENTION AND RESPONSE

In an earlier section, we quoted Nance (2003) who highlighted a key element for homeland security and for winning the fight against terrorism that needs to include "cooperative efforts among law enforcement and intelligence agencies, and resolving the root complaints of the terrorist-supporting population." Clearly, law enforcement agencies are not in a position to resolve the "root complaints" involved with any terrorist-supporting nation or community. Law enforcement agencies are, however, in an excellent position to prevent the erosion of positive community–policing relationships with the multicultural communities that might include community members who hold concerns of "root complaints" and other issues of unfairness, bias, and discrimination.

Training Law Enforcement Agencies in Multicultural Community Homeland Security Issues

Law enforcement professionals have recognized, especially as they have to work within multicultural communities on issues like homeland security, that prejudices and stereotypes left unchecked and acted upon can result in not only unfairness, humiliation, and citizen complaints, but also missed opportunities for building long-term police–community relationships important for homeland security. Social scientists have noted that stereotypes and prejudices become more pronounced when fear, danger, and personal threat enters the picture, as may happen in possible terrorism incidents. Training in understanding multicultural communities and in Terrorist Attack Pre-incident Indicators (TAPIs) might have prevented the following situation:

> Pavel Lachko, a Russian student at the University of Texas at Arlington, was in America for about a month when he received a rude cultural lesson he won't soon forget: In these post-September 11 times, young foreign men aren't allowed innocent mistakes. On September 6, Lachko and his roommate, fellow Russian student Boris Avdeev, wandered on their bicycles into the employee parking lot of the Arlington police station looking for someone to give them directions. Rather than giving them answers, police locked them in handcuffs, held them for questioning by an agent from the Department of Homeland Security and charged them with criminal trespassing. . . . "I heard the male officer say into his radio that we are Pakistanis," Lachko says. "We said, 'No, no, no. We are not Pakistanis. We're Russians.'" After about 20 minutes of standing with the police, he says, the officers took out their handcuffs and placed the men under arrest. . . . Johnson said he did not know whether the two young men were initially taken to be Middle Easterners, and he insisted the arrests had nothing to do with their nationality. "They were arrested because they violated the traffic control device. There is no access except through a traffic control device," he says. "Nationality played no role in the decision." The two Russians' American friends say that is difficult to believe. "The police were either para-

noid, which I doubt, or they were simply harassing foreigners," says Michael Dailey, a retiree taking graduate classes in German at the school. He says foreign students, who number about 3,000 at UTA, should be treated with more understanding. (Korosec, 2003)

Cultural awareness and understanding of the different multicultural populations of the community would have helped to prevent misidentifying the nationalities of the students. Moreover, training in TAPIs would have allowed the law enforcement officers in the example above to correctly recognize and identify some of the specific behaviors and cues of possible terrorists and discern the behaviors of likely nonterrorists.

Educating Multicultural Communities on Homeland Security

Most cities and states currently have websites and online information on homeland security for their communities. However, information and education regarding homeland security–specific actions for the prevention of terrorism are not available for most communities in the United States. This lack of information is even more pronounced for some of the multicultural communities with recent immigrants and refugees (including those from South and Central America, Asia, Eastern Europe, and the Middle East). The role of law enforcement officers in providing such information offers another viable avenue for developing positive relationships with multicultural communities and for community-policing efforts. Clearly, all communities are interested in acquiring specific information regarding activities of homeland security, as the following example illustrates:

> The East Side college has entered into a partnership with the American Institute of Homeland Defense to offer both continuing education courses and college-credit courses in homeland security and anti-terrorism preparation. Also, AIHD has designated St. Philip's as their Homeland Security Regional Center of Excellence for the San Antonio area. . . . "There's a great need for homeland security training for first responders," said John Carnes, dean of applied sciences and technology at St. Philip's. "That might mean that the first person on the scene could be someone from the fire department or the police department or a hotel employee." "Our (program) will be focused on first responders," added Ray Boryczka, director of continuing education for St. Philip's. "We're actually going to be training the people who will be the first ones on the scene." Boryczka said that since passing the word along about this new program, the college has received requests from organizations and individuals interested in what the program will offer. "Our phones have been ringing off the hook," he said. "It's a much bigger response than what we first expected, and these weren't fire departments, police departments or EMTs (emergency medical technicians). These were calls from the general public and from school districts and from businesses. This is a hot issue. The sensitivity is still there." (Conchas, 2003, p. H1)

Law enforcement agencies may also want to include into their Citizen's Police Academies information regarding homeland security and ways that the multicultural communities could participate and provide assistance to the public safety departments. Additionally, law enforcement agencies might utilize the nonsworn and CSO personnel to provide such information in a bilingual mode to ensure proper information to communities with large populations of immigrants and refugees. Community-based presentations at familiar neighborhood centers, associations, churches, mosques, and temples may facilitate greater multicultural population attendance and participation. Likewise, collaborative programs of law enforcement agencies and community-based organizations have resulted in positive dissemination of information and ongoing building of trust with multicultural communities (for example, see IRCO and Dial-911 in Chapter 6 and Spanish Police Academy in Chapter 7).

KEY ISSUES IN LAW ENFORCEMENT

Reluctance to Report and Participate in Homeland Security Efforts

Multicultural groups that have been stereotyped as possible terrorists (e.g., Arab and Middle Eastern Americans, Muslims, South Asians, Central Asians) may be reluctant to report crimes related to these stereotypes and may not seek police assistance and help for violations of their civil rights. Moreover, many may avoid contact with law enforcement agencies entirely with respect to homeland security efforts. Many of the multicultural groups may come from countries with extensive terrorism problems and may remember how police in their home countries have brutalized and violated them and others (in quelling terrorism). Sensitivity to the experiences of these multicultural groups and a knowledge of their history of being victimized by terrorists will be of positive value in gaining participation and cooperation in homeland security efforts. Another key challenge to effective cooperation with multicultural communities on homeland security issues is to help allay the fears and concerns expressed by community members with regard to their multiple interactions with law enforcement officers. Inquiries relating to homeland security, for example, may coexist with the investigation into other crimes and code enforcements like immigration, health, sanitation, housing, and welfare.

Victimization

Law enforcement agencies protect the safety and security of citizens in multicultural communities where harassment and discrimination resulting from being stereotyped as terrorist may lead to victimization. Documentation of such crimes against Arab and Middle Eastern Americans and Asian/Pacific Americans are provided in Chapters 5 and 9 and in Chapter 14 in this text. Some victims are harassed and attacked because of their attire or their appearance. For example, men from the Sikh religion wear turbans, and this is often stereotyped to be indicative of "foreign terrorists:"

> After 26 years of living in the United States, Thakar Basati of Palatine was rudely reminded that he is a foreigner here. Despite his American passport, Basati has had to endure interrogation at airports whenever he travels. On a routine traffic stop, he had to wait an hour for the police officer to write a citation. "Suddenly, I became a criminal," Basati said. "I've been a citizen for over 20 years." . . . Professor Sukhchain Singh, dean and administrator of the Sikh Religious Society, shared how post-Sept. 11 profiling had hurt his community. His group manages the largest Sikh religious center in the Midwest out of Palatine. "There are more than 250 recorded hate crimes against Sikhs in the United

States so far," he said attributing it to his group's unique religious attire. (Krishnamurthy, 2003, p. N1)

Victimization also includes being unfairly accused or identified as a possible terrorist. Those accused, or so identified, must be able to believe that the police and other public safety personnel are not against them, and that their well-being and safety are just as important as those of others who are not subject to these perceptions, assumptions, or stereotypes. Moreover, residents who are discriminated against or stereotyped as "terrorists" must be able to trust that prosecutors, judges, parole, and probation will utilize their full armamentarium to deter and jail terrorists, as well as those who unjustly terrorize, discriminate, and/or harass those who are *unfairly* stereotyped as terrorists, as seen in the next example:

> At an F.B.I academy meeting last year, in which strategies for gathering intelligence were discussed, one participant warned that officials were overlooking the effect that pursuing suspects has had on Muslim and other targeted groups.... Some early tips fell apart in highly public ways, as when a security guard named Ronald Ferry claimed to have found a ground-to-air radio in a certain room in a hotel across from the World Trade Center. The guest who was occupying that room, Abdallah Higazy, was jailed for nearly a month on suspicion that he had helped guide the hijackers who crashed airplanes into the twin towers. Mr. Ferry's falsehood was uncovered when an airplane pilot, who has not been publicly identified, came forward to claim the radio. A lawsuit Mr. Higazy has brought against Mr. Ferry and the F.B.I. says the agents who took the tip failed to press Mr. Ferry for a sworn statement, to subject him to a lie detector, or to interview a second guard who helped search the room, said Robert S. Dunn, a lawyer for Mr. Higazy. "They just took his word and ran with it," said Mr. Dunn. F.B.I. officials in New York declined to comment, citing the pending litigation. (Litchblau, 2003, p. A1)

As this example illustrates, it would be difficult for others who are from similar ethnic, religious, or cultural backgrounds of the accused to perceive that the criminal justice system would treat them fairly if the facts of the case example were found to be true as stated above.

Differential Treatment

In this chapter, as well as in the culture-specific chapters, we have provided examples of how members of multicultural communities have been treated unfairly because of law enforcement officers' perceptions of them as threats to homeland security or possible terrorists. Especially if a target is a possible terrorist, expressions of bias and prejudice in law enforcement agencies may go unchallenged. This is because of the tremendous fear of the potential terrorist threat, as well as the need to rally around the issues of homeland security. Often such bias and prejudice are expressed via inappropriate language and disrespectful terms such as, "rags," "suicidal rag-heads," "A-rabs," "Arab-bombers," "Muslim fanatics").

Under such circumstances, both law enforcement executive leadership and officers' professionalism will determine whether such bias and prejudices go unchecked or whether the treatment of a possible terrorist suspect will be fair and justifiable. Clearly, should the suspect not be a terrorist, then an injustice had occurred because of differential treatment. Moreover, the multicultural community of which the suspect is a member will begin to question their trust and reliance on the police agency that shows such bias and prejudice. Should the suspect indeed have been correctly identified as a possible terrorist, then any stereotypic and differential treatment may jeopardize the prosecution of the case as well.

Racial Profiling and Homeland Security

The issue of racial profiling, as noted in Chapter 14, is a major problem and concern for African Americans, Arab Americans, and Latino/Hispanic Americans. Citizens from different cultural and racial backgrounds believe that the determining factor in whether peace officers exercise their discretion in stopping a vehicle has to do with the driver's race and ethnicity. In the area of homeland security, current federal policy prohibits the use of "racial profiling" except under narrow circumstances to deal with terrorism and terrorist threats:

> The new policy, representing the first time that the federal government has imposed across the board guidelines on racial profiling, governs the conduct of 70 federal law enforcement agencies. A narcotics agent, for instance, cannot focus on a specific neighborhood simply because of its racial makeup, the policy states. In national security operations, however, the policy allows agents to use race and ethnicity in "narrow" circumstances to help "identify terrorist threats and stop potential catastrophic attacks," officials said. (Litchblau, 2003, p. A1)

The use of race and ethnicity is allowed under federal policy and guidelines for the identification of terrorist threats and to stop possible terrorist attacks. Law enforcement officers need to be cautious in the use of racial profiling for detecting terrorists and in homeland security matters. Hoffman (1998) has documented that terrorists will "do whatever it will take" to avoid detection and to accomplish a mission. Even though the use of racial profiling in circumstances involving terrorism is legal and justifiable, its use may result in actually not detecting the terrorist because the terrorist is knowledgeable about the racial profiling used.

Sustaining Police Services to the Multicultural Communities in Light of Homeland Security

One of the key challenges in developing and implementing law enforcement efforts in homeland security includes sustaining the community-policing and law enforcement services within multicultural neighborhoods. In times of scarce funding resources, on-the-street, community-policing efforts might take a back seat to homeland security and the fight on terrorism issues, as is shown by the following example:

> At Hartsfield, cutbacks by the federal government have trimmed six to eight officers per shift 24 hours a day, Peter Andresen said just before he was promoted from airport commander to deputy chief in August. Funding was cut in June. "We had to release people," Andresen said. "We still have people on every checkpoint, we just don't have the number that we had.". . . Councilman Ceasar Mitchell, chairman of the City Council's Public Safety Committee, says Atlanta should get help. "We're committed to safety, but at the same time those unfunded mandates are taking officers and dollars away from our streets," he said.

"I hope the federal government will say we're going to bring funding to the table so you can spend your allocated budget on tackling crime in your neighborhoods." (Bruner, 2003, p. JD1)

Since contact with multicultural communities will increase because of the emerging roles for law enforcement in homeland security, the need for additional bilingual officers and personnel will be paramount for the communities. As part of emergency preparation, the need to provide clear communications and to ensure understanding of emergency instructions will require bilingual personnel and translators in these diverse communities.

Increasing Multicultural Peace Officers for Homeland Security Functions

There is a significant underrepresentation of multicultural and bilingual personnel in federal, state, and local law enforcement and criminal justice positions. On all governmental levels, there have been extensive efforts at recruiting and filling law enforcement positions important for homeland security with multicultural and language-expert personnel. The small number of multicultural and language-expert officers has already hampered many departments in neighborhoods with multicultural populations in effectively serving those communities. When appropriate multicultural police services and bilingual expertise are not provided, the added roles and functions for homeland security further exacerbate the problems in serving multicultural communities.

A variety of reasons exist for such underrepresentation, including:

1. History of law enforcement relationships with multicultural communities

2. Image of law enforcement personnel in multicultural communities

3. Lack of interest by multicultural community members in law enforcement careers

4. Lack of knowledge about the different careers and pathways in law enforcement

5. Concern with and fear of background checks, physical requirements, and the application process

6. Concerns with roles assigned in these communities, especially in the areas of homeland security

7. Lack of advocates for law enforcement careers

With the growing need for multicultural and language-expert law enforcement personnel for homeland security roles and functions in areas throughout the United States, law enforcement agencies need to emphasize and be committed to the importance of "diversity" in their recruitment efforts.

Working with Immigration and Custom Enforcement

One of the key situations for a law enforcement agency involves decision making where the local public safety agencies and departments become involved in enforcing and working with the Immigration and Custom Enforcement (ICE) section, now a part of the Department of Homeland Security. The ramifications for multicultural community relationships and network-building are significant. The decision-making and strategic responses to terrorism on these collaborative and possible joint efforts are not clear-cut, nor "givens," for any law enforcement agency, as exemplified by the following law enforcement departmental stance:

> According to Homeland Security figures, 7 million immigrants are in the country illegally. About 87,000 illegal immigrants are in Massachusetts. More than 25,000 foreign-born people live in Worcester, according to the 2000 Census. Detective Lt. Robert F. Rich, Worcester Police liaison to anti-terrorism agencies, said that his department does not enforce immigration laws and does not foresee doing so. "We always cooperate with all law enforcement agencies," he said. "We work with ICE and federal agencies, and immigration law is strictly their purview." Lt. Rich said that there are times when police are trying to identify a suspect who has several aliases. They look for assistance from immigration agencies. "We look to identify who the individual is," he said. "Again, we don't get involved whether the person is legally here or not. We don't enforce that. We are enforcing criminal statutes in Massachusetts." (Echegaray, 2003, p. A2)

Immigration and Custom Enforcement cooperation with local law enforcement agencies is of particular concern for multicultural communities where there has been a history of legal as well as illegal immigration (e.g., Latino/Hispanic American, Asian/Pacific American, Arab and Middle Eastern American). Indeed, some multicultural community members will be prosecuted and deported. However, where no wrong has been committed, then law enforcement must keep a check on potential stereotyping and the prejudicial act of singling out individuals based on those stereotypes.

SUMMARY

The experience of law enforcement agencies involved in homeland security and the war on terrorism within multicultural communities is evolving. Likewise, the emerging roles and functions for law enforcement in homeland security present many challenges for the day-to-day work within the criminal justice system and the Federal Response Plan (FRP) against terrorism. Homeland security challenges for law enforcement agencies include the following: (1) detecting and preventing attacks of terrorism; these can be made more complex within multicultural communities because of the past histories of those communities with law enforcement in the United States, as well as in their native homelands; (2) avoiding stereotypes and possible biased perceptions based on ethnicity, culture, race, and religion that may be evoked within multicultural communities, and (3) working with multicultural community leaders regarding their perceptions of police actions and efforts in homeland security. Officers should realize that some citizens may have been victims of terrorism, as well as being harmed by the antiterrorism efforts within their native homeland (while innocent of any involvement with terrorism). These citizens carry with them stereotypes of police services as something to be feared and avoided. Law enforcement officials need to go out of their way to work with multicultural communities to establish trust, to provide outreach efforts, and to win cooperation in order to effectively accomplish their goals for homeland security efforts. Building partnerships focused on community collaboration in the fight against terrorism is important locally and nationally.

Attitudes and skills that enhance multicultural law enforcement include: (1) respecting cultural behaviors that may be different from one's own, (2) observing and understanding behaviors important to diverse communities, and (3) analyzing and interpreting diverse behaviors for services application within multicultural communities. These same multicultural attitudes and skills form the core elements, when coupled with an intelligence-based approach, in detecting and predicting terrorist actions and activities for homeland security.

Since the establishment of the Department of Homeland Security, law enforcement agencies have been receiving a variety of intelligence information, advisories, warnings, and other pertinent communications regarding the efforts and activities to be implemented within local communities. Local law enforcement agencies and officers, because of their knowledge of the existing multicultural communities and networks, have been called upon to aid in the data gathering and development of useful intelligence regarding possible terrorists. Such efforts have often produced a mixed reception by law enforcement agencies. When local law enforcement agencies and officers are requested to provide assistance for homeland security information-gathering and the interviewing of possible terrorist suspects, some of the following steps are recommended with the multicultural communities involved:

1. Contact with community leaders—Law enforcement officers need to work closely with community leaders to establish a cooperative plan for gathering the needed information. Community leaders could work with the law enforcement agencies' community relations office to develop a communication plan for the effective dissemination of information.

2. Utilize a communication plan—It is critical to have a well-developed communication plan to ensure that the proper messages are provided to the multicultural communities involved. This is particularly important when language translations and interpreting are necessary.

3. Define explicitly and spell out the implications for participation in the data-gathering process—Providing clearly defined procedures and information regarding how the data gathering and interviews would be used is most important. Additionally, if there are possible consequences (e.g., with the INS), these elements should be delineated to ensure an ongoing relationship of "trust" with members of the multicultural communities involved.

4. Utilize law enforcement personnel and translators/interpreters from the same or similar multicultural communities—Use of law enforcement personnel who are from the same or similar ethnic or cultural communities would contribute to maintaining relationships, building the trust necessary in such information-gathering processes.

Some multicultural community members, because of their past experiences with law enforcement, may be reluctant to participate in homeland security efforts. It is important for law enforcement departments and officials to build relationships and working partnerships with multicultural communities to ensure effective participation in combating terrorism and implementing homeland security.

A key challenge for law enforcement efforts in homeland security includes sustaining the community-policing and law enforcement services within multicultural neighborhoods. In times of scarce funding resources, on-the-street, community-policing efforts might take a back seat to homeland security and the fight on terrorism. Moreover, since contact with multicultural communities will increase because of the emerging roles for law enforcement in homeland security, the need for additional bilingual officers and personnel will be paramount for these communities. As part of emergency preparation, the need to provide clear communications and to ensure understanding of emergency instructions will require additional bilingual personnel and translators for these diverse communities.

DISCUSSION QUESTIONS AND ISSUES

1. ***Homeland Security Roles for Law Enforcement in Your Local Community:*** The chapter provided the six major goals of the Department of Homeland Security (DHS). Review the homeland security roles of law enforcement in your community using the six major DHS goals. List the special challenges and opportunities involved in implementing the top two or three DHS goals for law enforcement agencies in your community. What are some of the unique law enforcement challenges related to implementation of these six goals within multicultural communities?

2. ***Stereotyping and Biased Perceptions:*** Law enforcement officers and agencies must guard themselves from using a stereotype-based or racial profiling approach for detecting terrorism and in providing homeland security. Which groups or individuals in your community might be stereotyped as possible terrorists? What characteristics of these groups and individuals make them susceptible to stereotyping and biased perceptions? What are ways for professional peace officers to guard themselves against such ineffective practices?

3. ***Working with Multicultural Groups in Your Community on Homeland Security:*** The authors recommended some guidelines and approaches for collaborative efforts in information gathering and in implementing homeland security efforts within multicultural communities. Select one or more multicultural groups that are part of your community (or a part of a nearby community). How would you apply the suggested guidelines and approaches to working with these multicultural groups?

4. ***Recruiting and Using Multicultural and Language-Expert Law Enforcement Personnel:*** The authors noted the importance of having multicultural and language-expert personnel in working with multicultural communities. How would you go about recruiting and using such personnel in your local community? Do you see roles for the use of volunteers who have such backgrounds and language expertise in homeland security efforts? What are the advantages and disadvantages in using community volunteers in homeland security activities?

5. ***Victimization includes being unfairly accused or identified as a possible terrorist:*** What are ways to prevent and to help multicultural communities so that members would not be the recipients of unjust accusation and victimization? What approach would you suggest for your local law enforcement agencies to

prevent such victimization? What would you suggest that your multicultural community agencies do to prevent discrimination and harassment for those who are unfairly stereotyped?

WEBSITE RESOURCES

Visit these websites for additional information about multicultural law enforcement issues in responding to homeland security efforts.

Association of Former Intelligence Officers (AFIO)   http://www.afio.com

This website provides the *Weekly Intelligence News*, which summarizes some of the homeland security issues from the perspectives of the AFIO.

Central Intelligence Agency—Factbook: http://www.odci.gov/cia/publications/factbook/index.html

This website provides background and current information about groups and countries affecting the homeland security of the United States.

Department of Homeland Security (DHS)   http://www.dhs.gov/

This website provides extensive information regarding the DHS, as well as the threat level for the United States at any point in time. Suggestions and tips are provided for local communities in their preparation for homeland security.

Department of State—Travel Warnings and Consular Information   http://travel.state.gov/travel_warnings.html

This website highlights countries and areas around the world that might be of a terrorist threat to citizens of the United States and its homeland security.

Federal Bureau of Investigation   http://www.fbi.gov/

This website provides the latest annual report of terrorism incidents in the United States.

Federal Emergency Management Agency   http://www.fema.gov/

This website provides a range of useful information related to the management of community, state, and national emergencies and homeland security issues.

U.S. Army Chemical and Biological Defense Command (CBDCOM)
http://www.cbdcom.apgea.army.mil/cbdcom/

This website provides background and technical information on biological and chemical weapons that might be encountered by homeland security in a terrorist attack.

U.S. Coast Guard (USCG)   http://www.uscg.mil/USCG.shtm

The U.S. Coast Guard is responsible for the protection of all of our ports and waterways within the Department of Homeland Security. The website highlights many of the specific aspects of homeland security for a law enforcement agency.

REFERENCES

Bruner, T. K. (2003, September 11). "Homeland Security: Police get help but not at Hartsfield." *Atlanta Journal and Constitution*, p. JD1.

Conchas, E. (2003, October 22). "College gets homeland security nod; St. Philip's to offer anti-terrorism preparation classes." *San Antonio Express-News*, p. H1.

Dershowitz, A. M. (2002). *Why Terrorism Works: Understanding the Threat, Responding to the Challenge*. New Haven Conn.: Yale University Press.

Donohue, L. K. (2002). "Fear Itself: Counterterrorism, Individual Rights, and U.S. Foreign Relaions Post 9-11," Paper presented at the International Studies Association Convention, New Orleans, LA, March, 2002 (and parts published in "Bias, National Security, and Military Tribunals." *Criminology and Public Policy July, 2002).*

Echegaray, C. (2003, November 26). "More work awaits police if criminal alien bill passes." *Worcester Telegram and Gazette* (MA), p. A2.

Federal Bureau of Investigation. (1996). *Terrorism in the United States 1995*. Washington, DC: Terrorist Research and Analytical Center, National Security Division, Federal Bureau of Investigation (FBI).

FBI Bomb Data Center. (1999). *1999 Bombing Incidents*. General Information Bulletin 99-1. Washington, DC: Federal Bureau of Investigation.

Federal Emergency Management Agency (FEMA). (1997). *The Federal Response Plan Notice of Change: Terrorism Incident Annex*. Washington, DC: Author.

Ford, P. (2002, March 27). "Legal War on Terror Lacks Weapons." *Christian Science Monitor*, Section 4, p. 1.

Heymann, P. B. (2001). *Terrorism and America: A Commonsense Strategy for a Democratic Society*. Cambridge, MA: MIT Press.

Hoffman, B. (1998). *Inside Terrorism*. New York: Columbia University Press.

Howard, D. R., and Sawyer, R. L. (Eds.). (2004). *Terrorism and Counterterrorism: Understanding the New Security Environment*. Guilford, CT: McGraw-Hill/Dushkin.

Kleinberg, E., and Davies, D. (2001, October 19). "Delray Police Stopped Speeding Terror Suspect." *Palm Beach Post* (Florida), p. A1.

Korosec, T. (2003, September 25). "A Texas welcome: Two UTA students make a wrong turn, end up jailed in Arlington." *Dallas Observer*.

Krishnamurthy, M. (2003, August 12). "160 turn out for forum in Libertyville on immigration issues." *Chicago Daily Herald*, p. N1.

Litchblau, E. (2003, June 18). "Threats and Responses: Law Enforcement; Bush Issues Racial Profiling Ban But Exempts Security Inquiries." *New York Times*, p. A1.

Nance, M W. (2003). *The Terrorist Recognition Handbook*. Guilford, CT: Lyons Press.

"A Nation Challenged: The Terrorists; Hijacker Got a Speeding Ticket." (2002, January 9). *New York Times*, p. A12.

National Commission on Terrorism. (1999). *Countering the Changing Threat of International Terrorism*. Washington, D.C.: Author. Available: www.fas.org/irp/threat/commission.html

Norwitz, J. H. (2002). "Combating Terrorism: With a Helmet or a Badge?" *Journal of Homeland Security*, August (http://www.homelandsecurity.org/journal/articles/displayarticle.asp?article=72).

Pillar, P. R. (2001). "The Dimensions of Terrorism and Counterterrorism," in *Terrorism and U.S. Foreign Policy*. Washington, DC: The Brookings Institution Press.

Richardson, L. (1998). "Global Rebels: Terrorist Organizations as Trans-National Actors." *Harvard International Review, 20*(4).

Robbins, J. S. (2002). "Bin Laden's War," in D. R. Howard, and R. L. Sawyer, (eds.), *Terrorism and Counterterrorism: Understanding the New Security Environment*. Guilford, CT: McGraw-Hill/Dushkin.

Roig-Franzia, M., and Davis, P. (2002, January 9). "For Want of a Crystal Ball; Police Stopped Two Hijackers in Days Before Attacks." *Washington Post*, p. A13.

Smith, R. L., and Reed, E. (2001, November 29). "Local police to begin questioning visitors from Mideast." *Plain Dealer* (Cleveland, Ohio), p. A18.

Stern, J. (2004, January 4). "Women slip by radar with jihad agendas." *Contra Costa Times*.

"Trooper describes arrest 90 minutes after bombing." (1997, April 28). *Deseret News* (Salt Lake City), p. A2.

"Tipline or a Spy Force? Bush proposal for a hotline to report suspicious activity has met with skepticism in Madison and around the Country." (2002, July 21). *Wisconsin State Journal* (Madison, WI), p. B1.

"U.S. halts Arab registry effort." (2003, November 22). *St. Petersburg Times* (FL), p. A8.

Zamora, J. H. (2003, November 15). "$48 million in grants headed for Bay Area." *San Francisco Chronicle*, p. A20.

Part 4

RESPONSE STRATEGIES FOR CRIMES MOTIVATED BY HATE/BIAS AND RACIAL PROFILING

Part Four provides a detailed explanation of strategies for preventing, controlling, reporting, monitoring, and investigating crimes that are based on hate or bias because of the victim's race, ethnicity, national origin, religion, or sexual orientation. Criminal cases of these types have come to be known as bias or hate crimes; noncriminal cases are referred to as incidents. Some agencies refer to these acts as civil rights violations. The chapters that follow contain policies, practices, and procedures for responding to these types of crimes or incidents. We recognize that other groups, such as women, the elderly, the homeless, and the disabled, are sometimes victimized. However, in this book we focus primarily on hate crimes and incidents wherein the motivation was related to the victim's race, ethnicity, national origin, religion, or sexual orientation. The reasons for collecting data on crimes and incidents motivated by hate/bias committed by individuals or organized groups are included in Chapter 13. The end of that chapter provides examples to help students, members of the criminal justice system, and the community to develop sensitive and workable programs for handling these crimes and incidents. The recommended policies, training, practices, and procedures outlined in this text are currently in operation in most law enforcement agencies across the nation and are based on studies and recommendations by the U.S. Department of Justice's

Community Relations Service. The Commission on Peace Officer Standards and Training, found in all states of the nation, has been another major source of materials. The final chapter provides information about racial profiling for members of the criminal justice system. The type of policing reviewed in this unit is a civilizing process that will contribute to multicultural coexistence and cooperation. All law enforcement professionals should have a good working knowledge of the guidelines that follow.

Chapter 12

Hate/Bias Crimes: Victims, Laws, Investigations, and Prosecutions

OVERVIEW

This chapter focuses on hate/bias crimes and how they are investigated and prosecuted. The chapter first discusses the scope of the problem, providing historical perspectives and examples. We stress that the law enforcement professional must be aware of discrimination and hate crimes directed toward immigrants and people from different ethnic, national origin, racial, sexual orientation, and religious backgrounds. We present some aspects of urban dynamics as they relate to the economy, hate violence, move-in violence, and hate/bias crimes and incidents. In this chapter, while we devote some attention to crimes against new immigrants, the primary focus is on hate crimes against Jews, gays, and lesbians. We discuss the importance of hate crime investigations and treatment of the victims because of the unique impact on them as well as on the community. The chapter highlights the need for law enforcement officials to treat hate violence with the same degree of concern as heinous crimes such as rape and sexual assault. It presents information on special statutes that provide for not only the investigations of hate/bias crimes, but also increased penalties for the perpetrator.

COMMENTARY

Violence motivated by racial, religious, ethnic/national origin, or sexual orientation hatred has existed for generations in the United States and all over the world, and it seems to be on the rise. The criminal justice system and every community must address this problem. Consider the following:

> The institute estimates that a full 10 percent of the U.S. population is annually victimized by some form of ethnoviolence. That translates to more than 25 million victims this year [1991]. (National Institute Against Prejudice Violence, 1992, p. 2)

> But what happens when people of different origins, speaking different languages and professing different religions, inhabit the same locality and live under the same political sovereignty? Ethnic and racial conflict—far more than ideological conflict—is the explosive problem of our times. (Schlesinger, 1991, p. 27)

We can conclude that our environment contributes to our behavior. No social scientist would disagree. The issue becomes determining what social conditions contribute most to our behavior and to what degree "they" are responsible. Numerous studies show that the reduced space and increased stress of urban life give rise to increased incidence of violence. Economic levels have also been shown as paralleling the incidence of violence. (Fritsche, 1992, p. 13)

Following 9/11, there were many instances across the U.S. of discrimination against Americans who look different, who speak a different language, who worship differently: Arab Americans and Muslim Americans and even people who have nothing to do with Islam, Sikhs. It was a Sikh who was murdered in Arizona merely because he was dark skinned and wore a turban, required by his religion. A Pakistani Muslim grocer was shot to death in Dallas the same day. Others have died at the hands of "patriots." Hundreds of incidents have been reported and they are intensifying: beatings, vandalism, attacks on stores and mosques. Much of the hatred has been verbal. In some cases it has achieved terrorism's chief goal: It has made people afraid to go out in public. Throughout the region, Americans of Asian and Middle Eastern descent are declining to leave their homes or keeping their children at home, for fear of harassment, or worse. ("No room for bigotry," 2001, p. A23)

HISTORICAL PERSPECTIVE

Although civilization and technology have progressed, it does not appear that human behavior has evolved concurrently. Since the beginning of time people have gathered into tribes or groups with those of similar color, speech, and background for reasons of safety and commonality. Since that beginning, groups of people have been suspicious of others who are different from them. From such suspicions and discomfort about new neighbors came conflict, crimes, and even killings between an existing majority and the new minority interlopers; the territorial imperative to protect oneself from the "alien" became entrenched.

However, as civilization continued to progress, intermingling resulted in diverse mixtures of people in many countries. In the past half-century, with advances in communications and transportation, cross-border migration of ideas, travelers, and even settlements increased. Locals became less ethnocentric and less afraid of new arrivals and thought more in terms of the human family. But suddenly in the process of creating a world culture and a "global village" mindset, the world witnessed the breakup of superpowers and nation-states. The movement was then toward more local autonomy and separatism, often along the lines of ethnicity and religious fundamentalism: Canada saw conflict between its Anglo and French citizens, the Soviet Union crumbled and broke into separate republics, former central European satellite countries squabbled over borders as ancient rivalries flared, and Germany broke down the Berlin Wall in 1989 but experienced violence between neo-Nazis and opponents of their racist politics and actions.

In Yugoslavia, ethnocentrism and the reversion to tribalism resulted in civil wars between 1996 and 1998 among the former states, with Christian Serbs, Croats, Albanians, and Muslims engaged in wholesale slaughter of one another. "Ethnic cleansing" took place to oust members of other ethnic groups from targeted areas.

March 2004 saw continued struggles by NATO and the United Nations to stem a wave of ethnic violence in Kosovo and surrounding areas. In the predominantly

Albanian province including Kosovo, ethnic Albanians attacked Serbian neighborhoods, setting fires to houses and destroying Serbian Orthodox Churches. Most Albanians are Muslim, and some saw these acts as evidence that problems stemming from the 1997-99 war in Kosovo have not been resolved.

In 1994 the International Red Cross estimated that 800,000 Tutsis of Rwanda were murdered in what many referred to as genocide carried out by Hutu extremists. The Hutus used state resources and authority to incite—or force—tens of thousands of Rwandans to slaughter three-quarters of the Tutsi population of that country (PBS Online, 1999). Other conflicts occurred in the late 1990s and continued into the 21st century, such as the tragic events that took place in East Timor, a tiny half-island occupied by Indonesia. In addition to the fatalities, tens of thousands of people fled from their homes to refugee camps. Even U.N. peacekeepers were victims of the violence.

The many tribal factions in Afghanistan became the center of world attention in 2002 when the United States invaded that country to depose the ruling Taliban party, a group espousing an extreme and repressive version of Islam. The same year, Pakistan's dispute with India over Kashmir continued to fester. Conflict between the Hindu majority and the significant Muslim minority in India burst into the open in the western state of Gujarat, where rioting claimed many lives in continued religious and communal tensions. Then in 2003, the United States invaded Iraq and entered into what may be a long occupation of a country where rival Iraqi Muslim Sunnis and Shi'ites, as well as Kurds, who were long oppressed under Saddam Hussein, are still rivals for power. Not far away geographically, decades of violence in Israel between Palestinians and Israelis intensified in the new millennium.

Ancient animosities between groups of people in Asia, Latin America, and Europe may be brought with them as they relocate to North America. For example, Armenians, Turks, and Greeks in the United States keep alive ancient dislikes and distrusts; in 2000 anti-Semitic incidents in the United States took place, reflecting the turmoil in the Middle East between Israel and the Palestinians; and Serbs and ethnic Albanians living in the United States maintain their hatred due to events in Kosovo. In 1996, following the conflict in Bosnia between Serbs and Croats, the Saint Sava Serbian Church in Phoenix, Arizona, was vandalized with extensive graffiti espousing hate for the Serbs. The offenders were never brought to justice, but the evidence pointed to Croatian men still carrying hatred from historical events in Europe during World War II. Instead of newcomers adapting to their new opportunities and moving beyond cultural biases and old-country hatreds, these hatreds simply get transplanted.

In the United States, the so-called melting-pot society struggles not only with inhumanity toward new immigrants but also with the imported hatreds and racism brought by those new immigrants themselves. Law enforcement personnel must have some perspective on both the global and local situation when it comes to hatred and bias within the population they serve. Criminal justice system practitioners must be trained to counteract hate crimes and violence, as well as address their inhumane impact. The importance of local law enforcement officials' monitoring of such world events is discussed in Chapter 13. This is a major undertaking as we begin the 21st century because the United Nations is currently involved actively in peacekeeping efforts in 15 different countries.

There have been great strides in the area of civil rights and hate/bias crimes since the days when African Americans were terrorized and when lynchings and Jim Crow laws ruled parts of our country. No longer do we legally constitute an entire race as one-third human, or forbid fellow humans to share schools, lunch counters, restrooms, or bus seats. We have moved forward from times when interracial marriages were out-lawed in many states, when the small print in deeds forbade the sale of property to members of the "Negro" or "Mongoloid" races, when sports were segregated and African Americans were disenfranchised. It has been over 40 years since those days, although progress may have seemed slow to those victimized and to civil rights advo-cates and organizations. The authors believe that the Reverend Martin Luther King, Jr., would be pleased with the progress to date, but would say the job is far from complete. He had challenged us with the vision of creating a color-blind society. We are not there yet, but we remain convinced that the goal is indeed achievable and that we must keep working toward it.

THE HATE/BIAS CRIME PROBLEM

Introduction

Crimes motivated by hate in the United States have occurred for generations. Most of the immigrant groups that have come to America, including the Irish, Italian, Chinese, Polish, and Puerto Rican, to name a few, have been victimized. Although they are in-digenous peoples, Native Americans have not been immune to hate crimes. The de-scendents of African slaves continue to be victims of bias, discrimination, and crimes motivated by hate. This chapter, however, addresses only crimes motivated by hate in which the victims are Jewish or gay, lesbian, bisexual, or transgender individuals. There is brief mention in this chapter of Arab and Middle Eastern victims of hate/bias crimes following 9/11, but most of the issues related to other racial, ethnic, and reli-gious groups as victims of hate/bias are discussed in the culture-specific chapters (Chapters 5 through 9).

An unprecedented upward spiral of crimes motivated by hate began in the 1990s. Whether there was an actual increase or simply new documentation procedures is not known. In either case, the figures are disturbing. History has shown that increasing di-versity has led to intergroup conflict in countries throughout the world. This fact re-quires police to seriously consider their role in moderating complex intergroup relationships in the communities they serve. Consider the perspective offered by *Los Angeles Times* journalist Robin Wright when she wrote, "The world's now dizzying array of ethnic hot spots—at least four dozen at last count—starkly illustrate how, of all the features of the post–Cold War world, the most consistently troubling are turning out to be the tribal hatreds that divide humankind by race, faith, and nationality (p. A1). Wright indicates that fewer than 10 percent of the world's 191 nations are still ethni-cally or racially homogeneous. Fueled by widespread migration and cultural intermix-ing, "there are now between 7,000 and 8,000 linguistic, ethnic or religious minorities in the world. This mass migration is focused on cities. Its sheer magnitude in an in-creasingly complex and crowded world makes classes and conflict a virtually unavoid-able consequence of modern urban life" (p. A13). Wright identified four key factors that contribute to intergroup conflict: migration, power quest, insecurity, and limited resources. According to Wright:

> In the aftermath of migration, individuals or groups seeking power often exploit ethnic, religious and cultural differences. This drive for personal power and individual gain is characterized as a "power quest." Similarly, the transition that accompanies migration contributes to uncertainty, which can fuel ethnic and religious passions or rivalry. Coping with change, many people seek refuge within "their" group. When combined with limited resources, this heightened sense of group consciousness can exacerbate ethnic/cultural tensions. This economic dimension is critical and must be recognized by community police. (p. A13)

Minorities, already frustrated with their poor economic situation, are more prone to resentment and intolerance of actual or perceived racism and discrimination, especially when the police are suspect. The combination is often the triggering event for a riot.

Victims of hate/bias crimes are particularly sensitive and unsettled because they feel powerless to alter the situation since they cannot change their racial, ethnic, or religious background. Furthermore, the individual involved is not the only victim, because often fear of similar crimes can affect an entire group of citizens. A physical attack on a person because of race, religion, ethnic background, or sexual orientation is a particularly insidious form of violent behavior. Verbal assaults on persons because of others' perceptions of their "differences" are equally distressing to both the victim and society. And, unfortunately, these kinds of incidents can also occur in the law enforcement workplace among coworkers. Treating such occurrences seriously in law enforcement sends a message to community members that the local police agency will protect them. Doing the same within the law enforcement organization sends a vitally important message to all employees.

The criminal justice system, and especially local law enforcement agencies, will become the focus of criticism if attacks are not investigated, resolved, and prosecuted promptly and effectively. A hate/bias crime can send shock waves through the ethnic or racial community at which the act was aimed. These acts create danger, frustration, concern, and anxiety in our communities.

A 1993 study by Northeastern University determined that a large number of hate crime perpetrators are youthful thrill-seekers: 60 percent of offenders committed crimes for the thrill associated with the victimization. The second most common group responsible for hate crimes is reactive offenders who feel that they are answering an attack by their victims. The least common perpetrators, according to the report, are hardcore fanatics who are driven by racial or religious ideology or ethnic bigotry. These individuals are often members of or potential recruits for extremist organizations. Some perpetrators of hate crimes live on the U.S. borders and are petrified by what they consider to be "brown hordes" of Mexicans, Cubans, and Haitians who enter the United States both legally and illegally. They feel that if they cease their militant rhetoric and violence toward these immigrants that the country will be inundated with them. "Mexicans are the largest immigrant group in the country, accounting for 27 percent of foreign born. Their visibility makes them a magnet for anti-immigrant sentiment. Mexicans, being the most numerous, are taking the heat" ("Clinton seeks race dialogue, rhetoric needs to match deeds, say advocates," *Contra Costa Times,* Calif., June 15, 1997, p. A9). There are also many racists living near Native American reservations whose aim is to challenge, through violence, the few remaining treaty rights granted to native people.

Community awareness of hate violence grew rapidly in the United States during the late 1980s and 1990s. Many states commissioned special task forces to recommend ways to control such violence, and new legislation was passed. Despite the abundance of rhetoric deploring acts of bigotry and hate violence, however, few communities have utilized a holistic approach to the problem. Typically, efforts to prevent and respond to such crimes by local agencies have not been coordinated. Indeed, there are many effective programs that deal with a particular aspect of bigotry or hate in a specific setting; however, few models weave efforts to prevent hate violence into the fabric of the community.

Hate crimes are the most extreme and dangerous manifestations of racism. Law enforcement professionals, including neighborhood police officers (the best sources of intelligence information), must be aware of the scope of the hate/bias crime problem from both historical and contemporary perspectives.

A U.S. Commission on Civil Rights, Intimidation, and Violence (1990) report identified several factors that contribute to racial intimidation and violence, including the following:

- Racial integration of neighborhoods, leading to "move-in violence" (explained later in the chapter)
- Deep-seated racial hatred played on by organized hate groups
- Economic competition among racial and ethnic groups
- Poor police response to hate crimes

The unprecedented numbers of Latin American and Asian immigrants moving into neighborhoods that were unprepared for the social, economic, political, and criminal justice system consequences of multicultural living has also been a factor in some communities.

The Scope of Hate Crimes Nationally

Tracking hate crimes, which are typically underreported, did not begin in earnest until 1992. The federal Hate Crime Statistics Act of 1990 encourages states to collect and report hate crime data to the Federal Bureau of Investigation (FBI). The FBI, in partnership with local law enforcement agencies, began collecting data on such incidents and publishes annual reports as part of the Uniform Crime Reporting (UCR) Program. The collection of hate crime information is voluntary, however, and not all law enforcement agencies gather or submit data to the FBI. Making comparisons between years, therefore, may not clearly identify trends. The Bureau of Justice Statistics (BJS) takes the data collected by the FBI regarding hate crimes and prepares comparative reports every 3 years.

The 2002 BJS report reflected that hate crimes in the United States increased by 21 percent, from 8,063 in 2000 to 9,730 in 2001, as reflected in Exhibit 12.1. In 2001, most of the reported single-bias hate crimes were motivated by racial bias (45 percent), followed by biases against ethnicity or national origin (22 percent), religious intolerance (19 percent), and sexual orientation (14 percent), as shown in Exhibit 12.2. The data in the exhibit reflects the tremendous increase in bias-motivated crimes involving ethnicity or national origin following September 11, 2001. There were nine reported multiple-bias incidents that same year.

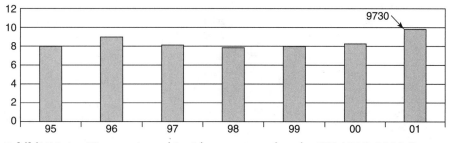

Exhibit 12.1 Bias-motivated incidents reported to the FBI 1995–2001 (In Thousands)
(*Source:* U.S. Department of Justice, Bureau of Justice Statistics, Hate Crime Statistics, 2002)

The report indicated that African Americans—with 2,899 victims of single-bias hate crimes counted in 2001—were by far the largest group of victims, as they have been since the FBI began gathering hate crime statistics. Hate crimes against African Americans rose slightly, from 2,884 incidents in 2000. Typically, among racially motivated incidents, 6 in 10 targeted blacks, 3 in 10 targeted whites, and the remainder targeted Asians or American Indians. After African Americans, the most victimized groups included Jews (1,043 victims), gay men (980 victims), and whites (891 victims) (see Exhibits 12.4, 12.5 and 12.6). The report also showed that 68 percent of hate crimes were committed against people and 32 percent against property, and that white people were the most common offenders in hate crimes—65.5 percent—followed by African Americans at 20.4 percent (BJS, 2002). The most dramatic change noted by the report

There were 8,019 single bias-motivated, criminal incidents reported (not including gender and disability) in 2000 and 9,686 in 2001. Of those, the number motivated:

	2000		**2001**	
	Number	Percent	Number	Percent
By racial prejudice	4337	53.7	4367	44.9
By bias towards ethnicity or national origin	911	11.3	2098	21.6
By religious intolerance	1472	18.3	1828	18.8
By sexual-orientation bias	1299	16.1	1393	14.3
Total	8019		9686	

Notes:
1. The term victim may refer to a person, business, institution, or society as a whole.
2. The term known offender does not imply that the identity of the suspect is known, but only that the race of the suspect has been identified, distinguishing him/her from an unknown offender.
3. A Multiple-bias incident is a hate crime in which two or more offense types were committed as a result of two or more bias motivations.

Exhibit 12.2 Single bias-motivation criminal incidents, 2000 and 2001
(*Source:* BJS, Hate Crime Statistics, 2001)

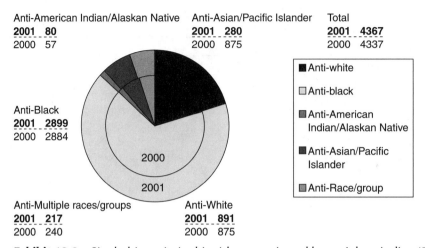

Anti-American Indian/Alaskan Native
2001 80
2000 57

Anti-Asian/Pacific Islander
2001 280
2000 875

Total
2001 4367
2000 4337

Anti-Black
2001 2899
2000 2884

- Anti-white
- Anti-black
- Anti-American Indian/Alaskan Native
- Anti-Asian/Pacific Islander
- Anti-Race/group

Anti-Multiple races/groups
2001 217
2000 240

Anti-White
2001 891
2000 875

Exhibit 12.3   Single-bias criminal incidents motivated by racial prejudice (2001 compared with 2000)
(*Source:* U.S. Department of Justice, Bureau of Justice Statistics, Hate Crime Statistics, 2000 and 2001)

was a more than 1,600 percent increase in reported hate crimes against Muslims—a jump from 28 incidents in 2000 to 481 in 2001; it is likely that this number is low, because most Arabs or Muslims in the United States do not report such crimes to authorities, according to Arab American advocates (see Exhibit 12.3).

As indicated above, following 9/11, the number of hate crimes directed against Muslims nationwide jumped dramatically, according to the FBI figures. Consider the following:

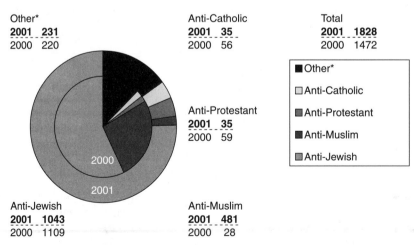

Other*
2001 231
2000 220

Anti-Catholic
2001 35
2000 56

Total
2001 1828
2000 1472

- Other*
- Anti-Catholic
- Anti-Protestant
- Anti-Muslim
- Anti-Jewish

Anti-Protestant
2001 35
2000 59

Anti-Jewish
2001 1043
2000 1109

Anti-Muslim
2001 481
2000 28

*Includes other religious groups, multiple-religion groups, anti-atheism, anti-agnosticism

Exhibit 12.4   Single-bias criminal incidents motivated by religious bias (2001 compared with 2000)
(*Source:* U.S. Department of Justice, Bureau of Justice Statistics, Hate Crime Statistics, 2000 and 2001)

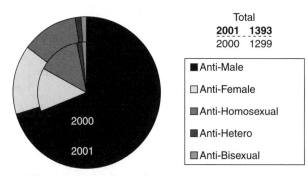

Total
2001   1393
2000   1299

■ Anti-Male

□ Anti-Female

■ Anti-Homosexual

■ Anti-Hetero

□ Anti-Bisexual

Exhibit 12.5   Single-bias criminal incidents motivated by sexual-orientation bias (2001 compared with 2000)
(*Source:* U.S. Department of Justice, Bureau of Justice Statistics, Hate Crime Statistics, 2000 and 2001)

Among the possible hate crimes being investigated by authorities are the fatal shooting Saturday in Arizona of a Sikh gas-station owner (killed for no other reason than he was dark-skinned, bearded and wore a turban and according to County attorney Richard Romley, "he was killed because of hate") and the shooting death the same day of a Pakistani Muslim grocer in Dallas. . . . Authorities nationwide have reported many other possible hate crimes in recent days, including assaults on individuals and attacks on Islamic-linked centers and shops. ("Hate crimes against Muslims rise," 2001, p. A14)

Hate crimes and other acts of vengeance against Muslims and other immigrants from the Middle East skyrocketed nationwide after the Sept. 11 attacks, according to a long-awaited FBI report. Areas with large Muslim populations, such as Southern California, Chicago, Detroit and Washington, reported the most incidents. [M]any immigrants, especially Arab, stayed home in the days after Sept. 11, afraid to go to work or school for fear of retaliation. In many cities, mosques were the target of vandalism. Many Muslims were afraid to report

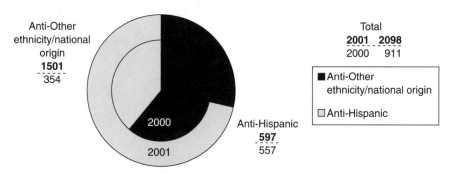

Anti-Other
ethnicity/national
origin
1501
354

Total
2001   2098
2000   911

■ Anti-Other
ethnicity/national origin

□ Anti-Hispanic

Anti-Hispanic
597
557

Exhibit 12.6   Single-bias criminal incidents motivated by ethnicity/national origin (2001 compared with 2000)
(*Source:* U.S. Department of Justice, Bureau of Justice Statistics, Hate Crime Statistics, 2000 and 2001)

hate crimes to the FBI out of fear the bureau would want to investigate them. ("Hate crimes against Muslims soared after 9/11, FBI reports," *Los Angeles Times,* November 26, 2002, p. A22)

In a unpublished study, completed by Bryan Byers in 2004, examining anti-Indian hate crime within the United States using UCR data from 1992-2001, he found:

1. Indians make up but a fraction of all hate crime reports in the United States at about one-half percent (0.5%)

2. Indians tend to identify their perpetrator as "White" more often than other victims (with others are combined) and they also tend to report fewer cases when the perpetrator's identity is "unknown."

3. Concerning location of victimization, it is noteworthy that Indians are more likely than other groups to experience victimization in "bars," in "fields or woods," at a "hotel/motel," and in/on a "highway/road/alley."

4. Conspicuously absent from the list of the 10 states with the most reported and processed Indian hate crime are some states with sizable native populations such as New Mexico (9.5% Indian), North Dakota (4.9% Indian), and South Dakota (8.3% Indian). (p. 8)

Byers indicates in his report that using UCR dataset to research anti-Indian hate crime is problematic, but he was able to make some tentative conclusions which need more study.

The Bureau of Justice Statistics released a report which indicated that "American Indians" experience the highest level of hate crimes per capita according to data from the National Crime Victimization Survey (NCVS). The NCVS study discovered that the overall rate of violent victimization (excluding homicide) for American Indians is 118.8 per 1,000, which is at least two-times the rate of any other racial group (Rennison, 2001, p. 10).

DEFINITION OF HATE CRIME AND HATE INCIDENT

Hate Crime

The federal definition of hate crime addresses civil rights violations under Title 18 U.S.C. Section 45. Although state definitions vary, in general a hate crime is considered to be:

- a criminal act or attempted act,
- against a person, institution, or property,
- that is motivated in whole or in part by the offender's bias against a
  - race,
  - color,
  - religion,
  - gender,
  - ethnic/national origin group,
  - disability status, or
  - sexual orientation group.

Definitions of hate crime often incorporate not only violence against individuals or groups, but also crimes against property such as arson or vandalism, in particular those directed against community centers or houses of worship.

Hate Incident

Hate incidents involve behaviors that, though motivated by bias against a victim's race, religion, ethnic/national origin, gender, age, disability, or sexual orientation, are not criminal acts. Hostile or hateful speech, or other disrespectful or discriminatory behavior, may be motivated by bias but is not illegal. Such incidents become crimes only when they directly incite perpetrators to commit violence against persons or property, or if they place a potential victim in reasonable fear of physical injury (IACP, 1999).

HATE CRIME SOURCE THEORIES

Urban Dynamics Theories

The relationships among the clustering of new immigrant groups, the economy, move-in violence, and hate/bias incidents and crimes in cities are well documented. It is important to understand that hate incidents and crimes often do not occur in a vacuum but are rather part of a larger social and economic interchange.

Clustering and target zone theory. Studies have shown that initially new immigrants tend to locate or cluster where people of their own ethnic and racial background are already established. They tend to congregate in the same areas of the country or within the city to be near relatives or friends; to have assistance in finding housing and jobs and in coping with language barriers; and to find the security of a familiar religion and social institutions. One study on new immigrant grouping by Steven Wallace for the University of California, San Francisco, noted that

> . . . for the first generation or two, ethnic communities are helpful because they provide a sense of continuity for immigrants while easing subsequent generations into American values and society. . . . The existence of an ethnic or immigrant community is obvious evidence that a group has not assimilated. A community represents a place where immigrants are able to associate with others like themselves. An immigrant community provides a safe place to engage in these activities that deviate from dominant norms such as speaking a language other than English, honoring "foreign" symbols of pride, and exhibiting other non-Anglo behavior. Commonly located in low-rent districts, ethnic communities are functionally found where members can afford to live while they work at low wage jobs. (1987, pp. 88–89)

Wallace indicates that the rewards of better education and jobs come with assimilation into mainstream society. Some groups of immigrants can be seen as "temporary inhabitants" of the inner city; they work toward and achieve their goal of moving into the suburbs as they improve their economic situation. As they gain wealth and education, they acquire the same economic and educational advantages as long-time Americans (Wallace, 1992).

Ron Martinelli, a criminologist and former San Jose, California, police officer, discusses a theory called "target zoning," or, as termed by sociologists, the concentric zone theory, shown in Exhibit 12.7. This model of urban ecology explains in simple terms what takes place when new ethnic minorities settle in an existing core area (inner city) that is often already economically depressed. These core areas are typically where low-socioeconomic-class whites, blacks, Hispanics, and established immigrants have settled because housing is cheap (or government subsidized), employment or welfare services are available, and there is some degree of comfort from living with people of one's own race or culture. These areas are often impoverished ghettos, with substandard, older housing, and they are frequently overcrowded, with a high incidence of social conflict and crime, including drug and gang activity. As new immigrants and members of racial and cultural groups move into the core area, they come into conflict with existing members of that community—a phenomenon that has been going on for generations. The newcomers and the established community members compete for housing, jobs, financial resources (e.g., welfare, food stamps), and education. When there is a collapse of affordable health services, lack of affordable housing, and reductions in benefits (cuts in social programs by federal and state authorities), as occurred in the 1990s and again in 2003, conflicts intensify among racial and ethnic groups. These circumstances magnify, and incidents of discrimination, bias, and hate violence increase (Shusta, 1987). Those who are more established want to move out, not just to improve their lot but to escape the conflict. Thus they move to the next ring in the concentric circle. The whole process is then repeated as those in the next circle move to outer circles. The result in many cases is "move-in violence," discussed later in this chapter. Similar processes have also been observed on the scale of entire states. States such as Texas, New York, and California have experienced large-scale immigration for several decades. More recently, a counterflow has been observed wherein native-born

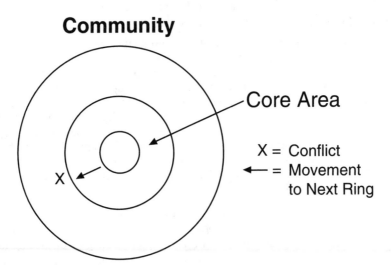

Community

Core Area

X = Conflict
⟵ = Movement
to Next Ring

Exhibit 12.7
Source: California Peace Officer Standards and Training Command College Independent Study: A Model Plan for California Cities Experiencing Multicultural Impact by Robert Shusta, 1987.

white families move from these states to neighboring states, such as Arizona, Oregon, Florida, and Nevada (Frey, 1998). This process can be seen as analogous to white migration to the suburbs, but on a much larger geographic scale.

The economy and hate violence. Poor economic times contribute greatly to hate violence (Wynn, 1987). In many areas of the country, when major industries such as steel and auto manufacturing have downturns, go out of business, or relocate, the likelihood of economic distress among low-skilled and unskilled workers increases. Scapegoating often results when blue-collar jobs are unavailable. The distress that accompanies unemployment and rising prices is often directed toward immigrants and minorities and manifests itself in harassment and violence.

Sociologists indicate that hate frequently stems from being deprived or having one's needs unsatisfied, so the poor despise the rich, the uneducated ridicule the intellectual, and the established ghetto inhabitant hates the new immigrant or refugee who moves into the area. Social scientists argue that the government definition of poverty does not measure the experience of being poor or the changes taking place in inner cities: not only has the number of ghetto poor increased but so has the severity of economic deprivation among them. Ghetto poverty and concentrations of diverse populations in one area often lead to conflict in these neighborhoods. The stresses of urban life, especially in inner cities, give rise to increased incidents of violence, especially in depressed economic conditions and reduced space.

Move-in violence. Move-in violence can occur when people of one ethnicity or race move into a residence or open a business in a neighborhood composed of people from a different race or ethnicity. It can also take place when the new resident is of the same ethnicity or race—for example, a Cuban moving into a Mexican neighborhood or a Caribbean black moving into an African American community. Changing community diversity and demographics can have a significant impact on the community because of hostility based on perceived and real group differences. However, the presence of new migrants or immigrants in a racially or ethnically different neighborhood does not automatically result in intergroup conflict or violence.

Historically, most cases of move-in violence have involved black, Hispanic, or Asian victims who locate housing or businesses in previously all-white suburbs or neighborhoods. Whites have not been the sole perpetrators, however, and have also been victims. For example, in Worcester, Massachusetts (in 1999), and in Sacramento, California (in 2000), Russian immigrants moved into nonwhite neighborhoods and community conflict occurred. New residents or business owners have moved into areas that are primarily black, Hispanic, or Asian and experienced friction with the original residents. According to the U.S. Department of Justice's Community Relations Service, there have been cases of Hispanic migration or immigration into communities that had been presided over for many years by black leaders. In some of these new mixed communities, such as the Los Angeles-area neighborhoods of Lakewood, Watts, and Pomona, Hispanic/Latino community members have sometimes perceived that their concerns are being ignored (Borquist, 2000). Other cases of conflict have involved communities with new immigrants from the Middle East and South Asia. For the past three decades, Middle Easterners have made up one of the fastest-growing immigrant groups in the country, their numbers increasing seven-fold since 1970 compared to a tripling of the overall immigrant population during that period. Nation-wide, the biggest newcomer groups from the Middle East consist of Iranians and Is-raelis, but there has also been a large number of Pakistanis from south Asia.

New immigrants, no matter where they are from, can meet with resentment, bi-ased treatment, and criminal victimization, especially if they appear to be different from the established community into which they move. Crimes directed at persons perceived as different and new to a neighborhood typically range from threats and vandalism to arson and fire bombings. Historically, most cases have involved racist whites attacking their victims out of a desire to preserve racial segregation in their communities. This trend still exists today, but with the changing demographics of the 21st century, we see perpetrators of crimes and victims from many different groups. According to Daryl Borgquist, Media Affairs Officer for the Department of Justice's Community Relations Service,

> White-on-black bias crime [of the] 1960s and 1970s does not reflect the dra-matic demographic changes in the country. The case work at the Community Relations Service has changed dramatically since the 1960s. Asian immigration has accounted for almost half of all U.S. immigration since the late 1960s, meaning that many Asians have settled in communities which never had Asians or only had a few. Cities such as Los Angeles, Houston, New York, and Wash-ington, D.C. (including Prince Georges County, Maryland), to name a few, have had a number of incidents of conflict between Korean grocers or market owners and the black communities in which their stores are located. For example, there has been a protest of a Korean store in D.C. that was firebombed in December of 2000. In Los Angeles, the Korean community was armed and formed a "se-curity group" to protect their stores from violence in the black community. (Borgquist, 2000)

Researchers and hate/bias enforcement officials have found that neighborhood in-tegration, competition for jobs and services, and issues involving "turf" create the pri-mary scenario for hate crimes (McDevitt, 1989; Southern Poverty Law Center, 1987). Social scientists and scholars from other disciplines have referred to "turf" as the "ter-ritorial imperative." Since the beginning of time, the drive to preserve and gain territory has characterized people's need to protect what they believe is their own (i.e., land, area, or family). A relatively homogeneous group feels threatened by the invasion of "others," whether they are refugees, job seekers, or immigrants in search of a better way of life. Suspicion, hostility, and even violence toward the "stranger" characterize human behavior, especially in bad economic times.

Research by Jack McDevitt (1989) found that over a 5-year period, the majority of confirmed bias crime cases in Boston took place when the victim was in a neighbor-hood where he or she "did not belong." "Young people in communities with exclusion-ary housing patterns often view themselves as guardians of the invisible walls that mark their community, and actively seek to drive away 'intruders' who are 'invading' their 'turf' " (New York State Governor's Task Force on Bias Crime Report, 1988, p. 13). Again, no one group has a monopoly on hate crimes: perpetrators of such offenses come from every racial, ethnic, and religious background. The criminal justice system must be sensitive to changing community demographics. It is important that new groups are assisted in their assimilation into the community.

Mini-Case Study: The Philadelphia Police Department Conflict Prevention and Resolution Team

The city of Philadelphia tested a way to prevent move-in violence in 1986 by utilizing a newly created police unit, which still exists, called the Conflict Prevention and Resolution (CPR) Team. The unit trains officers to investigate and prevent racial incidents. They work in partnership with detectives and other law enforcement officials to conduct a complete and thorough investigation of all hate-related incidents and crimes. Their goal is to maintain a proactive posture in the enforcement of Pennsylvania's Ethnic Intimidation Statute by investigating hate incidents that are motivated by a victim's race, color, religion, national origin, or sexual orientation. They also develop educational awareness and prevention programs that address bias crime, racism, and other forms of bigotry.

One of the most successful proactive programs undertaken by this unit is the Pre-Move Survey. The program involves CPR officers performing a door-to-door canvass in the neighborhood to communicate with the "majority" population prior to a "minority" family assuming residence. The program is predicated on the premise that potential conflict can be averted when people residing in a community see that the police are interested in the welfare and rights of new neighbors. The survey gauges the sentiment of the established residents toward the ethnic or racial group in question. It also alerts the local police district hierarchy of the potential for trouble in a given location. This proactive approach gives notice to potential antagonists that the police department and city government are aware of the situation and will not tolerate any criminality perpetrated against the new neighbors. The sources of information for the CPR unit about the possibility of a minority moving into a neighborhood with a different ethnic or racial majority are the Human Relations Commission, realtors, social services agencies, politicians, public servants, and other police officers. Certainly, many neighborhoods have been integrated without the unit's assistance and without incident. However, the Philadelphia Police Department is proud of the fact that there has never been an ethnically motivated criminal act perpetrated against new neighbors when the CPR unit has performed this procedure prior to the move-in. Philadelphia police officials do not claim that racial relations are significantly better because of the CPR unit, but they feel that their outreach approach has contributed to the reduction of racial violence in their city. The department has printed pocket guide cards to assist patrol officers and supervisors in explaining the ethnic intimidation laws to neighborhood residents. It has also produced and displayed multilingual posters within the community to explain CPR's functions and responsibilities.

VICTIMS OF HATE CRIMES

Targets of Hate Crimes

The psychocultural origin of hate crimes stems from human nature itself. To hate means to dislike passionately or intensely—to have an extreme aversion or hostility toward another person, idea, or object. Hate can have a benign manifestation, such as when one hates evil, or bad weather, or certain foods, or it can have an abnormal expression when it becomes obsessive or is wrongly directed at someone who has done no harm. People can be culturally conditioned to hate those who are different from them because of their places of origin, looks, beliefs, or preferences. As the song in the musical *South Pacific* reminds us, "We have to be taught to hate and fear. We have to be taught from year to year." Crimes and acts of hate serve as frightening reminders to vulnerable citizens that they may not take safety for granted. Collectively, they begin to develop a mentality that hate crimes can take place anywhere—in streets, in neighborhoods, at workplaces, and even in their homes.

There are innumerable examples of hate crimes that have victimized blacks, Asians, and Hispanics. Clearly, such hate goes back for many generations. These are discussed in Part Two: Cultural Specifics for Law Enforcement. The following sections will address Jews and lesbian, gay, bisexual, and transgender people as victims of hate or bias crimes.

JEWS AND ANTI-SEMITISM

Jews

Jews belong to a religious and cultural group, although they have sometimes been incorrectly labeled as constituting a separate racial group. Jews have experienced discrimination, persecution, and violence throughout history because their religious beliefs and practices set them apart from the majority. Even when they were totally assimilated (i.e., integrated into society), as was true in Germany early in the 20th century, they were still not accepted as full citizens and eventually experienced the ultimate hate crime—genocide. The term anti-Semitism means "against Semites," which literally includes Jews and Arabs. Popular use of this term, however, refers to anti-Jewish sentiment.

European anti-Semitism had religious origins: Jews did not accept Jesus Christ as the son of God and were portrayed as betrayers and even killers of Christ. This accusation gave rise to religious anti-Semitism and what Christians saw as justification for anti-Jewish acts. In the past three decades, there have been great strides by religious leaders to eliminate centuries of prejudice. For example, a 1965 Roman Catholic decree (the Nostra Aetate) stated that the church did not hold Jews responsible for the death of Christ. The decree, written by the Second Vatican Council under the leadership of the pope, encouraged people to abandon blaming Jews and instead work for stronger links and increased understanding between the religions. Despite some progress in ecumenical relations, there are still individuals who, 2,000 years after the birth of Christ, believe that Jews today are responsible for Christ's death.

Of more recent origin is another type of anti-Semitism, which falls under what some would label as anti-Zionism (i.e., against the establishment of the state of Israel as a homeland for Jews). Although politically oriented, this type of anti-Semitism still makes references to "the Jews" and equates "Jews" with the suppression of the Palestinian people. Finally, racially based anti-Semitism originated in 19th-century pre-Nazi ideology, which claimed that Jews were an inferior race. In their attempts to eliminate the Jewish "race," the Nazis considered people "impure" if one grandparent or even great-grandparent in their family was Jewish.

Prevalence of Anti-Semitic Crimes

In 2000, 44 states and the District of Columbia reported 1,606 (series 3 in exhibit) anti-Semitic incidents, according to the Anti-Defamation League (ADL), a 4 percent increase over 1999, as is shown in Exhibit 12.8. Anti-Semitic activity reported in 2000 comprised 877 (series 1 in exhibit) acts of harassment (intimidation, threats, and assaults) and 729 (series 2 in exhibit) of vandalism (property damage as well as arson and cemetery desecration). The small increase in anti-Semitic incidents is partly attributable to acts apparently related to the turmoil in the Middle East in 2000. According to the FBI's 2001 annual report on hate crimes, more than 75.3 percent of all crimes perpetrated on the basis of religion were directed against Jews and Jewish religious institutions (ADL, 2002). From 1987 to 1994, the annual ADL Audit totals showed a steady trend of annual increase. Since 1995, however, the annual totals have shown a general decline. Most recently, in the 4-year period 1997 to 2000, the annual totals have been confined within the range of approximately 1,550–1,600. Thus, despite the slight increase, the 2000 Audit maintains this recent pattern (ADL, 2000, 2001). The five states usually reporting the most anti-Semitic incidents are those with the largest Jewish populations and thus the most targets—New York, California, New Jersey, Massachusetts, and Florida.

Anti-Semitic Groups and Individuals. Several different types of groups in the United States have exhibited anti-Semitic attitudes, and some of the most extreme groups have committed hate crimes against Jews. The most glaringly anti-Semitic organizations are white supremacist groups, such as the Ku Klux Klan (KKK), the Aryan Nation, White

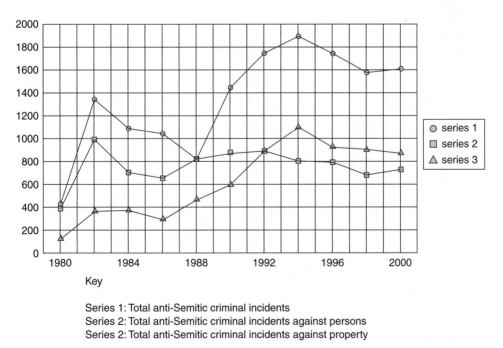

Key

Series 1: Total anti-Semitic criminal incidents
Series 2: Total anti-Semitic criminal incidents against persons
Series 2: Total anti-Semitic criminal incidents against property

Exhibit 12.8   Audit of anti-Semitic incidents year-by-year National totals 1980–2000

Aryan Resistance (WAR), the Order, the Posse Comitatus, the Covenant and the Sword, the Arm of the Lord, and neo-Nazi skinheads (discussed further in Chapter 13). These groups tend to hate all who are different from them but focus a great deal of attention on blacks and Jews. Some messianic individuals who believe that Armageddon (the end of the world) is imminent have been known to threaten Jews by phone or mail, but rarely have these threats been carried out. These people believe that Jews need to repent and see themselves as instruments of God, connected to the coming of the end of the world. Another aspect of anti-Semitism has been demonstrated by those who argued that it was this country's support of Israel that led to the September 11, 2001, attacks. Some hate groups used this argument to stir up anti-Jewish feelings and to erode sympathy and support for Jews and Israel at their organization's rallies and within the general public. In addition, those who are vehemently pro-Arab and anti-Israel may exhibit strong anti-Jewish attitudes. While it is not common for anti-Zionist attitudes to result in acts of violence against Jews in the United States as it is in Europe, Jewish Americans, like Arab Americans, can nevertheless become targets during Middle Eastern crises. Finally, in times of recession, Jews are often blamed for the economic decline, and the notion of Jewish "influence" (i.e., the baseless charge that Jews control the media, the banks, and even the world economy) provides a convenient scapegoat. It is not within the scope of this section to delve into these myths, but we point out that there is widespread harmful misinformation about Jews that anti-Semites continue to spread.

Jewish Community Concerns

Around the holiest days of the Jewish year (Rosh Hashanah and Yom Kippur, occurring in the early fall), there can also be heightened anxiety among some community members regarding security. Indeed, many synagogues hire extra security during times of worship over this 10-day holiday period. Acts of defilement can occur in synagogues and other Jewish institutions at random times as well. Acts of defilement and manifestations of prejudice bring back painful memories for Jews who experienced violent expressions of anti-Semitism in other countries, especially those who lived through the Holocaust; some of the memories and fears have been passed on to subsequent generations. At the same time, some people may overreact to an insensitive remark that stems from ignorance on the part of the speaker rather then malicious anti-Semitism. Some people may not understand that a swastika painted by teenagers on a building does not necessarily precede any acts of anti-Jewish violence. Yet a swastika almost always evokes a fearful reaction among many Jewish community members because of the historical significance of the symbol.

Police officers must understand that different segments of the Jewish community feel vulnerable to anti-Semitism, and therefore officers are advised to listen to and take seriously Jews' expressions of concern and fear. At the same time, they need to explain that sometimes acts of vandalism are isolated and are not targeting any group in particular (e.g., many skinheads or "thugs" are unhappy with their lot in life and tend to hate everyone). Finally, officers who take reports from citizens should reassure them that their local law enforcement agency views hate crimes and incidents seriously and that extra protection will be provided if the need arises.

What Law Enforcement Can Do. By discussing the concerns and fears of some Jewish community members, we do not imply that all Jewish citizens are overly concerned for their safety. In fact, a large percentage of American Jews do not even identify as Jews and do not share a collective or community consciousness with other Jews. At the other extreme are people who interpret events or remarks as anti-Semitic rather than as ignorance or insensitivity. Whatever the case, police officers should be aware that anti-Semitism has a long and active history, and, even if some fears appear to be exaggerated, they have a basis in reality.

Officers can take some steps to establish rapport and provide protection in Jewish communities when the need arises:

1. When an officer hears of an act that can be classified as a hate crime toward Jews, it should be investigated, tracked, and dealt with as such. Dismissing acts of anti-Semitism as petty crime will result in a lack of trust on the part of the community.

2. When hate crimes and incidents are perpetrated against other groups in the community (e.g., gay, African American, Asian American groups), officers should alert Jewish community leaders immediately. Their institutions may be the next targets.

3. Officers should be aware of groups and individuals who distribute hate literature on people's doorsteps. Publications such as *Racial Loyalty,* for example, target Jews and "people of color" and accuse Jews of poisoning the population. A book published by the same organization, *On the Brink of a Bloody Racial War,* has been left on many Jews' doorsteps. Even if no violence occurs, the recipients of such hate literature become very fearful.

4. In cooperation with local organizations (e.g., Jewish Community Relations Councils, ADL), officers can provide information through joint meetings on ways that individuals can heighten the security of Jewish institutions (e.g., information on nonbreakable glass, lighting of facilities in evenings).

5. Law enforcement officials should be familiar with the dates of the Jewish calendar, especially when the High Holidays (Rosh Hashanah and Yom Kippur) occur. Some people are concerned about safety and protection during events at which large groups of Jews congregate.

6. Finally, officers may contact a Jewish umbrella organization in the community to assist them in helping to send necessary messages to local Jewish institutions and places of worship. Two organizations in particular are worth noting: the national JCRC (Jewish Community Relations Council) and the ADL. The JCRC has representative organizations in almost every major city in the United States. This organization, the regional ADL organizations, and the Jewish Federations can be of great assistance to law enforcement in disseminating information to members of the Jewish community.

Because of their history, some Jews expect anti-Semitic incidents, and the reality is that there are still anti-Semites in our society. According to Riva Gambert, former associate director of the JCRC of the Greater East Bay December, 2003, whether an act is simply insensitive or whether it is indeed a hate crime, an officer still has to be responsive to generated fears and community concerns. An officer's ability to calm fears as well as to investigate threats thoroughly will result in strong relations between law enforcement officials and Jewish community members.

LESBIAN, GAY, BISEXUAL, AND TRANSGENDER VICTIMIZATION

Hate crimes targeting lesbian, gay, bisexual, or transgender (LGBT) individuals are distinct from other bias crimes because they target a group made up of every other category discussed within this textbook. In the United States today, there are organizations whose membership includes gay Jews, Catholics, Mormons, Buddhists, Armenians, Latinos/as, African Americans, Asians and Pacific Islanders, and virtually every other ethnic, racial, or religious group.

Homophobia

Gays and Lesbians Initiating Dialogue for Equality (GLIDE) defines homophobia as "an irrational fear, hatred, ignorance, or general discomfort with gay, lesbian, bisexual, or transgender persons, topics, or issues." Homophobia/homophobic acts can run the full spectrum from antigay jokes to physical battery resulting in injury or death. The former Executive Director of the National Gay and Lesbian Task Force stated that

> Racism and homophobia are byproducts of a society that does not value diversity. A climate exists in our country that devalues people of color as well as gay, lesbian, bisexual and transgender people. Racism and homophobia are symptoms of the same disease and the disease is named intolerance. ("Murder of Gay, African-American Man," 2000)

Homophobic Violence. Every year in the United States, thousands of LGBT persons are harassed, beaten, or murdered solely because of their sexual orientation or gender identity. According to the National Gay and Lesbian Task Force, hate violence against LGBT people has increased dramatically over the past decade, even when violent crime declined in the United States ("LGBT violence increase," 2000).

The FBI's "Hate Crime Statistics 2001" indicated that bias crimes based on sexual orientation made up 14.3 percent of all reported hate crimes, accounting for the fourth-highest category (after race, ethnic/national origin, and religion). This is an increase of almost 7 percent in the number of homophobic crimes from 2000. Relying on data from 12,122 law enforcement agencies in 48 states and the District of Columbia, the FBI reported 1,317 crimes motivated by sexual orientation bias. Significantly, the National Coalition of Anti-Violence Programs (NCAVP), relying on data from only 25 jurisdictions, reported 1,965 incidents of hate bias based on sexual orientation or gender identity, which indicates that serious underreporting takes place ("FBI Hate Crimes Data," 2001). NCAVP is a network of 26 antiviolence organizations that monitor and respond to incidents of bias, domestic, HIV-related, and other forms of violence affecting the LGBT community.

California reported the highest number of homophobic hate crimes, 23.1 percent of total hate incidents, compared to the third-highest, New York, with 7.3 percent. Along with New Jersey, Massachusetts and Michigan, these five states made up almost 50 percent of all the homophobic incidents reported in the United States.

Overkill. Anti-LGBT murders are often easily distinguished from other murders by the level of brutality involved. LGBT murder victims are often dismembered, stabbed multiple times, or severely bludgeoned ("Overkill," 2000). A 1994 study conducted by the NCAVP determined that almost 60 percent of the 152 anti-LGBT murders between 1992–94 involved "extraordinary violence." The following are just a few horrific examples of this phenomenon:

- The bodies of two women, ages 24 and 26, were found in 1996 at a secluded campsite in the Shenandoah National Park with their wrists bound and their throats slashed. A Virginia grand jury indictment in 2002 found that the killer had intentionally selected the victims based on his having stated that they "deserved to die because they were lesbian whores" ("NGLTF Applauds Federal Indictment," 2002).

- In 2002, the lead investigator in the murder of a 37-year-old Santa Barbara man stated that the suspect was charged with a hate crime because he had doused the victim with gasoline and set him on fire because of the suspect's hatred of gay people ("NGLTF and Pacific Pride Foundation," 2002).

- In 2003, the Alabama Supreme Court set an execution date for a death row inmate who helped two other men rob and kill a 60-year-old gay man, stabbing him 78 times before slashing his throat repeatedly, nearly decapitating him ("Alabama Supreme Court," 2003, p. 30).

- In 2000, a 20-year-old Los Angeles man fatally stabbed another man 138 times because he was gay ("News in Review," 2003).

- In 2002, two transgender women, 18 and 19 years old, were found in the front seat of the 19-year-old's car less than a block from her apartment by Washington, D.C. police. Each victim had been shot at least 10 times ("Task Force Calls," 2002).

As of 2003, 27 states and the District of Columbia have hate crime laws that include sexual orientation. There is no federal law that provides for an additional penalty enhancement for hate-motivated homophobic (anti-LGBT) crimes. However, in 1994, Congress passed the Hate Crimes Sentencing Act, which applies only to federal crimes. The Act allows judges to consider homophobia as a motive during sentencing.

The Phenomenon of Underreporting

Various reasons have been postulated for the phenomenon of LGBT hate crimes being seriously underreported to law enforcement, including the following:

Law enforcement is not required to collect and report LGBT hate/bias crimes.
Under the Hate Crimes Statistics Act, local law enforcement agencies are not required to report hate crimes to the FBI, although some states do mandate some type of statewide reporting. This is one reason that national statistics underreport sexual orientation hate crimes. For example, the FBI reported just three murders of gay and lesbian people motivated by hate. Yet the National Coalition of Anti-Violence Programs (NCAVP) reported that in Detroit alone, eight people were murdered because of their sexual orientation or gender identity. In further contrast, the NCAVP reported 29 murders motivated by homophobia ("FBI Hate Crimes Data," 2001).

LGBT individuals do not report being victimized. Unwillingness to "come out" (be identified as LGBT) by reporting these crimes to authorities is often cited in newspaper articles as a reason for underreporting (Berrill, 1986). If this were the only factor, then the phenomenon would not remain constant within metropolitan areas with large, open LGBT populations and organizations that provide outreach on such issues. In fact, data from the Los Angeles Gay and Lesbian Center, the primary agency that provides victim services and documentation of homophobic hate violence for L.A. County (including the independent city of West Hollywood, whose population comprises approximately 35 percent LGBT residents), clearly demonstrates that the underreporting of hate crimes is continuing into the new century. The truth is that many members of the LGBT community remain mistrustful of the police or suspect that their reporting of such incidents will not result in any significant action by law enforcement (Grobeson, 2003).

Other motivations for crimes. Though victims' advocates believe that a crime in which bias was a *primary* motivation should be classified as a hate crime, law enforcement officers are often unwilling to do so if there is any other motive in addition to bias (Choudhury, 2003). These advocates point out that law enforcement personnel have a practice of looking for "pick-up crimes." This refers to the tendency of some law enforcement personnel to drop the hate crime motivation of any incident in which an element of *any* other crime is involved (e.g., assault with a deadly weapon or robbery).

Conflicting police training policies. Another interesting facet of the issue of underreporting is that law enforcement personnel who receive training in the handling of hate crimes are often instructed *not* to ask about a person's sexual orientation, so assaults and batteries motivated by homophobia are often unclassified as hate crimes. The reluctance of some LGBT victims to reveal the homophobic component of a crime to police, either because of their being closeted or out of fear of double victimization, coupled with the numerous cases in which a victim reports a crime as bias-based but police refuse to classify it as such, leads to low criminal justice figures on homophobic hate crime (Choudhury, 2003). According to David S. Buckel, senior staff attorney for Lambda Legal, "Law enforcement is a key component in combating violence against lesbian, gay, bisexual, and transgender people. Like everybody else, we expect appropriate action when reporting an assault; no one should be worried that the police will make matters worse."

Transgender Hate Crimes

Transgender is an umbrella term that is used to encompass every group that involves gender identity or cross-gender presentation. These groups include cross-dressers, who are most often heterosexual men who cross-dress on occasion; queens and kings, who are homosexual men and women who may cross-dress occasionally or exclusively; and transsexuals, whose gender identity is different than their birth sex.

National attention was first drawn to the issue of transgender hate crimes during the 2000 Academy Award show, when the "Best Actress" award was given for the portrayal of Brandon Teena in *Boys Don't Cry.* Brandon, a 21-year-old woman living as a man, was brutally murdered on New Year's Eve in 1993. On Christmas Day 1993,

Brandon was kidnapped by two ex-cons, repeatedly raped, and brutally beaten in Nebraska. The men threatened to kill Brandon if he reported the crimes. The sheriff, referring to Brandon as an "it," did nothing to protect him. The men later hunted Brandon down, stabbing him in the stomach before executing him with a gunshot under the chin. The movies *Boys Don't Cry* and *The Brandon Teena Story* portrayed the hate and violence faced by those who do not conform to gender expectations.

Perhaps the most significant trend within national hate crime reporting is the increase in the number of incidents involving transgender individuals. There are several explanations, including increased visibility of this segment of the LGBT population, but the statistics are still disturbing. For example, in Los Angeles, incidents against transgender persons doubled between 2000 and 2001. Hate crime reports also clarify that the highest level of violence in homophobic crime is that perpetrated against those in the transgender population (Choudhury, 2003). In New York, 2001 statistics showed that transgender people increased to make up 13 percent of all victims reporting bias incidents (New York Anti-Violence Project Report, 2002). It is important to note that transgender individuals may be reluctant to report crimes against them because they believe that law enforcement personnel will treat them as a criminal rather than a victim (Manley, 2003).

Nationally, 2002 was the deadliest year for transgender persons in the United States, with a 30 percent increase in antitransgender murders over the previous year. Statistically, transgender people are 16 times more likely to be murdered than the general population and three times more likely than African American males, which is the next closest category ("Literary Stereotyping," 2003, p. 88). Of transgender murder victims in the United States, nonwhite youths are disproportionately represented (Manley, 2003).

Though there have been numerous hate crimes against transgender individuals throughout the United States, few have garnered the national media attention of the 2001 and 2002 murders of two transgender teenagers:

> In June of 2001, Fred Martinez, a 16-year-old "two-spirited" Navajo youth who was well known and liked within his small community, was chased down, brutally beaten and left to die of blood loss and exposure in Cortez, Colorado. The murderer was caught because he bragged to friends that he had "beat up a fag." ("The News," 2003, p. 17)

> Eddie Araujo, a transgender Newark teen, was killed by three men who found out he was anatomically male. The 17-year-old, 100-pound Araujo was beaten for hours and strangled in a garage then his body buried in a shallow grave near Placerville, CA, 150 miles away. From all witness accounts, the young men discovered that Araujo, whom they knew as "Lida," was anatomically male after a guest went into the bathroom with Araujo. ("No more arrests," 2002, p. A13)

Tools for Law Enforcement (Transgender Protocol). Most law enforcement personnel are unlikely to have had any significant contact with members of the transgender community prior to beginning their careers. The vast majority of problems for police officers in their encounters with transgender individuals involve lack of education, training, department policy and procedure, or protocol. Interactions between law enforcement and this community can be enhanced if protocols provide that officers are instructed to refer to the transgender person in the gender pronoun for which they are dressed or seeking to be perceived. This is particularly true of male-to-female transgender persons due to the length of time required for hormonal changes, because female-to-male transsexuals are often undetected due to facial hair growth, and because those agencies that enforce prostitution laws often have interaction with transgender (male-to-female) prostitutes. In training, a common-sense scenario is particularly effective: If someone spends hours each morning applying makeup, constructing a hairdo, and dressing in a manner to present themselves as a person of the opposite gender, then they consider it disrespectful and unprofessional when a law enforcement officer ignores their extended efforts (by referring to a transgender man in woman's attire as "sir" instead of "miss" or "ma'am," for example). Although transgender advocates point out that there is a great deal of verbal and physical abuse by officers, this simple solution addresses the single largest source of disputes between law enforcement and the transgender community (Grobeson, 2003). It is incumbent upon police administrators to ensure that people are treated properly.

If an agency is truly progressive, then policy should dictate that, for example, if an individual is living as a woman, the first paragraph of any narrative should state that the person is transgender, and then the individual should be referred to as "she" throughout the remainder of the report. (This does not include statistical or booking pages, which should be based upon genitalia.)

It is equally important that hate crime reports document the perspective of the perpetrator as well as the victim in attacks on transgender individuals. Most homophobic incidents targeting transgender individuals include epithets such as "You fucking queer." It is important for reporting, investigation, and accurate statistical data that these incidents be documented as targeting persons because they are gay, transgender, or both (Manley, 2003).

It is suggested that large police agencies have personnel specifically assigned to investigate hate crimes against LGBT individuals. Most agencies assign hate crimes to investigators, often to those assigned to handle "crimes against persons," as a corollary duty. "If you assign a robbery detective to investigate hate crimes, you will wind up with a robbery filing," says Grobeson. At the very least, agencies should ensure that those who investigate such crimes receive appropriate training.

Military Police

Despite the "Don't ask, Don't tell" policy put into place under former President Bill Clinton, the most horrific homophobic hate crimes to date have been committed by military personnel against fellow service members. Consider the following:

> In 2001, the military watchdog Servicemembers Legal Defense Network (SLDN) documented 1,075 cases of anti-gay harassment in addition to a record number of 1,250 discharges of men and women suspected of being gay, lesbian or bisexual. ("Operation Lift the Ban," 2002, p. 42)

> In 1999, Private First Class Barry Winchell was bludgeoned to death with a baseball bat by fellow soldiers while asleep in his bed in the barracks at Fort Campbell, Kentucky. Winchell had been harassed mercilessly by fellow soldiers for months prior to his murder, which occurred after an army sergeant violated the "Don't ask" policy and inquired about Winchell's sexual orientation. ("NGLTF Calls for Full Investigation," 1999)

The same year as the murder of PFC Winchell, the SLDN documented a 120 percent increase in reports of antigay harassment, including death threats, within the armed forces. The military's stated policy was eventually expanded to "Don't ask, Don't tell, Don't pursue, Don't harass."

It is important that FBI agents, military police, and law enforcement agencies that have adjacent military installations become familiar with organizations such as SLDN as well as updated policies issued by the Department of Defense (DOD). Military police officers should be aware that in response to the public outcry over the handling of the Winchell case, the DOD issued an action plan for each of the military services to address relevant (anti-LGBT) issues, including:

- Eliminating mistreatment, harassment, and inappropriate comments or gestures
- Training
- Reporting of harassment
- Enforcement of policies prohibiting harassment
- Measurement of antiharassment program effectiveness

Campus Police

Campus police need to be aware that many states have enacted "Safe Schools" laws mandating campus environments that are free of harassment and discrimination where no student is subjected to abuse or a hostile learning environment. In the last year, several students who were not protected by administrators or were subjected to unequal restrictions have sued their schools, holding administrators liable for failing to provide an environment free of hostility; these lawsuits have resulted in expensive verdicts. This liability is easily expanded to those campuses that maintain police or a security force. Take for example:

In a precedent-setting case, in 1996 a federal appellate court in Wisconsin ruled that a gay student's rights to equal protection were violated when school officials refused to protect him from anti-gay abuse. A federal jury found the school officials liable, and he subsequently was awarded over $900,000 in a settlement of the lawsuit. The young man had endured four years of brutal anti-gay abuse, including being subjected to a severe beating that required surgery, being assaulted and mock raped in class, and being shoved into a urinal and urinated on. School officials responded that if "you are going to be so openly gay, you have to learn to expect this." ("Wisconsin gay student," 1996)

In 2002, Washoe County School District in Reno, Nevada, paid out over $450,000 for failing to protect a gay student. Two students strung a lasso around his neck and threatened to drag him from their pick-up truck [as was done to African American hate crime victim James Byrd in Texas]; his school principal repeatedly demanded that he hide his sexual orientation, stating, "I won't have you acting like a fag"; two school police officers witnessed him being punched in the face six times by another student and then tried to discourage him from reporting the incident. ("Coming Down Hard on Hate," 2002, p. 46)

In 2002, the Titusville Area School District in Pennsylvania paid out $312,000 for failing to protect a gay student who suffered for five years from pervasive anti-gay abuse. ("Youth to Get Landmark Settlement," 2002)

According to a study by The National Mental Health Association (NMHA) in 2002, antigay bullying is widespread in America's schools, with more than half of the teens surveyed reporting that every day they hear other students being taunted. The study involved interviews of 760 youth ages 12 to 17 nationwide and found that antigay bullying occurs in many forms and is directed not only at students who are gay but also at students perceived to be gay. "For kids that are bullied, their mental health and education are at serious risk," said Michael Faenza, NMHA association president and CEO. "Gay and lesbian teens are at high risk because their distress is a direct result of hatred and prejudice that surrounds them." The harassment also increases the risk of bigger problems such as skipping school, running away, and even suicide, Faenza said. The study found that 85 percent of those polled said overweight kids are picked on the most, followed by gay students or those thought to be gay, 78 percent, and kids who dress differently, 76 percent ("Anti-gay bullying prevalent," 2002, p. A20).

It is important to note that law enforcement, particularly campus police, are becoming more involved in these situations, and are expected to complete official documentation regarding alleged violations and physical assaults based on a student's perceived or actual sexual orientation or gender identity.

It is imperative that officers be aware, both professionally and with regard to their own children, that across the United States the use of the word "gay" in a derogatory manner (as well as an upsurge in the use of "faggot") is the most common epithet on K–12 campuses. Activities, clothing, appearance, and actions that are viewed as "stupid," "bad," or "uncool" are referred to as "That's so gay!" or "Don't be so gay!"

All police agencies that have educational facilities within their jurisdiction need to be cognizant of the increasing trend of high schools to create safe environments for LGBT students. The creation of Gay–Straight Alliances (GSA) not only presents a quagmire of hotly contentious protests and debates that require peacekeeping, they often are a prelude to incidents of juvenile hate crimes. As of 2002, there were 1,681 GSA groups on high school campuses throughout the country, with 245 in California, 222 in Massachusetts, and 2 in Alabama ("Before, It Was Cute," 2003, p. 37).

Perpetrators of Homophobic Crime

Although there are many cases nationwide of individuals attacking LGBT person(s) verbally and/or physically, Grobeson suggests that most gay-bashing suspects fit specific profiles such as being a gang member or member of a white supremacist group. Sometimes gangs incorporate gay-bashing into their new member initiation. White supremacists (including neo-Nazi, skinheads, and the like) advocate violence against LGBT persons. It is important to note that those who engage in homophobic acts almost always engage in actions that discriminate against other groups as well.

Police Relations with Gay and Lesbian Communities

Historically, in most cities and counties in the United States, relations between the police and the gay and lesbian communities have been strained. Many LGBT persons believe that the police regard them as deviants, criminals, and second-class citizens who are unworthy of protection or equal rights. Because of this perception, many gay and lesbian crime victims do not report crimes to the police or cooperate with investigations. Even though negative attitudes and stereotypes will probably continue, progressive police departments have found that communication and mutual respect between the department and gay and lesbian communities are in the best interests of all concerned.

Examples of police departments in which outreach and communication have resulted in cooperation between the agencies and the gay community include San Francisco, Boston, New York, and Baltimore. These departments have observed a noticeable difference in reporting by lesbian and gay crime victims, fewer complaints of police abuse, and a general improvement in relations between law enforcement and gay and lesbian communities.

Researcher Kevin Berrill (1992) observed that there are numerous ways to improve relationships between the justice system and gay and lesbian groups. One of the keys to good relations, according to Berrill, is regular, institutionalized communication at the department, in committees and councils, and in public forums. In addition, he mentions the following:

- The creation of task forces and councils to establish ongoing dialogue and networking on important issues.

- Public forums that allow police officials to meet the LGBT community and help officials to recognize that they are a constituency with legitimate needs and concerns.

- The appointment of a police official to be a liaison with the LGBT community to respond to complaints and requests.

- The involvement of prosecutors in the development of policies, procedures, communications, and awareness training to improve relations between the criminal justice system and LGBT groups and individuals.

Almost every community has extremist and even militant segments, and the LGBT community is no exception. Some activists or activist groups, often those advocating for increases in local AIDS-related funding and research, may require additional attention and special interaction with local law enforcement. The goal of the agency liaison and management should be to avoid costly litigation and to communicate effectively with persons representing such groups. Departments should have an assigned liaison officer meet with these groups in an attempt to agree on acceptable behavior before any public demonstration occurs. Some groups obtain press coverage by orchestrating arrests by the police; in such cases, liaison and close monitoring by field supervisors, a press relations officer, a police video unit, and a department manager would be an absolute necessity.

This methodology has been successful with agencies in the San Francisco Bay Area, resulting in no physical confrontation with groups, no negative press or photos, and no legal action. However, even the best police outreach efforts may prove ineffective. For example, some activist groups have refused to communicate with police during their "actions." Nevertheless, police officers should not permit negative publicity from previous incidents with any group to stop them from attempting to make positive contact prior to scheduled public events. The willingness of the police to work with any community group, particularly LGBT activist groups, always results in positive publicity for police managers and their departments.

Conclusion

The handling and investigation of hate crimes require specialized and unique expertise. The epidemic of hate crimes will continue unabated as long as it is not addressed proactively by law enforcement management. It is important for law enforcement administrators to realize that they can be subjected to litigation and even punitive damages for the actions of their subordinates if they fail to provide proactive policies or take affirmative stances in regard to officer training or discipline (vicarious liability). It is equally important that military and campus police officers know the laws and establish protocol for preventing and investigating crimes motivated by hate for LGBT individuals. Kerry Lobel, former director of NGLTF, said, "When a hate crime occurs, every single one of us is diminished, regardless of our race, our religion, our sexual orientation. The very thing that separates hate crimes from other crimes of violence is that we are selected because of the community we represent. Hate crimes are meant to tear at the very fabric of our society" ("One Year," 1999).

WAR-RELATED HATE CRIMES

War-related hate crimes are not new in America. They took place during the French-Indian War, the Plains Wars against Native Americans, the Mexican-American and Spanish-American Wars, both world wars, and the wars in Korea and Indochina; in all these cases, Americans whose ancestry linked them with the enemy became victims of hate crimes.

Each year on the anniversary of the Pearl Harbor bombing, Japanese-Americans become targets of bias and, in some cases, hate violence; many Japanese-American parents are afraid to send their children to school on that day. The Gulf Wars in the early 1990s and in 2003 followed the patterns of previous wars with respect to the perceived enemy (i.e., Arab Americans were the targets of hate violence). There were many examples of Muslims reporting harassment and verbal abuse. Others reported not being able to wear their kufi, a small, round hat identifying them as Muslim, because they did not feel safe. The American Arab Anti-Discrimination Committee indicates that this unfortunate trend usually follows any conflict in the Middle East. More serious hate violence occurred in September 2001 immediately after the attacks by terrorists in New York and Washington when hundreds of incidents of beatings, vandalism, and attacks on stores and mosques were reported. The war on terrorism has made the observance of Islam a liability for a growing number of people in the United States Conservative pundits and religious leaders regularly label Islam a religion of terror. Most Americans, however, realize that the Muslims who were behind the attacks of September 11 were part of an extremist group and therefore not representative of the religion or the ethnicity as a whole.

HATE CRIME LAWS

Federal Laws

Federal laws provide criminal and civil causes of action for victims of hate crimes in the United States, regardless of whether they are citizens. Not all acts of hate violence are prohibited by federal law, however. Federal statutes forbid violence by private parties only when there is intent to interfere with a federally protected right—that is, one specifically guaranteed by a federal statute or the U.S. Constitution. Federal authorities can intervene only when a crime is motivated by race, religion, or national origin and at the time the crime is committed the victim is engaged in a "federally protected activity." Such activity includes voting, serving on a jury, going to work, or enrolling in or attending public school. Nevertheless, these rights are broadly interpreted when a perpetrator's motive is tainted by racial hatred. Similar protection is provided to victims of crimes motivated by sexual orientation, gender, or disability.

A victim of a hate/bias crime that violates a federal law can initiate criminal prosecution by reporting the crime to a local office of the FBI. That office then assigns an investigator to the case. A victim may also contact the local U.S. attorney's office or the criminal section of the Civil Rights Division at the U.S. Department of Justice in Washington, D.C. In addition to criminal prosecution, a victim can pursue a civil suit if the facts support a civil action under the federal statutes. The victim can seek both damages and injunctive relief in civil action against the perpetrator of violence that is motivated by racial hatred.

In general, the federal criminal statutes are intended to supplement state and local criminal laws. Procedurally, the U.S. Department of Justice (DOJ) will not become actively involved in prosecuting a particular action until local authorities have concluded their case. After a person is convicted or acquitted in state courts, the DOJ evaluates the result before determining whether to prosecute under federal statutes. There is no set time within which the Justice Department makes its decision.

Hate Crimes Prevention Act of 1999. The Hate Crimes Prevention Act of 1999, which provides federal authority to prosecute bias-motivated crimes, is, at this writing, in the process of being expanded. The Local Law Enforcement Enhancement Act (LLEEA) was introduced during the 108th Congress in May 2003 as Senate Bill 966. If passed, it would amend Section 245 of Title 18 U.S.C., expanding the federal criminal civil rights statute on hate crimes by removing unnecessary obstacles to prosecution. The legislation also provides authority for federal prosecution of crimes directed at individuals because of their gender, disability, or sexual orientation. The intent of the legislation is to eliminate gaps in the federal authority to investigate and prosecute bias-motivated hate crimes. The federal government's jurisdiction under the LLEEA would be limited to the most serious violent crimes directed at persons and to those cases in which local authorities are either unable or unwilling to investigate and prosecute. Until the bill becomes law, state and local law enforcement officials still play the primary role in the prosecution of hate violence.

State Laws

Almost every state and the District of Columbia have enacted laws that can be invoked to redress bias-motivated crimes. Many states have also enacted "penalty-enhancements" statutes, which were upheld unanimously by the U.S. Supreme Court in June 1993 in its decision of a Wisconsin case (*Wisconsin v. Mitchell,* 508 U.S. 476, 1993). Penalty enhancements are legal when the defendant intentionally selects his or her victim based on the victim's race, religion, national origin, sexual orientation, gender, or disability. Many states have also enhanced criminal penalties for vandalism aimed at houses of worship, cemeteries, schools, and community centers.

Why Special Laws?

There are some, including law enforcement leaders, who argue that there is no need for special laws dealing with hate/bias crimes because there are already statutes covering specific crimes. For example, an assault by one person on another is prosecutable in all jurisdictions. Therefore, the argument runs, why would such an assault be prosecuted differently even if it was motivated by a person's hate or bias toward victims because of their color, ethnic background, religion, sexual orientation, gender, or disability? Localities and states headed by leaders with this perspective have no system for identifying, reporting, investigating, and prosecuting hate/bias crimes. Thus, there are deficiencies in the way some law enforcement agencies and prosecutors process hate crimes.

First, incidents are not classified by racial, ethnic, sexual orientation, or religious motivation, making it virtually impossible to tabulate acts of hate violence, spot trends, perform analyses, or develop response strategies. Second, an inaccurate characterization of certain types of hate violence crimes occurs. For example, cross burnings are variously classified as malicious mischief, vandalism, or burning without a permit. Swastika paintings are often classified as graffiti incidents or malicious mischief. The reason for special hate/bias crime laws and penalty enhancement is that they send a clear message to the perpetrator and the public that these crimes will not be tolerated and will be treated as serious offenses.

There are some key differences that make hate/bias crimes more serious than standard offenses. Crimes of this sort deny the free exercise of civil rights, sometimes frightening the victim out of exercising freedom of speech, association, and assembly. Furthermore, these crimes tend to be more violent than other crimes. Often, the attacks are acts of terrorism intended to punish the victim for being visible (i.e., a person who looks or acts different is easy for a bigoted person to single out). Finally, these acts against individuals are also often meant to terrorize entire communities.

HATE/BIAS CRIME AND INCIDENT INVESTIGATIONS

Hate Crime and Incident Investigations

Criminal justice agencies must make hate/bias crimes a priority response, from the initial report through prosecution. To ensure that such crimes are treated seriously by all personnel, each agency must have written policies and procedures that establish protocol for a quick and effective response. Only when policies and procedures are in place, as well as feasible community programs, will society begin to control and reduce hate crimes.

Law enforcement agencies must provide training to investigators that includes such critical elements as understanding the role of the investigator, identifying a hate/bias crime, classifying an offender, interviewing a victim, relating to a community, and prosecuting an offender. When hate/bias crimes occur, they require investigators' timely response, understanding, and vigilance to ensure a careful and successful investigation. Investigators must have a comprehensive knowledge of the general elements and motivations behind hate/bias crimes and must recognize the potential of these crimes to affect not only the primary victim, but also the victim's family, other members of the victim's group, and the larger community.

There are general and specific procedures and protocols that should be used in response to crimes and incidents motivated by the victim's race, religion, ethnic background, or sexual orientation (RRES). These include actions to be taken by each of the following categories of personnel:

- Assigned officer/first responder
- Patrol field supervisor
- Watch commander
- Assigned investigator or specialized unit
- Crime prevention, community relations, or specialized unit
- Training unit

The actual guidelines may vary from jurisdiction to jurisdiction, but the basics are the same. Specific guidelines are available from federal and state organizations or police and sheriffs' departments. Some law enforcement agencies have model protocols that could be secured and used in the classroom or by departments who have not developed their own procedures.

Models for Investigating Hate/Bias Crimes

The following are suggested guidelines for law enforcement agencies without standardized protocol for follow-up of hate/bias crimes and incidents. The suggested formats are based on the size of the department.

Small department (agencies of 1 to 100 sworn). A small department may not have the staffing depth to have a specialized unit or investigator who can deal solely with hate crimes. Officers in small departments are usually generalists, meaning that they carry any type of case from the initial report through the investigation and submission to the district attorney. Therefore, all personnel should receive awareness training on cultural and racial issues and learn the requirements of handling crimes and incidents motivated by hate. The officer who takes the crime or incident report must have it approved by his or her supervisor. Some small departments have allowed patrol officers to specialize in the investigation of certain crimes; they might be involved in either providing advice and direction or actually taking the case and handling it to its conclusion. These officers are usually the ones allowed to attend training and conferences that will teach and update them on the investigations of these crimes and incidents. Some departments have a patrol supervisor perform the follow-up investigation and submit the case to the prosecutor's office. It is important that the officer and his or her supervisor keep command officers informed of major cases. Small agencies with a detective follow-up investigations unit must be sure that they are trained in aspects of dealing with crimes motivated by hate.

Medium-sized department (agencies of 100 to 500 sworn). The following is a model suggested for a medium-sized department with a crimes-against-persons investigations unit and an administration unit responsible for community relations or affairs. The format follows this protocol: The responding patrol officer takes the initial report and decides if what occurred was indeed a crime or incident motivated by hate or bias and then completes a preliminary investigation. Then the officer documents the findings on the department offense report form and follows the policy and procedure as established by the agency. The report (which may or may not already be classified as a hate/bias or civil rights violation, depending on department policy) is approved by the officer's supervisor and watch commander. Then it is forwarded to the investigations unit that follows up on such cases (usually the crimes persons unit). The report is reviewed by the investigations unit supervisor, who again evaluates whether a crime or incident took place. If it is decided that it is a hate/bias crime, the report is assigned to a crimes person investigator *who specializes in this type of investigation.*

A copy of the report is also forwarded (through the appropriate chain of command) to the administration or community relations unit for follow-up. The staff of the latter unit is also trained to handle hate/bias and civil rights violations investigations and to provide victim assistance. The administrative follow-up would include:

- Investigations required
- Referrals and support for the victim
- Conducting of public meetings to resolve neighborhood problems
- Conflict resolution
- Liaison with the diverse organizations in the community and victim advocates

Some cases may require that the criminal investigator and administrative officer work jointly to resolve the crime or incident under investigation.

Large departments (agencies of 500-plus sworn). Most large departments have enough staff that they can have a specialized unit. There are many advantages to having a specialized unit that focuses on crimes motivated by hate/bias or civil rights violations. The investigators become familiar and experienced with the law and special procedures required and can handle more complex, sensitive cases. Investigators who are allowed to specialize can form networks with victim advocate organizations, other police agencies, and community-based agencies. They work closely with the district attorney's office (probably with a special bias unit within that agency), establishing the working relationships and rapport important to successful prosecutions. The investigators develop a sense of pride in their efforts and a commitment to provide a competent investigative and victim assistance response. Since the primary function of the unit is hate/bias crime investigations, officers can sometimes develop knowledge of individuals and groups that commit such offenses and become more aware of where the incidents occur.

Detectives in departments who handle a multitude of cases do not have the time to track and monitor these crimes and therefore may not spot trends. Specialized units can evaluate the field performance of the patrol officers who have handled such crimes and can provide suggestions for improvement or commendations when the response has been effective or innovative.

There are also disadvantages to specialized units. Often, when there is a specialized unit, patrol officers believe that what is happening in the neighborhood in which they work is not their problem—it is the problem of the specialized unit. The officer takes reports and then transfers responsibility for resolution of problems. Patrol officers may be unaware of a problem or its magnitude or even what resources are being marshaled to resolve it unless there is good communication between them and the members of the specialized unit. These disadvantages are surmountable, however, especially if the department uses community-oriented policing strategies, which usually involve a higher degree of communication among agency units and with the community.

Hate crimes that fit certain criteria, to be discussed later, are investigated at the federal level by the FBI's Bias Crimes Unit and the Bureau of Alcohol, Tobacco and Firearms (BATF) church arson and explosives experts. BATF investigators also focus on regulating the illegal sale and possessions of firearms to potential perpetrators of hate crimes.

HATE/BIAS CRIME PROSECUTION

District Attorney's or Prosecutor's Office

Many district attorneys' offices in the United States now have attorneys and/or units that specialize in hate crime prosecution. These agencies have established policies and procedures designed to effectively and efficiently prosecute such crimes. There are compelling reasons for district attorneys to devote special attention and resources to these crimes. As the chief of community services of the Norfolk County, Massachusetts, district attorney's office wrote:

> A prosecutor has discretion to influence, if not determine, what might be called the public safety climate that citizens in the communities he serves will experience. . . . To establish a public safety climate that fosters the full enjoyment of civil and political rights by the minority members of our communities requires a focused political will directed to that end as well as resources and capacity. (Agnes, 1989, p. 3)

The most effective and successful approaches that build a climate of public safety have been those that:

- Established specialized hate crimes or civil rights violations units.

- Standardized procedures to prosecute hate crime cases (this standardization should include vertical prosecution of cases).

- Appointed attorneys to be liaisons with various ethnic, racial, religious, and sexual orientation groups in the community.

- Provided all attorneys on staff with cultural awareness or sensitivity training.

- Provided alternative sentencing programs aimed at rehabilitating individuals who commit hate-motivated crimes. (One example is the Anti-Defamation League's "The Juvenile Diversion Program: Learning About Differences," a 9-week series for students and sometimes parents on civil rights law, racism, anti-Semitism, the Holocaust, and the legacy of discrimination against minorities in America.)

District attorneys can play a major role in educating judges on the nature, prevalence, and severity of hate crime and in encouraging effective sentences for this offense. They can also be very effective in their working relationships with and encouragement of police officers investigating these crimes. The effort involves each member of the criminal justice system, but the prosecutor has one of the most important roles.

Special Problems in Prosecuting Hate/Bias Crimes

Prosecutors confront an array of issues when considering a potential hate crime. Ascertaining the real motivation for someone's behavior is difficult, and actually proving a person took an action because of hate can be an arduous task. Hate crime charges are the only ones for which proving motive becomes as important as proving modus operandi. Juries can often find it impossible to conclude with certainty what was going on in a suspect's mind during the crime. Attorneys who handle hate/bias crimes indicate that there are four potential obstacles to successful prosecutions:

1. Proving the crime was motivated by bias
2. Uncooperative, complaining witnesses
3. Special defenses
4. Lenient sentences

Prosecutors, given these obstacles, sometimes have difficulty deciding whether to file hate crime charges. Consider the following examples:

- A man recently got into an argument over napkins at a restaurant. He screamed his hatred for the Arab proprietors and later came back and bashed a clerk with a baseball bat. But there was no hate crime charge. The prosecutor said the argument over the napkins was more of a motive than anti-Arab prejudice.

- Prosecutors declined to file a hate crime allegation against a Hindu man who allegedly raped a Muslim coworker at a drug store. Police booked the Hindu man on hate and rape charges based on the victim's saying he had tormented her about her religion for months and called her a "stupid Muslim" right after the assault. But an assistant district attorney, who wrote a primer on hate crime prosecutions, said his office did not feel they could prove to a jury that his alleged hatred of Muslims was a substantial motivation in the charged crime.

As indicated, it is often difficult to identify hate-motivated crimes or incidents accurately. Usually, no single factor is sufficient to make the determination, and sometimes the incident is disguised by the perpetrator so that it does not appear to be a hate/bias crime. Even cases that have been well investigated may lack sufficient evidence to prove that the crime was motivated, beyond a reasonable doubt, by hate or bias. Generally, prosecutors follow established guidelines for determining whether a crime was bias related. Their criteria include:

- Plain common sense
- Perceptions of the victim(s) and witnesses about the crime
- Language used by the perpetrator
- Background of the perpetrator
- Severity of the attack
- Lack of provocation
- History of similar incidents in the same area
- Absence of any apparent motive

The National District Attorneys Association developed a comprehensive desk manual for prosecutors for identifying, responding to, and preventing hate violence. The desk manual, titled *Hate Crime: A Local Prosecutor's Guide for Responding to Hate Crime,* contains information about working with outside agencies and organizations, case screening and investigation, case assignment and preparation, victim and witness impact and support, trial preparation, sentencing alternatives, and prevention efforts. The manual could be useful in the development of a training curriculum specifically designed for prosecutors. How to order the desk manual can be found on their website, which is listed at the end of this chapter.

Objective Evidence: Bias Motivation

It is important that first responders and investigators properly identify and classify bias-motivated crimes. Officers unsure about identifying a potential hate/bias crime should consult with a supervisor or an expert (even outside the agency) on the topic. To help investigators determine whether an incident has sufficient objective facts to classify it as a hate/bias crime, the U.S. Department of Justice developed a document, "Summary Reporting System: Hate Crime Data Collection Guidelines," which contains a series of examples related to the reporting of hate crime incidents. These examples are intended to ensure uniformity in reporting data to the state and the FBI's UCR Section. The following are a few examples of guidelines:

- The offender and the victim were of different racial, religious, ethnic/national origin, or sexual orientation groups. For example, the victim was black and the offenders were white.

- Bias-related oral comments, written statements, or gestures were made by the offender that indicated his or her bias. For example, the offender shouted a racial epithet at the victim.

- Bias-related drawings, markings, symbols, or graffiti were left at the crime scene. For example, a swastika was painted on the door of a synagogue.

- The victim was visiting a neighborhood where previous hate crimes had been committed against other members of his or her racial, religious, ethnic/national origin, or sexual orientation group and where tensions remain high against his or her group.

- Several incidents have occurred in the same locality, at or about the same time, and the victims are all of the same racial, religious, ethnic/national origin, or sexual orientation group.

- A substantial portion of the community where the crime occurred perceives that the incident was motivated by bias.

For a complete list of guidelines recommended by the Department of Justice, the website where "Summary Reporting System: Hate Crime Data Collection Guidelines" can be ordered is listed at the end of this chapter.

Because of the difficulty of knowing with certainty that a crime was motivated by bias, the Hate Crimes Statistics Act stipulates that bias is to be reported only if the investigation reveals sufficient objective facts that would lead a reasonable and prudent person to conclude that the offender's actions were motivated, in whole or in part, by bias. The specific types of bias to be reported are as follows:

Racial Bias

Antiwhite

Antiblack

Anti-American Indian or Alaskan Native

Anti-Asian/Pacific Islander

Antimultiracial group

Religious Bias

Anti-Jewish

Anti-Catholic

Anti-Protestant

Anti-Islamic (Moslem)

Anti–other religion (Buddhism, Hinduism, Shintoism, etc.)

Antimultireligious group

Anti-atheist or anti-agnostic

Ethnicity/National Origin Bias

Anti-Arab

Anti-Hispanic

Anti–other ethnicity/national origin

Sexual Orientation Bias

Anti–male homosexual (gay)

Anti–female homosexual (lesbian)

Antihomosexual (gays and lesbian)

Antiheterosexual

Antibisexual

Antitransgender

(*Source:* U.S. Department of Justice, 1990, p. 15)

Training is available to help criminal justice agency personnel make decisions regarding hate/bias crimes. A few of those sources are:

- Office for Victims of Crime (OVC)
- Bureau of Justice Assistance (BJA)
- Office of Juvenile Justice and Delinquency Prevention (OJJDP)

All three sponsor grants to agencies to develop programs, and provide training seminars and technical assistance to individuals and local agencies regarding hate crimes.

OVC is working to improve the justice system's response to victims of hate crimes and OJJDP funds agencies to develop training for professionals and to address hate crimes through preventive measures and community resources. BJA has a training initiative for law enforcement agencies to generate awareness and to help in identifying, investigating, and taking appropriate action for bias crimes, as well as arming agencies with tools for responding effectively to incidents. Websites for all three agencies can be found in the listing at the end of this chapter.

In 2002, the Southern Poverty Law Center and Auburn University at Montgomery initiated an innovative online hate crime training program. The two organizations teamed up to develop the course, "Introduction to Hate and Bias Crimes," which is offered to law enforcement officers from the United States and Canada. Such training has been offered for years through a variety of agencies, both public and private, but constraints such as the expense of travel, time away from work, and the low priority given the matter by many police agencies have hampered officers' efforts to pursue it. The online course is a way to reach law enforcement officers in small towns and rural areas. Using material from the Federal Law Enforcement Training Center (FLETC), it introduces officers to the basics of hate crime, terminology, and categories of offenders. The course uses video clips, discussion boards, and online chats with veteran hate crime experts. Completion of the course earns students either one semester hour of college credit or 10 continuing education units. Information about the course schedule, future courses, and scholarship opportunities is available online at a website listed at the conclusion of this chapter.

Mini-Case Study

Discuss in class: What evidence would be required to prove the vandalism was bias motivated? What steps should the city, police, church, and community do to resolve this situation?

In October 2003 in the city of Pleasant Hill, California, vandals crushed two American Indian sweat lodges. The lodges—low, dome-shaped structures made of willows and covered with tarpaulins—contain fire pits and a few benches inside. The lodges are where local Indians from different tribes gathered several times a week for 10 years for ceremonies. The lodges are located behind a Lutheran Church in a residential neighborhood. In 1996, the Lutheran Church got a permit from the Pleasant Hill Planning Commission to build the lodges. The ceremonies have been the focus of a neighborhood controversy for at least 7 years and, in 1997, neighbors worked with Indians and the church to mitigate some of the smoke and noise. Run-ins with neighbors, who complain about the ceremonies going on too late, the singing being too loud, and about the smoke from the fires, continued. One nearby resident has accumulated a folder thick with papers documenting the neighborhood's fight against the sweat lodges.

After the vandalism, a few neighbors expressed to newspaper reporters their delight that the damage had been inflicted on the lodges. Leaders of the sweat ceremonies believe the vandalism was a hate crime. The police, as of this case study being prepared, had not completed their investigation but said that the incident could not be ruled a hate crime until they had proof it was bias motivated.

HATE/BIAS CRIME AND INCIDENT VICTIMOLOGY

Introduction

Meaningful assistance to victims of major crimes became a priority only in the 1980s. The growth of a body of "victimology" literature and the emergence of numerous victim advocate and rights organizations began at about that time, reflecting a growing concern about crime, the victims of crime, and their treatment by the criminal justice system. The public mood or perception had become (and may still be) that the criminal justice system cares only about the defendant. The perception was that the defendant's rights were a priority of the system, while the victim was neglected in the process.

Possibly one of the forerunners of the movement to improve the system was the President's Task Force on Victims of Crime, created by President Ronald Reagan in April 1982. The task force made 68 recommendations in its final report for addressing the problems of victims. The recommendations called for action by police, prosecutors, judges, and parole boards in making specified improvements in their respective operations. The preface included the following statement by the task force chairman, Lois Haight Herrington:

> Victims who do survive their attack, and are brave enough to come forward, turn to their government expecting it to do what a good government should—protect the innocent. The American criminal justice system is absolutely dependent on these victims to cooperate. Without the cooperation of victims and witnesses in reporting and testifying about crime, it is impossible in a free society to hold criminals accountable. When victims come forward to perform this vital service, however, they find little protection. They discover instead that they will be treated as appendages of a system appallingly out of balance. They learn that somewhere along the way the system has lost track of the simple truth that it is supposed to be fair and to protect those who obey the law while punishing those who break it. Somewhere along the way, the system began to serve lawyers and judges and defendants, treating the victim with institutionalized disinterest.

In 1982 the Omnibus Victim and Witness Protection Act, which, among other features, requires use of victim impact statements at sentencing in federal criminal cases, was signed into law. The legislation also provided, in federal cases, greater protection of victims and witnesses from intimidation by defendants or their associates, restitution by offenders to victims, and more stringent bail laws. In 1984 the Comprehensive Crime Control Act and the Victims of Crime Act authorized federal and state victim compensation and victim assistance programs. As a result of the task force recommendations, state and federal legislation, and other research by public and private organizations (most notably the National Institute of Justice), improvements were made in victim services and treatment as well as in the criminal justice system.

Law Enforcement and the Victim

For the most part, perpetrators of hate crimes commit them to intimidate the victim and members of the victim's community so that the victims feel isolated, vulnerable, and unprotected by the law. Many victims do not report their attacks to police out of fear and believe their best defense is to remain quiet. Other reasons, in addition to those outlined earlier in this chapter, include:

- fear of revictimization or retaliation
- fear of having privacy compromised
- for gays, lesbians, bisexual, or transgender individuals, fear of repercussions from being "outed" to family, friends, and employers
- fear of law enforcement and uncertainty about the criminal justice system responses
- for aliens, fear of jeopardizing immigration status, being reported to INS, or deportation
- humiliation or shame about being victimized
- lack of support system within the community
- cultural and language barriers

In the law enforcement field, courses in recruit academies and in-service advanced officer programs typically include training about victimization that covers such topics as sociopsychological effects of victimization, officer sensitivity to the victim, victim assistance and advocacy programs, and victim compensation and restitution criteria and procedures for applying. Classes normally stress the importance of keeping victims informed of their case status and of the criminal justice process. How patrol officers and investigators of such crimes interact with victims affects the victims' immediate and long-term physical and emotional recovery. Proper treatment of victims also increases their willingness to cooperate in the total criminal justice process. Because of such training, the victims of hate crimes began receiving special attention and assistance in progressive cities and counties all over the country.

Victims of hate/bias violence generally express three needs: (1) to feel safe, (2) to feel that people care, and (3) to get assistance. To address needs one and two, law enforcement agencies and all personnel involved in contacts with victims must place special emphasis on victim assistance to reduce trauma and fear. Such investigations sometimes involve working with people from diverse ethnic backgrounds, races, and/or sexual orientation. Many victims may be recent immigrants with limited English who are unfamiliar with the American legal system or have fears of the police rooted in negative experiences from their countries of origin.

> How immigrant and refugee communities generally perceive the criminal justice system is a principal factor in determining how best to serve those communities. These perceptions are often based upon the experiences of these groups with the criminal justice systems in their native lands. In many Asian countries, for example, there is a history of police corruption. The reporting of a crime may not only be futile but could invite unwanted and costly attention. The turmoil of war and the instability of political leadership have also dissuaded many from depending upon government institutions. (Ogawa, 1990, p. 14)

Therefore, the officer or investigator not only must be a skilled interviewer and listener but also must be sensitive to and knowledgeable of cultural and racial differences and ethnicity. He or she must have the ability to show compassion and sensitivity toward the plight of the victim while gathering the evidence required for prosecution. As with other crime victims, officers involved in the investigation must

- Approach victims in an empathic and supportive manner and demonstrate concern and sensitivity.
- Attempt to calm the victim and reduce the victim's alienation.
- Reassure the victim that every available investigative and enforcement tool will be utilized by the police to find and prosecute the persons responsible for the crime.
- Consider the safety of the victims by recommending and providing extra patrol and/or providing prevention and precautionary advice.
- Provide referral information such as counseling and other appropriate public support and assistance agencies.
- Advise the victim of criminal and civil options (Concord, California, Police Department, 1988).

The stress experienced by victims of hate/bias crime or incidents may be heightened by a perceived level of threat or personal violation. Just like the victims of rape or abuse, many become traumatized when they have to recall the details of what occurred. Sometimes transference takes place whereby the victim, because of what happened to him or her, transfers his or her anger or hostility to the officer. The officer must be prepared for this reaction and must be able to defuse the situation professionally without resorting to anger him- or herself. It is imperative that investigators and officers make every effort to treat hate crime victims with dignity and respect so that they feel a sense of justice. Insensitive, brash, or unaware officers or investigators may not only alienate victims, witnesses, or potential witnesses but also create additional distrust or hostility and cause others in the community to distrust the entire police department.

Addressing the victim's need to get assistance requires that the community have established resources that can assist the victim and the victim group (e.g., gays, Hispanics). Few communities have the resources necessary to offer comprehensive victim services. Even where resources are available, victims are often unaware of them due to poor public awareness programs or the failure of the criminal justice system to make appropriate referrals because of a lack of training or motivation. A key resource is the availability of interpreters for non-English-speaking victims and witnesses. Ideally, jurisdictions with large populations of non-English-speaking minorities should recruit and train an appropriate number of bilingual employees. If the jurisdiction does not have an investigator capable of speaking the same language, an interpreter system should be in place for immediate callout. Victims of hate-motivated incidents are encouraged to report the circumstances to the National Hate Crimes Hotline (1-800-347-HATE).

Readers wishing additional information about victims can refer to *Victims of Crime*, by Robert A. Jerin and Loura J. Moriarty (1997). It is a well-developed textbook for the field of victimology that has many criminal justice applications.

SUMMARY

Racism and crimes motivated by hate are two of the most challenging issues confronting the United States today. Our nation includes people from around the world who are guaranteed the rights to be free of discrimination, bias, and violence. Yet we continue to witness incidents of hatred manifested in violence toward people perceived as "different." Racism and the resulting hate violence, biased treatment, and discrimination cause divisions between people and deny them their dignity. Racism is a disease that devastates society. Police officers should be at the forefront in the battle to combat such criminal behavior within society. Law enforcement must lead in the protection of human and civil rights of all citizens.

The presence of hate/bias crimes and incidents is often attributed to changing national and international conditions, immigration, and ethnic demographic change translated to a local environment. As immigrants, persons of color, or persons of different religious beliefs or sexual orientation move into previously unintegrated areas, increased threat of hate/bias crimes can be expected. It is not just a problem for the criminal justice system, but rather must be addressed jointly by the whole community, including families, schools, business, labor, and social services. In taking the lead, law enforcement agencies can motivate other groups to join with them in their efforts to reduce hate violence.

Progress toward tolerance among peoples, mutual respect, and unity has been painfully slow in our country and marked with repeated setbacks. Criminal statutes and civil remedies to curb the problem in various jurisdictions across the nation have also been enacted slowly. Divisive racial attitudes, anti-immigrant sentiment, the increased number of hate/bias incidents, and the deepening despair of minorities and the poor make the need for solutions even more pressing.

DISCUSSION QUESTIONS AND ISSUES

1. ***Hate/Bias Crimes and Incident Reduction.*** Make a list of important elements in the design of a community-based program to reduce the number of hate/bias crimes and incidents in your area.

2. ***Move-in Violence.*** Discuss, in a group setting, what strategies might be used by a community to reduce the impact of move-in violence on a new immigrant.

3. ***Victims of Hate/Bias Crimes or Incidents.*** Have you been the victim of a hate/bias crime or incident? Share the experience with others in a group setting: the circumstances, the feelings you experienced, how you responded, and what action was taken by any community-based agency or organization.

4. Find out what resources exist in your community to assist victims of hate/bias crimes.

   a. Which groups provide victim assistance?

   b. Which coalition groups exist, and what types of community outreach programs are offered?

   c. What types of pamphlets or other written materials are available?

   d. Which groups have speakers' bureaus?

   e. Which groups are working with local law enforcement agencies with regard to response programs or cultural awareness training?

   f. Which groups are working with the district attorney's office?

   g. What types of legislative lobbying efforts are taking place, and who is championing the work?

WEBSITE RESOURCES

Visit these websites for additional information about hate crimes and victim assistance:

American-Arab Anti-Discrimination Committee (ADC):   http://www.adc.org

Information about the ADC's civil rights efforts and useful summary data about cases and complaints regarding hate crimes and discrimination involving Arab Americans.

Anti-Defamation League (ADL):   http://www.adl.org

A source of model policies and procedures for the investigation and tracking of crimes motivated by hate.

Bureau of Justice Statistics (BJS):   http://www.ojp.usdoj.gov.bjs

Data about crimes reported by law enforcement agencies across the nation to the FBI. BJA is also a resource center for justice topics such as training, technical assistance, publications, and grants.

National District Attorneys Association: http://www.ndaa.org

This website is a resource for information on many subjects. They produced a guide titled *Hate Crime: A Local Prosecutor's Guide for Responding to Hate Crime,* which covers several issues that arise during hate crime prosecutions. By highlighting model protocols and procedures from offices around the nation, the resource guide will help prosecutors' offices develop policies and procedures on handling hate crime investigations and prosecutions. It also will provide a comprehensive roadmap to individual prosecutors who are handling hate crime cases. Both prosecutors who are working on their first hate crime case and more experienced prosecutors of bias crimes will find the resource guide helpful.

National Gay and Lesbian Task Force (NGLTF):   http://www.ngltf.org

Information about lesbian, gay, bisexual, and transgender individuals as victims of crimes motivated by hate.

Office for Victims of Crime (OVC):   http://www.ojp.us.doj.gov/ovc

The site provides information about victims of crime and models for providing victim services. It also provides resources for training, publications, research, statistics, program funding, and grants pertaining to victims of crime.

International Association of Chiefs of Police: http://www.theiacp.org

An online resource for law enforcement issues publications including *Recruitment/ Retention of Qualified Police Personnel: A Best Practices Guide, December 7, 2001.*

National Office of Victim Assistance (NOVA):   http://nova.org

A good resource for victim assistance networks. The organization is based in Washington, D.C., and can be reached at (202) 393-6682.

Vera Institute of Justice: http://www.vera.org

The Vera Institute of Justice works closely with leaders in government and civil society to improve the services people rely on for safety and justice. Vera develops innovative, affordable programs that often grow into self-sustaining organizations, studies social problems and current responses, and provides practical advice and assistance to government officials around the world. They have publications on many law enforcement subjects.

Office of Juvenile Justice and Delinquency Prevention (OJJDP):   http://ojjdp
.ncjrs.org

OJJDP is a resource center for programs, publications, training, and grants regarding juvenile justice and delinquency prevention.

Southern Poverty Law Center (SPLC):   http://www.splcencter.org

An excellent resource for information about and statistics concerning hate organizations. As mentioned in this chapter, SPLC offers an online training course, "Introduction to Hate and Bias Crimes," for law enforcement officers from the United States and Canada. Information about the course is available at http://www.intelligenceproject.org

U.S. Department of Justice (DOJ):   http://www.doj.gov

U.S. Department of Justice developed a document, entitled "Summary Reporting System: Hate Crime Data Collection Guidelines," which contains a series of examples related to the reporting of hate crime incidents. These examples are intended to ensure uniformity in reporting data to the state and the FBI's UCR Section. The guidelines can be ordered either via their website or by calling (304) 625-4995. The FBI offers training for law enforcement officers and administrators on developing data collection procedures. For more information, contact the FBI at 1-888-UCR-NIBR. See also *Hate/Bias Crimes Train-the-Trainer Program,* conducted by the National Center for State, Local and International Law Enforcement Training, Federal Law Enforcement Training Center (FLETC), U.S. Treasury Dept. Contact FLETC at: 1-800-743-5382, x 3343.

REFERENCES

Agnes, Peter S. (1989). "Public Safety in the 80's: New Cultural Dimensions in Society. A Modern Prosecutor's Response to Challenges Posed by Cultural Diversity." Unpublished paper, Norfolk County, Massachusetts, District Attorney's Office.

"Alabama Supreme Court sets execution date for gay man's killer." (2003, March 27). *Gay & Lesbian Times,* p. 30.

Anti-Defamation League. (2001, 2002). *Audit of Anti-Semitic Incidents.* New York: Anti-Defamation League of B'nai B'rith, Civil Rights Division.

"Anti-gay bullying prevalent, study says." (2002, December 13). *Contra Costa Times,* p. A20.

"Anti-Native American Hate Crime." (2004, March). Bryan D. Byers, Department of Criminal Justice and Criminology, Ball State University, Muncie, Indiana. Presented at the annual meeting of the Academy of Criminal Justice Sciences, Las Vegas Nevada.

"Before, it was cute. Now, it's political." (2003, January 3). *Frontiers,* p. 37.

Berrill, Kevin. (1986, October 9). Testimony before the House Judiciary Committee on Criminal Justice: Second Session on Anti-Gay Violence, Serial no. 132.

Borgquist, Daryl. (2000, December 27). Media affairs officer, U.S. Department of Justice Community Relations Service, Washington, D.C., personal communication.

California Office of Criminal Justice Planning. (1989). "Emerging Criminal Justice Issue. When Hate Comes to Town: Preventing and Intervening in Community Hate Crime." Vol. 1, No. 4, p. 1.

Center for Democratic Renewal. (1992). *When Hate Groups Come to Town: A Handbook of Effective Community Responses,* Second Edition. Atlanta, GA.: Center for Democratic Renewal.

Choudhury, Progga. (2003). Victim Advocate and Outreach Director, Los Angeles Gay & Lesbian Community Services Center Anti-Violence Project. (Per personal communication with Mitchell Grobeson, February and April, 2003).

"Clinton seeks race dialogue, rhetoric needs to match deeds, say advocates." (1997, June 15). *Contra Costa Times,* p. A9.

"Coming down hard on hate." (2002, September 27). *Frontiers,* p. 46.

"FBI hate crimes data woefully underreports crimes against LGBT people." (2001, February 13). *National Gay and Lesbian Task Force News & Views.*

Frey, William H. (1998, June–July). "New Demographic Divide in the U.S.: Immigrant and Domestic Migrant Magnets." *Public Perspective, 9,* 14–15.

Fritsche, David. (1992, May). *America on Fire: The Anatomy of Violence.* Reno, Nev.: Dynamics Group.

Gambert, Riva. (2003). Former Associate Director of the Jewish Community Relations Council (JCRC) of the Greater (SF) East Bay, personal communication. (December, 2003)

Grobeson, Mitchell. (2003,). Sergeant (Ret.), Los Angeles Police Department, personal communication. (February, 2003).

"Hate crimes against Muslims rise." (2001, September 19). *Los Angeles Times,* p. A14.

"Hate crimes against Muslims soared after 9/11, FBI reports." (2002, November 26). *Los Angeles Times,* p. A22.

International Association of Chiefs of Police (IACP). (1999). "Responding to Hate Crimes: A Police Officer's Guide to Investigation and Prevention." Publications online: www.theiacp.org

Jerin, Robert A., and Loura J. Moriarty. (1997). *Victims of Crime.* Chicago, Ill.: Nelson-Hall.

"LGBT violence increase despite violence decrease." (2000, March 24). *National Gay and Lesbian Task Force News & Views.*

"Literary stereotyping." (2003, January). *The Blade—Transitions: Transgender News & Commentary,* p. 88.

Manley, Roslyn. (2003, March). Columnist, Transgender Activist (National Transgender Action Coalition). Personal communications with Mitchell Grobeson.

McDevitt, J. (1989, September). *The Study of the Character of Civil Rights Crimes in Massachusetts (1983–1987). Report of the College of Criminal Justice.* Boston: Northeastern University Press.

McDevitt, Jack. (1993). *Hate Crimes: The Rising Tide of Bigotry and Bloodshed.* New York: Plenum Press.

"Murder of gay, African-American man reflects twin disease of racism, homophobia, NGLTF says." (2000, March 24). *National Gay and Lesbian Task Force News & Views.*

National Institute Against Prejudice Violence. (1992, March). "10 Percent of U.S. Population Victimized." *Forum, 6*(1), 2–6.

New York Anti-Violence Project. (April 18, 2000). "Gay & Lesbian Anti-Violence Project Releases Report on Hate Incidents in 2001, *Media Release.*

New York State Governor's Task Force on Bias-Related Crime. (1988, March). Final Report. Albany: New York State Printing Office.

"No room for bigotry." (2001, September 21). *Contra Costa Times,* p. A23.

"The news affecting our community in 2002." (2003 January 3). *Frontiers,* p. 17.

"NGLTF applauds federal indictment in 1996 Shenondoah murders." (2002, April 10). *National Gay and Lesbian Task Force News & Views.*

"NGLTF calls for full investigation into brutal death of Army PFC." (1999, July 19). *National Gay and Lesbian Task Force News & Views.*

"NGLTF and Pacific Pride Foundation condemn hate-motivated Killing of Santa Barbara gay man." (2002, March 4). *National Gay and Lesbian Task Force News & Views.*

"No more arrests seen in teen's death." (2002, October 23). *Contra Costa Times,* p. A13.

"One year, twenty dead, no action." (1999, October 11). *National Gay and Lesbian Task Force News & Views.*

"Operation lift the ban." (2002, April 18). *Gay & Lesbian Times,* p. 42.

Ogawa, Brian. (1990). *Color of Justice: Culturally Sensitive Treatment of Crime Victims.* Sacramento: Office of the Governor, State of California.

President's Task Force on Victims of Crime. (1982, December). Final Report. Washington, D.C.: U.S. Government Printing Office.

Rennison, Callie. (2001). "Violent Victimization and Race, 1993–98." National Institute of Justice. Washington DC: Author.

800,000 Rwanda Tutsis murdered. (1999, April 23). Public Broadcasting Service, Frontline/World. www.pbs.org/

Schlesinger, Arthur, Jr. (1991, July 8). *The Cult of Ethnicity, Good and Bad.* Time, p. 27.

Shusta, Robert M. (1987). "The Development of a Model Plan for California Cities Experiencing Multicultural Impact." Class IV Post Command College, Sacramento, Calif.

Southern Poverty Law Center. (1987). *"Move-in" Violence: White Resistance to Neighborhood Integration in the 1980's.* Montgomery, Ala.: Southern Poverty Law Center, Klanwatch Project.

"Task Force calls for continued vigilance in solving murders of transgender women in SE Washington D.C." (2002, August 14). *National Gay and Lesbian Task Force News & Views.*

Turner, Nancy. (n.d.). "Responding to Hate Crimes: A Police Officer's Guide to Investigation and Prevention." Available at www.theiacp.org or from the National Criminal Justice Reference Service at 800-851-3420.

U.S. Bureau of the Census. (1980, 1990, 1994, 2003). *Distribution of the Population by Type of Residence and Race.* Washington, D.C.: Author.

U.S. Commission on Civil Rights, Intimidation, and Violence. (1990, September). *Racial and Religious Bigotry in America* (Clearinghouse publication no. 96). Washington, D.C.: U.S. Government Printing Office.

Wallace, Steven. (1987). "Elderly Nicaraguans and Immigrant Community Formation in San Francisco." Unpublished doctoral dissertation, University of California, San Francisco.

Wallace, Steven. (1992, November 9). Personal communication.

"Wisconsin gay student receives $900,000 in settlement." (1996, November). *Lambda Legal,* p. 1.

Wright, Robin. (1993, June 8). "Ethnic Strife Owes More to Present Than to History." *Los Angeles Times,* pp. A1, A 13.

Wynn, Dennis. (1987). Justice Department, Community Relations Unit, personal communication. (October, 1987).

"Youth to get landmark settlement on anti-gay harrassment case." (2002, January 17). *Erie Times News,* p. 2.

Chapter 13

Hate/Bias Crimes: Reporting, Monitoring, and Response Strategies

OVERVIEW

In this chapter, we discuss the nationwide reporting system and clearinghouse for hate crimes data collected from state and local police. Criminal justice leaders in every sector of the United States must utilize standardized and comprehensive statistics as one tool to analyze hate crime/bias trends. Using data, they must direct their resources more effectively against crimes of hate or bias and civil rights violations. In the first section of the chapter, we define the problem and establish why data collection is important. The second section continues with a discussion of the various organizations that monitor hate crimes and hate groups. The third section contains information about organized hate groups. In the fourth section, we explore conditions in communities requiring monitoring and subsequent deployment of law enforcement and community resources (community-oriented policing) that will prevent or reduce hate/bias crimes and incidents. The final section presents community response strategies to reduce hate crimes and incidents. The chapter considers the need for the community (religious institutions, schools, public agencies, private organizations, and neighborhood residents) to deal with the problem cooperatively because the challenge of hate crimes is not solely a law enforcement issue.

COMMENTARY

The need for quick and effective investigation and prosecution of hate/bias crimes combined with reporting and monitoring is exemplified in the following quotations:

> Victims of racially and religiously targeted incidents incur damage to their homes and property, injury to their bodies and sometimes death. In addition to physical suffering, being victimized because of one's race, religion, or national origin brings negative attention to one's differences, injures one's dignity and self-esteem, and makes one feel unwanted in the community, yet because most crimes against racial and religious minorities are not extremely violent, victims are usually not given any special attention or assistance. (National Organization of Black Law Enforcement Executives, 1986, p. 24)

> Hate crimes are anathema to a free and democratic society. The destruction and fear that these acts cause, not just for the individual victim but for an entire group of citizens, have ramifications well beyond the actual crime itself. This is why we must vigorously investigate, indict and punish those who unleash their

bigotry through cowardly acts of abuse, vandalism and violence. Local law enforcement agencies play a large role in combating and deterring hate crimes. Police training in how to identify a hate crime and how to deal with a victim's trauma is essential for an effective law enforcement response. (Anti-Defamation League, 1990, p. 2)

The FBI severely underestimates the number of crimes of bigotry and racism, from petty vandalism to murder, a report released Thursday says. The Southern Poverty Law Center said the FBI counts about 8,000 bias-motivated crimes in America annually, but the actual number may total 50,000. The national statistics are skewed because many police officers don't label offenses as hate crimes, and some states report having none. Even blatant discriminatory crimes often go ignored, the article said. "These statistics are the basics of public policy, and we cannot effectively address hate crime with these numbers [Southern Poverty Law Center spokesman Mark Potok] Potok said." The FBI acknowledges flaws in the data but says the system will improve as public and police awareness of bias crimes increases. ("Study," 2001, p. B7)

INTRODUCTION

Changing demographics in almost every part of the United States require that all localities deal with issues of intergroup relations. The ideal of harmony in diversity is offset by increased stress in the social fabric of a community, stress that often leads to bigoted or violent acts. Newspaper headlines across the country provide convincing examples of disharmony on a daily basis. Hate/bias crimes are not a new phenomenon; they have been present for generations. The need for law enforcement to maintain accurate and thorough documentation of such crimes is crucial.

Data must be collected at local levels and sent in a standardized fashion to state and national clearinghouses so that proper resources may be allocated to hate/bias crime investigations, prosecutions, and victim assistance. Such a system provides the necessary information not only to the criminal justice system but also to public policymakers, civil rights activists, legislators, victim advocates, and the general public. The data, if comprehensive and accurate, provide a reliable statistical picture of the problem. Agencies collecting data have also been able to strengthen their arguments and rationale for new hate crime penalty enhancements. In addition, the information is used in criminal justice training courses and in educating communities on the impact of the problem. The rationale for expending energy on tracking and analyzing these crimes was summed up in a report of the New York State Governor's Task Force on Bias-Related Crime: "A single incident can be the tragedy of a lifetime to its victim and may be the spark that disrupts an entire community" (1988, p. 32).

Increased public awareness of and response to such crimes has largely been the result of efforts by community-based organizations and victim advocate groups. By documenting and drawing public attention to acts of bigotry and violence, these organizations laid the groundwork for the official action that followed. It is extremely important that hate groups across the United States be monitored by criminal justice agencies. Documenting and publicizing a problem does not guarantee that it will be solved, but is a critical part of any strategy to create change. It also raises consciousness within the community and the criminal justice system. It is a simple but effective first step toward mobilizing a response.

HATE CRIMES REPORTING

Purpose of Hate/Bias Crime Data Collection

Establishing a good reporting system within public organizations (e.g., human relations commissions) and the justice system is essential in every area of the country. Hate/bias crime data are collected to help police:

- Identify current and potential problems (i.e., trends)
- Respond to the needs of diverse communities
- Recruit a diverse force
- Train criminal justice personnel on the degree of the problem and reason for priority response

When the police have information about crime patterns, they are better able to direct resources to prevent, investigate, and resolve problems pertaining to them. Tracking hate/bias incidents and crimes allows criminal justice managers to deploy their resources accordingly when fluctuations occur. Aggressive response, investigation, and prosecution of these crimes demonstrate that police are genuinely concerned and that they see such crimes as a priority. As departments visibly show their commitment to addressing hate/bias crime, the diverse communities they serve will be more likely to see police as responsive to their concerns. A secondary benefit for a responsive agency is that blacks, Asians, Hispanics, lesbians, gays, and women would be more apt to consider law enforcement as a good career opportunity.

The Boston Police Department began recording and tracking civil rights violations in 1978 when it created its Civil Disorders Unit. Boston was probably the first law enforcement agency in the United States to record and track such crimes. The Maryland State Police Department was also a forerunner when it began to record incidents on a statewide, systematic basis as part of a pioneering government-wide effort to monitor and combat hate violence in 1981. Agencies that implemented policies and procedures to deal with hate/bias crimes during the 1980s proved to be leaders in the field; in addition to Boston and Maryland, New York, San Francisco, and Los Angeles had forward-looking programs. The policies and procedures of these agencies have been used by other organizations as models.

Congressional Directive: Federal Hate Crime Legislation

In response to a growing concern and to understand the scope of the hate crime problem, U.S. Congress enacted the federal Hate Crimes Statistics Act (HCSA) of 1990 and subsequent acts that amended the directive. The Act requires the attorney general to establish guidelines, and collect and publish data about the prevalence of crimes motivated by bias or hate. The U.S. attorney general delegated his agency's responsibilities under the Act to the FBI. The Uniform Crimes Report (UCR) section of the FBI was assigned the task of developing the procedures for, and managing the implementation of, the collection of hate crime data. The national clearinghouse for hate/bias crime data enables the criminal justice system to monitor and respond to trends in those localities that voluntarily submit the information.

Uniform Crime Report System

The approach adopted by the U.S. Department of Justice incorporated a means of capturing hate crime data received from law enforcement jurisdictions into the already established nationwide Uniform Crime Report (UCR) program. As part of the UCR Program, the FBI publishes statistics in their annual publication, *Hate Crime Statistics.* The U.S. Department of Justice encouraged law enforcement agencies to follow the spirit of the federal legislation and voluntarily collect data. Only 2,771 law enforcement agencies of the approximately 16,000 in the United States that participate in the UCR program (out of nearly 17,000 total) submitted hate crime data voluntarily in 1991, the first year. The most recent available hate crimes statistics compiled by the FBI were for 2001 when, of all law enforcement agencies nationwide, a total of 11,987 reported, representing 49 states and the District of Columbia (Hate Crime Statistics, 2001). Only the state of Hawaii chose not to participate, and although Alabama submitted crime data, that state reported no hate incidents in 2001. Even though there was not 100 percent participation, the statistics represented almost 85 percent of the nation's population. However, because the number of agencies reporting hate crimes voluntarily varies each year, and because hate crimes are believed to be drastically underreported (see Chapter 12), it is not particularly useful to compare rates of hate crimes between years. The information collected does, however, offer perspectives on the general nature of hate crime occurrence. FBI hate crime statistics can be found on a website, which is cited at the end of Chapter 12.

The Southern Poverty Law Center (SPLC) issued a report in 2002 finding fault with the FBI's annual report on hate crimes. The SPLC maintains, based on their survey of all 50 states and the District of Columbia, that the system, already hobbled by the voluntary nature of reporting, is riddled with errors, failures to pass along information, misunderstanding of what constitutes a hate crime, and even falsification of data. The SPLC report suggests that while published hate crime totals have been running at approximately 8,000 cases a year, the real figure is probably closer to 50,000. They discovered that at least seven states had revealed to the FBI that they had inserted zeros for nonreporting agencies, implying that they had no hate crimes, when in fact those departments had chosen not to file reports at all. In other words, instead of putting a department into the nonreporting column, state agencies charged with reporting to the federal government simply categorized those departments as having no hate crimes. SPLC asserts that the deception has the effect of falsifying data, making states that submit false zeros look good at the expense of those that do not. They conclude that the dimensions of this problem are probably enormous; fully 83 percent of jurisdictions that reported in 1999 said they had no hate crimes. "These failings are a serious matter, because the FBI's numbers cannot tell you whether hate crimes have been going up or down nationally since the first statistics, covering 1991, were published. And they are nearly useless for public policy purposes because their quality is so poor" (SPLC Report, 2002). The SPLC proposes a list of policy suggestions that stress the importance of reinvigorated leadership from political and law enforcement officials and improved technical assistance and training for police to correct these deficiencies. As part of the attorney general's Hate Crime Initiative, the Bureau of Justice Statistics has examined ways to improve participation by law enforcement agencies in collecting and reporting hate crime statistics to the FBI and in profiling local responses to hate crime. The findings will assist the federal government in improving the accuracy of hate crime statistics and reporting practices and in developing a model for hate crime reporting.

Almost all states lack a central repository for police intelligence on hate crimes. That means an investigator working in one city of a state might not even know about a critical piece of information gathered in another location during a different incident. In 2000, California unveiled what it called the first high-tech database in the country aimed at combating hate crimes. The state implemented a computer system allowing police departments statewide to call up names, mug shots, and even the types of tattoos that identify particular individuals or groups linked to hate crimes.

HATE/BIAS CRIMES MONITORING

Monitoring Hate Groups

Monitoring extremist groups is an important obligation of law enforcement. Activities by these groups are tracked through a nationwide criminal justice reporting system and through nongovernmental organizations such as:

SPLC Report (formerly Klanwatch) and SPLC Intelligence Project. The SPLC Report and Intelligence Project are two products of the Southern Poverty Law Center located in Montgomery, Alabama. SPLC considers its primary responsibilities the monitoring of white supremacist groups on a national scale and the tracking of hate crimes. The group disseminates this information to law enforcement agencies through a bimonthly publication, the Intelligence Report. The center, which began as a small civil rights law firm in 1971, is now internationally known for its hate/bias publications, tolerance education programs, legal victories against white supremacist groups, and tracking of hate groups.

Anti-Defamation League. The Anti-Defamation League (ADL) was founded in 1913 "to stop the defamation of Jewish people and to secure justice and fair treatment to all citizens alike." The ADL has been a leader of national and state efforts in the development of legislation, policies, and procedures to deter, investigate, and counteract hate-motivated crimes. The organization is also respected for its research publications and articles dealing with such crimes. The ADL developed a recording system that has served as a model of data collection nationwide since its launch in 1979.

National Gay and Lesbian Task Force (NGLTF) and NGLTF Policy Institute. The NGLTF works to eradicate discrimination and violence based on sexual orientation and human immunodeficiency virus (HIV) status. The NGLTF was founded in 1973 to serve its members in a manner that reflects the diversity of the lesbian and gay community. In 1991 the task force was restructured into two organizations—the NGLTF and the NGLTF Policy Institute—to improve its lobbying efforts and expand its organization and educational programs.

Center for Democratic Renewal. The Center for Democratic Renewal (CDR; formerly the National Anti-Klan Network) is an organization that has tracked bias activity since 1982. CDR's strategy to end bigoted violence focuses on tracking bias activity, educating society through publications, and assisting victims through various programs.

Simon Wiesenthal Center. The Simon Wiesenthal Center, based in Los Angeles, is a human rights group named for the famed Nazi hunter. It monitors the Internet worldwide for tactics, language, and symbols of the high-tech hate culture. The center shares its information with affected law enforcement agencies. The organization, in some states, also operates Holocaust exhibits that are used as shocking examples of atrocities committed toward Jewish people during World War II. Police academies and in-service advanced officer training often use the exhibits for training on hate violence.

ORGANIZED HATE GROUPS

Knowledge of hate groups is essential when policing in a multicultural society. It is imperative for the criminal justice system to investigate (including the use of informants, surveillance, and infiltration), monitor, and control organized hate groups. Aggressive prosecution and litigation against these groups is also critical. Loretta Ross, Program Research Director of the Center for Democratic Renewal (CDR), summarized well the urgent need to address and effectively deal with the presence of hate groups in America:

> America has moved into a new era of white supremacy. The new tactics used by white supremacists and far right organizations must be exposed so that we can work together to mitigate their effectiveness. . . . The ground-breaking progress gained by the civil rights movement of the 1960s in the United States has steadily eroded over the past decade, and the issues and incidents of racism as well as anti-Semitism, homophobia, and violence against women are ones that need to be addressed with increasing urgency. (Ross, 1995, p. 1)

The White Supremacist Movement. "The white supremacist movement is composed of dozens of organizations and groups, each working to create a society totally dominated by white Christians, where the human rights of lesbians and gay men and other minorities are denied. Some groups seek to create an all 'Aryan' territory; others seek to re-institutionalize Jim Crow segregation" (Center for Democratic Renewal, 1992). While most of these organizations share a common bigotry based on religion, race, ethnicity, and sexual orientation, they differ in many ways. They range from seemingly innocuous religious sects or tax protesters to openly militant, even violent, neo-Nazi skinheads and Ku Kluxers. No single organization or person dominates this movement. Frequently individuals are members of several different groups at the same time. The increase in hate group membership, especially since September 11, 2001, leads many sources to confirm that white supremacism is on the rise.

Numbers of Hate Groups in the United States. The Southern Poverty Law Center (SPLC), as previously mentioned, tracks active hate groups in the United States. They identify hate groups by gathering information from their publications, citizens' reports, law enforcement agencies, field sources, and news reports. The number of groups known to be active is determined by surveying marches, rallies, speeches, meetings, leafleting, published literature, and criminal acts. Some white supremacist groups consist of only a few members, while others have tens of thousands. In 2002, SPLC documented 708 active hate groups, up 5 percent from 676 a year before and up 17 percent from 2000 (Intelligence Report, 2002, p. 38). The rise in numbers reflected a pattern of growth dating back to the mid-1990s.

Hate groups are categorized by the Center as Ku Klux Klan, Neo-Nazi, Racist Skinhead, Christian Identity, Black Separatist, Neo-Confederate, and Other. The Other category includes groups, vendors, and publishing houses endorsing a hodge podge of racist doctrines. A breakdown of how many groups are in each of the categories as of 2002 is:

Ku Klux Klan	133
Neo-Nazi	220
Racist Skinhead	18
Christian Identity	27
Black Separatist	82
Neo-Confederate	91
Other	137

Although the numbers of white supremacists in the United States are small in comparison with the total population, Loretta Ross explains why they should be taken seriously:

> Because the percentage of whites who actually belong to white supremacist groups is small, there is a general tendency to underestimate their influence. What is really significant is not the number of people actually belonging to hate groups, but the number who endorse their messages. Once known primarily for their criminal activities, racists have demonstrated a catalytic effect by tapping into the prejudices of the white majority. (1995, p. 7)

The following groups are described only briefly because there is constant change within them.

Neo-Nazis and Klans

The reason for concern about the activities of neo-Nazis and Klans should be obvious from such incidents as the 1993 breakup by the FBI of alleged plots among white supremacists, one to launch a race war in Los Angeles by placing a bomb in a prominent black church and the other to kill Rodney King. A seven-state crime spree in 1994–95 by members of the white supremacist Aryan Republican Army left behind pipe bombs in 22 banks from Nebraska to Ohio. In Wise County, Texas, in April 1997 federal officials arrested four Ku Klux Klan members who planned to blow up a natural-gas refinery and use the disaster as cover for an armored-car robbery. In San Diego in 2000, the FBI tape-recorded a member of a white supremacist group telling an informant how he might kill Morris Casuto, San Diego's regional director of the Anti-Defamation League, set fire to a synagogue, and shoot down an airplane ("Domestic Terrorism," 2000). The year 2003 saw the small rural town of Roy, Utah, inundated with ex-convicts and parolees who had joined white supremacist gangs while in prison, moving in because of the low police presence and generally tolerant neighbors. Police there grappled with a marked increase in crimes committed by the gang members ("Hate group influx," 2003, p. 18).

The largest of the neo-Nazi and Klan groups include the following:

Neo-Nazi-Type Groups	**Klan-Type Groups**
Aryan Nations	Alabama White Knights of the KKK
Knights of Freedom	America's Invisible Empire Knights of the KKK

Neo-Nazi-Type Groups	Klan-Type Groups
National Alliance	American Knights of the KKK
Nationalist Socialist Movement	Imperial Klans of America
World Church of the Creator (Creative Movement)	Invincible Empire Knights of the KKK
	Knights of the White Kamellia
	New Order Knights of the KKK
	White Shield Knights of the KKK

The ideology of Klan members, neo-Nazis, and other white supremacists has been clear since the formation of these groups. They commonly advocate white supremacy, anti-Semitism, homophobia, and racism.

The most violent groups are the neo-Nazi and their movements are growing in the United States and in countries such as Germany and Austria. Young people ages 13 to 25 who wish to join these organizations are required to commit a hate crime as part of the induction process. They openly idealize Hitler. In the 1990s they were responsible for nearly one-fourth of all bias-related murders in the United States. They have committed murders and hundreds of assaults and other violent crimes; most of their victims are African Americans, Latinos, Asian Americans, gays, lesbians, bisexuals, transgender individuals, and even the homeless.

World Church of the Creator or Creative Movement. The World Church of the Creator (WCOTC), classified as a neo-Nazi-type group, was founded in 1973 by Ben Klassen, who wrote the organization's manifesto, *The White Man's Bible*. The organization's existence ended in mid-1990 following the suicide of Klassen and the imprisonment of other leaders. In 1996, however, the WCOTC was reborn and has again become "America's most dangerous white supremacist group. . . . Based in Florida and North Carolina, the World Church of the Creator has been recruiting violent Skinheads from all across America. The group's rallying cry is 'Rahowa,' which stands for Racial HOly WAr" ("World Church," 1992, pp. 42–44). The group is also violently anti-Christian. A judge of the U.S. District Court in Chicago ruled in December 2002 that the World Church of the Creator, founded in Illinois, would have to surrender the name because an Oregon-based religious group already had a trademark on it. The group was also ordered to give up its website domain name and remove or cover up the phrase "Church of the Creator" on all its publications and other products. The group now calls itself the Creative Movement and has moved its headquarters to Riverton, Wyoming. The organization has not only a large membership active in many states, but also has one of the largest white prison gang memberships. It has been tough to control because of its religious facade, which allows its members to gather for meetings in prison.

Aryan Nations. The group Aryan Nations was formed in the early 1970s and operates out of northern Idaho. It is considered primarily an identity group but also embraces neo-Nazi philosophy. The organization preaches that God's creation of Adam marked "the placing of the White Race upon this earth," that all nonwhites are inferior, and that Jews are the "natural enemy of our Aryan (white) race" (Berkowitz, 1999).

The National Alliance. A neo-Nazi group, the National Alliance believes it is part of nature and subject to nature's laws only; therefore, members are able to determine their own destiny regardless of laws imposed by the government. They profess that those who believe in a divine control over mankind absolve themselves of responsibility for their fate. They also believe that they are members of the Aryan (or European) race and are superior to other races.

Racist Skinheads

Skinheads should also be considered dangerous. The 1993 bombings at the offices of the National Association for the Advancement of Colored People (NAACP) in Washington and California by members of a Skinhead organization is evidence of that fact. Membership of young adults in Racist Skinhead groups in the United States has grown considerably since the first group's inception in 1986. Racist Skinheads, easily recognized by their closely shaven heads, are transient and sometimes do not join with Skinhead groups. SPLC indicates their numbers are hard to assess because of this fact. The influence of adult white supremacist groups on Racist Skinheads and neo-Nazi skinheads has been substantial. The youth participate in adult hate group rallies and show a great deal of solidarity with them. Skinhead groups have developed their own leadership and appeal, distinct from adult Klan and neo-Nazi groups (Ross, 1995). The adult hate groups seek to replenish their membership ranks from the Racist Skinhead groups.

Identity

Identity describes a religion that is fundamentally racist, anti-Semitic, and antihomosexual. According to SPLC, the active Identity groups across the United States are organized under different names but with similar ideologies. The goal of Identity groups is to broaden the influence of the white supremacist movement under the guise of Christianity. They form their views of diverse people based on a particular interpretation of the Bible. For example, "[Identity] teaches that people of color are pre-Adamic, that is not fully human and are without souls; that Jews are children of Satan and that white people of northern Europe are the Lost Tribes of the House of Israel" ("World Church," 1992, pp. 42–44). The movement takes the position that white Anglo-Saxons—not Jews—are the real biblical "chosen people," and that blacks and other nonwhites are "mud people" on the same level as animals and therefore are without souls (Berkowitz, 1999). Identity followers believe that the Bible commands racial segregation. They interpret racial equality as a violation of God's law.

Christian Identity. Followers of this sect, founded in California by Wesley Swift after World War II, use the Bible as the source of their ideology. It is a quasi-theological movement of small churches, tape and book distribution businesses, and radio ministries.

Posse Comitatus. Another Identity group is Posse Comitatus, which means "power of the country" in Latin. The group is antitax and anti–federal government. The Posse believes that all government power is rested in the county, not at the federal, level.

Christian Patriots. The followers of this Identity group belong to many different organizations, all of which espouse white supremacy. The core beliefs are as follows:

- White people and people of color are fundamentally two different kinds of citizens, with different rights and responsibilities.

- The United States is not properly a democracy, but a republic in which only people with property should vote.
- Democracy is the same as "mobocracy," or mob rule.
- The United States is a Christian republic, with a special relationship between Christianity and the rule of law.
- Internationalists (usually identified as Jews) and aliens (sometimes identified as Jews, sometimes as immigrants and people of color) are attempting to subvert the U.S. Constitution and establish one-world socialism or, alternatively, the New World Order.
- The Federal Reserve banking system is unconstitutional and a tool of the "International Jewish Banking Conspiracy" (Center for Democratic Renewal, 1992).

Black Separatists

The SPLC has identified black separatist groups active in the United States under two different names: the House of David and the Nation of Islam. Black separatist groups are organizations whose ideologies include tenets of racially based hatred. Black separatist followers share the same agenda as white supremacists of racial separatism and racial supremacy. The two movements also share a common goal of racial purity and a hatred of Jews. One example of a black separatist, militant organization espousing hatred of Jews is the Black African Holocaust Council (BAHC). BAHC, based in Brooklyn, New York, was established in 1991. Membership is restricted to African Americans and Native Americans. The organization publishes a monthly magazine, the *Holocaust Journal,* which is replete with anti-Semitic and antiwhite rhetoric. BAHC holds monthly meetings and conducts weekly lectures and study groups on antiwhite or anti-Semitic issues.

Despite the differences between black extremists and white supremacists groups and their mutual contempt, these groups are able to join rhetorical forces to demean and slander Jews.

RESPONSE ALTERNATIVES TO ORGANIZED HATE GROUPS

Departments must actively work to fight and control organized hate groups, tracking their activities, establishing when they are responsible for crimes, and assisting in their prosecution. Intelligence gathering is crucial to efforts to reduce and prevent hate/bias crimes. Equally important is networking and sharing hate group information with other criminal justice agencies. Many have called this approach a cross-disciplinary coalition against racism. It involves state and regional commitments by criminal justice agencies with other public and private entities, including the Internal Revenue Service. All the institutions jointly develop and implement components of multitiered intervention strategies targeting enforcement, education, training, victim assistance, media relations, political activism and advocacy, and ongoing self-evaluation.

The fight begins with an assessment of the size and scope of the various supremacist groups, their movements, their leaders, and their publications. When hate crimes are perpetrated against one group in the community, law enforcement must immediately alert any other potential organizations that may be targeted. When a synagogue in Sacramento, California, was firebombed, Jewish community leaders were critical of law enforcement, contending that they should have disseminated warnings after an NAACP headquarters in Tacoma was bombed and another in Sacramento gutted by arson. One synagogue president pointed out: "Had we learned [about the NAACP bombing] we would have notified all other congregations, the NAACP and other minority organizations. This was something that could have potentially been prevented if law enforcement had the sensitivity, the direction and the competence to advise us" ("Jewish Community," 1993, p. A20).

One example of networking on the West Coast is the Bay Area Hate Crimes Investigators Association (BAHCIA), which provides training on hate crimes investigations and disseminates information on crimes, hate groups, and individuals active in their respective jurisdictions. Membership includes persons who specialize in hate crime cases from law enforcement, district attorneys, public agencies, and private organizations from the nine San Francisco Bay Area counties. The association was formed "to address the dramatic increase in the incidence of hate violence, and the special needs of law enforcement officers and investigators who work on hate crime cases." The association's bylaws mention that the mission of BAHCIA is to establish a cooperative effort among local, state, and federal agencies, with the purpose of eliminating hate crime in the greater Bay Area. Besides monthly meetings, it sponsors annual Hate Crimes Investigators' Conferences. (Contact the San Francisco Police Department Hate Crime Unit at (415) 553-1133 for more information.)

CASE STUDY: LEWISTON, MAINE, 2003

An excellent example of how a community and the police can organize around diversity and counter the actions of hate groups occurred in Lewiston, Maine, in early 2003. A rally was planned at a college by the World Church of the Creator (WCOTC) and the National Alliance in connection with a controversy regarding a growing Somali immigrant community in the town. More than 1,000 Somalis had moved into Lewiston, and by the fall of 2002, tensions had risen. Somali leaders and others thought racism was surfacing in the community. WCOTC and the National Alliance saw this as an opportunity to come to the town to organize the community against the Somalis.

The city of Lewiston and police department created a steering committee for a new group, the Many and One Coalition, with 200 members. Utilizing advice from the Southern Poverty Law Center (especially its publication *Ten Ways to Fight Hate: A Community Response Guide*) and other local and national human rights groups, they planned the community's response to the pending rally. An outreach coordinator for the SPLC Tolerance Project arrived in Lewiston days prior to the rally to help the town organize its efforts. The day before the rally, the college hosted a forum on issues of tolerance and diversity. The following day, about 5,000 townspeople showed up for a separate rally in support of diversity and the Somali community. Only 30 people turned out for the hate rally (SPLC Report, 2003).

TRENDS AND PREDICTIONS FOR ORGANIZED HATE GROUPS

Some experts predict that white supremacists will continue to commit traditional crimes (e.g., cross burnings, vandalism) but will venture into high-tech activities such as computer system infiltration and sabotage. Their political activism will include "white rights" rallies, protests, and demonstrations; election campaigns by racist candidates; and legislative lobbying. These activities are expected to incite countermovements and will create very labor-intensive situations for law enforcement to handle (Rosenfeld, 1992).

Observers of hate groups have also noted the shift in tactics by white supremacists in the United States. Discovering that supremacists could no longer effectively recruit members using the ideology of open racism with the focus on persons of color, Jews, immigrants, and the like, they are now targeting lesbians and gays. Loretta Ross, in an article titled "White Supremacy in the 1990s," indicates that hate groups since the mid-1990s have been refocusing their energies because

> [t]hey are worried that they can never convince the majority of white Americans to join them in their netherworld. While many whites may share their prejudices, very few are willing (any longer) to act on them by openly carrying a Klan calling card or an Uzi. This situation demands a new strategy that combines old hatreds with new rhetoric. White supremacists desperately need to reinvigorate their movement with new recruits by manipulating white fears into action. (1995, p. 2)

This new approach does not imply that supremacists no longer hate people of color, Jews, and so on. Rather, it means that they are refocusing their energies; that they are exploiting white fear of change; and that they have adopted not only homophobia as a prominent part of their new agenda but also anti-abortion, anti-immigration, and so-called pro-family and pro-American values, in addition to their traditional racist and anti-Semitic beliefs. Ross (1995) says that the broadening of issues and the use of conservative buzzwords have attracted the attention of whites who may not consider themselves racist but do consider themselves patriotic Americans concerned about the moral decay of "their" country.

One disturbing trend is the age and gender of new members of supremacist groups. They are younger than in the past (including teenagers) and many are young women. Organized hate is no longer the exclusive domain of white men over 30 years of age. According to Ross,

> Since the 1980s, women have joined the racist movement in record numbers. . . . This new and dangerous increase accounts for nearly one-third of the membership of some hate groups. The increase in the number of women, coupled with a strategic thrust to reform the public image of hate groups, has expanded women's leadership. These new recruits do not fit the stereotypical image of wives on their husbands' arms. In fact, many of them are college-educated, very sophisticated, and display skills usually found among the rarest of intellectuals of the movement. (1995, p. 7)

To recruit new membership, radical right groups around the country are staging "European" festivals. It is an attempt to draw ethnic whites into their racist movement. Many attendees at festivals have been shocked to learn that the coordinators are members of racist organizations. One such festival, held in Sacramento, California, in February, was advertised as "Euro-Fest 2003." The literature about the event described Celtic music, ethnic food, and activities. According to SPLC, however, organizers

> had Mein Kampf and little baby blankets in blue and white with little swastikas all over them. Women in knee-length skirts and Bavarian bustiers sold copies of *ABC: Arian Beginnings for Children,* along with *Talk Back,* a publication of the White Student Alliance. At a nearby table, photos were on sale of two beautiful young blonde girls giving the Nazi salute. A fellow with a black T-shirt bearing a swastika strolled by; near him, another man's shirt urged "David Duke for Senate." Over at the table of the neo-Nazi National Alliance, women's thongs with the Alliance symbol embroidered on the front, available in green, pink, yellow, white and red, were moving briskly. (The Southern Poverty Law Center's Intelligence Report, 2003)

Organizations and officials tracking hate groups have offered other predictions on the evolution and future of hate groups. These experts believe that groups that have traditionally shunned or actively opposed each other for ideological reasons will join forces against their "common enemies." For example, Tom Metzger of White Aryan Resistance, a "pure racist" who has always shunned religion, has been associating with Christian Identity groups such as Aryan Nations (Anti-Defamation League, 1999). Black separatists have associated with white supremacists at events where they shared the same ideology. Evidence of additional, unusual associations of common enemies became glaringly apparent following the September 11 terrorist attacks when an axis developed between neo-Nazis in North America and Europe and Islamic extremists in the Middle East and elsewhere. Although neo-Nazis have long despised Arabs and Muslims, they have increasingly allied with Arab and Muslim extremists against common enemies, most often Jews. American neo-Nazis have also been increasingly working with their counterparts in Europe (SPLC Report, 2002). The Southern Poverty Law Center provides some additional insights:

> 2001 was a year that saw the expansion and solidification of America's hate movement. New alliances between groups were made. Unity was clearly a goal for many groups and their leaders. Across the board, there seemed to be a hardening—a Nazification—of the ideology of right-wing revolutionary groups. Abandoning old rivalries and inter-group hatreds, neo-Nazis, racist Skinheads and others attended concerts and held rallies to raise funds and espouse their politics of hatred. (SPLC Report, 2002)

> As the United States becomes even more globalized and multicultural, it is said to be fueling the rise of ethnic nationalism and the growth of hate groups. The Intelligence Project found that "the latest increase in hate groups was accounted for almost entirely by rises in neo-Nazi and softer-line neo-Confederate groups." Although t.hese groups differ greatly, both see multiculturalism as undermining white society. For the neo-Nazis, the "international Jew" represents all that threatens ethnically pure nations. For the neo-Confederates, the enemy is non-white immigration and the ideology of multiculturalism. (SPLC Report, 2002)

The tragic events of September 11 also are said to have caused an increase in the number of hate groups and membership within them, aided by new recruitment drives. According to a report, "State of Hate: White Nationalism in the Midwest 2001–2002,"

White supremacy groups have used images of the burning World Trade Center towers on fliers as a way to argue that America needs to close its borders to new residents. "White nationalist organizations are really trying hard to capitalize on the events of Sept. 11," said Devin Burghart, author of the report. "They are beginning to gain some footing. They are actively out there seeking to use the issue as a recruiting tool." ("Study: U.S. hate groups," 2001, p. A20)

Those who study hate groups observed that as the first months of 2003 began to unfold, the radical right was in turmoil because of the death of one founder and the incarceration of another of two of the major white supremacist groups. Several groups were also torn apart by internal battles. The arrests of key leaders (including raids on their homes and headquarters), lawsuits and jury verdicts, defections, deportations, and desperate finances reflect that the criminal justice system and other organizations that target extremists are having an impact on such groups.

The Internet and Hate Groups

The Internet has become the medium of choice for recruiting young members to hate groups and for disseminating hate dogma and racist ideology. The Internet enables people to spread hate instantaneously and anonymously around the world. The medium provides hate groups the ability to send unwanted mass e-mailings simultaneously into millions of homes, some seeking to recruit today's affluent and educated youth to their cause. Their websites entice viewers with online games, comic strips, and music, or simply a friendly pitch from another kid. College and university sites are being bombarded with messages and lures from hate groups. In some areas the Internet is also being used to provide tips on how to target groups' opponents with violence. The Southern Poverty Law Center emphasizes the danger of the Internet, indicating that "there are now over 250 million people on the worldwide Web with 150,000 more signing up every day. Increasingly what they find when they log on is hate. The gospel of hate is being projected worldwide, more cheaply and effectively than ever before, and it is attracting a new demographic of youthful followers to the Neo-Nazi movement" (SPLC Report, 2000, p. 7). As of 2002, SPLC was tracking over 443 hate sites, up from 405 in 2001 and 350 in 2000. SPLC has developed its own website with a special online campaign, "Hate Hurts," about the impact of hate.

HATE/BIAS CRIME AND INCIDENT CONTROL

Hate/bias crimes and incidents can be controlled only through the combined efforts of the community (schools, private organizations, government agencies, churches, service organizations, and families), federal and state legislatures, and the criminal justice system—a holistic approach. It is important to profile communities to determine if they are at risk of strife or conflict caused by the social, economic, and environmental conditions that can result in hate crimes and incidents. Academic authorities on hate crimes identify three types of offenders: the thrill seeker, the reactive offender, and the hard-core offender (Levin, 1993). They describe the reactive offender as one "who grounds his attack on a perceived transgression, such as an insult, interracial dating, or neighborhood integration." The hard-core is typically a member of some racist organization, although statistics reveal that most hate/bias crimes are not committed by hate group members. According to national and regional statistics, juveniles commit approximately 50 percent of all hate crimes in which the perpetrators are known. This fact must be addressed within all communities.

Trend Monitoring in Multicultural Communities

Monitoring conditions in a community provides useful information for forecasting potential negative events and preparing accordingly. Former FBI agent William Tafoya has suggested that responsible forecasting should go beyond issue identification. He and others contend that the framework for evaluating any predictions should include an analysis of economic circumstances, social and cultural conditions, and the political environment. Tafoya warns:

> It is a grave error for law enforcement executives to dismiss social maladies as being not within their purview. These conditions constitute the setting within which police officers must daily cope. They not only exacerbate, but are breeding ground for crime, drug use and violence. It is also a mistake to sweep aside such concerns as a function of bias and bigotry alone. Indeed, racism is a major component of the problem. But there are other ingredients in the witches' brew that transforms the essence of equity today. (1990, p. 21)

For this reason, most law enforcement agencies in the United States have established some form of what is called community-oriented policing (COP). Enlightened police executives recognized that they had not been operating as partners with the communities and neighborhoods that they serve and began doing so through COP.

Identifying Communities at Risk

Community profiling. Law enforcement agencies experiencing demographic changes in their communities are well advised to perform an analysis of what is taking place: community profiling. Community profiling involves a demographic analysis of the community with regard to ethnicity/national origin, race, religion, and sexual orientation groups. Such a profile must include a sense of time: What can the community and law enforcement personnel expect from profiled groups with regard to the observance of holidays and religious or cultural ceremonies?

Progressive agencies send out listings to their patrol officers of religious and cultural holidays and world crisis events that could affect the area they serve. If officers wait to identify at-risk communities until hate crimes are committed, they are not fulfilling their professional responsibilities. Knowing how to identify at-risk communities and then committing resources to resolve problems is proactive police work and is crucial to preventing conflict. While this involves more departmental time and personnel initially, the ultimate savings in terms of preventing community disruption is well worth the effort.

Neighborhood and police partnership. Neighborhoods (citizens and all those local institutions encompassed by the term) together with the police are the best means of identifying communities at risk. The term "at risk" refers to communities having a high level of criminal activity or disorder and usually a higher number of incidents of civil rights violations—hate/bias crimes, discrimination, racism, and bigotry. How does a city determine if a neighborhood is at risk? Who is responsible for the assessment? What strategies can be utilized to reduce the at-risk status? The best approach is community policing, described in Chapter 1, whereby police help the community protect itself and enhance the quality of life of those within. Officers and citizens meet to discuss the neighborhoods' most serious problems and work together to resolve them.

> Community policing strategies can certainly be applied to efforts to reduce racial tension. Mike Scott, director of administration at the Ft. Pierce, Florida, Police Department, said: "Officers often recognize some kind of racial tension going on in a part of their city, but they can't seem to pinpoint it. They can feel it, they can see the incidents occurring on the streets, and people whispering about it, so there's a vague sense of tension. Unfortunately, that's where a lot of officers are left hanging." (Parker, 1991, p. 11)

Community policing encourages officers to delve into such observations and feelings to determine not only what is happening but also who is involved, what their motivation is, and where they are from. Officers should consider themselves as first-line intelligence assets for their community. For example, they should watch for graffiti and/or other materials posted on walls, fences, telephone poles, and buildings. These markings could signal a racist operation in progress or a locally active hate group. In addition, to be effective, officers who patrol highly diverse areas must have some grasp of cultural awareness and cross-cultural communication. Morris Casuto, director of the San Diego Regional Office of the Anti-Defamation League and instructor at both the San Diego Police Academy and the San Diego County Sheriff's Training Academy, stresses: "If officers are scrambling to understand communities only after a crime is committed, it is a terrible indictment of their lack of professionalism."

Additionally, officers must know neighborhood leaders and ways to locate them quickly in the event that they are needed to provide general assistance or to control rumors or people. Neighborhood leaders can provide invaluable help when it comes to dealing with victims who distrust police. Rana Sampson, a community policing training coordinator for the Police Executive Research Forum (PERF), stresses that a problem-focused approach provides officers with a solid understanding of social, economic, and environmental problems in the community. Sampson indicates that "when officers start understanding the problems of the community, it means they're starting to work with the community. . . . When they start working with the community, they realize that 80 percent of the people are really good. A much smaller percentage of people are actually engaged in negative behavior" (Parker, 1991, p. 12).

There are limits to what the police can do without community help. In many communities, however, police first have to overcome their traditional role identification as independent crime fighters before they can become an integral part of the team that works together to solve local problems. However, when officers patrol neighborhoods daily, they can interact with citizens to engender trust and can be the best resources to monitor activities. Herman Goldstein, University of Wisconsin law professor and the architect of the problem-oriented policing (POP) concept, said that "the police department, more than any other agency of government, must have a bird's eye view of the dynamics within its community, including the demographics, agendas of various groups, and an in-depth understanding of the hopes, aspirations and frustration of various groups. This will give the police a feel for the mood and tensions that exist within a community" (Parker, 1991, p. 13).

Role of human relations commissions (HRCs). Many cities and counties nationwide have established community human relations commissions. Created as independent agencies, they are responsible for fostering equal opportunity and eliminating all forms of discrimination. These objectives are accomplished by means of investigating, mediating, and holding public hearings on problems that arise from discrimination prohibited by federal, state, and local laws. Most HRCs will not investigate incidents of discrimination where such a function is preempted or prohibited by state or federal legislation. In cases where there is a violation of state or federal law, the HRC refers the complainant to the appropriate agency. It then monitors the progress of the complaint. Each HRC has established procedures that govern how it receives, investigates, holds hearings on, and mediates and resolves complaints. Confidentiality is a protected right of the complainant in discrimination cases reported to HRCs. As established by state or federal law, the names of the parties may not be made public, with few exceptions, without the written consent of both. Human relations commissions should also be part of the community–police partnership in which they all take responsibility for educating their community about its diversity. This includes serious and sustained efforts to bring people together for dialogue.

Community Relations Service (CRS). The Community Relations Service, an arm of the U.S. Department of Justice, is a specialized federal conciliation service available to state and local officials to help resolve and prevent racial and ethnic conflict, violence, and civil disorder. When governors, mayors, police chiefs, and school superintendents need help to defuse racial or ethnic crises, they turn to CRS. This service helps local officials and residents tailor locally defined resolutions when conflict and violence threaten community stability and well-being. Created by the Civil Rights Act of 1964, CRS is the only federal agency dedicated to preventing and resolving racial and ethnic tensions, incidents, and civil disorders. CRS gathers data in seven areas: demographic balance, administration of justice (particularly police–community relations), employment, education, housing, health and welfare, and community relationships. The statistical data is then used to assess six critical factors:

1. Relationship of minorities to the administration of justice system

2. Impact of the economy

3. Level of minorities' inclusion in and/or exclusion from the system and the number of minorities serving as elected officials

4. Quality of intergroup relationships

5. Level of violence currently in the community/neighborhood and/or city

6. Basic demographic influences

It is time-consuming to perform this type of analysis and develop a program based on the findings. Police departments have access to the same kind of data and a great deal of experience and expertise to complete the same type of analysis within neighborhoods if they choose to do so.

TRENDS TO MONITOR: STEEP TYPOLOGY

The acronym STEEP stands for "social, technological, environmental, economic, and political." There is often a connection between the economy, social conditions, and politics and the numbers of hate/bias crimes that occur. This relationship is explained in Chapter 12. It is important for agency personnel and officers involved in community-oriented policing to understand the basic economic, social, and political issues contributing to social unrest.

Economic Circumstances

Crime, social unrest, riots, and disturbances have often occurred during depressed economic times. Waves of immigrants (both legal and illegal) also affect the scramble for available jobs and services. Internationally, poverty, overcrowding, and wars have been pressuring more people to migrate than ever before, laying the conditions for what the United Nations called "the human crisis of our age." In Florida, for example, refugees from Cuba and Haiti flooded the state in the 1980s and 1990s. Many areas experienced real conflict as established residents who were already struggling now had masses of people competing with them for services and jobs. California continually experiences legal and illegal immigration from Mexico and Central and South America. The new immigrants (the weakest group) become the target for people's frustrations as their own sense of well-being decreases. The established ethnically and racially mixed groups in neighborhoods see what they perceive as preferential treatment for the newcomers and react accordingly: "People who come from other countries are welcomed and treated better than people who have lived here for many years," commented one black leader (Preston, 1989, p. A1).

Federal decisions that lead to settlement of immigrants into economically depressed communities have frequently taken place without regard to the capacity of local resources to handle the influx. Polls reflect a subsequent increase in anti-immigrant attitudes. Eventually, police and community problems evolve as a consequence of these well-meaning national policies that have not been thoroughly worked through. Tracking influxes of immigrants into communities plus an awareness of political decisions should keep law enforcement executives and officers alert to relocation and acculturation problems of newcomers in their communities. Tracking also provides an opportunity to work with the community to develop transition management plans as well as preventive programs for keeping the peace. National immigration policies and politics have a tremendous impact on cities and counties, and therefore criminal justice agencies must monitor them and plan accordingly.

As Henry DeGeneste and John Sullivan wrote in *Fresh Perspectives,* a Police Executive Research Forum publication,

> Urban tensions are fueled by a combination of . . . wealth disparity and the pressures of large scale migration, which are present not only in American cities, but in cities worldwide . . . . [Robin] Wright [a journalist for the Los Angeles Times] notes, "[T]ensions in cities are often complicated by another dimension—racial or ethnic diversity." . . . [M]inorities are increasingly left stranded in urban outskirts—slums or squatter camps—excluded politically and financially. Their ensuing frustrations contribute to the volatility of urban life.

Conflict (such as riots) resulting from urban decay, overcrowding, poor social services and ethnic tension has occurred in cities world-wide and can be expected to continue, particularly as swelling migrant populations flock to cities. (1997, p. 2)

Political Environment

Executives of criminal justice agencies must monitor legislation, sensitive court trials, and political events that affect not only the jurisdictions they serve, but also the nation and the world. Often what goes on outside of the United States has an impact on local populations. Law enforcement must be aware of foreign political struggles and their potential to polarize ethnic and racial groups in their community, leading to conflict. Police must have the ability to recognize potential problems and strive to prevent or mitigate intergroup conflict. Only by acknowledging their primary role in preventing and mediating conflict in the community can peace officers begin to remediate long-standing and emerging tensions. The criminal justice system cannot operate as though in a vacuum.

Social and Cultural Conditions

Typically, poverty and frustration with the system, the perception of racism, and unequal treatment are conditions for social unrest. Diverse peoples living in close proximity can also create potentially unstable social conditions. Furthermore, on familial level, a decline in the cohesiveness of the nuclear family (including divorce) adds to stresses within micro units in the society. Unemployment, especially among youth, is another social condition with potentially dangerous consequences. "Some authorities believe that an alarming proportion of youth lack basic skills necessary to compete in an increasingly technologically-oriented job market. How will the frustration and joblessness of young people manifest itself tomorrow?" (Tafoya, 1990, p. 15).

And, finally, gangs and the heavy use of illegal drugs and their impact on neighborhoods make social and cultural conditions ripe for explosive events. None of these elements alone, however, account for community violence. But all these factors, in combination with political and economic conditions, contribute to discontent. Officers frequently are frustrated that they cannot undo decades of societal precursors that set the stage for upheavals.

LAW ENFORCEMENT RESPONSE STRATEGIES

Public confidence and trust in the criminal justice system and law enforcement in particular are essential for effective response to hate/bias crimes. Residents in communities where people of a different race, ethnic background, religion, or sexual preference reside must be able to trust that they will be protected. They must believe that the police are not against them, that the prosecutors are vigorously prosecuting, that the judges are invoking proper penalties, and that parole, probation, and corrections are doing their share to combat crimes motivated by hate or bias. If people believe that they have to protect themselves, tensions build, communication breaks down, and people try to take the law into their own hands.

Community Programs to Reduce and Control Hate Crimes

Some solutions to reduce hate/bias crimes involve going back to basics, involving grassroots institutions such as families, schools, workplaces, and religious organizations. Partnerships between the criminal justice system and these institutions are often more successful in crime reduction programs than is the criminal justice system alone. However, some institutions that once built positive values or exercised some control over people are no longer working or have diminishing influence. The broken or dysfunctional family, for example, contributes significantly to society's problems, including the increase in criminal activity.

An effort must be made to reinstitute values that reinforce noncriminal behavior; law enforcement must be an integral part of that movement. The status quo policing approach (reactive) will not work anymore. "People have clearly begun to recognize that our strict law enforcement arrest approach isn't getting the job done," notes Darrel Stephens, former executive director of the Police Executive Research Forum (personal communication, December 2000). Progressive criminal justice executives and communities realize that crime has many complex causes and that police departments are not the first or the only line of defense. If crime is to be controlled, there must be a community alliance or partnership and the causes must be attacked on multiple fronts.

Generic Community Resources and Programs

Community resources and programs that are available or can be established include:

- *Victims' hotline:* Similar to those available for domestic violence and rape victims and suicide prevention. The staff is trained to provide victim assistance in terms of compassion, advice, referrals, and a prepared information package.

- *Human relations commission:* The staff provides assistance to victims of hate crimes or incidents, holds hearings, and provides recommendations for problem resolution.

- *United States Department of Justice Community Relations Service:* The Community Relations Service (CRS), with headquarters in Washington, D.C., has 14 regional and field offices and provides services to every state. The Justice Department has trained staff who, when notified of a problem, will participate and mediate in community meetings in an attempt to resolve conflicts. Many individual states have similar justice agencies that perform these services.

- *Conflict resolution panels:* Specially trained staff of a city or county who can assist agencies and/or victims (including groups) in the resolution of conflict, such as that caused by hate or bias.

- *The media:* Cooperation in building public awareness on the problem of hate/bias violence via articles on causes and effects, resources, and legal remedies is essential.

- *Multilingual public information brochures:* These can be provided by government agencies on the rights of victims, services available, and criminal and civil laws related to hate and bias.

- *Police storefronts:* Police substations, established in the neighborhoods of communities with high concentrations of ethnic minorities, that are staffed by bilingual officers and/or civilians. The staff takes reports and provides assistance to the members of that community.

- *Community resource list:* List of organizations that specialize in victim assistance. Examples are the Anti-Defamation League of B'nai B'rith, Black Families Associations, Japanese-American Citizens Leagues, the National Association for the Advancement of Colored People, and the Mexican-American Political Association, to name a few. National organizations that might be contacted as a resource are listed in Appendix C. The importance of having established networks with minority leaders and organizations cannot be overstressed. These leaders are extremely important for criminal justice agencies and should be identified and cultivated in advance to assist in a timely fashion with investigations, training, victim aid, and/or rumor control. If an agency experiencing serious hate/bias problems does not react quickly and effectively, victims and their community groups gain media attention because they publicly question an inadequate response or resolution. Only when a system involving trust and respect is already in place will such a network prove its worth if violence occurs in the agency's community. A good relationship with representatives of diverse communities is essential because it can help broaden the department's understanding of different cultures, ethnicities, and races. The same is true of members of gay and lesbian groups. When community members are utilized within departments, they can also help convince reluctant victims and/or witnesses to cooperate with investigators. Furthermore, they can encourage more victims to report incidents.

The key to a successful law enforcement response to hate crimes is building a partnership with victimized communities. There are many components and processes in building such a partnership. Other activities and events characterizing a joint effort would include educating the public at large, providing organizational networking opportunities, monitoring the media, and implementing federal, state, and county programs. The activities for each are described in the following sections.

Educating the Public at Large. Prejudice and bias, which can ultimately lead to violence, is often the result of ignorance. In many cases the biased individual has had little or no firsthand exposure to the targeted group; thus the bias may be due to learned stereotypes and negative media images.

One key to combating ignorance is to educate the public as well as criminal justice system employees about the history, diversity, cultures, languages, and issues of concern of the various groups within the community. This can be accomplished through neighborhood forums, workshops, and speakers' bureaus. The speakers' bureaus should be composed of people who are well versed on the issues and are available to speak at community meetings, schools, and other forums. Criminal justice employees, of course, would be trained in the workplace and/or in in-service or academy-based training courses. Most cities and counties have organizations that represent community groups that can assist in developing and implementing such education at local elementary and secondary schools, in churches, and on college and university campuses. To check the accuracy of material presented, organizers of educational programs should have at least two or three minority community members provide input on the content of the program to be delivered. Preferably, they would represent the different sub-groups within the community. Neighborhoods and communities should be encouraged to observe their various heritages through the celebration of holidays and other special days via fairs and festivals. Calendars show that there are more holidays for different religions and cultures in the United States than anywhere else in the world.

Organizational Networking. National and local organizations must network to share information, resources, ideas, and support regarding crimes motivated by hate. The list of potential organizations would include the NAACP, the ADL, the Committee against Anti-Asian Violence, the National Gay and Lesbian Task Force, and the National Institute against Prejudice and Violence. Such advocacy organizations can furnish an invaluable bridge to victim populations and assist in urging citizens to come to the police with information about hate crimes. Most of these organizations have publications and reports covering such topics as how to respond to bigotry, trends in racism, and community organizing. Through networking, organizations or groups learn who their allies are, increase their own resources and knowledge about other minority groups, and form coalitions that make a greater impact on the community and the criminal justice system. They can also assist criminal justice agencies in dealing with community reactions to hate violence and help the victims of violence cope with the experience.

The Phoenix, Arizona, Police Department offers a good example of organizational networking. In 1994 a hate crimes advisory board with representation from most of Phoenix's ethnic groups was created. The knowledge that members have and share about their communities, cultures, and potential hot spots is highly beneficial. The board has since expanded into the Central Arizona Hate Crime Advisory Board to reflect its growth. The board is the police department's conduit to the community. These partnerships between human rights groups, civic leaders, community leaders, and law enforcement can advance police–community relations by demonstrating a commitment to be both tough on those responsible for hate crimes and aware of the special needs of hate crime victims.

Monitoring the media. Minority organizations and the criminal justice system must monitor the media, which can be a foe or an ally. The media must be used strategically for education and publicity about hate/bias crimes and incidents, about multicultural and multiracial workshops, and about festivals and other cultural events. They must be monitored in terms of accuracy of reporting and must be asked to publish corrections when warranted. Negative editorials or letters to the editor pertaining to an affected group should be countered and rebutted by an op-ed piece from management within the involved criminal justice agency. Organization leaders or their designated spokespersons should become the primary sources of information for reporters to contact.

Federal, state, and county programs. Police executives should seek out every source of federal, state, and county law enforcement assistance programs and make the information available to investigators and/or task forces investigating or preventing hate crimes.

Churches, mosques and synagogues. Where the usual support organizations (e.g., ACLU, NAACP, ADL) do not exist and sometimes even where they do, churches, mosques, and synagogues often are advocates for people facing discrimination and/or who are victims of a hate incident or crime. For example, the Concord (California) Hispanic Ministry acts frequently as an advocate for Latinos with tenant–landlord problems in addition to providing Spanish-language masses, family counseling, and religious classes.

Communities with Special Programs

Some jurisdictions have used a community approach to decrease the numbers of crimes and incidents of all types, including those motivated by hate/bias. Some exemplary programs include the following:

- *Block watch volunteers program:* The Northwest Victim Services (NVS), a non-profit organization created in 1981 in Philadelphia, formed a partnership with police in the city's highest-crime-rate districts (the 14th and 35th) that utilizes an organized block watch program. Carefully selected, screened, and trained block watch volunteers not only perform the usual functions of neighborhood watch (crime prevention) but also perform a vital victim assistance role. They provide emotional support for victims who are often frightened or unfamiliar with the criminal justice process and accompany them to the various stages of the trial.

- *Task force on police–Asian relations:* In localities that have large Asian populations, task forces have been created that consist of criminal justice members, educators, victim/refugee advocates, volunteer agencies, and representatives from each Asian group living or working in the community. The purposes are several: to train criminal justice employees on communication techniques that improve relations and make them more effective in dealing with the Asian community; to prepare Asians on what to expect from the various criminal justice components, especially the police; to open lines of communication between law enforcement and Asians; and to encourage Asians to report crimes and trust the police. Agencies in California that have created such task forces and could be contacted for additional details are the San Francisco, Westminster, Garden Grove, Anaheim, Fresno, San Jose, and Huntington Beach Police Departments. These task forces could certainly be adapted to other ethnic and racial groups as well. The city of Boston and other cities have effectively used the task force approach to resolve neighborhood problems, and have found them to be effective for exchanging information and curtailing rumors; identifying problems and working on solutions; and, perhaps most important, allowing citizens to help with and approach problems on a joint basis.

- *Rapid response strategy:* The Boston Police Department also has a program to address any problem that shows a pattern. The strategy has been particularly effective in preventing and reducing civil rights violation crimes. The police department first identifies the problem from police reports, interviews with known victims, attendance at community meetings, and discussions with informants. If a pattern includes a particular day and time for incidents, the department gathers a group of area residents where the incidents are occurring. They are asked to observe (sometimes anonymously) the vicinity in which the incidents are taking place and are provided with a special hotline number, rather than the usual police emergency line, to report activities. The hotline is staffed by a police officer or civilian (with an interpreter available, if necessary), who is equipped with a walkie-talkie. One or more unmarked police vehicles are strategically placed on the periphery of the target area, along with any other officers needed, depending on the seriousness of the crime or activity expected. Calls coming from the observer to the base station are logged, and officers are dispatched when necessary via the walkie-talkies. Response time is generally less than 2 minutes, thus many crimes are prevented and/or the perpetrator is caught in the act or shortly thereafter. The effectiveness of this approach is due to the minimum amount of police staffing required for maximum coverage and the fact that some of the burden is placed on community members, who share in their own protection.

- *Citizens' patrol:* Following a series of attacks (including one fatal) on gays and lesbians in the Hillcrest community of East San Diego, California, the police responded by appointing a task force to investigate the crimes and providing more officers to patrol the area's streets. They also organized a citizens' patrol, whose volunteer members began driving Hillcrest's streets, watching for and reporting suspicious activity. Even when the task force was disbanded after the arrest of the suspect, the citizens' patrol remained. The patrol's membership even increased, and two-citizen teams with cellular telephones regularly drive problem-area streets. Both police and community leaders say there has been a noticeable decrease in violent street crimes and a feeling that Hillcrest is safer.

- *Mobile crisis unit:* A pioneering program in Arizona involved a mobile crisis unit. The unit is available 24 hours a day to counsel victims at crime scenes, transport victims, console families, make referrals to social services agencies, and provide instant information on the criminal justice process. The staff monitors police and sheriff radio frequencies and responds when requested.

- *Network of neighbors:* The human relations commission in Montgomery County, Maryland, has a "memorandum of understanding" with the police that when a hate crime occurs, the police department immediately notifies the commission. The commission in turn contacts the volunteer of the Network of Neighbors who lives closest to the victim. The network member visits the victim as soon as possible to assure the person of community support and to assist with other needs. The volunteers receive training on victim assistance and referrals. The New York City Police Department modeled a similar Good Neighbor Program after Montgomery County's.

- *STOP program:* The Montgomery County, Maryland, Office of the Human Relations Commission (OHRC) has a program that educates juvenile perpetrators of hate violence about the impact of their behavior on victims and the entire community. The program, which began in 1982, sends first offenders to the STOP program instead of through the court system. The OHRC staff requires that juvenile perpetrators and their parents attend five 2.5-hour sessions. Sessions include written and experiential exercises, discussions, films, and homework relating to their specific incident and the impact of hate and violence in general. Juveniles are also required to perform 40 hours of community service.

- *School Programs:* The Maine Office of the Attorney General's Civil Rights Team Project, created in 1996 with the help of a U.S. Department of Justice, Bureau of Justice Administration grant, uses teams of students and faculty members to promote awareness of bias and prejudice in its public high schools, middle schools, and elementary schools. Their stated mission is that no student in the state should have to experience anxiety, fear, or terror in school because of the color of their skin, their religion, their gender, their sexual orientation, their disability, or any other aspect of themselves that makes them different from other students. Law enforcement works together with teachers and administrators to empower students to stand up for civility and respect. The teams are made up of three or four students per grade, plus two or three faculty advisers. The teams have two formal responsibilities: (1) to promote awareness of bias and prejudice within their schools and (2) to organize forums for students to talk about harassment. If a team receives information about harassment, it is charged with forwarding that information to a responsible teacher or administrator. The Attorney General's office assigns a community adviser to each team to serve as liaison between the team and the Office. Annually the Attorney General's office provides full-day training for new and returning civil rights teams and for faculty and community advisers. This training includes

- a presentation on the type of hate crimes committed in Maine schools
- interactive exercises on the role of degrading language and slurs in escalating a situation to serious harassment and violence
- a presentation by a Holocaust survivor or a victim of bias and prejudice
- role-playing exercises on how to run effective civil rights team meetings
- small-group work on real-life scenarios

All participating schools agree to host Attorney General's office staff for a half-day workshop for faculty, administrators, and staff. The workshop gives teachers and other school staff a better understanding of the destructive impact of degrading language and bias-motivated harassment and teaches them how to intervene when students engage in such behavior. A similar project within the schools was created in Massachusetts.

Such community models, including those of churches and synagogues, can play a vital role in reducing violence in neighborhoods, schools, and the workplace. Successfully implemented programs can reduce individual violence, ranging from street crime to domestic abuse to drug-related crimes. Civil unrest, which can often include gang violence and open confrontations between various segments of society, can also be reduced. Building bonds of trust between the police and the community also allows community-oriented policing to contribute to the goal of promoting color-blind policing, where citizens and their police form new partnerships that offer the promise of reducing the potential for civil unrest.

Stephen Wessler, for the Bureau of Justice Administration (BJA), prepared a research paper, "Addressing Hate Crimes: Six Initiatives That Are Enhancing the Efforts of Criminal Justice Practitioners." The monograph highlights six BJA-funded projects that demonstrate the creativity and deep commitment of local, state, and federal law enforcement agencies in leading the nation's effort to combat bias-motivated crime. It identifies projects that support police and prosecutorial agencies in responding to hate crimes and supplies sources for additional information. To obtain a copy of this monograph (NCJ 179559), contact the National Criminal Justice Reference Service at (800) 851-3420. Their website is listed at the end of this chapter.

SUMMARY

The changing demographics of our communities, coupled with a bleak economic environment, constitute significant factors resulting in an increase in crimes motivated by hate or bias. It is clear that a national, standardized data collection process is essential so that the criminal justice system and respective communities served can grasp the scope of the problem and allocate resources accordingly. Such a system would enhance the prospects for developing an effective response to crimes motivated by hate or bias. Similar monitoring approaches must also be utilized by schools and businesses to ensure that acts of bigotry are tracked and resolved quickly and effectively.

The degree to which the criminal justice system, especially law enforcement agencies, responds to acts of hate and bias intimidation, violence, or vandalism sends a message to victims, communities (especially the groups to which the victims belong), and perpetrators that racism, discrimination, and crimes motivated by hate will not be tolerated. If the criminal justice system reacts swiftly and effectively or is proactive, perpetrators will know that their actions will result in apprehension and prosecution. Those sympathetic to perpetrators may be deterred from similar hate/bias actions. The fears of the victims' groups will be calmed, and trust toward the criminal justice system will be established. Other members of the community who are sensitive to the impact of hate/bias crimes and incidents will also react favorably when state and federal laws are vigorously enforced, leading to long-term benefits for all.

DISCUSSION QUESTIONS AND ISSUES

1. *Hate Crimes Monitoring Systems.* Does your law enforcement agency (where you work or in the community in which you reside) have a system in place for monitoring hate/bias crimes and incidents? If yes, obtain a copy of the statistics for at least the past 5 years (or as many years as are available) of the hate/bias crimes and determine the following:

   a. What trends are noticeable in each category?

   b. Do the categories measure essential information that will assist your law enforcement agency in recognizing trends?

   c. What would improve the data collection method to make it more useful in measuring trends and making predictions?

   d. Has your law enforcement agency actually used the data to track the nature and extent of such crimes and incidents? Did it deploy resources accordingly? Provide the class with examples.

2. *Trend Monitoring.* Make a list of specific community social, economic, and political conditions and events occurring within the law enforcement jurisdiction in which you work or live. Which ones, if any, could potentially be connected to crimes motivated by hate? For each condition listed, make a "Comments" column. Suggest what specific factors a peace officer or criminal

justice practitioner should look for in the community that would assist the agency in forecasting trends and events.

3. ***Resources.*** Find out what resources exist in your community to assist victims of hate/bias crimes.

   a. Which groups provide victim assistance?

   b. Which coalition groups exist, and what types of community outreach programs are offered?

   c. What types of pamphlets or other written materials are available?

   d. Which groups have speaker bureaus?

   e. Which groups are working with local law enforcement agencies with regard to response programs or cultural awareness training?

   f. Which groups are working with the district attorney's or prosecutor's office?

4. ***Role of Your District Attorney's Office.*** Assess the role of your district attorney's or prosecutor's office by determining the following:

   a. Does it have a special hate crimes or civil rights unit?

   b. Do hate crimes cases receive special attention?

   c. Are misdemeanor and felony hate crimes prosecuted differently?

   d. How does the office determine if it will prosecute a hate crime case?

   e. What types of training do assistant district attorneys receive regarding hate crimes?

   f. What types of community outreach does the office provide regarding hate crimes?

5. ***Victim Assistance.*** Identify avenues of victim assistance in your area. Research and document the following:

   a. Does your state have a crime victims' assistance program? Does it offer victim compensation? What about a victim's bill of rights?

   b. What services does the local department of mental staff offer?

   c. Do any community groups, rape crisis centers, or crime victim services agencies in the area offer counseling to hate crimes victims?

   d. Are any mental health care professionals willing to donate their services to victims of hate crimes?

6. ***Human Relations Commission.*** What is the role of the human relations commission (HRC) if one exists in your area?

   a. Does it have a specific task force on hate crimes?

   b. Does it have any type of tracking system for recording statistics on hate crime?

   c. What is its relationship with local law enforcement agencies and district attorneys' offices regarding hate crime?

   d. What is its relationship with community organizations concerned with hate crimes? Has it produced any brochures, pamphlets, or other materials on hate crimes?

    e. Does it provide multicultural workshops or sensitivity training regarding different ethnic, racial, or lifestyle groups?

    f. Have there been occasions when the HRC has gone beyond the scope of its charter or stated goals that resulted in negative exposure or media attention? Describe the circumstances.

REFERENCES

Anti-Defamation League. (1990). Special report by former U.S. Attorney General Richard Thornburgh. Available: www.adl.org

Anti-Defamation League. (2001). *ADL 2000—Audit of Anti-Semitic Incidents.* Available: www.adl.org

Berkowitz, Howard. (1999, September 14). Hate on the Internet, Congressional testimony.

Casuto, Morris. (1992, November 2). Director of the San Diego Regional Office of the Anti-Defamation League and instructor at the San Diego Police Academy and the San Diego County Sheriff's Training Academy, personal communication.

Center for Democratic Renewal. (1992). *When Hate Groups Come to Town: A Handbook of Effective Community Responses.* Atlanta, Ga.: Author.

DeGeneste, Henry I., and John P. Sullivan. (1997, July). "Policing a Multicultural Community." *Fresh Perspectives.*

"Domestic terrorism alleged in Lemon Grove." (2000, December 11). *San Diego Union Tribune,* p. A3.

"Hate group influx seen in northern Utah towns." (2003, April 6). *Contra Costa Times,* p. 18.

"Jewish community critical of law enforcement lack of notification," (1993, July 29). *San Francisco Cronicle.* p. A20.

Levin, B. (1993). "Bias Crimes: A Theoretical & Practical Overview," *Stan. Law & Pol'y Rev.* 4:165.

New York State Governor's Task Force on Bias-Related Crime. (1988). Final Report. Albany: New York State Printing Office.

Parker, Patricia A. (1991, December). "Tackling Unfinished Business: POP Plays Valuable Position in Racial Issues." *Police, 19,* pp. 5–9.

Preston, Julia. (1989, January 18). "Trouble Spreads in Troubled Black Areas." *Washington Post,* p. A-1.

Rosenfeld, Henry O. (1992, June). "Establishing Non-Traditional Partnerships to Mitigate the Future Impact of White Supremacist Groups." Sacramento, Calif.: Peace Officer Standards and Training.

Ross, Loretta. (1995). "White Supremacy in the 1990s." *Public Eye,* pp. 1–12.

Southern Poverty Law Center. (2002). *Intelligence Report,* Issue 109.

Southern Poverty Law Center. (2003). "In Sheep's Clothing," *Intelligence Report,* Issue 110, pp. 20–24.

SPLC (Southern Poverty Law Center) Report. (2003, March). "Maine town's diversity rally outdraws hate-group gathering." Vol. 33, No. 1, p. 8.

SPLC Report. (1992, February). *Klanwatch Intelligence Report.* Issue 59.

SPLC Report. (2000, September). *Klanwatch Intelligence Report,* Issue 99.

SPLC Report. (2002, April). "FBI hate crime statistics ignore thousands of victims." Vol. 32, No. 1, p. 4.

Stephens, Darrel W. (2003). Chief of Police, Charlotte-Mecklenburg Police Department, Charlotte, North Carolina. personal communication.

"Study: FBI undercounts hate crimes." (2001, November 30). *Contra Costa Times,* p. B7.

"Study: Hate groups capitalizing on attacks." (2001, November 11). *Contra Costa Times,* p. A20.

Tafoya, William L. (1990, December–January). "Rioting in the Streets: Déja Vu?" *C. J. the Americas, 2*(6), 21.

U.S. Department of Justice. (1990). *Summary Reporting System: Hate Crime Data Collection Guidelines.* Washington, D.C.: U.S. Government Printing Office.

"World Church of the Creator America's most dangerous supremacist group." (1992, September 21). Southern Poverty Law Center Newsletter, pp. 42–44.

Chapter 14

Racial Profiling

OVERVIEW

This chapter addresses the topic of racial profiling—a current, central, and controversial area of law enforcement. It provides the core knowledge important to students and professionals within the criminal justice system, including a conceptual definition of "racial profiling," "profiles," and "profiling." The chapter also presents historical and background information on the effects of racial profiling on minorities as well as on different ethnic, cultural, and religious groups as a consequence of the current war on terrorism. The chapter contains a discussion and examples of manifestations of racial profiling and associated elements such as "bias-based policing." There is, additionally, an examination of diverse points of view and perceptions of racial profiling, and its impact upon minority communities, citizens, and law enforcement agencies along with statistical data from research on the issues. The chapter includes a section comparing "profiling" as a legitimate tool of law enforcement with "racial profiling" as a bias-based aberration of the tool. These conceptualizations of profiling are defined and presented with field examples and illustrations from several different law enforcement agencies. The chapter includes suggestions for preventing racial profiling in law enforcement.

COMMENTARY

Actual or perceived racial profiling by law enforcement officers affects blacks, Hispanics, Arab Americans, and other minority groups from every walk of life, every vocation, and every level of the socioeconomic ladder. The extent to which race, ethnicity, and/or national origin can be used as factors in targeting suspects for stops, searches, and arrests has been a concern of citizens and law enforcement for some time. The controversy over racial profiling is compounded by the unsupported assumption that the officer making traffic and field-interrogation stops of nonwhite citizens is making a race-based decision rooted in racial prejudice. These concerns became even more critical since the "War on Terrorism" began on September 11, 2001. Consider these excerpts from the media and how their content impacts law enforcement in general:

> **Bush issues ban on racial profiling by federal authorities.** President Bush issued the first broad ban on racial profiling by federal law enforcement agencies but included exceptions permitting use of race and ethnicity to combat potential

terrorist attacks. The new policy covers about 120,000 officers at 70 federal agencies with law enforcement powers. It prohibits the use of "generalized stereotypes" based on race or ethnicity, and allows officers to consider them only as part of a specific description or tip from a reliable source. ("Bush bans racial profiling," 2003, p. A14)

ACLU of New Jersey Wins $775,000 for Victims of Racial Profiling by State Troopers. Newark, N.J. *The State of New Jersey has agreed to pay more than $775,000 to motorists who were victims of racial profiling to settle lawsuits brought by the American Civil Liberties Union of New Jersey, the group announced at a news conference today.* ("Racial profiling," American Civil Liberties Union, January 13, 2003)

Racial-profiling class-action suit is settled by California Highway Patrol. *The California Highway Patrol settled a racial-profiling lawsuit yesterday by agreeing to extend a ban of some car searches and require officers to specify the reason for each drug-related traffic stop beyond just a hunch about wrongdoing. The settlement, filed in federal court, also requires the highway patrol to track all stops and constantly review that database to spot whether any officer is pulling over a disproportionate number of black or Hispanic motorists. The highway patrol also must pay $875,000 in legal fees and damages.* (2003, p. A4)

Three Students Charge Illinois State Police with Racial Profiling in Vehicle Stop. Peoria, Illinois. *What should have been a routine traffic stop in November 2000 degenerated into an unlawful detention and search of three African American high school students in which a state trooper uttered a racial slur, according to a federal lawsuit filed by the American Civil Liberties Union of Illinois today.* (Press Release, American Civil Liberties Union, May 8, 2002)

Studies Find Race Disparities in Texas Traffic Stops. *Black and Hispanic motorists across Texas are more than twice as likely as non-Hispanic whites to be searched during traffic stops while black drivers in certain rural areas of the state are also far more likely to be ticketed.* (Headline, The New York Times, October 7, 2000)

DEFINITIONS

Over the past few years, there have been hundreds of articles and publications in which "racial profiling" has been defined, yet no single definition dominates the national conversation about this issue. The debate has troubled not only those involved in the criminal justice system, but also concerned citizens and communities, scholars, researchers, civil rights organizations, and legislators. With no agreed-upon criteria for what does or does not constitute racial profiling, it has been difficult to clarify and resolve the issues. Variation among definitions means that interested parties are often talking at cross-purposes, unwittingly discussing different types of police practices, behavior, and stops. For this reason, proposals to prohibit racial profiling are difficult to develop and carry out. Depending on the definition of racial profiling used, some police activities would be considered acceptable and others would not. We cannot make an act illegal if we cannot define it. Data collected cannot even be interpreted properly. The criminal justice system and state legislatures must choose an appropriate definition that would be accepted not only statewide, but also nationally. The definition should have explicit standards that specify what actions are allowed and not allowed by law enforcement officers. There should be fewer gray areas in which officers and agents do not know if their procedures and tactics are legal or not.

This textbook utilizes the following definitions.

Racial Profiling

The authors will use the definition developed by the U.S. Department of Justice and the National Organization of Black Law Enforcement Executives (NOBLE). According to these organizations, racial profiling is any police-initiated action that relies on the race, ethnicity, or national origin rather than the behavior of an individual or information that leads the police to a particular individual who has been identified as being, or having been, engaged in criminal activity. Racial profiling, also known as Driving While Black or Brown (DWB), has been ruled illegal by the courts and is considered improper police practice by law enforcement officers and agencies.

Profile

A "profile" is typically a document that contains explicit criteria or indicators issued to officers to guide them in their decision making. It is usually based on data collected and interpreted to signify a trend or suggest that, given a particular set of characteristics (behavioral or situational commonalties), a person could believe that something may result based on that particular cluster of characteristics. A profile relies upon expert advice provided to law enforcement agencies to identify perpetrators of criminal activities. It can be an outline or short biographical description, an individual's character sketch, or a type of behavior associated with a group. It is a summary of data presenting the average or typical appearance of those persons or situations under scrutiny. Officers use these indicators of behavioral or situational commonalties to develop reasonable suspicion or probable cause to stop subjects.

Profiling

Any police-initiated action that uses a compilation of the background, physical, behavioral, and/or motivational characteristics for a type of perpetrator that leads the police to a particular individual who has been identified as being, could be, or having been engaged in criminal activity.

Racially Biased Policing

Racially biased policing occurs when law enforcement inappropriately considers race or ethnicity in deciding with whom and how to intervene in an enforcement capacity (PERF Report, 2001). Racially biased policing is illegal. The authors will use the term "racial profiling" throughout this chapter instead of racially biased policing because it is a more commonly recognized term, although "racially biased policing" is a much better description of the phenomenon.

Bias-Based Policing

The act (intentional or unintentional) of applying or incorporating personal, societal, or organizational biases and/or stereotypes in decision making, police actions, or the administration of justice.

Race or Ethnicity

A particular descent, including Caucasian, African, Hispanic, Asian/Pacific, or Native American.

Reasonable Suspicion

A police officer may briefly detain a person for questioning or request identification only if the officer has a reasonable suspicion that the person's behavior is related to criminal activity. The officer, however, must have specific and articulable facts to support his or her actions; a mere suspicion or "hunch" is not sufficient cause to detain a person or to request identification. Reasonable suspicion can be based on the observations of a police officer combined with his or her training and experience, and/or reliable information received from credible outside sources.

Suspect-Specific Incident

An incident in which an officer is lawfully attempting to detain, apprehend, or otherwise be on the lookout for one or more specific suspects who have been identified or described in part by national or ethnic origin, gender, or race.

HISTORICAL BACKGROUND OF THE TERM RACIAL PROFILING IN LAW ENFORCEMENT

During the 1990s, concerns about the police use of racial profiling as a pretext to stop, question, search, and possibly arrest people became a major focus of minority individuals and communities, politicians, law enforcement administrators, scholars, and researchers. National surveys in the last decade revealed that the majority of Americans, white as well as black, believed racial profiling was commonly used in the United States, but 80 percent of those surveyed opposed the practice. They believed that police were routinely guilty of bias in their treatment of racial and ethnic minorities, and also that such behavior had been going on for a long time. What is the source of racial profiling as both a term and as a law enforcement practice? Before addressing that question, it is useful to examine how people use prior events or information to make decisions in everyday life.

People routinely form mental images or tentative judgments about others and the surrounding circumstances or situation, both consciously and subconsciously, which is also a form of stereotyping. This sort of stereotyping, or looking for what one perceives to be indicators, provides a preliminary mental rating of potential risk to a person encountering a particular event or person.

It involves (see Senge's "Ladder of Inference" discussed later in this chapter) conscious and unconscious thought processes whereby an individual: (1) makes observations and selects data) born out of that person's past experiences, (2) adds cultural and personal meaning to what he or she observes, (3) makes assumptions based on the meanings that he or she has attributed to the observation, (4) draws conclusions based on his or her own beliefs and, finally, (5) takes action. This process comprises basic decision making in life by all people and because it guides a person's interpretation of events. A person's socialization, including parental upbringing, plays a major role in determining decisions he or she makes and the actions taken accordingly in both professional and personal settings.

Profiling in law enforcement is used by officers to look for characteristics that indicate the probability of criminal acts or factors that tend to correlate with dangerous or threatening behavior. For officers, most of these characteristics have been internalized based on experience and training. If they have had dangerous encounters while on duty, these experiences prepare them for future, similar events—as the old saying goes, *better safe than sorry!* The professional training that leads to the development of indicators or common characteristics comes from many sources, beginning with the police academy and in-service training under the supervision of a field-training officer. Informal education may include mentoring by an older partner and pressure from peers on how to do the job, and more formal training continues via advanced officer courses on various subjects. All of these help establish the common practice of profiling. If an official profile of a suspect is used by an agency, and the perpetrator is caught, we say, "he or she fits the profile," thus validating this perspective. When serial bombing suspect Eric Robert Rudolph was finally apprehended in June 2003, for example, FBI profiling experts immediately confirmed that the notorious fugitive did indeed *fit their profile.* Training and experience provide officers with indicators to look for not only to prevent harm to themselves, but also to identify those people or events that are suspicious and warrant closer attention. This attention then helps civilians and police officers decide what action is prudent to take when confronted by a similar person or situation. This doesn't necessarily mean the person using profiling in this way is biased or prejudiced. Fulbright professor Ira Straus, in an article for United Press International, suggests that some degree of profiling can be appropriate and even necessary as long as it is not abusive. In the article, he is not using the term profiling to mean the same as the definition used in this textbook, but using "profiling" meaning stereotyping.

> Profiling is universal. Every person relies on it for a preliminary rating of their risks with each person they run into. If people do not profile explicitly, they do it implicitly. If they do not do it consciously, they do it unconsciously. But they go on doing it. They could not live without it.
>
> Do police do it too? Of course they do. All police and investigative efforts involve working from two ends, direct and indirect. The direct end means following the trail of specific leads and informants. The indirect end means profiling; that is, finding a social milieu or pool to look in and ask around in—a milieu where there are more likely to be informants, leads, and criminals answering to that crime.
>
> To profile is morally risky. The dangers of unfair and unreasonable profiling— that is, profiling based on unfounded prejudices such as racism—are well known. They are widely discussed, guarded against, and proscribed. (2002, pp. 1–2)

Professor Straus implies profiling (or in his context, stereotyping) is not always based on accurate information or data. When the meanings placed on observations are faulty or biased, the assumptions and conclusions, therefore, may be incorrect, thereby leading to inappropriate attitudes, behavior, and actions.

Law enforcement officers, airport security personnel, customs and border patrol agents, and some other occupations use profiles because, in the absence of conclusive, specific details, that is the only way to narrow the amount of information from which to make decisions, including whether or not to stop a person for further investigation.

Although there are other historical examples of racial profiling, the first use of the term appears to have occurred in New Jersey, where troopers were trying to stem the flow of illegal drugs and other contraband into and across their state. In the early 1990s, a relationship developed between the Drug Enforcement Administration (DEA) and the New Jersey State Patrol (NJSP). Training was provided to the NJSP on what the DEA had determined to be common characteristics of drug couriers along Interstate 95 from Miami through New Jersey. The characteristics included the types of cars preferred (Nissan Pathfinders), the direction of travel, and the use of rental vehicles from another state. In addition, it was common to find that a third party had rented the vehicle, the driver was licensed in a different state than the one where the rental took place, and there were telltale behavioral cues (such as nervousness or conflicting stories). The profile also noted that the national origin of many of those involved in drug-trafficking organizations was predominantly Jamaican.

The NJSP used "pretextual stops" (that is, using some legal pretext, such as failing to signal a lane change or having a missing license plate or faulty brake light) on I-95 to determine the potential criminality of a car's driver and occupants. The officer(s) would then attempt to establish a legal basis to search for illegal drugs. Many argued, and the courts agreed, that these pretextual stops were also based on the fact that the driver and occupants were black or dark-skinned. In other words, they had been racially profiled—targeted because of the color of their skin. The resultant studies determined that blacks and Hispanics on I-95 were stopped disproportionate to their numbers on that road. Due to the controversy and subsequent court decision and punitive judgment against the New Jersey State Patrol, they no longer distribute a typical felony offender profile to their officers "because such profiles might contribute to what the state's attorney general calls 'inappropriate stereotypes' about criminals" (Will, 2001). New Jersey, like other states, has also created legislation making racial profiling illegal, with criminal sanctions for officers using the practice.

PROFILING CHALLENGES IN THE WAR ON TERRORISM

Prior to September 11, 2001, the use by law enforcement agencies of profiles that included race, ethnicity or national origin, or the act of profiling using the same criteria, had come to be generally frowned upon, or even condemned, in the United States. But an attitude change occurred after the horrendous attacks on the World Trade Center in New York City and the Pentagon. One outcome of that event was the establishment of the U.S. Department of Homeland Security and the attempt to coordinate law enforcement agencies and the military in national defense of the citizenry and infrastructure. The scope of the state of emergency created by the hijackers has altered both public opinion and government policy concerning profiles and profiling based on national origin and ethnicity, especially regarding both the legitimacy and necessity of the practices. Given the ongoing and complex conflicts in the Middle East, plus the global terrorist threat from al-Qaida and other Islamic extremists, the issue became more charged and complicated. Police at the national and local level had to develop strategies for detecting and apprehending terrorists. Tentative profiles were quickly developed on the basis of obvious characteristics and experience.

Since all the terrorists involved in the September 11 incidents were Islamic males from the Middle East, the issue became whether law enforcement and security personnel could target or profile suspicious men with similar backgrounds for stops, searches, or increased questioning. Profiling, using those profiles, began to be employed on the basis of several factors common to these particular terrorists, who were

- young males who were Arab in appearance

- primarily citizens of Saudi Arabia

- trained in fundamentalist religious and/or al-Qaida training camps in Afghanistan or Pakistan

- adherents of Islam who had been inspired to religious extremism by fundamentalist clergy, especially with regard to *jihad* (see Glossary)

- harboring a deep hatred, in general, of Western decadence, materialism, and immorality, which they perceived as undermining the values and stability of their societies, and in particular, of America for its interference in Middle Eastern affairs.

In the aftermath of September 11 and the emergency federal legislation enacted in response to it, there were mass round-ups of individuals of Middle Eastern origin and descent in the United States and abroad based on profiles. In many cases, the rights of those apprehended may have been violated. Instances of persons of Middle Eastern or South Asian descent (or who appeared to be Arab or Muslim) removed from planes and subjected to detention, questioning, and search have been reported where there was no reasonable suspicion or probable cause that they might have harbored criminal intentions. Consider the following incidents reported in the media:

> **Passengers kicked off flights sue airlines, allege profiling.** Five minority flyers who were forced off airplanes after Sept. 11 accused airlines of racial profiling in lawsuits filed Tuesday that heighten the sensitive debate over how to prevent terrorist attacks. The American Civil Liberties Union filed the suits that claim the passengers, who looked Middle Eastern or Asian, passed rigorous security checks but were kicked off their flights after other passengers or crew members said that they "felt uncomfortable" with them on board, according to the ACLU. ("Passengers kicked off flights," 2002, p. D1 and back page)

> **Airline Racism.** ADC [American-Arab Anti-Discrimination Committee] has received over 60 cases in which passengers, both men and women, perceived to be Arab have been expelled from an aircraft during or after boarding on the grounds that passengers or crew do not like the way they look. ADC has also received dozens of complaints from passengers subjected to extreme security measures, such as women wearing the hijab, or religious head scarf, being made to remove it in public, even after passing through security without incident. (ADC Fact Sheet: The Condition of Arab Americans Post-9/11, Washington D.C., March 27, 2002)

Initially, there was little outcry among the general public against these actions and others. Recall that prior to September 11, 80 percent of Americans opposed racial profiling. After that day, however, "there [was] an immediate reversal of public opinion," says Michelle Alexander of the American Civil Liberties Union (ACLU) of Northern California. Polls taken soon after the attack showed that 70 percent of Americans believed that some form of profiling was necessary, and acceptable, to ensure public safety. It is apparent that the public was willing to give up certain freedoms in exchange for helping the government reduce the opportunity for terrorists to operate in the United States. Members of the American Association for Public Opinion Research, at a May 2002 meeting, offered a historical perspective. They said that while civil liberties usually have broad public support, the public has been willing to tolerate substantial limits on those freedoms when there are serious threats to security and safety within the United States and to Americans abroad. Their report cited the decline in support for civil liberties after Pearl Harbor and again at the height of the Cold War. Other than the American Civil Liberties Union and the National Association of Arab Americans, there were few who spoke out against detentions of Middle Easterners and South Asians after September 11 at security areas in airports and elsewhere. These organizations questioned the use of what appeared to them to be racial profiling and abuse of civil rights, generally and specifically. However, many citizens argued that proactive law enforcement and enhanced security measures at airports were necessary to prevent or reduce opportunities for terrorist acts and to investigate and bring to justice those involved. Discovering terrorists and their missions, prior to another attack, became a matter of urgency.

The researchers added, however, that support for civil liberties has always resumed when the threat subsides. This certainly was the case as time passed after September 11 without additional terrorist acts in the United States. Between 2001 and 2003, membership in the ACLU *increased* 15% (2003, p. A23). The increase suggests that despite the war on terrorism and potential for terrorist acts, many Americans remain troubled by the potential for the federal government overreaching that is embodied in such antiterrorism measures as the USA Patriot Act (increasing the FBI's wiretapping and search powers), which expands the powers of the criminal justice system.

The use of profiles and profiling in law enforcement requires a balancing of morality, legality, efficiency, equality, liberty, and security concerns. It has the potential to affect millions of innocent people in the United States who are or may appear to be of Muslim, Arab, Middle Eastern, or South Asian descent, or Sikh. It is important that law enforcement officials and security agents avoid hasty judgments and not condemn all Muslims, those of the Islamic faith, or Middle Easterners for the crimes of a few. Officers, agents, and those who protect airports and other public facilities should seek to learn more about both Islam and Arab civilization (see Chapter 8).

Reality Check

How does law enforcement balance the need to reduce crime, and especially terrorism, against the potential for accusations of discrimination, race biased policing, and stereotyping? It is a challenging and complex problem for officers, especially for those strongly committed to nonbiased practices who believe in proactive policing. The real issues with any type of law enforcement profiling or the development of profiles are:

(1) Who is doing the profile construction and on what basis? Does that person have some expertise (for example, in behavioral science)? Is the profile creator objective, unbiased, and nonjudgmental in formulating a particular profile? (2) Who is interpreting the profile? Is that person sufficiently trained in its application? and (3) Is the officer who is using profiling doing so legally? Is it based on departmental policy rather than his or her acting on personal biases, attitudes, and beliefs?

Criminal justice agencies are facing major challenges regarding the issue and impact of the use of profiles and profiling, especially after September 11. Law enforcement personnel are charged with: (1) Protecting the rights of those who are the subject of stereotyping, harassment, and discrimination (i.e., those who are *misidentified* as a result of profiles or profiling); (2) Identifying and bringing to justice those who are terrorists and criminals (i.e., those who are *correctly identified*); (3) Not missing terrorists and/or criminals who do not fit a particular profile or stereotype; and (4) Not being so hampered by one's personal stereotypes, attitudes, beliefs, perceptions, and knowledge (or lack thereof) that innocent people are detained and terrorists are not apprehended in the course of law enforcement.

POLICE AND CITIZEN PERCEPTIONS OF RACIAL PROFILING

Myth, Misperception, or Reality?

There are some police officers, government administrators, and others who maintain that racial profiling is a myth or a misperception. They argue that the majority of officers do not stop or detain people based on their race, ethnicity, or national origin, but on their behavior, location, circumstances, and other factors. Officers contend that those who are stopped often do not understand police procedures, or are overly sensitive, or are using the allegation that bias was involved in their stop, questioning, search, and/or arrest to cast aspersion on the action taken in an attempt to nullify it.

Although these observers claim that racial profiling doesn't exist, an abundance of anecdotes and statistics document that it does. As mentioned, national surveys have indicated that the majority of white, as well as black, Americans believe that racial profiling is widespread across the nation. The complaints about racial profiling now extend to Arab and Middle Eastern people or those who appear to be from that region of the world.

> Current research on racial profiling has suggested that in some jurisdictions, officers disproportionately stop nonwhite citizens. Some studies have characterized these stops as discrimination, while others have only acknowledged that a disparity exists and correctly noted that inferences as to the cause of the disparity cannot be appropriately made with the data available. (Engel, 2001 p. 269)

Researchers studying allegations of racial profiling need also to explore discretionary decision making of individual officers, a subject that has long been the object of study by those doing research in the criminal justice field.

> Most of the research on criminal justice has documented that the impact of racial prejudice on criminal justice agents' decision making has been decreasing in prevalence and importance for at least 30 years. Prior to the 1970s, racial prejudice was still the basis for many state and local laws. Since that time, po-

lice departments have made continuing serious managerial efforts to reduce and eliminate prejudicial behavior by police officers, and recent research is no longer consistent with earlier research on the extent to which race per se directly influences police decisions. This recent research suggests that police officers' behavior is predicted primarily by legal and situation-specific factors and that the influence of race and other extra-legal factors is diminishing. (Engel, 2001, pp. 251–252)

Police Perceptions

What are the police's perceptions of allegations that all race-based decision making by them is motivated by their own prejudice?

Most law enforcement officers would maintain they are not biased, prejudiced, or using racial profiling in their policing methods. Proactive policing sometimes involves using legitimate profiling based on officer experience and training or using profiles provided by their agency. Sometimes, however, officer experience can mean a lot of things. If the experience leads to faulty assumptions and conclusions, then the officer might engage in inappropriate behavior and take the wrong action. (See the "Education and Training" section of this chapter for a discussion of the sources of officers' beliefs and attitudes.)

Officers use profiling (behavioral commonalities or indicators) or written profiles to identify those they should investigate to determine if they are committing or about to commit a crime. Profiling is done on a daily basis by police officers, not just in high crime areas where gangs congregate or highway corridors where drug runners operate, but in all communities. It also takes place in predominantly white communities when officers see out-of-place or suspicious-looking members of minority groups. The officer in this situation would argue that he or she would find reason to check out anyone, regardless of color, who did not seem to fit the area or time of day, especially if he or she were acting suspiciously. Profiling also takes place when an officer sees a white person in a predominantly minority area, especially if the area is one in which drug sales or prostitution take place. The officer checks out the individual if reasonable suspicion is present that a crime might be taking place. Most officers would emphatically deny they are biased or prejudiced when using such profiling.

Officers also insist that their agency and the community in which they work pressure them to reduce crime in the neighborhoods, and that profiling (not racial profiling) is a tool to accomplish a reduction in some crimes. If officers believe that their agency supervisors and managers want them to be aggressive on the streets by stopping vehicles and pedestrians to determine if there is potential criminal activity leading to a search and arrest, officers will do so, especially if this behavior is rewarded within their organization. Reward structures within agencies include such things as favorable evaluations, shifts, assignments, and even promotions. Unfortunately, if officers come to believe that minority citizens are more likely to be involved in criminal activity of some sort and that aggressively stopping their vehicles will result in more searches and arrests, they are more likely to stop them (referred to as the expectancy theory), especially if the department encourages and rewards the practice.

Sometimes, however, departments targeting criminal activity can cause a backlash. Take, for example, the Oakland, California, "Riders" case. During a 3-week period ending July 3, 2000, four officers of the Oakland Police Department were accused of beating and framing suspects by planting drugs and writing false police reports. The officers' attorneys used the defense that top Oakland police brass promoted the practice of "attacking" suspects and having a "hostile" relationship with suspected drug dealers because of one program implemented by the department—Project SANE (Strategic Application of Narcotics Enforcement). The program involved redirecting about 57 officers, particularly during overnight hours, to target drug dealing. In his courtroom testimony, Police Chief Richard Word defended his department's aggressive policing policy and maintained that the effort to target street-level drug dealing did not cause the behavior of the officers who became known as "The Riders." He added that officers should know the difference between proactive police work and violating civil rights and the Riders had exceeded directives. Reducing crime in Oakland had become Word's top priority soon after he was promoted to chief. He, along with the city's mayor and manager, set a goal of a 20 percent reduction in crime. The officers were cleared in eight police misconduct counts and a mistrial was declared September 30, 2003, on 27 more charges. They had denied all charges but, according to one defense attorney, "they acknowledge[d] they were aggressive on the job and say their behavior was rewarded. They were told push the line, stretch the law, but don't break it . . . [A] lot of stops were questionable, but these guys were told to push it" ("Oakland's police chief angry," 2003, p. A5). There was a civil settlement of $10.9 million with the 119 plaintiffs and the City of Oakland had to pay $3.6 million to contract with an independent monitoring agency that will oversee police reforms over a 5-year period ("Oakland to analyze," 2003, p. A4).

As indicated above, some police officers and city or county administrators deny the existence of racial profiling. They claim that those who believe that they are the victims of racial profiling may not be aware of other factors that the officer may have considered. Traffic stops are the most common situations leading to complaints of racial profiling. A 1999 nationwide survey regarding police contact with the public by the U.S. Bureau of Criminal Justice Statistics determined that speeding was the most common reason for being pulled over, accounting for 51.2 percent of all traffic stops. The majority of drivers stopped by police (84.3 percent) felt they had been stopped for legitimate reasons.

The Police Executive Research Forum (PERF) undertook an extensive study of racial profiling. They chose to avoid the term "racial profiling," preferring "racially biased policing." They indicate in the report that "racial profiling" was defined so restrictively that the term does not fully capture the concerns of both police and citizens. For example:

> Racial profiling is frequently defined as law enforcement activities (e.g., detentions, arrests, searches) that are initiated *solely* on the basis of race. Central to the debate on the most frequently used definitions is the word "solely." In the realm of potential discriminatory actions, this definition likely references only a very small portion. Even a racially prejudiced officer likely uses more than the single factor of race when conducting biased law enforcement. For example, officers might make decisions based on the neighborhood and the race of the person, the age of the car and the race of the person, or the gender and the race of the person. Activities based on these sample pairs of factors would fall outside the most commonly used definition of racial profiling. (PERF, 2001, p. 3)

Using this common definition of "racial profiling," then, provides a very narrow meaning for the term. Those who define the practice so narrowly (i.e., race as the only reason for stopping, questioning or arresting someone) that we can imagine only the most extreme bigots engaging in it. Using such a definition, racial profiling is easy to both denounce and deny (Barlow & Barlow, 2002).

In the study, the PERF staff conducted meetings around the country with citizens and police line and command staff regarding occurrences and perceptions of biased policing. (Note: The Police Executive Research Forum has produced a video and guide to facilitate police–citizen discussions on racially biased policing. To order free copies, see the "Website References" section of this chapter for their address. The subsequent report, *Racially Biased Policing: A Principled Response,* revealed that the police in the study were using the narrow definition of "racial profiling" (stops based *solely* on race or ethnicity) and thus could declare vehemently that police actions based solely on race were quite rare. The citizens in the study, however, were using a broader definition, one that included race as one among several factors leading up to the stop of the individual.

> Many of our law enforcement participants did express skepticism that "racial profiling" was a major problem, exacerbating some citizens' frustration. It became clear to staff that these differing perceptions among citizens and police regarding racial profiling's pervasiveness were very much related to the respective definitions they had adopted. The citizens equated "racial profiling" with all manifestations of racially biased policing, whereas most of the police practitioners defined "racial profiling" as stopping a motorist based *solely* on race. Presumably, even officers who engage in racially biased policing rarely make a vehicle stop based *solely* on race (often ensuring probable cause or some other factor is also present). (PERF Report, 2001, p. 15)

Other Factors in Police Stops. Those concerned about racial profiling must also recognize that when a stop or detention by officers is not self-initiated, it was most likely to have been generated because a witness or victim had provided a description of a person or event that they felt required police action—a suspect-specific incident or due to computer-generated information. This is the case in the majority of contacts police make with citizens. If the complainant describes a suspect of a certain race, ethnicity, or national origin, that is what the officer will search for. For example, if police receive a report of possible criminal activity, and reliable information indicates that he is 5'8", lean, long-haired, and Asian, then "Asian" may be considered, along with the other demographics, in developing reasonable suspicion or probable cause to detain. If, however, the citizen is reporting the activity of a minority because of his or her own biases, the police should attempt to ensure the legitimacy of the complaint and not be an agent of what might be racially charged paranoia. In Brooksfield, Wisconsin, dispatchers were trained to gather more information from callers to determine if the call is legitimate. If not, they then can explain this fact to the caller and not trigger a potentially volatile police–citizen encounter.

Some allegations of racially motivated stops are clearly not reasonable. In some cases, officers cannot discern the race or ethnicity of the driver and/or occupant prior to the detention. For example, some cars have tinted or darkened windows or a head rest on the back of the seats. Obviously at nighttime, it is challenging to identify drivers or passengers in detail. (Readers of this textbook should try to identify the occupants of a vehicle in front of them to test this argument.)

Policing during the 1990s and into the present day has been driven by two forces: (1) data developed and analyzed by specialists (crime analysts) that provides officers with predictions on where crimes might occur (including time of day and even generalized suspect information), and (2) "Problem-Oriented Policing (POP)" or "Community-Oriented Policing (COP)" approaches, wherein neighborhood representatives tell officers about problems, including potential suspects, in their communities. In the latter case, members of the community demand that officers take enforcement action against drug dealers, prostitutes, gang members, those disturbing the peace, and suspicious persons regardless of their race or ethnicity. Take, for example, the following case study:

MINI CASE STUDIES: CULTURE AND CRIME

Mini-Case Study 1: Arlington County, Virginia

In 2000, Ed Flynn, chief of police for Virginia's Arlington County, responded to the demands of his city's black community for stricter drug enforcement. "We had a series of community meetings. The residents said to us, 'Years ago, you had control over the problem. Now the kids are starting to act out again.' They even asked us, 'Where are your jump-out squads [officers who observe drug deals from their cars, then jump out and nab the participants]?'" So Flynn and his local commander put together an energetic strategy to break up the drug trade. They instituted aggressive motor-vehicle checks throughout the problem neighborhood, stopping and questioning those who were driving too fast or who had cracked windshields, too-dark windows, or expired tags. "We wanted to increase our presence in the area and make it quite unpleasant for the dealers to operate," Flynn says. The Arlington officers also cracked down on quality-of-life offenses like public urination, and used undercover surveillance to take out the dealers.

By the end of the summer, the department had cleaned up the crime hot spots. Community newsletters thanked the cops for breaking up the dealing. Chief Flynn observed, however, "We had also just generated a lot of data showing 'disproportionate' minority arrests. We are responding to heartfelt demands for increased police presence," he says. "But this places police departments in the position of producing data at the community's behest that can be used against them" (Mac Donald, 2001).

Another example of urban policing using race-neutral, data-driven methods is New York's innovative COMPSTAT (Computerized Statistics) program. COMPSTAT involves computer-generated crime analysis that allows police commanders to focus enforcement strategies on specific crimes and problem areas in the city. Officers are held accountable for reducing the specific crime in that area. If robberies are up in a certain precinct, officers are deployed to locate and arrest those responsible. If the neighborhood they are assigned to is a minority part of the city, those contacted will likely be members of minority groups. Race is irrelevant to this sort of policing. When Russian immigrants in New York dominated the Ecstasy trade, law enforcement efforts targeted (profiled) them, and ultimately their illegal activities were reduced. Arrests are most often the result of criminal intelligence, computer-generated data, and good police work, not racism.

There are some who argue that the use of racial profiling is justified and should be legal because the demographics of crime demonstrate a relationship between the numbers of blacks and Hispanics stopped, searched and arrested, and incarcerated and the numbers of crimes committed—that is, that members of those minority groups do commit more crime than whites or Asians (MacDonald, 2001). Others argue that this sort of rationalization perpetuates the problem through a vicious cycle. Studies have been used to both prove and disprove this hypothesis. It is open to question whether officers stop minorities because they believe this hypothesis, they are biased, or both.

Victim and Civil Rights Advocates' Perceptions

The claims and counterclaims about the existence and prevalence of racial profiling have been made for years and they should not be dismissed as misperceptions or misunderstandings. We have to regard them as indicators of a very real social phenomenon. There have been a few attempts to reliably estimate the degree to which blacks, Latinos, Arabs, and Asians have been victims of the practice.

According to a national study by Richard Lundman and Robert Kaufman, professors of sociology at Ohio State University, black men are 35 percent more likely than white men to report being stopped by police for a traffic violation. The researchers analyzed data from the National Crime Victimization Study conducted by the U.S. Department of Justice in 1999. The study indicated that "African Americans who are stopped for traffic violations are less likely than whites to believe the police had a legitimate reason to stop them, and more likely to believe they were mistreated" (Lundman & Kaufman, 2003).

Other studies, past and present, have discovered almost parallel findings. A Montgomery County, Washington D.C., traffic stop study showed that black drivers were stopped at a rate higher than their proportion of the county population or registered drivers ("Most Recent Traffic Stop Data," 2002, p. T3). The same was concluded in Boston after studies reported in the *Boston Globe* ("Boston to Track," 2003).

The *Boston Globe* studies included a three-part, investigative report series. The investigation involved an analysis of Massachusetts state records of traffic stops for speeding wherein clear disparities regarding race, gender, and age were documented. Police officers tended to give a ticket to some and a written warning to others. The *Globe*'s investigative analysis "found clear patterns in who gets a break and who does not when it comes to traffic enforcement:

- In cities and towns across the state [Massachusetts], Latino and black men were most likely to be ticketed. In Boston, for example, 42 percent of white women, 53 percent of white men, 58 percent of minority women, and 68 percent of minority men were ticketed when cited for speeding 15 m.p.h. over in a 30 m.p.h. zone. Whites and women enjoyed an even larger advantage, on average, in suburbs and small towns.

- Older drivers are less likely to get ticketed—especially if they are white. The records show that, as drivers age, their chances of getting a warning increase. But this deference to age tends to be denied to blacks and other minorities.

- The racial and gender disparities persist no matter how egregious the speeding offense. For example, when local police cited drivers for going 25 m.p.h. over the speed limit, 89 percent of minority drivers were ticketed, versus 82 percent of whites ("Race, Sex, and Age Drive Ticketing," 2003, p. A1; "Troopers Fair," 2003, p. A1).

The report indicated, however, that disparities in tickets and warnings do not prove intentional bias or racial profiling by police.

Blacks are not the only Americans who say they have been the targets of racial or ethnic profiling by law enforcement. Hispanic men reported they were more likely than white men to question why they were stopped and how they were treated (Lundman & Kaufman, 2003). Also, just as "driving while black or brown (DWB)" has been used by civil rights advocates to demonstrate racial profiling of African Americans or Hispanics, in recent years, "flying while Arab" has been used to describe the targeting of Arabs, South Asians, and Middle Easterners. The complaints of racial profiling are most often at airports and other places where there is a concern about the potential for terrorist attack. Civil rights advocates say that Arabs, South Asians, and Middle Easterners, most of them loyal American citizens, have become victims of the new war on terrorism. It is a difficult issue and one in which officers and security agents are damned if they do and damned if they don't.

The American-Arab Anti-Discrimination Committee (ADC) of the National Association of Arab Americans reported that "following the appalling September 11 attacks on the United States, the Arab-American community has experienced an unprecedented backlash in the form of hate crimes, various forms of discrimination and serious civil liberties concerns" (ADC Fact Sheet: "The Condition of Arab Americans Post-9/11," March 27, 2002). The ADC had also received many complaints from Arab and Middle Eastern individuals reporting that they had been subjected to extreme security measures—being searched and questioned for no apparent reason other than their appearance. See further discussion of this issue in Chapter 8 and Chapter 12.

Minorities complain that they are not only more likely to be stopped than whites, but they are also often pressured to allow searches of their vehicles. *The New York Times* reported that a 1997 investigation by New Jersey police of their own practices found that "turnpike drivers who agreed to have their cars searched by the state police were overwhelmingly black and Hispanic." It was found that, under pressure, these groups were more likely than whites to allow searches of their vehicles and even signed waivers stating that they consented ("Racial Profiling Routine," 2000, p. A1).

The many accounts from people who have been stopped by police on questionable grounds and subjected to disrespectful behavior, intrusive questioning, and disregard for their civil rights lend credibility to the reality of the practice. Data collected by police departments to refute such claims often reveal that, without further analysis and interpretation, minority drivers are stopped in numbers far out of proportion to their presence on the road.

The PERF report mentions the reactions of non-Hispanic white officers upon hearing their fellow officers, who are minority and within the study group, describing their own experiences:

After a white officer in the group downplayed the scope of the problem, a minority officer would speak up and describe his or her personal experience with being pulled over by police. In several cases, it was clear to the facilitators that white officers were surprised by these stories. Their peers' experiences seemed to impact them in a way that the citizens' stories conveyed in press accounts did not. (PERF Report, 2001, p. 15)

A study by professors David and Melissa Barlow surveyed African American police officers of the Milwaukee Police Department to determine if they felt they had been racially profiled at any time in their life, and if so, to what extent. The researchers wanted to discover the opinions of black officers on the legality of the circumstances under which they had been stopped by police. Because the subjects of the survey were themselves police officers, their views could not be easily dismissed.

The personal experiences of people of color who have been victims of racial profiling are often rejected as being anecdotal, uninformed or overly sensitive. ... [P]olice executives attempting to address the problem of racial profiling suggest that many incidents are simply problems of perception, because the public does not understand the intricacies, strategies and techniques of law enforcement. What appears to be racial profiling to the general public may be nothing of the sort. (2002, p. 2)

The survey defined racial profiling as "when race is used by a police officer or a police agency in determining the potential criminality of an individual" (Barlow & Barlow, 2002, p. 14). Of the 2,100 sworn personnel of the Milwaukee Police Department, 414 were designated as "black." One-hundred-fifty-eight of those officers responded to the survey, producing a response rate of 38 percent. Over 99 percent were over 25 years of age and had been sworn police officers for at least 1 year. The percentage of male respondents was 83.5 while the percentage of female respondents was 16.5.

Exhibit 14.1 shows that the majority of those who responded to the survey believed they had been racially profiled. Note that the percentages drop off rapidly as the survey proceeded from questions about being stopped and questioned to questions about being arrested. The researchers suggest that the numbers fall off rapidly because the officers would have identified themselves as such upon being stopped and thus avoided further action. It should be noted that some of those surveyed reported that

	Yes	No
Stopped	69%	31%
Questioned	52%	60%
Searched	19%	81%
Ticketed	21%	79%
Arrested	7%	93%

Exhibit 14.1   Question: In your professional opinion, do you believe that you have ever been stopped, questioned, searched, ticketed, or arrested as a result of racial profiling as defined above?
(Source: Barlow & Barlow, 2002, p. 14)

they were on duty but in plain clothes when they were stopped. From their findings, the Barlows conclude that black men are more likely to be the victims of racial profiling than black women by a ratio of three to one.

In their research, the Barlows also asked the sworn police officers of the Milwaukee Police Department whether they personally used racial profiling in the performance of their job. They found that most (90 percent), of the respondents do not use racial profiling nor believe it is a necessary or legitimate tool for law enforcement. The researchers concluded, "Although many white Americans, members of law enforcement and government officials deny the existence of racial profiling or racially biased policing, the findings from the study suggest that it is a reality" (2002, p. 15).

The following mini-case studies involve descriptions of actual events as described by the victims. The issues and implications of each should be discussed in class, especially the question of whether the police behavior is proper, justified, legal, or necessary.

MINI CASE STUDIES: CULTURE AND CRIME

Mini-Case Study 2: You Decide—Racial Profiling?

It is early in the morning, and a well-dressed young African American man driving to a job interview in his Ford Explorer on I-95 is pulled over for speeding. The officer, instead of simply asking for a driver's license and writing a speeding ticket, calls for backup and is joined by another trooper. The young man is told to leave his vehicle, as the troopers announce their intention to search it. "Hey, where did you get the money for something like this?" one trooper asks mockingly while he starts the process of going through every inch of the Explorer. One of the officers pulls off an inside door panel and more dismantling of the vehicle follows. They say they are looking for drugs, but in the end find nothing. After ticketing the driver for speeding, the two officers casually drive off. Sitting in his now-trashed SUV, the young man weeps in his anger and humiliation (Callahan, 2001).

1. Do you believe police officers do in fact pull over and search the vehicles of African Americans disproportionately to their numbers?

2. Are there racial or ethnic characteristics on which officers can legitimately focus during an investigation or to prevent criminal activity?

3. Should profiling only include the actions, behavior, and activities of the person(s) observed by the officer?

4. How can law enforcement leadership and trainers teach officers to distinguish between behavioral profiling and racial profiling?

5. Are those who argue that the "demographics of crime" justify racial profiling using data that is biased? Does this sort of rationalization perpetuate the problem through a vicious cycle?

MINI CASE STUDIES: CULTURE AND CRIME

Mini-Case Study 3: Does the War on Terrorism Give License to Law Enforcement to Engage in Racial Profiling?

An Arab American says he was racially profiled recently on his way to Washington, D.C. He was pulled out of line at the Orange County, California, airport, questioned, and searched. "It was done in front of everyone's staring eyes," he said. "That made it a humiliating experience. They want to give a message to non-Arab Americans, that they're doing something about 'it.' This has nothing to do with security" (Polakow-Suransky, 2001).
Discuss the following:

1. Passengers who appear "Arab-looking," which has included South Asians and Latinos, have been asked to leave airplanes because fellow passengers and crew members refuse to fly with them. How can airline security and management justify these actions?

2. Sikh men have been denied the right to board aircraft because they refuse to fly without their turbans, which equates with asking a woman to fly without her skirt.

3. Has the war on terrorism or the conflict in the Middle East provided the opportunity for officers and security personal to use racial profiling tactics?

4. What options are available for officers and security personnel to provide security and safety to the public they serve?

5. Did the general public have a different attitude toward racial profiling following 9/11? What has been the nature and degree of the backlash for Middle Easterners and others who may have a Middle Eastern appearance?

Racial bias, or the perception of same, distorts attitudes toward civil authority. It also impacts the victims' quality of everyday life. In addition to actual bias, the perception of bias is a substantial barrier to good police–community relations. The victims of racial profiling maintain that police use this practice because there are officers who believe that having black or brown skin is an indication of a greater risk of criminality, and they therefore view minorities as potential criminals. Skin color becomes evidence: the upshot is that African Americans and Hispanics become suspects every time they engage in the most common and prototypically American act—driving (Harris, 2000).

PROFILING AS A LEGAL TOOL OF LAW ENFORCEMENT

Profiling and profiles have long been used as legitimate law enforcement tools to look for signs of potential criminal activity. They are tools utilized by law enforcement in almost every country in the world, although the people profiled will vary by country. For example, the constabularies in Northern Ireland and England have profiles that help them identify extremists among members of the IRA. Religion and national origin would be factors in this profile, not race or ethnicity. In Israel, the police have profiles of Palestinian terrorists. Now the criminal justice community in many parts of the world is using profiles to locate and arrest members of Al-Qaida. In the United States, a profile used by airport and homeland security agents of a potential terrorist might include such factors as: (1) a man in his 20s or 30s who comes from Saudi Arabia, Egypt, or Pakistan; (2) probably living in one of six states—Texas, New Jersey, California, New York, Michigan, or Florida; (3) likely to have engaged in some sort of suspicious activity, such as taking flying lessons, traveling in areas of possible targets, or getting a U.S. driver's license. Meeting some of these criteria—not necessarily having a certain skin color—is enough to instigate questioning by law enforcement authorities.

The Police Executive Research Forum (PERF) created policy intended for adoption by police departments across the nation. The policy clearly delineates what is legal profiling. The policy discusses the U.S. Constitution Fourth Amendment provision that officers shall *not consider* race/ethnicity to establish reasonable suspicion or probable cause except when based on trustworthy, locally relevant information that links a person or persons of a specific race/ethnicity to a particular unlawful incident(s). The policy

- disallows use of race as a general indicator for criminal behavior
- disallows use of stereotypes/biases
- allows for the consideration of race *as one factor* in making law enforcement decisions if
  - trustworthy and locally relevant information
  - links specific suspected unlawful activity to a person(s) of a particular race/ethnicity
- relies on *descriptions* of actual suspects, not general *predictions* of who may be involved in a crime

For example, an officer observes the following: (1) The tail light is burned out on a vehicle with a white driver; (2) It is midnight; (3) The car is in a minority neighborhood where drugs are known to be sold; (4) The driver pulls up to the curb and talks briefly to someone standing there; (5) An exchange takes place; (6) The driver drives away; (7) The driver makes furtive movements as if hiding something under the seat when police pull him over. Although not a representative example because the driver is white, race was used as a part of the decision to pull the driver over.

PERF recommends that the following principle be applied: "Race/ethnicity should be treated like other demographic descriptors. Police can use race/ethnicity as one factor in the same way that they use age, gender and other descriptors to establish reasonable suspicion or probable cause." The organization recommends the best test for officers to use is (1) Would I be engaging this particular person but for the fact that this person is white? (2) Would I be asking this question of this person but for the fact that this person is [fill in the demographic descriptor] (PERF Report, 2001)?

What is needed in assessing the use of profiles and profiling is a combination of common sense and fairness, a balance between effective law enforcement and protection of civil liberties. The authors believe that profiles and profiling need not upset such a balance if it is used judiciously, fairly, and within the law. Most officers understand that profiling, not *racial profiling,* is an acceptable form of proactive law enforcement, and the courts agree. The U.S. Customs Service, the U.S. Border Patrol, and the Drug Enforcement Agency (DEA) have long used profiles as a tool to detain and investigate persons fitting the "drug courier profile." Such a profile is based on behaviors, actions, traits, demeanor, intelligence information, carrier routes, statistical evidence, and other factors (not just a single characteristic like race or ethnicity). The U.S. Border Patrol obviously links race to incidence of crime on the border with Mexico. It is only logical to assume that most people attempting to illegally enter the country are of Hispanic/Latino or Mestizo descent. The use of profiles in this context appears to be legal and acceptable. A border patrol profile, however, not only includes the ethnicity of the individual but also such factors as their proximity to the border, erratic driving, suspicious behavior, and the officers' previous experience with alien traffic.

Now airport police and security agents, and other officials within Homeland Security, use profiles to identify those who might be a threat to security in their respective jurisdictions. For example, the Computer Assisted Passenger Prescreening System (CAPPS II), developed in 1998 and first tested in 2003 by the Federal Aviation Administration, is a nationwide preflight computer system used to check personal information on every airline passenger. Under the program, an airline passenger provides name, birthday, address, and phone number when getting a flight reservation. That information is checked against commercial databases (credit reports and consumer transactions) and a score is generated indicating the likelihood that the passenger's identity is authentic. The personal information is also checked against a government database to determine if the person is on a terrorism watch list or represents a security risk. Those deemed to be an "elevated" or "uncertain" risk are required to undergo secondary screening with a handheld wand. Anyone deemed a high risk is supposed to be brought to the attention of law enforcement. The system also screens passengers based on where they're flying and how they purchase their tickets—not on how they look. None of the profile information, on face value, involves the race, ethnicity, or national origin of the persons checked. CAPPS II seeks to streamline the airport screening process by flagging only those passengers deemed potential security risks. That will benefit the vast majority of travelers by ensuring fewer are stopped. Critics of CAPPS II, however, see the system as having the potential for unconstitutional invasions of privacy and government snooping. They also are concerned that people may be falsely identified as terrorists.

A computer system developed in Florida called Matrix (Multistate Anti-Terrorism Information Exchange) came on line in that state in 2002. The system enables investigators to find patterns and links among people and events faster than ever before, combining police records with commercially available collections of personal information about most American adults. It is described as a powerful new tool to analyze billions of records about both criminals and ordinary citizens. For example, it would let authorities instantly find the name and address of every brown-haired owner of a red Ford pickup truck in a 20-mile radius of a suspicious event. In 2003, the system was being made available to law enforcement nationwide. The Justice Department provided $4 million to expand the Matrix program to states and will provide the computer network for information sharing among them. The Department of Homeland Security pledged $8 million to help. The Matrix system, however, has drawn the attention of some civil-liberties groups who fear that it will dramatically lower the threshold for government snooping because other systems don't permit investigators to search criminal and commercial records with such ease or speed. Matrix is another example of the ongoing post–September 11 debate about the proper balance between national security and individual privacy.

Legitimate Use of Race/Ethnicity

An important question is whether race can *ever* be a valid consideration when conducting law enforcement activity. In the *Travis* opinion, the majority concluded that "race or ethnic background may become a legitimate consideration when investigators have information on the subject of a particular suspect" (Travis, 62 F. 3rd at 54). Simply put, the suspect described and being sought is of a certain race or ethnicity (refer to the definition of suspect-specific incident in this chapter). Court decisions have allowed officers to consider the totality of the circumstances surrounding the subject of their attention in light of their experience and training, which may include "instructions on a drug courier profile" (*Florida v. Royer,* 460 U.S. at 525, note 6). Actually, many courts have upheld the use of drug courier profiles as the sole determinant of a stop or cause for suspicion. Therefore, profiles combined with other facts and circumstances can establish reasonable suspicion or probable cause. Race or color may be a factor to consider during certain police activity (*U.S. v. Brignoni-Ponce,* 442 U.S., 837, 887,1975). The Whren decision by the Supreme Court enhanced the already extensive power of police to detain individual citizens under the banner of the war on drugs by allowing pretext stops through the "objective" standard test (Bast, 1997; Harris, 1997, 1999).

Some see the Whren decision (*Wren v. United States*) "objective standard" ruling as opening the door for police abuse. They argue that in the Whren case, it did not matter to the court that the officers lied about their intent, that they were violating departmental policy to make the stop, or that they really wanted to stop the car because it contained two African American men who sat at a stop sign for 20 seconds in an area known for drug dealing. They are concerned that the Whren decision clearly opens the door for racial profiling because it allows police officers to stop anyone without reasonable suspicion or probable cause, thus providing a mechanism for circumventing the Fourth Amendment requirements of the U.S. Constitution. Because minor traffic violations are numerous, they argue, to limit stops to the observation of traffic violations is no limitation at all. If a police officer wants to stop a car, but does not have the legal authority to do so, all the officer has to do is to follow it until the driver gets nervous and at some point turns right without a turn signal, drifts across the center line, or simply fails to come to a complete stop at a stop sign. Upon observing a minor traffic violation, the police officer can stop the driver and attempt to pressure him or her into giving consent for the car to be searched. Under this "objective" standard, the motivation of the officer and previous enforcement patterns become irrelevant (Barlow & Barlow, 2000).

The courts said that the burden that "brief detentions" place on law-abiding minority citizens is a minor and necessary inconvenience in the war on crime, suggesting that little damage is done by the practice of profiling. However, those who advocate making the standard for brief detentions more restrictive insist that these court decisions have failed to acknowledge that these detentions grow into regular occurrences, breeding resentment and anger both in the citizens stopped and the police officers who confront hostile persons of color. Just because race is couched within other factors does not mean that there is no racial discrimination (Kennedy, 2000). When police officers use race as a factor in criminal profiling based on presumed statistical probabilities they contribute to the very statistics upon which they rely (Hughes, 2000, Harris, 1999).

The Supreme Court has made it clear that as long as the government can show that police searches and seizures are objectively reasonable (that is, based on probable cause or reasonable suspicion), they do not violate the Fourth Amendment, regardless of the officer's subjective (actual) motivation for the search or seizure. That does not mean, however, that objectively reasonable searches and seizures can never violate the Constitution. Officers motivated by prejudice who lawfully search or seize only members of certain racial, ethnic, religious, or gender groups are still subject to claims of constitutional violations (i.e., racial profiling).

Police officers who undertake searches of persons or vehicles not incident to an arrest must have reasonable suspicion or probable cause to perform such a search. An officer who does not have reasonable suspicion may ask for a consent to search (except in those states or localities where it is illegal) and even have the motorist sign a waiver to that effect. Sometimes, however, evidence of racial bias may be discovered when there is a repeated pattern of minorities being subjected to consent searches much more often than whites. Law enforcement agencies must monitor the data they collect on discretionary consent searches to ensure that the discretion is not applied more often to minorities. Where more minorities are being asked to agree to consent searches, it can be a "strong indication of how race or ethnicity affects thinking about who's suspicious enough to be searched," said profiling expert David Harris (2002). An explanation for the disparity, says a prominent researcher in racial profiling, John Lamberth (1996), a private consultant in Wilmington, Delaware, is that minorities may be more nervous around police and officers may misinterpret that as suspicious behavior.

Far-reaching authority for searches was granted to law enforcement when on October 26, 2001, President George W. Bush signed the USA Patriot Act (USAPA) Presidential Executive Orders into law. The law gave sweeping new powers to both domestic law enforcement and international intelligence agencies. The provisions of the law, aimed at terrorism, expanded surveillance capabilities (in effect, searches) and allowed for nationwide wiretaps under certain circumstances. Many aspects of the new law are still being tested and questioned by those concerned about the potential for government intrusion into the lives and civil rights of innocent people. The USAPA will be discussed more fully in Chapter 10 and Chapter 11.

Illegitimate Use of Race/Ethnicity

Courts have held that matching a profile *alone* is not the equivalent of the reasonable suspicion or probable cause necessary to conduct an investigative detention or arrest (see, for example, *Reid v. George*, 448 U.S. 438, 1980, and Royer at 525, note 6). There are no circumstances under which officers may stop citizens based solely on their race, sex, religion, national origin, or any other demographic feature. Officers must base their stops of persons, whether in a vehicle or on foot, on reasonable suspicion or probable cause that a violation of the law has been or is about to be committed based on facts and information that they can articulate.

Some states, via legislation, have banned consent searches where there is no clear reason for suspicion. The mere nervousness of the motorist or occupant(s) is not sufficient reason to ask for a consent search. The Fourth (banning unreasonable search and seizure) and Fourteenth (equal protection of the laws) Amendments to the U.S. Constitution provide a framework for the protection of drivers from being indiscriminately targeted by the police via traffic stops. To prove this type of claim, the claimant must produce facts or statistics showing that they were targeted solely because of their race. The burden then shifts to the police to provide evidence that they did not act solely on the basis of the defendant's race.

Weeding out the illegitimate uses of profiles or profiling by police officers is the only way law enforcement can maintain credibility within the communities they serve. The authors believe that the majority of officers know not to act on any prejudices they might hold.

PREVENTION OF RACIAL PROFILING IN LAW ENFORCEMENT

To formulate measures to prevent the practice of racial profiling and inappropriate behavior and actions on the part of officers, the criminal justice system should consider the following seven areas:

- Accountability and supervision
- Agency policy to address racial profiling
- Recruitment and hiring
- Education and training
- Minority community outreach
- Professional traffic stops
- Data collection on citizens' race/ethnicity

Accountability and Supervision

Preventing the use of racial profiling or biased policing in law enforcement is critical. Police executives need to reflect seriously on this and respond to both the reality of, and the perceptions of, biased policing. Law enforcement executives, managers, and supervisors must send a clear message to all personnel that using race, ethnicity, or national origin alone as the basis for any investigative stop is not only unacceptable conduct but also illegal. It can lead to termination from employment and possibly prosecution. If convicted, the officer(s) could be fined and/or incarcerated depending on the laws of the particular state.

Police managers and supervisors, in order to identify officers who might be biased, should monitor such indicators as: (1) high numbers of minority citizen complaints; (2) high numbers of use-of-force or resisting incidents involving minorities; (3) large numbers of arrests not charged due to prosecutors finding improper detentions and/or searches; (4) perceptible negative attitude toward minorities; (5) negative attitudes toward training programs that enhance police–community relations or cultural awareness.

Prevention of racial profiling also involves other components of the criminal justice system such as prosecutors and courts. Legislators are also an integral part of the process. For example, the following took place in New Jersey:

Nearly five years after New Jersey state troopers shot three unarmed minority men and ignited a furor over racial profiling, the State Legislature passed a bill making it a crime for the police to use race as the primary factor in determining whom to stop and search. The General Assembly passed a bill that would make such profiling punishable by five years in prison and a $15,000 fine. A similar bill has already cleared the Senate, and Gov. James E. McGreevey immediately announced plans to sign the bill. ("New Jersey adopts ban," 2003, p. A1)

According to one law enforcement executive, however, supervision and legislation alone will not root out rogue officers:

> In his first extensive public comments on racial profiling, Cincinnati Police Chief Tom Streicher said Monday any proposed solution must "get at what's in the officer's heart." "What's in his heart manifests itself someplace in his conduct. It's in there. We have to figure out a way to get at that," the chief said. "We would have a national model here."
>
> It's not enough to just log the race of drivers stopped by police, Chief Streicher told City Council's law committee. Crucial to solving the problem of racial profiling, whether it's real or perceived, is a broader approach, he said, a program that would review other contacts officers have with residents, not just in traffic stops.
>
> A "bad apple" cop isn't going to admit his biases just because City Council passes a resolution ordering him to, Chief Streicher said. ("Officers' hearts," 2001, p. 3)

Law enforcement agencies must convey to their communities that they, as citizens, will be protected from such abuses and that abuses are not tolerated or advocated. Preventing the use of racial profiling by law enforcement officers not only is crucial to maintaining credibility within the community, but also reduces exposure to civil liability on the part of the departments and officers.

The authors of this text believe that the majority of law enforcement officers, supervisors, and managers within agencies across the country are hard-working men and women who are committed to serving all members of our communities with fairness and respect. These professionals know that racial profiling is unacceptable and conflicts with the standards and values inherent in ensuring that all people are treated equally regardless of their race or ethnicity. They know that racial profiling can expose a police department to costly lawsuits and ruin minority relations. They are intolerant of the use of racial profiling and willingly partner with their communities to address the issues involved and develop approaches to eradicate either confirmed acts of racial profiling or the perception that it is taking place within their agency.

Agency Policies to Address Racial Profiling

Law enforcement agencies must have clear policies and procedures to address racial profiling and the perceptions thereof. Most departments in the United States have developed such general orders to cover not only traffic stops but also the temporary detentions of pedestrians and even bicyclists. The policies usually address the Fourth Amendment requirement that investigative detentions, traffic stops, arrests, searches, and property seizures by officers must be based on a standard of reasonable suspicion or probable cause officers can support with specific facts and circumstances. The policy must include: (1) No motorist, once cited or warned, shall be detained beyond the point where there exists no reasonable suspicion of further criminal activity; (2) No person or vehicle shall be searched in the absence of probable cause, a search warrant, or the person's voluntary consent. The policy should specify that in each case where a search is conducted, this information shall be recorded, including the legal basis for the search and the results. It is strongly recommended that consent searches only be conducted with written consent utilizing the agency forms provided.

According to the International Association of Chiefs of Police (IACP), departments without a policy should look at as many models addressing racial profiling as possible before they select one that meets their needs. Agencies should also involve community members, especially minorities and civil rights advocates, in the development and implementation of the policy. The policy must communicate a clear message to law enforcement personnel and the people they serve that racial profiling and other forms of biased-based policing are not acceptable practices. The statement should include what discipline (including criminal prosecution where such laws exist) could result if officers violate the provisions of the policy. A general order most often contains such language as factors such as the person's race, sex, sexual orientation, age, dress, or unusual, disheveled, or impoverished appearance do not alone justify even a brief detention, a request for identification, or an order to move on, nor do general complaints from residents, merchants, or others. Officers, however, must have specific facts and be able to articulate them to support their actions; a mere suspicion or "hunch" is not sufficient cause to detain a person or to request identification.

The San Francisco Police Department created a general order that outlines their policy for policing without racial bias. It states that "To maintain that trust, it is crucial for members of our Department to carry out their duties in a manner free from bias and to eliminate any perception of policing that appears racially biased." It clarifies the circumstances in which officers can consider race, color, ethnicity, national origin, gender, age, sexual orientation, or gender identity when making law enforcement decisions.

> *Policy*: Investigative detentions, traffic stops, arrests, searches and property seizures by officers will be based on a standard of reasonable suspicion or probable cause in accordance with the Fourth Amendment of the U.S. Constitution. Officers must be able to articulate specific facts and circumstances that support reasonable suspicion or probable cause for investigative detentions, traffic stops, arrest, nonconsensual searches and property seizures. Department personnel may not use, *to any extent or degree,* race, color, ethnicity, national origin, age, sexual orientation or gender identity in conducting stops or detentions, or activities following stops or detentions *except* when engaging in the investigation of appropriate suspect specific activity to identify a particular person or group. Department personnel seeking one or more specific persons who have been identified or described in part by any of the above listed characteristics may rely on them in part only in combination with other appropriate identifying factors. The listed characteristics should not be given undue weight.
>
> • Except as provided above, officers shall not consider race, color, ethnicity, national origin, gender, age, sexual orientation or gender identity in establishing reasonable suspicion or probable cause.
>
> • Except as provided above, officers shall not consider race, color, ethnicity, national origin, gender, age, sexual orientation or gender identity in decid-

ing to initiate even those consensual encounters that do not amount to legal detentions or to request consent to search. (San Francisco Police Department General Order 5.17, 07/17/03)

The legislature of Massachusetts enacted laws pertaining to racial profiling and the collection of data relative to traffic stops in 2000. The various involved government agencies, including the Criminal Justice Training Council and minority advocates, then developed and adopted uniform, statewide general orders, policies, and guidelines pertaining to racial and gender profiling—its identification and its prevention. There are many other departments with excellent general orders concerning racial profiling that could be used as models for agencies designing their own, including the Chicago Police Department; the Fort Worth, Texas, Police Department (General Order: 321.06 Racial Profiling); the Kentucky State Police, and the Tucson, Arizona, Police Department. The Chief of the Chicago Police Department even required the entire command staff to sign a pledge to enforce the provisions of their policy. The department organized a media campaign to educate Chicago residents about the issue, the general order, the training provided, and how citizens could contact the police department if they had a complaint. The general order, entitled "Prohibitions Regarding Racial Profiling and Other Biased Based Policing," defines the terms, states a clear policy for the department, and establishes training protocols to ensure that both recruits and veteran officers are fully aware of department policy. Additionally, the Chicago general order specifically holds both individual officers and supervisors accountable for their actions. Notably, the general order requires that officers are able to clearly articulate the specific police or public safety purpose of any traffic or street stop. The policy was largely the product of a task force that included members of the department and a group of leaders from the African American and Hispanic communities. The goal was to improve overall community and race relations, communications, and understanding.

Recruitment and Hiring

Police agencies can reduce racial bias by recruiting and hiring officers who can police in a professional way. Within legal parameters, the department should hire a workforce that reflects the community's racial and ethnic demographics. Those hired should be expected to carry out their duties with fairness and impartiality. Having such a workforce increases the probability that, as a whole, the agency will be able to understand the perspectives of its racial/ethnic minorities and communicate effectively with them.

The officers that departments should be recruiting are those who are aware of and capable of managing their own ethnic, racial, and cultural stereotypes and biases in a professional way. These qualities are essential to reducing bias in policing. The multiple testing stages that applicants for law enforcement positions go through help weed out those who are unable to control their biases. Interviews, polygraphs, psychological tests, and background investigations are all intended to identify those who are biased to the point that they might act on their prejudices (see Chapter 1). It should be noted that the possibility of bias is not limited to white officers. Members of minority groups can have biases against white people, against members of other minority groups, or even against members of their own race/ethnic group. In 2003, the *Boston Globe* analyzed 20,000 citations by Boston police; it was discovered that "minority officers here are at least as tough as whites on minority drivers, and sometimes tougher" ("Minority Officers," 2003, p. A1). Police recruitment messages, verbal and written, must emphasize that those who are prejudiced, regardless of their race or ethnicity, who cannot distinguish between appropriate and inappropriate behavior and actions, will not be hired. As mentioned earlier in this chapter, no one is completely free of bias, but the recruitment effort should be targeted at those who understand and control their biases.

The impact of affirmative action laws and consent decrees upon the ability of an agency to recruit a racially/ethnically representative workforce goes beyond the scope of this chapter (see Chapter 3). Agencies must know how they can legally go about recruiting and hiring a diverse and racially unbiased workforce. Affirmative action laws vary by state and continually change.

Hiring officers who understand and empathize with the various cultures and socioeconomic conditions of their community will result in more effective street policing. Police executives, mid-managers, and supervisors involved in the recruitment and testing process should monitor and/or audit the system to ensure that it is meeting the department's mission statement and goals.

Education and Training

Law enforcement agencies need to provide training and education to enable officers to effectively utilize legal enforcement tools so they can perform their work professionally and effectively within today's multicultural communities. Some departments have utilized effective, interactive simulation training exercises to train officers on professional traffic stop procedures, and especially those involving agitated citizens. Clearly, most law enforcement officers know not to act on the prejudices and stereotypes they might hold. However, the nature of prejudice is such that some people are not aware of their prejudices or biases. Therefore, they make inferences and take actions toward certain groups based on these biased perceptions. Training that provides accurate information concerning groups about which officers might have prejudices and stereotypes is one of the approaches police departments should use to prevent racial profiling.

What is the mental process that takes place when an officer makes a stop based on race, ethnicity, or national origin? Officers who have a biased belief system observe and collect certain "data" that in turn reinforces that belief system. Meanings are added to make sense of the observations ("I notice minorities more and stop them more because of my biased beliefs about them"). Based on these meanings, assumptions are made that fill in for missing data ("This motorist is carrying drugs on him"). The officer draws conclusions (based on beliefs) and then takes action (decides to stop African American and Hispanic motorists much more frequently than whites). These steps in our thinking take place very quickly. Most of us are not aware that this process goes on all the time (see the section in Chapter 1 on prejudice in law enforcement).

In his book, *The Fifth Discipline Fieldbook: Strategies and Tools for Building a Learning Organization,* management specialist Peter Senge and his coauthors provide a clear and simple model called the "Ladder of Inference" that illuminates most people's typical patterns (and flaws) of thinking. The authors' discuss thinking and decision-making processes using the ladder to describe, from the bottom up, how people select data, add meanings, make assumptions, draw conclusions, adopt beliefs, and ultimately take action (see Exhibit 14.2). They maintain that

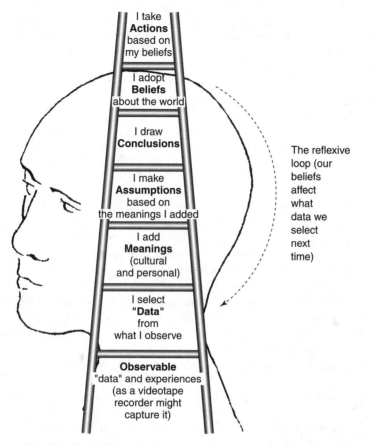

The reflexive loop (our beliefs affect what data we select next time)

I take **Actions** based on my beliefs

I adopt **Beliefs** about the world

I draw **Conclusions**

I make **Assumptions** based on the meanings I added

I add **Meanings** (cultural and personal)

I select **"Data"** from what I observe

Observable "data" and experiences (as a videotape recorder might capture it)

Exhibit 14.2
(*Source:* Senge, Kleiner, Roberts, Ross, and Smith, 1994, pp. 242–246.
Reproduced with permission of Peter Senge)

We live in a world of self-generating beliefs that remain largely untested. We adopt those beliefs because they are based on conclusions, which are inferred from what we observe, plus our past experience. Our ability to achieve the results we truly desire is eroded by our feelings that:

- Our beliefs are the truth
- The truth is obvious
- Our beliefs are based on real data
- The data we select are the real data (Senge, 1994, p. 242)

The authors explain that most people no longer remember where their attitudes and beliefs came from (i.e., what data or experiences led to their assumptions and conclusions). Therefore, they may not understand the basis of the actions they take. Peter Senge and his coauthors (1994) discuss "leaps of abstraction" in which our minds literally move at lightning speed . . . because we immediately "leap" to generalizations so quickly that we never think to test them. . . . [L]eaps of abstraction occur when we move from direct observation (concrete "data") to generalization without testing. Leaps of abstraction impede learning because they become axiomatic. What was once an assumption becomes treated as a fact. He says that we then treat generalization as fact (pp. 192–193).

How do you spot leaps of abstraction? First, by asking yourself what you believe about the way the world works. . . . Ask "what is the 'data' on which this generalization is based?" Then ask yourself, "Am I willing to consider that this generalization may be inaccurate or misleading?" It is important to ask this last question consciously, because, if the answer is no, there is no point in proceeding. (p. 194)

In intensive training conducted by Senge nationwide, police and other corporate executives are able to learn about the models above and relate them to issues and challenges in their own organizations. The models provide some insight into what may be going on in officers' minds as they stop members of minority groups. Thus the models can help officers better understand their actions vis-à-vis racial profiling. It is natural for people to substitute assumptions for what is not known, but in the case of racial profiling, this is a very dangerous proposition. Officers have to recognize when they are converting their biases into "facts" and when their assumptions substitute for real data.

Training and education provide departments an opportunity to inform officers of the penalties for not adhering to policies and laws on the subject. Many state legislatures have created laws barring law enforcement officers from engaging in racial profiling. Such legislation also requires that every law enforcement officer participate in expanded training regarding racial profiling. This training is typically coordinated, monitored, and controlled by the Commission on Peace Officer Standards and Training, an agency that is found in every state. These state commissions should, if they haven't already, integrate the topic of racial profiling into their diversity training for both entry-level and in-service programs. Law enforcement agencies should consult local chapters of their community's minority group organizations to obtain accounts and examples of actual or perceived racially biased policing for use in training programs. Such programs should also cover:

1. Definitions of key terms involved, such as profile, profiling, racial profiling, racially biased policing, probable cause, and reasonable suspicion

2. Identification of key indices and perspectives that signal cultural differences among residents in a local community

3. The negative impact of biases, prejudices, and stereotyping on effective law enforcement, including examination of how historical perceptions of discriminatory enforcement practices have harmed police–community relations

4. History and role of the civil rights movement and its impact on law enforcement

5. Specific obligations of officers in preventing, reporting, and responding to discriminatory or biased practices by fellow officers

6. Various perspectives of local groups and race-relations experts regarding cultural and police–community relations

Training should also involve constitutional law and ethics. Every state will have different requirements, but here is an example from the Commission on POST of Missouri:

1. All commissioned, licensed peace officers, who have the authority to enforce vehicle/traffic laws, must attend a minimum of one hour of racial profiling training each year.

2. Individuals who have *no authority* to make traffic stops are *exempt* from this annual requirement.

3. All racial profiling training used to meet the requirement must be obtained from a licensed training center, an approved provider of continuing education, or a course approved by POST.

The law enforcement community is more capable than ever of effectively addressing biased policing. In the past few decades, there has been a revolution in the quality and quantity of police training, the standards for hiring officers, and accountability.

Minority Community Outreach

Every police and community interaction requires a strong, ongoing link to community groups and civil rights organizations. Links might be established when community-oriented policing, which became popular in the 1990s, is used to address neighborhood problems. A link is also established when community task forces are assembled to address issues, especially of racial profiling and the perception thereof. These steps demonstrate respect for the minority community and create shared responsibility for whatever action is taken. The police hold primary responsibility for community outreach on every level, but the community is also responsible for becoming involved in activities that form positive relationships with the police. Policing within the community can function only in an environment of mutual engagement and respect. In the context of racial profiling or biased policing, outreach to the community is imperative. For constructive dialog to take place, therefore, police executives must remain open to discussions of racial profiling or the perception thereof within their jurisdictions.

Although there are many examples of police departments collaborating with the minority community to discuss and resolve issues pertaining to racial profiling or racially biased policing, the Chicago Police Department could serve as a positive example. In 2000, Chicago's police superintendent sponsored a series of meetings between the police and residents of the minority community to address racial tensions and concerns about police racial bias. The forums included community activists and the police department was represented by staff of all ranks. Prior to the first meeting, participants were surveyed for their opinions, perceptions, and observations about racial profiling and racially biased policing. The questionnaire also asked them to rate the department's strengths and weaknesses regarding minority outreach, and for their ideas about how to improve police–minority relations and resolve issues. The forums were moderated by an independent facilitator. At the first meeting, community members shared their thoughts, experiences, and concerns, and police staff was asked to listen but not respond. Later in the day, the police shared their thoughts and reactions to the morning session, and the citizens were instructed to listen and not respond. During the final session of the day, all participants joined in a discussion of the issues and ideas raised earlier. The meetings continued over a period of time until the participants identified specific actions to be taken by both the police and community members to address the issues raised (PERF Report, 2001, p. 104).

Professional Police Traffic Stops

The reason for every stop made by a law enforcement officer must be legally defensible and professional. Major Grady Carrick (2000), a Florida Highway Patrol troop commander in Northeast Florida, gives the following advice:

> To implement professional police traffic stops, agencies must adopt a three-dimensional approach: organizational policy, officer training, and data collection. These dimensions represent the essential ingredients of a comprehensive agency strategy.

The following are key points involved.

- *Organizational/agency policy.* Agencies must develop a well-structured policy concerning professional traffic stops, outlining the conduct of officers and the prohibition of discriminatory practices.
- *Officer training.* Agencies should include a component on racial profiling into existing in-service training programs. Special workshop discussions on the issue of racial profiling can also be scheduled.
- *Data collection.* See below for a discussion on data collection.

The authors would add a fourth element not mentioned by Major Carrick, but thought to be a crucial factor:

- *Accountability/supervision.* Law enforcement supervisors and managers must hold officers accountable for adhering to the policy. They must bring the message personally to employees, as well as to the public, that biased policing will not be tolerated and could result in discipline, possibly including prosecution or termination. Managers, supervisors, and the entire workforce must embrace and adhere to the policy.

The Highway Safety Committee of the National Highway Traffic Safety Administration believes that there are core elements that must be included in policies guiding professional police traffic stops. These include:

1. Definitions of "racial profiling" and "reasonable suspicion."
2. A clear statement that race or ethnicity alone cannot constitute a reason for a traffic stop, unless it is related to a specific, detailed description pertaining to a specific crime.
3. A requirement that all persons be treated with the utmost courtesy in traffic stops.
4. A provision for adequate training and supervisory oversight.

Deputy Chief Ondra Berry (Reno, Nevada, Police Department), in diversity training he conducts nationwide and in communications with his own officers, offers the following advice: "When contemplating stopping a motorist, ask yourself, "Is there a possibility that I may be making an assumption about this driver based on race? Am I moving from my own personal 'data' and making a leap of extraction about this vehicle or about this person?" Officers need to recognize that this is a possibility. Berry further advises, "Do not take race into account when deciding who to stop. Use your good policing skills. Again, if you are normal, you have unbalanced views about people who are different from you" (Berry, 2000).

Data Collection on Citizens' Race/Ethnicity

When racial profiling became an issue throughout the United States, many law enforcement jurisdictions began collecting data on the race/ethnicity of people stopped and/or searched by police. Some did so voluntarily while others did so because of court decrees or community pressure. The purpose of collecting data is to address racially biased policing and the perceptions thereof to determine whether it is taking place. The use of data collection requires officers to complete a form following each traffic stop.

Research by the Police Executive Research Forum (PERF, 2001) examined the arguments for and against data collection:

Arguments in Favor of Data Collection

Data collection helps agencies:

1. Determine whether racially biased policing is a problem in the jurisdiction.
2. Convey a commitment to unbiased policing.
3. "Get ahead of the curve."
4. Effectively allocate and manage department resources.

Collecting data and interpreting them, if done correctly, reflects accountability and openness on the part of the agency. The process helps to improve police–community relations. Departments doing so identify problems and search for solutions. The data gathered can be informative to department management about what types of stops and searches officers are making. Managers and supervisors can then decide not only if these practices are the most efficient allocation of department resources but also if biased policing is taking place. Without the collection and analysis of data, departments can have a difficult time in court defending their practices if challenged.

Arguments against Data Collection

1. Data collection does not yield valid information regarding the nature and extent of racially biased policing.
2. Data could be used to harm the agency or its personnel.
3. Data collection may impact police productivity, morale, and workload.
4. Police resources might be more effectively used to combat racially biased policing and the perceptions thereof.

Many departments still resist record keeping. They argue, for one, that the mere collection of "racial" statistics may imply that biased policing is taking place. These agencies maintain that the raw data, when first collected and before analysis and comparison with benchmarks, could enhance the public's negative perceptions of the agency at the cost of both the morale and effectiveness of officers. At the same time, some departments have expressed concern that any data that they do collect could be used against them in court. These law enforcement executives question the ability of data collection systems to provide valid answers about the nature and extent of racially biased policing within their departments. The simple collection of data will neither prevent racial profiling nor accurately identify if it is taking place. The process alone does not protect agencies from public criticism, scrutiny, and litigation because the data collected is open to interpretation. The raw data collected represent meaningless numbers unless put into a relevant context using statistical benchmarks (to be discussed later), so there is a legitimate means of comparison. Standing alone, the data collected can be used to make or defend any position that someone may adopt about racial profiling. Law enforcement agencies, therefore, must take additional steps to ensure that the numbers they collect accurately reflect reality (Kruger, 2002). Each department must evaluate its specific circumstances. For agencies that have had no community complaints and/or already closely monitor officer behavior in other ways, undertaking data collection may not be the most efficient use of resources.

Another argument used against data collection has been the observation that, within some law enforcement agencies, officers discontinued or reduced the number of self-initiated traffic stops and pedestrian contacts they made when data collection became a requirement. Officers, resentful or concerned about being monitored, ceased to initiate stops in order to avoid the possibility of being perceived as racially biased. Some agencies do not require the officer to reveal his or her identity on the data form. The identity of the individual(s) detained is never documented on the form. Some city/county administrators and law enforcement executives are also concerned about the time and costs associated with the collection and analysis of data.

Thus, data collection has its advantages, disadvantages and limitations. PERF recommends that police agency executives, in collaboration with citizen leaders, review the pros and cons of the practice. They must factor in the agency's political, social, organizational, and financial situation to decide whether or not to either initiate data collection or to allocate available resources to other approaches to racially biased policing and the perceptions thereof.

Data Collection Elements. The data elements that both the U.S. DOJ Resource Guide and PERF recommend that law enforcement agencies collect are

- Date/time/location
- Characteristics of the individual(s): Age/gender, Race/ethnicity/national origin
- Reason for stop: penal or vehicle code violation or infraction; reactive (call for service) or self-initiated
- Search or no search: if search, the search authority (including consent [if consent involved]) and results (what, if anything, was recovered)
- Disposition: arrest, citation, verbal warning, written warning, or no action

There is a rationale and justification behind each of the elements recommended for inclusion. The elements selected are designed to measure not only who police are stopping, but also the circumstances and context of the stops. "In effect, we are trying to collect 'circumstantial' data to tell us the real reasons citizens are being stopped—which should reflect the motivations of the officers and/or the impact of agency policies and practices" (PERF Report, 2001, p 121). In completing the characteristics of the individual section of the form pertaining to race, ethnicity, or national origin, officers are expected to use their best judgment based on their observations, training, and experience and not ask the person detained. It is also possible to rely on driver licensing agencies, in some states, for race and ethnicity identification data on persons stopped. It is recommended that the data collected be sufficient to allow for meaningful analysis. This means that there must be a statistically significant number of stops documented over a specific period of time to adequately appraise the circumstances surrounding the types of stops that officers make.

Activities to Target for Data Collection. Most agencies collect data only on traffic stops (moving or mechanical violations) because of their frequency and also because this is where there is the greatest potential for police racial bias (or perception thereof) to occur. Another source of data is *vehicle stops or general investigative stops* of drivers. This sort of stop involves officer discretion (wherein the officer should have reasonable suspicion or probable cause to conduct an investigative stop) and is also an important source of information to analyze. Collecting data on *detentions* encompasses not only traffic and vehicle stops, but also pedestrian or bicyclist stops. A fourth source of data is *nonconsensual encounters,* in which an officer is not detaining the citizen, but is questioning him or her. PERF recommends that agencies collect data on all vehicle and traffic stops. Their recommendation does not include pedestrian stops or nonconsensual encounters that do not amount to detentions. Exhibit 14.3 shows a series of concentric circles that represent the types of activities police departments might target for data collection.

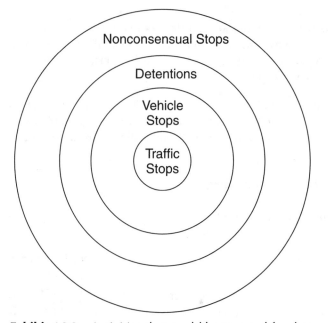

Exhibit 14.3   Activities that could be targeted for data collection
(*Source:* PERF Report, p. 121)

Data collection would be different for municipal and highway policing. The job of city police and county sheriffs is mostly responsive in nature in that they answer to calls for service from victims or witnesses to events. The officers' enforcement patterns depend on the character of the neighborhoods that they serve, and thus the race/ethnicity of the persons they contact will vary. This must be taken into account during data analysis and interpretation. Comparative benchmarks must be utilized for each differing community and area of the city or county. Highway policing, in contrast, involves more self-initiated activity and more discretion on the part of officers. Moreover, it may prove useful for the collection and analysis to distinguish between low and high discretion stops (U.S. Department of Justice, 2000).

Statistical Benchmarks or Base Rates. Statistical benchmarks or base rates are the comparative populations or groups with which the data collected are going to be analyzed and interpreted. Racial profiling analysis requires developing an appropriate benchmark and is the most important methodological decision made by researchers. The selection and development of benchmarks is a very complicated process often requiring the assistance of specialists in the field so that the right interpretation of the data collected is achieved. There is no agreement on what constitutes a reliable benchmark.

Research on the subject of benchmarks identified three different methods:

1. **Resident population of the community** that is policed by the department under consideration—probably the most common.

2. **Field observation of drivers** at randomly selected sites during randomly selected times. Normally filed observers attempt to identify the race, ethnicity and approximate age of each driver.

3. **Accident records for not at fault drivers** to estimate the qualitative features (e.g. racial composition) of actual roadway users. Information arising from accident statistics is commonly used by traffic engineers to develop qualitative benchmarks of actual road users.

There are advantages and disadvantages to each of the types of benchmarks mentioned. None of the benchmarks mentioned are universally adaptable to every racial profiling evaluation. The following is a brief explanation of the advantages and disadvantages of each.

Resident Population of the Community
Advantages:
- Population estimates are readily available

- Inexpensive

- Benchmarks based on population do not limit the researcher to an analysis of traffic enforcement patterns

- If enforcement policy is consistent can be valid methodology. For example, an individual driving ten miles over the speed limit is just as likely to be stopped by a police officer on one beat as one on another.

- If number of officers in enforcement area is consistent can be valid methodology

Disadvantages:
- Method measures only the static and not the transient population
- System does not account for people counted but who don't drive
- Population estimates are often inaccurate (e.g., undocumented persons living in area not counted or undercounted)

Field Observation of Drivers
Advantages:
- Randomness can produce a relatively accurate sample of actual users of the roadway
- System can account for those people who are just passing through a community and do not live there
- Accounts for various driving exposure
- Method is not hampered by the under reporting problems associated with population estimates.

Disadvantages:
- Expensive and time consuming
- Cannot transfer findings from one area to other areas of the community
- Nighttime observations are difficult due to lighting and tinted windows on vehicles
- Observation area may require security or safety precautions for observers. Some researchers have utilized cameras to record drivers image and speeds and been able to estimate race or ethnicity and approximate age from photos at a safe location later.

Accident Records for not at Fault Drivers
Advantages:
- Easy and inexpensive to develop
- Accounts for transient population and non drivers
- Can be applied to an entire community
- Race or ethnicity can be verified by cross checking the state's department of motor vehicles database. Many states, however, do not document race or ethnicity on driver's licenses

Disadvantages:
- Lack of validation to date of this methodology
- Not at fault driver not always determined correctly
- Some non-English speakers don't communicate well enough, so fault not determined
- Many communities do not document non-injury or low damage accidents.

One criminal justice researcher, Brian Withrow, however maintains that:

> A benchmark comparison alone cannot measure the factors that influence a po-
> lice officer's decision to initiate a traffic stop. We cannot even determine
> whether or not the officer even knew the race of the individual prior to the stop.
> In other words, benchmark comparisons only tell us who gets stopped, not why
> (Withrow, 2004, p. 23)

The benchmarks selected must be able to help measure if individuals are being
stopped on the basis of their race, ethnicity, or national origin. One question to be
asked is, in a similar situation, would a person who was not a member of a minority
group have been stopped? In other words, the correct comparison is not to the people
living in the neighborhood or driving on the highway who did not engage in the same
conduct as the person stopped, but to those who did engage in the same conduct but
were not stopped because they were not of a minority race (U.S. Department of Justice,
2000). One can see how difficult a task it is to develop statistical benchmarks.

Unfortunately, most research and analysis of collected data on traffic and field in-
terrogation stops (detentions) do not take into consideration the decision-making
processes of the officer(s) involved. Most data collection efforts have neglected the
need to explain how and why officers make decisions pertaining to traffic or other
stops when studying racial profiling. Research designs should also allow for the investigation of officers' decision making after stops have been initiated (Engel, Calnon, &
Bernard, 2000, p. 261).

Data Analysis and Interpretation. Once the data have been collected, what do they
show? This is the most difficult part of the process—the analysis and interpretation of
the statistics compiled. Ultimately, the problem with interpreting results is that these
traffic and field-interrogation data have been collected without the guidance of any theoretical frameworks. Researchers have simply counted things—the number of traffic
stops, citations, and searches conducted by police against white and nonwhite suspects.
Instead, the research should be conducted under the larger theoretical context of explaining behavior. Problems with the interpretation of empirical data are due partially
to data collection efforts that have not addressed why officers might engage in decision
making based on citizens' race (Engel et al., 2000, p. 259).

Robin Engel and her coauthors (2000) state in their report that research on racial
profiling should include consideration of three dependent variables:

1. The behavior of the individual police officer
    a. Why do police officers in general stop more black citizens than white citi-
       zens? How and why do officers make decisions?
    b. Why do some officers exhibit more racial disproportionality while others
       exhibit less?
    c. Have there been changes in racial disproportionality over time?
2. The behavior of different police departments. Do some police departments
   have high rates of racial profiling and others have low rates? If so, what explains these differences?

3. The aggregate rates of officer and departmental behavior. Has race-based decision making been transformed in the past 40 years from one based primarily on individual racial prejudice to one based mainly on race-based departmental policies? (p. 261)

As explained, statistical benchmarks must be developed for comparison with the raw data collected by agencies. Among the decisions that must be made are:

1. Are the statistics collected compared with the city's racial makeup as determined by the nationwide census?

2. Are they compared with licensed drivers living in the city's jurisdiction?

3. Are they compared with the racial composition of the drivers on the roads, if that could be determined?

4. Are situational characteristics (e.g., suspects' characteristics, characteristics of the police–citizen encounter, and legal characteristics) considered and collected?

5. Are officers' characteristics (e.g., sex, race, experience, and attitudes) considered and collected?

6. Are organizational characteristics (e.g., formal and informal policies and attitudes and preferences of administrators and first-line supervisors) considered and collected?

7. Are community characteristics (e.g., demographic, economic, and political) considered and collected?

Data interpretation can be done internally by the law enforcement agency involved if the community political climate is good and there is trust that the analysis will be credible. However, since this is not usually the case, and to avoid the findings being considered suspect, most agencies obtain the services of an independent analyst. It is important that the analyst not only have some general knowledge of law enforcement procedures, but also be knowledgeable on the selection and development of statistical benchmarks or base rates.

Community Task Forces for Development and Implementation. Citizen input is critical to the success of data collection and interpretation. Community group representatives must be involved with police personnel of all ranks to form a task force. The task force members, including in most cases an independent analyst, work together to decide: (1) if data collection will be collected about the race/ethnicity of persons contacted by officers, (2) the design of benchmarks to utilize in the interpretation of the data, and (3) the response or action to be taken based on the interpretation. Representatives might include members of local community groups such as the National Association for the Advancement of Colored People (NAACP), the Urban League, the American Civil Liberties Union (ACLU), the Latino Unity Coalition, and Pan Pacific Asian representatives. Police departments should take their input and implement the appropriate recommendations in subsequent phases of the project. Task forces and community-oriented policing are beneficial to a department's efforts to investigate and solve problems associated with allegations of racial profiling. Task forces not only help ensure that the process addresses specific concerns of the community, but also help improve police–community relations. PERF suggests how to get started:

1. Unless mandated, decide, with citizen input, whether data collection should be one component of the jurisdiction's overall response to racially biased policing and the perceptions thereof.

2. Communicate with agency personnel as soon as a decision is made to start collecting data. The executive should provide a rationale for data collection and address anticipated concerns.

3. Set up a process for listening to personnel's concerns, and have personnel develop constructive ways to address them.

4. Develop a police–citizen group to serve in an advisory capacity.

5. Develop the data collection and analysis protocol. Ensure that the interpretations will be responsible, based on sound methodology and analysis.

6. Field test the data collection system for three to six months, and use that test to make modifications before implementing the system jurisdiction-wide. (PERF report, 2001, pp. 143–144)

MINI CASE STUDIES: CULTURE AND CRIME

Mini-Case-Study 4: Biased Policing (Racial Profiling)

Denver, Colorado, Police Department

The Biased Policing Task Force is a community–police collaboration that began in November 2000 to address the national issue of racial profiling. The name, Biased Policing Task Force, was selected to reflect that the issues addressed by the project go beyond race/ethnicity to include any discriminatory actions that were based on age, gender, sexual orientation, or gender identity.

Mission Statement:

To promote and enhance a healthy relationship between the Denver Police and the community through mutual accountability, which promotes open communication and fosters respect and trust.

In order to accomplish this we will do the following:

*   Ensure that biased profiling does not occur
*   Compile statistical data as to the nature of police contacts
*   Develop policies that reflect this position
*   Create training programs for the community and the police
*   Develop standards and monitor compliance
*   Value safe neighborhoods and support policing to ensure the safety of elders, youth, the disabled, and all individuals

Task Force Committees:

- Policy/Procedures
- Data Collection
- Training
- Youth Issues

State Legislation

Members of the Task Force also worked with members of the Colorado General Assembly to craft House Bill 01-1114, concerning profiling in connection with law enforcement traffic stops.

Policy/Procedures

On June 1, 2001, 7 months of work culminated in the announcement of the Denver Police Department's policy regarding biased policing and the procedures to collect data on all officer-initiated citizen contacts, both traffic and pedestrian. Officers now complete a Citizen Contact Datasheet for every officer-initiated contact where the person was detained based on reasonable suspicion or probable cause.

Data Analysis

The Task Force Data Analysis Subcommittee concluded that a meaningful analysis of contact data requires the collection of information for no less than 1 year. This will allow for the compilation of an adequate amount of citizen contact data and comparative benchmark measures. This time frame will also average out the effects of special events or directed patrol activities (DUI enforcement campaigns), as well as seasonal variations in crime and enforcement activities. In addition, this is the same reporting period prescribed by the new state law.

(*Source:* Denver Police Department, 1331 Cherokee St. #406, Denver, Colorado 80204)

Unintended Results of Data Collection. In some agencies, when mandatory data collection was instituted, the number of traffic tickets dropped precipitously as officers, wary of being accused of racial profiling, stopped fewer people. This occurred in Houston and in Cincinnati. In other agencies, officers refused to fill out the forms or made mistakes, which made the data unusable. The officers complained that the collection process was a waste of time and that the data collected might be used against them. Some argued that officers who use racial profiling because they are prejudiced will never fill out the form. There are examples of cities in which police officers are so fearful of the possibility of being accused of being racist if they stop a person of color that they avoid making contact, even if a violation or minor crime is being committed. If accusations begin to control policing, public safety suffers. Some agencies have equipped their patrol vehicles with video cameras and audio recording devices to provide evidence of the actions of their officers in the event of complaints.

SUMMARY

Citizen discontent and lawsuits against law enforcement can originate as a result of racial profiling or use of profiles or profiling that appears to have been based on bias. Law enforcement professionals need to be critical and introspective when analyzing this problem of racism and prejudice in the profession. They need to reflect seriously on the issues involved and respond to both the reality of, and the perceptions of, biased policing. It is imperative that members of the criminal justice community and government officials understand the strong feelings about racial profiling, especially the feelings of those who have been targeted. Racial profiling or racially biased policing must stop, not only because it is illegal, but also because it leads to distrust by the minority community, litigation with expensive settlements, and the results are not worth the negative public opinion. No one of any race should have to fear being stopped or detained by police purely on the basis of skin color, ethnicity, or national origin.

One of the first assignments of those involved in addressing the issues would be to agree on a definition of terms. Hopefully, the definitions are uniform standards, adopted statewide. Law enforcement executives should review complaints of racial profiling covering a period of time (5–10 years) to get a handle on the existence and/or perception of the problem and its scope. They should also conduct a series of meetings with community spokespersons and representatives of civil rights groups to elicit and listen to stories and accounts of racial profiling and perceptions of same. If racial profiling is identified as having occurred and appears to have been carried out by a small number of officers, immediate and appropriate action should be taken—an investigation either confirming or refuting claims. The problem should be acknowledged and the public informed that it has been corrected. If a larger problem is identified, then other processes must be set into action to study its scope and how it can be resolved. This is often accomplished through the use of a police–community task force, because racial profiling is not solely a law enforcement problem, but rather one that can be solved only through partnerships that are based on mutual trust and respect. Data collection and its proper interpretation can be one part of a police response to determine if biased policing is taking place and to what degree. The agency executive must work with community leaders to develop a multifaceted response tailored to the needs of the jurisdiction. Resolution would not only include data collection and analysis, but also training, education, supervision, monitoring, and recruitment within the agency. Every law enforcement agency must adopt a policy that specifies the circumstances in which race or ethnicity can be used as a factor in making enforcement decisions. That policy should indicate not only that officers are to patrol in a proactive manner, to investigate aggressively suspicious person(s) and circumstances, and to actively enforce the motor vehicle laws, but also that citizens will only be stopped or detained when there exists reasonable suspicion to believe they have committed, are committing, or are about to commit an infraction of the law.

DISCUSSION QUESTIONS AND ISSUES

1. *Law enforcement agency policy on racial profiling.* The student can determine if a police department in the area meets recommended standards regarding policies pertaining to racial profiling:

   a. Does the policy clearly define acts constituting racial profiling using the definition provided at the beginning of this chapter?

b. Does the policy strictly prohibit peace officers employed by the agency from engaging in racial profiling?

c. Does the policy provide instructions by which individuals may file a complaint if they believe they were a victim of racial profiling by an employee of the agency?

d. Does the agency provide public education relating to their complaint process?

e. Does the policy require appropriate corrective action to be taken against a peace officer employed by the agency who, after an investigation, is shown to have engaged in racial profiling in violation of the agency's policy? What benchmarks are utilized and who interprets the data?

f. Does the agency require the collection of data relating to traffic stops in which a citation is issued and to arrests resulting from those traffic stops, including information relating to:

1) The race or ethnicity of the individual detained

2) Whether a search was conducted and, if so, if it was based on the consent of the person detained

g. Does the agency policy require them to submit a report on the findings and conclusions based on the data collected to a governing body of the county or state for review and monitoring purposes?

2. *Actual incident for discussion:* In a city in Indiana, an African American police officer driving an unmarked police car was pulled over by an officer not from his agency. The officer was wearing a uniform at the time, but he was not wearing his hat that would have identified him as a police officer. According to a complaint filed, the trooper who pulled the man over appeared shocked when the officer got out of the car. The trooper explained that he had stopped the man because he had three antennas on the rear of his car. Discuss the following:

1) Do you think the officer who pulled over a colleague was guilty of racial profiling?

2) Do you think the officer was being honest when he said the reason for the stop was the multiple antennas? Is having multiple antennas a crime?

3) Can complaints of being racially profiled be dismissed as the exaggerations of hypersensitive minorities or people who do not understand the job of a police officer?

WEBSITE RESOURCES

Visit these websites for additional information about racial profiling and related issues:

American-Arab Anti-Discrimination Committee (ADC):   http://www.adc.org

This website provides information about the ADC's civil rights efforts and useful summary data about cases and complaints regarding discrimination involving Arab Americans.

American Civil Liberties Union (ACLU):   http://www.aclu.org

This website contains multiple locations for information about many issues, including racial profiling.

Asian American Legal Defense and Education Fund (AALDEF):
http://www.aaldef.org

> This website provides information about civil rights issues with Asian/Pacific Americans and highlights issues of immigration, family law, government benefits, anti-Asian violence and police misconduct, employment discrimination, labor rights, and workplace issues.

Mexican American Legal Defense and Education Fund (MALDEF):
http://www.mldef.org

> This website is a good source of Latino civil rights issues and publications.

National Organization of Black Law Enforcement Executives (NOBLE):
http://www.noblenatl.org

> This website is a good source of information on many subjects including recommended police policy and procedure, NOBLE publications, press releases and training material, resources, and classes.

Police Executive Research Forum (PERF):   http://policeforum.org

> This website has an abundance of information about racial profiling and model programs. PERF produced a free video and guide to facilitate police–citizen discussions on racially biased policing. They also produced a helpful guide, *Racially Biased Policing: A Principled Response.*

REFERENCES

Barlow, David E, and Melissa Hickman Barlow. (2002). "Racial Profiling: A Survey of African American Police Officers." *Police Quarterly,* 5(3), 334–358.

Barlow, David E, and Melissa Hickman Barlow. (2000). *Police in a Multicultural Society: An American Story.* Prospect Heights, IL: Waveland Press.

Barlow, Melissa. (1998). "Race and the Problem of Crime in *Time* and *Newsweek* Cover Stories, 1946–1995." *Social Justice, 25*(2), 149–181.

Bast, Carol M. (1997). "Driving While Black: Stopping Motorists on a Subterfuge." *Criminal Law Bulletin. 33,* 457–486.

Berry, Ondra. (2000). Deputy Chief, Reno, Nevada Police Department. Interview, December, 2000.

"Bush bans racial profiling." (2003, June 18). *Washington Post,* p. A14.

"Boston to track all stops by police." (2003, July 20). *Boston Globe,* p. A1.

Callahan, Gene and William Anderson. (2001, August-September). "The Roots of Racial Profiling: Why are Police Targeting Minorities in Traffic Stops?" *Reason,* p. 1.

Carrick, Grady. (2000, November). "Professional Police Traffic Stops: Strategies to Address Racial Profiling in Perspective." *FBI Law Enforcement Bulletin,* pp. 8–10.

Davis, Nicole. (2001, December). "The Slippery Slope of Racial Profiling." Applied Research Center.

"A Comparative Analysis of Commonly Used Benchmarks in Racial Profiling: A Research Note." (2004, March). An unpublished paper submitted to the Academy of Criminal Justice Sciences by Brian Withrow, Wichita State University, School of Community Affairs, Wichita, Kansas.

Davis, Ronald L., IDA GILIS, AND MAURICE FOSTER. (2001, May). *A NOBLE Perspective: Racial Profiling—A Symptom of Bias-Based Policing.* National Organization of Black Law Enforcement Executives, Alexandria, VA.

Engel, Robin S., Jennifer M. Calnon, and Thomas J. Bernard. (2002). "Theory and Racial Profiling: Shortcomings and Future Directions in Research." *Justice Quarterly, 19*(2), 249–273.

Harris, David A. (1999). "Driving While Black: Racial Profiling on our Nation's Highways." American Civil Liberties Union. Available: www.aclu.org/prfiling/report/index.

Harris, David A. (2000, March). "Hearing on Racial Profiling Within Law Enforcement Agencies, United States Senate Subcommittee on the Constitution, Federalism and Property Rights." Written Testimony.

Harris, David A. (2002). *Profiles in Injustice: Why Racial Profiling Cannot Work.* New York: New York University Press.

Hughes, Johnny. (2000, March). "Some Straight Talk on Profiling." *Law Enforcement News, 26*(530), 15.

Kruger, Karen J. (2002, May). "Collecting Statistics in Response to Racial Profiling Allegations." *FBI Law Enforcement Bulletin,* pp. 8–12.

Kurlander, Neil. (2000, July). "Software to Track Traffic Stop Data." *Law Enforcement Technology, 27*(7), 148–153.

Lamberth, John. (1996). "A report to the ACLU." New York: American Civil Liberties Union.

Lundman, Richard J., and Robert Kaufman. (2003, February). "Driving While Black: Effects of Race, Ethnicity, and Gender on Citizen Self-Reports of Traffic Stops and Police Actions." *Criminology, 41,* 195–220.

Mac Donald, Heather. (2001, Spring). "The Myth of Racial Profiling." *City Journal, 11*(2) pp. 1–5.

"Minority officers are stricter on minorities." (2003, July 20). *Boston Globe,* p. A1.

"Most recent traffic stop data show little change—Black drivers still stopped at higher rate." (2002, June 6). *Washington Post,* p. T3.

NCJRS. (2001, Spring). "Recommendations from the First IACP Forum on Professional Traffic Stops." *3*(1).

"New Jersey adopts ban on racial profiling." (2003, March 21). *News India-Time,* New Jersey, p. A1.

"Officers' hearts hold racial profiling solution." (2001, March 6). *Cincinnati Inquirer,* p. 3.

Oliver, J. A., and A. R. Zatcoff. (2001, July). "Lessons Learned: Collecting Data on Officer Traffic Stops." *Police Chief,* pp. 23–24.

Fridell, Lorie, Robert Lunney, Drew Diamond, and Bruce Kubu. (2001). Police Executive Research Forum Report (PERF): "Racially Biased Policing: A Principled Response." *Police Executive Research Forum,* Washington, D.C.

International Association of Chiefs of Police. (2003). "Sample Professional Traffic Stops Policy and Procedure." Publication available online at www.theiacp.org

International Association of Chiefs of Police. (2003). "Recommendations from the First IACP Forum on Professional Traffic Stops." Publication available online at www.theiacp.org

"Oakland to analyze police reform deal." (2003, July 15). *Contra Costa Times,* p. A4.

"Oakland's police chief angry with Rider story." (2003, May 2). *Contra Costa Times,* p. A5.

"Passengers kicked off flights sue airlines, allege profiling. Lawsuits seek balance between greater national security and civil liberties." (2002, June 5). *Contra Costa Times,* p. D1.

Polakow-Suransky, Sasha. (2001, November). "Flying While Brown." *American Prospective,* p. 21).

"Race, sex, and age drive ticketing." (2003, July 20). *Boston Globe,* p. A1.

"Racial profiling routine, New Jersey finds." (2000, November 28). *New York Times,* p. A1.

Ramirez, Deborah, Jack McDevitt, and Amy Farrell. (2000, November). "A Resource Guide on Racial Profiling Data Collection Systems: Promising Practices and Lessons Learned." Washington, D.C.: U.S. Department of Justice.

Senge, Peter, Art Kleiner, Charlotte Roberts, Richard Ross, and Bryan J. Smith. (1994). *The Fifth Discipline Fieldbook: Strategies and Tools for Building a Learning Organization.* New York: Currency Doubleday.

Senge, Peter M. (1994). *The Fifth Discipline: The Art & Practice of the Learning Organization.* New York: Currency Doubleday.

Schott, Richard G. (2001, November). "The Role of Race in Law Enforcement." *FBI Law Enforcement Bulletin,* pp. 24–32.

Strandberg, Keith. (1999, June). "Racial Profiling." *Law Enforcement Technology,* 26(6) 62–66.

Straus, Ira. (2002, October). "Commentary: Profile to Survive," *United Press International.* United Press International. Available: www.upi.com

U.S. Department of Justice. (2000). *A Resource Guide on Racial Profiling Data Collection Systems: Promising Practices and Lessons Learned.* Washington D.C.: Author.

"Troopers fair, tough in traffic encounters." (2003, July 22). *Boston Globe,* p. A1.

Will, George F. (2001, April). "Exposing the 'Myth' of Racial Profiling." *Washington Post,* p. A19.

Part 5

CULTURAL EFFECTIVENESS
FOR PEACE OFFICERS

Part Five concludes this text by highlighting some of the themes from previous chapters, while discussing broad concepts on the emerging role of peace officers within a 21st-century multicultural society.

Chapter 15 analyzes these changes primarily from the perspective of altering the reader's image of law enforcement and understanding the impact of this shift on one's behavior as a public servant. We examine why those who serve the public are expected to be more tolerant and less ethnocentric in their outlook and dealings with citizens than in the past. The chapter reinforces the meaning of cultural sensitivity and provides a model for understanding cultural differences. It also considers peace officer professionalism and peacekeeping in a diverse society by first defining and presenting the interwoven concepts of leadership, professionalism, and synergy. The analysis focuses on cooperation in statewide and regional law enforcement. One section links professionalism to ethics and interactions with diverse groups, emphasizing the special obligation that peace officers have in upholding respect for human dignity.

Chapter 16 considers all the emerging and changing issues confronting the peace officer in his/her peacekeeping roles and in the use of high technology in multicultural law enforcement. Peace officers need to be competent to deal with their increasing roles in multijurisdictional crime-solving efforts (beyond homeland security and terrorism like the DC sniper, stolen identity, multistate crime scams). Moreover, the role of peace officers in assisting and communicating with multicultural communities in disasters, terrorism, controlling rumors resulting from regional events (e.g., anthrax fears), requires additional resources, skills, and the use of new law enforcement tools. Modern law enforcement requires an operating value and culture of improved intra-agency communication, as well as supportive relations with multicultural communities.

In addition to the Instructor's Manual for this text, further resource material is provided here in the form of four appendices. These supplementary aids correspond to various chapters in the book. They include assessment instruments as well as a listing of consultants and services related to the content of this text.

Chapter 15

Peace Officer Image, Cultural Sensitivity, and Professionalism

OVERVIEW

This chapter considers the changing role and image of peace officers that will result in increased cultural awareness and effectiveness in law enforcement in the 21st century. Given the impact of greater diversity on both peacekeeping and law enforcement, we explore how cultural understanding can be translated into more effective community policing. To increase cultural awareness, readers are provided with a simple model for quick analysis of differences in various cultures, ethnic groups, and generations. The content strengthens the case that improved police performance and professionalism are dependent on cross-cultural skills and sensitivity among peace officers.

COMMENTARY

The following quotes exemplify the diverse images of law enforcement, the importance of professionalism, and the necessity that today's peace officers have technical knowledge and skills:

> In the sense that image has a profound impact on the actual human interactions, sensitivity to how people perceive police is a very positive indicator. . . . The alternative available to police, which is to isolate themselves from public opinion, is to seek more favorable public opinion. . . . If the police and general community were to agree that keeping the peace was the law enforcement job, the problem would continue in that reality dictates that police arrest law violators and enforce laws in general, not merely keep the peace. (Coffee, 1990, p. 245)

> In a paper presented to the Commission on "Recruitment, Selection, Promotion, and Civil Service," A.C. Germann outlined the criteria for a profession in general, and law enforcement in particular. These included being service-oriented; highly competent, being allowed autonomy and authority in the exercise of that competence and accomplishment; valuing of free inquiry and loyalty to the profession which relates more to the opinion of professional peers than to hierarchical supervisors; determination to influence change by actions to eliminate or ostracize all incompetent members of the organization. (President's Commission on Law Enforcement and the Administration of Justice, 1967)

Explosive growth in Internet commerce, e-mail, and electronic networks have expanded the capabilities of criminals to commit crime. Hackers have proven themselves capable of major disruptions of electronic businesses and of inflicting considerable financial losses. Online pedophiles and stalkers prey on youngsters in chat rooms. White collar criminals are adept at electronic money laundering. Electronic developments are changing the face of crime. Investigators in every type of law enforcement agency in the nation are now confronted with electronic evidence that demands a high order of technical knowledge and skill. Computer forensic science is the process of extracting information and data from computer storage media and guaranteeing its accuracy and reliability. Like traditional crime investigation, cyber forensics involves gathering an assortment of physical evidence, interviewing witnesses, and determining suspects—but it also involves a knowledge of software options and computer media. (Office of Justice Programs, 1999)

These commentaries underscore a common reality—the image of law enforcement projected to the public by police officers, their organizations, and the media (Hancock & Sharp, 2000). In the first quotation, a noted criminal justice author has emphasized the importance of the public image created by law enforcement agencies and their personnel. The third quote highlights the emerging and changing roles and skills in information and high technology that peace officers must have in law enforcement to be peacekeepers in the 21st century.

IMPACT OF IMAGE ON HUMAN BEHAVIOR

People create images, both accurate and inaccurate, of themselves and others, as well as images of their roles. Our behavior is then influenced by these mental pictures, and others respond to what we project, which may not necessarily reflect reality. The most powerful of these images is the one we have of ourselves, followed by those formed about our multiple roles. Similarly, we also create images of our organizations, our nation, and the criminal justice system and its activities.

Police officers today are both knowledge and service workers who must focus on effective performance, according to Norman Boehm, former director of the California Commission on Peace Officer Standards and Training. Thus, he believes police departments must become both learning organizations and enforcement agencies. Boehm maintains that the former have the responsibility to provide officers with the new knowledge, skills, and behaviors to be effective on the job. "Smart cops," in every sense of the word, are becoming the norm (Barlow, 2000; Cromwell & Dunham, 1997).

Such an image of peacekeepers may explain why so many justice agencies are mandating a 2- or 4-year college degree for entering recruits and why the report of the Police Executive Research Forum, *The State of Police Education: Policy Direction for the 21st Century* (Carter, 1992), describes in detail the benefits of an educated officer. Brainpower, not brawn, is what will make for effectiveness in the vastly changing world of this new millennium.

Exhibit 15.1 differentiates between perceptions of the disappearing and emerging police work culture. Contrasting the two views helps to explain why, within the criminal justice field, a different image of law enforcement must be created of the peace officer and then projected to the public. This is but a synopsis of the transition under way

TRADITIONAL WORK CULTURE	EVOLVING WORK CULTURE
Attitude Reactive; preserve status quo	Proactive; anticipate the future
Orientation Enforcement as dispensers of public safety	Enforcement and peacekeeping as helping professionals
Organization Paramilitary with top-down command system; intractable departments and divisions; centralization and specialization	Transitional toward more fluid, participative arrangements and open communication system; decentralization, task forces, and team management
Expectations Loyalty to your superior, organization and buddies, then duty and public service; conformity and dependency	Loyalty to public service and duty, and one's personal and professional development; demonstrate leadership competence and interpersonal skills
Requirements Political appointment, limited civil service; education—high school or less	Must meet civil service standards; education—college and beyond, lifelong learning
Personnel Largely white males, military background and sworn only; all alike, so structure workload for equal shares in static sharply defined slots	Multicultural without regard to sex or sexual preference; competence norm for sworn and unsworn personnel; all different, so capitalize on particular abilities, characteristic, potential
Performance Obey rules, follow orders, work as though everything depended on your own hard efforts toward gaining the pension and retirement	Work effectively, obey reasonable and responsible requests; interdependence means cooperate and collaborate with other; ensure financial/career future
Environment Relatively stable society where problems were somewhat routine and predictable, and authority was respected	Complex, fast-changing, multicultural society with unpredictable problems, often global in scope, and more disregard of authority, plus more guns/violence even among juveniles.

Exhibit 15.1   Law enforcement role transitions.

in the world of work and law enforcement, which in turn alters our views of various justice roles. In the latter, the shift and trends seem to be away from the traditional approaches—from reactive to proactive; from just enforcement and crime-fighting toward prevention and detection of criminal activity, toward preserving the public peace and service, and toward protecting life and property; and from just public-sector policing to synergistic security services by both public and private sectors working in cooperation (Hunter, Mayhall, & Barker, 2000).

Darrel Stephens, former director of the Police Executive Research Forum (PERF), put the situation quite simply: "Mechanically bean counting of arrests and putting squad cars on the street is no longer enough." These observations are from one who has served as chief of police at many large departments. He has demonstrated his position on preventive, community-oriented policing. In a graduation address to police executives at California's POST Command College on January 15, 1993, Stephens stated his conviction that citizens are the first line of defense in preventing and fighting crime, not the crime fighter who reacts after the crime is committed. Therefore, he advocates a problem-solving type of law enforcement that collaborates with the varied community groups within departmental jurisdiction.

Image Projection

Within this larger context, comprehending the significance and power of image and its projection becomes critical for would-be peacekeepers. Image is not a matter of illusion or mere public manipulation of appearances. Behavioral scientists have long demonstrated the vital connection between image and identity, between the way we see ourselves and our actual behavior. Realists among us have always known that life's "losers," many of them convicted felons, lack an adequate sense of identity and suffer from feelings of poor self-worth. Some people raised in dysfunctional families go so far as to engage not only in self-depreciation and abuse but in self-mutilation as well. Aware of these factors, California established a special commission to promote self-esteem among school youth, so as to curb crime and delinquency.

Behavioral communication may be understood in terms of senders and receivers of messages. Exhibit 15.2 suggests that we view the multiple images we form in terms of concentric or spiraling circles, centered on the all-important self-image at the core (Harris, 1994). As we see ourselves, we project an image to which people respond. Normally, we are in control of the reactions and treatment we receive by the image we project. Our self-concept has been long in development, the outcome not just of life experience but of others' input to us. If a child continuously receives negative feedback from parents and teachers, he or she begins to believe in personal worthlessness. Usually, these young people fail to achieve unless an intervention calls into question their distorted concept of self. Such persons are likely to project weak images that often prompt others to take advantage of them. On the other hand, if they have self-confidence and project a positive image, both verbally and nonverbally, an acceptable response from others is probable. (The exception would be with bigoted persons who reflect an inner bias and refuse to accept people different from themselves, as with frustrated youth known as skinheads. In this case, the problem and conflict are caused by feelings of low self-worth.) The best antidote to underachievement or even racism is for a person to have a healthy self-image.

Furthermore, if a person is confused about identity, as is often the situation with adolescents, people tend to respond in an uncertain way toward that person. Therefore, in the selection of police candidates, law enforcement officials seek those with a strong self-image and self appreciation. Police academy training should reinforce, not undermine, this self-confidence. Police supervisors are advised to provide regular positive reinforcement of their officers' sense of self.

Multiple Images

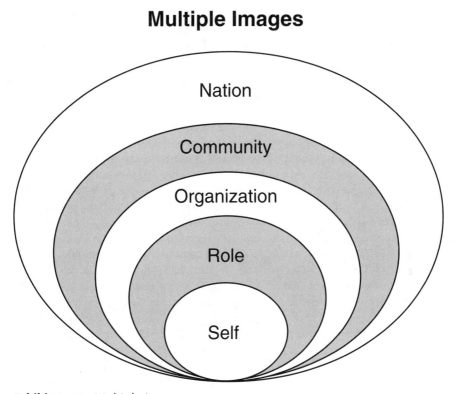

Exhibit 15.2   Multiple images

We play many roles in the course of life—male or female, married or single, child or parent, student or mentor. However, our concern here is specifically on work and professional roles within the criminal justice system and the changing images projected by its practitioners. In terms of behavioral communication theory, police officers project an image to the public based on how they see themselves, and citizens usually respond to that image (see Langworthy & Lawrence, 1999).

Two examples—one old, one new—illustrate this point. In 1829 Sir Robert Peel established the London Metropolitan Police, projecting an image of a paid, professional force to which the British public responded positively, calling them "peelers" or "bobbies." Rejecting the old adage "employ a thief to catch a thief," he recruited these new police from the military (rather than from criminal backgrounds, as was then the custom) and compensated them with adequate salaries so they would be less inclined to accept bribes or indulge in other irregularities (Gilbert, 1990).

Since then, the role of police has evolved as society has changed its perceptions of values and priorities, justice and criminality, law and enforcement (Carter & Radalet, 1999; Champion & Rush, 1997). Currently, for example, the average citizen seems less concerned about police enforcement of vice and traffic laws and more concerned about their combating gang and domestic violence, especially physical abuse of children, spouses, and the aged, and even more recently, terrorism. Understandably, the American public today, particularly among minorities and the disenfranchised, has high expectations about being treated humanely and fairly when encountering police in an economically developed country. However, new arrivals to the United States and Canada, whether through legal or illegal entry, come with their own cultural perceptions and perspectives from their homeland. These can include negative images of police there, which may be that of oppressors and bribe takers. For these citizens, professional police in the new homeland may need to go out of their way to help them overcome the mental barriers they carry due to their cultural background.

The second example involves how modern media have a powerful influence on how the public perceives police. It begins with fictional police as depicted in novels and mystery stories, expands to reports of police activities in newspapers and magazines, and extends to radio and television broadcasts about policing. Today U.S. movies and television "cop shows" are viewed internationally. The range of media impact on images of law enforcement is extensive.

With the coming of the information age and its new communication technologies, local police actions may become international incidents. With the help of satellites, television, and computers, the inhabitants of our planet react as a global village. The ultimate embarrassment to law enforcement's image occurred worldwide in 1991. This was the watershed case that took place with the beating of African American Rodney King by a few members of the Los Angeles Police Department. This unfortunate event was captured on videotape and played repeatedly over the airways internationally. It underscores another new reality: criminal justice representatives are now subject to extra scrutiny and accountability when citizens use camcorders to capture their activities for possible review, even on the Internet. In 2000, just before the Republican Convention, Philadelphia's municipal administration was embarrassed in this, "the City of Brotherly Love," when police were again caught on video severely beating a minority criminal. The only mitigating factor in the undermining of that police force's image on the national media is that both white and black officers were involved in applying what they thought was "reasonable restraint." Furthermore, that department did admirable policing during the actual convention.

The principal lesson to be learned from any controversial police action is that the organizational image of a reasonable and effective agency can be undermined by the unprofessional and illegal actions of a relatively small percentage of officers (see Palmiotto, 2001). It is not enough for a peace officer to be a competent professional; he or she must also assist by preventing or reporting wrongdoing by colleagues.

"PEACE OFFICER" IMAGE

Adopted in various American states, the term peace officer, which we utilize in this book, is a concept that might reverse negative publicity. Law enforcement personnel must take pride in the term and internalize its meaning. By projecting this image and its corresponding behavior, police are more likely to make a favorable impression on people. Interestingly, it is terminology that was very popular in the old west and often used in old cowboy movies. This term is also in use nationally within the U.S. Department of Justice, as well as within certain regions. For example, the California code (section 830) defines a peace officer as including sheriffs, police, marshals, constables, inspectors, investigators, district attorneys, state highway patrol and police division, state university and college police, designated personnel in the departments of justice, corrections, fish and game, parks and recreation, and forestry. This broad definition applies to members of the National Guard when on duty during states of emergency, as well as to U.S. federal marshals. It can encompass a wide range of related criminal justice occupations, such as arson investigators; park rangers; coroners; investigators of child support and fraud; security officers in municipal and public utilities; harbor, port, and transportation security officers; and public housing security. Similarly, in the state of Texas, the term peace officer is in widespread use; its Commission on Law Enforcement Standards and Training uses the term for constables, sheriffs, city police, specialized police, and the Texas Rangers. But do practitioners appreciate the implications of this nomenclature by which they are widely known?

Within this wide spectrum of peace officers, the image is strengthened by their being "sworn" to uphold the law, their adherence to standards and training, their badge and weapon, and sometimes their uniforms and insignia. But the true significance of the words "peace officer" has yet to be fully realized by most who operate under the umbrella term.

Influencing the Public Positively

Psychologists remind us that the image we have of our role affects not only our behavior but also the behavior of those to whom we project this image. The U.S. Marine Corps, for example, is currently undergoing a change of image from warriors to peacekeepers and humanitarians. What if all those described previously under the definition of peace officer actually saw themselves as such, thus projecting that image to the public? What if they were actually to become peace practitioners rather than symbolic enforcers of authority? A change in role image and actions among agents of the law might prompt the majority of the law-abiding community to perceive them more positively—as peace officers in fact as well as in name. Rather than fear police, citizens would turn to them as resourceful problem solvers. Neighborhood police who interact with the community are more likely to improve public perception of law enforcement, in contrast to police who rarely leave their squad cars or come into difficult areas as members of special units. There is much to be said for "cops" from the past who knew and patrolled their neighborhoods on foot.

Changing Police Cultures

In the article "Taking Police Culture Seriously," law professor Andrew Goldsmith (1990) of Melbourne, Australia, makes these astute observations:

> Police culture tends to be seen negatively, as a contrary and perverse influence on "proper" exercise of police discretion. It is seen as often subversive of the ideals and demands of legality. Yet most modern societies are essentially dependent upon rule-based forms of police accountability. Police culture needs to be approached more positively, as a potential resource in the formulation of rules governing police powers and practices. This requires that police administrators and officers participate in negotiated rulemaking, a process similar to collective bargaining, in which police cultural perspectives are drawn upon.

Traditional police cultures transitioned away from the more rigid military and bureau-cratic cultures of the past to a more flexible, corporate-like, proactive, and high-tech culture. Law enforcement leaders became change agents in this 21st-century process. To facilitate the changeover, many police administrators and managers applied meth-ods of cultural analysis to their own unique work environment.

Ways of Analyzing Cultures

There are many ways to study a culture, such as a systems approach that might analyze it in terms of kinship, education, economics, politics, religions, associations, health, and pastimes. However, Harris and Moran (2000) provide a simple model that will en-able those in law enforcement to get a grasp of a culture, whether on a large or small scale, irrespective of the grouping. These 10 benchmarks can be used to better compre-hend a foreign organizational or local culture, especially that of a minority or ethnic group. Exhibit 15.3 summarizes these characteristics for cultural analysis, first in terms of cultures in general and then specifically in the context of police culture.

---

1. **Sense of self and space.** Examine how people in this cultural group perceive themselves and distance themselves from others. Culture not only helps to confirm one's identity but provides a sense of space, both physical and psychological. Such cultural conditioning of behavior may dictate a humble bearing in one culture or macho posturing in another. Some cultures support rugged individualism and independent action, while others teach that self-worth is attained in group conformity and cooperation. In some cul-tures, such as American, the sense of space dictates more physical distance between individuals, while in Latin/Asian cultures, less distance is desirable. Some cultures are very structured and formal, while others are more flexible and informal. Some cultures are very closed and determine one's place very precisely, while others are more open and dynamic. Each culture validates self in unique ways.

Police culture, for example, expects officers to project a sense of authority and assertiveness, to be respected and in control, to be curious and suspicious, to act with social appropriateness and a sense of duty, to uphold the law, and to serve the common good. Sense of space is experienced in terms of a precinct or district, a patrol area ("beat"), or a neighborhood in community-based policing.

2. **Communication and language.** Examine the communication system in the culture, both verbal and nonverbal. Apart from the national or regional language that might be spoken, study the dialects, accents, slang, jargon, graffiti, and other such variations. For example, there are differences in the way the English language is spoken in England and within the British Isles and Commonwealth nations; in North America, between the Canadians and the Americans (and within the latter between regions and groups, such as black English). Levine reminds us to go Beyond Language to comprehend the full com-munication by seeking the meanings given to body language, gestures, and signals.

The police culture has its own jargon and code system for communicating rapidly within the field of law enforcement; organizational communications dictate a formal system for reporting, for ex-changes with superior ranks, for dealing with public officials and the media. A code of silence may exist about speaking to outsiders concerning police business and personnel.

3. **Dress and appearance.** Examine the cultural uniqueness relative to outward garments, adorn-ments, and decorations or lack thereof; the dress or distinctive clothing demanded for different occa-sions (e.g., business, sports, weddings or funerals); the use of color and cosmetics; the hair and beard styles, or lack thereof; body markings.

Exhibit 15.3   Characteristics for cultural analysis.

In police culture, policy, regulations and even custom may determine a uniform with patches and insignia of rank, plus certain equipment to be worn and even the length of hair permissible. Exceptions may be permitted for those in administration, detective, or undercover work.

4. **Food and eating habits.** Examine the manner in which food is selected, prepared, presented, and eaten. According to the culture, meat, like beef or pork, may be prized or prescribed, or even forbidden all together—one person's pet may be another's delicacy. Sample national dishes, diverse diets, and condiments for tastes do vary by culture (realize that cultural groups can be conditioned to accepting some food or seasoning that your own body would not tolerate without reactions. Feeding habits may range from the use of hands or chopsticks to the use of utensils or cutlery (e.g., Americans and Europeans do not hold and use the fork in the same manner). Subcultures can be studied from this perspective (as in soldier's mess, executive dining rooms, vegetarian restaurants, prescriptions for females, etc.). Even drinking alcohol differs by culture—in Italy, it is more associated with eating a meal, while in Japan and Korea it is ritualized in the business culture as part of evening entertainment and strengthening business relations, sometimes done to excess.

In police culture, the emphasis has been on fast foods, hearty meals (preferably "complimentary," although official regulations require payment by officers for all such services); customs include that the patrol car sets the eating time for both partners, as well as off-duty relaxation and comradery in a "cop's drinking hole," sometimes marked by too much alcoholic consumption. The new generation of police is more concerned about healthy foods, keeping physically fit, and stress management—including diet, exercise, no smoking, and no substance abuse.

5. **Time and time consciousness.** Examine the time sense as to whether it is exact or relative, precise or casual. In some cultures, promptness is determined by age or status (e.g., at meetings—subordinates arrive first, the boss or elder last). Is the time system based on 12 or 24 hours? In tribal and rural cultures, tracking hours and minutes is unnecessary, for timing is based on sunrise and sunset, as well as the seasons, which also vary by culture (e.g., rainy or dry seasons vs. fall/winter/spring/summer). Schedules in the postindustrial work culture are not necessarily 8 hours; businesses may operate on a 24-hour basis because of telecommunications and electronic mail. Chronobiologists are concerned under such circumstances about the body's internal clock and performance, so analyze body temperature and composition relative to sleepiness, fatigue, and peak periods (e.g., as with jet fatigue when passing through time zones).

The police culture operates on a 24-hour schedule with sliding work shifts that do affect performance; some departments adopt the military time-keeping system of 24 hours. Normally, promptness is valued and rewarded; during police operations, timing is precise, with watch synchronization of all involved.

6. **Relationships.** Examine how the culture fixes human and organizational relationships by age, sex, status, and degree of kindred, as well as by wealth, power, and wisdom. In many cultures, marriage and the family unit are the most common means for establishing relations between the sexes and among parents, children, and other relatives. In the Far East, this is accomplished through an extended family that may involve aunts, uncles, and cousins living in the same household. Many cultures also operate with the male head of household as the authority figure, and extend this out from home to community to nation, explaining the tendency in some countries to have dictators. In traditional cultures, custom sets strict guidelines about boy—girl relations prior to marriage, about treatment of the elderly (in some cultures, they are honored, in others ignored), about female behavior (wearing veils and appearing differential to males in contrast to being considered an equal). "Underworld" or criminal cultures sometimes adopt a family pattern with the "godfather" as the head and various titles to distinguish roles.

In police culture, organizational relations are determined by rank and protocol, as well as by assignment to different departmental units. Although policy may dictate that all fellow officers and citizens be treated equally, unwritten practice may differ. The partnership system usually forgoes close relations and trust between individuals whose life and welfare is dependent upon the other. Postindustrial policing is moving more toward developing team relationships.

7. **Values and norms.** Examine how the culture determines need satisfaction and procedures, how it sets priorities, and values some behavior while decrying other practices. Thus cultures living on a survival level (e.g., homeless) function differently from those which are affluent. In some Pacific Island cultures, for instance, the more affluent one becomes, the more one is expected to share with the group. Cultural groupings with high security needs value material things (e.g., money and property), as well as law and order. In the context of the group's value system, the culture sets norms of behavior within that

society or organization. Acting upon a unique set of premises, standards of membership are established affecting individual behavior—for example, the conventions may require total honesty with members of one's own group but accepts more relaxed behavior with those from other groups. Other standards may be expressed in gift-giving customs, rituals for birth/marriage/death, and guidelines for showing respect, privacy, and good manners. The culture determines what is legal or illegal behavior through a codified system or custom; what may be legal in one culture may be illegal in another.

In police culture, for instance, subordinates are expected to show respect for officers of superior rank, while the reverse may be tolerated for those who have broken the law. Publicly and by departmental regulations, a code of ethics is in place in which bribery and corruption are punishable offenses. A department of internal affairs ensures that alleged transgressors of such norms are investigated and tried or exonerated. This culture also espouses traditional American values of duty, loyalty, patriotism, and so on.

8. **Beliefs and attitudes.** Examine the major belief themes of a people and how this affects their behavior and relations among themselves, toward others, and what happens in "their world." A cultural "universal" seems to be a concern for the supernatural, evident in religious adherence and practices, which are often dissimilar by group. "Primitive" or tribal cultures are described as "animists" because they experience the supernatural in nature (e.g., "Indians" or Native Americans)—a belief to which modern environmentalists resonate. The differences are apparent in the Western cultures with Judeo-Christian traditions, as well as Islamic, in contrast to Eastern cultures, dominated by Buddhism, Confucianism, Taoism, and Hinduism. Religion, or the lack of it, expresses the philosophy of a people about important realities of life's experiences. Some cultural groups are more fundamentalist and rigid in their religious beliefs, while others are more open and tolerant. The position of women in a society is one manifestation of such beliefs—in some, the female is enshrined, in others treated like an equal by the male; in others, she is subservient to the male and treated like chattel. A people's belief system is often dependent on their cultural stage of human development—hunting, farming, industrial, or postindustrial; advanced technological societies seems to substitute a belief in science or cosmic consciousness for more traditional beliefs.

In police culture, for example, there has been a strong belief in group loyalty, pragmatism, power, and public service. God and religion have been acknowledged in oaths, in religious societies of police officers, by appointment of department chaplains, and during burial ceremonies of officers who die in the line of duty. Until recently, the law enforcement culture tended to be "chauvinistic," but that is changing with the introduction of more female officers and education of the workforce on diversity issues.

9. **Mental processes and learning.** Examine how some cultures emphasize one aspect of brain, knowledge, and skill development over another, thus causing striking differences in the way their adherents think and learn. Anthropologist Edward Hall suggests that the mind is internalized culture and involves how a people organize and process information. Life in a particular group or locale defines the rewards and punishments for learning or not learning certain information or in a certain way. In some cultures, the emphasis is on analytical learning—abstract thinking and conceptualization, while in others it is upon rote learning or memorization; some cultures value logic, while others reject it; some cultures restrict formal education only to males or the wealthy, while others espouse equal education for all. While reasoning and learning are cultural universals, each culture has a distinctive approach. However, the emergence of the computer and telecommunications as learning tools are furthering the globalization of education.

In police culture, recruit academies and other forms of in-service training may differ by locality as to content, instructional emphasis, and method. Anti-intellectualism among some police is being undermined by professional development and standards established by the federal/state governments and their credentialing processes, as well as by criminal justice curricula in higher education. As a result, modern police are moving from a more reactive, pragmatic, action-oriented behavior based on feelings and experience toward a proactive, thoughtful, analytical, and informed response. Professional competence is judged now by high performance and level of learning, not just by years on the job and connections.

10. **Work habits and practices.** Another dimension for examining a group's culture is their attitude toward work, the types of work, the division of work, the dominant work habits and procedures, and the work rewards and recognitions that are provided. Some cultures adopt a work ethic that says it is desirable for all to be so engaged in worthwhile activities—even sports and the arts, while others preclude labor for income. Work worthiness is measured differently by cultures as to income produced, job status, or service to the community. In Japan, for example, cultural loyalty is transferred from the family to

the organization, which is dependent upon the quality of individual performance. Classification of vocational activity is somewhat dependent on the culture's stage of development—a people can be characterized primarily as hunters, farmers, or factory or knowledge/service workers, with the trend away from physical labor toward use of mental energy aided by new technologies. The nature of work, as well as the policies, procedures, and customs related to it, are in transition. In the postindustrial culture, there is more emphasis on the use of advanced technologies, such as automation and robotics, as well as upon quality of working life—from compensation and benefits to stress management or enhancement of one's potential on the job. In conjunction with work, a culture differs in the manner and mode of proffering praise for good and brave deeds, outstanding performance, length of service, or other types of accomplishment. Promotions, perks, and testimonials are all manifestations.

In police culture, a hierarchial structure has organized work into specializations, divisions, and other such operational units engaged primarily in law enforcement and crime fighting. Job performance varied from "workaholics" to those who just put in time. Today the trend is toward peacekeeping and crime prevention, toward teamwork and community-based policing, toward obtaining citizen cooperation. Rewards and recognitions in the past have been largely commendations, advancement in rank, and retirement dinners, but now are being expanded to include assignments for professional development, interagency exchanges, and even sabbatical leaves for educational advancement.

Source: Excerpted with permission from Philip R. Harris and Robert T. Moran. (2000). *Managing Cultural Differences* (5th ed.). Boston: Butterworth-Heinemann. This parent book with *Instructor's Guide* is part of the 12 titles in the MCD Series of volumes available from Butterworth-Heinemann (225 Wildwood Ave, Woburn, MA 01801; 781-904-2500; Web site: www.BH.com).

A police officer in emergency situations is obviously not going to have the time to do an in-depth cultural analysis. However, especially in community-policing types of situations, the officer can undertake some preparation before beginning an assignment in a given area where citizens will largely be from unfamiliar ethnic groups. Most people have preconceived notions or only a stereotypical understanding of cultural groups with which they have not previously had contact. The categories listed in Exhibit 15.3 are areas where one often finds predictable cultural variations. The more information an officer or agent can gather about the cultural patterns of a distinctive community group, the less likely he or she is to make false assumptions about people. Knowledge of these cultural patterns would help the officer understand the behavior and actions of groups and contribute to an overall ability to establish rapport and gain trust.

Admittedly Exhibit 15.3 offers only 10 general classifications for cultural analysis, whether a nation, an organization, a profession, a group, a generation (e.g., youth or seniors), or an ethnic or racial group. There are other dimensions of culture, but the categories provided here help peace officers more quickly and systematically comprehend cultures, such as those described in Part Three of this book. The same approach can also be applied to study the "underworld" or criminal culture and its various subcultures (e.g., bank robbers, car thieves, hijackers, drug pushers, or sexual perverts). Furthermore, during international travel, whether on duty or on vacation, these same major characteristics can be observed to make the intercultural experience more meaningful. When law enforcement officers from other countries visit, these guidelines are useful for encouraging them to talk about their national or police cultures. All of the aspects of culture noted are interrelated; there is a danger in trying to compartmentalize this complex concept and miss the sense of the whole.

Using Culture to Create Positive Police Images

If the representatives of law enforcement are more culturally aware and sensitive, they are more likely to project to the public a positive image as peacekeepers. Following are examples of actual newspaper headlines affecting the image of the department involved. Although the media do not always accurately report what happened, we know that there are still instances of police insensitivity and that even inaccurate news reports leave deep impressions in the minds of viewers. Some negative headlines have included statements such as the following:

- "Report on Police Cites Racism, Excessive Force"
- "Law Enforcement: Officials Deny That Deputies Are Using Excessive Force as Agency Faces More Turmoil"
- "Policewomen Call Sexual Harassment Endemic in Their Department"
- "On the Beat, Police March to a Changing Set of Rules"
- "Police Abuses Laid Bare, but Solutions Fall Short"

More positively, there are numerous reports of law enforcement agencies engaged in constructive cross-cultural communication with the communities they seek to protect. One story concerned a special unit established by the San Diego Sheriff's Department to patrol Native American reservations, which are being overrun from the outside by drugs and violence. Federal Public Law 280 transferred criminal jurisdiction and enforcement on reservations to some states. In this instance, the tribal chairmen requested the deputies to patrol their rural, remote areas, which had become a kind of no-man's land. Word spread among the inhabitants of the reservation that the "law is back in town and he's not so bad." Terry Lawson's experience on the Barona Indian Reservation underscored the importance of culture underscoring knowledge and sensitivity when he said, "We're learning things the hard way, and I'm sure we're going to step on ourselves a lot more. When something bad happens, you're going to have a deputy who knows the tribal chairman by his first name, and who the Indians know by his first name. We're talking about personalized service ("Law is back in town and he's not so bad," Los Angeles Times, June 17, 1991, p. 17).

But do deputies have to learn about Native American cultures or other cultures the hard way? The issue is how much cross-cultural training is provided to officers for unique assignments (refer back to Chapter 9). If police are culturally sensitized, as suggested by the methods of cultural analysis, they will more likely achieve their goals with positive interactions.

Throughout this book the underlying message to law enforcement has been that patrolling or observing on the basis of one's own cultural background may result in distorted perceptions. Instead, peace officers should try to better understand the unique world of the community being served. For example, gestures have different meanings in varied cultures. In India, men and women do not usually hold hands in public. Men may hold hands, and women in some rural areas may walk behind the men. When asking questions of some people, especially from southern India, the gesture of rolling the head from side to side (which is similar to the "no" head movement in the West) signifies "I'm listening" or "I'm in agreement." Now transpose this gesture into a North

American urban area where a native of southern India is stopped by a police officer for running through a red light. The officer asks, "Did you see that red light?" If not yet acculturated to the ways of the United States or Canada, the response from the immigrant may be a head roll from side to side, a gesture that means "yes" in India. This response would probably confuse the officer, who may presume the Indian to be lying (i.e., the officer would interpret the Indian's head movement as "no").

POLICE CULTURE

In addition to ethnic or racial cultures, the police institution has a unique organizational culture. Hence, there is a distinct police subculture throughout the world evident in agencies and departments. This is an important consideration when seeking interagency cooperation on a case or project; although all may be in the field of law enforcement, each entity has a unique organizational culture that can encourage or discourage collaboration. It is also possible to analyze the cultural differences of specialization within the criminal justice field. Although the cultures of police, sheriffs, marshals, and correctional officers have much in common, there are also distinct differences caused by the nature of their law enforcement duties. Finally, the workplaces of some agencies are locked into a traditional industrial or military model, whereas others are attuned to a more innovative, team-oriented, post-industrial work culture (Harris, 1998; Senn & Children, 1999).

Occupational groupings worldwide have a commonality of culture, whether military, managerial, or police. During the 1960s, the National Commission on the Causes and Prevention of Violence commented on the U.S. police force as being mostly white, upwardly mobile, lower middle class, conservative in ideology, and resistant to change. Therefore, the commissioners observed that young police officers of that decade, sharing the attitudes and biases of the majority culture, might experience (1) fear and distrust when dealing with minorities and (2) mild cultural shock when working in the urban ghettos of America, especially if faced with militant hostility.

Commenting on this disappearing law enforcement subculture, Coffee (1990) confirms that it consisted largely of Caucasian men from working- or middle-class backgrounds, many with military service backgrounds. Coming from a conventional culture with limited contact with diverse groups, recruits experience a process of occupational socialization whereby they become identified with police associates and with their procedures, problems, and values. In other words, they adopt the cultural outlook or mindset of their colleagues in law enforcement, developing their own secure mini-world or cultural oasis. Immersed daily in this police micro culture with its humor and pathos, its peak energy highs and boredom, its stresses and dangers, this culture shapes their perceptions and attitudes, their role views and sense of responsibility, and their commitment to safeguard one another. It often leads to a "we (police)/they (public)" attitude. Readers can decide for themselves whether this socialization process and outlook is still present among justice personnel in the 21st-century in their locality. What is evident throughout North America is that police departments are recruiting more educated and diverse personnel.

Furthermore, police constantly interact with the criminal subculture, the hazardous "underworld" of the unsavory, the deviant, and the brutal. When engaged in undercover work, police temporarily assume the characteristics, dress, language, and behavior of criminals. Sometimes, they become so immersed in this illegal subculture that they lose their own sense of identity and perspective, adopting the role of the rogue cop. Furthermore, some police retreat into a "we/they" isolation—"they" being not only the perpetrators of crime but also all nonsworn officers and civilians. Thus, many police are more comfortable with "their own kind," whether they come from another agency, another state, or another nation. However, with increasing professionalism and education, as well as the recruitment of more women and diverse groups, police culture everywhere is being altered rapidly. Peace officers are becoming more comfortable and skillful in interacting with a variety of peoples and cultures at all levels of society. This adaptation and integration of cultural knowledge into daily interactions help maintain important levels of professionalism vital to the success of law enforcement.

POLICE LEADERSHIP IN PROFESSIONALISM AND SYNERGY

Lack of professionalism and inadequate personnel development can be very costly to any organization. But when it occurs within the public sector, it can prove damaging to both individuals and their careers, as well as to agencies and society. The following subsections cover three key concepts, which will be defined especially because of their implications for law enforcement and peacekeeping within a multicultural society (see Barlow, 2000; Dantzker, 2000).

Leadership

Leadership is exercised when one takes initiative, guides or influences others in a particular direction, and demonstrates how a process or procedure is performed. Leaders are said both to possess a good balance of conceptual, technical, and professional competence and to demonstrate judgment and people skills. Leaders are not only creative change agents but practical futurists, exercising foresight and the capacity for the "big picture" and the "long view" (see McGregor, 1991; Sullivan, 2000; Tamayo, 1999). Today, as we transition into a new information age and multicultural work environment, leaders need to be both transformational and transcultural. That is, such high performers innovate in

- Transforming workplaces from the status quo to appropriate environments
- Renewing organizations and becoming role models by transmitting intellectual excitement and vision about their work
- Helping personnel to manage change by restructuring their mindsets and values

Leaders help to improve their organizations by preparing the next generation of supervisors and professionals. They do this primarily through the human resource development program that they initiate and/or supervise (Harris, 1998). At a more personal level, they become mentors and coaches to high-performing personnel with organizational potential (Lynn Learning Labs, 1998).

In terms of the intercultural aspect, such leaders deal with all persons fairly, regardless of gender, race, color, religion, or cultural differences. A leader seeks to empower a more diverse workforce in law enforcement to be reflective of the communities served by this workforce. Furthermore, culturally sensitive leaders cut across cultural barriers while combating prejudice, bigotry, or racism wherever found in the organization and community (Simons, Vazquez, & Harris, 1993). Police supervisors, for example, exercise this leadership through anticipatory thinking, strategic planning, creative decision making, and effective communications (Moran, Harris, & Stripp, 1993; Whisenand & Ferguson, 1996). Similarly, chiefs of police provide leadership when they annually present their departmental goals both orally and in writing for the benefit of the city council and their agency workforce, ensuring over the year that these goals are systematically achieved.

Professionalism

Professionalism means approaching an activity, such as one's occupation or career, with a sense of dedication and expertise. In contrast to an amateur, a professional is a committed high performer. A professional possesses integrity and demonstrates competence—regardless of the role, career activity, or sport in which he or she is engaged. Following is a description of some of the characteristics of professionalism, particularly with reference to law enforcement. A professional in criminal justice systems is concerned about:

- Doing an effective job or rendering an effective service

- Developing and maintaining his or her career skill or competency level

- Exhibiting ethical and sensitive behavior and ensuring that other departmental members do the same

- Capitalizing on diversity in people and organizations and seeking to develop human potential with regard to diversity

- Being aware of the latest developments in the criminal justice field

In law enforcement, professionals would make it a point to understand the law and legal system in which they work, as well as the key issues in the criminal justice field (Barlow, 2000; Calvi & Coleman, 2000; Schmalleger, 2001).

To increase their competence, these professionals are familiar with aspects of criminology and criminal and deviant behavior (Barkan, 2001; Bartol, 1999; Goode, 2001). Whether writing a report, conducting an investigation or an interview, or commanding a police action, professional peace officers do the work consistently well (Adams, 1998; Gabor, 1994; Wallace, Robertson, & Steckler, 2001). They are high performers who meet their own goals and targets, not just for self-advancement or to please command officers, but because of the important nature of their duties. Their performance observes the code of ethics expected of public employees (Goodman, 1998; Leighton & Reiman, 2001; Sonnenberg, 1995). With growing multiculturalism in both the community and workforce, law enforcement professionals support policies and programs that promote collaboration among people of diverse backgrounds (Harman, 1992). Furthermore, they work with colleagues or the community to rectify any divisiveness, intolerance, discrimination, and even violence in the workplace (Peak & Glensor, 1999; Twilling, 1995). And, as will be noted in Chapter 16, competent with the emerging computer technology, digital communication, and research tools necessary in law enforcement today.

Synergy

Synergy implies cooperation and the integration of separate parts to function as a whole and to achieve a common goal. Synergy occurs through working together in combined action, attaining a greater total effect than a sum of the individual parts. Cultural synergy builds on the differences in people to promote mutual growth and accomplishment. Through such collaboration, similarities, strengths, and diverse talents are shared to enhance human activities and systems. For team management and teamwork, synergistic relations are essential (Moran & Harris, 2005). In law enforcement, synergistic leaders

- Facilitate interagency and interprecinct cooperation.

- Create consensus, which enables disparate people and groups to work together by sharing perceptions, insights, and knowledge.

- Promote participation, empowerment, and negotiation within an organization or community so that members work to mutual advantage and are committed to teamwork and the common good over personal ambition or need.

- Demonstrate skills of facilitating, networking, conflict resolution, and coordination.

- Are open-minded, effective cross-cultural communicators.

Synergistic leaders give priority to the professional development of subordinates, especially through training and team building (Justice & Jamieson, 1999).

Thus leadership, professionalism, and synergy are three powerful, interrelated concepts. When combined within the criminal justice system in general, or law enforcement and peacekeeping in particular, they may alter one's role, image, and performance. The following descriptions demonstrate the application of these concepts to real situations. Leadership, professionalism, and synergy are illustrated at both the organizational and individual levels in the context of the new work culture (Harris, 1994).

REGIONAL OR STATEWIDE COOPERATION IN LAW ENFORCEMENT

Society and communities today are so complex and interdependent that individual departments can best deal with certain enforcement challenges and crime problems through cooperation among criminal justice entities at all levels of government. This is most certainly true with enforcement challenges like terrorism and homeland security, and crime problems that are multijurisdictional in nature like identity theft. Although cooperation is certainly more efficient and effective, for many traditional public safety agencies, it may require a paradigm shift in the thinking of its members. Effecting change means exercising a type of law enforcement leadership that actively promotes specific information interchanges, joint ventures, and task forces that operate on a statewide or regional basis. It would be contrary-thinking and unprofessional behavior not to work with another agency because of jurisdictional jealousy and fear as to who will get the credit for success in the operation, or because of distorted desires to protect one's agency territory and budget. The overriding concern should be the public good by agencies working together to prevent and counter criminality in the community, while promoting the common good and civility. Perhaps Hawthorne, a police execu-

Reduced funding, increased demands for public services, technological advances in law enforcement, and the regional nature of crime in the '90s have all been identified as factors that could entice some communities to merge law enforcement agencies with those of neighboring communities. These mergers, however, could lead to a loss of community identity, reduced level of local control over the police, and the political perception that the city cannot take care of itself. This study examines the opportunities for the functional consolidation of certain law enforcement support services to achieve the benefits of consolidation, without the perceived negative impacts of full law enforcement mergers. It includes a guideline for conducting a feasibility study to determine possibilities for consolidation in any given area, as well as a transition management plan to aid in the implementation of such a project. Common pitfalls and success factors are also identified to assist in the successful implementation of a regional approach to any law enforcement support function. (Hawthorne, 1995)

Exhibit 15.4   Regional law enforcement consolidation of services.

tive, has summed up the need and problems best in his research, which is summarized in Exhibit 15.4.

Within the larger criminal justice system, there are already many commissions, councils, and other structures for promoting interagency collaboration. Law enforcement leaders with a sense of professionalism and synergy would ensure that all their command is committed to such collaborative action (see Langworthy & Lawrence, 1999). As a case in point, many matters of police training are best dealt with at a statewide or regional level, but with local agency input and participation (Pierce, 1997). For example, there are such joint, interagency programs for training with other public-sector personnel in human behavior, cultural diversity, affirmative action, terrorism, and homeland security. Again, in large metropolitan areas with several police jurisdictions, a consortium might be established to create an alliance for that locality to address specific law enforcement problems (e.g., ethnic gangs, juvenile delinquency, or emergency preparedness). Similarly, a regional, collaborative approach in peacekeeping might involve joint problem solving and activities on such concerns as hate crimes or recruitment of more women and minorities into criminal justice careers (Justice Research Association, 2000). Probably the greatest area for improvement of synergistic relations is between and among federal, state, and local law enforcement.

Agency representatives come from differing organizational cultures. Therefore, any interagency collaboration or merger requires the practice of the kind of cross-cultural communication skills described in Chapter 4. Another illustration directly related to this book's theme would be in a border city with a twin urban area in another country (Johnson, 1994). For the United States, this synergy could be along the northern border with Canada or the southern border with Mexico, requiring international cooperation among public agencies that have similar missions but different cultural contexts and legal systems. In such situations, local police departments of both nations should routinely share information and should cooperate in combating crime or facilitating cross-border traffic. How much more could be accomplished if the many law jurisdictions along the American–Mexican border, for example, were to enter into informal or formal arrangements to cooperate and advance the professional development of each other? For instance, within the sister cities of Juarez, Texas, and Ciudad Juarez,

Mexico, the Mexican police could be most helpful to their northern colleagues in terms of language and cultural training, particularly with reference to those of Mexican origin living in Texas. In return, the Texas peace officers might assist in the technical and professional preparation of their Mexican counterparts. This cooperation might contribute to more humane treatment of U.S., Mexican, and Canadian citizens who break the law when south of the border. Under Mexican law, based on the Napoleonic law system, the supposed transgressor is considered guilty until proven innocent, the opposite of the U.S. legal system, which is based on English Common Law.

For American, Canadian, and Mexican police, there are numerous other ways to be mutually supportive, ranging from information exchanges on criminology and specific criminals and groups to promotion of better bilateral relations and border law enforcement management. With the North American Free Trade Agreement (NAFTA), we should expect increasing exchanges and transfers between the citizens of Canada, the United States, and Mexico (Moran & Abbott, 2000). With the cooperation of law enforcement in all three countries of North America, that process is facilitated. To overcome cross-cultural barriers, police jurisdictions and their personnel in adjoining countries have more to gain by thinking in terms of synergy across borders. One place to begin is to learn about the differences in each nation's legal system. Therefore, something is to be gained by joint training projects, such as, for example, a collaborative effort of customs service or border patrol agents of one or all three nations, especially during these times with the problems of international terrorism and homeland security.

Police Professionalism, Ethics, and Diversity

Police professionalism, according to Hunter, Mayhill, and Barker (2000), requires self-awareness and a positive self-image. For professionalism to grow in law enforcement, the late Pamela D. Mayhill advocated not only greater technical skill training but also higher educational attainments, along with the setting of goals for career development. To reduce stress within the working environment of modern police, this criminal justice professor advocated an atmosphere of improved intra-agency communication, as well as supportive relations with the community (Anderson, Swenson, and Clay, 1995).

Police Professionalism. The principal purpose of criminal justice education, whether in universities, colleges, or academies, is to improve performance and to increase professionalism among those in law enforcement. What, then, seem to be the characteristics of a police professional? Some answers have been provided throughout this book, including earlier in this chapter when we discussed the concept of professionalism in general. A law enforcement professional is

- One who is properly educated and public service oriented.
- One whose behavior and conduct on the job is appropriate and ethical, avoiding clear conflicts of interest.
- One who respects the dignity and humanity of everyone contacted in the course of his or her duties by treating all fairly and with equal justice.
- One who is culturally sensitive to the differences and potential of others.
- One who is aware of the impact of agency culture on the professional behavior of officers.

- One who is a lifetime learner concerned about personal and career development for both self and others.

The Florida Criminal Justice Executive Institute recently issued a monograph entitled *Against Brutality and Corruption.* It discusses how these twin evils can be countered within law enforcement by officers who demonstrate integrity, wisdom, and professionalism. Its author, Edwin J. Delattre (1991a), observes, "We tend nowadays to neglect the immorality of professional incompetence! Many people who discuss ethics in different walks of life, whether in business or public service or the traditional professions, seem to believe that behaving honestly on the job and having the 'right' attitudes about race, sexual orientation, and the environment are all that ethics requires. This view ignores our plain duty to be professionally competent and good at our jobs."

In the Teacher's Guide for another volume, Delattre (1991b) emphasized to police academy instructors that because all police training is directly relevant to ethics, instruction should include competent performance components. We not only reinforce that observation, but add to it: All police professional development should contain adequate preparation in the understanding of culture and the attainment of cross-cultural skills. Our position is that ethical behavior by law officers also encompasses respect for human dignity, concern for human rights, and value for diversity in the human family (Hurst, 1993; Miller, 1996; Ortega, 1993). Unethical behavior is present when officers are deliberately racist, acting with discrimination, prejudice, bigotry, and intolerance toward a fellow officer, citizen, or foreign visitor. Such actions by public employees are simply unprofessional and unacceptable. The public will no longer overlook or tolerate such behavior by peace officers (Goodman, 1998; Leighton & Reiman, 2001).

Although the criminal justice system has made significant progress in recruiting and promoting women and members of diverse groups within the past decade, discrimination still exists within some law enforcement agencies and in the treatment of the public by their representatives.

Police Ethics. As a concept, ethics is closely associated with professionalism. Codes of ethics are vital to guide the behavior of practitioners of the learned professions (e.g., law or medicine) and to punish those who do not adhere to the agreed, enunciated conduct of behavior for those vocations. For peace officers, such codes promote self-regulation and discipline within a law enforcement agency (Boyd, 1993). Often these codes are written and sometimes are summarized within an agency mission statement. To be a professional implies not only competence and expertness, but adherence to higher standards of professional conduct (Bowman, 1991; Gellermann et al., 1990; Lewis, 1991).

In the best sense, professionalism implies having more than technical skills and refers to the moral contributions that professionals make in a complex, democratic society—the ethic of the calling. The ethical person is perceived as someone who has courage and integrity, is willing to resist corruption and unprincipled people by upholding humanity, justice, and civility. Such a peace officer tries to be loyal to his or her own conscience and avoids unprofessional behavior (e.g., use of excessive force, adherence to the blue code of silence during investigations, biased policing or expressions of bias and bigotry, or acceptance of bribery).

This goal area is being included to emphasize our continuing obligation to deliver the highest quality police service in a manner that is seen as fair, impartial, and professional . . . Our objectives in this area for the coming year are:

1. Continued dedication to the principles of policing as articulated in our Mission, Vision, and Principles, and also in the Code of Ethics

2. To continue following the maxim of treating others as you would desire to be treated. . . . In each contact, whether internal or external, treating others in a respectful, professional manner is our first obligation and enduring concern

3. Continue to focus on building trust throughout the organization

4. Supervisors and managers should know the principles articulated in the City Leadership Statement, then act in a manner consistent with that directive Organizational leaders will be evaluated, in part, on their ability to carry out that directive (Memorandum to Members of the Police Department, January 25, 2000, from Chief of Police Bob Harrison, City of Vacaville)

Exhibit 15.5   Professionalism.

To conclude this section, we provide in Exhibit 15.5 an excerpt from a departmental memorandum of the Chief of Police in Vacaville, California, which underscores our message.

At the core of professionalism should be one's sense of ethics (Muraskin & Muraskin, 2001). This may be manifested individually or through a group, such as society in general or a profession in particular, such as those sworn to uphold the law. Ethical practices are cultural expressions of a society, an organization, or a profession. The *Random House Dictionary* defines the term ethics as "a system of moral principles; the rules of conduct recognized in respect to a particular class of human actions within a particular culture as expressed by a group (e.g., medical ethics, police ethics, or Christian ethics), or by an individual (e.g., personal ethics)." The alternative definition is "a formal classification for study as a branch of philosophy dealing with values relating to human conduct, with respect to rightness and wrongness."

Certain ethical standards are cultural universals, generally accepted by humankind; other ethical practices are culturally specific, dependent on the attitudes and traditions of a particular group. Some ethical expectations are overt or open, while others are covert or hidden. For example, in parts of rural India, if an automobile driver were to hit someone, the expectation would be for the driver to not stop but to proceed to the nearest town where the incident would then be reported to the police. This practice does not condone hit-and-run driving, but faces a reality of an inadequate justice system in this developing country so people might be tempted to take action themselves and with immediacy. Thus the driver, whether at fault or not, escapes to police in the next village to admit the accident. In contrast, in American culture the legal and ethical action for those involved in a car accident is to exchange information and/or to call the police and report the matter immediately from the site of the accident. Leaving the scene of a reportable accident before the arrival of police, in most circumstances, is a crime in the United States. The culture universal is that drivers must report accidents in which they are involved; the culture specific is that the procedure for doing this differs in national cultures. Police professionals should be aware of such differences.

Police and Diverse Community Groups. Nowhere is law enforcement's sense of professionalism and ethics challenged more than the manner in which we treat diverse ethnic and racial group members, whether citizens or visitors. Apart from the indigenous Native Americans, immigrants from the 15th through the 19th centuries were mainly from Europe and Africa, were gradually assimilated into the mainstream population. But in the 20th century, the newcomers were primarily from Asia, the Middle East, and the countries of the former Soviet Union; for them, the process of acculturation is still ongoing.

While most immigrants to the United States concentrate on becoming Americans, there are new groups who have come as refugees, fleeing persecution, strife, and distant wars. Their minds and efforts are directed to their native countries and their suffering peoples. These include the Tamils of Sri Lanka, the Eritreans and Ethiopians of eastern Africa, the Congolese and Sierra Leoneans of western Africa, the Kurds of Iraq and Turkey, the Afghans from Afghanistan, the H'mong tribesmen of Laos, the Muslims from the Middle East, and even the followers of the Falun Gong sect from China, along with thousands of others, such as Serbs and Kosovars from Yugoslavia. These people usually arrive poor and live together in less desirable urban centers of the United States, striving to preserve their traditional cultures, especially their languages and music. Often such desperate peoples are at the agricultural or rural stage of human development, largely from peasant stock. Normally, they have little knowledge of English but are hard working and take jobs that more prosperous Americans no longer want. Their common concern is for relatives and friends in their homeland. Thus, they frequently send back a portion of their meager earnings, take out bank loans, buy bonds, or engage in all kinds of voluntary relief work to assist the citizens of their native countries. They seek information about those left behind through newsletters and newspapers in their native language, or even by using the Internet and maintaining Websites.

Those left behind in the old country are very dependent on the generosity of these new immigrants; the economies of some of their Third World countries are entirely sustained on gifts from these exiles. For example, 35 groups support the destitute Sri Lankan Tamils who are totally dependent on their expatriates abroad. One Tamil bank takes in $350 billion a year in this way, about half as much as the Sri Lankan government's war budget.

The downside is that some of these American funds go to support divisions left behind from past misunderstandings, including civil wars. Of the 30 groups designated by the U.S. State Department as terrorists, most are doing their fundraising in this country. In July 2000, 200 police officers in Charlotte, North Carolina, arrested a man suspected of raising money for the Hezbullah extremists in Lebanon and Palestine. Furthermore, some of the old-country rivalries and feuds have been exported to the United States, often on the basis of clan loyalties—to further their narrow cause, conferences, petitions, and protests are organized, even online. All this contributes to furthering ethnic tensions, and sometimes to illegal activities. For instance, the large Afghan community in Flushing, New York, is split between the supporters of the Taliban back home and their opponents. The 70,000 rural-mountain-type Hmongs in Minnesota fought with the Americans in the Vietnam War. They have thriving farmers' markets, but cooperation among themselves is undermined by clan divisions, along with arguments between moderates and radicals over military action in Laos against the still existing Communist government.

While most of these contemporary immigrants are law abiding, hard working, family oriented, and dedicated to education for their children, the realities described have great implications for law enforcement. Such upwardly mobile peoples are vulnerable to victimization by U.S. criminals, as well as by the lawbreakers among their own. The illegal activities of Russian–American Mafia in Bensonhurst, Brooklyn, confirm this unpleasant factor. (Adapted from "There Is Another Country," *Economist,* August 19, 2000, pp. 26–27.)

Exhibit 15.6   New migrant communities

What constitutes the term "minority group" is becoming increasingly debatable. For example, in some states (e.g., California) and cities (e.g., Miami, Florida), the Hispanic or Latino "minority" has become or is becoming the majority, while Caucasians will become the minority group in such areas. One strategy for improving relations is to bring more diverse members into law enforcement, a phenomenon that is taking place slowly in North America (see Muraskin, 2000).

Any new group integrating into the United States will present new law enforcement challenges that require changes in police tactics and behavior in the 21st century. Exhibit 15.6 describes one such emerging issue in the next decade. For law enforcement organizations, human resource development (HRD) starts with recruitment and selection of qualified candidates. Apart from testing and basic qualifications, future peace officers have stable personalities, are willing to be educated further, are career growth oriented, and are representative of the multicultural communities in which they serve. In previous chapters, we have reviewed this challenge.

The ideal recruit should possess the potential to become the police professional described earlier in this chapter and in Chapter 3. Furthermore, the academy curriculum must be relevant and constantly altered to prepare newcomers for the realities of their actual duties on the job in an ever-changing society. Just as a culture changes, so do the laws that officers enforce and the duties they perform. For example, because of the diversity of the New York City population, its police academy, like others in the East and Midwest of the United States, devotes a third of the study time to learning from the social sciences; a large part of this segment deals with cross-cultural issues. Harris designed a similar program for the Philadelphia Police Department entitled "Police Development and Human Behavior," which provided academy students with the key concepts from the behavioral sciences of psychology, anthropology, and sociology. This program is encapsulated in his book *High Performance Leadership* (Harris, 1994).

ORGANIZATIONAL TRENDS IN LAW ENFORCEMENT

In concluding this section, it is useful to present two organizational trends that provide increasingly important changes to effect law enforcement agencies. Change must come from within the department before all personnel can demonstrate effectiveness and sensitivity in the community (Wagner, 1994).

Trend One: Transforming the Organizational Culture

The culture of law enforcement agencies must internalize changes and accept diversity within both the department and the community. In the past this culture typically was dominated by white males, principally of Irish or Italian backgrounds, who were often military veterans. With the influx of a multicultural workforce into the criminal justice fields, system change is necessary if the organizational culture is to reflect the needs and concerns of this new generation from a culturally diverse society (Simons et al., 1993).

One of the nation's leading diversity consultants, Elsie Cross, confirmed the reality of organizations' need to change. Throughout 20 years of working with many large corporate clients, this African American consultant recognized that most corporate cultures have actually been white male cultures, in which the majority controlled the power in the organization by dominating meetings, making all key decisions, establishing exclusive information loops, and choosing their own successors. To compensate for the past discrimination and to increase organizational effectiveness, Elsie Cross Associates recommends the following strategies for managing diversity and valuing differences (White, 1992):

- Introduce culture change to overhaul policies and procedures by means of focus groups and workshops that define basic assumptions, written codes, and rituals; incorporate this feedback into a revised mission statement that becomes a proclamation of the "new organizational culture vision and values."

- Identify the barriers that block individual or group diversity goals; identify the champions capable of building broad, internal coalitions around cultural awareness and group action against discrimination and for planned change.

- Require that the top command make at least a 5-year commitment of resources to redefining the agency culture toward more effective management of diversity.

- Hold managers accountable for implementing the diversity changes through regular evaluation of their efforts.

- Confront the pain of racism and sexism at the personal and group level in the organization.

This management model has proven successful, and Cross credits the National Training Laboratories for Applied Behavioral Sciences for helping her to develop it. The strategy is invaluable to would-be law enforcement leaders in a multiracial and multicultural society.

Trend Two: Organizations Must Move beyond Awareness to Meet Today's Multicultural Challenges

Law enforcement leaders should ask themselves this question: Does our agency provide adequate training for officers in cultural awareness? When a law enforcement agency has provided the basic training in cultural awareness and inaugurated effective equal employment and affirmative action policies, it is time to adopt another strategic plan that moves the law enforcement agency toward cultural competence. George F. Simons, a consultant on diversity, believes we must move beyond mere avoidance of ethnic, racial, and gender discrimination or sexual harassment. Police supervisors and managers should not have to "walk on eggshells" while at work trying not to offend women and minorities. For managing or training in a multicultural environment, this expert counsels that advanced diversity training that teaches people the skills to communicate and collaborate effectively with each other as colleagues, especially through mixed-gender, mixed-ethnic, and mixed-racial groups, should be conducted. Dr. Simons (Simons & Abramms, 1999) offers the following advice:

- Organizational policy that supports productive partnerships and creative sharing with diverse membership of representatives from majority and minority groups should be developed.

Pluralistic leaders:

1. Look for ways to serve as catalysts for changing the work environment and community to welcome and value diverse people
2. Are committed to eliminating all the various "isms" (racism, sexism, etc.) that exist in their immediate work environment or neighborhood and speak to the greater concerns for equality, fairness, and other democratic ideals
3. Help diverse people to be seen fairly and to be valued in the work environment and broader community
4. Accept feedback about how to improve their relationships with those who are different by remaining open to change and growth
5. Acknowledge their own prejudices or stereotypes and see the limitations that these will bring to their work
6. Take time to assess their individual progress toward achieving the qualities and characteristics of a pluralistic leader
7. Mentor others who need to gain sensitivity toward diversity
8. Value differences among people and cultures as one of the great treasures of the human family and global community

Exhibit 15.7 Police pluralistic leaders.
Source: MGH Consulting, © 1993, reprinted with permission of MGH Consulting, 2454 Cameron Drive, Union City, CA 94587.

- Executives and other leaders should participate in special coaching programs that include assessment, mind management, and communications training that enables them to model behavior and values that inspire their associates to work ingeniously with differences.

To further promote police officer professionalism and peacekeeping strategies in a diverse society, officers must be able to look up to leaders who are not ethnocentric and biased in their manner of leading their agency and responding to the communities they serve. For a peace officer to reflect cultural awareness and understanding of all peoples, as well as to apply the principle of fair treatment to every police action and communication, he or she must have role models at all levels of the chain of command, especially at that of police chief. The police chief should explicitly demonstrate pluralistic leadership and ideally be "an ambassador for diversity" with his/her department. Early in this chapter, we discussed peace officers who are cosmopolitan or pluralistic in approach. Attaining this outlook cannot happen consistently without direction from the top. For this reason, we reprint, in Exhibit 15.7 a list of characteristics and attributes of a pluralistic leader developed by MGH Consulting.

SUMMARY

For professionals in any facet of the criminal justice system, change begins with leadership modeling the role, and second with the practitioners' image of their role, which is then projected to the public. In the evolving new work culture, adhering to the image of peace officer is appropriate and requires that those in public service become more culturally sensitive in their outlook and approach. Effectively dealing with cultural issues within the field of law enforcement then becomes a means for exercising leadership that demonstrates that sensitive peacekeepers respect cultural uniqueness.

Professional law enforcement leaders must take the initiative to guide their departments to ones that are culturally competent. Also, leaders must capitalize on the diversity of people within the organization and community, establish synergy, and seek to develop human potential for the betterment of both. The challenges for law enforcement, in particular, are to recognize and appreciate diversity within both the community and the workforce, while using such insights advantageously. Human diversity must become a source of renewal rather than tolerable legislated requirements within our agencies, communities, and society. To accomplish this goal within criminal justice systems, multicultural awareness and skills training must become an integral part of the human resource development of peacekeepers (Moran et al., 1993; Wederspahn, 2000). The type of peacekeeping advocated in this chapter also requires competent supervision and management with police administration (Holden, 1999; Whisenand & Rush, 1998). It is also important that departments, regionally or statewide, work together to prevent and counter criminality in the community at the same time promoting the common good and civility. There must be a interagency collaboration, synergy, in regard to not only fighting crime, but also training, information exchange, and recruitment within a cultural and diversity context.

DISCUSSION QUESTIONS AND ISSUES

1. ***Cultural Impact.*** Consider the long-term influence of the institution of slavery on the African American family in general and their male youth in particular. What is the implication of this negative heritage for today's black citizens as a whole and its influence within the subcultures of police officers and criminals? Identify hopeful trends that repair or redress the damage of slavery and discrimination on this valuable segment of the American population.

2. ***Extended Families and the Law.*** Many Asian, Near Eastern, and Middle Eastern cultures function with an extended rather than a nuclear family. When such immigrants come to North America, they attempt to carry on this larger family tradition (e.g., food preparation of large meals, working hard in a family-owned business, remodeling and enlarging houses or estates, acquiring several automobiles or a fleet, intermarriage with relatives). Consider how such customs may cause the new arrivals to violate local laws and regulations relative to killing animals, child labor, multiple-family dwellings and occupancy, multiple-car parking on public streets, and so forth. Have you observed anything in this regard about Indo-Chinese, Cuban, Haitian, Asian, Indian, Pakistan, or other immigrants? What can a patrol officer do to help these newcomers from breaking laws of which they are unaware?

3. ***Culture and Crime.*** With inadequate border management and increased illegal entry, a criminal element from abroad slips into the United States and preys on the vast majority of law-abiding immigrants from the "old country," particularly through extortion. Earlier in this century, such thugs and "crime families" were mainly from Europe; today they come in increasing numbers from the

former Soviet Union, Latin America, Caribbean Islands, and Asia. Consider how law enforcement nationally can share information and tactics to combat such threats (e.g., from Hong Kong triads, Salvadoran death squads, Russian black marketers, Jamaican Mafia, and Asian gangs). At the same time, how can peace officers gain the confidence of the law-abiding immigrants, many of whom have been culturally conditioned against police in their homelands? What insights can you share on these matters of concern to law enforcement?

4. **Police Culture.** Every group, whether ethnic, racial, vocational, or professional, has characteristics defining its culture. The police organizational culture is no exception. People who do not belong to a particular in-group often develop myths and stereotypes about another group in an attempt to categorize behavior they may not understand. Make a list of myths and stereotypes about police officers that exist among community members. After you have compiled and shared your list with others, discuss the following:

   a. How did these myths or stereotypes arise?

   b. Is there any truth to the myths or stereotypes?

   c. Do they in any way affect communication with citizens or prevent you from doing your job well?

   d. Do any of the stereotypes or myths create special difficulties or challenges with people from diverse backgrounds? If so, how?

   e. What can a modern, professional police force do to counter or lessen the influence of such myths and stereotypes in the community?

REFERENCES

Adams, T. E. (1998). *Police Field Operations.* Upper Saddle River, N.J.: Prentice-Hall.

Anderson, W. D. Swenson, and D. Clay. (1995). *Stress Management for Law Enforcement Officers.* Upper Saddle River, N.J.: Prentice-Hall.

Barkan, S. E. (2001). *Criminology: A Sociological Understanding.* Upper Saddle River, N.J.: Prentice-Hall.

Barlow, D. E., and Barlow, M. H. (2000). *Police in a Multicultural Society—An American Story.* Prospect Heights, Ill.: Waveland Press.

Barlow, H. D. (2000). *Criminal Justice in America.* Upper Saddle River, N.J.: Prentice-Hall.

Bartol, C. R. (1999). *Criminal Behavior: A Psychosocial Approach.* Upper Saddle River, N.J.: Prentice-Hall.

Bartol, C. R., and Bartol, A. M. (1998). *Delinquency and Justice: A Psychosocial Approach.* Upper Saddle River, N.J.: Prentice-Hall.

Bowman, J. S. (Ed.). (1991). *Ethical Frontiers in Public Managment.* San Francisco: Jossey-Bass.

Boyd, T. (1993). "A Model for Development of Police Officers' Understanding and Adherence to Ethical Standards" (Order 16-0313). Sacramento, Calif.: POST Commission.

Calvi, J. V., and Coleman, S. (2000). *American Law and Legal Systems.* Upper Saddle River, N.J.: Prentice-Hall.

Carter, D. L. (1992). *The State of Police Education: Policy Direction fo rthe 21st Centry,* Washington, D.C.: Police Executive Research Forum.

Carter, D. L., and Radalet, L. A. (1999). *The Police and the Community.* Upper Saddle River, N.J.: Prentice-Hall.

Champion, D. J. and G. J. Rush. (1997). *Policing in the Community.* Upper Saddle River, N.J.: Prentice-Hall.

Coffee, A. (1990). *Law Enforcement: A Human Relations Approach.* Upper Saddle River, N.J.: Prentice-Hall.

Crews, G. A., and Montgomery, R. H. (2001). *Chasing Shadows: Confronting Juvenile Violence in America.* Upper Saddle River N.J.: Prentice Hall.

Cromwell, P. J., and Dunham, R. J. (1997). *Crime and Justice in America: Realities and Future Prospects.* Upper Saddle River, N.J.: Prentice-Hall.

Dantzker, M. L. (2000). *Understanding Today's Police.* Upper Saddle River, N.J.: Prenctice-Hall.

Delattre, E. J. (1991a). *Against Brutality and Corruption: Integrity, Wisdom, and Professionalism.* Tallahassee: Florida Department of Law Enforcement/Criminal Justice Executive Institute.

Delattre, E. J. (1991b). *Character and Cops: Ethics in Policing.* Washington, D.C.: American Enterprise Institute for Public Policy Research.

Gabor, T. (1994). "Generalist or Specialist: What Will Be the Status of the Police Professional by the Year 2003?" (Order 17-0349). Sacramento, Calif.: POST Commission.

Gilbert, E. L. (Ed.). (1990). *The World of Mystery Fiction.* Bowling Green, Ohio: Bowling Green State University/Popular Press.

Goldsmith, Andrew. (1990). "Taking Police Culture Seriously." *Policing and Society, 1* (2), 91–114.

Goode, E. (2001). *Deviant Behavior.* Upper Saddle River, N.J.: Prentice-Hall.

Goodman, D. J. (1998). *Enforcing Ethics: A Scenario-Based Workbook for Police and Corrections Recruits and Officers.* Upper Saddle River, N.J.: Prentice-Hall.

Hancock, E. W., and Sharp, P. M. (2000). *Public Police: Crime and Criminal Justice,* Upper Saddle River, N.J.: Prentice Hall.

Harman, P. (1992). *Cultural Diversity Training for the Future: Is California Law Enforcement on Track?* (Order 14-0274). Post Commission, Sacramento, C.A.

Harris, P. R. (1994). *High Performance Leadership: HRD Strategies for the New Work Culture.* Amherst, Mass.: Human Resource Development Press.

Harris, P. R. (1998). *The New Work Culture: HRD Transformational Management Strategies.* Amherst, Mass.: Human Resource Development Press.

Harris, P. R. (2005). *Managing the Knowledge Culture.* Amherst, M.A.: Human Resources Development Press.

Harris, P. R., and Moran, R. T. (2000). *Managing Cultural Differences Instructor's Guide.* Boston: Gulf Publications Series/Butterworth-Heinemann.

Harrison, Bob. (October 5, 2000). Chief of Police, Vacaville, Calif., personal communication.

Hart, L. B. (1999). *Learning from Conflict.* Amherst, Mass.: HRD Press.

Holden, R. N. (1999). *Modern Police Management.* Upper Saddle River, N.J.: Prentice-Hall.

Hunter, R. D., P. D. Mayhall, and T. Barker. (2000). *Police Community Relations adn the Administration of Justice.* Upper Saddle River, N.J.: Prentice-Hall.

Hurst, N. (1993). "Managing Cultural Diversity in Law Enforcement by Year 2003" (Order 16-0318). Sacramento, Calif.: POST Commission.

Johnson, J. (1994). "What Role Will Mid-Size Law Enforcement Agencies Play in Managing an Open Border between the United States and Mexico by the Year 2003?" (Order 17-0343). Sacramento, Calif.: POST Commission.

Justice, T., and Jamieson, D. (1999). *The Complete Guide to Facilitation: Enabling Groups to Succeed.* Amherst, Mass.: Human Resource Development Press.

Justice Research Association. (2000). *Your Criminal Justice Career: A Guidebook.* Upper Saddle River, N.J.: Prentice-Hall.

Langworthy, R. H., and Lawrence, F. T. (1999). *Policing in America: A Balance of Forces.* Upper Saddle River, N.J.: Prentice-Hall.

"Law is back in town and he's not so bad." (1991, June 17). *Los Angeles Times,* p. 17.

Leighton, P., and Reiman, J. (2001). *Criminal Justice Ethics.* Upper Saddle River, N.J.: Prentice-Hall.

Lewis, C. W. (1991). *The Ethics Challenge in Public Service.* San Francisco: Jossey-Bass.

Lynn Learning Labs. (1998). *Mentoring: Passing the Torch.* Amherst, Mass.: Human Resource Development Press.

McGregor, E. B. (1991). *Strategic Management of Human Knowledge, Skills, and Abilities.* San Francisco: Jossey-Bass.

Miller, S. (1996). "Communicating Effectively with Non-English-Speaking Customer Population in Mid-Size California Cities by Year 2005" (Order 22-0455). Sacramento, Calif.: POST Commission.

Moran, R. I. and J. Abbott. (2000). *NAFTA: Best Practices.* Boston: Gulf Publications Series/Butterworth-Heinemann.

Moran, R. T., Harris, P. R., and Stripp, W. G. (1993). *Developing Global Organizations: Strategies for Human Resource Professionals.* Boston: Gulf Publications Series/Butterworth-Heinemann.

Muraskin, R. (2000). *It's a Crime: Women and Justice.* Upper Saddle River, N.J.: Prentice-Hall.

Muraskin, R., and Muraskin, M. (2001). *Morality and the Law.* Upper Saddle River, N.J.: Prentice-Hall.

Office of Justice Programs. (1999). "Enhancing Technology's Use in Addressing Crime." Fiscal Year 1999 Annual Report Available: http://www.ojp.usdoj.gov/99anrpt/chap8.htm

Ortega, D. (1993). "The Impact of an Ethnically Diverse Workforce on the Role of the Field Training Officer by Year 2002" (Order 16-0322). Sacramento, Calif.: POST Commission.

Palmiotto, M. J. (2001). *Police Misconduct: A Reader for the 21st Century.* Upper Saddle River, N.J.: Prentice-Hall.

Peak, K. J. (2000). *Policing America: Methods, Issues, Challenges.* Upper Saddle River, N.J.: Prentice-Hall.

Peak, R. J., and R. W. Glensor. (1999). *Community Policing and Problem Solving: Strategies and Practices.* Upper Saddle River, N.J.: Prentice-Hall.

Pierce, S. (1997). "What Will Be the Impact of Regionalized In-Service Training on the Davis Police Department by the Year 2002?" (Order 24-0500). Sacramento, Calif.: POST Commission.

President's Commission on Law Enforcement and the Administration of Justice. (1967). Washington, D.C.: U.S. Government Printing Press.

Schmalleger, F. (2001). *Criminal Justice Today: An Introductory Text for the 21st Century.* Upper Saddle River, N.J.: Prentice-Hall.

Senn, L. E., and J. R. Children. (1999). *The Secret of a Winning Culture.* Boston: Gulf Publications Series/Butterworth-Heinemann.

Simons, G. F., and Abramms, B. (1999). *The Questions of Diversity: Reproducible Assessment Tools for Organizations and Individuals.* Amherst, Mass.: Human Resource Development Press.

Simons, G. F., Vazquez, C., and Harris, P. R. (1993). *Transcultural Leadership: Empowering the Diverse Workforce.* Boston: Gulf Publications Series/Butterworth-Heinemann.

Sonnenberg, R. (1995). "How Will Law Enforcement Respond to Ethnic Dilemmas within Changing Cultural Diversity?" (Order 19-0396). Sacramento, Calif.: POST Commission.

Sullivan, S. (2000). *Mastering Leadership* [Audiovisual workshop]. Amherst, Mass.: Human Resource Development Press.

Tamayo, R. (1999). "What Will Be the Leadership Training Subject Delivery System for Middle Managers by the Year 2003?" (Order 26-0539). Sacramento, Calif.: POST Commission.

Twilling, G. (1995). "What Will Be the Role of Law Enforcement in Workplace Violence by the Year 2004?" (Order 19-0398). Sacramento, Calif.: POST Commission.

Wagner, L. (1994). "What Will Be the Status of Community-Oriented Policing and Problem Solving in a Mid-Size Agency by Year 2002?" (Order 18-0391). Sacramento, Calif.: POST Commission.

Wallace, H., Roberson, C., and Steckler, C. (2001). *Written and Interpersonal Communication Methods for Law Enforcement.* Upper Saddle River, N.J.: Prentice-Hall.

Wederspahn, G. H. (2000). *Intercultural Services: A Worldwide Buyers Guide and Sourcebook.* Boston: Gulf Publications Series/Butterworth-Heinemann.

Whisenand, P. M. (1998). *Supervising Police: The Fifteen Responsibilities.* Upper Saddle River, N.J.: Prentice-Hall.

Whisenand, P. M., and Ferguson, F. (1996). *The Managing of Police Organizations.* Upper Saddle River, N.J.: Prentice-Hall.

White, J. P. (1992, August 9). "Elsie Cross vs. the Suits: One Black Woman Is Teaching White Corporate America to Do the Right Thing." *Los Angeles Times Magazine,* pp. 14–18, 38–42.

Chapter 16

Emerging Strategies, Roles, and Technology for Peace Officers in Multicultural Law Inforcement

OVERVIEW

This chapter focuses on emerging and changing issues in the strategies and roles confronting the peace officer in multicultural law enforcement today. Peace officers now need to be able to manage and adapt to innovations and advanced technology within their increasing roles in local community policing and in multijurisdictional crime-solving efforts such as homeland security. The role of peace officers has increased in functions to encompass assistance to and communication with multicultural communities in disasters, terrorism, and controlling possible community confrontations resulting from global/regional events (e.g., celebration of Israeli Independence Day). The emerging roles for peace officers are highlighted as they pertain to working with multicultural special populations such as minority and immigrant youths and people with mental health problems. Curtailing litigation against law enforcement agencies is a key challenge for law enforcement leaders and officers, requiring changes in police policies, training, and practices. Training and preparation of future law enforcement personnel will require changes in the curriculum of the police academies, as well as the ongoing and continuing education of law enforcement officers.

COMMENTARY

Perhaps the biggest challenge facing law enforcement officers and leaders of the 21st century will be to develop law enforcement organizations and services that can (1) effectively recognize, relate to, and operate within the multicultural and global shifts in culture, (2) utilize technological advances, and (3) adapt to community/governmental expectations. As highlighted by the First Leadership Conference of the International Association of Chiefs of Police (IACP, 1999):

> Forces in the community, the police agency, local government, and global trends are profoundly altering expectations and requirements for leading police agencies successfully.

Today's law enforcement organizations will need to embrace innovations and technological advances through appropriate training, education, and preparation of its officers. This is particularly important in the training curricula and processes within the police academies. Emphasis is critically needed in the area of working with multicultural communities, and in the overall knowledge bases of diversity, basic psychology, interpersonal relations, and communications.

> Numerous current studies clearly demonstrate that the training of American police is deficient. Many police academies have a training curriculum consisting of approximately 400 hours. . . . Even when an academy is well structured . . . the curriculum concentrates on the law enforcement task, which occupies a relatively small portion of the police officer's time. Although most of the officer's time is devoted to service activities, training in the service function is, for the most part, de-emphasized or ignored at police academies. . . . Dedicated and responsible officers may be placed on the street unprepared for the experience they will face. They do not have a clear understanding of the true attitudes of the public they are policing. They may not have an appreciation of the historical factors that shaped the larger community and its neighborhoods. They may not understand the sources of the fears and prejudices of the people in the community, including themselves. They may not be trained in the techniques necessary to defuse dangerous situations with finesse or to seek alternatives to arrest. Unfortunately, they are too often taught to respond to threats or hostility with force. Lack of training in such subjects as introduction to social theory, basic psychology, human development and behavior, constitutional law, minority history, ethnic studies, interpersonal relations and communications skills allows communication blocks to remain intact. (Hunter, Mayhall, & Barker, 2000, pp. 194–195)

Law enforcement officers and their organizations will need to continually update and increase their sophistication with advanced technology and scientific innovation to work within multicultural communities.

> As criminals become more sophisticated in their use of advanced technology to perpetrate crime, criminal justice professionals must have equally sophisticated tools to prevent, investigate, and prosecute those crimes, to better track and manage offenders, and to protect the public. (Office of Justice Programs , 1999)

THE FUTURE OF PEACEKEEPING STRATEGIES IN MULTICULTURAL COMMUNITIES

Those who would uphold law and order in the 21 century will need to be more proactive and less reactive (Thibault, Lynch, & McBride, 2001). The new generation of peace officers must not only increase their knowledge in such matters but also promote positive law enforcement innovations, as noted in this chapter. In this next section, we focus on a few strategies for agencies to consider in their efforts to keep community peace in a multicultural society.

Within multiracial communities facing the myriad challenges of transition and integration, economic constraints, and rising crime, representatives of the justice system need to act proactively, sensitively, and knowledgeably. If social order is not to be replaced by chaos, law enforcement representatives of all types not only need to be culturally sensitive but also must actively avoid racist, sexist, and homophobic behavior that may trigger violent social protest. Police researcher Neil Lingle (1992), in his futurist study a decade ago on ethnic groups and culture, identified programs that can promote a cooperative and interactive relationship between peace officers and the community that are still applicable today. His recommendations for law enforcement include the following:

- More cultural awareness and sensitivity training of personnel
- More recruitment and promotion of minorities and ethnics with the help of police unions
- More information to officers on external factors affecting their performance (e.g., influence of wealth and economic power, as well as racial or ethnic and political power)
- More study of institutional racism, organizational diversity, and the impact of minority employment and promotion on police policies and practices in the future

The recommendations from the President's First Leadership Conference of the International Association of Chiefs of Police reinforced similar emphases for the future (IACP, 1999):

> The influx of new ethnic groups and sizable increases in the population of present groups require police leaders to possess and operationalize heightened degrees of cultural awareness and an ability to tailor leadership behavior to a richer and more varied set of subcultures. They must also ensure that these ethnicities are properly represented in the workforce. Population shifts are creating pressures on executives in suburban jurisdictions, urbanizing counties, sheriffs, and state police. The comparative tranquility of rural areas can no longer be taken for granted. (pp. 9–10)

Community-Based Policing

The last two decades of the 20th century brought problems to law enforcement that forced strategic changes within agencies. Because of greater population diversity in many communities, reduced budgets, increased illegal immigration, social disorder, and domestic terrorism, criminal justice entities were subject to increased scrutiny and public review. Progressive law enforcement executives embraced a strategy of community-based policing to meet many of these challenges (see Chapters 1 and 14, this volume; IACP, 1999; Peak & Glensor, 1999). The Philadelphia Police Commissioner's Council vigorously voiced the transition to this strategy in 1987, and its application has emerged with ever-increasing importance to multicultural law enforcement:

> A key concept . . . is that the police abandon the image of themselves as a "thin blue line," standing between the "good citizens" of the community on the one hand, and the "bad guys" on the other. Rather, they should favor an image of themselves as partners to the community in a joint effort to produce freedom from fear and victimization. . . . Finally, this concept acknowledges that unless the police work at establishing and maintaining a proper relationship with the community, they themselves can be seen as victimizers and troublemakers, rather than as peacekeepers. (pp. 4–5).

Law enforcement agencies adopting the community policing strategy have not only become partners within a community but advocates for public well-being. As a result, the role of the peace officer, especially at the line level, changes dramatically in those cities and counties using community-based policing. In addition, with increased contact between community members and police, there will be opportunities to educate the public as to the difficult practices and decisions that police have to make continually. The following example illustrates the community's review of racial profiling within local police citation practices for traffic violations:

> The Northeastern researchers cautioned that traffic tickets cannot identify the motives of police officers. But records can show patterns and identify disparities that should be discussed. "The goal here is to have police departments and communities discuss whether the level of disparity is explainable," said Jack McDevitt, director of the Northeastern's institute. . . . The state task force— composed of police officials, minority community leaders, and civil liberties groups—has met for six months without any consensus on what level of disparity should result in a community being monitored by the state. The lead researcher said despite that, communities should begin carefully reviewing patterns in ticketing in their own departments. "Police departments have had two opportunities to review their data now: the *Boston Globe* study, and our study," McDevitt said. "Those with the greatest disparities, I would think it would be in their interest to look at this issue now, instead of waiting for community members to ask why it took so long. You can't eliminate this behavior overnight." ("Profiling Study," 2004, p. A1)

To accomplish effective community policing, methods must be developed to facilitate problem identification and problem-solving dialogue. Mastrofski and Greene (1991) emphasized that "if police are to increase a neighborhood's involvement in determining how it is policed, then three issues must be addressed: (1) to what extent should the community be organized, (2) who should be represented, and (3) what should the community do?" (p. 16)

In July 2000, Harris visited the old New York City neighborhood of Flushing, New York. While awaiting a plane change at nearby LaGuardia Field, he was surprised at how this once Caucasian area had completely changed into a largely Asian community, dominated by Chinese and Korean immigrants. When a nearby fast-food restaurant was invaded by outsiders who wounded seven customers, killing two, the new business leaders entered into a dialogue with their local precinct commanders. One outcome of improved community relations is that some larger enterprises in the vicinity, such as hotels, are utilizing off-duty police to strengthen their security forces.

Critical to the success of any community-based policing program is the resolution of two issues: (1) How willing are citizens to accept some responsibility for community law enforcement? and (2) How willing are police officers to relinquish the social isolation of police cars to become involved with neighborhood citizens in police–community programs? These issues must be a part of a strategic, long-term plan by the chief executive desiring to implement community policing (CP) in his or her community. Chief Darrel W. Stephens of Charlotte-Mecklenburg, North Carolina, maintains that community- or problem-oriented policing is the future of law enforcement and is the next stage in the evolution of this profession.

How is this transition to this community orientation to be made? Typically, it takes an agency 5 to 7 years to go from traditional policing to community policing. As a start, some departments have created citizen police academy programs that provide knowledge of the CP partnership between the community and the law enforcement agency (see Chapters 5 and 7 for several examples). As part of the citizen's program, community members also learn some of the requisite skills and resources to do problem solving. Other communities hold neighborhood forums to accomplish the same objectives. As with change for most people, it takes time to transform the attitudes of typical officers toward such modern policing. Some have the mistaken notion that there are community-oriented police officers—and then there are all those other real cops.

For long-term CP success, departments must recruit people who exhibit compassion, have good communication skills, and are problem-solvers. Job descriptions and evaluations should be rewritten to emphasize and reward such abilities. Furthermore, community policing also requires obtaining personnel, whether sworn or not, who have the local foreign-language skills to reach out to new ethnic communities.

This law enforcement approach is not incident or technology driven. Officers work in the neighborhoods on a decentralized basis, stressing regular contacts with citizens. They report back to their supervisor, who in turn transmits the information to the chief executive and his or her staff so that additional resources can be deployed as necessary. In addition to tactical plans, the agency should have a plan that calls for consulting with key community leaders before merely reacting in the event of a major crisis. Too often, police reaction has been the stimulus event for riots. Obviously, community policing cannot function in a vacuum. It needs the support of not only the public but also other government agencies. Eldrin Bell, an African-American and the chief of police for Atlanta, Georgia (at a conference hosted by the National Organization of Black Law Enforcement Executives), declared, "We cannot get to community-oriented policing until we have community-oriented government." Chief Bell suggested that government be decompartmentalized, cleaned up, and made more community-directed through use of community councils. He contended that in doing so community members and government employees work together to solve problems. Police senior leadership needs to be a driving force in the process, "Community policing is forcing executives to develop a new knowledge base, perfect change management skills, and, most profound for some, to jettison a number of historical fundamental professional beliefs and values. The evolution of Community-Oriented Policing (COP) is far from complete. As it continues to evolve, the leadership role is destined to evolve with it. The role must always be viewed as dynamic" (IACP, 1999).

Community-oriented policing is proactive, and it is based on the neighborhood and the police identifying problems within the community and directing resources to solve them. For example, as the police move more into the world of high technology, we see officers with laptop computers using them to collect information and to analyze what is occurring in their neighborhood (e.g., recording and analyzing hate/bias crimes). Community-based policing involves additional expenses in cities or counties with already tight budgets. Public administrators and legislators must support ongoing CP efforts, lest they experience the dilemma of "pay me now" (providing budget for such strategies) or "pay me later" (the aftermath of lawsuits, riots, disturbances, distrust, and so forth).

A key, continuing learning process and role function in community-based policing is the ongoing monitoring of important local and global events that might affect multicultural law enforcement. Public events such as the anniversary of September 11, Earth Day, Double Ten Independence Day, Israeli Independence Day, Pakistan and Indian political demonstrations, and Israeli or Palestinian political rallies all have the potential for multicultural community conflicts and confrontation (although the majority of these events have been peaceful). Police presence is required at such events, but as with other situations, excessive police presence can escalate hostilities and decrease community partnership efforts. Law enforcement officials need to be well informed about current events around the globe, as conflicts outside the United States often have a ripple effect across the world and may have an impact on local events. The monitoring of world events and community trends will help police officers take a preventive posture that can ultimately help to avoid confrontation between various multicultural groups in this country (also see Chapter 13).

Crime Prevention among Minority and Immigrant Youth

If it is to succeed, community-oriented policing must focus on positive relations, contact, and communications between young people and peace officers. This approach not only counters but actually prevents juvenile delinquency (Bartol & Bartol, 1999; Goode, 2001). A related challenge today is how to train officers to be successful role models for the benefit of young people, especially those from immigrant or "ghetto" groups (for example in Chapter 1, the Bosnia Youth and IRCO programs). One aspect of this effort should be to make the case for equal justice in law and order from the perspective as perceived by minority and immigrant young people, so as eventually to attract some of these youth into law enforcement careers (Shiner, 1996).

However, before such a goal can be realized, police officers have to change how they perceive deprived or disturbed youth and how they deal with them as human beings. David Cole, a professor of law at Georgetown University, in his book about examining how the criminal justice system handles troubled youth from the underclass, provided an example of an African American youth's reactions to his encounters with law enforcement:

> Equal justice? How would you feel if the police regularly stopped you, for no apparent reason, demanding to know who you are and where you are going? Further, suppose they often search your car or belongings without sufficient cause because they consider your ethnic group more prone to criminality. How would you feel as the target of such frequent questioning and suspicion, especially if you can ill afford a lawyer to protect your rights? To make matters worse when charges are leveled against you, you may spend months languishing in jail, until an often incompetent, public attorney is assigned to you; then he or she usually advises you to plead guilty. Should you get a jury trial, it will not be composed of your peers or those from your ethnic group. In reality, if I am a young man from my ethnic group, the statistics prove that in the U.S., our rate of imprisonment is seven times that of the general population, for my kind are automatically thought by police as inclined to violence and crime. People of color like me are arrested, convicted and killed more often than other citizens. In fact, among young persons within my group from the age of 20–29 years, one in three is in prison, on parole or probation. And who am I?—a black youth supposedly living in a democracy lauded as the home of the free and the brave. . . . Even when members of my group have an education and a job, we may be stopped by officers for "walking or driving while black." If white citizens were treated like we are by law enforcement, there would be a public outcry! For the vast majority of our people who have been stopped by police are subsequently proven innocent. There are no equal rights for my kind when it comes to search and seizure! (2000, p. 31)

Cole (2000) provides some sobering thoughts for planned change with respect to the way the criminal justice system treats youth from diverse racial and ethnic groups. But how about young people in general, what is the situation and what is working? Consider two cases:

Schools. Some law enforcement agencies contract with school districts to provide officers on a daily basis for security purposes, as well as to offer role models. Many officers get involved in educating youth on a voluntary basis in a variety of ways. Sworn officers are rightly proud of sponsoring projects such as the Police Athletic League (PAL), which involves neighborhood kids in constructive teamwork, or the Police Explorer Scout programs. Future studies by police executives propose a variety of youth strategies for this purpose, ranging from a police high school curriculum to police cadet programs (Office of Justice Programs, 1999). So far police in schools and increased security in these facilities have not deterred violence in random actions by alienated students against classmates, as occurred at Columbine High School in Littleton, Colorado, in 1999. It would seem that more preventative programs to identify violence-prone youth have to be developed by both police and educators through cooperative efforts (see Meadows, 2001; Small, 1996).

Gangs. Perhaps the biggest challenge would appear to be in preventing or counteracting rising youth violence, especially among males between the ages of 12 and 24 in the nation's inner cities, where unemployed, disadvantaged youths seek identity and support through destructive gang participation (Britz, Rush, & Barker, 2001). As such, gangs declare truces and work together among the different ethnic, racial, and cultural communities, or link up with gangs in other cities for criminal activity. They can become a real threat to community stability if members' energies are not redirected.

Effective management of gang activities include improved educational opportunities, job training, and gang prevention programs. Organizational system planning and interventions are also needed (Britz, et al., 2001):

1. Develop a countywide master plan for helping youth at risk of joining gangs, especially among minorities and immigrants.

2. Overhaul the juvenile justice system, which often serves as a recruitment and training program for the gangs.

3. Focus on the 10 to 15 percent of gang members who are hard-core criminals.

4. Develop cooperative, private-industry programs to provide training and jobs for inner-city youth.

Law enforcement studies, such as those cited earlier, point out a number of antigang and youth-oriented strategies:

- Cooperation with the local clergy who maintain effective relations with gang members. For example, a coalition of Protestant and Catholic churches have formed the Southern California Organizing Committee, which promotes a "Hope in Youth" campaign. This is a 5 year, public–private investment in a $20 million fund. With it, teams were formed in their church congregations to work with youth. One team member would be an outreach worker with a caseload of

25 youths at risk, leading them away from gang involvement to alternative education or training and drug rehabilitation; a second team member would work with individual parents of gang members, while a third would develop parent unions to empower them with respect to their children's education. Each church then would sponsor and mentor gang members in transition to a more mature way of life.

- Assistance to local ethnic business organizations that wish to work with gangs in community ventures and job development. One such association was formed between the Korean-American Grocers Association and two Los Angeles African American gangs, the Bloods and the Crips. Gangs will increasingly occupy law enforcement time, and agencies must be creative in devising nonarrest approaches to a community's disadvantaged youth, particularly in conjunction with other community organizations.

- Creation of ethnic police benevolent associations to provide role models and programs for disadvantaged youth of similar cultural heritage who are in gangs or who are potential recruits. Hence, the African American police groups are involved with young, male African Americans, while the Hispanic police officers' groups focus on young Latino males, and the Asian American officer's groups direct services toward young males from Chinese, Vietnamese, Korean, and Japanese backgrounds. The same strategy can be extended to ethnic police organizations for Italian Americans, Irish Americans, Polish Americans, and so forth.

  Forward-looking officers encourage and participate in a community task force that "gangs up" on the problem by brainstorming on how to defuse the danger by providing positive places and group experiences for local youth. Social activities, sports, voluntary service, and other constructive mechanisms are emphasized. The goal should be to divert present-day gangs into team programs engaging in community rebuilding, while offering a gang alternative to youth who have not yet joined gangs but seek some group identity. Community conservation or ecology corps provide one example of how young adults can be involved constructively in their communities. The plan for the annual National Youth Service Day (NYSD) is another. NYSD is the largest service event in the world, mobilizing millions of young people to identify and address the needs of their communities through service. NYSD is also an opportunity to recruit the next generation of volunteers and educate the public about the role of youth as community leaders. Junior Achievement has already proved what businesspersons can do to involve youth positively in productive ways. Even bored, middle-class or affluent youth would benefit from such outlets for their energies, in contrast to "hanging out" or "mall hopping." Such endeavors take a combination of public and private investment and personnel, and peace officers could provide needed leadership in this area.

- Counteracting hate groups that reach out to a troubled generation of alienated white youth from urban, suburban, and even rural areas. White supremacists groups often become surrogate families to angry, disaffected young men and women, some of whom are from the underclass, and may have parents in jail as well (1.5 million U.S. parents are in prison). Often their members are products of dysfunctional families and perceived of as outside mainstream activities. Skinheads are enlisted to engage in hate crimes against racial, ethnic, religious, or gay groups that these dysfunctional youth have learned to despise. Many of these young people have themselves already been in prison, where they were recruited by such gangs as the Nazi Low Riders (NLR). Some, too, are frustrated middle-class kids who use the Internet Web hate sites to absorb neo-Nazi propaganda. Others are lower-middle-class youths discontented with society because of socioeconomic conditions. Wanting to protest, they may begin by getting together for something like graffiti tagging but end up engaging in hate crimes against their scapegoats. The problem is global in scope. Europe has its own violent, young skinheads who attack immigrants. To undercut the white supremacists gangs (sometimes fueled by drugs and alcohol abuse) schools and colleges have begun programs to teach tolerance. What is needed is for both active and retired members of law enforcement to reach out in positive endeavors to help redirect the energies of these hate-filled youth into constructive enterprises.

- Apprenticeships or internships for youth in law enforcement have long involved interested young people on a part-time basis or during summer vacations (Taylor, 1999). Some have been at the high school level, organized through traditional police youth groups. However, with the increase of criminal justice studies in colleges and universities, innovative projects attempt to give these students some on-the-job, real-world experience in police, corrections, and justice activities. As a case in point, the criminal justice internships at New York's St. John's University are highly organized under a supervisor, Professor John McCabe, formerly chief of patrol in the New York Police Department. Those who have completed a majority of their criminal justice studies courses and meet the criteria can become interns. Student interns get hands-on experience and gain valuable insights into segments of the justice system, from juvenile justice and the district attorney's office to the U.S. marshals or drug enforcement agencies. The program to jump-start criminal justice careers provides three academic credits if successfully completed and has proved invaluable to the participants. St. John's University students (juniors or seniors) who qualify are required to complete 120 hours, or 8 hours a week, at the internship sponsor site. The program runs for 15 weeks, or one semester. The youth also must attend orientation sessions, as well as keep a daily log of their intern activities, verified and signed by their site supervisor. At the end of the process, participants prepare a term paper on their field experience and receive a letter grade. Some interns who work for a police department or federal agency are offered full-time positions upon graduation. Obviously, these internships not only facilitate the transition to a criminal justice job but also help the person to determine whether this is his or her preferred career field. The benefits to the law enforcement entities that employ such interns are numerous.

Crime Prevention among People with Mental Illness

In June 1999, the White House convened the first-ever Conference on Mental Health to address ways of reducing the stigma of mental illness and discrimination against people with mental disorders. The Attorney General chaired a session on mental health and the criminal justice system to address the recurring cycle of people with mental disorders being incarcerated for crimes (often having only committed minor offenses) and receiving only minimal or no treatment for their underlying mental health problems. The session focused on legislative proposals to address these issues, including a mental health court proposal and other proposed legislation to improve services to the mentally ill within correctional settings.

Following up on the White House conference, the Office of Justice Programs and the Department of Health and Human Services (DHHS) Center for Mental Health Services hosted a July 1999 conference on the treatment of people with mental disorders within the justice system. Issues included the challenges of integrating criminal justice and mental health systems, diverting mentally ill offenders to appropriate treatment through mental health court programs, improving mental health services in the juvenile justice system, and creating community partnerships to respond to the needs of people with mental disorders.

The Bureau of Justice study, released at the time of the July conference, estimated that 283,800 mentally ill offenders were held in the nation's state and federal prisons and local jails at mid-year 1998, and an additional 547,800 mentally ill people were on probation in the community. Other findings included:

- Offenders identified as mentally ill were more likely than other offenders incarcerated or on probation to have committed a violent offense. Nearly 1 in 5 violent offenders in prison or jail or on probation were identified as mentally ill.

- When compared with other inmates and probationers, the mentally ill inmates and probationers reported higher rates of prior physical and sexual abuse and higher rates of alcohol and drug abuse by a parent or guardian while they were growing up.

- Since admission, 61 percent of the mentally ill state and federal prison inmates and 41 percent of the local jail inmates said they had received treatment for a mental condition in the form of counseling, medication, or other mental health services. Fifty-six percent of mentally ill probationers had received treatment since beginning their sentences.

- More than three-quarters of the mentally ill inmates had been sentenced to prison, jail, or probation at least once prior to their current sentence. Half reported three or more prior sentences. The mentally ill inmates were more likely than other prisoners to have a prior sentence for a violent offense.

- While incarcerated, the mentally ill were more likely than other inmates to be involved in fights and to be charged with breaking prison and jail rules (Office of Justice Programs, 1999).

Law enforcement strategies to deal with the problems of people with mental health issues within the criminal justice system include:

- Cooperation with the cultural leadership, local clergy, and other community-based agencies (e.g., homeless shelters, food banks, social services) to provide a network of support for people with mental health problems.

- Assistance to local ethnic business organizations that wish to work voluntarily with mental health issues within the community.

- Creation of specific police training and educational materials for working with people with mental health problems.

- Development of procedures and policies within the law enforcement agency for dealing with mental health problems.

Professional officers encourage the development of and participation in community task forces and committees on mental health issues. Brainstorming on how to defuse the stigma of mental illness and promote the well-being of people with mental health problems through positive support, services, and community connectedness is critical in task force effectiveness.

Curtailing Litigation against Police Agencies and Officers

Much innovation is necessary so that police responses will satisfy citizens rather than provoke them to lawsuits against officers and their departments, especially in multicultural communities. Nonviolent peacekeeping is particularly critical in ethnic, immigrant, and racially diverse communities, where misperception and miscommunication may occur because of language barriers, along with differences in body language and nonverbal interactions. Moreover, "mounting local, state, and federal legislation complicates analytical and planning decisions processes and multiplies the workload required to ensure that policies, protocols, training, and workforce behaviors are consistent with new legislative initiatives" (IACP, 1999). The principal problem in this regard relates to the use of force by law enforcement at the time of arrest; that is, whether it is perceived as excessive or deadly. Agencies that analyze citizen complaints against officers usually find that this area receives the most negative community feedback, especially from persons who feel disenfranchised.

America is a very litigious society. Throughout the United States, the last two decades of the 20th century witnessed a dramatic increase in individual and class-action suits against law enforcement agencies for mistreatment and killing of citizens by police officers. The scope of this national problem can be appreciated by citing statistics from one other city, Detroit. Between 1997 and 2000, that municipality had to pay $32 million because of lawsuits brought against the police. A city council analysis showed that 78 percent of the money so expended involved cases with only a small number of officers; 261 officers were named in more than one suit. The issue is what the city administration should do with such repeat offenders. Furthermore, are the officers guilty of unprofessional behavior and maltreatment or simply the victims of legal strategies by lawyers?

The City of Los Angeles had to pay $14,658,075 in 1991, as a result of settlements, judgments, and awards related to excessive force litigation against its police. Then, in 1994, a jury awarded Rodney King $3.8 million to compensate for police actions. A federal judge ruled on August 28, 2000, that the Los Angeles Police Department (LAPD) can be sued as a racketeering enterprise in the so-called Rampart corruption scandal. This unprecedented decision, subject to judicial review by higher courts, could open this municipality to scores of lawsuits capable of bankrupting the city. U.S. District Judge William Rea ruled from the bench on a civil suit brought against the LAPD by a man who claims he was beaten and framed in 1997 for a crime by rogue police officers in the LAPD's Ramparts Division. Such illegal actions by officers within the Ramparts Division caused 100 cases to be dismissed, resulting in five officers being charged with both conspiracy and even attempted murder. This latest ruling cleared the plaintiff to pursue the case under the federal racketeering statutes against conspiracies. His lawyers maintain the innocent man was a victim of a police conspiracy to deny him of his lawful rights as a citizen.

Many lawsuits against police agencies and their members are frivolous or unsubstantiated and are thus thrown out of court or are decided in favor of law enforcement. However, too many lawsuits result from inadequately screened or trained officers whose behavior on the job is not just unprofessional and unethical but outright biased and criminal. With greater public access to improved communications technology and increased information, citizens are fighting back when police abuse their human or civil rights. When they win these legal suits, taxpayers ultimately have to pay for the insufficiencies or mistakes of their public servants in the criminal justice system.

Some analysts believe the problem is exacerbated because personnel in too many agencies operate more like soldiers than like peace officers (e.g., growth of Special Weapons and Tactics [SWAT] teams in departments). For 150 years, police departments have been organized based on the military model. As noted in the Police Leadership in the 21st Century Conference, "The transition to participatory management seems irreversible. It is, less and less, a choice that the chief executive can control. In the empowerment environment of contemporary organizations, chiefs are less able to function entirely through hierarchical structures, especially to effect change" (IACP, 1999). In the 21st century the move to organizations in which power is increasingly shared and accountability required at all levels of the law enforcement agency will continue to be emphasized because of increasing public dissatisfaction with law enforcement agencies, highlighted by legal settlements against officers. Public dissatisfaction, in turn, is reflected in jury decisions, as exemplified by the following excessive force case:

> Ventura County must pay more than $2 million in damages to a Fillmore man shot in the back by a rookie sheriff's deputy two years ago as the man tried to disarm his intoxicated son at a wedding reception, a jury ruled Monday. The verdict came after a day of deliberations in U.S. District Court in Los Angeles, where retired Fillmore police officer Anthony Morales, 54, sued the county for violating his civil rights and demanded compensation for injuries sustained in the May 2000 shooting. In July, jurors held Deputy Tonya Herbst, 31, liable for battery, negligence and civil rights violations after concluding that she used excessive force when she shot Morales as he wrestled a gun away from his son, Chad. The panel awarded $2,073,000 in compensatory damages following a separate damages phase that began last week. . . . "They were not pleased with this officer," Williamson said. "They did not find her credible. They specifically told us afterward that they did not believe her story." During the trial, Oxnard defense attorney Alan Wisotsky told jurors that Herbst believed her life and the safety of others were in danger when she saw the younger Morales raising the gun. He argued that Morales had not disarmed his son and had moved into the path of the bullet during a struggle for control of the weapon. He also noted that Herbst's actions were deemed justified by the Ventura County district attorney. But Williamson told jurors that Herbst ignored instructions from a training officer and recklessly fired her weapon after Morales had defused the situation. Attorneys sought about $3 million in compensation. (Wilson, 2003, p. B1)

On the other hand, what of the officer's rights when accused of misconduct during a legal action? Brian Harris, a homicide detective of the Houston Police Department, noting that in our judicial system the accused is presumed to be innocent until proven guilty, argued that under such circumstances, the public should afford sworn officers the same rights as the supposed victim. Until the evidence is presented and an inquiry commission or court has rendered a verdict, the public and media should not presume guilt. Furthermore, there is the issue of intent. When an officer's life or well-being is threatened, he or she may not intend to hurt a perpetrator while defending him- or herself. Again, this is where training comes in, so that discipline and control are maintained in very difficult situations that police increasingly find themselves in while patrolling and seeking to ensure law and order in the community. Detective Harris concludes that training in basic police practice and its implementation by supervisors are the keys to effective performance on patrol: "When police create time and distance between themselves and the suspect, then they can conduct a safer encounter."

Emerging Technology and Multicultural Law Enforcement Innovations

Attempts are being made by the new generation of law enforcement leaders to develop innovative strategies, structures, and services that meet the changing needs of communities (IACP, 1999; Office of Justice Programs, 1999). Many innovative peacekeeping strategies have already been described in this book. And each year, new opportunities unfold, such as using biometric technologies for rapid computerized identification of possible terrorists through their fingerprints at U.S. borders (the Immigration and Customs Enforcement's US-VISIT Program) and the identification of people by their eyes, smell, and other body characteristics ("New Ways," 2000, pp. 85–91), as well as DNA profiles as evidence (Dwyer, Neufeld, & Scheck, 2000).

Advancement in technology may require law enforcement agencies to abandon some of their tried-and-true methods. For example, the delay in information dissemination and communications to multicultural communities in the DC snipers' case affected not only those who became suspects, but also citizens of multicultural communities with fears and apprehensions about being possible victims in the case:

> After panic erupted over the first shootings, FBI trainees were brought in to staff the telephone tip lines at the Montgomery County, Md., police headquarters. The FBI, scorning the technological revolutions of the last half-century, relied on the same tried-and-true methods the bureau used to catch targets like John Dillinger in the 1930s. The *Washington Post* reported: "Authorities said information is taken down by hand on forms that make multiple carbon copies. Copies are sorted and marked 'immediate,' 'priority' or 'routine.' Tips that concern Montgomery County are put in one pile, Fairfax in another, Richmond in a third. FBI employees then drive the paperwork out to police in those locations." The *Post* noted complaints by numerous lawmen that "the FBI's problems handling thousands of phone tips are slowing and hampering the probe." When the FBI trainees were not laboriously scrawling down the latest tip, they were busy hanging up on the snipers. In a note attached to a tree after the ninth shooting, the snipers complained that tip line operators had hung up on them five times. The note denounced police "incompitence" [sic] and declared: "We have tried

to contact you to start negotiation. These people took [our] calls for a hoax or a joke, so your failure to respond has cost you five lives." Shortly after the arrest of the two suspects, D.C. Police Chief Charles Ramsey publicly confessed: "We were looking for a white van with white people, and we ended up with a blue car with black people." (Bovard, 2003, p. A21)

Some agencies have established an innovation task force made up of the most creative officers from all units of a department. In this approach, the chief asks the group to discover ways for police to encourage a "climate of understanding within the community, and combat a climate of fear." To that end, the innovation team, along with community focus groups (described next), might study together new ideas of promise and develop action plans to implement them. Following are some examples of such innovations:

- Ongoing contact (in the form of both structured and unstructured meetings) with members of all minority and immigrant community organizations (including church leaders, business and civic leaders, school officials, and so forth). The ongoing nature of the program must be emphasized because, typically, law enforcement only meets with community leaders after a crisis.

- Bicycle or scooter bike patrols in problem and recreational areas; officers then interact with community members, especially where there are large concentrations of minority and immigrant youth.

- Crises management strategies not only for emergencies and disasters, but also for homeland security and working with neighborhoods at risk (see Chapters 10 and 11).

- Neighborhood or shopping mall storefront police substations.

- Police concentration on repeat offenders and repeat locations for criminal activities.

- Law enforcement strategies with the homeless and those with mental health problems.

- Teams consisting of officers from diverse backgrounds regularly meeting with inner-city youth, engaging them in such activities as sports, mentoring, and finding new ways to become role models.

- Preventative programs with schools to reduce school violence. For example, a Federal Bureau of Investigation (FBI) report issued in 2000, "The School Shooter: A Threat Assessment Perspective," lists personal traits in teenagers that may lead to violence. Police and educators need to use this profile to help identify high-risk youth who manifest poor coping skills, access to weapons, drug and alcohol abuse, alienation and narcissism, inappropriate humor, and no parental or guardian monitoring of television or Internet use. In addition to these characteristics, be alert to dysfunctional family situations, as well as poor interactions in school on the part of the troubled youngsters.

- Development of neighborhood child protection plans to reduce incidents of child abuse. Such plans should include constructive opportunities for youth to network with each other and with positive adult role models in their community. Such plans should also include business, civic, and religious organizations and the adoption of a particular high-risk neighborhood in which the police, community leaders, and family members make a commitment to protecting their youth. Such efforts would include collaboration in proactive research efforts, as noted in the following example:

> Research into child abuse and neglect needs to address parents' day-to-day concerns and try to solve them, J. Robert Flores, a U.S. Department of Justice administrator, said yesterday . . . most research into social problems comes too little, too late to be used to formulate policy, as he must do, he said. The result is that many policy makers, police officers and judges believe that "research just tells you about the problem after it happens," he said. "It doesn't contribute to solving the problem in the future." Flores spoke at the eighth annual International Family Violence Conference. Flores said a lot of current research proves its critics right. Even the most recent studies cover statistics from at least three to four years ago, despite the fact that the situation already may have changed. Meanwhile, his office must make policy on a "minute-to-minute basis," he said. "At the end of the day, if there's a vacuum of information, policy still needs to be set," Flores said. As an example, Flores highlighted the summer of 2002, when a number of widely reported child abductions occurred. People wanted to know if there was a trend towards this kind of crime, and how to protect their children if there was, he said. But research had not yet explored those topics, he said, leaving parents struggling for answers. (Yates, 2003, p. A3)

- A program, in conjunction with other public service agencies, to protect the elderly from victimization by both economic and violent crimes (Bentz, 1996; Froom, 1996; Phelps, 1992).

- Innovative strategies by police to counteract hate crimes within their communities (see Chapters 12 and 13).

Police supervisors in their departments should be actively encouraging the innovations described in this chapter, as well as police innovators who contribute to cultural synergy and peacekeeping. For example, agencies might have an award for the Innovative Officer of the Month and display the person's picture in the squad room with a description of his or her innovative practice on or off duty. Central to the use of innovation in multicultural law enforcement is the ability of officers and leaders to manage the forces of change (IACP, 1999):

> The nature and implications of the forces that are changing police leadership are only partially understood. Further dialogue and eventual consensus must top the leadership research agenda. Unfortunately, practitioners do not have the luxury of awaiting the results of scholarly study. Every day they must manage the impacts of and seize the opportunities presented by changing forces. (p. 11)

SUMMARY

Law enforcement officers and leaders of the 21st century will have to develop criminal justice organizations and services that can effectively recognize, relate to, and operate within the multicultural and global shifts in culture, technological advances, and community/governmental expectations. This chapter has highlighted the emerging issues confronting the peace officer in adapting innovations and advanced technology to changing strategies and roles in multicultural law enforcement. Law enforcement officers in the 21st century will need to be more proactive and less reactive. The new generation of peace officers must not only increase their knowledge bases, but also promote positive law enforcement innovations, as noted within this chapter, to include: (1) Increasing awareness and skills within multicultural communities and special populations like minority and immigrant youths, elderly, and people with mental health problems; (2) Embracing and using Community-Oriented Policing practices; (3) Curtailing litigation against law enforcement agencies; and (4) Utilizing the innovations and advanced technology available to law enforcement agencies. The functional role of peace officers has increased to involve assistance to and communication with multicultural communities in disasters and terrorist events, as well as controlling possible community confrontations resulting from global or regional events. Training and preparation of future law enforcement personnel for services to multicultural communities will require changes in the curriculum of the police academies, as well as the ongoing and continuing education of law enforcement officers.

In this final unit and chapter, as throughout *Multicultural Law Enforcement,* the authors have shared information and insights about improving public service in diverse communities. Our intention has been to help readers become more proactive with regard to the changing population, while anticipating future developments in both the law enforcement agency and society. The basic premise is that the personal and professional development of modern peace officers requires cultural awareness training that reinforces creative agency policies and practices on this diversity or multicultural issue. Part One of this book was devoted to the impact of increasing cultural diversity on the community, peacekeeping, and the law enforcement agency. Part Two centered on cross-cultural training and communication for peace officers. Part Three reviewed cultural specifics relevant to officers when they interact with people from Native American, African American, Asian/Pacific Islander, Hispanic/Latino, or Middle Eastern backgrounds. Part Four examined the matter of culturally and racially motivated hate crimes and response strategies (as well as the issues involved with profiling and racial profiling).

Finally, in Part Five, we have offered an overview of how peace officers can improve their effectiveness in a multicultural workforce and community by practicing greater cultural sensitivity. Numerous concepts, methods, and anecdotes were provided to promote innovative, futuristic professional development of sworn officers and their associates. With the human family in profound transition during the 21st century, futurists expect further social disturbances. Thus, our analysis focused on planned changes in the image, operations, services, and skills of law enforcement practitioners within rapidly changing workforces and societies.

Readers are challenged to examine the concepts and techniques presented in these pages, as well as to implement those that are feasible within local agencies and communities. If the strategies proposed here are adopted, the law enforcement field will indeed provide more professional, diverse leadership within the public sector, while presenting positive models in that regard to the private sector. For the professionally minded who will go beyond the content of this book, several appendixes and the Instructor's Manual complement the main content of this text.

DISCUSSION QUESTIONS AND ISSUES

1. *Increase Awareness and Skills with Multicultural Communities Involving Special Populations:* The chapter emphasized the importance of training and education for skills in working with multicultural communities involving special populations (e.g., minority and immigrant youth, elderly, people with mental health problems). What are the groups or individuals in your multicultural community that might be considered as special populations? What are some of the specific skills and resources for law enforcement needed to address these special populations in your community?

2. *Emerging Technology and Multicultural Law Enforcement Innovations:* Law enforcement officers and agencies need to embrace and to utilize the innovations and emerging advanced technologies that are available for effective work in multicultural communities. Using the list of innovations as a starting point, brainstorm other innovations and advanced technology that you think would be important to multicultural law enforcement. In what ways will the items in your brainstormed list have a positive impact on multicultural communities? Would there be any negative impact on those communities?

3. *Curtailing Litigation against Police Agencies and Officers:* The authors noted that much innovation is necessary so that a police response will satisfy citizens rather than provoke them to lawsuits against officers and their departments, especially in multicultural communities. Select one or more multicultural groups that are part of your community (or a part of a nearby community) and discuss how nonviolent peacekeeping is particularly critical in ethnic, immigrant, and racially diverse communities. What does it mean to say that police officers should do their duties with honor and integrity?

WEBSITE RESOURCES

Visit these websites for additional information about strategies and roles related to emerging innovation and technology issues in multicultural law enforcement.

The Center for the Study of Technology and Society   http://www.tecsoc.org

This website provides information on the application of technology for law enforcement organizations, including the implication that the use of such technology has on multicultural communities and the diverse society as a whole.

International Association of Chiefs of Police (IACP)   http://www.iacp.org

This website provides information and reports by the IACP highlighting emerging law enforcement issues and technology that might have an impact on multicultural communities.

Police Executive Research Forum (PERF)   http://www.cpdny.org/Chief/police.html

This website provides information for improving policing and advancing professionalism through research and involvement in public policy debate.

Social Technology Future Consortium: www.socialtechnologies.com
This website provides information for keeping up with and anticipating new developments in science and technology as these affect organizational strategies.

REFERENCES

Bartol, C. R., and Bartol, A. M. (1999). *Delinquency and Justice: A Psychosocial Approach.* Upper Saddle River, N.J.: Prentice-Hall.

Bell, E. (1992, September 28). Keynote speech at the conference sponsored by the National Organization of Black Law Enforcement Executives (NOBLE), the Police Executive Research Forum (PERF), and the Reno Police Department, Reno, Nev.

Bentz, D. (1996). "How Will a Medium Sized Police Agency Provide for the Needs of the Elderly Population by Year 2007?" Sacramento, Calif.: POST Commission.

Bovard, J. (2003, October 3). "Concrete lesson of the snipers." *Washington Times,* p. A21.

Britz, G. S., Rush, J., and Barker, T. (2001). *Gangs: An International Approach.* Upper Saddle River, N.J.: Prentice-Hall.

Cole, D. (2000). *No Equal Justice: Race and Class in the American Criminal Justice System.* New York: Free Press.

Dedman, B. (2004, January 21). "Profiling Study Cities Dozens of Locales." *Boston Globe,* p. A1.

Dwyer, J., Neufeld, P., and Scheck, B. (2000). *Actual Innocence.* New York: Doubleday.

Froom, R. (1996). "Preparing to Meet the Challenges of a Growing Elderly Population." Sacramento, Calif.: POST Commission.

Goode, E. (2001). *Deviant Behavior.* Upper Saddle River, N.J.: Prentice-Hall.

Hunter, R. D., Mayhall, P. D., and Barker, T. (2000). *Police Community Relations and the Administration of Justice.* Upper Saddle River, N.J.: Prentice-Hall.

Lingle, N. (1992). "People of Color and Culture: the Future of California Law Enforcement" (Order 13-0247). Sacramento, Calif.: POST Commission.

International Associations of the Cheirs of Police (IACP) (1999). *Police Leadership in the 21st Century: Achieving and Sustaining executive success.* Recommendations from the President's First Leadership Conference (http://www.theiacp.org/document/)

Mastrofski, S. D., and Greene, J. R. (1991). "Community Policing and the Rule of Law," in David Weisburd and Craig Uchida (Eds.), *The Changing Focus of Police Innovation: Problems Of Law, Order, and Community* (pp. 120–128). New York: Springer-Verlag.

Meadows, R. J. (2001). *Understanding Violence and Victimization.* Upper Saddle River, NJ: Prentice-Hall.

"New ways of identifying people." (2000, September 9), *Economist,* pp. 85–91.

Office of Justice Programs. (1999). *Office of Justice Programs Annual Report for Fiscal Year 1999.* Available: http://www.ojp.usdoj.gov/99anrpt.htm

Peak, K. J., and Glensor, R. W. (1999). *Community Policing and problem solving: Strategies and Practices.* Upper Saddle River, N.J.: Prentice-Hall.

Phelps, P. B. (1992). "The Development of an Elderly Victimization Management Strategy for Law Enforcement." Sacramento, Calif.: POST Commission.

"Profiling study cities dozens of locales." (2004, January 21). *Boston Globe,* p. A1.

Shiner, D. (1996). "How Can Small Law Enforcement Agencies Achieve Ethnic Diversity With Their Command by Year 2000." Sacramento, Calif.: POST Commission.

Simpson, D. (2003, October 30). "Laptops to speed crime follow-up, aid trend-spotting." *Atlanta Journal and Constitution,* p. JA1.

Small, K. (1996). "Youth Violence Prevention: A Cost-Effective Strategy for Law Enforcement." Sacramento, Calif.: POST Commission.

Taylor, D. (1999). *Jump starting your career: An internship guide for criminal justice.* Upper Saddle River, NJ: Prentice-Hall.

Thibault, E. A., Lynch, L. M., and McBride, R. B. (2001). *Proactive Police Management.* Upper Saddle River, N.J.: Prentice-Hall.

Wilson, T. (2003, September 16). "Man Shot by Deputy Awarded $2 Million; Jury finds the rookie officer liable for negligence and civil rights violations." *Los Angeles Times,* p. B1.

Yates, R. (2003, July 16). "U.S. official says child abuse research trails need." *Union Leader* (Manchester, NH), p. A3.

Appendix A

Multicultural Community and Workforce:

Attitude Assessment Survey*

The first set of questions ask for your opinions about how certain segments of the community view the police. Using the response sheets (Attitude Assessment Survey Response Sheet) on pages 505–508, put the number of the response that you think best describes each group's perception. Remember, give the response based on how you feel each group would answer the statements.

1. In your opinion, how would this group rate the job this police department does? (See response sheet.)

2. This group generally cooperates with the police.

3. Overall, this group thinks that police department acts to protect the rights of individuals.

4. This group feels that the current relationship between the police and the community is described by which of the following?

5. Overall, this group feels this department responds to citizen complaints about officers in an objective and fair manner.

6. This group thinks most contacts with police are negative.

The next questions ask for your opinions about procedures and practices within the police department.

7. Overall, police supervisors in this department respond to citizens' complaints about employees in an objective and fair manner.

8a. Most police officers in this department are sensitive to cultural and community differences.

8b. Most civilian employees in this department are sensitive to cultural and community differences.

9a. This department adequately prepares officers to work with members of the community who are of a different race or ethnicity than the majority of the population.

*Adapted with permission from the Alameda, California Police Department, March 1993.

503

9b. This department adequately prepares civilian employees to work with members of the community who are of a different race or ethnicity than the majority of the population.

10. The police administration is more concerned about police–community relations than it should be.

11a. Special training should be given to officers who work with community members who are of a different race or ethnicity than the majority population.

11b. Special training should be given to civilian employees who work with community members who are of a different race or ethnicity than the majority population.

12. Special training should be given to assist officers in working with which of the following segments of the community?

13. How often are racial slurs and negative comments about persons of a different race or ethnicity expressed by personnel in this department?

14a. Persons of a different race or ethnicity in this city are subject to unfair treatment by some officers in this department.

14b. Persons of a different race or ethnicity in this city are subject to unfair treatment by some civilian employees in this department.

15a. Prejudicial remarks and discriminatory behavior by officers are not tolerated by line supervisors in this department.

15b. Prejudicial remarks and discriminatory behavior by civilian employees are not tolerated by line supervisors in this department.

16. Transfer policies in this department have a negative effect on police–community affairs.

17. Citizen complaint procedures in this department operate in favor of the citizen, not the employee.

18. Internal discipline procedures for employee misconduct are generally appropriate.

19. The procedure for a citizen to file a complaint against a department employee should be which of the following?

20. With regard to discipline for misconduct, all employees in this department are treated the same in similar situations, regardless of race or ethnicity.

21. What kind of discipline do you think is appropriate for the first incident of the following types of misconduct? (Assume intentional.)

This section examines your views about police–community relations training and community participation. Please circle the response that best describes your opinion.

22. Do you think training in police–community relations was adequate to prepare you to work with all segments of the community?

23. How often do you have opportunities to participate in positive contacts with community groups?

24. Do you think this department has an adequate community relations program?

25. What subject areas related to community relations would be helpful on an in-service training basis?

26. What do you think is the most important thing that citizens need to understand about the police?

27. How can the police department best educate the public about police policies and practices?

28. Listed are steps that police departments can take to improve police services as they relate to community relations.

Attitude Assessment Survey Response Sheet

Place the number that corresponds to your response in each column.

	Business community	Minority resident	Community leaders	Most residents	Juveniles
Question 1:					
(1) Very good					
(2) Good					
(3) Fair					
(4) Poor					
(5) Very Poor					
Question 2:					
(1) Most of the time					
(2) Sometimes					
(3) Rarely					
(4) Never					
Question 3:					
(1) Strongly agree					
(2) Agree					
(3) Disagree					
(4) Strongly disagree					
Question 4:					
(1) Very good					
(2) Good					
(3) Fair					
(4) Poor					
(5) Very poor					
Question 5:					
(1) Strongly agree					
(2) Agree					
(3) Disagree					
(4) Strongly disagree					
Question 6:					
(1) Strongly agree					
(2) Agree					
(3) Disagree					
(4) Strongly disagree					

Place check in column corresponding to your response for each question.

	Strongly agree	*Agree*	*Disagree*	*Strongly disagree*	*Don't know*
Question 7:					
Question 8a:					
Question 8b:					
Question 9a:					
Question 9b:					
Question 10:					
Question 11a:					
Question 11b:					

Check one response for each group.

Question 12:	Strongly agree	Agree	Disagree	Strongly disagree
African American/black (includes Caribbean, Haitian, and so forth)				
Asian				
Hispanic				
Homosexual				

Circle your response.

Question 13:	(1) Often	(2) Sometimes	(3) Rarely	(4) Never

Place check in column corresponding to your response for each question.

	Strongly agree	Agree	Disagree	Strongly disagree	Don't know
Question 14a:					
Question 14b:					
Question 15a:					
Question 15b:					
Question 16:					
Question 17:					
Question 18:					

Circle one response.

Question 19:
(1) Citizen sends complaint in writing to department.

(2) Citizen telephones complaint to department.

(3) Citizen comes to department.

(4) Any of the above are acceptable means.

(5) None of the above are acceptable means.

Please explain.

_____

_____

Question 20: (1) Strongly agree (2) Agree (3) Disagree (4) Strongly disagree

Check one response for each.

Question 21:

Type of misconduct	Verbal warning	Training/ counseling	Oral reprimand	Formal reprimand	Suspension	Termination
Excessive force						
False arrest						
Discrimination						
Use of racial slurs						
Criminal conduct						
Poor service						
Discourtesy to citizen						
Improper procedure						

Please circle the response that best describes your opinion.

Question 22: (1) Yes (2) No (3) Did not receive training
If no, please describe why the training was not satisfactory.
Please explain._____

_____

_____

Question 23: (1) Frequently (2) Sometimes (3) Rarely (4) Never

Question 24: (1) Yes (2) No (3) Don't know
Please explain._____

_____

_____

Question 25: _____

_____

_____

Question 26: What do you think is the most important thing that citizens need to understand about the police?

_____

_____

_____

Question 27:

Circle one only.
(1) Through patrol officer contacts with citizens
(2) Through public meetings
(3) Through the media
(4) Selected combinations of the responses above
(5) Other (explain): _____

_____

_____

(6) Don't know

Please indicate how important you think each of the following should be to this administration by placing the number that best describes your response next to the appropriate question.

Question 28:	1 Somewhat important	2 Important	3 Not at all important
Hire more police			
Focus on more serious crime			
Improve response time			
Increase salaries			
Provide more training			
Raise qualifications for potential applicants			
Be more courteous to public			
Increase foot patrols			
Reduce discrimination			
Provide dedicated time for community involvement			

Appendix B

Cultural Diversity Survey: Needs Assessment*

ANONYMOUS QUESTIONNAIRE

There has been a great deal of discussion in recent years about whether the job of police officer has been changing. Some of the discussion revolves around issues related to contact with people from different cultural, racial, or ethnic groups. Please check or enter one answer for each question.

1. Comparing the job of officer today with that of officer a few years ago, I think that today the job is
   ( ) a lot more difficult
   ( ) somewhat more difficult
   ( ) about the same in difficulty
   ( ) somewhat easier
   ( ) a lot easier

2. When I stop a car with occupant(s) of a different racial or ethnic group than myself, I must admit that I am more concerned about my safety than I would be if I stopped a car with the same number of white occupant(s).
   ( ) strongly agree
   ( ) agree
   ( ) disagree
   ( ) strongly disagree

3. If an officer notices a group of young people gathering in a public place and the young people aren't known to the officer, they should be watched very closely for possible trouble.
   ( ) strongly agree
   ( ) agree
   ( ) disagree
   ( ) strongly disagree

*Adapted with permission: police department wishes to remain anonymous.

4. If an officer notices a group of young people from another racial or ethnic group gathered in a public place, the officer should plan on watching them very closely for possible trouble.

( ) strongly agree

( ) agree

( ) disagree

( ) strongly disagree

5. How often do you think it is justifiable to use derogatory labels such as "scumbag" and "dirtbag" when dealing with possible suspects?

( ) frequently

( ) some of the time

( ) once in a while

( ) never

6. When I interact on duty with civilians who are of a different race, ethnicity, or culture, my view is that

( ) they should be responded to a little more firmly to make sure that they understand the powers of the police

( ) they should be responded to somewhat differently, taking into account their different backgrounds

( ) they should be responded to the same as anyone else

7. When I encounter citizens of a different race, ethnicity, or culture who have committed a violation of the law, my view is that

( ) they should be responded to a little more firmly to make sure they understand the powers of the police

( ) they should be responded to somewhat differently, taking into account their different backgrounds

( ) they should be responded to the same as anyone else

8. When interacting on duty with civilians who have a complaint or a question and who are of a different race, ethnicity, or culture, I try to be very aware of the fact that my usual gestures may frighten or offend them.

( ) strongly agree

( ) agree

( ) disagree

( ) strongly disagree

9. When interacting on duty with offenders who are of a different race, ethnicity, or culture, I try to be very aware of the fact that my usual behavior may frighten or offend them.

( ) strongly agree

( ) agree

( ) disagree

( ) strongly disagree

10. How often have you run into a difficulty in understanding what a civilian was talking about because of language barriers or accents?

    ( ) frequently

    ( ) once in a while

    ( ) hardly ever

    ( ) never

11. How often have you run into difficulty in understanding what an offender was talking about because of language barriers or accents?

    ( ) frequently

    ( ) once in a while

    ( ) hardly ever

    ( ) never

12. How often have you run into some difficulty in making yourself clear while talking to a civilian because of language barriers or accents?

    ( ) frequently

    ( ) once in a while

    ( ) hardly ever

    ( ) never

13. How often have you run into some difficulty in making yourself clear while talking to an offender because of language barriers or accents?

    ( ) frequently

    ( ) once in a while

    ( ) hardly ever

    ( ) never

14. How important is it that the police department provide training to make its members aware of the differences in culture, religion, race, or ethnicity?

    ( ) extremely important

    ( ) very important

    ( ) fairly important

    ( ) not too important

    ( ) not important at all

15. Personally, I believe that the training I have received on group differences is

    ( ) far too much

    ( ) somewhat too much

    ( ) about the right amount

    ( ) too little

    ( ) virtually nothing

16. The training in the area of group differences has been

    (   ) extremely helpful
    (   ) very helpful
    (   ) somewhat helpful
    (   ) not too helpful
    (   ) not helpful at all

17. My own view is that our department's quality of service could be improved by

    (   ) placing greater emphasis on hiring on the basis of the highest score obtained on the entrance exam, making no attempt to diversify by race, ethnicity, or gender
    (   ) placing greater emphasis on diversity by race, ethnicity, or gender and somewhat less emphasis on the numerical rank obtained on the entrance examination
    (   ) giving equal weight to both the score obtained on the entrance examination and diversification by race, ethnicity, or gender

18. What percentage of civilian or internal complaints against employees are adjudicated equitably?

    (   ) over 80 percent
    (   ) between 60 and 80 percent
    (   ) between 40 and 60 percent
    (   ) between 20 and 40 percent
    (   ) less than 20 percent

19. Some civilian or internal complaints are adjudicated more favorably toward people from diverse groups rather than toward the majority population.

    (   ) strongly agree
    (   ) agree
    (   ) disagree
    (   ) strongly disagree

20. I think that employees of a different race or ethnicity receive preferential treatment on the job.

    (   ) strongly agree
    (   ) agree
    (   ) disagree
    (   ) strongly disagree

21. The racial diversity of my coworkers has made it easier for me to see issues and incidents from another perspective.

    (   ) strongly agree
    (   ) agree
    (   ) disagree
    (   ) strongly disagree

22. To think that employees of a different race or ethnicity than myself receive preferential treatment on this job

( ) bothers me because I do not think it is justified

( ) does not bother me because I think it is justified

( ) is fair only because it makes up for past discrimination

( ) I do not believe minorities get preferential treatment

23. In certain situations, having a partner of a different race or ethnicity than myself is more advantageous than having a partner of my same race or ethnicity.

( ) strongly agree

( ) agree

( ) disagree

( ) strongly disagree

24. I have received negative feedback from members of the community regarding the conduct of other officers.

( ) strongly agree

( ) agree

( ) disagree

( ) strongly disagree

25. I have received negative feedback from members of the community regarding the conduct of officers who are of a different race or ethnicity in particular.

( ) strongly agree

( ) agree

( ) disagree

( ) strongly disagree

26. I have received more negative feedback from members of the community regarding the conduct of officers from different races and ethnic backgrounds than about the conduct of white officers.

( ) strongly agree

( ) agree

( ) disagree

( ) strongly disagree

27. In terms of being supervised

( ) I would much rather be supervised by a man

( ) I would somewhat rather be supervised by a man

( ) I would much rather be supervised by a woman

( ) I would somewhat rather be supervised by a woman

( ) It does not make a difference whether a man or a woman supervises me

28. In terms of being supervised by a man
    - ( ) I would much rather be supervised by a nonminority
    - ( ) I would somewhat rather be supervised by a nonminority
    - ( ) I would much rather be supervised by a minority
    - ( ) I would somewhat rather be supervised by a minority
    - ( ) It does not make a difference to which group my supervisor belongs

29. In terms of being supervised by a woman
    - ( ) I would much rather be supervised by a nonminority
    - ( ) I would somewhat rather be supervised by a nonminority
    - ( ) I would much rather be supervised by a minority
    - ( ) I would somewhat rather be supervised by a minority
    - ( ) It does not make a difference to which group my supervisor belongs

If this questionnaire is being used for a training class, please check the one answer in the following questions that best applies to you.

30. What is your sex?
    - ( ) male
    - ( ) female

31. What is your race?
    - ( ) white
    - ( ) African American or black
    - ( ) Hispanic
    - ( ) Native American
    - ( ) Asian American
    - ( ) other

32. How many years have you been employed by the police department?
    - ( ) 0 to 5 years
    - ( ) 6 to 10 years
    - ( ) 11 to 20 years
    - ( ) more than 20 years

33. What is your current rank?
    - ( ) officer
    - ( ) sergeant
    - ( ) lieutenant
    - ( ) captain or commander
    - ( ) deputy chief
    - ( ) chief

34. What is the highest academic degree you hold?

(   ) high school

(   ) associate's degree

(   ) bachelor's degree

(   ) master's degree

Appendix C

Listing of Consultants and Resources

The following is a partial list only of consultants who may be useful to law enforcement agencies (current as of January 2004). Please note that we are not personally familiar with each of the following and are, therefore, unable to endorse their services. The most complete listing of consultants and resources can be found in *Intercultural Services,* Boulder, CO, Butterworth-Heinemann (see next page).

CROSS-CULTURAL DIVERSITY CONSULTANTS AND RESOURCES

Aaron T. Olson, Education, Training and Organization Consultant, P.O. Box 345, Oregon City, OR 97045. Telephone: (971) 409-8135. Coauthor of the *Instructor's Manual for Multicultural Law Enforcement: Strategies for Peacekeeping in a Diverse Society (Third Edition).* Also Oregon State Police Patrol Supervisor, Oregon Public Safety Academy and Regional Instructor and a Criminal Justice Department Instructor at Portland Community College, Portland, Oregon. Provides multicultural training, consulting, and workshops to public safety personnel, education, and community organizations. Website: http://www.atolson.com. E-mail: information@atolson.com

The Backup Training Corporation. 421 E. Coeur d'Alene Avenue, Coeur d'Alene, Idaho. Telephone: (800) 822-9398 or (208) 765-8062. Provides CD-ROM training courses on cultural diversity, community policing, and other topics for law enforcement. Website: http://www.thebackup.com.

ChangeWorks Consulting (CWC). 28 South Main Street, #113, Randolph, MA 02368. Telephone: (781) 986-6150. CWC specializes in workplace and community diversity, organizational change, leadership development, conflict resolution, and social justice education. CWC's goal is to work with clients to create safe, equitable, and productive relationships, workplaces, and communities through the exploration of the impacts of race, ethnicity, gender, class, age, sexual orientation, physical abilities, and other aspects of diversity. Website: http://www.changeworksconsulting.org

Deena Levine & Associates. P.O. Box 582, Alamo, CA 94507. Telephone: (925) 947-5627. Coauthor of *Multicultural Law Enforcement: Strategies for Peacekeeping in a Diverse Society.* Cross-cultural consultant for businesses and organizations. Website: http://www.dlevineassoc.com. E-mail: dlevine@telis.org

Defense Equal Opportunity Management Institute (DEOMI), Patrick Air Force Base, Cocoa Beach, FL 32391. Telephone: (407) 494-6976. DEOMI offers a variety of courses related to equal employment opportunity, civil rights, diversity, and human relations for the U.S. armed services. Training includes law enforcement, regulatory aspects, and legal compliance. Website: http://www.patrick.af.mil/deomi/

Elsie Y. Cross Associates, Inc. 7627 Germantown Avenue, Philadelphia, PA 19118. Telephone: (215) 248-8100. Website: http://www.eyca.com

ExcelForce. A diversity training and consulting group staffed by faculty made up entirely of sworn officers and civilian law enforcement professionals. They provide consultant and training services to organizations engaged in managing a diverse workforce, addressing staff development challenges, strengthening police–community relations, promoting equal opportunity, creating inclusive work teams, recruiting and retaining across gender, racial, and ethnic lines, and implementing reform strategies to better serve and protect our multicultural communities. 5448 N. Kimball Ave., Chicago, IL 60625. Telephone: (773) 463-6374. E-mail: info@excelforce.com. Website: http://www.excelforce.com

George Simons International. 236 Plateau Avenue, Santa Cruz, CA 95060. Telephone: (888) 215-3117. Consulting practice of George Simons, leading diversity author and producer of videos and instruments on this subject. Website: http://www.diversophy.com

The GilDeane Group, Inc. 13751 Lake City Way, NE, Suite 210, Seattle, WA 98125. Telephone: (206) 362-0336. Maintains a computer data bank and referral service for cross-cultural consultants. Also operates a book service and publishes a newsletter on diversity training. Website: http://www.gildeane.com

Herbert Z. Wong & Associates. One Broadway, Suite 600, Cambridge, MA 02142. Telephone: (781) 749-2997. Dr. Herbert Z. Wong is coauthor of *Multicultural Law Enforcement: Strategies for Peacekeeping in a Diverse Society* and *Multicultural Law Enforcement: Concepts and Tools in Practice.* Herbert Z. Wong & Associates' consultants engage in organizational surveys, cultural assessments, and workforce diversity training. The consulting firm specializes in diversity training and the assessment of organizational culture for implementing the strategic advantages of diversity. Federal law enforcement and regulatory agency diversity assessment and training are also provided. Website: http://www.MulticulturalLawEnforcement.com

Managing Cultural Differences (MCD) Authors' Network. 2702 Costebelle Drive, La Jolla, CA 92037. Telephone: (858) 453-2271 or (800) 231-6275. Ten authors and editors who produced the 12 volumes of the MCD Series for Butterworth-Heimann Publishing. All experienced cross-cultural consultants. Website: www.bh.com-management/

Multicultural Law Enforcement Training Resources Center. One Broadway, Suite 600, Cambridge, MA 02142. Telephone: (617) 489-1930. Multicultural law enforcement and diversity training and educational resources are provided by Herbert Z. Wong and Aaron T. Olson, two of the coauthors of the *Instructor's Manual (and CD-ROM) for Multicultural Law Enforcement: Strategies for Peacekeeping in a Diverse Society.* Educational training materials are provided to augment the text for classroom teaching (e.g., videotapes, films, course outlines, exercises, and case studies). Resources also include the Training-of-Trainers Programs for Multicultural Law Enforcement and Diversity Training. E-mail: Info@MulticulturalLawEnforcement.com. Website: http://www.MulticulturalLawEnforcement.com

ODT Inc. P.O. Box 134, Amhurst, MA 01004. Telephone: (800) 736-1293. Principal distributor of diversity and upward management materials; consulting network. Website: http://www.odt.org

Ondra Berry Law Enforcement Cultural Diversity Training. Reno, Nevada, Police Department. Telephone: (775) 334-2197. Reno Police Department, P.O. Box 1900, Reno, NV 09505-1900. Website: http://www.betances.com/consultants.htm

Pelikan Associates. 6501 Bannockburn Drive, Bethesda, MD 20817. Telephone: (301) 229-8550. Helen Pelikan's public and customized training programs on use of the Meyer–Briggs Type Indicator (MBTI). MBTI is a tool for working constructively with individual differences in a multicultural society.

PowerPhone, Inc. P.O. Box 1911, 1321 Boston Post Road, Madison, CT 06443. Telephone: (800) 537-6937. Can provide a 2-day, interactive workshop for law enforcement officers and dispatchers on race relations and cultural awareness. Website: http://www.powerphone.com

San Diego Regional Training Center (RTC). 10455 Sorrento Valley Road, Suite 202, San Diego, CA 92121. Telephone: (858) 550-0040. Susanne Foucault, Executive Director. A joint powers organization developing training, organizational consulting, and other resources. Provides the cultural awareness, train the diversity trainer, and leadership courses for law enforcement agencies in the southern California area. Website: http://www.sdrtc.org

Simulations Training Systems. P. O. Box 910, Del Mar, CA 92014. Telephone: (800) 942-2900 and (858) 755-0272. Produces simulation games in cross-cultural and team management based on the research of Dr. Garry Shirts. Website: http://www.simulationtrainingsystems.com

U.S. Commission on Civil Rights, 624 9th Street N.W., Washington, D.C. 20425. Telephone: (202) 376-8312. The U.S. Commission on Civil Rights: (a) investigates complaints alleging that citizens have been deprived of their right to vote resulting from discrimination, (b) studies and collects information relating to discrimination on the basis of race, color, religion, sex, age, disability, or national origin; (c) reviews federal laws, regulations, and policies with respect to discrimination and equal protection under the law; and (d) submits reports to the President and to Congress on civil rights issues. Website: http://www.usccr.gov

ANTI-BIAS ORGANIZATIONS AND GOVERNMENT AGENCIES

American-Arab Anti-Discrimination Committee (ADC)
4201 Connecticut Avenue, NW, Suite 500
Washington, D.C. 20008
(202) 244-2990
Website: http://www.adc.org

Anti-Defamation League (ADL)
442 Park Avenue South
New York, NY 10016
(212) 684-6950
Website: http://www.adl.com

U.S. Department of Justice
Bureau of Justice Statistics
810 Seventh Street, NW
Washington, D.C. 20531
(800) 732-3277

Center for Democratic Renewal National Office (CDR)
P.O. Box 50469
Atlanta, GA 30302-0469
(404) 221-0025
Website: http://www.cdr@igc.apc.org

Coalition against Anti-Asian Violence
c/o Asian American Legal Defense and Education Fund
99 Hudson Street, 12th Floor
New York, NY 10013
(212) 966-5932

Congress on Racial Equality (CORE)
30 Cooper Square
New York, NY 10003
(212) 598-4000
Website: http://ww.core-online.org

Equal Employment Opportunity Commission (EEOC)
1801 L Street, NW
Washington, D.C. 20507
(202) 663-4400
Website: http://www.eeoc.gov

Gay & Lesbian Alliance against Defamation (GLAAD)
150 West 26th Street, Suite 503
New York, NY 10001
(212) 807-1700
Website: www.glaad.org

Jewish Community Relations Advisory Council (JCRC)
National Office
823 United Nations Plaza
New York, NY 10017
(212) 490-2525

Museum of Tolerance, Los Angeles
(313) 553-8403

National Asian Pacific American Legal Consortium
1140 Connecticut Ave., NW, Suite 1200
Washington, D.C. 20036
(202) 296-2300
Website: http://www.napalc.org

National Association for the Advancement of Colored People (NAACP)
Washington Bureau
1025 Vermont Avenue, NW
Washington, D.C. 20009
(202) 638-2269
Website: http://www.naacp.org

National Conference for Community Justice
Regional Offices—see Website
Website: http://www.nccj.org

National Congress of American Indians (NCAI)
2010 Massachusetts Avenue, NW, 2nd Floor
Washington, D.C. 20036
(202) 466-7767
Website: http://www.ncai.org

National Council of La Raza (NCLR)
1111 19th Street, NW, Suite 1000
Washington, D.C. 20036
(202) 785-1670
Website: http://www.nclr.org

National Gay and Lesbian Task Force
1734 14th Street, NW
Washington, D.C. 20009
(202) 332-6483
Website: http://www.ngltf.org

National Hate Crime Reporting Hot-Line
(800) 347-HATE

National Institute against Prejudice and Violence
712 W. Lombard Street
Baltimore, MD 21201
(410) 706-5170

National Organization for Women (NOW)
1000 16th Street, NW, Suite 700
Washington, D.C. 20036
(202) 331-0066
Website: http://www.now.org

National Organization of Black Law Enforcement Executives (NOBLE)
908 Pennsylvania Avenue, SE
Washington, D.C. 20003
(301) 352-0842

The Prejudice Institute
132 Stephens Hall Annex
Towson State University
Towson, MD 21204
(410) 830-2435

Southeast Asia Resource Action Center (SEARAC)
1628 16th Street, NW, 3rd Floor
Washington, D.C. 20009
(202) 667-4690
Website: http://www.searac.org

Southern Poverty Law Center
400 Washington Avenue
Montgomery, AL 36104
(205) 264-0286
Website: http://www.splcencter.org

U.S. Department of Justice Community Relations Service Headquarters
810 Seventh Street, NW
Washington, D.C. 20531
(202) 305-2935

Appendix D

Self-Assessment of Communication Skills in Law Enforcement:

Communications Inventory

The following is adapted for law enforcement from Dr. Phil Harris's Communications Inventory in High Performance Leadership (1992). As you answer the questions, think about your cross-cultural communication with both citizens and coworkers in your department. (Many of these questions also apply to communication with people of the same background.) Find your areas of strength and your areas of weakness and make it a point to improve those areas. To check whether your perceptions of your communication are correct, have a coworker or partner fill out the questionnaire for you. Part of knowing where to improve involves self-awareness and an honest appraisal of your strengths and weaknesses.

Instructions: Circle the word that best describes your approach to the communication process.

1. In communicating, I project a positive image of myself (e.g., voice, approach, tone).
   Seldom   Occasionally   Often   Always

2. When appropriate, I try to show my "receiver" (the person with whom I am communicating—for example, victims, citizens making complaints, suspects, witnesses, and coworkers) that I understand what is being communicated from his or her point of view. I do this by restating this point of view and by showing empathy and concern.
   Seldom   Occasionally   Often   Always

3. I am sensitive to culturally different usages of eye contact and I establish eye contact where appropriate, but avoid intense eye contact with people for whom less eye contact is more comfortable.
   Seldom   Occasionally   Often   Always

4. I am aware of when my own emotions and state of mind affect my communication with others. (For example, I know my own needs, motives, biases, prejudices, and stereotypes.)
   Seldom   Occasionally   Often   Always

5. I refrain from using insensitive and unprofessional language while on the job (including language used in written and computer communications).
   Seldom   Occasionally   Often   Always

6. I try not to let the person with whom I am communicating push my "hot buttons," which would negatively affect my communication (e.g., cause me to go out of control verbally).
   Seldom   Occasionally   Often   Always

7. When speaking with individuals from groups that speak English differently from the way I do, I try not to imitate their manner of speech in order to be "one of them."
   Seldom   Occasionally   Often   Always

8. With non-native speakers of English, I try not to speak in an excessively loud voice or use incorrect English (e.g., "You no understand me?") in an attempt to make myself clear.
   Seldom   Occasionally   Often   Always

9. I am aware that many immigrants and refugees do not understand police procedures and I make special efforts to explain these procedures (including their rights).
   Seldom   Occasionally   Often   Always

10. I check in a supportive manner to see if people have understood my message and directions and I encourage people to show me that they have understood me.
    Seldom   Occasionally   Often   Always

11. With non-native speakers of English, I make a special point to simplify my vocabulary, eliminate the use of slang and idioms, and try to use phrases that are not confusing.
    Seldom   Occasionally   Often   Always

12. I make extra efforts to establish rapport (e.g., show increased patience, give more explanations, show professionalism and respect) with individuals from groups that have typically and historically considered the police their enemies.
    Seldom   Occasionally   Often   Always

13. I am sensitive to cultural or gender differences between me and the receiver.
    Seldom   Occasionally   Often   Always

14. I convey respect to all citizens while on duty regardless of their race, color, gender, or other difference from me.
    Seldom   Occasionally   Often   Always

15. When using agency communication channels or media, I communicate professionally, avoiding inappropriate or derogatory remarks.
    Seldom   Occasionally   Often   Always

Participant's initials _____

[Source: Adapted with permission from the Alameda, California, Police Department, March 1993.]

Glossary*

Acculturation: The process of becoming familiar with and comfortable in another culture. The ability to function within that culture or environment, while retaining one's own cultural identity.

Affirmative action: Legally mandated programs whose aim is to increase the employment or educational opportunities of groups that have been disadvantaged in the past.

Alien: Any person who is not a citizen or national of the country in which he or she lives.

Al-jihad: Struggle (literal translation in Arabic). The term has also been used by some to mean "holy war" against infidels or nonbelievers.

Al-Qaida: Also spelled al-Qaeda. A multinational group that funds and orchestrates the activities of Islamic militants worldwide. It grew out of the Afghan war against the Soviets, and its core members consist largely of Afghan war veterans from all over the Muslim world. Al-Qaida was established around 1988 by the Saudi militant Osama bin Ladin. Bin Ladin used an extensive international network to maintain a loose connection between Muslim extremists all over the Arab world, as well as in Europe, Asia, the United States, and Canada.

Anti-Semitism: Latent or overt hostility toward Jews, often expressed through social, economic, institutional, religious, cultural, or political discrimination and through acts of individual or group violence.

Assimilation: The process by which ethnic groups that have emigrated to another society begin to lose their separate identity and culture, becoming absorbed into the larger community.

Awareness: Bringing to one's conscious mind that which is only unconsciously perceived.

Bias: Preference or an inclination to make certain choices that may be positive (bias toward excellence) or negative (bias against people), often resulting in unfairness.

Bias-based policing: The act (intentional or unintentional) of applying or incorporating personal, societal, or organizational biases and/or stereotypes in decision making, police actions, or the administration of justice.

Bigot: A person who steadfastly holds to bias and prejudice, convinced of the truth of his or her own opinion and intolerant of the opinions of others.

B-NICE incident: An acronym for any terrorist incident involving Biological, Nuclear, Incendiary, Chemical and/or Explosive weapons of mass destruction.

---

*Glossary adapted in part from *Transcultural Leadership: Empowering the Diverse Workforce.* Houston, Texas: Gulf Publishing Company. Permission granted from authors: George Simons, Carmen Vazquez, and Philip Harris (1993).

Consent decree: An out-of court settlement whereby the accused party agrees to modify or change behavior rather than plead guilty or go through a hearing on charges brought to court. [Source: CSIS Project Glossary @ (http://csisweb. aers.psu.edu/glossary/c.htm)]

Cosmopolitan: Literally, "a citizen of the world." A person capable of operating comfortably in a global or pluralistic environment.

Cross-cultural: Involving or mediating between two cultures.

Culture: A way of life developed and communicated by a group of people, consciously or unconsciously, to subsequent generations. It consists of ideas, habits, attitudes, customs, and traditions that help to create standards for a group of people to coexist, making a group of people unique. In its most basic sense, culture is a set of patterns for survival and success that a particular group of people has developed.

Cultural competence: A developmental process that evolves over an extended period of time; both individuals and organizations are at various levels of awareness, knowledge, and skills along a continuum of cultural competence. Culturally competent organizations place a high value on the following: (1) Developing a set of principles, attitudes, policies, and structures that will enable all individuals in the organization to work effectively and equitably across all cultures; and 2) developing the capacity to acquire and apply cross-cultural knowledge and respond to and communicate effectively within the cultural contexts that the organization serves.[(Adapted from Cross, T., Bazron, B.J., Dennis, K.W., and Isaacs, M.R. (1989).) *Toward a culturally competent system of care. Volume 1: Monograph on effective services for minority children who are severely emotionally disturbed.* Washington, DC: CASSP Technical Assistance Center, Georgetown University Child Development Center].

Department of Homeland Security (DHS):   The cabinet-level federal agency responsible for preserving the security of the United States against terrorist attacks. This department was created as a response to the 9/11 terrorist attacks.

Discrimination: The denial of equal treatment to groups because of their racial, ethnic, gender, religious, or other form of cultural identity.

Diversity: The term used to describe a vast range of cultural differences that have become factors needing attention in living and working together. Often applied to the organizational and training interventions in an organization that seek to deal with the interface of people who are different from each other. Diversity has come to include race, ethnicity, gender, disability, and sexual orientation.

Domestic terrorism   involves groups or individuals whose terrorist activities are directed at elements of government, organizations, or population without foreign direction.

Dominant culture: Refers to the value system that characterizes a particular group of people that dominates the value systems of other groups or cultures. See also **Macroculture/majority or dominant group.**

Emigre: An individual forced, usually by political circumstances, to move from his or her native country and who deliberately resides as a foreigner in the host country.

Ethnic group: Group of people who conceive of themselves, and who are regarded by others, as alike because of their common ancestry, language, and physical characteristics.

Ethnicity: Refers to the background of a group with unique language, ancestral, often religious, and physical characteristics. Broadly characterizes a religious, racial, national, or cultural group.

Ethnocentrism: Using the culture of one's own group as a standard for the judgment of others, or thinking of it as superior to other cultures that are merely different.

Glass ceiling: An invisible and often perceived barrier that prevents some ethnic or racial groups and women from becoming promoted or hired.

Heterogeneity: Dissimilar; composed of unrelated or unlike elements.

Immigrant: Any individual who moves from one country, place, or locality to another. An alien admitted to the United States as a lawful permanent resident.

Homeland security: Federal and local law enforcement programs for gathering, processing, and application of intelligence to provide the United States with a blanket of protection against terrorist attacks.

International terrorism: Involves groups or individuals whose terrorist activities are foreign-based and/or directed by countries or groups outside the United States or whose activities transcend national boundaries.

Jihad: See **Al-jihad.**

Macroculture/majority or dominant group: The group within a society that is largest and/or most powerful. This power usually extends to setting cultural norms for the society as a whole. The term majority (also minority, see below) is falling into disuse because its connotations of group size may be inaccurate.

Microculture or minority: Any group or person who differs from the dominant culture. Any group or individual, including second- and third-generation foreigners, who is born in a country different from his or her origin and has adopted or embraced the values and culture of the dominant culture.

Multiculturalism: The existence within one society of diverse groups that maintain their unique cultural identity while accepting and participating in the larger society's legal and political system.

Paradigm shift: What occurs when an entire cultural group begins to experience a change that involves the acceptance of new conceptual models or ways of thinking and results in major societal transitions (e.g., the shift from agricultural to industrial society).

Parity: The state or condition of being the same in power, value, rank, and so forth; equality.

Pluralistic: The existence within a nation or society of groups distinctive in ethnic origin, cultural patterns, religion, or the like. A policy of favoring the preservation of such groups with a given nation or society.

Prejudice: The inclination to take a stand for one side (as in a conflict) or to cast a group of people in a favorable or unfavorable light, usually without just grounds or sufficient information.

Profile: A "profile" is typically a document that contains explicit criteria or indicators issued to officers to guide them in their decision making. It is usually based on data collected and interpreted to signify a trend or suggest that, given a particular set of characteristics (behavioral or situational commonalties), a person could believe that something may result based on that particular cluster of characteristics. A profile relies on using expert advice provided to law enforcement agencies to identify perpetrators of criminal activities. It can be an outline or short biographical description, an individual's character sketch, or a type of behavior associated with a group. It is a summary of data presenting the average or typical appearance of those persons or situations under scrutiny. Officers use these indicators of physical, behavioral, or situational commonalties to develop reasonable suspicion or probable cause to stop subjects.

Profiling: Any police-initiated action that uses a compilation of the background, physical, behavioral, and/or motivational characteristics for a type of perpetrator that leads the police to a particular individual who has been identified as being, could be, or having been engaged in criminal activity.

Race: A group of persons of (or regarded as of) common ancestry. Physical characteristics are often used to identify people of different races. These characteristics should not be used to identify ethnic groups, which can cross racial lines.

Racially biased policing: Occurs when law enforcement inappropriately considers race or ethnicity in deciding with whom and how to intervene in an enforcement capacity.

Racial profiling: Any police-initiated action that relies on the race, ethnicity, or national origin rather than the behavior of an individual or information that leads the police to a particular individual who has been identified as being, or having been, engaged in criminal activity.

Racism: Total rejection of others by reason of race, color, or, sometimes more broadly, culture.

Racist: One with a closed mind toward accepting one or more groups different from one's own origin in race or color.

Refugee: A person who flees for safety and seeks asylum in another country. In addition to those persecuted for political, religious, and racial reasons, "economic refugees" flee conditions of poverty for better opportunities elsewhere.

Scapegoating: The practice of blaming one's failures and shortcomings on innocent people or those only partly responsible.

Stereotype: To believe or feel that people and groups are considered to typify or conform to a pattern or manner, lacking any individuality. Thus a person may categorize behavior of a total group on the basis of limited experience with one or a few representatives of that group. Negative stereotyping classifies many people in a group by slurs, innuendoes, names, or slang expressions that depreciate the group as a whole and the individuals in it.

Subculture: A group with distinct, discernible, and consistent cultural traits existing within and participating in a larger cultural grouping.

Suspect-specific incident: An incident in which an officer lawfully attempts to detain, apprehend, or otherwise be on the lookout for one or more specific suspects identified or described, in part, by national or ethnic origin, gender, or race.

Synergy: The benefit produced by the collaboration of two or more systems in excess of their individual contributions. Cultural synergy occurs when cultural differences are taken into account and used by a multicultural group.

Terrorism: A violent act or an act dangerous to human life, in violation of the criminal laws of the United States or any segment to intimidate or coerce a government, the civilian population, or any segment thereof, in furtherance of political or social objectives (U.S. Department of Justice, 1997).

Terrorist attack Pre-Incidence Indicators (TAPIs): A term used by the intelligence community to describe actions and behaviors taken by terrorists before they carry out an attack (Nance, 2003).

Transgender: The term "transgender" covers a range of people, including heterosexual cross-dressers, homosexual drag queens, and transsexuals who believe they were born in the wrong body. This term includes those who consider themselves to be both male and female, or intersexed, as well as those who take hormones to complete their gender identity without a sex change.

Weapons of Mass Destruction (WMD): Three types of weapons are most commonly categorized as WMD: (1) nuclear weapons, (2) biological weapons, and (3) chemical weapons. The subcategories of WMD include activities that may be labeled as "agro terrorism," which is to harm our food supply chain and "cyber terrorism," which is to harm our telecommunication, Internet, and computerized processes and transactions.

White supremacist group: Any ongoing organization, association, or group of three or more persons, whether formal or informal, having as one of its primary activities the promotion of white supremacy through the commission of criminal acts.

White supremacy: Helan Page, an African American anthropologist, defines white supremacy in the United States as an "ideological, structural and historic stratification process by which the population of European descent . . . has been able to intentionally sustain, to its own best advantage, the dynamic mechanics of upward or downward mobility or fluid class status over the non-European populations (on a global scale), using skin color, gender, class or ethnicity as the main criteria" for allocating resources and making decisions [Source: Ross, Loretta (1995). *White Supremacy in the 1990s.* The Public Eye. Sponsored by the Political Research Associates. (www.publiceye.org/eyes/whitsup.html) Somerville, MA, p. 6].

Index